JUDITH MILLER

The Illustrated
Dictionary of
ANTIQUES
& Collectibles

A BULFINCH PRESS BOOK
LITTLE, BROWN AND COMPANY
BOSTON • NEW YORK • LONDON

A Marshall Edition
Conceived, edited and designed by
**Vista 2000 Ltd. and
Marshall Editions**
The Orangery
161 New Bond Street
London W1S 2UF

www.marshallpublishing.com

Project Editors	Sue Harper, Theresa Lane
Project Art Editor	Caroline Hill
Editors	Caroline Behr, Wendy Dear, Anna Fischel, Nicola Munro, Emily Salter, Julie Targett
Designers	Anne Fisher, Clair Watson
Editorial Assistants	Victoria Cookson, Ben Horslen
Picture Research	Jessica Curtis, Pernilla Pearce
Proofreader	Constance Novis
Managing Editor	Julie Brooke
Editorial Director	Ellen Dupont
Art Director	Dave Goodman
Editorial Coordinator	Gillian Thompson
Production	Angela Couchman, Anna Pauletti, Liz Yorke
Photography Coordinators	Caroline de Kerangal, Sophie Mortimer
Illustrators	International Artworks Ltd.
Photographers	A & J Photographics
	Philip de Bay
	Chris Linton
	Mike Newton
	Graham Rae
	Steve Tanner

Compilation copyright © 2001 by Marshall Editions Developments Ltd.
Text copyright © 2000 Vista 2000 Ltd.

Photograph of Judith Miller by Adrian Weinbrecht.

Front cover: tl RW/CL, tcl CI, tcr PC/GR, tr BON/MN, bl SPL,
bcl Sotheby's/AJ, bcr CI, br SPL;
back cover: t DL/AJ, tc L/CL, bc SAS/ST, b BAL/Royal Geographic Society.

First North American Edition
ISBN 0-8212-2746-7
Library of Congress Control Number 00-111503
Bulfinch Press is an imprint and trademark of Little, Brown and Company (Inc.)

Originated in England by Graphic Facilities Group

Printed and bound in Germany by MOHN Media Mohndruck GmbH

Contents

Cross-references in the text are indicated by
the use of SMALL CAPITALS

Consultants

Judith Miller (General Editor)

George Archdale (General Consultant)
John Axford (Oriental)
Fiona Baker (Arts and Crafts, Art Nouveau and Art Deco)
Miles Barton (Prints, Posters and Printed Ephemera)
John Benjamin (Jewellery),
Alexis Butcher (Silver)
Nicholas Couts (Cameras and Optical Toys)
Jonathan Darracott (Watches)
Nicholas M. Dawes (American Antiques)
Audrey Field (Lace)
Joseph Gonzalez (Maps)
Leigh Gotch (Toys)
J.W.F. Harriman (Militaria)
Jeanette Hayhurst (Glass)
Mark Hill (Precision Instruments and Miscellaneous)
Charles Kewley (Sporting Memorabilia)
Ann Knox (Dolls, Teddy Bears and Automata)
Jo Marshall (Ceramics)
Mike and Sue Richardson (Toys)
Rebecca Scott (Textiles)
Jeremy Smith (Furniture)
Catherine Southon (Scientific, Medical and Marine Instruments)
Michael Turner (Clocks and Barometers)
Jonathan Wadsworth (Rugs and Carpets)

Chief Contributors
Jill Bace, Frankie Leibe, Sarah Yates

M
Y INTEREST IN ANTIQUES began when I was at school in the Scottish Borders in the 1950s and 60s. We were taken on frequent trips to the wonderful stately homes in the area and I was transfixed by the wealth of antiques in them: furniture, ceramics, glass, silver, carpets and rugs, toys and weapons. My interest grew when I became a student at Edinburgh University in the late 1960s and began to collect "old plates" from the junk shops there. The names on the backs of the plates fascinated me and I tried to find out more about them. And that is the start of a journey of discovery that continues today.

There have been two major developments over the last 30 years that have made *The Illustrated Dictionary of Antiques and Collectibles* even more needed. The first is the vast expansion of what is called antique. When I started to collect, an antique had to be at least 100 years old and many antique dealers and fairs would only allow pre-1840 items. This meant that slightly "newer" items were condemned to a lower status and could often be found in junk shops. They were also thought less worthy of research. Over the years this has changed dramatically, with many items from the 20th century now being eagerly collected. This means that there is a far greater choice of items for people to collect and discover – many with very strange names and strange associated terminology.

"He ain't my guv'nor, but I'm follerin' 'im 'cos he's the only blinkin' bit of shade about!"

The second, and probably more important, factor is the vast increase in interest in antiques and collectibles, fuelled by many successful TV series, with shows like *The Antiques Roadshow*, in the UK and the US, gaining top viewer ratings. Suddenly more and more people want to find the answers to questions such as what Granny's vase actually is, and when was it made? The chair that everyone in the family said was made by Gustav Stickley – who was he? Rococo – what was that? And what would you do with a scarificator?

As you will find when you start to use the book, this is much more than a simple dictionary. We have approached top experts in their fields to ensure that the information is of most use both to the experienced collector and the person who is starting out. It will give you the details of styles, periods, great craftsmen and women, explain what a piece is, how it was used and when it was most fashionable. It will explain methods of construction and decoration and give a general price guide for items illustrated. It will give details of the "movers and shakers" of the world of antiques and collecting from kings to architects and from inventors to religious sects.

The main philosophy behind the book is to provide the one essential, authoritative and accessible reference book for anyone who is interested in antiques and collecting. I have needed a book like this for 30 years.

Happy hunting!

Judith Miller

Periods and styles

Date	Britain	France	Germany	Italy
			Reformation triggered by Martin Luther (1521)	Renaissance Italy divided into Naples and Milan (under Spanish rule), the Papal States and Florence
1550	Elizabeth 1 (1558–1603)			Cosimo I de Medici becomes Grand Duke of Tuscany (1570)
				Battle of Lepanto leads to the defeat of the Turks (1571)
1600	James I (1603–25)	Louis XIII (1610–43)	Thirty Years' War (1618–48)	
	Commonwealth (1649–1660)	Louis XIV (1643–1715)		
1650	Charles II (1660–1685)			Venice loses Crete to the Turks (1669)
	William & Mary (1688–1694)		Louis XIV of France invades the Rhineland (1689)	
	William III (1694–1702)			
1700	Queen Anne (1702–1714)	Régence (1715–23)		Austria rules Milan, Naples and Sardinia (1713)
	George I (1714–1727)	Louis XV (1723–74)		Venetian maritime empire ends (1718)
	George II (1727–1760)		Ascendancy of Prussia under Frederick II (1740–86)	Kingdom of the Two Sicilies becomes independent (1735)
				Medici line ends in Florence (1737)
1750	George III (1760–1820)	Louis XVI (1774–93)	Seven Years' War (1756–63)	
		Directoire (1793–99)		
1800	George IV (1820–1830)	Empire of Napoléon I (1799–1815)	Napoléon I unites W. Germany (1806)	Napoléon I crowned king of Italy (1805–15)
	William IV (1830–1837)	Restauration (1815–30)		Guiseppe Mazzini initiates the Risorgimento (1830s)
	Victoria (1837–1901)	Louis Philippe (1830–48)		War of Independence against Austria (1848)
1850		2nd Empire of Napoléon III (1848–70)	Under Kaiser Wilhelm I and Bismarck, German Empire conquers Austria and France (1870)	Guiseppe Garibaldi unifies Italy under Victor Emmanuel II of Sardinia (1861)
		3rd Republic (1871–1940)		Florence is capital of the new kingdom (1865–71)
				Italian forces occupy Rome (1870)
				Italy invades Ethiopia (1885)
1900	Edward VII (1901–1910)		Establishment of Weimar Republic (1918)	
	George VI (1936–1952)			
1950	Elizabeth II (1952–)			
			Berlin Wall demolished (1989); West and East Germany united (1990)	

Scandinavia	United States	Landmarks in applied arts
Gustavus Vasa reigns in Sweden (1523–40)		Discovery of Nero's Golden House in Rome inspires Grotesque style (1488) Council of Trent stimulates the Baroque movement (1545)
		Benvenuto Cellini publishes his *Autobiography* (1558)
Denmark's Golden Age under Christian IV (1588–1648)		Roman catacombs discovered (1578)
Gustavus Adolphus (1611–1632) Sweden at war with Denmark (1643–45 and 1657–58)	Colonial period (c.1600–1780) Dutch found settlement on Manhattan Island called New Amsterdam (New York) (1611) Pilgrim Fathers land at Plymouth (1620)	Tea is first shipped to Europe from China (1609) Inigo Jones designs the Queen's House, Greenwich (1616–18) and the Banqueting House, Whitehall (1619–22) English traders establish a factory in Canton (1637)
	Quakers found Pennsylvania (1682)	Château of Versailles built (1660–1715) Gobelins factory founded (1667) Revocation of Edict of Nantes triggers spread of Huguenot craftsmen (1685)
Great Northern War: Sweden versus Denmark, Poland and Russia (1700–21) Era of Liberty in Sweden with parliamentary government (1719–72)		Böttger discovers the secret of hard-paste porcelain (1709) Excavation of Herculaneum begins (1738)
Gustav III reintroduces absolutism in Sweden (1789)	Declaration of Independence (1776) War of Independence (1775–83) Federal period (1780–1830) US Constitution (1787)	Publication of Chippendale's *Gentleman & Cabinet-Maker's Director* (1754) Publication of Robert Adam's *Works in Architecture* (1773–1822) Napoléon I invades Egypt (1798)
Sweden loses Finland to Russia (1809) Sweden annexes Norway from Denmark (1814) The French marshall Bernadotte becomes king of Sweden as Karl IV Johan (1818)	War with England (1812–14)	Thomas Hope publishes *Household Furniture and Decoration* (1807) British Houses of Parliament designed by Charles Barry and A.W.N. Pugin (1840–1852)
	Civil War; slavery abolished (1861–65) Battle of Wounded Knee: last major battle between native Americans and whites (1890)	Great Exhibition in London (1st international trade exhibition) (1851) 1st exhibition of Japanese art in Europe (London, 1854) William Morris's Red House designed by Philip Webb (1859) Chicago Exhibition (1st international trade show in US) (1893)
Norway becomes independent under King Haakon VII (1905)	Wall Street crash (1929)	Paris Exposition (1900) Bauhaus established (1919) Le Corbusier publishes *L'art décoratif d'aujourd'hui* (1925) Design Council inaugurated in UK (1944)
		Robert Venturi publishes *Complexity and Contradiction in Architecture*: the "Bible" of Post-Modernism (1966)

A

Aalto, Alvar (1898–1976)
A Finnish architect and designer
considered one of the giants of
20th-century design. A leading
exponent of the MODERN
MOVEMENT but with a
Humanist outlook, Aalto
favoured a more organic
approach to design. He
preferred to use natural birch
and laminated birch plywood rather
than modern materials
such as tubular steel,
because he felt they were
more sympathetic to the
physical and psychological condition of
people. He characterized these needs as
"psychophysical". One of his most highly
regarded architectural projects was the
Paimio Sanitorium for Tuberculosis in
Finland (1929–33), where he designed
the interior furnishings as well as the
building itself.

Examples of Alvar Aalto's furniture
were first seen outside Finland in 1933 in
Milan, at the V Triennale Exhibition, and
in London at Fortnum & Mason's shop.

Alvar Aalto chair,
c.1945 [J]

In the latter case a company, Finmar, was
established to import Aalto's furniture
designs into England. The firm
Wohnbedorf was established in
Switzerland for other European imports.
Aalto formed a production company
called Artek in 1935 with Harry
Gullichsen, Nils Hahl and his wife Aino
Marsio Aalto (1894–1949).

Although renowned as an architect
and furniture designer, he also turned his
hand to glass and designed a range of
vases in 1938 for Karhula-Iittala, Finland.
These were characterized by their
asymmetrical form and organic
appearance and have the same fluid
outline as Aalto's chairs.

Alvar Aalto plywood chair
and table, c.1930 [J]

Aaron's rod A term used by plasterers
in the 18th and early 19th centuries to
designate a leaf-entwined staff. It can also
refer to the caduceus, a winged
staff coiled with two
serpents. In Classical
mythology, it is an
attribute of Mercury, the
messenger god of the
Roman pantheon (in
Greek, Hermes).

Abacus The flat
moulding on the top of
a capital that supports
the entablature.
Occasionally the abacus is
decorated with simple ornament, such as
chamfered borders or slight indentations.

Abacus moulding

Abalone shell The shell of a tropical
mollusc, one of several yielding MOTHER-
OF-PEARL, used to decorate jewellery and
metal during the RENAISSANCE. In the
17th century it was adopted as an inlay for
furniture and often embellished PAPIER-
MÂCHÉ furniture in the 19th century.

Abbotsford style Nineteenth-century
furniture inspired by the decoration of
Abbotsford (1824), the Scottish home of
Sir Walter Scott, and characterized by
ELIZABETHAN and GOTHIC motifs such as
STRAPWORK, cusps and spiral columns.

Abrahams, Robert Frederick
(1827–95) An English painter who studied
in Paris and Antwerp and exhibited at the
Royal Academy in 1846–51. He went to
COALPORT in 1855 as a porcelain
decorator. In 1863 he left Coalport and
went to the Hill Pottery and then in
1865 he became art director at COPELAND
AND GARRETT.

Abrash Variations in tone and saturation found within a single colour in a carpet sometimes deliberately to create a lively shimmer. It can be pronounced when a weaver has run out of one dyed batch of wool and resorts to a new batch.

Abstract Expressionism A term first used in 1919 to describe certain paintings by Wassily Kandinsky. It is applied today to a movement in American painting and

Abstract Expressionist porcelain
cup and saucer, c.1955 [Q]

studio ceramics from *c*.1942, which was highly influential in the 1950s and early 1960s. The work of potters Peter Voulkos and John Mason is notable. Features include apparently random compositions with gestural marks and holes.

Abtsbessingen pottery A faience factory in Thuringia, Germany, producing a fine white-glazed faience. In business from 1747–91, it was one of the best 18th-century faience factories and at the start the painter Joseph Philipp Dannhofer worked there for three years. The usual mark was a motif like a tuning fork, sometimes with the decorator's initials.

Acacia *(Robinia pseudacacia)* A strong, durable hardwood, varying in colour from pale yellow to golden brown with deeper brown markings. Used mainly for inlay and banding but also for some rural furniture in the 18th and 19th centuries.

Acanthus A Mediterranean plant, *Acanthus spinosus*, with fleshy, scalloped leaves. From antiquity it was widely used for carved ornament, such as decorative

mouldings and Corinthian and Composite capitals. In the 18th century it was a popular motif for furniture and metalwork.

Acanthus

Accordion pleat A series of folds like those of the bellows of an accordion, particularly fashionable in 1950s dressmaking.

Achromatic lens A twin lens combination discovered in the mid-18th century that removed the distorting colour fringes from images seen through telescopes. This also enabled telescopes to become smaller and more portable. Patented in 1758 by the Englishman John Dollond, the combination was applied at the end of the century to microscopes.

Acid-etching A technique for decorating glass such as CAMEO GLASS. The pattern is marked out and protected by a special resist. The vessel is then submerged in HYDROFLUORIC ACID, which eats through the unprotected area. The longer the piece is exposed to the acid, the deeper the relief. The principle is the same for PRINTS except the medium is copper, zinc or mild steel sheets.

Acid polishing Dipping cut glass into a mixture of sulphuric and HYDROFLUORIC ACID to produce a lustrous, shiny surface that, in the late 19th century, replaced hand and mechanical polishing.

Acid-etching

Acier, Michel-Victor (1736–95) A French sculptor and modeller of groups and figures at SÈVRES, appointed to the MEISSEN Porcelain Factory in 1764 and pensioned off in 1781. Particular themes of his were children, and allegorical and mythological scenes. He set a style between ROCOCO and Classical.

Ackermann, Rudolph (1764–1834) A German carriage maker from Stollberg, Saxony, who moved to London where he worked from 1783–86, designing the funeral carriage of Horatio Nelson. From 1809–28, Ackermann published a monthly magazine called *The Repository of Arts*. It included furniture designs by, among others, George BULLOCK and George SMITH, later published as *Fashionable Furniture*.

Acoma pottery Nineteenth-century Native American pottery from the south-west US, in unglazed terracotta, painted with geometric patterns in earth tones.

Acorn The fruit of the oak tree. In Roman, Celtic and Scandinavian art the acorn symbolized fecundity and immortality. The acorn features widely on JACOBEAN oak furniture, was common for brass drop handles on late 17th-century and American furniture and was adopted for GOTHIC REVIVAL metalwork. Cords for curtains and blinds had turned wood acorns well into the 20th century.

Acorn cup An English silver STANDING CUP with a bowl and cover in the form of an acorn and a tree-trunk stem, made from *c*.1580 to *c*.1620.

Acorn flagon An English, particularly Yorkshire, pewter flagon, mostly made from *c*.1700 to *c*.1750, with a wide base and tapering bulbous body like an acorn. It usually has a domed cover.

Acorn knop A finial on the end of silver or base metal spoons taking the form of an acorn. One of the earliest forms of medieval spoon, from *c*.1300 to *c*.1500.

Act of Parliament clock See TAVERN CLOCK.

Acupictura A term for embroidery which imitates painting. Sometimes called needle painting, the subject is represented in the most accurate detail achievable.

Adam, Robert (1728–92) A Scottish architect and designer, the son of William Adam, a leading Scottish architect. Together with his brothers John and James, Robert inherited his father's practice in 1748. In 1754 he embarked on an architectural GRAND TOUR and, during his stay in Rome, cultivated potential aristocratic patrons and became an accomplished draughtsman, absorbing the principles and motifs of Roman antiquity and the NEO-CLASSICAL style that he studied assiduously. In 1758 he set up as an architect in London and by the early 1760s had become the leading British architect of the day, also designing interiors, architectural fittings – ranging from chimney-pieces to door handles and escutcheons – and all types of furniture, metalwork and textiles in the light, delicate Neo-classical style that bears his name. His designs were executed by leading craftsmen, such as Thomas CHIPPENDALE. The furniture, often painted or gilded, depended more on ornament than form for effect. Wall mirrors, pier tables, commodes and girandoles were decorated with classical motifs such as rams' heads, husks, palmettes and festoons. The popularity of the Adam style peaked in Britain in

the 1760s and 1770s. The *Works in Architecture of Robert and James Adam* was published in Britain in 1773–78 and helped to spread the style to France and the US.

Robert Adam drawing of fireplace, c.1770 [G]

Adams, George (1704–72) An English craftsman producing precision instruments of fine quality. He established his workshop in 1735 and gained a high reputation. In 1746 he invented the New Universal Single Microscope, which incorporated the system of using single lenses of various powers set in a revolving disc under the barrel. George Adams provided James Cook with instruments for his journey to inspect the transit of Venus from the Pacific Ocean in 1769. He and his son George Adams Jnr (1750–95) were appointed to the positions of mathematical instrument-makers to George III in 1760 and produced a number of scientific instruments for the king's collection.

Sextant by George Adams, 18th century [H]

Adams, Robert (1809–70) An English firearms designer. In 1851, he was in partnership as Deane, Adams and Deane and obtained a British

master patent for a solid frame, self-cocking percussion REVOLVER. Shown at the GREAT EXHIBITION in 1851, it was adopted by the army as the first service revolver and used by officers during the Crimean War (1853–56). In 1856, Adams became director and manager of the London Armoury Company but the demand for guns declined in the early 1860s and he went bankrupt in 1864.

Adams, William There were several potters of this name during the 18th and 19th centuries in Staffordshire, all related to a greater or lesser degree. The first recorded William established Adams & Co. in 1769 in Greengates, Tunstall, and made EARTHENWARE, BASALTES, JASPER and PARIAN until 1800. Another William Adams was based in Stoke in the early 19th century and made much blue printed earthenware between 1804 and 1840. Toward the end of the century another company called William Adams & Co. made railway commemorative wares.

Adams and Company A late 19th-century American glass-maker, established in Pittsburgh in 1851 as a union of two older firms: Adams, Macklin and Company and Stourbridge Flint Glassworks. Adams made mostly clear pressed and cut FLINT GLASS of heavy type, until the end of the 19th century.

Adler glass A tall, cylindrical German drinking glass or HUMPEN, sometimes with a cover, also called an *Adlerhumpen* (German: "eagle beaker") or *Reichs-adlerhumpen* ("imperial eagle beaker"), with enamelled decoration of a double-headed eagle with the symbols of the Holy Roman Empire on its wings. Made in Germany and Bohemia from the mid-16th century, such glasses were used to drink toasts and were much reproduced in the HISTORISMUS movement.

Robert Adam design window seat, c.1775 [A]

Aesthetic Movement

In the late 19th century, a number of English artists, architects and critics reacted against the art and design popular at the time, which was based on realism or meant to convey moral values, in favour of works of art whose only justification was their intrinsic beauty.

Art for art's sake

The movement was largely an English phenomenon, although it spread to the US in the latter part of the century, and in its turn influenced both the ARTS AND CRAFTS and ART NOUVEAU styles. The word "aesthetic" came into common usage in the latter part of the 19th century. Both the movement and the names popularly associated with it – the American painter James Abbott McNeill Whistler (1834–1903), the writer Oscar Wilde and the architect E.W. GODWIN – received much newspaper coverage, with both Whistler and Wilde involved in famous court cases. Gilbert and Sullivan's operetta *Patience* made fun of the movement and of "aesthetes".

Minton earthenware
wall plaque, c.1877 [N]

The sources of inspiration of the movement were diverse and included many "exotic" arts such as JAPONAISERIE, Egyptian and Moorish, the GOTHIC REVIVAL and the QUEEN ANNE REVIVAL. Japanese art had a major influence on Western art after Japan opened its doors to the West in 1853. The leading architect whose work clearly shows his appreciation of Oriental simplicity and subtlety was E.W. Godwin and the work of the English illustrator Aubrey Beardsley also shows a marked Japanese influence. The Queen Anne Revival was attributed to the architects Richard Norman Shaw and William Eden Nesfield, along with William MORRIS. The Gothic style also had some 0 impact having been brought to prominence by A.W.N. PUGIN. Egyptian influences can be seen, for example, in a THEBES STOOL made by LIBERTY & CO.

Silver and ivory teapot
with Japanese motifs
in Aesthetic style, c.1880 [I]

Some of the best pieces from this period can be seen in the work of E.W. Godwin. The more commercial pieces in ceramic or silver may be overtly Oriental looking, i.e. made as if from bamboo, or they may have conventional shapes but be decorated in an Oriental style with flowers, birds and insects. Furniture was often ebonized and featured spindles or had gilded highlights or painted panels. In the US, in the late 19th century, the influence of the Aesthetic style can be seen in early interior decoration of Louis Comfort TIFFANY, the silverware of the GORHAM MANUFACTURING COMPANY and in the beginnings of ART POTTERY by various makers including ROOKWOOD POTTERY.

Recognizing the style

Aesthetic style took many of its forms from nature, at first using "honest" simple forms, but later these natural forms became exaggeratedly sinuous and "decadent".

Bamboo
motif

Cherry blossom
motif

Sunflower motif

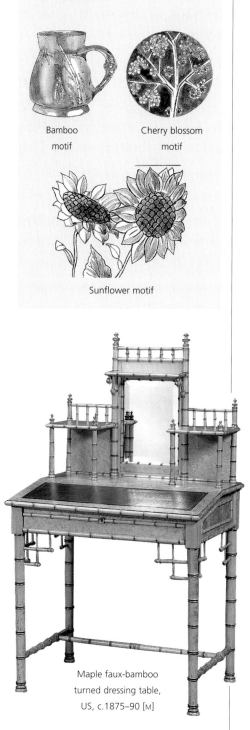

Maple faux-bamboo
turned dressing table,
US, c.1875–90 [M]

Aedicule From the Latin *aedicula*, a shrine within a temple, framed by two COLUMNS supporting a pediment and entablature and containing a statue. The term is also applied to the frame of a window, door or niche formed by two PIERS, PILASTERS or columns supporting a PEDIMENT and entablature, a gable, lintel or plaque.

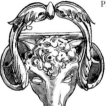

Aegricanes

Aegricanes In Classical architecture, the head of a ram or goat. They were frequently used in temples. Swags or garlands are often attached to the horns, sometimes curving into VOLUTES reminiscent of an Ionic capital. Revived as an ornamental motif in the Renaissance, it was a popular device in the 18th century, combined with festoons for repeating frieze decoration in the style of Robert ADAM. Aegricanes were also used for handles in ceramics and metalwork, and on furniture combined with cloven hoof MONOPODIA for tripods and side tables.

Aerograph A mechanical atomizer or spray gun used to apply a coloured ground to lesser quality porcelain or pottery from the 1890s onward and often used more recently to apply glazes.

Aerography A technique in which a coloured ground was applied to porcelain or pottery using a mechanical apparatus, such as an AEROGRAPH, instead of a more traditional method such as using a carefully moderated layer of oil to hold the colour to the surface.

Aesthetic Movement See p. 13.

Affleck, Thomas (1740–95) A Scottish-born American cabinet-maker and chair specialist active in Philadelphia from 1763. Affleck's work is among the most highly prized of all American Chippendale furniture. Typical pieces include mahogany chairs carved in the manner of early George III examples, showing a restrained Rococo influence.

Afshar rug, south-west Persia, c.1890 [J]

Afshar carpets Carpets from a Turkic-speaking nomadic and partly settled tribal group based in South Persia near Kerman, who made (and continue to make) fine and coarse rugs with geometric designs in which jewel-like shades of red and blue predominate. Products include pile rugs, KILIMS and SOUMAK carpets.

Agate An opaque and banded variety of chalcedony, agate is a member of the quartz family and has been used as an ornamental hardstone for centuries. Frequently stained, the layers of contrasting colour are ideal for carving into cameos, where the black and white variety is called onyx and the red and white kind, sardonyx.

Agate glass An opaque, marbled glass that was used to imitate vessels made from semi-precious stones such as agate, chalcedony and jasper. Known from Roman times, it was made by mixing together two or more colours of molten glass. It was further developed in the late 15th century by Venetian glassmakers who developed "chalcedony" glass, and refined still further in the 19th century by Bohemian glassmakers such as Friedrich EGERMANN. See also LITHYALIN GLASS.

Agate ware A ceramic imitation of the natural stones of agate and marble. Made by kneading together variously coloured clays, or sometimes by painting. When kneaded, the striations of colour go through the BODY and this is called "solid agate". Particularly used by WEDGWOOD and other Staffordshire potteries in the 18th and 19th centuries. Also used on the Continent, notably at the APT factory.

Agra carpets Agra was the capital of the Mogul Empire in 16th and 17th centuries and an important carpet-weaving centre from *c.*1850 to *c.*1910. Carpets, mainly with wool pile, were made in commercial workshops and in the city's jail. Formal curvilinear designs are based upon earlier Persian Classical models. The traditional red and blue threads are dominant in the design; ivory ground carpets are also seen but are rare.

Aide-mémoire Fashionable in 18th-century France, and popular generally throughout the 19th century, these memory aids were decorative cases on clips or chains, which open to reveal ivory leaves (latterly, paper) and a pencil for jotting notes. They were often crafted in gold or silver and decorated with enamel, jewels and tortoiseshell.

Aigrette A decorative hair ornament especially popular in the 18th and 19th centuries. Mounted in gold or silver and frequently set with diamonds, gems or pearls, the most popular designs included feathers, plumes and sprays of flowers.

Air beading A decoration most commonly used in the stems of wine glasses, in the form of small bubbles or "beads" of air that form a continuous line.

Air twist A decoration used in the stems of 18th-century English drinking glasses in which bubbles of air were deliberately introduced into the glass and elongated and twisted as necessary to form an internal pattern.

Air twist stem, English, c.1765 [L]

Ajouré (French: "allowing light through") A term for metal sheet with a pierced openwork pattern, used especially in jewellery.

Akerman, John (*fl.*1719–55) An English glasscutter and retailer, based in London. His advertisement *c.*1719 in the *Whitehall Evening Post* was the first to offer cut glass for sale in England, possibly made by a Bohemian glasscutter employed by his firm. From *c.*1740–48 he was master of the Glass Sellers' Company that had sponsored George RAVENSCROFT during the development of lead glass.

Akstafa A village in the Caucasus, the name being applied to a distinctive type of rug made by tribal weavers in the region in the 19th and early 20th centuries. The rugs are finely knotted, with cotton weft and woollen warp. They are immediately recognizable by the presence of large fan-tailed birds (possibly peacocks) which always flank a column of star-shaped medallions, supported by flower-heads and zoomorphic motifs. Designs are always geometric and multicoloured with extensive and effective use of white.

Aksu A region in East Turkestan known for the production of carpets and rugs. See also KHOTAN and YARKAND.

Alabaster A soft form of gypsum with fine grains and a white, or yellowy-white, translucent appearance. It can be polished to a waxy finish but scratches easily and is most often used for small sculptures. Until the mid-16th century, it was frequently used for religious statuary.

Alabastron The Greek name for a small bottle or flask used for storing unguents and cosmetics. It had a rounded base, slightly elongated form and usually two small loop handles on the sides. Early glass examples (*c.*300 BC–AD 100) were CORE FORMED and often had coloured trailed decoration. See also PERFUME BOTTLE.

Mediterranean alabastron, 600–500 BC [O]

Albany pattern First mass-produced in the 1880s, this popular style of silver FLATWARE and cutlery is characterized by fanned and fluted handles. They were an affordable alternative to the 18th-century ONSLOW pattern.

Albany slip A rich brown glaze added to the interior of an American CROCK to render the vessel impervious to liquid. Named after the upstate New York capital city, but used throughout the north-eastern states.

Albarello An Italian word of obscure origin given to pharmacy jars, usually of waisted cylindrical shape. Probably originating in the Middle East, they were made from tin-glazed earthenware in Italy, Spain and the Netherlands from the 15th century onward. They usually had a label bearing the name of the drug contained inside and were often made in sets for the pharmacies of monasteries. Some had a groove round the neck so that a parchment cover could be tied on.

Maiolica albarello, Italy, c.1580 [G]

Albert A watch chain, usually with oval links, each twisted to allow the chain to lie flat, named after the Prince Consort, Queen Victoria's husband. Often each link is graduated in size to give a tapered appearance. The term is frequently used to describe any watch chain that attaches a watch to a waistcoat.

An Albert watch chain, c.1870 [J]

Albert pattern Named after Prince Albert and produced from 1840 onward, this classic style of silver FLATWARE and cutlery has simply a border of scrolls around the handles, which terminate in foliate motifs.

Albisola potteries A north Italian centre of MAIOLICA and FAIENCE production that started from the 17th and 18th centuries with the nearby towns of Savona and Genoa. Although little is known of their products, the Grossi, Corradi and Levantino families are known to have worked there, producing wares decorated in a free and flowing way and polychrome figures in landscapes with flowers and trees. In the early years, blue and later HIGH TEMPERATURE COLOURS were used. The mark was a "pharos" or "lighthouse". Maiolica is still made in the area.

Album quilt with Stars and Stripes for the Union, mid-19th century [i]

Album quilt Also known as friendship or autograph quilts, album quilts were made in the mid-19th century US. They were made up of a number of separate sections of patchwork, worked by various individuals. Often each block was designed by its creator. The finished quilts were frequently made for presentation.

Alcaraz An important carpet-weaving centre from the mid-15th to the end of the 17th century in south-west Spain. Famous for the 15th-century "Admiral" heraldic carpet, woven for Don Fadrique Enriquez, 26th Admiral of Castille, which bears his armorial in three square panels. Typical features include Anatolian geometric motifs, kufic script and armorials of Spanish nobility. Turkish carpets from the 15th and 16th century were also imitated. Examples exist with Holbein designs. In the 16th century, patterns became more European in character, featuring wreaths of oak leaves and acorns, vines and crowns. Italian and contemporary 16th-century textiles were also a great influence. Yellows, blues and ivory are typical colours. The knot in these carpets is distinctive and is tied round alternate single warps in offset rows.

Alcock, Samuel & Co. Based at Cobridge, Staffordshire, 1828–53 and at Burslem 1830–59. The firm made general pottery and porcelain and some good PORCELLANEOUS animal models. It used printed, painted and impressed marks of Samuel Alcock & Co., S.A. & Co. and S. Alcock & Co.

Staffordshire Alcock bowl and cover, c.1840 [L]

Alcora faience "blackamoor" candlestick, c.1750 [G]

Alcora pottery This Spanish factory started by making faience c.1727 and the French potter and painter Joseph Olerys from MOUSTIERS worked there from 1727 to 1737. Lustred pottery was made from 1749 to a recipe brought from Manises in Valencia. A great variety of wares was produced, the earliest in the style of Moustiers, particularly *style Bérain* including table centrepieces, candlesticks, cornucopiae, statues, animals and table services.

The factory continued to make faience until 1780, after which it made cream-coloured earthenware in the English style. In the 19th century, the factory turned to making TRANSFER-PRINTED ware but closed in 1895. The mark was a capital A, impressed and painted in red, brown and black. A mark "Fab. De Aranda A" in colours is also known.

Alder (*Alnus glutinosa*) A durable hardwood from a wetlands tree native to northern Europe. The pale brown wood carves well and was used for 18th- and 19th-century country furniture, occasionally for the turned members of WINDSOR CHAIRS and for TREEN and the soles of clogs.

Ale glass A type of English drinking glass with a funnel bowl designed to hold small quantities of the very potent ale of the time. Early 17th-century examples had short stems and were known as short or dwarf ale glasses; from the late 17th century, they became taller, with longer stems.

English ale glass, c.1800 [R]

Alençon A centre for French needle lace in the 18th century, making pretty, delicate fashion lace designed with minutely detailed flowers and foliage on a simple twisted ground, used for caps and lappets, sleeve ruffles and frills, until the French Revolution. The industry was revived briefly in the mid-19th century.

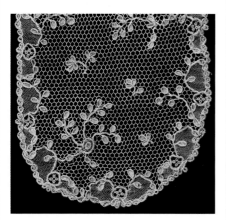

Alençon linen needle lace lappet, c.1770 [o]

Alentours A style of tapestry-weaving first introduced at the GOBELINS factory in the early 18th century, becoming popular by the mid-18th century. Typically, a central figurative scene, characteristically feathery in appearance, is surrounded by a wide, elaborately scrolling border featuring floral swags and architectural elements.

Ale warmer A copper or brass pan with wooden or iron handles that was put in a fire to prepare mulled ale. It is usually boot-, shoe- or cone-shaped and was introduced in the 18th century in England. Examples from the 19th century are more common today.

Alexandrite A variety of chrysoberyl, alexandrite is a rare and valuable gemstone because it changes colour from bluish-green in daylight to raspberry-red in artificial light. Principal sources of alexandrite include Russia, Brazil, Sri Lanka and Tanzania. Synthetic corundum is frequently described as "alexandrite" and can be mistaken for it.

Alexandrite glass Late 19th- and early 20th-century decorative glass, with a multicoloured surface, shading through amber and blue to deep pink at the extremities, which are successively reheated to create the effect. It was named after the ALEXANDRITE hardstone that appeared to change colour depending on the light. The glass was manufactured in Britain by Thomas WEBB & Son.

Alhambresque An adjective from the name of the palace in Granada, southern Spain, built for the Moorish kings during the 13th and 14th centuries. It refers to large vases with pear-shaped bodies and double wing handles, decorated in blue and gold lustre in Arab style that were known at the Alhambra.

Alla certosina A geometric mosaic inlay, named after the Certosa di Pavia monastery in Italy, using polygonal pieces of wood, ivory, bone, metal and mother-of-pearl. Popular in northern Italy in the 15th century and revived in Italy in the mid-19th century when it was often used on furniture in the Moorish or North African style.

Allen, Robert (1745–1835) An English porcelain painter who started work at the LOWESTOFT porcelain factory when he was only 12 years old, as a painter in underglaze blue. He later became foreman of the factory and was "acquainted with all the various processes". Eventually, Allen became manager of the works, possibly in 1780.

Allison, Michael (*c*.1785–1855) An American cabinet-maker of the FEDERAL period, active in New York City from *c*.1800 to 1847. His work combines the elegance of French taste with the grace of English Regency influence and is often compared with

Alexandrite glass bowl, c.1920 [P]

that of his better known rival, Duncan PHYFE. Examples are rare and highly prized.

Alloa glassworks
Established in 1750 in Alloa, Scotland, the factory's main period of production was the mid-19th century. Its main ware is STIPPLE-ENGRAVED commemorative bottles and FRIGGERS in the NAILSEA style, with the later addition of engraved tablewares.

American Hepplewhite secretary bookcase attributed to Michael Allison, c.1795 [A]

Alloy Two or more different metals mixed together chemically to produce a "new" metal with more suitable or tailored physical properties. Almost all metals found in the decorative arts are alloys, including various gold alloys, STERLING SILVER, BRASS, BRONZE and PEWTER.

Altenburg pottery
A type of STONEWARE made at Altenburg, Saxony, from the early 17th to the mid-18th century. Typical wares include tankards and jugs decorated with allegorical reliefs and coats of arms, sometimes with a characteristic pale brown glaze and applied bead decoration.

Early 18th century Altenburg tankard, c.1710–20 [M]

Aluminium A silvery white metal extracted from bauxite. Lightweight, malleable and resistant to corrosion, it was first discovered in 1827 and used for jewellery from the 1850s. In the 1920s it was used for such items as ART DECO cocktail equipment and ashtrays, and in the 1930s for Modernist furniture (e.g. by Donald DESKEY).

Amatory jewellery
Jewels of sentiment and love, common from the 17th to the late 19th century. Early symbolism included the true lovers' knot, Cupid shooting arrows, flaming hearts, the POSY RING and the "fede" ring, where several bands enclose a heart beneath hands clasped in troth. Amatory jewels especially popular in the early 1800s included jewelled padlocks with keys and serpents with their tails in their mouths, representing eternity and eternal love.

Amatory diamond brooch, English 1880 [C]

Amber A soft fossilized resin exuded from coniferous trees that grew in the Oligocene age (30–50 million years ago). The principal variety is Baltic, ranging in colour from a cloudy yellow to a rich orange/red, and from opaque to translucent in clarity. Other examples include Burmese, Sicilian and Romanian. It is prized for its beauty and magnetic qualities, as it attracts small particles when it is warm and rubbed. From antiquity to the 17th century it has been used for jewellery, *objets d'art* and the decoration of furniture. Amber declined in popularity in the 18th century but was revived in ART NOUVEAU jewellery.

Amberg, Adolf (1874–1913)
A German sculptor and metalworker, now remembered mainly for his work as a designer of sculptural porcelain figures. Between 1894 and 1904 he worked at Bruckmann & Sohn of Heilbronn, Germany, where he designed decorative ornaments and silver tableware. At the International Exhibition in Paris in 1900, a large silver fountain designed by Amberg in association with the architect Otto Rieth was displayed. In 1904 he designed 16 exotic figures for the "marriage procession" themed table centrepiece made for the wedding of the German crown prince. The designs were later made by the BERLIN Porcelain Factory and exhibited to acclaim at the 1911 Berlin Art Exhibition.

Amberg pottery
A FAIENCE factory founded in Bavaria, Germany, in 1759 by Simon Hetzendörfer. From 1790 cream-coloured EARTHENWARE and HARD-PASTE PORCELAIN were produced. In c.1850 they acquired moulds from the LUDWIGSBURG porcelain works, from which they made reproductions. The pottery closed in 1910.

Amberina Coloured glass used for tablewares and decorative pieces, usually shading from light amber at the base to dark ruby at the extremities, which are reheated to produce the distinctive colour. Patented by Joseph LOCKE in the US in 1883, the majority of American "Amberina" glass was made by the LIBBEY GLASS CO. The cased "Plated Amberina" patented by Locke in 1886 was largely produced in the US by the NEW ENGLAND GLASS CO., who licensed SOWERBY'S ELLISON GLASSWORKS to produce it in Britain.

Amboyna (*Pterocarpus indicus*)
A decorative hardwood, varying in colour from light reddish brown to orange, with a mottled figure and tightly curled grain. It was imported from the Moluccas in the Malaysian archipelago and used for BANDING, INLAY and VENEERS on high-quality 18th- and early 19th-century furniture; from the mid-19th century it was in more common use and was found on medium-quality pieces.

Amelung, Johann Frederick (active 1784–95) A German glass-maker who emigrated to the US and founded the Amelung Glassworks in New Bremen, Maryland, in 1784. The small works produced mostly window glass and, from c.1785, some freeblown vessels in slightly smoky glass, including rare engraved and coloured examples comparable to contemporary BOHEMIAN glass. The works closed in 1795 owing to commercial failures.

Amen glass An item of JACOBITE GLASS: a mid-18th-century wine glass with DIAMOND-POINT ENGRAVED decoration of a crown, verses from a Jacobite hymn, and the word "Amen". Only about 24 genuine "Amen" glasses are known to exist. Numerous copies have been produced.

Amberg pottery vessel, c.1770 [M]

American Belleek See BELLEEK, AMERICAN.

American China Manufactory
See BONNIN AND MORRIS.

American Chippendale An innovative style of formal furniture unique to North America, with makers active from *c.*1750 to the War of Independence. The name derives from Thomas CHIPPENDALE who achieved renown through publication of his design ideas in the *Gentleman and Cabinet-maker's Director*, first circulated in 1754 and widely read in the US. Many American makers interpreted the style, ignoring most of Chippendale's "Gothick" details, such as blind-fret carving and cluster column legs, and chinoiseries such as pagodas and "Chinamen". The result was a genre that compares to contemporary George III mahogany furniture, but is slightly larger, with carved Rococo elements which are

American Chippendale chest-on-chest, c.1770 [D]

bolder and more pronounced than on English furniture. Standards of manufacture are generally high but vary widely by region and individual maker. The timbers used, the techniques and the treatment of such details as BALL-AND-CLAW feet also vary to a greater of lesser extent between cabinet-makers and regions. Such variations are the subject of considerable documentation.

American Chippendale furniture varies widely in the possibility of attribution – some makers were well-known but many were country cabinet-makers who are now unknown. Some pieces may also have American patriotic associations.

The introduction of BLOCK-FRONT form by the school of John GODDARD in Newport, Rhode Island, exemplifies the early development of this style, which was fully developed by cabinet-makers in New England, particularly Boston and Salem in Massachusetts, New York City and Philadelphia. By the 1760s, Philadelphia had over 100 cabinet-makers, notably Thomas AFFLECK, Benjamin RANDOLPH and William SAVERY, and produced some of the finest American Chippendale furniture, particularly chairs. The term is used less today than in the past and many scholars prefer more precise terms, including "American Rococo".

American Colonial
See COLONIAL STYLE.

American Federal See FEDERAL STYLE.

American Flint Glassworks
An American glassworks established in 1769 by Henry William STIEGEL (1729–85), a German ironmaster and glass-maker who emigrated to the US and established three glassworks in Pennsylvania in the 1760s, including the Mannheim Glassworks (est. 1763). The factory closed in 1774 when Stiegel was sent to debtors' prison. Examples of Stiegel glass are difficult to authenticate

and widely faked. Forms are comparable to contemporary Bohemian vessels, made in low-lead, greenish grey glass.

American football memorabilia
See FOOTBALL, AMERICAN.

American Pottery Company A small factory established in Jersey City, New Jersey, by the Scottish immigrant David Henderson and his brothers in 1828, and active until 1854. The main products were useful wares in robust EARTHENWARE with yellow or ROCKINGHAM (streaky brown) glaze, and some printed ware. Products are normally unmarked.

American Pottery Co. moulded yellow ware pitcher, c.1840 [O]

Amorino (pl. *amorini* Italian: *"little cupids"*) Winged CHERUBS, used in Italian RENAISSANCE ornament and BAROQUE work, commonly on porcelain, bronze and wood-carving. Sometimes only the winged head is used. Derived from Classical sources: a well-known series appears on a Pompeii wall-painting.

Amphora (Greek: *amphoreus*) A two-handled jar with a narrow neck and double handles, used in Classical times to carry oil, wine and water. Jars of amphora shape were made in the Rhineland from AD 720–1190, to export Rhenish wine. With the rediscovery of Classical sites in the early 18th century, the shape appears as a decorative motif, for instance in NEO-CLASSICAL silverware and on furniture.

Attic black figure amphora, c.400 BC [F]

Amphora pottery and porcelain
A German factory founded in 1892 in Turn-Teplitz as Riessner, Stellmacher & Kessel (R.S.K.). The factory made porcelain figures but was chiefly known for earthenware Art Nouveau vases. The factory ceased production at some time during World War II.

Ampulla The Latin name for a type of small vessel made throughout the Roman Empire and used for storing oils and perfumes. Typically, it has a flat base, a round or ovoid body and an elongated neck with one or two handles.

Amstel porcelain factory A porcelain factory in WEESP was bought and moved to Oude Loosdrecht in the Netherlands, in 1771 by Johannes de Mol. When he died in 1782, the factory became a limited company; it was moved to Amstel in 1784 where it continued until 1820. Sometimes called Oude Amstel, it made fine porcelain in the style of Meissen and Sèvres and used "Amstel" as a mark.

Amstel plate, c.1800 [Q, a pair]

Anchor escapement An escapement mechanism of a CLOCK incorporating an arm with two pallets shaped like an anchor. Developed in the mid-17th century, it was used in combination with the PENDULUM in most clocks by c.1800, as a more accurate form of regulation than the VERGE ESCAPEMENT.

Anchor motif An ornamental motif associated with a marine or commercial activity. Also seen as a repeating dart or arrowhead device frequently used in the enrichment of OVOLO or ASTRAGAL mouldings. See also EGG AND DART. With a rope, it is called a "fouled anchor".

Fouled anchor

Pair of cast iron baseball player andirons, American, c.1900 [I]

Andirons (or fire-dogs) Forerunners of the fire basket, two large iron rests that stand in a hearth to contain logs, their fronts often made in reflective material, such as silver, brass, polished steel or PAKTONG. Silver examples are known dating back to the 1660s but are rare.

Anemometer by Negretti & Zambra, England, c.1900 [N]

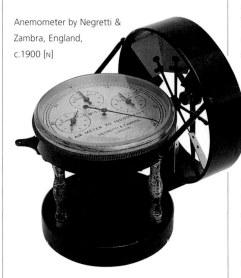

Anemometer/air meter A small circular instrument with eight or twelve blades arranged in a fan or occasionally a circlet of cups and a central dial used for measuring the velocity or the pressure of wind. Portable anemometers were developed in the 19th century.

Aneroid barometer A type of BAROMETER that does not use fluid but has a small vacuumed metal capsule that rises and falls with changes in atmospheric pressure. Invented by the French engineer Lucien Vidie in 1843, this barometer became more popular than the earlier mercury barometer from the late 19th century.

Angarano pottery A group of factories active in the 18th century until the 1780s near Bassano in northern Italy, producing creamware groups and figures. Family names involved include Manardi and Moretti. See also NOVE.

Angell family An English 19th-century firm of silversmiths. Joseph II (d.c.1852) was made a freeman of the Goldsmiths' Company in 1804 and entered his first mark in London in 1804. His best-known work is the "Battle of Issus" Shield (1828), richly embossed and chased with a scene representing the battle (333 BC) between Alexander the Great and Darius of Persia. Joseph III (c.1816–c.1891), his son, took over the family firm in 1849. He specialized in chased and enamelled table centrepieces, tea and coffee sets, claret jugs and other domestic pieces, typically decorated with such motifs as scrolls and strapwork.

Angle barometer A type of barometer made in the 18th century, in which the upper part of the mercury-filled tube is set horizontally at an angle. A modified form of the STICK BAROMETER, the angle barometer gives a more accurate reading since the mercury has to move over a greater distance for the same change in atmospheric pressure. Surviving items are rare as this barometer was never very popular because of its awkward shape.

Angling memorabilia Fishing with rod and line has been practised from earliest times but surviving items tend to date from the 19th century at the earliest. This covers a great variety of items including reels, artificial spinning baits, flies, trade catalogues, art (paintings and prints from the 17th century to present day), carved wooden trophies, stuffed fish in cases, rods and accessories.

Angling memorabilia: tin of salmon-fishing flies, English c.1930 [R]

Anglo-Indian furniture A term used to describe European furniture types – chairs, tables and case furniture – that were made in India from the mid-18th century, notably for Robert Clive (governor of Bengal 1755–60 and 1765–6) and throughout the 19th century, for both wealthy Indian and European clients.

Anglo-Indian table, 19th century [J]

Although English in shape, the furniture was made from local hardwoods, such as EBONY, and often extensively carved with such Indian-inspired motifs as elephants and elaborate foliage, and decorated with ivory inlays. See also VIZAGAPATNAM.

Anglo-Japanese furniture A type of furniture made from c.1870 in Europe when Japan was re-opening to the West, and which reflected the ensuing contemporary fashion for Japanese prints and artifacts. It formed part of the AESTHETIC MOVEMENT and was often made of BAMBOO or EBONIZED wood, with mother-of-pearl inlay and painted panels incorporating Japanese motifs such as birds and blossom and flowers. One of the best-known exponents was E. W. GODWIN, who made exclusive ebonized furniture. At the other end of the market were inexpensive bedroom suites, writing tables and chairs that incorporated Japanese motifs.

Anglo-Moorish furniture A type of furniture produced in Britain in the late 19th century in response to the fashion for smoking rooms and exotic Moorish interiors, as seen at Leighton House, London. Pioneered in Britain by H. & J. Cooper (est. 1875) who produced chairs with elaborately carved panelled backs. By 1884 LIBERTY'S were retailing Anglo-Moorish chairs and tables, and the style was also applied to such pieces as hat stands.

Angoulême porcelain
A factory started in 1780 in the Rue de Bondi in Paris under the protection of the Duc d'Angoulême. Porcelain with simple decoration was made but also some more elaborate pieces, with jaspered decoration simulating agate and tortoiseshell with gilt borders. The factory closed in 1828.

Angoulême sprig cup and saucer, c.1810 [R]

Angoulême sprig A name given to a simple pattern of cornflowers, often found on Parisian "Angoulême", but also used in other factories, especially at the English DERBY factory. While most porcelain factories were not permitted to copy the rich SÈVRES style, the Paris factory of the Duc d'Angoulême was one of nine Parisian studios exempted, and combined several colours and gilding.

An hua A term used in Chinese ceramics meaning "secret" or "veiled" decoration; the designs being visible through transmitted light. Produced either by INCISING the design into the porcelain before GLAZING and FIRING or by painting in white SLIP on the porcelain body. The technique was used in the early MING DYNASTY (1368–1644) and revived in the QING DYNASTY (1644–1912) particularly in the reign of the YONGZHENG emperor (1723–35).

Aniline dye The first synthetic dye, accidentally discovered by British chemist William H. Perkin in 1856. Produced from the oxidization of aniline, a by-product of coal tar, the first artificial colours produced using these dyes were violets through to deep pinks, including the so-called "Perkin's mauve".

Animal furniture A type of furniture made in the late 19th century, in which taxidermists and furniture-makers collaborated to create furniture from dead animals and birds, for example, hollowed-out elephants' feet as waste-paper bins, hall lamps made from bears and monkeys, and lamp bases made from dead birds.

Bronze figure of a horse by Pierre-Jules Mêne (1810–79), 19th century [J]

Anthemion

Animaliers, Les A group of mid-19th-century French sculptors, led by Antoine-Louis BARYE, who specialized in naturalistic representations of animals. Produced in cast-bronze limited editions, these works reacted against the Classical themes then dominating French sculpture. One of the most prolific and successful Animalier sculptors was Pierre-Jules Mêne. The term may now describe any sculptor making small animal bronzes.

Annaberg potteries
A group of factories in Saxony, Germany, in the 16th century, known for a dark brown SALT-GLAZED STONEWARE enamelled in colours over relief-moulded decoration, produced from c.1630 until the early 18th century. Typical shapes are HUMPEN and APOSTLE JUGS, often with ARMORIAL motifs. Wares are often confused with those of the earlier factory of Kreussen, near Bayreuth.

Annamese ware See VIETNAMESE POTTERY.

Annealing A process for strengthening glass or metal. Objects are heated in an "annealing" oven and allowed to cool at a gradual and uniform rate. This alters the arrangement of molecules in the material and makes it more resistant to cracking.

Annulet An architectural term for a narrow flat FILLET or band encircling a COLUMN. It is also used in heraldry for a small ring in a coat of arms.

Ansbach factory Both faience and porcelain were produced in Ansbach, Bavaria, south of Nuremberg (its 18th-century name was Onolzback). Faience of fine quality had been made here since 1710, but in 1757 the Margrave Karl Alexander opened a porcelain factory, bringing in the expertise of some MEISSEN workers. It was soon successful and in 1762 moved into the princely hunting lodge, Bruckberg. Johann Friedrich Kändler, a cousin of the famous Meissen modeller Johann Joachim KÄNDLER was the artistic director and the factory flourished between 1758 and 1777 making good porcelain figures. The porcelain body has a brilliant whiteness and the painting, by such artists as Scholhammer and Stenglein, is particularly good. Flower painters included such artists as Kahl and Schreimuller. Ansbach also sold large amounts of porcelain to the factory at The Hague (1777–90), where it was marked with their signatory stork. The business was in private ownership from c.1807 and finally closed in 1860.

Ansbach pastoral group, c.1768 [Q]

Anthemion A Classical ornament based on the ACANTHUS flower, but similar to a type of PALMETTE resembling the honeysuckle flower and leaf. It was commonly used in Greek and Roman architecture for ornamental banding on friezes, architraves, cornices and the necks of Ionic capitals. Frequently combined with other motifs, it enjoyed renewed popularity in the 18th century and was fashionable for the decorative arts during the NEO-CLASSICAL period.

Antimacassar A covering cloth thrown over the backs of upholstered sofas and chairs, as protection and as ornament. It takes its name from macassar oil, a hair treatment for men during the 19th century and was particularly fashionable during the mid-19th century.

Antimagnetic watch A watch made of non-magnetic metal or in which the MOVEMENT is protected from magnetic flux by a soft inner case. Many parts of a movement are made from steel and are therefore subject to being magnetized or affected by magnetism. This can have an adverse effect on the accuracy of a watch.

Antwerp lace See FLEMISH LACE.

Aogai A Japanese lacquerwork technique introduced c.1620. Small pieces of MOTHER-OF-PEARL from the *Haliotis* mollusc are inlaid into a LACQUER surface. Pieces are selected for their attractive blue/green iridescent hues.

Apostle jug A jug moulded in relief with figures of the Twelve Apostles in niches around the body, found especially in 17th-century German earthenware (e.g. Kreussen) and in the 19th century during the RENAISSANCE REVIVAL period.

Apostle spoon A silver spoon (pewter and brass examples also exist) whose stem ends in the small cast figure of one of the Twelve Apostles or the "master" (Christ).

Rare documentary sets of 13 exist but individual spoons are far more commonly available today. Each saint holds an emblem or symbol of his martyrdom (e.g. St Peter with a key), but these are often damaged or missing. Size and poor quality casting can also make identification difficult. They were made throughout Europe *c.*1500–1700. However, many "apostle" coffee spoons were mass-produced in Britain in the 19th and 20th centuries.

Silver apostle spoon
featuring St Thomas, 1615 [G]

Apothecary jar A glass or earthenware jar used in an apothecary's or chemist's shop, or in early times in the "apothecary" of a monastery. Globular jars with a handle and a spout were for "wet" drugs and those of cylindrical shape were for "dry" drugs. The name of the drug was given on a label. See also ALBARELLO.

Apple wood See FRUITWOOD.

Appliqué (French: "applied") A decorative technique in which pieces of one material are laid onto a foundation of a different material. The seams round appliquéd motifs are often hidden by the use of braids or decorative stitching.

French satin coverlet appliquéd with silk and velvet by the Bernheimer family, early 19th century [G]

Aprey pottery A faience factory in the Haute Marne region of France, founded in 1744 by Jacques Lallemont, Baron d'Aprey and Joseph Lallemont de Villehaut (who is said to have also produced porcelain, but this is not authenticated). The painter Protais Pidoux from MENNECY was responsible for lively floral decoration. The best wares date from *c.*1770–90 with the work of François Olliver from NEVERS and the decorators Jacques Jarry and Antoine Mege. In the mid- to late 19th century earlier moulds were re-used. Marks are Ap, APR, AP and, rarely, APREY. The factory closed in the late 19th century.

Aprey pottery chinoiserie
plate, c.1770 [O]

Apron (also known as a skirt) A shaped, often carved, pierced or decorated, piece of wood found beneath the seat rail of a chair or settee, the FRIEZE rail of a table, or the base of the framework of a piece of CASE FURNITURE.

Apt pottery A French faience and earthenware factory founded in 1728 by César Moulin at Le Castelet, making wares in the English style, including figures and yellow and brown "marbled" and AGATE WARES. It remained in the Moulin family until its closure in 1852. Products were of fine quality, with shapes often inspired by silver wares. Other potteries opened in the area, the best known being those of Elzéar Bennet and La Veuve Arnoux. The area is still a pottery-making centre today.

Aquamanile A medieval bronze or brass EWER, to hold water for washing the hands during meals or religious ceremonies. The finest examples were produced from the 11th to 15th century in the Meuse valley, northern France, and are in the form of lions, stags, mythical beasts such as dragons and GRIFFINS, or mounted knights.

Aquamarine A variety of beryl ranging in colour from pale sea-green to the valuable deep sea-blue, frequently obtained by heating. Aquamarine is highly transparent. Fine crystals are mined in Brazil; other sources include Zambia and Mozambique. Imitations include synthetic blue spinel, blue topaz and glass.

Aquatint of a pastoral scene from
Works of British Artists, 1825 [H, for the book]

Aquatint A popular printing technique from the 1770s onward, particularly for landscapes, so named because the overall effect is of a watercolour wash. Fine speckled gradations of tone are achieved by evenly coating the printing plate with powdered resin prior to immersion in acid. Lighter areas are achieved by stopping the acid attack on the plate with varnish, the darker areas by the greater exposure to or biting of the acid.

Arab Hall, The See ARABIAN STYLE.

Arabesque A pattern of stylized interlaced foliage using fanciful and intricate combinations of flowing lines, flowers, tendrils, spirals, knots and zigzags. Contemporary with STRAPWORK, developed at Fontainebleau, France, in the mid-16th century, the arabesque originates from the Near East and features strongly in European decorative ornament until the early 17th century. Craftsmen came from all over the Middle East and settled in Venice, producing densely decorated engraved and inlaid metalwork. Known as Venetian Saracenic, the style spread through published engravings and was used to decorate metalwork, pottery, marquetry furniture, jewellery and lace.

Arabesque

Arabian style Ornament fashionable in 19th-century Europe, featuring motifs drawn from north African and Middle Eastern cultures. Decorative patterns such as ARABESQUES from Islamic metalwork, textiles and ceramics had been used in Europe since the Renaissance, but interest was renewed in the mid-19th century following the visits of such leading painters as Frederick, Lord Leighton (1830–96) to Arab countries. The best-known Western interpretation of an Islamic interior is the Arab Hall at Leighton House, London (1877–79), featuring vividly coloured and patterned tiles and richly carved wooden screens.

Arabian style table in oak, English, c.1905 [N]

Arad, Ron (b.1951) An Israeli architect and designer who now lives in England and is currently head of furniture design at the Royal College of Art. For "One Off Design" (with Dennis Groves) he made furniture from existing but altered items, e.g. car seats as chairs. His work is now more sculptural and bold and such pieces are made by his own company, Ron Arad Associates. He works mostly in metal, but also with glass and concrete.

Arbor A small revolving shaft or spindle, usually made of steel, in a CLOCK or watch mechanism and on which a PINION or lever is mounted.

Arcade Manufacturing Co. A prolific American manufacturer of CAST IRON toys in Freeport, Illinois, from the 1920s until World War II. Arcade specialized in neat, highly detailed road vehicles whose accuracy was ensured by deals with the full-size manufacturers. Over 250 different toys, usually single or two-piece castings (riveted together), were each made in a variety of sizes, fitted with turning wheels and usually finished with a single colour paint scheme decorated with their name on a paper sticker.

Arcadian pottery The trade name used on "souvenir" wares made by the firm Arkinstall & Sons Ltd, of Trent Bridge Pottery, Stoke on Trent, Staffordshire (1904–24). They made inexpensive wares in the style of W.H. GOSS, were taken over by Robinson & Leadbeater 1908, then by A.J. Robinson & Sons and later by Cauldon Ltd in 1925. The Arcadian mark disappeared in 1937.

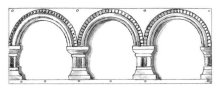

Arcadian dish with racehorse, English, 1921 [S]

Arcading A series of linked arches – pointed, round-headed and occasionally interlaced – supported on COLUMNS or piers. The arcade may be free-standing, as in covered walks and cloisters, servng a decorative and structural purpose. Blind arcades, which are attached to a wall, are purely decorative, and are also a popular ornament on chair backs and applied on the panels of chests.

Arches and piers making up arcading

Arcanist In alchemy, a general term meaning an initiate into a secret sought by alchemists, originally the search for a method of synthesizing gold. After the discovery of PORCELAIN in Europe by BÖTTGER in the early 18th century it was used in particular in reference to the formula for making porcelain.

Archambo, Peter A HUGUENOT of unknown birthplace and date (*d.*1759) who became a "Free" Goldsmith (silversmith) in London in 1720. An important maker, producing a range of high quality, domestic silver until *c.*1750 when his son Peter (1724–68) entered his first mark after his apprenticeship with Paul De LAMERIE.

Architect's table A type of specialized table, most commonly made in walnut or mahogany, introduced in the early 18th century for artists and draughtsmen. They were made with hinged leaves or retractable slides and incorporated either an adjustable, often double-hinged top, an easel top or an adjustable rising top. The tables also often had circular brass candle stands that could swing out to provide extra light.

Architrave A term that describes the lowest section of the upper part, or entablature, of an architectural order and can also refer to the MOULDING round a window, door or other opening in a building or a piece of furniture.

Argand lamp A type of lamp invented in Switzerland in 1784 by Aimé Argand and subsequently manufactured in France, Britain and the US. The tubular hollow wick, covered with a chimney and fed with oil by a tube from the reservoir, ensured a plentiful air supply, which in turn ensured that the oil burned quickly, producing a bright light.

Argentan lace FRENCH NEEDLE LACE from Argentan in Normandy. This fine 18th-century lace has delicate floral designs on a hexagonal ground. It was used for the fashion and boudoir flounces popular before the French Revolution.

Argyll, Argyle Any small container for gravy, often made in silver or old Sheffield plate, with some means of retaining or producing heat e.g. hot iron, burner or hot-water jacket. Named after one of the Dukes of Argyll who had an aversion to cold gravy, these vessels are first recorded *c.*1760 and enjoyed great favour during the reign of King George III (1760–1820).

Silver Argyll, English, 1783 [E]

Argy-Rousseau, Joseph-Gabriel (1885–1953) A French glass-maker particularly renowned for his PÂTE-DE VERRE and pâte-de-cristal. Such pieces are usually signed "G. Argy-Rousseau". However, he also produced vessels in clear glass decorated with coloured enamels, which are signed "G.A.R". He is best known for his ART DECO figures and vases.

Argy-Rousseau pâte de verre vase, c.1910 [G]

Ariel glass First introduced in 1930 by the Swedish glass firm ORREFORS. The glass centre is sandblasted with INTAGLIO patterns of abstract, figurative or animal subjects. These are then cased in another layer of clear glass leaving the pattern as an air pocket or bubble. Sometimes the patterns are highlighted with colours.

Arita porcelain factories
In the early 17th century, Korean potters settled in and around Arita, in the Hizen province of Japan. Finding abundant local CHINA CLAY and fuel, they established kilns for producing STONEWARES and PORCELAIN. The earliest Arita porcelains (*c.*1620–40) imitate contemporary Chinese wares of the late MING DYNASTY (1368–1644) as well as

Korean stonewares. The ware produced before exports began is known as Shoki-Imari.

In the late 17th century, Arita became increasingly important, producing BLUE AND WHITE, IMARI and KAKIEMON porcelain for export to Europe. These were transported to the port of Imari, shipped to the Dutch trading centre at Nagasaki and then to Europe. Wares include GARNITURES of large vases, dishes, bowls, plates, EWERS, figures and animals. The trade reached its zenith *c.*1700. With increasing competition from the Chinese kilns at JINGDEZHEN and changing tastes in Europe, Japan's export trade declined in importance although pieces continued to reach the West throughout the 19th century, including wares from other important centres in the Arita region such as HIRADO and NABESHIMA.

Arita octagonal porcelain jar, c.1680 [C]

Ark A piece of English storage furniture, first made in the 13th century and used until the 19th, in the form of a wooden bin or chest, constructed usually from pegged split boards of oak or elm, with a canted or roof-shaped lid and used for storing meal or flour.

Art Deco style

Elegance, innovation, excitement: these are some of the words associated with the Art Deco style. Originating before World War I, it was officially launched in Paris in 1925. Over the next decade, its stylized, geometric forms spread throughout the decorative arts, especially in the US.

Inspiration and originality

The term Art Deco was used from the 1960s to describe, in retrospect, the style identified from the landmark *Exposition Internationale des Arts Décoratifs et Industriels Modernes* held in Paris in 1925. The exhibition was dedicated to works that showed "new inspiration and real originality". It had initially been planned for 1915, but was postponed because of the outbreak of World War I. The Art Deco style had been gradually evolving from *c*.1908 and many items now accepted as pure Art Deco, for instance furniture and objects by Jacques-Emile RUHLMANN and Paul IRIBE, were of pre-war design.

The exhibition attracted several million visitors. Over 150 exhibition stands or pavilions were constructed in central Paris: the fact that they were only temporary inspired widespread use of new materials such as laminates and plastics. The Citröen company lit the Eiffel Tower with thousands of electric light bulbs (an extravagant novelty at the time), while the couturier Paul Poiret, based on his barge *Amour* moored in the Seine, played a "perfume piano" which gave off intoxicating perfumes that varied with every tune played. Works by the leading French designers, such as Ruhlmann, René LALIQUE and André GROULT were shown to acclaim, as was silver by Jean PUIFORCAT and Charles CHRISTOFLE and glass by BACCARAT. In contrast to such luxury goods, the pavilion designed by the Swiss-born LE CORBUSIER exemplified his vision of a new, minimalist architecture, filled with mass-produced furniture.

The British stand was mainly ARTS AND CRAFTS influenced and attracted little interest. The contribution of British design to Art Deco is generally considered to be the late style of Charles Rennie MACKINTOSH, including his geometric designs of 1916 for Derngate, a house in Northampton.

Art Deco bookcase in calamander wood
French, c.1925 [c]

Silvered-bronze figure of "Amazon"
by Marcel-André Bouraine, a leading French
Art Deco sculptor, c.1930 [H]

This silver fruit dish with glass liner by Ercui
illustrates French enthusiasm for tableware
in Art Deco style, 1930s [P]

Recognizing the style

Early Art Deco designs of c.1925 featured rounded and oval shapes in motifs such as formalized baskets of flowers, rosebuds, leaping deer and strings of pearls. Tightly whorled spirals, tassels, stylized sunbursts and lightning bolts were also popular. As the style developed, motifs became increasingly geometric, or reflected an enthusiasm for jazz, travel and abstract art.

Deer in stylized setting

Sunburst motif

Geometric motif in a brooch

The origins of Art Deco were diverse. Movements in art such as post-Impressionism, Cubism, Fauvism and Futurism all had an impact on the style. Also contributory were the BALLETS RUSSES, the new jazz music, the excavation of Tutenkhamen's tomb, the exotic cultures of Africa and South America, and the machine, in particular new forms of transport such as the automobile and aeroplane.

Clean geometric lines

The best Art Deco is characterized by a clarity of form that is angular and clean, with stylized striking decoration and stunning quality. The manufacturers at the upper end of the market concentrated on high quality pieces veneered in exotic woods such as AMBOYNA and Macassar EBONY, combined with IVORY, SHAGREEN, ENAMEL and LACQUER. After *c.*1925 they also used new materials such as tubular steel, but continued to work in a traditional style. The French liner *Normandie*, launched in 1932 and later destroyed in World War II, epitomizes French Art Deco style at its finest, with lavish interiors by Jules Leleu, panelled glass and mirrors by Lalique, ironwork by Edgar BRANDT and hundreds of chairs upholstered in AUBUSSON tapestry with an Art Deco design of flowers from the French colonies.

Art Deco wine or cocktail glass, c.1930 [s]

Art Deco in the US

The US declined to take part in the 1925 Paris exhibition, on the grounds that it could not meet the entry requirements. However, touring exhibitions of Art Deco soon reached US museums and department stores and its styles were also brought over by immigrant architects and designers. At first, copies of French pieces were made. But by the late 1920s, "Deco" style, as it came to be known, was seen in a more purely American idiom in furniture by such influential designers as Donald DESKEY and Eero SAARINEN.

It was above all in the architectural triumph of the "skyscraper" and its associated products that Deco was assimilated. Exterior shapes were echoed on doors, light-fittings and murals, and also on furniture such as Paul Frankl's 1930s' "Skyscraper" line, where maple, plastics and metallic finishes were applied on multi-functional units which, ideally suited for New York apartments, combined cupboards, display units and bookcases. A coffee service made by the GORHAM MANUFACTURING COMPANY used triangles of contrasting metals and was named "The Lights and Shadows of Manhattan" in tribute to the silhouettes of New York's tallest buildings.

A further phase of Art Deco in the US was exemplified by the "streamlining" designs of Norman BEL GEDDES. In 1934 it was proposed to President Roosevelt that streamlining should be adopted as a symbol of the restructuring of the US economy after the Depression. The World Fair Exposition of 1939 became a public affirmation of this development.

Coffee-pot by the British Art Deco designer Clarice Cliff, 1930 [L]

New technology

An alternative to the luxury Art Deco style developed, especially in Germany where from 1919 members of the Bauhaus designed pieces for industrial production using new materials such as plywood, tubular steel and aluminium. This influence spread to the US, where designers used these and other new materials to create unique pieces of furniture and prototypes for mass-produced items such as electric lights, vacuum cleaners, radios and refrigerators.

Bauhaus-inspired table lamp, c.1930 [M]

Vase by Weller of Zanesville, Ohio, with typical low-relief decoration and sherbet-pink glaze, c.1930 [o]

Armada chest
A 19th-century term to describe a heavy iron-bound strongbox, often with complicated locks and hidden keyholes, that was made in Germany, Austria and Flanders in the 16th and 17th centuries.

Armadio An Italian term to describe a cupboard, originally derived from a CASSONE or chest with two doors instead of a lid. From the 16th century, the armadio developed into a two-storey cupboard with PILASTERS.

Armet A type of helmet that completely enclosed the head, used during the 15th and 16th centuries. It comprised a skull, visor, cheekpieces and sometimes a circular guard at the back called a rondel.

Armillary sphere
A skeletal globe in which rings represent the poles, equator, ecliptic and tropics of Cancer and Capricorn, with a central sphere representing the Earth or the Sun. Used for teaching and demonstrating astronomy, globes were often made from pasteboard or brass. Models vary in size from floor-standing to small portable examples.

Gilt-brass armillary sphere, Italian 17th century [C]

Armoire A French term that appears to have been used as early as the 13th century for a storage cupboard. From the

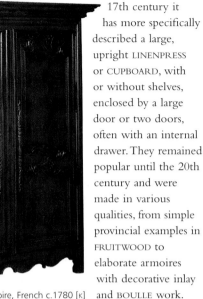
Provincial armoire, French c.1780 [K]

17th century it has more specifically described a large, upright LINENPRESS or CUPBOARD, with or without shelves, enclosed by a large door or two doors, often with an internal drawer. They remained popular until the 20th century and were made in various qualities, from simple provincial examples in FRUITWOOD to elaborate armoires with decorative inlay and BOULLE work.

Armoire à deux corps A French term for a type of CASE FURNITURE made in two sections for ease of transport. It consisted of two cupboards – a larger, lower cupboard on which sits a narrower, recessed upper one – both with two doors.

Armorial ware Ceramics decorated with a coat of arms. Armorials have been popular on European pottery from the RENAISSANCE with examples seen on Italian MAIOLICA, SLIPWARE, English and Dutch DELFT, and on porcelain from the 18th century. The term is most often associated, however, with CHINESE EXPORT WARE, often decorated with the arms and crests of Europeans and Americans from the late 17th century through to the 19th.

Armour Equipment made to protect the body during combat, originally from natural materials such as wood, hide, horn, bone and textiles. Metals were used from the Bronze Age. The use of armour declined with increasing use of firearms and artillery from the 1650s and the development of tactics demanding swift deployment of forces.

Chinese export porcelain armorial plate, c.1720 [F, for 6]

Arnhem pottery Founded by Johannes van Kerckhoff in 1755, this factory at Arnhem in Holland was taken over by J. Hanau in 1756. Arnhem pottery made a type of TIN-GLAZED EARTHENWARE usually decorated in blue and formerly attributed to Amsterdam. Active until 1773, it produced wares in the manner of DELFT, using a deep blue and a good quality manganese, as well as wares similar to those of STRASBOURG painted with ENAMEL COLOURS. Scenes after ROCOCO prints were decorated in HIGH-TEMPERATURE COLOURS. The mark is a cockerel – not to be confused with a similar mark used by CANTAGALLI.

Arnold, John An eminent English clock- and watchmaker (1736–99). In 1764 he presented to King George III a watch with repeating work mounted into a finger ring. His career was dedicated to the advance of accurate horology and he invented a form of spring detent ESCAPEMENT used in CHRONOMETERS. He was succeeded by his son John Roger Arnold, also a clock- and watchmaker.

Arnoux, Joseph-Léon F. See MINTON.

Arraiolos A Portuguese carpet-making centre for the production of woollen embroidered carpets in the Alentejo. The earliest and rarest examples are from the 17th century. Production declined in the 19th century but revived in the 20th century and continues today. Carpets display a range of floral and folkloric motifs, birds and animals.

Arras porcelain factory A factory in the Pas de Calais, France. It was founded in 1770 by Joseph-François Boussomaert of Lille who made SOFT-PASTE porcelain intending to compete with Tournai, but produced only medium quality tableware, mostly decorated in UNDERGLAZE blue. It closed in 1790.

Art furniture oak buffet
by Godwin, c.1870 [A]

walnut or oak, that reacted against historical revival styles and depended on form rather than decoration. It anticipated the ARTS AND CRAFTS movement and also had strong links with the AESTHETIC movement. Early pieces often used ebonized or black woods. Major exponents were E.W. GODWIN and COLLINSON & LOCK.

Art glass A term used from the mid-19th century for glass that is primarily decorative rather than functional, with an emphasis on high quality materials, design and craftsmanship. It also describes the contemporary fashionable coloured glass, e.g. AMBERINA and BURMESE, which was produced in the US in the last quarter of

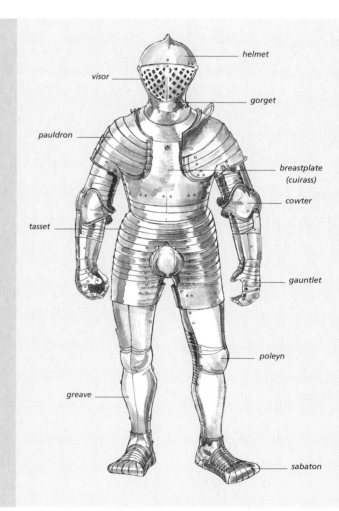

Art-glass vase by de Vez, French c.1890 [K]

the 19th century. Both DAUM FRÈRES' and Émile GALLÉ were influenced by art glass.

[1]Articulated A term used to describe the eyes in Classical sculpture when the pupils are clearly delineated rather than being blank and smooth.

[2]Articulated The body of a doll or figure with jointed limbs.

[3]Articulated A type of jewellery held together by armour jointing.

Artificial porcelain See SOFT-PASTE PORCELAIN.

Arras tapestry factories Arras, an ancient tapestry-weaving town in northern France, was once capital of the province of Artois in Burgundy. The term "thread of arras" came to mean the finest quality thread from which tapestries were made. The town was producing HIGH-WARP tapestries as early as the 11th century. The first written reference comes in 1311 when a Countess of Burgundy ordered "figured cloth" in Arras. In 1394 Arras came into the possession of Burgundian Dukes, who became patrons of the tapestry-weaving industry. The term "Arras" has become synonymous with Gothic wall hangings; so valuable were they that in 1396 Arras tapestries were traded with Bajazet Sultan of Turkey for the lives of captured Burgundian and French nobles. Arras workshops went into decline after the town was sacked by the French in 1477 and finally closed in the early 16th century.

Art Deco See pp.26–27.

Art furniture A term introduced in the 1860s in Britain and America – coined by Charles EASTLAKE – to describe simple architect-designed furniture, usually in

Armour

The development of armour has always been a trade-off between protection and weight versus mobility. From the 12th century European knights wore metal helmets and heavy chain mail consisting of looped metal rings. It was expensive to make so a thick leather breastplate was often worn instead. Chain mail and scale armour gave good protection as well as being flexible. Plate armour (as shown right), which was introduced in the 14th century, gave better protection but was heavier and reduced mobility. The pieces had to be either separate or articulated at the joints to allow movement.

helmet
visor
gorget
pauldron
breastplate
(cuirass)
cowter
tasset
gauntlet
poleyn
greave
sabaton

Mahogany cabinet with "naturalistic" motifs on the panels by Stuttgart Möbel Fabrik, German c.1880 [E]

Theresienthal liqueur glass with transparent enamelling, c.1900 [N]

Art Nouveau

One of the most appealing of styles, Art Nouveau was both a European and an American phenomenon. From around 1890 to 1914 this international style strove to be consciously radical.

Origins of the style

The name Art Nouveau, which came to mean all design that was organic, sinuous and asymmetric, was taken from the title of the shop of one of the style's leading exponents and entrepreneurs, Samuel Bing, whose Maison de l'Art Nouveau opened in Paris in 1895. Other countries had their own names: in Germany it was Jugendstil ("youth culture"), in Holland it was Nieuwe Kunst, in Spain it was Modernista and in Italy it was called Stile Liberty after the London store.

The major sources of inspiration came from nature, Symbolist painting and literature, the ARTS AND CRAFTS MOVEMENT, Japanese art, the ROCOCO period and the GOTHIC REVIVAL. There were also national characteristics: for example, Celtic art was influential in Britain and Holland was inspired by its Indonesian colonies.

However, for all those differences there was one unifying factor and that was nature. This sprang from the 19th century's advances in the science of natural history, which were accessible to a wider public due to increased availability of magazines and books. Travellers were going further afield and rare and exotic plants were exhibited in heated glasshouses in many of the major cities. Several leading designers were also botanists (Emile GALLÉ, Christopher DRESSER, who was a doctor of botany, and Eugene Grasset).

Nature could be represented in a literal way such as in a "Wisteria" or "Dragonfly" lamp by Louis Comfort TIFFANY, or the effects of the natural world could be copied for decorative effect, as in his LAVA GLASS. The iridescent finishes of LOETZ-WITWE and Tiffany were inspired by ancient glass excavated from the ground that had acquired a mother-of-pearl-like sheen. Art Nouveau furniture used natural forms in elaborate inlays, although the best uses the organic form in its structure rather than as mere decoration. Jewellers such as René LALIQUE – who also made glass – created the most wonderful designs inspired by nature, depicting flora, fauna and figures in semi-precious and precious stones, gold and enamels.

Daum Frères cameo-glass vase, c.1890 [L]

The influence of Symbolism

The 19th-century literary movement of Symbolism, with its mystical and spiritual content, provided the power behind Art Nouveau emblems. In the 1880s, Symbolist writing and painting came together and numerous magazines sprang up to show this new affinity, including *La Plume* (1888) in France and later in England, *The Yellow Book* (1894), which featured the work of the illustrator Aubrey Beardsley. Symbolist art is not just about what can be seen, it

Liberty silver and enamel
picture frame in Celtic style
by Archibald Knox, 1904 [I]

is as much about what cannot, the suggested and the implied. France was the chief home of the Symbolist Movement and Paul Gauguin is perhaps the most well known painter, although Gustav Klimt, Odilon Redon, Jan Toorop, Ferdinand Khnopff and Edvard Munch were also Symbolist painters.

Art Nouveau often displays an erotic or sensual quality. This comes from a combination of nature and fantasy, mixing beast and human, or human and plant forms together. One of the most commonly seen motifs is the "Art Nouveau Maiden", with her long diaphanous robes and flowing hair. This female form was used in all media. The German metalwork company WMF draped her around the side of picture frames and fashioned her into candlesticks and candelabra. René Lalique made her as part-dragonfly and part-woman in gold, PLIQUE-À-JOUR enamels, chrysoprase (an apple-green gemstone), MOONSTONES and diamonds. Alphonse MUCHA's posters are resplendent with these beautiful women with their long hair and perfect figures. Raoul Larche, the sculptor, immortalized the US dancer Loïe Fuller in gilt bronze, capturing the movement of her many long scarves as she danced at the Folies-Bergères. The erotic dancer Isadora Duncan was another inspiration.

Outstanding Art Nouveau designers

The Frenchman Émile Gallé is one of the best known of the virtuoso glass-makers. A keen botanist and patriot, he took much of his inspiration from his beloved province, Lorraine. His best designs for glass are remarkable and make use of a wide variety of glass-decorating techniques such as CAMEO, wheel carving, *marquetrie-sur-verre* (in which coloured lumps of glass are pressed into the heated body of the piece) and MARTELÉ. He also designed furniture, particularly excelling in marquetry. Hector GUIMARD (who designed the entrances to the Paris Metro) and Louis MAJORELLE are two of the greats of Art Nouveau design, their work being highly organic yet tightly controlled. Elsewhere, Belgian architects Victor Horta and Henry VAN DER VELDE, Charles Rennie MACKINTOSH and the MACDONALD sisters in Scotland, Josef HOFFMANN and the WIENER WERKSTÄTTE in Austria, the Germans Richard RIEMERSCHMID and August ENDELL, Louis SULLIVAN and Louis Comfort TIFFANY in the US, Archibald KNOX and J.S. HENRY in England, and Antoni GAUDI in Spain all brought their own unique artistry to the style.

Hot enamel Art Nouveau
Revival pendant
necklace with
characteristic
insect motif,
1970s [R]

Recognizing the style

Art Nouveau took many of its motifs from nature, but nature seen through eyes looking for the sensuous and erotic – exotic animal and insect shapes and languid figures of women. Plant motifs in particular capture a sense of movement and growth with entwined stems and buds depicted at the point of bursting into bloom.

Femme-fleur

Dragonfly
motif

Sinuous flower stem

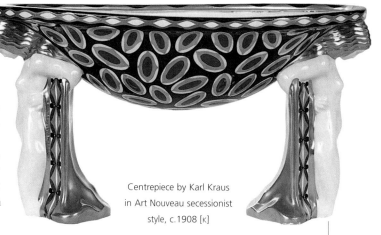

Centrepiece by Karl Kraus
in Art Nouveau secessionist
style, c.1908 [K]

Arts and Crafts

The Arts and Crafts Movement began in England in the second half of the 19th century. Based on aesthetic and moral principles, it had a deep impact on the applied arts in Europe and America, both now and then.

Workshop of the world

The term "Arts and Crafts" comes from the Exhibition Society of the same name that held its first show in 1888. The idea of such an exhibition was said to stem from a letter that the art and social critic John Ruskin (1819–1900) wrote to William MORRIS. The ART WORKERS' GUILD sponsored the Society.

In the middle of the 19th century Britain was the most advanced industrialized nation in the world. When London staged the Great Exhibition of 1851, for which half the exhibits came from Britain and her colonies, it was a celebration of the productivity of man and machine. For many, such a show was a marvel and over three million people viewed it. However, some were not so impressed. Mechanical advances had provided consumer goods for the burgeoning middle classes, but had separated the buyer from the craftsman. Now the manufacturer made the decisions. John Ruskin and William Morris, among others, pointed out the lamentable lack of design quality. Most of the exhibits were over-decorated versions of earlier styles. Protesters also objected to factory methods, which they believed were soul-destroying and undermined the creative process and pride of workmanship.

It was architects who first rose to the challenge. Most of the important designers of the movement – Philip WEBB, C.R. ASHBEE, C.F.A. VOYSEY, W.R. LETHABY, Ernest GIMSON, Sidney and Ernest BARNSLEY and William BENSON – had architectural training. William Morris began his career articled to architects G.E. Street.

One of the design cornerstones of the movement was "fitness for purpose". This meant that the purpose or function dictated the design. There was no point, for example, in heavily decorating the legs of a dining table if it was to be surrounded by chairs and people or in making a chair with an elaborately carved SPLAT if it was uncomfortable. The Movement was not against decoration as such, but insisted that it should be appropriate. In the case of furniture, for instance, they often used the construction methods of MORTISE AND TENON or butterfly joints as decoration. Before machinery had usurped the craftsman, artisans had taken pride in concealing the evidence of their own hand, but now to be visibly handmade became a sign of quality.

Coffeepot by Benham & Froude, designed by Christopher Dresser, to combine easy pouring with uncluttered and aesthetic lines, c.1885 [J]

Pilkington Royal Lancastrian monochrome bowl designed to be simple, beautiful and functional by W.S. Mycock, c.1900 [N]

Recognizing the style

The Arts and Crafts Movement revived many motifs from the Middle Ages. They incorporated ornament and designs from medieval churches and castles and English motifs such as daisies, roses and rabbits into patterns.

Stylized
heraldic beast

English
wild rose

Sturdy but elegant Arts and Crafts oak chair, c.1900 [N]

Art pottery The term for handmade and/or hand-decorated ceramics. It is often used for late 19th-century and also 20th-century pieces such as POOLE. The Victorian era saw the increased mechanization of the STAFFORDSHIRE POTTERIES and wares were mass-produced, moulded and printed. A premium was therefore placed on hand-crafted pieces. The work of small potteries such as MARTIN BROTHERS and William DE MORGAN became sought after. The larger factories, noting their success, introduced their own handmade ranges. DOULTON and MINTON proved particularly successful. In the US, companies such as ROOKWOOD and FULPER produced art pottery from the start of the 20th century.

Poole pottery earthenware vase designed by Ruth Pavely, 1956–57 [o]

Art Union, The Art Unions were societies established in Britain to promote fine and applied art. The Art Union of London was founded in 1836. Artists were awarded prizes and subscribers received their works via a lottery system.

Art Workers' Guild A group established in 1884 in London by like-minded architects, artists and craftsmen. Nearly all the major figures of the ARTS AND CRAFTS Movement, including William MORRIS, were members. The guild still exists.

Art Workers' Guild of America Modelled on the English ART WORKERS' GUILD, the US guild was established in Providence in 1885 by John Aldrich (industrialist), S. Burleigh (artist and designer) and C.W. Stetson (painter).

Aryballos A small ancient Greek vase to hold oil or perhaps perfume. It had a globular body and short narrow neck with a disc-shaped top and a flat vertical handle.

Aryballos

Arzberg porcelain factories There were four factories at the industrial centre of Arzberg in Bavaria, Germany. The first was founded in 1839 but it was nearly a century later that the area came to prominence. In December 1928 the Arzberg Porcelain Factory began making simple, timeless tableware and vases. The "Arzberg 1382" service, designed by Hermann Gretsch (1895–1950) in 1931, is still produced today.

Ash (*Fraxinus excelsior*) A wood varying from a light honey colour to mid-brown. It bends well when steamed and is used for inexpensive country furniture, chairs in particular. Many WINDSOR chairs have ash members. Few pieces in ash have survived from before the 18th century as the wood is susceptible to worm.

Ash, Gilbert (1717–85) A cabinet-maker in New York City, specializing in WINDSOR and other chairs including MAHOGANY ones of high ROCOCO style. Some have survived, bearing the maker's label. Ash was succeeded by his son, Thomas (d.1815).

Ashbee, Charles Robert (1863–1942) An English architect, designer, romantic socialist, teacher and writer. He was a major figure in the ARTS AND CRAFTS Movement. He taught in the East End of London and founded the Guild and School of Handicrafts (1887–95). The Guild and School was re-formed in

C.R. Ashbee silver porringer and cover, c.1900 [i]

Chipping Campden, Gloucestershire as a community (1902–08). Ashbee believed in the integrity of the craftsman and all artifacts were handmade to a high standard. He was the principal designer and excelled in silver and jewellery and, to a lesser extent, furniture. After the closure of the Guild, Ashbee focused more on architecture.

Ashbury metal An alloy of TIN with antimony and zinc, resembling PEWTER. It was used in the late 18th and early 19th century for spoons, small boxes, buttons and buckles.

Ashtead Potteries Ltd Factory founded in Surrey after World War I to provide employment for disabled servicemen. Professional potters tutored the production of tableware and smaller decorative EARTHENWARE pieces. It made Winnie the Pooh nursery wares from c.1920 and figurative subjects c.1930. The factory closed in 1935.

Ashworth & Bros, George L. A ceramic company based at Broad Street, Hanley, Staffordshire, 1862–1968. They made EARTHENWARE and ironstone. The firm succeeded Morley & Ashworth (1858–60), which had acquired the rights to the MASON patent for ironstone, the Mason moulds and other materials on the formation of G.L. Ashworth & Bros.

In 1860 they mostly produced Mason-type earthenwares decorated with TRANSFER PRINTS and coloured, although the firm is listed in some 19th-century directories as making porcelain. In March 1968 the old mark was replaced by Mason's Ironstone China Ltd and since 1973 the company has been part of the WEDGWOOD group.

Asparagus tongs A silver or silver-plated 18th- and early 19th-century utensil, either scissor-like or of U-section, with narrow, corrugated grips to hold on to slippery asparagus spears.

Silver asparagus tongs, English 1808 [K]

Aspidistra stand A deliberately "rustic" container supported on three or four legs designed to hold a plant pot. Made of brightly coloured pottery, varnished wood and bamboo, they were introduced in the last quarter of the 19th century, when the fashion for aspidistras was at its height.

Asprey A firm of jewellers and silversmiths with royal warrants, established in New Bond Street, London, c.1804, retailing high quality merchandise. In the 1990s it opened new premises in New York and Hong Kong. It amalgamated with Garrards, the crown jewellers, after the collapse of the Far East markets c.1998.

Assay The testing of gold or silver, to determine the standard of purity and safeguard against adulteration. As pure silver or gold is too soft for general use it must be mixed with other metals. Testing assesses the alloy for accepted or legal minimum fineness, body of known weight and properties. Sophisticated chemical analysis is carried out today but traditional methods used comparisons with control samples of known physical properties such as weight. The removal of a tiny piece of silver for assaying may leave a wriggly groove known as the assay groove. See also HALLMARK.

Assyrian motifs Originating in Assyrian architecture (c.721–633 BC) and playing a key role in Classical Greek ornament, these include the lotus, ROSETTE, winged bull, lion and eagle, the Tree of Life, and the DIAPER. Filtered through Greek prototypes, they indirectly influenced decoration in the NEO-CLASSICAL period. Popular interest followed archeological discoveries published in the mid-19th century and Assyrian motifs were used in jewellery, metalwork, furniture and architecture.

Astbury, John (1686–1743) A potter from Staffordshire who, with his son Thomas, from c.1720 applied coloured "sprigging" (separately made relief ornament, such as trailing vines) onto a red or brown body, which was then covered with a traditional lead glaze. "Astbury" is occasionally found incised or impressed on red earthenwares of c.1760–80. The term "Astbury ware" describes earthenware models of horses, figure jugs and useful wares covered with the same lead glaze of yellowish tone, made c.1730–80. Other potters of this name worked in Staffordshire; most wares are unmarked.

Asprey silver desk clock, 1902 [L]

Astbury–Whieldon A generic term for 18th-century Staffordshire figures associated with John ASTBURY and Thomas WHIELDON, decorated in relief and lead-glazed.

Astragal (also known as bead moulding) A small MOULDING with a semicircular section used on furniture and metalwork, often enriched with BEAD AND REEL ornament. The shaped profile is used to underscore a difference in planes, or to provide decorative bands of light and shade as an accent or embellishment. Bead mouldings side by side evolve into REEDING. The glazing bars of bookcases are often of this shape.

Brass astrolabe, 1691 [D]

Astrolabe A flat circular, usually brass, instrument used to measure the altitude of the Sun, Moon and stars, introduced to Europe by Islamic peoples in the 10th century. There are two types: spherical (only one complete example is known to exist) and planispheric. The outer edge has a scale divided 0–360° with an alidade, or rule, fixed to the centre with a pair of sighting vanes. It also has a rotating fretted disc (rete), containing a number of star pointers.

Astronomical dial
See EQUINOCTIAL DIAL.

Asuka period A Japanese period (AD 538–645), noted for the cultural advances championed by the Buddhist scholar and statesman, Prince Shotoku (573–621).

Athénienne Originally a Classical incense burner in the form of a three-legged tripod, sometimes with a lidded basin. It was adapted in the late 18th century for use as a TORCHÈRE or JARDINIÈRE. Developed as part of the NEO-CLASSICAL vogue, they remained popular into the early 19th century. During the REGENCY, wooden examples were often painted to resemble bronze or marble. See also CASSOLETTE.

Athénienne, English early 19th century [H]

Atlas A bound collection of MAPS named after a Titan in Greek mythology who was forced to bear the heavens on his shoulders. Although manuscript sea charts (portolans) had been bound together from the 14th century, the earliest printed atlas was the 1477 Bologna edition of PTOLEMY'S *Geographia*. In the mid-16th century, various Italian publishers issued collections of maps, but the first truly modern atlas – with up-to-date and uniformly scaled maps – was ORTELIUS' 1570 *Theatrum Orbis Terrarum* (Theatre of the World). MERCATOR'S 1585 *Atlas* was the first book to use the word "Atlas". A highpoint of atlas production was the BLAEU *Atlas Maior* (Grand Atlas) of 1662.

Atmos clock A type of clock patented in 1913 in Switzerland, in which the MOVEMENT is powered by slight variations in atmospheric pressure or temperature. Made from 1926 by the Swiss firm Jaeger-le-Coultre, it was developed primarily as an extremely accurate timekeeper.

Atterbury & Co. A US glassworks founded in 1859 in Pittsburgh, making clear PRESSED and CUT GLASS tablewares. Also known as the White House Works, it closed in 1893.

Attick A supplementary architectural order used on the highest storey, supported with COLUMNS, PILASTERS or sculpted figures. It often features as the open loggia of Renaissance *palazzi*.

Attwell, Mabel Lucie
(1879–1964) An English illustrator of annuals and gift books. From 1911–64 she designed postcards for Valentine's of Dundee. She developed a genre of "chubby" children in situations with adult overtones. Her designs for ceramics were made by SHELLEY.

"Boo-boo" Pixie milk-jug by Attwell, 1928 [N]

Aubusson carpets Carpet-weaving began *c*.1740 in this French town with SAVONNERIE-style piled carpets, but these were of inferior quality. In 1771 Aubusson began to weave the *tapis ras* (FLATWEAVE carpets) for which it became famous. During the First Empire (1804–15) motifs from Classical antiquity, BEES and military TROPHIES were used. Under Louis Philippe (1830–48) designs were more intricate and used stronger colours: brown, dark red, olive green and gold. The Second Empire (1852–70) heralded softer colours. Late 19th-century examples have pink and beige floral designs, often within a red surround. Aubusson, in the Massif Central, continues to produce fine carpets, often for specific commissions.

Aubusson tapestries Small workshops grouped into guilds wove tapestries in Aubusson from the early 16th century. In 1665 the town was granted the title of royal manufactory, but unlike GOBELINS or BEAUVAIS, it provided for a local clientele, producing less expensive LOW-WARP tapestries. Made in a simpler style in coarser yarns, the tapestries were known as *rustique* and depicted verdures and some biblical and mythological subjects. By the mid-18th century Aubusson's simpler style was in tune with middle-class taste. Tapestries are still produced and restored by hand in Aubusson.

Audran, Claude III (1658–1734) A French designer and decorator. From 1696 he designed elegant and exuberant decorations for the royal palaces of Louis XIV. He designed the suite of GROTESQUE ornament for the GOBELINS tapestries *Portières des Dieux* (1699–1711) and the *Douze Mois* grotesques for the Dauphin at Meudon (1708).

Audubon, Jean Jacques F. (1785–1851) A French ornithologist, artist and naturalist who went to America in 1803 to enter business but concentrated on

Aubusson tapestry, 18th century [H]

sketching North American birds. In 1826 he went to Europe to seek patrons and publishers. In London he attracted a subscription from King George IV for his renowned illustrated volumes of *The Birds Of America*. His reputation established, he settled in New York working on further ornithology print books until his death.

Plate of Roseate Spoonbill from drawings for *The Birds of America* by Audubon, 1827–38 [A, for set of 435]

Auffenwerth, Johann (d.1728) A German enameller in Augsburg. He was a HAUSMALER artist, painting in his own workshop decorating both Meissen and Priental porcelain and faience, predominantly in gold and sometimes silver, with CHINOISERIE subjects. His daughters, Sabina and Anna Elisabeth Auffenwerth (later Wald), were also "outside decorators".

Augarten factory
Formerly the State Porcelain Works in Vienna (closed 1864), the Wiener Porzellanfabrik Augarten was set up in 1922 as the successor to the former Imperial company. It makes figures and porcelain, mostly reproductions of earlier VIENNA porcelain, and uses the banded shield or beehive mark with a crown and the words "Augarten Wien".

Augarten porcelain figure, c.1930 [P]

Augsburg A city in southern Germany, superseding Nuremberg in the mid-16th century as the most important German centre for gold, silver and brass production and a major influence on the rest of Europe during the 17th and early 18th centuries. Guilds of artists and craftsmen were established at an early period in Augsburg and BAROQUE and ROCOCO pieces with fine engraving were much in demand. The workshops of Augsburg artisans supplied the courts and royal households of Europe with mirrors, guéridons, reliquaries and statues, as well as fine tableware.

Augsburg silver-gilt sponge box, 1751 [B, a pair]

Auguste, Henri (1759–1816) A French goldsmith, son of Robert-Joseph AUGUSTE. He became a master goldsmith in 1785 and succeeded his father as court goldsmith to Louis XVI, creating NEO-CLASSICAL silver dinner services and other plate for the royal family until the Revolution. He later worked for Napoleon, producing the Empire-style ewer and basin used at the emperor's coronation but went bankrupt in 1809.

Auguste, Robert-Joseph
(c.1723–1805) A French goldsmith and jeweller. Apprenticed to François-Thomas GERMAIN, he became a master goldsmith in 1757 and was appointed goldsmith to the court of Louis XVI. He is best known for grand dinner services commissioned by European royalty, including Gustav III of Sweden, Catherine the Great of Russia, Joseph I of Portugal and George III of England. The earliest are in the ROCOCO style, but pieces from the 1770s are more elegant and restrained, decorated with Neo-classical FESTOONS, SWAGS and BEADING. Auguste also made gold boxes and the gold crown, chalice and other regalia (destroyed during the Revolution) for the coronation of Louis XVI in 1774. His workshop was taken over by his son Henri AUGUSTE, c.1785.

Augustus the Strong See FRIEDRICH AUGUSTUS I.

Auliczek, Dominicus
(1734–1804) A sculptor and porcelain-modeller born in Bohemia (Czechoslovakia), died in Munich. In 1763 he succeeded

Nymphenburg model by Auliczek, c.1770 [K]

BUSTELLI as master modeller at the NYMPHENBURG factory in Munich. He modelled many animal and bird figures and groups, often with a hunting theme, and several series of mythological figures. As Court sculptor he modelled statues for the park of Nymphenburg Castle. Auliczek became factory inspector in 1773, and retired in 1797.

Ault, William (b.1841) An English potter who worked in the Staffordshire Potteries from the age of 15 and became manager at T.G. Green's Church Gresley Pottery. In partnership with Henry Tooth, he founded BRETBY ART POTTERY (1883–1920) and in 1887 established Ault Pottery in Derbyshire, which he ran until the early 20th century. Between 1892 and 1895, the output of Ault Pottery included pieces designed by Christopher DRESSER.

Aumbry A term originally used to describe a medieval cupboard that housed provisions given as alms to the poor. By extension it soon came to be used for most types of early food cupboards with solid or, occasionally, pierced doors.

Aurene glass A type of ART GLASS with an iridescent metallic surface produced by spraying with tin or lead chloride to produce "Gold Aurene", and with added cobalt oxide to produce "Blue Aurene". It was developed by Frederick CARDER, whose signature appears on the base of the pieces, at the STEUBEN GLASSWORKS, and was registered in 1904.

Auricular style
Ornament in a rippling, undulating style (also known as "lobate"), supposedly based originally on the human ear. It is found in

Auricular style

17th-century silver and furniture. It was inspired by contemporary scientific interest in anatomical dissection and was developed by the VAN VIANEN family of silversmiths, of Utrecht in the Netherlands. The most characteristic example is a silver-gilt ewer of 1614, in the Rijksmuseum, Amsterdam, made by Adam van Vianen (*c*.1569–1627), formed as a crouching monkey supporting fleshy scrolls and shells.

Automaton A device that mimics the movement of humans or animals for the enjoyment and entertainment of adults and children. From earliest times man has tried to add movement to images of himself and his surroundings. Egyptians and Greeks created articulated statuettes, which could be animated by strings. The earliest surviving treatise on automata was written by Hero of Alexandria, in the second century BC. Hero used animated models to illustrate physical properties such as the laws of hydraulics and mechanics.

The invention of the spring-driven clock movement in the 15th century provided a portable source of motion with differently shaped cams determining the type of movement. Elaborate animated displays were often connected to public clocks or were created for the amusement of royal patrons. From the

Automaton by Gustave Vichy, "Egyptienne à Genoux", c.1890 [E]

18th century onward, automata became increasingly popular throughout Europe, either as circus attractions or as exhibits in highly individualistic museums. One well-known example is the silver swan automaton made by the watchmaker James Cox, now in the Barnard Castle Museum, Durham.

Whereas the automata of the 18th century were usually one-offs, the 19th century introduced workshop- or factory-made automata. One of the first mass-produced automata was the AUTOPERIPATETIKOS.

Nowadays, automata are usually associated with the various artists working in the Marais district in Paris around 1900. They reflected Parisian life and entertainment of that time, with characters such as pierrots, clairvoyants, musicians, magicians and performing circus animals. They moved to popular tunes generated by one or more cylinders and combs. The automata usually had papier-mâché or BISQUE heads supplied by companies such as JUMEAU and were dressed in either imitations of contemporary clothes, or romantic interpretations of period costumes. Jean Roullet (d.1907) was one of the greatest makers of the period. He founded a company in 1865 and was later joined by his son-in-law, Ernest Descamps. Roullet & Descamps continued to produce automata until 1972. Other well-known makers were G. Vichy, Blaise Bontemps, Leopold Lambert and the company Phalibois.

The fashion for automata gradually subsided with the mood of austerity brought about by World War I.

Automaton clock A clock featuring automata or mechanical figures or devices such as rocking ships or windmills, often in combination with complex striking or musical work. Automaton clocks were produced from the 16th century, especially in Germany, but most examples found today date from the 19th century.

Automobile mascot See CAR MASCOT.

Autoperipatetikos ("walking-about-by-itself") The earliest form of walking doll, invented by Enoch Rice Morrison and patented in 1862. The autoperipatetikos is a china or papier-mâché SHOULDER-HEADED doll with an integral conical-shaped cardboard skirt housing a mechanism that causes the cast metal boots under the skirt to move up and down alternately, thus simulating a walking movement.

Aventurine A type of translucent dark-brown glass incorporating golden specks of oxidized metal that give it the sparkling appearance of a type of quartz known in Italian as *avventurina*; the other possible source of the name is from *per avventura* (Italian: "by chance"), a reference to the accidental nature of its discovery (or rediscovery – a similar, if not identical, process had been used in ancient times) at the MURANO glassworks in the early 17th century. Minute metallic flecks are formed when copper oxide is added to the molten glass. Aventurine can also be used as a glaze, and in some lacquerwork a similar effect is achieved by sprinkling metal particles onto the wet lacquer.

Venetian Revival aventurine glass, late 19th century [R]

Avisseau, Charles-Jean (1796–1861)
A French potter who founded a pottery
at Tours, France, in 1842. He successfully
imitated the pottery of Bernard PALISSY
and also copied Henri Deux and SAINT-
PORCHAIRE wares. His tradition was
carried on by his descendants until the
early 20th century.

Axminster carpet factory Established
in Devon, England, in 1755 by Thomas
Witty to rival French SAVONNERIE carpets.
Its wool-pile carpets were hand-knotted
using a TURKISH KNOT, with linen or
cotton warps and wefts. Motifs were similar
to those on contemporary French carpets
– fans, floral garlands, roundels, PATERAE –
but English features such as strawberry
plants and TUDOR-STYLE rose medallions
were often included. Some 18th-century
examples have a dark brown background.
By the early 19th century, the factory was
the main centre of British carpet-weaving,
with most of its fashionable products

based on French and oriental designs. In
1835 production ceased due to a fire. The
looms were transferred to WILTON where
production had continued to this day.

Aynsley, John An engraver of prints for
ceramics and a maker of creamware from
1780 to 1809 at Lane End, Staffordshire.
His mark was "J. Aynsley/Lane End".

Aynsley, J. & Sons A pottery making
printed and coloured china table services
from 1864 to the present day at the
Portland Works in Longton, Staffordshire,
founded by John Aynsley, a lustreware
maker, and later run by his grandson John
Aynsley (1823–1907).

Cup, saucer and plate by J. Aynsley & Sons, 1930s [R]

Aynsley, H. & Co. A pottery making
stoneware, lustre and painted ware at the
Commerce Works, Longton, Staffordshire,
from 1873 to the present day.

Ayrshire work Fine early 19th-century
WHITEWORK made in Scotland and Ireland,
with small flowers and NEEDLELACE detail.
It decorated ladies' muslin collars c.1800–30
and was later used for christening gowns.

Azmalyk A pentagonal camel trapping,
often made in pairs to adorn each side of
a bride's camel, woven by the Hekke and
Yomut tribal groups of West Turkestan.

Azulejos (Spanish/Portuguese: "tiles") From
the 14th century in Spain tiles were used
as wall decoration and for facing doorways.

B

Baby house A term used for all DOLLS'
HOUSES up to the early 19th century.
They were mainly
commissioned from a
carpenter or joiner
and were often
intended for adult
amusement.

**Baccarat
Glasshouse** (est. 1764)
A French glasshouse
founded at Saint-
Anne, Baccarat,
Lorraine. From the
19th century on it was a
leading producer
of high quality
CUT GLASS
tableware.
From the mid-
19th century it
also produced a
range of OPALINE
GLASS and
outstanding
PAPERWEIGHTS. After
several changes it is
now known as the
Compagnie des Cristalleries de Baccarat.

"Flaçon de chemise"
by Baccarat,
c.1844 [J]

Bacchus, George & Sons An English
glass manufacturer established in
Birmingham and known by this name
from 1840. In the 1830s the company
made pressed glass. It showed CASED
GLASS at the 1851 GREAT EXHIBITION in
London, was one of the first to use
transfer-printing, and for a brief period
made high quality paperweights and
engraved glass. The company was taken
over by Stone, Fawdrey & Stone in 1860
but the Bacchus name was still used
until the 1890s.

Bacchus motif A decorative motif
associated with Bacchus, the Roman god
of wine and fertility and his Greek
counterpart Dionysus. A popular subject

Axminster hand-knotted carpet, c.1800 [F]

for Classical and RENAISSANCE decoration, the theme of Bacchus and his companions – the wildly dancing Maenads and a drunken Silenus – was taken up again by decorators in the late 18th century. The myth of the god's discovery of wine was used in dining-room furniture, ceramics and silver tableware. Bacchus's attributes include the GRAPEVINE, IVY, LAUREL, DOLPHIN and panther. In the 19th century the motif was taken up by hotels and drinking establishments and Bacchus was shown accompanied by *putti* trailing vine garlands and bunches of grapes on drinking vessels and serving accessories.

Bacchic ornament

Bachelor's chest A chest of drawers, typically of walnut or mahogany, that evolved from the beginning of the 18th century. Its small size and narrow proportions, combined with a versatile drawer arrangement and size and fold-over top or BRUSHING SLIDE, made it suitable for bachelors' apartments.

Backboard The unpolished wooden boards at the back of a piece of CASE FURNITURE or a framed mirror. They were often made from a soft wood such as PINE and simply nailed on, although they may be panelled on good quality furniture from the late 18th and the 19th century. From the 20th century onward they were often made of PLYWOOD.

Backplate The rear of the pair of metal plates encasing the MOVEMENT in a clock or watch. Backplates are generally made of brass and are often

Backplate of a clock by
Thomas Tompion, c.1680 [c]

engraved with the name of the clock or watchmaker along with decorative motifs such as SCROLLWORK or flowers.

Back screen A detachable woven cane or WICKERWORK screen introduced in the mid-19th century, that was clipped onto the top rail of a dining-room chair to protect the sitter from the heat of the fire.

Backstaff A navigational instrument composed of two scaled arcs – one arc of 30°, the other of 60° – set at the opposite ends of a straight staff. Invented by English sea captain John Davis in 1594, they are usually constructed from ebony or rosewood with boxwood arcs, a moveable shadow vane and pinhole sighting piece. The user stood with his back to the sun and aligned one scale with the horizon and the other on the shadow cast by the sighting piece. The two readings added together gave the solar altitude. The advantage was that the

Rosewood and boxwood backstaff,
English 1744 [G]

sun could be observed without looking directly at it. The backstaff was superseded by the OCTANT.

Back stool A small armless three- or four-legged stool, sometimes fully upholstered, fitted with a back, introduced in the late 16th century. In the early 18th century it became known as a SIDE CHAIR.

Bacon cupboard A piece of farmhouse furniture, known from the Middle Ages until the middle to late 18th century. It consisted of a SETTLE with drawers beneath, fitted with a tall closed cupboard forming a high back to the seat, which could be used for hanging up joints of bacon.

Carved mahogany side chair
by Badlam,
1790–1800 [M]

Badlam, Stephen (1751–1815) An American cabinet-maker of the FEDERAL period, active in Dorchester, near Boston, Massachusetts. Badlam produced high quality NEO-CLASSICAL mahogany furniture in high style, some featuring detail by the Boston carver Simeon Skillin. Badlam's work is rare and sometimes labelled. He was suceeded by his son of the same name (1779–1847), who moved the business to Boston.

Baff The Farsi word for "knot", often combined with a further description of a rug's origin. Thus, *bibi-baff* are very fine rugs knotted by a Persian princess (*bibi*).

Bail handle A drawer handle in the form of a cast or moulded loop, shaped like a horizontal capital C between two small knobs and sometimes mounted on a back plate. First used from *c.*1690.

Baillie Scott, Mackay Hugh
(1865–1945) An English architect and designer. Baillie Scott designed furniture for the palace of the Grand Duke of Hesse in Darmstadt, Germany, in 1898 and also worked with the Dresdener Werkstätte für Handwerkkunst. He used ART NOUVEAU motifs to decorate his furniture designs, which were otherwise in the ARTS AND CRAFTS style.

Bain, Alexander (*c.*1811–77) A Scottish scientist and clockmaker who, with a clockmaker called Barwise, patented one of the first ELECTRIC CLOCKS in the 1840s. Powered by an earth battery, this clock had a magnetized PENDULUM, the swing of which was maintained by electrically charged coils on either side of the case. Some of his grandfather clocks are still in existence. In 1846 he installed electric clocks in Edinburgh and Glasgow railway stations, synchronized by a cable between the two buildings.

Baize A coarse woollen fabric with a characteristic long nap. It is used chiefly for coverings and linings and is commonly used to line billiard and snooker tables. In some countries it is also used for articles of clothing such as ponchos, cloaks and even skirts.

Bakalowits floral glass,
c.1899 [P]

Bakalowits, E. & Söhne
An Austrian glass retailer established in Vienna in 1845 and still going. Bakalowits himself produced designs for iridescent glass for the LOETZ, WITWE glassworks and persuaded Josef HOFFMANN and Ludwig Koloman MOSER to do likewise.

Bakelite A revolutionary synthetic early PLASTIC, patented by the Belgian Dr Leo Baekeland in 1907 from a phenolic resin and formaldehyde. This hard, non-flammable plastic could not be remoulded once set. It had a limited colour range, principally mottled brown or black, but also green and blue. When rubbed, bakelite gives off a benzene-like smell. Bakelite became popular in the 1920s and 1930s when it was used for domestic items, jewellery and electrical fitments.

Bakelite desk set,
1930s [R]

Bakewell Glassworks An American glass factory in Pittsburgh founded by Benjamin Bakewell and his partner, Benjamin Page, in 1808. The factory produced a greyish CUT GLASS and, from about 1825, a variety of PRESSED GLASS until its closure in 1882.

"Daffodil" oak dresser by Baillie Scott, c.1904 [F]

Bakhtiari carpets Carpets made to the present day by a formerly nomadic tribal group in southern Persia. Fine-quality carpets, rugs, flatweaves, saddlebags and saltbags are made in strong polychrome colours. A rectangular compartmented field enclosing flora is a favourite design. Warps and wefts are normally of cotton.

Bakhtiari carpet, west Persia
late 19th century [E]

Balance spring From the late 1600s this flat spiral spring enabled portable timepieces to gain an accuracy only previously seen in PENDULUM CLOCKS. The spring sits above the oscillating balance wheel and is usually connected to a balance cock (the wheel's support) and the balance itself. Ideally, it takes the same amount of time for a small oscillation of the balance as for a large one, which makes the watch very accurate.

Baldric A strap or belt, usually leather, worn from one shoulder diagonally across the chest, to support a sword, shield or musical instrument.

Ball, Tompkins and Black A New York City silversmith and jeweller, founded in 1839 as the successor to Marquand and Company (1801). Heavily chased sterling silver hollowware in Neo-Rococo taste is typical and may bear a mark. In 1876, the firm became BLACK, STARR & FROST.

Ball-and-claw foot
A termination for furniture legs that became popular in the early 18th century, derived from Chinese bronzes where the dragon holds a flaming pearl of wisdom. In Europe, the claw of an eagle was sometimes substituted for the dragon's claw.

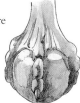

Ball-and-claw
foot

Ballets Russes The Russian Ballet was established by Serge Diaghilev in 1909. Its exotic and colourful sets and costume designs by Leon Bakst had an impact on ART DECO style and on French art.

Ball foot A turned spherical foot used largely on oak and walnut case furniture and chairs from the late 17th/early18th century and revived in the early 19th century. Faded from fashion *c*.1850.

Ball-jointed doll A doll with turned wooden spheres at the shoulders, elbows, hips and knees, held in place between two concave surfaces, so able to simulate natural movements to some extent.

Balloon back A round or oval open chair back, associated with ROCOCO REVIVAL style side chairs and popular in Britain from *c*.1835–70.

Balloon clock A BRACKET CLOCK with a waisted or balloon-shaped case, popular in England from the late 18th to the early 19th century. Probably derived from French styles, it is usually of satinwood or mahogany with a convex or flat dial.

Satinwood balloon clock,
English c.1800 [E]

Ball turning A wooden member, shaped on a lathe into a row of "ball" shapes, that was often used used for the centre rails of chair backs. Popular in northern Europe and America in the late 17th century, it was revived in the 19th century as an ornament on furniture.

Baluch A Sunni Muslim partly nomadic tribal group who still weave rugs in the Pakistan province of Baluchistan and on the Afghan Persian border. Products include carpets, rugs, flatweaves and artifacts. Wool is mostly used for the pile and foundation. Designs are geometric in form and the colours tend to be sombre.

¹Baluster A small turned or carved upright vase- or pear-shaped column, pillar or post that was often imitated in chair legs and used as a central support for a table or as a SPINDLE for a gallery.

²Baluster shape Describes various wares shaped like turned balusters such as drinking glasses with knopped stem made in England *c*.1700–30, and coffee-pots.

Balustroid A lighter form of the BALUSTER glass, developed in England in the mid-18th century. It had a tall, thin stem with several knops.

Bamboo furniture
Furniture made from *Bambusa arundinacea* in East Asia and imported into Britain in the 18th century. It was copied in the early 19th century in the vogue for CHINOISERIE and inexpensive and flimsy bamboo furniture was popular later in the century.

Bamboo table,
English c.1890 [J]

Band See FILLET.

Bandai A post-World War II Japanese toy manufacturer. They originally made TINPLATE vehicles, in particular models of American cars, but also exported large numbers of tinplate mechanical robots in the 1950s and 60s, and plastic ones from the 1960s onward. Bandai are still producing toys, marking them with a "B" or a small figure with outstretched limbs.

Bandelwerk See LAUB-UND-BANDELWERK.

Banding A decorative narrow band of INLAY of contrasting wood, used round the edge of drawer fronts, table tops and panels. There are three major forms: CROSSBANDING, HERRINGBONE BANDING and straight banding, which is cut along the length of the grain.

Banding

Bangle See BRACELETS AND BANGLES.

Banister A term derived from BALUSTER, used from the 18th century to describe both the upright elements that make up a balustrade and the vertical bars in seat furniture – as found in the mid-18th-century banister-back chair.

Banjo barometer A type of WHEEL BAROMETER with a banjo-shaped wooden case. Introduced in Britain in the late 18th century by Italian craftsmen, the banjo barometer features a silvered brass DIAL, and sometimes also a spirit level, thermometer, clock, convex mirror and/or a HYGROMETER. Some ANEROID BAROMETERS have also been made with banjo-shaped cases.

Banjo clock An American WALL CLOCK with a banjo-shaped case, invented in 1802 by Simon Willard (1753–1848) of Massachusetts. The long trunk, with a rectangular base, usually has VERRE ÉGLOMISÉ panels and curved brass frets. Only 4,000 clocks were made.

Bank See SAVINGS BANK.

Banko ware Japanese pottery made from the mid-18th century, originally inspired by the work of Numanami Shigenaga (1718-77) who used the seals *banko* (everlasting) and *fujiki* (changeless) for his wares. The wares are typically decorated with human figures, monkeys or other animals picked out in enamels or glazes. Banko ware was revived in the 19th century, made of grey stoneware and often in the form of a lotus or flowers.

Banquette A French term for a long, low rectangular bench, supported on six or more legs, the seat of which was often upholstered with tapestries. It was developed in France in the late 17th century, when banquettes were used in state rooms and state bedrooms. It remained largely a French type of furniture, although some four-legged English versions are known.

Bantam work See LACQUER.

Bar back (or rail back) A term that describes the multiple straight or shaped uprights that run between the chair seat and top RAIL. They were used to make up certain styles of chair back, for example, the 18th-century shield back.

Barbeau (French: "cornflower") A blue, pink or green cornflower sprig that was a popular decorative motif on French ceramics in the 18th and 19th centuries. It was reputedly introduced for

Chinese Kangxi barber's bowl, c.1720 [J]

Queen Marie-Antoinette of France at SÈVRES and is also found on the wares of the PARIS, CHANTILLY and NIDERVILLER porcelain factories. The motif was adopted by English porcelain decorators, who named it the ANGOULÊME SPRIG, as it was a recurring design at the Paris manufactory established in 1781 by the Duc d'Angoulême.

Barbedienne, Ferdinand (1810–92) The leading 19th-century French bronze-founder, working for BARYE and other sculptors; also a furniture-manufacturer. He was originally a wallpaper manufacturer. In 1838 he went into business with Achille Collas and by 1850 Collas & Barbedienne was one of the leading foundries in Paris, producing bronzes for leading sculptors and manufacturing high-quality furniture in various styles – GOTHIC and LOUIS XVI, as well as RENAISSANCE REVIVAL. In the 1880s he made JAPONAISERIE furniture and bronzes.

Barbedienne candalabrum, late 19th century [J, a pair]

Barber's basin or bowl A round bowl used by barbers from the 16th to the 19th centuries, with a semicircular segment removed to fit around a customer's neck. They are found especially in English DELFTWARE and French and Spanish FAIENCE. Large numbers of porcelain examples were imported from China and Japan in the early 18th century.

Barbie doll Probably the most successful doll ever produced, with sales of several million since it was first launched in 1959 in the US. Barbie was developed by the Californian company Mattel Inc. from a "Lilli" doll, inspired by a mid-1950s cartoon character in a leading German newspaper. Pre-1961 examples of Barbie are the most popular.

Barcelona chair See Ludwig MIES VAN DER ROHE.

Bargello (flame stitch, Florentine stitch, Hungarian stitch) A simple needlework technique in which stitches are worked in a zigzag or flame pattern on canvas using a range of shaded colours to create an all-over design in silk or wool. Introduced from Hungary during the Middle Ages, the technique later spread throughout Europe and was used particularly for wall hangings, upholstery and curtains.

Barge ware Brown-glazed EARTHENWARE pottery wares produced in Derbyshire c.1860–1910 for the barge-owners who transported ceramics from Staffordshire by canal. It was usually applied with white panels inscribed with the names of purchasers, dates, mottos and verses, and brightly decorated with green,

Barge ware teapot, c.1880 [P]

blue and pink bird and flower motifs. The most common wares are highly utilitarian: teapots, jugs and CHAMBER POTS.

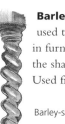

Barley-sugar twist A term used to describe spiral TURNING in furniture-making, named from the shape of a barley-sugar stick. Used from the late 17th century.

Barley-sugar twist

Barlow, Arthur, Florence and Hannah Leading British ceramics artists, a brother and sisters who worked for DOULTON Lambeth making ART POTTERY stonewares. Arthur (c.1845–1909) is known for his incised foliage, Hannah (1859–1913) for her incised depiction of animals, and Florence (d.1909) for her PÂTE-SUR-PÂTE decoration, often depicting birds. Their works were marked with their respective initials; ABB, HBB and FEB.

Barnack, Oscar (1879–1936) A German microscope designer and inventor of the Leica camera. He worked for Leitz, the leading manufacturer of microscopes. He realized the potential of using a small camera with cine film, the difficulty being to produce a high-quality enlargement from a small negative. He built two prototype cameras, later known as the UR Leicas and, following many modifications, the first Leicas were made in 1924–25, revolutionizing camera design. The model continued with subsequent improvements. Today the name is synonymous with precision cameras of high-quality.

Barnsley, Sydney (1865–1926) and **Ernest** (1863–1926) Brothers who were members of the ARTS AND CRAFTS movement. Sydney founded Kenton & Co. in 1890 with W.R. LETHABY, Ernest GIMSON and others. After it closed in 1892 the brothers established a workshop which later became the COTSWOLD SCHOOL, in Gloucestershire. They later moved to Froxfield, Hampshire, where their furniture design was continued by Sydney's son Edward (1900–87). An educational trust promotes their work today.

Barograph An instrument that records the changes in atmospheric pressure over a period of time. Usually fitted into a glass-fronted wooden case, it features a pen or stylus – recording barometer readings on successive days on a paper chart – attached to a mechanism driven by a clock MOVEMENT. The earliest barographs, developed in the 19th century, were of the mercury type, but those with ANEROID mechanisms are more common.

Barometer An instrument for measuring atmospheric pressure and therefore forecasting changes in the weather. It was invented in 1643 by the Italian philosopher and mathematician Evangelista Torricelli, although the first barometers for domestic use only appeared in the late 17th century. The earliest type was the STICK BAROMETER. The WHEEL BAROMETER was the most popular type from the 18th century, and the ANEROID BAROMETER from the 19th. Pocket aneroid barometers, used by travellers and climbers, were produced c.1860 by the London firm of NEGRETTI & ZAMBRA. For household use barometers were set in cases made by cabinet-makers or clockmakers. These were either wall-hung or free-standing, and reflected the style of contemporary furniture and clock cases.

Ebonized and ormolu-mounted wheel barometer by Negretti & Zambra, 19th century [H]

Baroque style

Named after the Portuguese *barroco*, meaning an irregularly shaped pearl, the Baroque style with its exuberant grandeur swept Europe from the 1620s for nearly 100 years in all areas of the decorative arts.

Baroque wooden statuette of Ceres, the goddess of autumn, holding a horn of plenty, in Spanish Colonial style, c.1640–60 [L]

Painterly magnificence

Baroque style originated in Italian painting, sculpture and architecture, during the course of the 17th century and became the dominant style in the European decorative arts. In furniture, it is evident in the use of such Classical architectural and sculptural elements as pediments, PUTTI, heavy scrolls and VOLUTES, thick fronds of ACANTHUS, SWAGS, vases and TROPHIES, while the overall effect of grandeur is enhanced by bulbous, monumental forms and elaborate mouldings and carving, often of mythological figures such as mermaids, tritons and cupids. Luxurious materials were preferred, including rich velvet, BROCADE and DAMASK upholstery, SEMI-PRECIOUS STONES and IVORY.

The style spread during the mid-17th century from Italy to France, where it reached its height during the reign of Louis XIV (see LOUIS XIV STYLE), particularly at the palace of Versailles, near Paris, where the magnificent unified scheme of decoration symbolized the power of the French monarchy.

Generally, Classical architecture and sculpture were the dominant influences, mingled with exotic elements, in particular CHINOISERIE, resulting in a fashion for imported LACQUERWORK panels and furniture, motifs such as pagodas and Chinese figures, and especially blue and white porcelain.

Baroque silverwork frame, with a typical decoration of elaborate acanthus motifs, c.1650 [A]

The distinctive French Baroque style was disseminated throughout Europe in the late 17th and early 18th centuries. Books of engraved ornament by leading French designers such as Jean Le Pautre (1617–82) and later Jean BÉRAIN (1639–1711) circulated the style and HUGUENOT craftsmen fleeing France after the Revocation of the Edict of Nantes in 1685 spread Baroque form and ornament farther. Many Huguenots settled in the Protestant Netherlands and later in England, where the style was also made fashionable by King William III and Queen Mary II (see WILLIAM AND MARY STYLE).

In the early 18th century, Baroque was gradually replaced by a lighter style that prefigured the ROCOCO. During the 19th century, enthusiasm for historical styles led to its revival, particularly in France during the SECOND EMPIRE (1852–70).

Recognizing the style

The Baroque style was characterized by rich and sometimes heavy ornamentation, much of it based on plant forms, such as the acanthus, and animal or human forms such as putti, tritons, dolphins and eagles, usually intertwined in complex forms.

Basket of flowers   Leafy scroll

Italian Baroque embroidered cope, made for a priest, lavishly worked in gold spun thread, c.1670 [I]

Baroque pearl An irregularly-shaped pearl that is less valuable than a round pearl, but which has been used in jewellery for centuries since its appearance frequently suggests natural or organic forms. In modern times imitation baroque pearls are widely used in COSTUME JEWELLERY.

"Baroque" pearl necklace by Miriam Haskell, 1950s [Q]

Baroque Revival A style of decoration reviving motifs and forms of the BAROQUE style and fashionable in Europe and the US in the second half of the 19th century. While incorporating Baroque elements, e.g. scrolling foliage, figural sculpture and luxurious materials, forms and ornament are larger, more exaggerated and curvaceous.

Barovier glasshouse A leading manufacturer of Venetian glass, based on the island of Murano, near Venice. First established as Fratelli Barovier in 1878 by three brothers of the Barovier family, a dynasty of well-known glassmakers. In 1942 the family firm merged with another glassmaking dynasty to become Barovier & Toso, which, thanks largely to the talented designer Ercole Barovier (1889–1974), went on to specialize in brightly coloured and innovative art glass. The firm remains one of the most notable producers of Venetian glass today.

Barr, Flight & Barr See WORCESTER PORCELAIN FACTORY.

Barrel A drum-shaped device in a CLOCK or watch mechanism. In weight-driven clocks, the cord to which the weights are attached is wound round the barrel; in watches and spring-driven clocks the barrel contains the coiled spring, the force of which is often equalized by the FUSEE in high-quality movements. A "going" barrel is a type of barrel in spring-driven clocks with teeth around the edge transmitting the power of the spring directly to the TRAIN, without a fusee.

Barry, Joseph B. (1757–1838) An Irish-born American cabinet-maker of the FEDERAL period active in Philadelphia, from c.1810 to c.1822. Barry's work shows both NEO-CLASSICAL and Egyptian influence. Examples are highly prized and rank with the work of his US contemporaries Charles-Honoré LANNUIER and Antoine-Gabrielle QUERVELLE.

Barum ware A type of ART POTTERY made from c.1879 at Barnstaple, Devon, under the direction of C.H. BRANNAM, typically made of red clay with a rich, shiny blue and green glaze. Production continues today under the name Candy & Co., who took over the firm in 1979.

Barye, Antoine-Louis (1796–1875) The finest sculptor of the French ANIMALIER school, working in the spirit of the Romantic movement. Barye's animal figures are characterized by violent movement and tense

Barye bronze model of a stallion, c.1850 [C]

stances. He also excelled in equestrian and mythological subjects. A collection of his work can be seen in the Louvre Museum, Paris.

Basal rim (also called a chime or foot rim) A slightly projecting ring on the bottom of a vessel, utensil or plate made of silver, ceramic or glass, which raises the bottom of the object above the surface on which it stands.

Basaltes ware teapot and cover, c.1815 [R]

Basaltes ware A stoneware body coloured black and unglazed, to imitate basalt which in its natural state is a fine-grained volcanic rock. The term was used by Josiah WEDGWOOD in the 1760s when he was experimenting with different earthenware substances, and was influenced by the discoveries of Herculaneum and Pompeii. Widely copied by other manufacturers, a contemporary term for it was "Egyptian black".

Bas d'armoire A type of low cupboard originating in 18th-century provincial France as a substitute for the more elaborate COMMODE. During the EMPIRE period it was commonly made in mahogany, and decorated with typical gilt-bronze motifs of NEO-CLASSICAL or Egyptian inspiration.

Baseball memorabilia:Joe DiMaggio's
Yankee Road jersey, 1940s [A]

Baseball memorabilia Memorabilia
and equipment associated with this game
– evolved from the Knickerbocker Base
Ball Club of New York in the mid-1840s.
These may take the form of bats, balls,
trading cards, clothing, pennants, gloves,
programmes, figurines and photographs.
Any of the above is enhanced in value if
signed or used by a notable player. See
also ANDIRON.

Base metal Any of the common metals
such as copper, tin and lead, as opposed to
the precious metals like gold, silver and
platinum. The term is often used of plated
articles when it is not obvious which
metal has been plated over, as in "a silver-
plated base metal teapot".

Basket glass Decorative glass that takes
the form of an open basket with a
handle, used for holding fruit or
sweets. Baskets were
popular decorative and
novelty items and were
made in a variety of
types of glass, from
cased, coloured and
cut lead glass to the
verre de soie baskets produced
by the STEUBEN GLASSWORKS.

Basket-top clock An early BRACKET
CLOCK with an elaborately pierced metal
top, often with a carrying handle, made in
England from the 1660s.

Basketweave (or ozier, from
the German for "willow")
A decorative pattern imitating
interwoven rushes, cane, willow or
straw. With the fashion for pastoral
decoration, basketweave patterns were
popular for ceramics and metalwork from
the early 18th century. The MEISSEN
factory introduced porcelain plates
decorated with wickerwork borders in
relief and silver baskets made of woven
metal wire became fashionable.
Basketweave patterns continued to be
popular in metalwork, ceramics and
pressed glass throughout the 19th century.

Bas-relief Low relief, that is, carved or
built-up work not raised very high above
the ground. A decorative technique
derived from sculpture but also widely
used in panels on furniture and
metalwork to give definition to design,
producing effects of light and shadow.

Basse taille Originating in the Middle
Ages, basse taille is a method of
enamelling whereby the gold or silver
field is ENGRAVED or ENGINE-TURNED
with a scene or design and the cavities
filled with translucent enamel. Shallow or
deep engraving will reduce or intensify
the overall appearance to create a three-
dimensional effect.

Bassett-Lowke clockwork
locomotive, English, 1931 [o]

Bassett-Lowke Company Founded in
1899 by Wenman Joseph Bassett-Lowke
in Northampton producing model trains
with a painted finish. From 1910 they
started importing specially commissioned

lithographed toy trains from Gebrüder
BING of Nuremberg for the English
market. They also included general
imported products from CARETTE and
MÄRKLIN in their own catalogue with no
acknowledgement. The emphasis was
always on accuracy of detail and products
ranged across all gauges from "00" to
"IV", and used steam, electric or
CLOCKWORK power. The company
concentrated on "0"-gauge from the
1930s and production ceased in 1971
when a 45-year run of their most well-
known steam driven "0"-gauge Mogul
ended. They were responsible for the
introduction of the first "H0/00"-gauge
electric trains in 1935, made by Trix, first
in Germany, and from 1938 in England.

Bassinet A type of cradle consisting of a
long wickerwork basket with a hood.

Batavian ware A class of CHINESE
EXPORT PORCELAIN decorated using a
brown or "café-au-lait" glaze in
conjunction with
underglaze blue
or FAMILLE ROSE
enamels. Named
after Batavia
(modern Jakarta), the
Dutch East India   Batavian punch bowl,
Company trading   Qianlong, c.1740 [i]
centre in South East
Asia. The wares were produced for export
throughout the first half of the 18th
century and include vases, teapots, tea
bowls and saucers and other useful
wares. The style was also
copied by MEISSEN and by
other European factories.

Bateman & Co. An English
silversmithing family. Hester (1708–94)
continued her huband John's business in
London after his death with her sons
Peter and Jonathan. They produced
flatware and tea and coffee wares in the
Neo-classical style, often with bright cut
decoration. William Bateman, the son of
Jonathan, continued the business into the
late 19th century.

Bates, Elliott & Co. A factory at Dale Hall Works, Burslem, Staffordshire, from 1870–75, then Bates, Walker (1875–1878), Bates Gildea & Walker (1878–81), Gildea & Walker (1881–85) and finally James Gildea until 1888. They made domestic earthenware, STONEWARE tea urns and some JASPER WARE vases in John TURNER's old moulds and marked "Turner Jasper Ware".

Bath metal A cheap bronze-like alloy that was used from the late 18th century to make small boxes and particularly buttons. (It had also been used earlier in the century to make unofficial coinage.)

Batik kain panjang (loin cloth), Java, c.1940 [s]

Batik The ancient Japanese art of decorating fabric using a wax-resist technique. Wax is applied in patterns to undyed fabric, the exposed fabric is then dyed and the wax removed, revealing the pattern. The process could be repeated, depending on the number of colours and complexity of design required. First introduced to Europe by the Dutch EAST INDIA COMPANY in the 17th century, batik patterns were produced in Europe from 1842 by the Swiss textile company P. Blumer and Jenny.

Bat printing A method of TRANSFER-PRINTED decoration in English ceramics, in which the impression of the STIPPLE ENGRAVING was taken onto soft flexible glue sheets or "bats". The bats were used to transfer tiny drops of oil onto the

porcelain, the design was dusted with powdered pigment and then fired. Commonly used in Staffordshire in the early 19th century.

Battam, Thomas (d.1864) Battam & Sons of Gough Square, London, were ceramic decorators 1830–70. Thomas Battam Snr was at one time art director at Copelands and he also formed the Ceramic & Crystal Palace Art Union in 1858. His son continued the trade and his paintings in the style of LIMOGES ENAMELS were included in international exhibitions, especially in 1862 and 1871.

Battersea Enamel Factory Founded by Stephen Theodore Janssen in London in 1753, the factory produced enamelled items with the first TRANSFER-PRINTED designs, often in puce on white enamel over a copper base, a technique invented by John BROOKS, the manager. The colours are painted onto an engraved metal plate, printed onto paper and transferred to the object. The factory mainly produced small items, many decorated with landscapes or flowers or imitating designs on MEISSEN porcelain. It only lasted until 1756 but influenced factories in Birmingham and Staffordshire.

Battersea enamel snuffbox, 1754 [D]

Battery mechanism The use of a low voltage electric motor powered by a battery to drive a toy. The battery may be fitted inside the toy, or connected to it by a remote cable and hand control-box.

Baudouine, Charles A. (1808–1895) An American cabinet-maker of French extraction active in New York City by

Baudouine side table, 1840s [I]

1830. He produced large quantities of rosewood parlour furniture using a variation of the laminating process patented by his rival, John Henry BELTER. In the 1840s, he was associated with Anthony Kimbel, best known through his partnership with Joseph Cabus as KIMBEL AND CABUS. Baudouine furniture is typically in elaborate ROCOCO REVIVAL style. Chairs and sofas have pierced, richly carved backs of laminated rosewood, which, unlike Belter's work, may be composed of two elements joined in the centre. His attributed pieces are of less value than those of Belter.

Baudry, François (1791–1859) A French cabinet-maker. Born in Nantes, by 1822 he was making furniture in Paris where he became *Ebéniste du Roi* to Louis-Philippe (furniture-maker to the king). He produced a range of luxurious furniture that was exhibited in Paris.

Bauer, Adam (*b*.1743) A German porcelain modeller, a pupil of François Lejeune, whom he succeeded as sculptor to the Duke of Württemberg in south-west Germany c.1770–75. Bauer worked at the LUDWIGSBURG porcelain factory (owned by the Duke), producing groups and figures until 1771. He then became master modeller in the FRANKENTHAL factory 1777–9 and later worked in VIENNA and Sterzing-an-Brenner.

Bauhaus

Founded in Weimar, Germany, in 1919 by the Modernist architect Walter Gropius, the Bauhaus trained artists and craftsmen to design high quality goods specifically for industrial production. Its functional, geometric styles are still a source of inspiration for today's designers.

Building for the future

The Bauhaus, whose name is derived from the German words *bauen* (to build) and *Haus* (house), is generally considered one of the most influential design schools of the 20th century. It was founded by Walter GROPIUS (1883–1969), when he was appointed to succeed Henry VAN DE VELDE as director of the Art School and the School of Arts and Crafts in Weimar. The courses at the Bauhaus focused on practical experimentation with materials and the importance of colour and form, as opposed to academic theory and the study of fine art.

One of the main founding principles of the school was the unification of art, architecture and applied arts and the importance of co-operation between art and industry. The Hungarian-born architect and designer Marcel BREUER (1902–81) experimented with the new material of chromium-plated tubular steel to create innovative, lightweight frames for furniture, as seen in his "Wassily" armchair of 1925, named after the artist Kandinsky who admired it. It was made by such firms as Standard-Möbel Lengyel & Co. of Berlin and THONET of Vienna. Among the most successful Bauhaus designs put into commercial production were the glass, brass and steel lamps designed in the school's metal workshop by Marianne Brandt (1893–1983) and Wilhelm Wagenfeld (b.1900), manufactured by the Leipzig firm of Korting and Mathiesen in the late 1920s and early 1930s. Brandt was also known for her geometric hemispherical teapots and ashtrays in silver and brass. Innovative furnishing textiles were developed in the textile department under Gunta Stolzl, while the typefaces created by Herbert Bayer (1900–85) in the advertising department had a lasting impact on poster and typographic design. In 1925 the school moved to Dessau and it was here that the signature Bauhaus style became particularly apparent under the guidance of modernist designer Laszlo Moholy-Nagy (1895–1946). Gropius resigned in 1928, one of his successors as director being Ludwig MIES VAN DER ROHE. The Bauhaus then moved to Berlin in 1932 before being closed down by the German National Socialists in 1933.

The overall success of the school in making design of good quality available to everyone was limited and many products were still in fact made by hand even though their austere, geometric forms suggested machine production. Consequently, original pieces from the 1920s or early 1930s are rare. Since the 1960s, many Bauhaus furniture pieces have been re-issued by the US firm Knoll and the Italian company Cassina, while from the 1980s the Italian design firm Alessi has also manufactured some of Brandt's metalwork designs from the 1920s.

The dramatic and geometric style of the Bauhaus is typified by this copper and silver teapot by Marianne Brandt, c.1924 [H]

Synchron double-sided electric clock designed by Peter Behrens for AEG, Berlin, c.1910 [M]

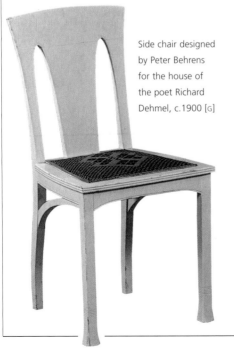

Side chair designed by Peter Behrens for the house of the poet Richard Dehmel, c.1900 [G]

Tin and enamel napkin holder, stamped Ruppel, c.1930 [R]

Baumgarten tapestry factory
Set up in New York City in 1893 by William Baumgarten, a successful interior decorator, under the directorship of Jean Foussadier, previously head weaver at the English Royal Windsor Tapestry Manufactory. Baumgarten initially concentrated on seat-covers worked in simple floral patterns, and later also produced tapestries in the French taste. The factory closed in 1912.

Baxter, Thomas (1782–1821) A fine ceramics painter. He worked at his father's studios in London, on French, Chinese and COALPORT blank wares. He attended art classes at the Royal Academy under Henry Fuseli and was influenced by Greek and Roman vase painting. He returned to WORCESTER to work for BARR, FLIGHT & BARR c.1814, and founded an art school there. In 1816 he moved to SWANSEAthen back to Worcester in 1819. He is especially known for his figure subjects and atmospheric landscapes.

Baxter print A colour print produced by George Baxter (1804–67), which combined the use of an INTAGLIO or engraved steel plate, often in AQUATINT,

Baxter print of Queen Victoria, c.1850 [Q]

for the image, and colour from a range of wood blocks. They represent some of the earliest colour prints and achieved huge commercial success. In 1837, his book *The Picture Album or Cabinet of Painting* illustrated the merits of his process, which was soon licensed to other printers and widely used into the 1870s. All original Baxter prints are inscribed with his name.

Bayeux porcelain factory Founded in 1812 by Joachim Longlois in Bayeux, Normandy, France, the factory produced industrial and decorated wares. These included porcelain figures and tablewares in the most popular 19th-century styles, particularly EMPIRE and JAPONAISERIE. The ownership changed frequently, as did the marks, but most incorporated the name of the town. Operations ceased at the factory in 1951.

Bay leaf motif See LAUREL.

Bayonet A knife or DAGGER fitted to the barrel of a firearm for close range fighting, introduced in the second quarter of the 17th century and still used today. It is believed to have originated in the French city of Bayonne where *bayonette* meant a large knife.

Bayreuth pottery and porcelain
A German faience factory founded in 1714 near Bayreuth in north-west Bavaria, allegedly with the help of a MEISSEN worker Samuel Kempe. Stoneware in the style of J.F. BÖTTGER was made before 1726. The finest wares date from c.1728 to c.1744, when the factory was owned by a merchant, Johan Georg Knöller, and the pottery produced outstanding blue-painted ARMORIAL WARES. HARD-PASTE porcelain was produced from 1760, maybe earlier, and from 1788 to 1806 cream-coloured earthenware was made as well as faience.

The factory closed in 1852. It was followed by the porcelain factories of Siegmund Paul Meyer, founded in 1900, and Anton Weide, founded in 1920.

Bayreuth faience teapot, c.1740 [E]

Baywood See MAHOGANY.

Bead and reel A decorative motif, originating in Classical antiquity, of round bead forms alternating with small, oblong shapes resembling reels. It is frequently used as a form of decoration on furniture, and was popular for engraved ornament on 18th-century silver. It was also adopted by cabinet-makers and particularly favoured for architectural mouldings in the NEO-CLASSICAL period.

Bead and spindle

Bead and spindle A decorative motif of round bead and long spindle forms, used in a variety of combinations for woodwork and mouldings. It was especially popular in the 17th century. It enjoyed a revival in the 19th century, when it commonly featured on furniture, especially on chair-backs.

Bead edge A type of border work, characterized by small round beads of the same, or graduated size, arranged in a neat single row. A Classical decoration used particularly on silver FLATWARE and CUTLERY in the late 18th century and second half of the 19th century, it is still widely used.

Bead edge on a silver fork, continental 1900 [S] ▶

Beading

Beading A type of ornament comprised of a line of tiny cylindrical beads, resembling a necklace. Originating in ROMANESQUE decoration, beading was commonly used for MOULDINGS and in the 18th century was a popular decorative motif for silver, furniture and ceramics.

Bead moulding See ASTRAGAL.

Beadwork cushion, English, c.1870 [K]

Beadwork A form of embroidery in which small glass beads are threaded onto silk and stitched to a fabric ground, or threaded onto wire, which is then shaped. It was fashionable in the 17th century for pictures, mirror frames, and small cabinets and later in the 19th and 20th centuries for ladies' handbags.

Beaker A cylindrical drinking vessel made since prehistoric times, of pottery, porcelain, glass wood or silver. Usually tapering, with or without a cover, with no handle or stem, and decorated in various ways.

Beatty & Sons A US glasshouse founded c.1850 by Alexander J. Beatty in

Steubenville, Ohio. Beatty produced clear and coloured table glass, specializing in goblets. The factory closed in the late 19th century.

Beauvais carpet A pile- or flat-woven carpet made from the late 18th to the early 19th century at the BEAUVAIS TAPESTRY FACTORY. The designs and colouration are similar to those of the AUBUSSON and SAVONNERIE factories.

Beauvais (Beauvaisis) potteries
A group of potteries around Beauvais in Normandy, France, whose best-known wares were produced from the late 14th to the mid-16th century. Objects were made for both domestic and religious use, the latter including 16th-century "Passion dishes", glazed in a typical colour palette of yellow and green.

Beauvais tapestries The town of Beauvais in Normandy, France, was a weaving centre from the 16th century onward. Initial production centred around LOW-WARP *verdures* (hangings worked with designs of leafy plants). In 1664 it was established as a royal factory by Louis XIV's chief minister, Jean-Baptiste Colbert, and produced tapestries of outstanding quality. A series designed by Jean BÉRAIN featuring mythological figures known as "Grotesques" was particularly popular. In 1734 the animal painter Jean-Baptiste Oudry became director of the factory, employing François BOUCHER, whose designs helped Beauvais to acquire a reputation throughout Europe. Soft furnishings made en suite with tapestries became a speciality. Toward the end of the 18th century the increasing popularity of wallpaper, together with the upheavals of the French Revolution, led to a decline in the factory's fortunes. It was amalgamated with the GOBELINS factory in 1940.

Beauvais tapestry, Louis XIV period [A, for set of 4]

Meissen beaker and cover, c.1730 [C]

Beaux Arts style Found in late 19th- and early 20th-century French and US architecture and decorative arts, this style is characterized by an academic interpretation of ancient Greek and Roman architecture. It was named after the Ecole des Beaux Arts in Paris, the French national school of architecture, painting and sculpture, which promoted the Classical ideal.

Bébé A French BISQUE-headed doll popular between 1860 and 1900, distinguishable from the FASHION DOLL by its child-like torso with protruding tummy and shorter, stubbier limbs. Pierre François JUMEAU claimed to have invented the bébé in 1855.

Jumeau Bébé doll, c.1890 [H]

Bedfordshire lace English East Midlands BOBBIN LACE fashionable from the mid-19th century, made with decorative BOBBINS, some inspired by MALTESE LACE wheat-ear pattern.

Bedstead A framework, made of wood or metal, that supports bedding. Early bedsteads were often built into the wall (see BOX BEDSTEAD). The first free-standing examples appeared in the 16th century and, in northern Europe, were usually made of oak, often heavily carved and, from the mid-16th century, with a tester or canopy (see HALF-TESTER). From the 17th century, the drapery on four-poster beds became increasingly elaborate. From the mid-18th century, the emphasis was on elaborately carved bed posts and cornices, often gilded and painted in the NEO-CLASSICAL style. In France, under the influence of the EMPIRE STYLE, new types such as the LIT-EN-BATEAU appeared; furniture-makers in the US and UK favoured beds with two posts at the head and a canopy, as well as tubular brass and cast-iron bedsteads. Most surviving early examples are state or royal beds; few ordinary examples have survived.

Beech (*Fagus sylvatica*) A tree native to Britain and northern Europe that produces a pale straw-coloured softwood with a close, fine straight grain that is easy to carve. It features in furniture-making in the 18th century in Britain, and particularly in France, where it was elaborately carved and gilded. It was used extensively in England in the early 19th century, when it was often painted to resemble more expensive woods such as ROSEWOOD.

Bee motif In ancient Greek, Chinese, and occasionally Christian art, a device representing industry and order, and less frequently, rebirth and immortality. It was adopted as an emblem by the powerful Barberini family in Rome, ornamenting the buildings commissioned by the Barberini Pope Urban VIII in the 17th century. It was also adopted by Napoleon in the lavish decoration of textiles, furniture and architecture glorifying his reign. Bees appeared on ceramics and silver from the mid-18th century, and until the 1920s were a popular motif on tableware designed to contain honey.

Behrens, Peter (1868–1940) A German architect, designer, teacher and influential design practitioner. Walter GROPIUS, Ludwig

Peter Behrens table silver, 1902 [H, the set]

Beilby wine glass, c.1770 [H]

MIES VAN DER ROHE and LE CORBUSIER all worked for him at the start of their careers. In 1907 he was a founder member of the avant-garde Deutscher Werkbund (an organization set up to bring together the arts and industry for mutual benefit). His designs for the turbine factory of the giant German industrial concern AEG (1909), with its use of glass walls, are considered particularly influential.

Beilby, William (1740–1819) **and Mary** (1749–97) An English brother and sister team of glass decorators and the leading British exponents of enamelling in the second half of the 18th century. They worked in Newcastle upon Tyne, decorating wine glasses, goblets and decanters with white and bluish white enamel decoration.

Beinglas (German *Bein*: "bone") A type of semi-opaque white glass, often decorated with enamelling, also known as MILK GLASS and "water glass". It derives its name from the bone ash added to the ingredients. The main areas of production were Bohemia and Thuringia, from the mid-18th to the mid-19th centuries.

Belfast Glassworks An Irish glasshouse operating from 1803–40, one of several established between 1780 and 1825 in Ireland to avoid the heavy glass tax imposed by British Excise Acts. It made jugs, bowls, decanters and vases in the heavy greyish lead crystal associated with Anglo-Irish glass.

Bel Geddes, Norman (1893–1958) A US industrial designer, who worked as a commercial illustrator before moving to theatre and industrial design, where his work became internationally recognized. He was a leading exponent of "streamlining", a particularly American emphasis in 1930s design (see ART DECO), and the teardrop shape that he believed was a perfect example of it.

Bell A small metal dome on a clock emitting a note when struck (see STRIKING systems). Bells have been used on mechanical clocks since the early Middle Ages, when – because early clocks had no dials – they indicated the hours of prayer in churches and monasteries. They are generally made of a specific alloy of copper and tin known as bell metal, which produces a clearer sound than other metals, though many modern clock bells are made of steel. Tubular bells, which have a purer pitch, are hollow metal tubes struck with leather mallets.

German armorial
bellarmine, c.1613 [H]

Bell, John (*c*.1811–95) A leading English Victorian sculptor, born in Suffolk. In 1829 he attended the Royal Academy Schools. He exhibited marble statues and busts in the Royal Academy Exhibition from 1833 to 1877. He made models for Sir Henry COLE's Summerly's Art Manufacturers and also for MINTON's Parian body from 1847, including the figures of Dorothea, Clorinda and Una and the Lion. Some bear his name as part of the mark.

Bell and baluster A turned bell shape above a slender BALUSTER. The bell and baluster form was generally applied to the legs of English and Dutch furniture from the late 17th and 18th centuries.

Bellangé, Pierre-Antoine (1758–1827) A French cabinet-maker and founder of a dynasty of furniture-makers. By 1788 he was a *maître* ÉBÉNISTE and was employed by royal households, primarily that of Louis XVIII, for whom he produced imposing EMPIRE STYLE furniture. He also executed furniture commissions for the American White House.

Bellarmine A type of German salt-glazed STONEWARE wine or beer flagon, moulded below the rim with a bearded face of a man said to be Cardinal Bellarmine (1542–1621) who was intensely disliked in Protestant countries. The shape originated in Cologne in the mid-16th century and was made in the Rhineland, Flanders and London until the end of the 17th century.

Belleek, American A term given in the US to late 19th- and early 20th-century porcelain of US manufacture that was inspired by Irish BELLEEK PORCELAIN or, more commonly, contemporary Royal WORCESTER art porcelain. The name "Belleek" was used as a trademark and may be printed on the wares of the OTT & BREWER PORCELAIN FACTORY of

American Belleek vase
by Ott & Brewer, c.1900 [N]

Trenton, New Jersey, its successor, the LENOX PORCELAIN CO. and the Willets factory, also of Trenton.

Belleek porcelain factory Founded in County Fermanagh, Northern Ireland, in 1863 by David McBirney and Robert Armstrong. The delicate porcelain of PARIAN type with an iridescent glaze manufactured by Belleek was used for vases (often shell-shaped) and dishes. Other typical products are baskets with openwork lattice

1863–91

Irish Belleek porcelain basket,
1863–90 [H]

sides applied with roses, shamrocks and daisies. The history of the factory has been divided into periods and the marks change accordingly. The factory also made earthenware for household wares. The Belleek factory is still operating today.

Belle époque A French term for the period of comparative peace and prosperity from the end of the 19th century until the outbreak of World War I in 1914. The style was epitomized by the paintings and posters of French artist Henri de TOULOUSE-LAUTREC.

Belle Vue Pottery Established in 1869 by Frederick Mitchell (d.1875) in Rye, Sussex, England. It lasted under the family ownership until World War II in 1939. The Sussex pig, hops and sprigs were popular motifs. Glaze colours were usually brown or green, the latter obtained from powdered brass left over from pin-making.

It was re-opened as the Rye Pottery by John C. Cole in 1947 and is still active, renowned for its hand-painted figures.

Belleek vase, early
20th century [P]

Bellflower A term used mainly in American decorative arts to describe the pendant flower commonly termed a HUSK in England, used in the European NEO-CLASSICAL period from about 1775. Bellflower images are derived from Greco-Roman fresco painting and appear mainly as inlay in American furniture of the FEDERAL period, particularly examples made in Baltimore, and chased on silver.

Bellflower

Bellin, Jacques Nicolas (1703–72) A French cartographer and publisher, the French Navy's first hydrographic engineer. He carried out major coastal surveys of France and other parts of the world. Bellin is renowned for his many large-scale, high quality sea charts. He also produced the decorative maps in Prévost's 1746 book of travel narratives, *Histoire Générale des Voyages*.

Bell metal Alloys of copper and tin in different proportions yield progressively bronze, gun metal, bell metal and brass. Bell metal is pale yellowish because of the relatively high proportion of tin (about 25 per cent). When struck, bell metal resonates sonorously and is therefore ideally suited to the casting of bells.

Bell-top case A type of wooden case found on 18th-century English BRACKET CLOCKS in which the top is shaped like a bell, with convex mouldings above and concave mouldings below.

Bell toys A more or less elaborate young child's toy, popular in the US. They were made in TINPLATE from the late 19th-century, CAST IRON in the early 20th and pressed steel in the later 20th century. The toys consist of a simple

mechanism in which a bell is operated by a cam and chimes as the toy is pulled – or pushed – along on its wheels.

Belper pottery A producer of STONEWARE in Belper in Derbyshire, from 1809 to 1834. The name "Belper" is usually impressed into the body. It was owned by the BOURNE family of Denby and was transferred there in 1834. The Bournes also acquired the Codnor Park pottery and the "Codnor Park" mark was used from 1833 until 1861 when the workmen were moved to the DENBY POTTERY.

Belter, John Henry See p.54.

Benares brasswork A term for domestic brassware such as large trays and salvers, made by hand in Benares (Varanasi), India, and exported to the West in large quantities in the 19th century. Imitations were manufactured in Birmingham, England, sent to India and re-imported, but authentic Indian pieces can be identified by their engravings depicting scenes and deities from Hindu mythology.

Bendigo pottery An Australian pottery founded in 1857 at Bendigo in Victoria by a Scot,

US bell toy, late 19th century [L]

George Guthrie. The pottery made domestic ware until 1914, then developed a line of portrait jugs of military personnel. It is still in production today.

Bends The curved pieces of wood, also called runners, that join the front and back of a rocking chair and allow it to rock.

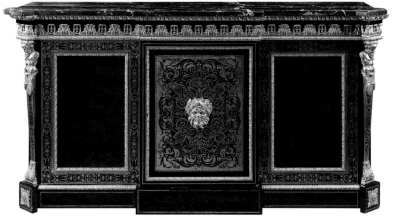

Guillaume Beneman side cabinet, c.1775 [A]

Beneman (or Benneman), Guillaume (d.1811) A French cabinet-maker, probably born in Germany. He was working in Paris *c.*1784 and by 1785 he was a *maître* ÉBÉNISTE, making furniture for the royal household of Louis XVI, including a writing desk for the king, based on the famous Bureau du Roi made for Louis XIV by Jean-Henri RIESENER and Jean-François OEBEN. He succeeded Riesener as Court cabinet-maker and became responsible for all the furniture made for the royal palaces. However, he went on to become better known for his furniture in the DIRECTOIRE and EMPIRE styles, some after designs by Charles PERCIER, that he made for Napoleon I.

Bennett, John (1840–1907) A Staffordshire ceramics decorator who worked for the DOULTON POTTERY AND PORCELAIN factory before emigrating to the US in 1877. In New York, he sold MORRIS- and ISLAMIC-style pieces, decorated with colourful UNDERGLAZE painting, to TIFFANY & CO. among others.

John Henry Belter (1804–63)

The German furniture-maker Johann-Heinrich Belter emigrated to America in 1840 and produced furniture in New York City from 1844. His pieces catered for a rapidly expanding middle class in the US, where there was an enormous furniture-making industry by the mid-19th century.

New techniques for new styles

From the beginning of his career in New York, Belter focused on the production of seat furniture designed for use in the "parlour", or formal living room that became a fixture in American and European suburban homes following the railway boom of the 1840s. Belter's "parlour suites" typically consisted of one or two sofas, a chaise-longue or *récamier*, armchairs for ladies and gentlemen, side chairs, side tables and a centre table.

Belter's success was largely due to his patent process of laminating sheets of rosewood into a ply that could then be bent in complex curves by steaming into lightweight but sturdy forms. The process was first patented by him in 1847. By the time of his death, it was widely copied, mostly by rival firms in New York, notably Anthony BAUDOUINE and Joseph MEEKS, leaving a legacy of American furniture still generically referred to as "Belter". The laminating and bending technique had been used in Germany in the 1830s and Belter may have seen the process or even learned it from the work of the German furniture-maker Michael THONET in Coblenz.

The process proved ideal for seat backs in richly carved and pierced extravagant ROCOCO REVIVAL furniture. This genre was extremely popular in a rapidly expanding American market, particularly after it was displayed at the New York City "Crystal Palace" International Exhibition of 1853, and Belter went on to open an extensive furniture-making factory on Third Avenue in 1854. His furniture is, however, rarely found outside North America. Belter furniture is typically of parlour type, in dark brown laminated rosewood. The laminates are thinly cut and tightly glued together, including up to 12 layers of rosewood. Seat backs are extremely thin, less than one inch in most cases, and feel sturdy with a natural springiness, despite being heavily pierced. Decoration is typical of the art of immigrant craftsmen who had recently arrived from central Europe.

The style of the furniture is heavily influenced by Rococo Revival, popular in Europe at the time, and Belter probably used imported French and English pattern-books. Popular motifs are richly carved fruit, floral bouquets and cartouches, which could follow the elaborate S-scrolls of a chair or sofa back or a cabriole leg. Belter furniture has grown in popularity and demand over the last 20 years, to a point where the best examples rival Federal furniture in value. Much of it shows evidence of neglect from being largely ignored by dealers and collectors for most of the 20th century, however, and more common examples in poor condition are of less value. Belter's factory was briefly continued by his brother-in-law, Springmeyer, but closed due to bankruptcy in 1867.

Rococo Revival laminated rosewood side chair, upholstered in damask, c.1845–65 [H]

Rococo Revival ebonized rosewood centre table with marble top, c.1845–65 [I]

Rococo Revival carved rosewood sofa with pierced serpentine crest, c.1850–1860 [B]

Bennett Pottery An American pottery founded by English-born James Bennet in East Liverpool, Ohio (now part of Pittsburgh), in 1839 to make inexpensive, useful pottery. In 1841 he was joined by his three brothers, Daniel, Edwin and William, and the range later expanded to include PARIAN porcelain. Edwin went on to found a successful pottery in his own name in Baltimore in 1846, which made a wide range of ware, including majolica and art pottery, until 1936.

Bennington treacle-glazed lion, 1850 [K]

Bennington pottery The largest manufacturer of ceramics in the US during the 19th century was founded by John Norton as a brickworks in Bennington, Vermont, in 1793. It remained largely in the control of the Norton family until closure in 1894. Early production at Bennington was mostly crude redware and salt-glazed stoneware vessels of a type known in the US as crocks, which include large storage vessels for water, maple syrup and liquor. Crocks are typically of pale grey or buff colour with impressed manufacturers' marks, and may be decorated with cobalt blue folk art designs. In 1842, the Norton family took Christopher Webber Fenton as a partner who, together with English immigrant workers from the COPELAND factory, began the production of PARIAN porcelain including statuary, pitchers and mantelpiece vases. They also used a colourful mottled variety of ROCKINGHAM GLAZE termed "flint

enamel" or, when it was brown, "treacle glaze". This ware was known as Rockingham ware in the US. From 1849 until 1858 the works was known as the UNITED STATES POTTERY COMPANY.

Benson, William Arthur Smith (1854–1924) An architect by profession, Benson became a renowned late 19th-century English metalwork designer and also designed furniture. In 1880 he opened his own workshops followed by a factory in 1883 (closed in 1923). Benson was a friend of William MORRIS, a director of furniture at Morris & Co. from 1896 and a founder member of the ART WORKERS' GUILD. His showroom in Bond Street was well regarded for his useful but aesthetic electric lamps and other domestic metalwares.

Bent limbs As the name suggests, a baby doll's COMPOSITION limbs moulded at a slight angle at elbows and knees, used to assemble the so-called five-piece baby body.

Bentwood furniture Michael THONET developed his bentwood furniture in 1842, using steam to bend the frame. It was very successful and, when his patent ran out in 1869, many firms were eager to repeat his success. One rival firm, J. & J. Kohn, had the foresight to commission leading designers such as Josef HOFFMANN from the WIENER WERKSTÄTTE. Thonet's furniture won him many medals including one at the Great Exhibition in 1851 in London. The chairs could be flat-packed for export and re-assembled on arrival.

Bérain, Jean (1639–1711) A leading French architect and designer at the court of Louis XIV. The son of a gunsmith, he was employed as an engraver by the French court from 1670 and progressed to become chief designer to Louis XIV by 1690. He is best known today for his engraved designs, published as a collection in 1711, for furniture, chimney pieces and other interior decoration featuring light and elegant grotesques, incorporating figures of satyrs, bandwork, acanthus, festoons, birds and sometimes Chinese figures and monkeys (see SINGERIE). Such ornament is found on BOULLE MARQUETRY furniture, BEAUVAIS TAPESTRIES, goldsmiths' work and French FAIENCE of the time.

Bergama An important Turkish carpet-weaving area (formerly Pergamon), where village workshops have been producing rugs since the 13th century. Quality varies from coarse to fine wool pile on wool warps. The weft is usually reddish brown. Designs are geometric and strongly influenced by the Caucasus and Turkoman products. Harmonic shades of terracotta, blues and apricot are typical. See also TURKISH CARPETS.

Bentwood rocking chair, English 1930s [O]

Berlin porcelain factory

The Royal Porcelain Factory in Berlin reflected the power and prestige of the Prussian throne in the late 18th and 19th centuries and supplied the royal family and nobility with ornate tableware that reflected their status.

Floral painted cabinet plate, made for display, c.1820 [N]

The beginnings

Wilhelm Kaspar Wegely set up the first porcelain factory c.1751. He recruited workers from MEISSEN and HÖCHST and produced both figures and useful wares, inspired by Meissen and Vienna. However, Wegely went bankrupt in 1757. A merchant, Johann Ernst Gotzkowsky, set up a new factory, having bought the "secret" of porcelain-making from one of Wegely's workers. F.E. Meyer was appointed modelling master in 1761 and two landscape painters from Meissen were also employed.

Gotzkowsky in turn went bankrupt and the company was sold to Frederick the Great in 1763 and became the Royal Porcelain Manufactory with the king himself taking an active interest. The famous service made for his palace Sans Souci, with oriental figures within a yellow border, is a fine example of German ROCOCO taste. Frederick ordered many services for his castles, as well as snuff-boxes as presents for his generals and visitors. The style of the wares was strongly influenced by Meissen. The brothers Elias and Christian Meyer were in charge of modelling. In 1789 Karl Friedrich Riese produced classical-style figures. In 1771 a fine KAOLIN clay had been found in Brachwitz, near Halle, which the factory still uses. The porcelain produced in the BIEDERMEIER period, often to the designs of Karl Friedrich Schinkel (1781–1841), was of high quality. Large vases with fine landscape painting are particularly noteworthy, as well as richly decorated "cabinet" wares. The painter Alexander Kips became artistic director in 1886 and for 22 years exerted great influence.

Solitaire set decorated with classical figures and trophies, c.1890 [G]

In the late 19th century, Berlin produced large porcelain plaques, often finely painted with copies of famous paintings. At the turn of the century, the sculptor and modeller Paul Scheurich worked at the factory for a short time producing Rococo-style figures in contemporary dress. The factory was destroyed in World War II (in 1943) but the porcelain collection and library had been moved to Selb. After various other moves, the Berlin and Selb works were reunited in 1955–57. Since 1918 it has been styled Staatliche Porzellan Manufaktur Berlin.

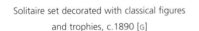

Factory marks

Through the history of the factory the mark most used is the sceptre in underglaze blue, with KPM (for Königliche Porzellan-Manufaktur) in the mid-19th century.

KPM	**W**	*Gf*	✝	**KPM**
From 1832	Wegely 1752–57	Gotskowsky factory 1761–63	Royal factory 1763–1823	1823–1837

Ovoid milk jug, 19th century [Q]

Caned mahogany bergère, c.1810 [I]

Bergère A type of informal and comfortable EASY chair, of generous proportions with upholstered or caned back and sides and a deep seat with a SQUAB CUSHION. First made in France in the 18th century, the bergère was copied throughout Europe both at the time and into the 19th and 20th centuries.

Berlin ironwork Cast-iron jewellery and other small objects made in Berlin and popular from the early to the mid-19th century. It was first made c.1813–15, during the war with France, when wealthy Prussian women were given iron jewellery in exchange for gold and silver pieces, to help the war effort. Such items as brooches, necklaces, rings and fans had delicate OPENWORK designs often with NEO-CLASSICAL, and later GOTHIC, motifs.

Berlin potteries There were several faience factories in Berlin and north-west Germany, producing good faience decorated in both underglaze blue and colours, from the late 17th century to the end of the 18th. The earlier styles copied Chinese porcelain both in shape and in decoration. By the 18th century it had a more German flavour and beer-tankards were produced in quantity. Among known factories were those of Gerhard Wolbeer (1678–1770), Cornelius Funcke (1699–1767) and Karl Friedrich Lüdicke (1756–79).

Berlin tapestry factory Set up in 1685 by Pierre Mercier (d.1729), a Huguenot weaver from AUBUSSON. Most notable among early production was a series of histories of the Great Elector, Frederick William of Brandenburg. In 1714 Jean Barraband (1687–1725) took over, joined in 1720 by Charles Vigne. Under their influence production changed to incorporate the fashionable CHINOISERIES, COMMEDIA DELL'ARTE, hunting and genre scenes. The factory closed in 1769.

Berlin woolwork Embroidery worked in coloured wools on a canvas background, either in plain TENT STITCH or CROSS STITCH with designs and wools originally imported from Berlin. It was a popular home craft in 19th century England. The designs were available on squared paper to be transferred to the canvas by the embroiderer or worked from a kit. Patterns available included slippers, bags and fire screens. Pictures and sampler motifs were fashionable from the 1830s to the 1880s.

Bernberg pottery A pottery started by Johann David Kratzenberg in the town of Bernberg in north-west Germany in 1725. It produced faience decorated in Chinese blue and white style often with LAUB-UND-BANDELWERK and coats of arms. The factory probably closed c.1774.

Bertoia, Harry (b.1915) An American graduate of the CRANBROOK ACADEMY,

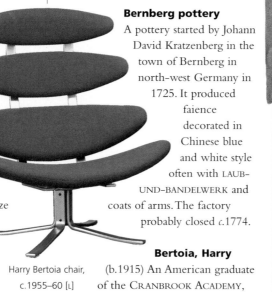

Harry Bertoia chair, c.1955–60 [L]

metal sculptor and furniture designer. He is best known for chairs of "Organic Modernist" forms, made in wire mesh and tubular steel for KNOLL.

Bessarabia An area in the borders of Moldavia and Romania known for weaving rugs, carpets and KILIMS from the 18th century onward. Loose piled weavings were based upon French SAVONNERIE designs, double-wefted with a TURKISH KNOT. Piled weaving ceased at the outbreak of the Crimean war in 1854. Kilims were made throughout the 19th century, designs were simple and uncrowded, with a mixture of naturalistic floral forms in pastel shades on an ivory or black background.

Bessarabian kilim, 19th century [E]

Bevel A sloped or slanting edge of a flat surface, generally referring to glass or wood. Bevelled glass has a chamfered corner, made by cutting away the edge where the two flat surfaces meet at a right angle. This is seen, for example, on the edges of mirrors, which are usually bevelled to protect against chipping. In furniture, the term may also refer to an applied MOULDING.

Ludwigsberg fisher girl by J.C.W. Beyer, c.1760 [H]

Beyer, Johann Christian Wilhelm

(1725–1806) One of the leading German porcelain modellers of the 18th century. Born in Thuringia, Germany, he trained as an architect, painter and sculptor in Dresden, Paris and Rome. From 1759 he worked for Duke Karl of Württemberg at the LUDWIGSBURG porcelain factory, where he produced a series of outstanding figures, with elements of both ROCOCO and NEO-CLASSICAL styles. In 1768 he was appointed court painter and sculptor in Vienna, where he spent the rest of his working life.

Bi (or pi) A Chinese term for a flat disc of jade of various colours, with a hole in the centre, used for ritualistic or emblematic purposes until the abdication of the last Manchu emperor in 1912. The earliest examples are undecorated and date from the Neolithic age (*c*.9000–*c*.2000 BC), while later examples become more highly decorated. They represent the sun or heaven.

Bianchetto A buff pottery covered with a coating of fine white clay or SLIP, which is fired and then decorated with painted designs and covered with a soft lead glaze. It preceded MAIOLICA at FAENZA and other Italian potteries.

Bianco (or bianchi) di Faenza A type of white MAIOLICA introduced at FAENZA from *c*.1550, sometimes elaborately modelled and lightly decorated with coloured motifs. Instantly popular, it replaced ISTORIATO wares and was adopted by other Italian and European potteries, until the 19th century.

Bianco-sopra-bianco (Italian: "white over white") A technique originating in Italian MAIOLICA wares from the early 16th century, denoting painting in opaque white over, or on, a greyish white ground. From the mid-18th century, the technique was adopted by other European potteries such as RÖRSTRAND, LAMBETH and BRISTOL.

Bibelot A small, principally decorative object, such as a SNUFF-BOX or ETUI, either carried on the person or displayed on chimneypieces and/or furniture.

Bible box A type of box, usually of oak, used in Britain from the late 16th century and throughout the 17th, to hold a bible and important family documents. They had simple hinged lids, often sloping. Bible boxes were made during the Colonial period in the US and were often set on a stand – a precursor of the HIGHBOY.

White jade bi disc, 18th century [K]

Bidet A small bath, basin or bowl supported on a wooden stand, first made in the early 18th century in France and designed to allow women in particular to wash the lower part of the body. The basin might be SILVER, METAL or PORCELAIN; the stand was often of WALNUT or a rare wood. Unusual outside France, although designs by SHERATON exist.

Bidri A type of Indian metalwork, originating in Bidar in the 17th century but now made throughout northern India. SPICE BOXES, hookah bases and other wares are cast from an alloy of zinc, blackened by immersion in a mixture of sal ammoniac and saltpetre, then inlaid with DIAPER, FLORAL or LEAF patterns in silver, brass or gold. Imported to Europe during the 19th century.

Biemann intaglio cut glass portrait paperweight c.1830 [K]

Biemann, Dominik (1800–57)

A leading Bohemian glass engraver. Born in Novy Svet (now part of Czechoslovakia) he trained at the Novy Svet glassworks on the estates of the counts of Harrach, where he acquired a mastery of INTAGLIO engraving that earned his reputation as one of the finest engravers in the BIEDERMEIER STYLE. He later worked largely in Prague and from 1826 was known for engraved intaglio portraits on glasses, beakers and plaques.

Biennais, Martin-Guillaume

(1764–1843) A leading French silversmith and cabinet-maker. By 1789 he had set up business as a cabinet-maker and dealer in Paris, but after the dissolution of the guild system in 1797 began manufacturing and dealing in silver and jewellery. He produced large quantities of silver, in particular NECESSAIRES for Napoleon and his family and Greek Revival dinner services for the Russian, Austrian and Bavarian courts, as well as the regalia for Napoleon's coronation.

Biedermeier style

A style of decorative arts popular in Germany, Austria and Scandinavia from c.1815 to the 1840s. Its development was associated with the revival of the German furniture trade after the defeat of Napoleon and, most importantly, the increasing power and prosperity of the middle classes.

Chair in typically light-coloured maple, c.1820 [N]

Bourgeois virtues

The style was named after Gottlieb Biedermeier, the pseudonym of a 19th-century German author of comic poems, and derives from *bieder* (plain, honest) and Meier, a common German surname. It is most evident in furniture, which is characterized by simple, symmetrical and classical forms generally derived from EMPIRE and REGENCY furniture. The overall effect is one of solidity and comfort, especially with the invention of coil-spring upholstery, the patent for which was taken out by a Viennese upholsterer, Georg Junigl, in 1822. Cabinet-makers favoured the use of large plain areas of VENEERS, in light-coloured woods, especially MAPLE, CHERRY and BIRCH, revealing the intrinsic beauty of the wood grain, and often contrasted with sparing use of contrasting inlay in EBONY. Motifs are generally NEO-CLASSICAL, for example COLUMNS, PILASTERS and LYRES, as well as geometric, such as circles, stars and ovals. Much Biedermeier furniture was made by anonymous craftsmen, although leading makers such as Josef Danhauser (1780–1829) of Vienna, employed by the Archduke Charles of Austria, also designed furniture in this style.

The Biedermeier style also appeared in German and Austrian glass and ceramics. In glass, makers such as Dominik BIEMANN produced finely engraved pieces, decorated with classical portrait busts or religious scenes, while the new techniques of coloured glass such as LITHYALIN were used to embellish traditional forms such as tumblers and beakers. These also appeared with topographical views, often intended as souvenirs for the growing tourist trade.

Beaker by Egermann in Liithyalin glass c.1830 [K]

At the porcelain factories of BERLIN and VIENNA, single decorative pieces or small services were produced for the middle-class market, replacing the large table services previously made for royalty and aristocracy. Typical products were decorated with profile portraits or topographical views of such buildings as the Berlin Opera House or Royal Palace, framed by gilt borders.

As in furniture, ceramic forms were based on classical prototypes, for example urns and KRATERS for vases, but shapes are heavier and more rounded or flaring than in the Neo-classical period. From the 1840s the Biedermeier style declined in fashion, as ornament became richer, incorporating shells, fruits, flowers and other elements of the ROCOCO REVIVAL style. Its simplicity and restraint, however, inspired avant-garde designers in the late 19th and early 20th centuries and many copies continued to be made.

The enduring legacy of Biedermeier: a 1920s Danish copy of an 1840s original [K]

Biedermeider style used the traditional ornamentation of 18th century furniture in simplified form. It particularly favoured urns, shells and lyres, and also restrained geometric shapes.

Shell motif

Table of simple geometric shape

Biggin A coffee pot or hot-water jug in silver or SHEFFIELD PLATE with a stand and spirit burner, attributed to the 18th-century silversmith George Biggin. Introduced *c*.1790 and made through the 19th century, they were designed for portability, for example while conducting parliamentary campaigns. They are often cylindrical with a lip spout, minimal decoration and a detachable cover.

Bigot, Alexandre (1862–1927) A French artist potter, important in the growth of ART POTTERY in Paris. He experimented with FLAMBÉ GLAZES and was interested in incorporating ceramics as a decorative feature in architecture.

Bilbao mirror A type of mirror, framed with marble or marble and wood, popular in the late 18th century. They were named after the port of Bilbao in Spain from where the mirrors were exported.

Billet A moulding ornament of rounded or squared blocks. In ROMANESQUE STYLE architecture, the billet was typically spaced in a regular pattern along a moulding. A series of billets used together is sometimes known as a "billet frieze".

Pinxton trio painted with William Billingsley landscapes, late 18th-century [J]

Billingsley, William (1758–1828) An important English porcelain decorator, son of a decorator at the Chelsea factory. He was apprenticed as a painter at DERBY when he was 16 years old. From Derby he went to PINXTON. He was at Mansfield from 1799 to 1802 and at WORCESTER in 1808. In 1813 he went to Wales and worked at SWANSEA and NANTGARW, being largely responsible for the success of these factories. In 1819 he went to John ROSE's factory in COALPORT. His flower painting is in a soft, naturalistic style with the highlights added by brushing out the enamel colours; "Billingsley rose" is a famous motif. He also painted landscapes and was a talented gilder on porcelain.

Bilsted (*Liquidambar styraciflua*) A wood used as an alternative to mahogany in 18th-century American furniture-making.

Bilston enamel factories A group of factories in Bilston and Wednesbury, Staffordshire, UK, producing enamelled snuff-boxes, scent bottles, small decorative plaques for jewellery and other OBJECTS OF VERTU, from the mid-18th century to the early 19th. The largest firm was established by Benjamin Bickley in 1749. The enamel-on-copper wares, imitating MEISSEN and CHELSEA, feature typically Rococo-style painted decoration, such as landscapes, floral bouquets and exotic birds in pale colours, often embellished with gilding. Great quantities of the ware were exported to Europe and the US. The last factory closed in 1831.

Bilston enamel étui with Rococo decoration and portrait, 18th century [L]

Bilston japanning factories A group of factories at Bilston, Staffordshire, UK, manufacturing JAPANNED wares such as snuff-boxes made from tin-plated sheet iron and decorated with CHINOISERIE patterns or flowers. The earliest pieces date from the 1690s but production continued until the 19th century.

Japanned metalware tends to be generically called PONTYPOOL WARE or tole. (See also TOLEWARE.)

Binche lace A Flemish centre for fine BOBBIN LACE from the late 17th century and densely patterned STRAIGHTLACE used for narrow fashion trimming in the early 18th century. It is similar to VALENCIENNES lace.

Gebrüder Bing stationary steam engine, c.1902 [L]

Bing, Gebrüder A German toy and bear company founded in 1865 by the brothers (Gebrüder) Ignaz and Adolf Bing in Nuremberg, using the trademark GBN. They began making tinplate toys in the early 1880s, prospering particularly during the 1920s but foundering in the world slump in 1932. Their vast catalogue of STEAM, CLOCKWORK and ELECTRICALLY powered toys and models included stationary steam engines, ships, railways and accessories, dynamos, MAGIC LANTERNS and telephones. They manufactured for Germany, France, England and the US, tailoring the toys and their finishes to each market. Bing produced their first teddy bears in 1907. They resembled those produced by STEIFF and even had a metal button to identify them. Bing bears often had mechanical abilities, for example some could even turn somersaults. The company closed in 1932.

Gebrüder Bing bear, c.1920 [H]

Bing, Samuel (Siegfried) (1838–1905) An influential dealer, collector, publisher and promoter of ART NOUVEAU and Japanese art in Paris. He opened his famous shop, the Maison L'Art Nouveau, in 1895 and sold pieces by leading designers of the style – Emile GALLÉ, Louis Comfort TIFFANY and René LALIQUE. He also commissioned work directly from designers such as Edouard Colonna, Georges de Feure, Leon Jallot and Eugene Gaillard.

Bing & Grøndahl A porcelain factory in Copenhagen, Denmark, founded in 1853 by Harold Bing, whose products rivalled the COPENHAGEN PORCELAIN FACTORY. In 1885 Pietro Krohn took over as art director, and in 1888 designed the "Heron" service. The company exhibited at the Paris Exhibition of 1900, in particular models by Kai Nielsen (1882–1924) and Jean Gauguin, son of the artist Paul Gauguin. At the end of the 19th century, the company began the tradition of annual Christmas and Easter plates, which continues to this day. Later designers for the factory included Henning KOPPEL.

Bing & Grøndahl vase painted by Fanny Garde, c.1908 [N]

Binns, Charles Fergus (1857–1934) An English-born American educator, technologist and potter, the most influential figure in US ceramics in the first quarter of the 20th century. In 1900 he became the first director of the New York School of Clay Working at Alfred University, which later became the New York State College of Ceramics, and was director for 35 years. It was the leading institution for ceramic education and research in the US. He worked in high-fired stoneware of simple design, inspired by Chinese porcelain.

Birch (*Betula alba*) A tree native to northern Europe that produces a golden wood with a reddish tinge, often used as a substitute for SATINWOOD. From the late 18th century, furniture-makers – especially Russian and eastern European – used birch in the solid for chairs and other furniture. It was also used as a veneer.

Birdcage support

Birdcage support A structure used from c.1740–65 on high quality English and American TILT-TOP TABLES, consisting of four small pillars between a small square top and a base. This "cage" is hinged to the top of the table and allows the top to be tilted vertically for storage. It provides a solid support for the table when it is in use and sufficient depth so that the table top can be held rigidly to its central support by a wedge.

Bird's-eye maple A variant of MAPLE wood (*Acer* spp.), a tree native to northern Europe, the US and Canada, that has a figuring of light brown rings that resemble birds' eyes. It became fashionable as a VENEER in the late 18th century and in the REGENCY period, and was used from the mid- to late 19th century for bedroom furniture. The bird's-eye figure is also found in other timbers.

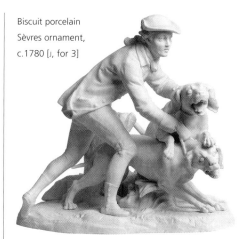

Biscuit porcelain Sèvres ornament, c.1780 [J, for 3]

Biscuit porcelain A term used to denote the porcelain BODY after its first firing, when it is white and with a matt appearance, and before it is glazed. It was used for making small sculptures at the end of the 18th century and beginning of the 19th century at SÈVRES and MEISSEN especially, and also at DERBY.

Biscuit tin The famous British biscuit makers Huntley & Palmer first used tins to house biscuits for sale c.1837. Early handmade tins were soon replaced by machine-made tins, and the 1877 development of off-set LITHOGRAPHY introduced a riot of bright colours and designs to biscuit tins. They were produced in a wide range of novel and attractive shapes including cars, trains and books, sometimes in honour of events such as royal jubilees.

English biscuit tin, c.1900 [S]

German bisque doll, 1890s [R]

Bisque An unglazed porcelain mainly used between 1860 and 1925 to make DOLLS' heads. Bisque is fired twice, initially at a high temperature, before the surface is painted and re-fired at a lower temperature.

Bizarre silk A style of European woven silks produced in the late 17th and early 18th centuries. Asymmetrical designs often incorporated elements from Chinese, Japanese and Indian floral patterns with architectural devices. The fashion for "bizarre" elements virtually disappeared by c.1725 but was revived by Clarice CLIFF in her "Bizarre" pottery range of 1928.

Bizen potteries Located at Imbe in the Bizen province and one of the "Six Old Kilns" of Japan where, in the 12th to 14th centuries, many of the technical advances in Japanese ceramics were made. Bizen wares were one of the first types of Japanese pottery used for TEA CEREMONY articles. Main characteristics are a high-fired body, unglazed coarse texture and warm, reddish brown colour which varies with "chance" effects produced when oxygen is allowed into the kiln. In the 17th and 18th centuries a smooth ware imitating Chinese YIXING stoneware was made. Production continued through the 19th and 20th centuries.

Bizen moon-shaped wall-hanging vase, c.1860–1900 [N]

Black, Starr & Frost Silversmiths, jewellers and retailers active in New York City from 1876 until c.1940. The firm suceeded BALL, TOMPKINS & BLACK and operated mainly as a retailer, rivalling TIFFANY & CO. Stamped marks appear on silver and metal mounts.

Black basaltes See BASALTES WARE.

Blackamoor A Venetian decorative device in the form of a life-size carved figure of a black slave dressed in an exotic multicoloured costume. Blackamoors were in popular use as a pedestal supports for such pieces as TORCHÈRES from the 18th century through to the early 20th.

Black Forest clock, late 19th century [Q]

Black Forest clock A type of weight-driven WALL CLOCK made in the Black Forest region of Germany since the mid-17th century. Early examples were made almost entirely of wood by local craftsmen, but from the mid-19th century mass-produced ones usually had steel or brass movements. CUCKOO CLOCKS and TRUMPETER CLOCKS were also made.

Black jack A sturdy drinking tankard or flask of stout or tapering form made from plain or decoratively tooled rigid leather, often with silver or pewter mounts or linings. Some black jacks are large, holding a gallon of beer. They are known since the 17th century, but were almost certainly used much earlier.

Black marble clock, 19th-century [O]

Black marble clock A type of mass-produced 19th-century French MANTEL CLOCK with a case made in or faced with black marble. Inexpensive versions feature polished black slate instead of marble.

Blackwork Also known as Spanishwork, blackwork is a monochrome embroidery technique usually using black thread and sometimes embellished with metal thread. Blackwork was introduced into Europe by the Moors via Spain, becoming a particularly fashionable decoration on costume during the 16th century.

Blaeu, Willem Janszoon (1571–1638) **and Joan** (1596–1673) Willem Blaeu was the founder of one of the leading Dutch map-making firms of the 17th century. He produced important individual maps as well as a sea ATLAS and a series of world atlases that culminated in the publication, by his son Joan, of the *Atlas Maior* (Grand Atlas) in 1662. Issued in various languages and editions between 1662 and 1672 (when a disastrous fire destroyed the plates and ruined the firm), the *Atlas Maior* is a masterpiece of Dutch "Golden Age" cartography and arguably the most magnificent atlas ever published. A work of art, it is prized for its superbly engraved maps, enriched by decorative CARTOUCHES and flowing calligraphy.

Blanc-de-Chine
figure of Guanyin,
18th century [c]

Bleu celeste
A turquoise glaze used
at the SÈVRES porcelain
factory as a ground colour.
Introduced in 1752, it was
developed by Jean Hellot
(1685–1766), decorator and
chemist at Sèvres from 1745–1766. Also
used on 19th-century copies of Sèvres.

Vincennes bleu
celeste seau à
liqueur, 1754 [c]

Bleu de roi A blue (royal blue) glaze first
used at VINCENNES *c.*1749, then at
SÈVRES. It was also used on English
porcelain at CHELSEA and WORCESTER.

Bleu persan A dark blue glaze on a
pottery body, copying Chinese and
Persian styles. Designs of foliage, lace or
ironwork in opaque white enamel
contrast with the solid blue background.
A technique much used at the French
faience factory at NEVERS and copied on
early English DELFTWARE (late 17th and
early 18th centuries).

Blind tooling The process whereby
impressions are made in the cover
material of books, principally leather,
with stamps or tools, sometimes with the
addition of heat. The impressed design
remains plain with no gilding, foil or
colour. The tool firstly "strikes" the
material to create the impression and is
secondly pressed and rocked to polish and
set the impression. Blind tooling has been
used to decorate books and other leather
items since the 7th or 8th centuries.

Blind tracery Ornamental decoration
with flowing lines derived from
GOTHIC architecture and applied as
carved wood to furniture from the 14th
century onward. Unlike PIERCED
DECORATION, blind
tracery has a
solid backing.

Block-front In American furniture, a
form of serpentine front in which the
outer edges of wide drawers protrude,
used mainly in AMERICAN CHIPPENDALE
style for chests of drawers and kneehole
desks. The best block-fronts are carved
from a solid piece of mahogany.

Block-front drawers

Blonde lace Delicate, mainly French and
Spanish, blonde silk BOBBIN LACE
fashionable from the mid-18th to early
19th centuries. Black blonde lace was also
made. See also CHANTILLY LACE.

Bloom Dulling of the surface of old glass
from exposure to damp, smoke and fumes,
an excess of alkali in the ingredients, or
extreme abrasion or total erosion of
gilding and enamelling. Also the powdery
residue left on furniture stripped in a
tank. See also CRIZZLING (in lead glass).

Blowing One of the earliest methods of
making glass in which a blob of molten
glass is gathered on the end of a hollow
rod. The glass-maker then blows through
the rod forcing the glass into either a freeblown or a mould-blown shape.

Blanc-de-Chine A type of Chinese
porcelain, usually white, made at DEHUA
in the Fujian province from the MING
DYNASTY (1368–1644) to the present day.
Wares include crisply modelled figures,
cups, bowls and joss stick-holders. Blanc-
de-Chine was exported to Europe and
copied in the 17th and 18th centuries.

Blanket chest A wooden chest,
sometimes called a coffer, coffre or joined
chest, known as storage furniture since the
Middle Ages. Usually of oak, the first
simple construction was of boards nailed
together. Panelled construction began in
the 15th century. Some chests have inlaid
or LINENFOLD panels or carvings.

Bleeding bowl A shallow bowl in silver,
pewter or ceramic, with one flat pierced
handle. Made in the 17th
and early 18th centuries,
they were used by
surgeon barbers when
bleeding patients. Some
bowls had a semi-circular
segment removed (see BARBER'S
BASIN). In the US bleeding bowls
are known as porringers.

Silver bleeding
bowl by John
Duck, 1683 [H]

Chinese porcelain blue and white
bowl and cover, c.1648 [N]

Liverpool porcelain teapot
with Chinese motifs, c.1765 [M]

Transfer-printed pottery
beaker with chinoiseries, c.1850 [Q]

Blue and white

The term "blue and white" denotes decoration in underglaze blue on the white body of both pottery and porcelain, whether Oriental, European or American, hand-painted or printed.

Oriental inspiration

The first blue and white was Chinese porcelain, which by the 13th century had been perfected to a white translucency, and was painted with cobalt blue. The Chinese technique was just to dry the porcelain body, rather than hardening it in a kiln, before painting. The blue was mixed with water and applied with a brush. It was then glazed and fired in the kiln. Production continued through the centuries, but the blue and white of the Ch'ing dynasty emperor Kangxi (1662–1722) is considered to be the finest technically.

By the beginning of the 17th century China was exporting porcelain to Europe. In the 17th and 18th centuries, Oriental blue and white porcelain was highly prized in Europe and America. Enhanced by fine silver and gold mounts, it was collected by kings and princes. When BÖTTGER made his discovery of porcelain-making at MEISSEN in 1707–09, Chinese porcelain (and stoneware) was the inspiration. The Meissen factory was not initially successful with blue and white but, once it had conquered the technique, it produced its ONION PATTERN, based on a Chinese design and still made today. When England started making SOFT-PASTE PORCELAIN nearly 40 years later, blue and white Chinese porcelain was again the inspiration. WORCESTER made both hand-painted and printed designs, inspired by Chinese patterns and CHINOISERIES. All the other English porcelain-producers followed suit, as did many other European factories. Throughout the 17th century blue and white pottery was made copiously in DELFT and in England as English DELFTWARE.

Oriental blue and white porcelain was copied all over Europe and the US by the 19th century and was used in everyday as well as stately and royal surroundings. European copies were themselves exported all over the world. Blue and white printed wares were an important part of the Staffordshire factories' production. Both painted and printed patterns were used on PEARLWARE, STONEWARE, IRONSTONE CHINA and EARTHENWARE. In the 20th century cargoes of blue and white porcelain were recovered, which had been on their journey from China to Europe in the 17th–19th centuries when they were shipwrecked. The blue and white cargoes were used as ballast in the ships bringing tea to Europe.

Cobalt blue

The Mongolian Yuan dynasty (1280–1358) is famous for introducing a particularly pure cobalt ore from Persia. The finest blue was imported to China and known as "Mohammedan" blue. It was used throughout the Ming dynasty (1368–1660), though supplies were low during the reigns of the emperors Cheng Hua (1465–87) and Wan Li (1573–1619) and later.

Nanking blue and white porcelain meat dish
made in Jingdezhen, c.1780 [N]

English delft blue-dash charger,
c.1690 [G]

Blue-dash charger Charger is a word derived from the Middle English "chargeour" (a large flat dish for carrying things). Made of pottery, it was also a dish to hang on a wall or be placed on a DRESSER or BUFFET as decoration. The term was applied to English dishes made of TIN-GLAZED EARTHENWARE with blue dashes on the rim, and coined by A.E. Downman in his book of 1919.

Blue john A variety of fluorspar, blue john is a violet-blue banded HARDSTONE, which has been used in ornamentation for centuries. Indigenous to the Castleton area of Derbyshire, it is frequently called Derbyshire Spar.

Blue mazarin See MAZARIN BLUE.

Blunderbuss A short, large-calibre gun with a flared muzzle, used from c.1640 to the 1850s. Blunderbuss probably derives from the German *Donnerbuchse* ("thunder-gun"). Loaded with a heavy charge of lead pellets, it was devastating at close range and was greatly favoured by mailcoach guards and on board ship.

Brass-barrelled mariner's
blunderbuss, c.1800 [K]

Boarded chest A crudely constructed chest in which the front and back are made of planks of wood attached with nails to the vertical end pieces rather than by MORTISE AND TENON joints as in a joined chest.

Bobbin A slender wooden or bone spool or reel to hold thread ready to unwind for making BOBBIN LACE. Some are inscribed or weighted with glass beads. See also LACE.

Bobbin lace This lace-making method required the aid of a parchment pattern marked with pins on a hard pillow. Threads wound on BOBBINS were passed round the pins. A ribbon of lace emerged as the pins were moved, resulting in "straightlace". Alternative lace motifs called "part lace" were made separately and then assembled. Italy led the way but centres for making bobbin lace were formed throughout Europe in the 17th and 18th centuries, notably FLANDERS.

Bobik A small table, made in Russia in the late 18th century, with a distinctive kidney-shaped top, often decorated with MARQUETRY, and straight-edged on the inner side.

Bob pendulum A type of PENDULUM consisting of a brass or steel rod with a disc-shaped metal weight (bob) at the end, in use in LONGCASE CLOCKS from c.1660. The timekeeping of a clock can be accelerated or slowed by altering the height of the bob so that the pendulum swings at a different rate.

Bocage A mass of trees or shrubs from a 14th-century French word *bosc*, or in literary English "bosky", meaning bushes or a wood. When used in ceramics it denotes bushes and/or branches around a figure, springing from supporting tree-trunks.

Derby group with bocage and Commedia dell'Arte figures, c.1765 [H]

Boch Frères A ceramic firm founded by Pierre-Joseph Boch (*d*.1818) in Luxembourg in 1767 and continued by subsequent generations of the same family. It merged to become VILLEROY AND BOCH in 1836. When Belgium and Luxembourg were partitioned in 1839 the Belgian branch of the family set up a factory at Keramis in 1841 and traded as Boch Frères, making Art Deco pottery in the 1920s and 30s. The factory is still going.

Boch Frères Art Deco
pottery vase, c.1930 [O]

Body The composite material from which the various types of ceramics – POTTERY, PORCELAIN, EARTHENWARE and STONEWARE – are made. The term refers both to the fired or unfired material. Porcelain body is sometimes known as PASTE.

Boehm, Edward Marshall (1913–69) A US porcelain-maker, founder of Edward Marshall Boehm Inc. in Trenton, New Jersey, in 1950. The firm specialized in realistic animal and bird sculptures in naturalistic BISCUIT porcelain, comparable to the work of Dorothy Doughty at ROYAL WORCESTER, modelled by Boehm. The firm continues, owned by Helen Boehm, wife of the founder.

Bohemian glass

This area of Eastern Europe had a flourishing glass industry from the 15th century owing to its wealth of timber for furnaces and variety of minerals. This was aided by the patronage of Rudolf II, who became Holy Roman Emperor in 1576 and established his court at Prague.

From woodland craft to industry

The numerous factories began by producing WALDGLAS but were quick to learn new techniques. Rudolf II employed craftsmen such as Caspar Lehmann (1570–1622) who adapted gem-engraving techniques for use on glass and began the tradition of wheel-engraved Bohemian glass. In the late 17th century, the development of POTASH GLASS made possible a whole new range of CUT GLASS decorated with engravings of mythological, allegorical and figural scenes. By the end of the 18th century, Bohemian glass dominated world production.

In the 19th century, Bohemia became a centre for the production of new types of coloured glass. Jirí, Count von Buquoy (1781–1851), produced c.1817 an opaque black glass in imitation of Wedgwood's BASALTES WARE and, in 1819, HYALITH, an opaque glass in either red or black, which was often gilded. In 1818, Friedrich EGERMANN invented a yellow glass STAIN. In the 1820s and 1830s, exhibitions at Prague inspired further experimentation: Bohemian glass-makers produced a distinctive ultramarine c.1826; in 1829 Egermann developed the opaque glass LITHYALIN and in the 1830s perfected a rich red ruby stain. Also in the 1830s Josef Riedel used uranium to produce *Annagrün* (greenish-yellow) and *Annagelb* (yellowish-green) clear glass. Bohemian glass-makers produced a range of heavy, richly coloured cased and stained pieces, in particular goblets, with cut and engraved decoration. Many new glassworks were opened during this period, including the Loetz factory that was to become the LOETZ, WITWE glassworks, in particular in Haida (now Novy Bor) and Karlsbad, where Bohemian glass-makers such as Ludwig Moser (1833–1916) continued the tradition of fine engraving.

In the 20th century, while designers such as Koloman MOSER established an ART GLASS studio, many Bohemian glass-makers concentrated on producing high-quality copies of other European glass. In the 1920s and 1930s, they produced copies of 19th-century British styles such as IRIDESCENT GLASS, as well as a range of now rare heavy cut lead glass vases, bowls and decanters in ART DECO styles. Glass is still produced in Bohemia today.

Glass in Annagrün yellow-green, produced by the addition of uranium to the batch, c.1840 [F]

Bohemian drinking glass, with coloured glass medallions on the base, c.1850–65 [N]

Bohemian liqueur glass in the rich ruby colour developed by Egermann, c.1880 [S]

Spa glass

Bohemia is rich in natural springs and in the 18th and 19th centuries spa towns such as Carlsbad, Warmbrunn and Franzensbad became fashionable resorts for wealthy people to take cures. Elaborately decorated and coloured glasses were used to take the waters and served as mementoes.

Lithyalin spa glass from the workshop of Egermann, 1836 [I]

Boiserie designs from Versailles, 17th century

Boelen, Jacob (1657–1729) A Dutch-born American silversmith active in New York City from *c*.1680. His pieces, which may bear the maker's mark IB within a shield, include tankards and cups and are extremely rare.

Böhm, August (1812–90) A Bohemian glass-engraver. Born in Meistersdorf, he was one of the leading engravers of the BIEDERMEIER period (1820s–40s). He travelled widely, working in London and STOURBRIDGE in Britain, Hamburg and the US, engraving goblets and plaques with portraits, as well as religious subjects and battle scenes.

Bois de rapport A term used for wood cut across, rather than along, the grain to create a distinctive marked figure that is then used for decorative veneering or other inlaid decoration.

Bois durci A type of simulated EBONY, patented in 1856 by François Charles Lepage, made from sawdust bound together with the protein albumen from egg or blood. It was applied to furniture in the form of decorative medallions and rosettes and was popular in England and France from *c*.1855 to 1900.

Boiserie A French term for a type of carved wood panelling used on the walls of the rooms of substantial buildings and houses. Often elaborately decorated with carved foliage and painted with gold ornament, it was used particularly in 17th- and 18th-century France and reflected the fashions for ROCOCO and NEO-CLASSICISM. Examples survive in Paris and Versailles. Furnishings in the same style matched the panelling.

Bokhara A town in central Asia (now Uzbekistan) that was a major exporting centre for Afghan and Turkoman carpets, rugs and textiles in the 19th century. Many Turkoman tribal carpets are erroneously described as Bokhara but this term should refer only to carpets made by the TEKKE tribe and should be called Tekke Bokhara.

Bole A soft reddish variety of clay, found in eastern Mediterranean countries and used as a pigment. It was used by J.F. BÖTTGER in the stoneware he developed in 1707 at MEISSEN. It is also used in the compounding of ENAMEL COLOURS and as a ground for gilding on furniture. It is a relatively pure clay consisting basically of kaolinite plus iron oxide.

Bolection moulding A MOULDING, usually with an S-shaped section, used to cover the joint between two elements whose surfaces are not level and often found as a framework round panels.

Bologna potteries Bologna was the centre in Italy for LEAD-GLAZED earthenware from the 15th to the 18th century. The usual decorative technique was SGRAFFITO – incising the white slip coating to expose the buff or red clay

body underneath and filling in the grooves with metallic pigments. Kiln-wasters from 1450–80 have been found at Bologna, some pieces bearing heraldic coats of arms of Bolognese families.

Italian bombé commode, c.1760 [E]

Bombé (French: "puffed out", "blown out") A term used in the early 18th century to describe the swelling convex shape on two or more axes used on the front of chests-of-drawers made in France from the RÉGENCE period until the fashion for classical furniture in the reign of Louis XVI; the US term is "kettle shape".

Bonbon dish, c.1900 [S]

Bonbon dish An open sweetmeat dish on a base for small sugared dessert items, made in glass or porcelain from the mid-18th century to the 19th century.

Bonbonnière (French *bonbon*: "a sweet") A box with a lid to hold small sweets. Enamel bonbonnières in animal forms were made in imitation of MEISSEN porcelain in the 1770s and 1780s.

Bone ash The product of ground calcined bones, usually cattle bones. This pure white substance is sometimes used in porcelain production. "Bone china", which contains 45–50 per cent bone ash, was first patented by Thomas Frye of the BOW factory in England in 1748.

Victoria and Albert bone china
dessert plate, c.1850 [s]

Bone china A British PORCELAIN in
which calcined ox bone is added to the
BODY, which gives a very white colour.
This was first used by Thomas Frye of
BOW in 1748 to make a type of SOFT-
PASTE PORCELAIN. In the late 18th
century, Josiah SPODE adopted it mixed
with china clay and stone to make a
harder version to compete with the
importation of Oriental porcelain. It is
first fired to a translucent state without a
glaze at 1280°C (2336°F) and then glaze-
fired at a lower temperature below
1080°C (1976°F).

Bonheur, Isidore-Jules (1827–1901)
The sculptor brother of ROSA BONHEUR,
known for his life-like bronzes of sheep,
cattle and horses and more animated wild
animals. Many bronzes complemented his
sister's works. One of the leading French
ANIMALIERS, his first important work was
shown at the Paris Salon in 1848.

Bonheur, Rosa (1822–99) A leading
19th-century French animal painter and
sculptor who exhibited at the Paris Salon
from 1841. Depicting life-like lions, tigers
and horses, her most famous work is the
vast *Horse Fair* of 1853.

Bonheur-du-jour A type of ladies' small
writing desk with a flat writing surface at
the front, an arrangement of small

drawers, cupboards or shelves at the back,
and a drawer below. An established form
by the late 1760s, it was interpreted in
different styles and with a variety of
decoration throughout Europe during
the 19th and the early 20th centuries.

Bonnet top A term used in American
furniture of the mid-18th century to
describe a domed or "broken" arched
top found mainly on early and better
examples of the HIGHBOY. The form is
derived from WILLIAM AND MARY style,
and can also be a double arch, or "double
bonnet" top. Later bonnet tops are
sometimes added to plain highboys to
enhance their value.

Bonnet top

**Bonnin and Morris porcelain
factory** A partnership of Gouse Bonnin
from England and George Anthony
Morris of Philadelphia, who in 1770
established the American China
Manufactory in Southwark, Philadelphia.
The experiment was unsuccessful, closing
in November 1772 when the works and
contents were sold at public auction.
Products, which are very rare and
desirable, are limited to blue and
white painted or (rarely) printed
wares of useful type, comparable
to some BOW. Marks include a
blue painted P (for Philadelphia)
or S (Southwark).

Bontemps, Georges
(1799–1884) A French glass-maker.
From 1823–48 he was director at the
Choisy-le-Roi glassworks, Paris, where he
initiated several important technical
developments, including OPALINE GLASS.

In 1848, he moved to England to work at
the Spon Lane glassworks in Smethwick,
Birmingham, and wrote a technical glass
treatise – *Guide du Verrier* – in 1868.

Boote, T. & R. Of Waterloo Pottery (and
other addresses) in Burslem, Staffordshire,
1842 to the present day. They made useful
wares in earthenware, also figures in
PARIAN WARE and tiles, frequently printed
in brown. Wares have printed marks, from
1890 to 1906 including the firm's name
and often the name of the pattern.
Waterloo Pottery closed in 1906 and the
firm concentrated on making tiles, being
famous, among other things, for tiling the
Blackwall Tunnel in London.

Booze bottles Initially, the bottles
designed to hold whisky made for
Edmund G. Booz of Philadelphia by the
Whitney Glassworks; thereafter a general
term used for spirit bottles not of flask
form, mostly made during the second half
of the 19th century.

Bordeaux potteries A group of
FAIENCE factories in south-west France
from the early 18th century. The first one
known was founded by Jacques Hustin
and made domestic ware and larger pieces
from 1729 until 1783. Eight faience or
porcelain factories were listed in 1790.
There are still active potteries in the
Bordeaux area.

Bordeaux faience plate, c.1780 [o]

Boreman, Zachariah (1738–1810)
A good painter of landscapes at the
CHELSEA porcelain factory until 1783 and
at the DERBY porcelain factory
from 1784 until 1794, when he
left to become an OUTSIDE
DECORATOR in London. He
specialized in monochrome (black
or brown) landscapes, often of
Derbyshire scenes.

Borne, La Stoneware was produced
in this centre in the Loire, France,
from the mid-16th century. Later, a
series of studio potters settled in the
area, including Henri-Paul-Auguste
Beyer (1873–1945), Vassili Ivanoff
(1897–1973) and the sculptor and
potter Elisabeth Joulia (b. 1925).

Borussia-Glas A type of clear lead
glass, with engraved black and white
overlay, made at the Haida glassworks
in Bohemia in the early 20th century.

Boselli, Giacomo (1744–1808) Also
known as Jacques Borelly or Boselly, a
French manufacturer of FAIENCE at
Marseilles until 1779
when he moved to
the Italian town of
Savona near Genoa.
He made earthenware
pieces decorated with
enamel colours and
figures in soft-paste
porcelain.

**Boston & Sandwich
Glass Company**
One of the largest
commercial
glassworks in North
America, founded in
1826 in Sandwich,

Boston & Sandwich
Glass Co.
candlestick,
c.1845–70 [G]

Cape Cod, Massachusetts, by Deming
Jarves (1760–1869) who had previously
founded the NEW ENGLAND GLASS
COMPANY. Until closure
in 1888, the company
produced an enormous
variety of useful and
ornamental ware,
including cut and blown
pieces and, later, pressed
and flashed (CASED)
glass in colourful
artistic designs of
the "fancy" type,
which is often
generically referred
to in the US as
"Sandwich glass".

Boston rocker
An American form
of rocking-chair
popular in Boston,
Massachusetts, and throughout New
England from about 1820. It resembles a
conventional WINDSOR CHAIR with
spool-turned elements, a seat which turns
up at the back and a scrolling back. The
term is used commonly in the US for
rocking-chairs of this form. Some
examples are signed and can be of high
value, but most show heavy restoration
or wear and tear.

Boston rocker

Botanical flowers A type of porcelain
decoration, in which true-to-life flowers
were painted from the scientific floras of
the 18th century. It was used on the
famous "Flora Danica" service, made
c.1800 by the COPENHAGEN porcelain
factory, after the studies of plants by the
Danish botanist Linnaeus. The English
factory of CHELSEA produced a series
from Sir Hans Soane's designs in the mid-
18th century and DERBY also favoured
this form of decoration – copying the
designs from books of engravings.

Boteh A tear drop or leaf-shaped motif
frequently seen in Oriental rugs, carpets
and textiles. Curvilinear and geometric
versions exist in nomadic and urban

pieces, often arranged in
infinitely repeating
patterns in the main
field, and also seen as
secondary ornaments. The
exact origin of the motif
is unclear.

Boteh motif

Bott, Thomas
(1829–70) An English
painter and designer working at the
WORCESTER porcelain factory, where he
was responsible for the so-called LIMOGES
ENAMEL style, inspired by the medieval
enamels made in that French city. The
style was revived in the 19th century,
predominantly with figures in white
enamel against a dark, usually blue,
background. His son, Thomas John Bott
(1854–1932), was also employed at the
Worcester porcelain factory for some
years painting in the same style as his
father, before moving to COALPORT.

**Böttger, Johann
Friedrich**
(1682–1719) The
German ceramicist
and ARCANIST
responsible for the
invention of
European HARD-
PASTE PORCELAIN.
He thought he
could turn base
metal into gold
and persuaded the
King of Prussia to
employ him to do so. But sensing failure,
he fled to Dresden in Saxony. There he
was imprisoned by Augustus the Strong,
who was an obsessive collector of
Oriental porcelain. Böttger worked with
the scientist Von Tschirnhaus and they
finally made porcelain in 1708.
Tschirnhaus died in that year. Böttger
continued alone, making a fine red
stoneware, white porcelain and lustre. The
Royal Saxon Porcelain Manufactory at
MEISSEN was established in 1710 with
Böttger as director but by then his health
was broken. He died in 1719.

Böttger stoneware
tankard, c.1710 [C]

Böttger lustre A delicate pink-lilac lustrous glaze for ceramics invented by J.F. BÖTTGER, often used in the gilt-edged surrounds of CHINOISERIE subjects.

Bottle glass An unrefined, commonly found glass, known also as "green glass" because of its dark green or dark brown colouring, which results from the addition of iron compounds to sand. It was used in England from the mid-17th century for bottles and, with the addition of coloured flecks, for NAILSEA-type glass from the early 19th century.

Bottle ticket
See WINE LABEL.

Chinese Qianlong bottle vase, 1736–95 [K]

Bottle vase A shape with a globular or ovoid body and tall "bottle" neck, so combining the characteristics of both a bottle and a vase. The shape originated in China, posibly in the late TANG dynasty.

Boucher, François (1703–70) A French painter and designer who studied in Rome. Elected to the French academy in 1734, he became Court painter in 1765. His painting was enormously influential on 18th-century European tapestry and ceramics. In 1736 he designed a series of cartoons for BEAUVAIS – *Les fêtes Italiennes* – the first of over 40 he was to produce for Beauvais. In 1755 he became artistic director of GOBELINS. His interest in Chinese porcelain inspired him to design groups of Chinese figures for CHELSEA and MEISSEN and his pastoral scenes were to greatly influence decoration at SÈVRES. He became factory designer there in 1754.

Boudeuse (French *bouder*: "to sulk") A type of French 19th-century SOFA also known as a "conversation piece", with a central backrest that separates the two occupants.

Boudoir doll Made in France and Spain *c.*1920 to *c.*1930 to adorn beds and boudoirs, boudoir dolls represent seductive, long-limbed ladies. Their bodies are covered in silk, cotton or a knitted fabric called stockinet, with painted facial features including languishing eyes, and applied bobbed silk hair.

Bough pot A European ceramic pot or vase, usually semicircular, with a flat back and removable top pierced with holes to hold cut flowers or bulbs. Delft TULIPIÈRES are specialized examples. Josiah WEDGWOOD referred to his examples as "rootpots".

Louis XIV ormolu-mounted commode attributed to André-Charles Boulle, late 17th century [A]

Bouillotte lamp A type of brass or gilt-bronze table-lamp made in France from the 18th century. Named after a card game (and probably developed to illuminate the small tables on which it was played), it has a wide, dish-shaped base and a stem with candle brackets and a metal shade.

Boulle, André-Charles (1642–1732) A French cabinet-maker. In 1672 he was appointed *ébéniste du Roi* and designed furniture and superb clockcases for the court of Louis XIV and other European rulers and rich patrons. Although his furniture is unstamped, pieces can usually be identified by provenance and by the use of superb gilt-bronze ornaments and the eponymous elaborate, showy tortoiseshell and brass marquetry. Earlier pieces by Boulle were decorated with wood marquetry.

Boulle marquetry A type of decorative inlay used on 17th- and 18th-century furniture, developed by André-Charles BOULLE. Sheets of tortoiseshell or turtleshell (often backed with coloured foil) and brass were glued together. They were then cut into

French tapestry (from the Louvre), designed by Boucher, c.1745–50 [D]

decorative patterns with a fretsaw to provide matching brass and tortoiseshell designs and grounds that could be combined or contrasted at will. These were known as *première* and *contre partie* and were used on matching pairs of commodes or side cabinets.

Sheffield plate candelabrum designed by Boulton, c.1810 [K]

Boulton, Matthew (1728–1809) An English metalworker and silversmith, born in Birmingham. He began in his father's business making buckles and buttons. In 1762 he built a manufactory in Soho, Birmingham, and went into partnership with John Fothergill producing buttons, toys, buckles and a wide range of domestic ware in SHEFFIELD PLATE. He later made silver and fine ormolu in the ADAM style. He was a major campaigner in establishing the Birmingham Assay office in 1773. With James Watt he developed a steam engine to aid mass-production and expanded the business to produce coins and medals. After he died the company continued until the mid-19th century.

Bourdalou(e) An oval ladies' chamber pot, made from both porcelain and pottery by leading continental and English factories, and even in China for export back to Europe. WEDGWOOD made them in creamware, and referred to them as "coach pots"; other sources say that ladies carried them concealed in their muff. The name is derived from Louis Bourdaloue, a French preacher at the court of Louis XIV at Versailles who was so popular that

English Spode bourdalou, c.1820 [L]

ladies had to queue for hours to be admitted to the church where he was to preach. Their use survived into the 19th century for long coach jouneys.

Bourne & Son A family firm owning potteries at BELPER from 1812–34 and at DENBY from 1834 to the present. Earlier products included salt-glazed stoneware jugs with hunting scenes in relief and with greyhound handles; most of their products were utilitarian. The factory now specializes in simply designed but well-made fireproof kitchen wares.

Boutet, Nicholas Noel (1761–1833) A French gunmaker, appointed artistic director of the Versailles Arsenal in 1793. He concentrated on luxury arms for presentation to foreign dignitaries. His guns showed little technical innovation, but were made and decorated to the highest standards. He is the only gunmaker ever to have signed his work "Directeur Artiste".

Bovey Tracey Pottery See WEMYSS WARE.

Bow front A design feature primarily associated with mid-18th-century furniture, predominantly sideboards and chests-of-drawers, where the front of a piece of CASE FURNITURE forms a continuous convex curve.

Bow porcelain factory
A manufactory founded *c.*1744 in Stratford, east London (at that time in the parish of Bow). A patent, dated December 1744, was granted to "Edward Heylyn a merchant, and Thomas Frye a portrait painter" for a new method of manufacturing a material whereby a ware might be made of the same nature as china or porcelain. In November 1749 another patent was granted in the name of Frye alone. The

pre-1760

1760–76

"new method" refers to the inclusion of a substantial amount of BONE ASH in the body of the porcelain, making it very heavy. The factory was called New Canton and a printed advertisement appeared in August 1748 stating that "useful and ornamental china" was for sale. In the beginning Bow made blue and white wares in a vibrant blue; documentary pieces are inkwells inscribed "Made at New Canton 1750". It also made tea wares, plates, jugs, mugs and cutlery handles, which were made throughout the history of the factory. Its white wares with prunus decoration in relief were inspired by the so-called BLANC-DE-CHINE made at Dehua in China. Inspiration also came from the FAMILLE ROSE wares of China, as well as Japanese KAKIEMON porcelain – the "two quail pattern" was particularly popular. European-style subjects included botanic drawings and painted flowers and birds in the style of MEISSEN and SÈVRES. The Bow enamel blue is especially distinctive. The factory also made many figures, which often reflected a strong local interest, or topical subjects such as the actress Kitty Clive and the actor Henry Woodward. Some of the earliest figures have a distinctive style with small heads; these are

Bow "Sphinx" by the "Muses Modeller", c.1750–60 [i]

attributed to the "Muses Modeller" after a set of the classical Muses. Bow also copied Meissen figures. Its models of animals are naïve but charming. In 1775 the factory closed and the moulds and tools were transferred to DERBY.

Bowie knife A large hunting knife, said to take its name from the US frontiersman James Bowie who was killed at the Alamo, Texas, in 1836. They normally have broad, single-edged blades, with sharply angled points. Although they originated in 19th-century America, many were made in Sheffield, England.

Box back A commercially made English DOLLS' HOUSE from the late 18th century to the 1930s, based on the style of a typical town house, with a flat façade projecting from a rectangular box.

Box bedstead A type of northern European bed, built into the corner of a room and enclosed by a wooden canopy and curtains or sliding wooden panels that matched the wall panelling. They were popular in Scandinavia, Germany and the Low Countries in the 17th century, where they were known as closets or cupboard beds. They were used in rural areas until the 19th century.

Kodak Bull's Eye
no.2 Box Brownie, 1898 [S]

Box Brownie In 1898, the US inventor George Eastman and the camera designer and manufacturer Frank Brownell designed the Box Brownie as a low-cost easy-to-use camera. It was launched in 1900 and for 80 years was linked with modern popular photography. The name was last used in 1980.

Boxlock A type of FLINTLOCK or PERCUSSION LOCK where the moving parts were centrally mounted in a box-shaped housing (as opposed to sidelocks where the housing was to one side). The mechanism was in use from *c*.1710 until the latter half of the 19th century.

Box stool A low miniature square or rectangular 17th-century oak stool with a box underneath the seat.

Boxwood (*Buxus sempervirens*) A tree native to northern Europe and Asia, the timber from which is pale yellow, sometimes brown or orange, with a close, even grain. Boxwood was used from the late 17th century onward for decorative inlay, turned members, TREEN, tool handles, carving and blocks for engraving.

Bracelets and bangles A bracelet is a length of continuous joined links or articulated sections or a flexible strap while a bangle is inflexible and often hinged. Bracelets have been worn throughout history and were particularly popular in the 19th century. REGENCY and early VICTORIAN designs included broad gold meshwork straps with CANNETILLE clasps and clusters of SEMI-PRECIOUS STONES and diamonds in cartouches. The 1840s and 1850s were characterized by coiled serpents, enamel straps and knot motifs, the 1860s and 1870s by Classical and Renaissance Revivalist influences, and the latter part of the century by mass-produced half hoops, clusters and horseshoes of diamonds, pearls and gems, as well as cheaper nine-carat gold and silver cuff bangles. In the 20th century, PLATINUM came into general use. Bracelets in the ART DECO period were linear and introduced Egyptian and Oriental themes and geometric sections of diamonds, rubies, emeralds and sapphires. In the 1940s and 1950s, broad gold and gem-set straps were often

Bracket foot on
mahogany kneehole desk,
George III period [G] ▶

decorated with bold three-dimensional motifs. Bracelets of the 1960s and 1970s were often abstract or set with continuous lines and clusters of diamonds and gems in white gold and platinum.

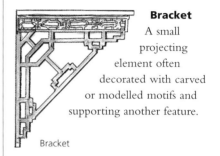

Bracket
A small projecting element often decorated with carved or modelled motifs and supporting another feature.

Bracket

Bracket clock A spring-driven clock originally designed to stand on a wall bracket but later on a shelf or table and also known as a MANTEL or TABLE CLOCK. Such clocks were introduced after the invention of the PENDULUM in the mid-17th century. British bracket clocks usually have wooden cases but French and later American examples feature a more diverse range of materials.

Bracket foot A support for CASE FURNITURE, in use from the late 17th century and especially popular in the 18th century, in the form of two brackets mitred and joined at the corner. The early form was usually straight-sided; from around 1730–40 the OGEE bracket foot was also used, joined, at the end of the 18th century, by the splayed bracket foot.

Bracquemond, (Joseph-Auguste) Felix (1833–1914) A French ceramic designer, painter and engraver. His designs are among the first to show Japanese influence, after he saw a book of Hokusai's work in 1856. He worked for Criel-Montereau, J.T. DECK, SÈVRES and C.F. Haviland (1872–80), then opened his own studio.

Bradbury & Sons, Thomas A firm originally founded in 1769 in Sheffield, England, trading as Matthew Fenton & Co. and making Old Sheffield plate and silver, especially flatware. It opened its first showroom in London *c.*1820 and by 1900 had become one of the best-known manufacturers of silver and plate. Thomas Bradbury was also known for his pocketbook of date letters on English silver.

Braganza foot A rectangular ribbed and scrolled foot used on chairs and tables. Originating in England in the 17th century and named after Catherine of Braganza, Charles II's Spanish queen, it often replaced the bun foot in William and Mary's reign.

Braganza foot

Brameld family See ROCKINGHAM.

Brampton potteries A small group of Derbyshire factories from the early 18th to the early 20th century, which made brown domestic stoneware. The main factories were those of S. & H. Briddon and J. Oldfield, who also made toffee-coloured wares with relief decoration and Toby jugs in salt-glazed stoneware. See also DERBYSHIRE POTTERIES.

Brandt, Edgar (1880–1960) A French ART DECO designer and metalworker. He exhibited at the 1900 Paris Exhibition, provided work for the ocean liner *Normandie* and showed his work at the 1925 Paris Exposition. He opened showrooms in London and New York under the name of Ferrobrandt.

Brandy bowl A one- or two-handled silver bowl usually on a foot of oval or polygonal outline, often silver-gilt or with a gilded interior. It was used to warm drink, including brandy, in the embers of a fire. Brandy bowls were made in large numbers in Europe, and particularly in Holland, in the 17th and 18th centuries.

Brangwyn, Sir Frank (1867–1956) A Belgian-born painter and designer, brought up in England where he worked with William MORRIS. He also worked in Paris with Samuel BING, and designed textiles, carpets, stained glass and furniture as well as dinnerware for Royal Doulton.

Brannam, Charles Hubert (1855–1937) The Brannam family were potters in Devon from the late 18th century. Thomas Brannam exhibited jugs at the GREAT EXHIBITION of 1851. C.H. Brannam took over his father's pottery in Barnstaple, North Devon, in 1879 having studied art. He continued to produce traditional slip and sgraffito-decorated pottery. He introduced more fashionable designs under the name BARUM WARE, sold through Howell & James, LIBERTY & CO. and HEAL & SON. His sons continued in the pottery, which is still in business today, although it moved to a new site in Barnstaple in the 1980s.

Brass An alloy of copper and zinc, first known in the 2nd millennium BC. The ratio of the two metals alters the

English brandy bowl, c.1790 [G]

characteristics of the alloy – it becomes progressively whiter as more zinc is added. Ductile and easily cast, brass has been used since medieval times for household wares, such as bowls, candlesticks, cooking pots and fireplace furnishings. In the Middle Ages the main production centres were the Low Countries and Germany but, from the 18th century, Birmingham, England, was dominant, mass-producing buttons, buckles, door-knockers and furniture mounts.

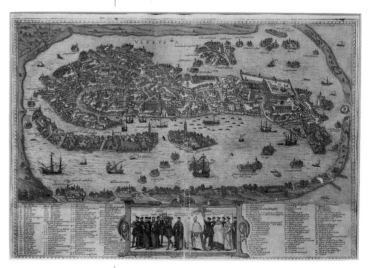

Map and plan of Venice, coloured engraving by Braun & Hogenberg, 1572 [M]

Braun, Georg (1541–1622) **and Hogenberg, Frans** (*c.*1536–88) A German topographer and an engraver who published the first ATLAS of town plans and views, the six-volume *Civitates Orbis Terrarum* (Cities of the World), in various editions from 1572 to 1617. It eventually included more than 500 detailed plans and bird's-eye views, many with portraits of local inhabitants in typical dress.

Bread basket A silver basket designed to hold bread, often oval and pierced to imitate wicker. Seventeenth-century examples are rare and tend to have two handles. Those from the 1730s have a central swing handle, mounted at either side. Their weights vary but average size is 30cm (12in) long. Bread baskets were also made in plate and other materials.

Break-front (or broken front) A term for 18th-century case furniture with a projecting or protruding centre section, as often seen on furniture in the CHIPPENDALE and LOUIS XVI styles.

Break-front

Breech The rear end of the barrel of a firearm, which contains the chamber where the gunpowder charge is ignited. As it has to withstand great pressure on firing, it is always of heavier construction than the rest of the barrel.

Breechloading action A firearm loaded from the BREECH. Made from the 15th century onward, breechloading guns were never really effective because of leakage of gas from the barrel joint. In the 19th century, their performance was improved with the development of the self-contained CARTRIDGE.

Breguet, Abraham-Louis (1747–1823) An eminent French clock- and watchmaker, credited with many inventions including a shock-resisting

system to protect the vulnerable watch balance, a form of BALANCE SPRING that still holds his name, and a modification to the LEVER ESCAPEMENT. He also made the first carriage clock for Napoleon I *c.*1798.

Breloque A French term for a small decorative object in gold or enamel such as a figurine, locket or seal, with a small ring for suspending from a watch chain or CHATELAINE.

Bretby vase by Christopher Dresser, c.1890 [K]

Bretby Art Pottery An English pottery founded in Woodville, Derbyshire, by Henry Tooth and William AULT in 1883. AULT left in 1887, the pottery then became known as Tooth & Co. and still exists. Two of its most popular ranges were Oriental subjects in relief and simulated copper and metal wares with jewelled ornament in the ART NOUVEAU style. It closed in 1920.

Breuer, Marcel Lajos (1902–81) A Hungarian architect-designer who studied in Vienna and at the BAUHAUS, and worked in Germany, England (1935) and the US (from 1937). He was head of carpentry at the Bauhaus (1925–1928) where he produced his first tubular steel chair designs (Wassily, 1925). In England, he designed in plywood for Isokon, producing his famous and elegant chaise-longue. In the US he practised as an architect while also designing furniture.

Brewster, Elisha An American clockmaker. From *c.*1844 he worked in partnership with Elias and Andrew Ingrahams at Bristol, Connecticut, producing inexpensive SHELF, MANTEL and WALL CLOCKS with veneered wooden cases in a variety of designs, such as the "steeple" clock with a pointed gable.

Brewster chair An American open armchair form of Elizabethan inspiration, first made in Massachusetts in the mid-17th century. Brewsters are typically made of ash, maple or hickory with woven rush seats and are a distinctive large early version of the more familiar PILGRIM CHAIR of COLONIAL America. Few original Brewsters exist but some excellent fakes are recorded. See also CARVER CHAIR.

Brezová The more recent Czech name for the porcelain manufacturing town of Pirkenhammer, in what was formerly Bohemia. The factory was started in 1802 by Friedrich Holke and J.G. List and had many changes of owners, including Fischer & Mieg in 1857. It is still in existence. The mark is two crossed hammers, with or without the name of the town.

Bright cut decoration A form of engraving on silver, primarily from *c.*1770–1800. The engraver's tool removes V-shaped chips or facets of metal in simple patterns often from

Breuer laminated birch chair, 1936 [G]

around the borders of a piece. The result is a glistening or sparkling effect as these facets reflect light at different angles.

Brilliance See BRILLIANT CUT.

Brilliant cut The ideal form of cutting for diamonds. A brilliant consists of 58 facets; 33 above the girdle or crown of the stone and 25 below on the pavilion. Nineteenth-century brilliants tended toward a cushion-shape and were often ill-proportioned; modern stones are perfectly symmetrical and thus display maximum "brilliance".

Briqueté A term used to denote a form of decoration simulating a brick wall.

Brisé fan A folding fan made from ivory, metal or wood where the leaf of the fan is formed by the sticks themselves rather than having a paper or silk panel applied to the sticks.

Ivory brisé fan, French 1880 [M]

Bristol glasshouses The numerous glasshouses active in Bristol from the 17th century. Initially known for the production of window and BOTTLE GLASS, they later became famous for decorative enamelling and gilding, opaque white glass and finally high-quality coloured glass. These late 18th and early 19th-century Bristol blue glasses and decanters (also in green and amethyst) were coloured with COBALT imported from Germany via Bristol.

Bristol porcelain factories The earliest porcelain made here was a soft-paste porcelain by Benjamin Lund and William Miller of Redcliff Backs. Lund

Bristol porcelain vase, c.1770 [D]

had taken out a licence to mine SOAPSTONE in 1748–49. Figures of a Chinese man and some sauceboats are known, moulded with "Bristol" or "Bristoll" as a mark and some are dated 1750. In 1752 the Lund-Miller concern was bought by the WORCESTER Porcelain Company. In its short life this factory made some attractive products – now rare and much in demand.

The second factory in Bristol, from 1770–81, was moved there from Plymouth where it had been founded by William COOKWORTHY in 1768, and made HARD-PASTE PORCELAIN. Richard Champion became manager and bought the business in 1773. The patent expired in 1775 and Champion sold his right to the Society of Staffordshire Potteries in 1781. The Champion factory made simply decorated ware for utilitarian use, but it also made some finer examples in the style of Sèvres and Derby. Champion also made some armorial services. They used a simple X mark and later copied the mark of Meissen. "Wreathing" or low spiral ridges in the paste is a characteristic of the BODY.

Bristol potteries A number of potteries were known in the area from the late 17th century, producing TIN-GLAZED EARTHENWARE AND BLUE-DASH CHARGERS. The 19th-century factory of Pountney & Co. was originally known as the Bristol Pottery. It made tableware for domestic use and later for hotels and WEMYSS WARE from 1904.

Bristol Potteries tile, c.1750–70 [R]

Britain "9th Lancers" lead soldiers, 1920 [R]

Britain Ltd, William William Britain (1828–1906) set up a family mechanical toy business at his home in London in 1847. William's eldest son (also William) developed the HOLLOW CAST method for producing lead figures that weighed less and were cheaper to produce. This revolutionized the toy figure market and many companies copied them. Model soldiers, mostly in boxed sets, dominated their production but they also made farm figures. Figures were made for other companies, for example, BASSETT-LOWKE. Horse-drawn army units followed, also vehicles and some planes. Lead in toys was outlawed in 1966 and the company currently uses plastic and mazak DIECAST alloys for their reproduction sets.

Early figures are unmarked but are recognizable by their oval bases and the excellent quality of the casting and painting, with strict attention to accuracy in the soldiers' uniforms and weapons. From 1900 paper labels were stuck to the base; cast lettering was used from c.1905. After 1907 the toy figures had square bases.

Britannia metal A soft alloy of tin, copper and antimony similar to pewter but without lead, which will temporarily take a high polish. Made in Britain from 1790, it served as a cheaper alternative to silver and Old Sheffield plate but was softer, less durable and prone to perishing. During the Victorian period it was widely used as a base for electroplated articles.

Broad glass A type of flat window or pane glass, also known as "cylinder" or "muff" glass because it was made from a large cylindrical-shaped piece of blown glass cut down the length, reheated and flattened. The technique was first used in the Lorraine area of France in the 12th century. It was adapted by Venetian glassmakers in the 16th century to make mirrors, and further refined in 19th-century Britain. Production of broad glass is now fully mechanized.

Broadsword A general term originating during the 17th century for a heavy double-edged sword designed as a cutting weapon, principally for cavalry soldiers. Similar single-edged swords are known as "backswords".

Broadsword, English
c.1640 [H]

Brocade A woven textile ornamented with a raised design formed by additional weft threads. Weaving was slow and expensive, hence many early brocades use silver and gold thread. Because brocading thread was used only for the pattern and was not integral to the structure of the fabric, brocades tend to be light and therefore ideally suited for various items of costume.

Silk brocade, French
19th century

Brocard, Philippe-Joseph (d.1896) A French STUDIO GLASS artist inspired by Islamic mosque lamps, which he copied. He also made enamelled and gilded dishes, vases and ewers and exhibited work at the 1878 Paris Exhibition.

Brocart A French term for BROCADE.

¹ Brocatelle A woven fabric, usually in silk and wool with a relief pattern, the background having a satin-like appearance, widely used in 18th-century upholstery.

² Brocatelle A type of variegated marble used for the tops of 18th-century tables.

Brocot, Achille (1817–78) A French clockmaker who invented the BROCOT ESCAPEMENT and the Brocot suspension, a method of regulating a clock by inserting a key through the front of the dial to adjust the length of the PENDULUM spring.

Brocot (or pin-pallet) escapement A type of DEADBEAT ESCAPEMENT invented by A. BROCOT in the early 19th century. Used mainly in 19th-century French clocks, it features pallets consisting of cylindrical hardstone or steel pins.

Broderie anglaise A WHITEWORK embroidery with bold punched stylized patterns to decorate ladies' underwear and children's clothes. Used from the mid-19th-century until the present day.

Brogden, John (active 1842–85) An English goldsmith whose designs were inspired by RENAISSANCE, Moorish and ASSYRIAN themes, and who used GRANULATION and FILIGREE motifs. He incorporated CAMEOS, enamel and bold GEMSTONES such as garnet and turquoise.

Bronchit Glassware with a matt black enamelled geometric decoration on clear or matt glass, designed by Josef HOFFMANN c.1910 and made in Vienna by J. & L. LOBMEYR.

Bronze An alloy of copper and tin, with small amounts of other elements such as silver, zinc, aluminium or lead. Developed in western Asia in the 4th millennium BC, it has been used throughout the world for weapons, coins and utilitarian household items, owing to its strength, hardness and durability. Its fluidity when molten makes it one of the most suitable mediums for CASTING sculpture and decorative objects.

Bronze d'ameublement (French: "bronze furnishing") A small domestic item such as a clock case, ANDIRON or lighting fitting cast in bronze and usually gilded. The finest examples, in the ROCOCO and NEO-CLASSICAL styles, were made in France in the 18th century, from models supplied by leading sculptors.

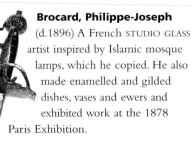

Bronze d'ameublemont: bronze, marble and ormolu candlestick, French c.1800 [J, a pair]

Bronzite See BRONCHIT.

Brooch Of all the forms of jewellery worn since earliest times, the brooch is the most functional. The basic need to secure a garment led to the development of the *fibula* – a twisted safety pin used by the Romans and Etruscans 2,000 years ago. During the Middle Ages, simple gold ring brooches were given as tokens of betrothal, and in the 16th century hat badges, usually gem-set or enamelled, conveyed wealth, status and authority. In the 17th and 18th centuries, the brooch became a decorative accessory due to improvements in gemstone cutting and the rise in popularity of the diamond. It underwent many changes in design; a brief outline follows:

18th century: Silver-mounted naturalistic sprays; bouquets of flowers; tied bows. *Early 19th century:* Romantic gold brooches with gems conveying messages; NEO-CLASSICAL designs influenced by Napoleon's France. *1820s–30s:* Maltese crosses; naturalistic sprays; CANNETILLE goldwork set with foiled gems such as pink topaz and amethyst. *1840s–50s:* Increasing use of gold settings; TREMBLANT designs with flowerheads on coiled springs; large semi-precious gems such as garnet; knots; coiled ribbons; serpent motifs. *1860s–70s:* Archaeological revivalism; yellow gold frames set with MOSAIC, cameos and hardstones (see CASTELLANI). RENAISSANCE REVIVAL; enamels, pearls and coral (see GIULIANO). *1880s–90s:* Mechanization and mass-production; stars, crescents and flowerheads; insects and dragonflies; novelty and sporting themes; bar and silver name brooches. *1900–10:* Sensuous naturalistic ART NOUVEAU forms of LALIQUE; platinum; large, valuable coloured stones and fancy diamonds in delicate BELLE ÉPOQUE settings; bows and latticework; Garland Theme. *1920s–30s:* Flowing lines gradually replaced by linear ART DECO forms; double clips worn on both lapels or brooches worn on the shoulder; detachable Jabot pins; fob brooches and novelties in vivid contrasting colours such as onyx and coral; fancy cuts for all gems; multi-gem-set clips by CARTIER. *1940s–50s:* Floral sprays in yellow gold with large semi-precious gems such as citrine and aquamarine;

Diamond, sapphire, ruby emerald and onyx brooch, English 1925 [A]

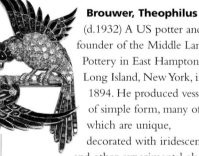

Gold, pearl and amethyst brooch, English c.1890 [Q]

asymmetrical and three-dimensional naturalistic and abstract forms; novelties. *1960s–70s:* Multi gem-set abstract forms; gold comical birds and animals; stylized diamond bows, floral sprays and matching sets; experimental crystal forms in bark finish settings.

John Brooks (*c.*1710–60) The manager of the BATTERSEA ENAMEL FACTORY who tried to take out three patents in England in the 1750s, claiming to have "discovered the art of printing on Enamel, Glass, China and other ware". He lived in Birmingham, the centre of the enamel trade, and later in London.

Brouwer, Theophilus

(d.1932) A US potter and founder of the Middle Lane Pottery in East Hampton, Long Island, New York, in 1894. He produced vessels of simple form, many of which are unique, decorated with iridescent and other experimental glazes. Marks may feature a whale jawbone centering an "M", and incised "Brouwer".

Brown & Co., George W. An American tin toy manufacturer who founded a factory in Forestville, Connecticut, in 1856. Credited as one of the earliest producers of clockwork toys in the US, he made hand-painted tin horse-drawn toys, trains and boats. Production ceased towards the end of the 19th century.

Brown-Westhead, Moore & Co. A British maker of dinner services and MAJOLICA ornamental wares based from 1862 at Cauldon Place, Staffordshire. It was previously known as RIDGWAY Bates & Co. (1856–58) and Bates, Brown-Westhead & Moore (1859–61). The company became Cauldon Ltd in 1905, and Cauldon Potteries Ltd from 1920–62.

Brown Bess British military flintlock, c.1790 [I]

Brown Bess A nickname for the British FINTLOCK MUSKET used *c.*1710–1840. It probably derived from the German *Buchse* meaning gun, and the browned finish of the barrel designed to prevent rust.

Brown ware A term used to describe both Chinese brown-glazed STONEWARE of the Song Dynasty (90–1279 AD) and English brown salt-glazed stoneware made at Brampton, Derbyshire, from early in the 18th century and throughout the 19th century.

The main Brampton potter was William Bromley who was succeeded by Robert Bambrigge & Co. Other 19th-century factories include Mrs Blake's, formerly worked by her husband, and subsequently part of the Luke Knowles' works (later Matthew Knowles & Son), which made stoneware bottles, kegs and barrels. William Briddon founded a factory in 1790 which was continued by his family. Thomas Oldfield went into business in 1810 and formed Oldfield & Co. in 1826, making jugs, figures, twisted pipes, PUZZLE JUGS and TOBY JUGS. John Wright's factory near St Thomas's Church was still in the family in 1878.

Brown EARTHENWARE with yellow or orange TRANSFER-PRINTED designs of pseudo-Chinese scenes was made from *c.*1800 to the 1850s in STAFFORDSHIRE and possibly Swansea and Liverpool, but the factories are unidentified.

Bruges tapestry factory Situated in Western Flanders (modern-day Belgium) on the River Reie, Bruges was not one of the largest centres of Flemish tapestry-weaving, but it flourished from *c.*1300 until the 17th century. Outdated cartoons discarded by the more important centres were often used. Verdures, GROTESQUES, historical and religious tapestries were made in monastic and private workshops.

Bru Jeune et Cie One of the most important Parisian manufacturers of bisque-headed FASHION DOLLS and BÉBÉS. The firm was established by Léon Casimir Bru in 1866 and sold to Henri Chevrot in 1883. Bru dolls are marked with "Bru (Jeune)" or a circle and dot. Bru was one of the founding members of the SOCIÉTÉ FRANÇAISE DE FABRICATION DE BÉBÉS ET JOUETS in 1899, which produced Bru dolls from the original moulds until the 1950s.

Brunswick pottery A German FAIENCE factory, founded in 1707 by Duke Anton Ulrich, with Johann Philipp Franz as director. Heinrich C. von Horn rented it and in 1711 went into partnership with J.G. von Hantelmann until 1744. Thereafter it changed hands frequently. Its earliest products were in blue and white, but it soon used polychrome colours and shapes such as fruit on plates and tureens in the form of birds, fish and bunches of grapes. It closed in 1807.

Brush pot A cylindrical container for calligraphers' or artists' brushes, from China and Japan. Can be made from a section of bamboo or from porcelain and decorated with calligraphy or blue and white scenes. Known examples date from the 16th century and these pots are still made today.

Brushing slide
A retractable shelf, often covered in green baize, fitted to the top of a chest of drawers. It can be pulled out and used for brushing or folding clothes or for writing.

Brussels lace Flemish 18th-century fine LACE with realistic flowers and fruit and detailed raised work. CHINOISERIE designs gave way in the 19th century to simpler scattered floral motifs on a plaited, or *vrai droschel*, ground. Machine-made nets were used as a ground for applied Brussels lace. *Point de gaze* NEEDLE

Brussels point de gaze handkerchief lace, c.1880 [N]

LACE was introduced at the GREAT EXHIBITION. Duchesse bobbin lace and *point de gaze* were combined for a type of mixed fashion lace in the 19th century.

Brussels pottery and porcelain
Faience was made here in several factories from the mid-17th century. In 1705, a factory was started by Corneille Mombaers and Thierry Witsenburg that made tureens in bird, fish and fruit shapes. A second factory was founded in 1802 by the brothers Van Bellinghen and closed in 1866. Porcelain was also produced in several factories in the late 18th century but they appear to have all closed by 1803.

Brussels tapestry factories
Under the patronage of the Dukes of Burgundy, Brussels became an important tapestry-weaving centre in the 14th century. In 1515, Pieter Coecke van Aelst (*d.*1550) undertook a commission from Pope Leo X for a series of tapestries, *The Acts of the Apostles,* from cartoons by Raphael. Hung in the Sistine Chapel, they gave Brussels a first-class reputation and marked a major change of creative control from weaver to artist. Tapestries were made into the 18th century – the last workshop closed in 1794.

Buckle Shoes and breeches commonly used buckles as a fastening in the 18th century, made from steel or pinchbeck set with paste or simply engraved. Waist buckles were popular at the start of the 19th century and the ARTS AND CRAFTS movement inspired colourful naturalistic themes.

Budai A Buddhist monk and god of Contentment, usually represented seated and grinning, exposing his bare fat belly, sometimes with a sack. He was a popular

Brussels tapestry depicting an episode from the Trojan wars, late 16th century [F]

subject in Chinese art, modelled in BLANC DE CHINE or decorated in FAMILLE ROSE enamels. In Japanese he is called Hotei.

Buddy L Fred Lundahl ran the Moline Pressed Steel Co. in Illinois, USA. In 1922, he started to make pressed-steel toy vehicles. The large-scale range, strong enough to sit on, was named after his son Buddy. The firm now makes steel and plastic vehicles, some with action and sound.

Buddy L pressed steel mechanical shovel, c.1930 [Q]

Buen Retiro porcelain factory When King Carlos IV of Naples and Sicily inherited the Spanish throne in 1759 he moved his royal porcelain factory from Naples (CAPODIMONTE) to the garden of the royal palace in Madrid. He took the artists and workmen, and even some of the clay, with him, so that the early wares are indistinguishable from those of Capodimonte. In 1804 KAOLIN was discovered in Madrid and so hard-paste porcelain – quite different from the soft paste of Capodimonte – was introduced. The factory closed in 1808.

Buen Retiro workshop Spanish PIETRE DURE and MOSAIC workshop from 1763–1808, specializing in elaborately decorated tabletops. It was founded at the Palace of Buen Retiro in Madrid by Charles III of Spain with workers from the Naples Royal Pietre Dure Factory.

Buffet A type of heavy, 16th-century doorless cupboard with tiers of shelves for displaying plate. The buffet went out of fashion from the end of the 17th century to the early 19th, when it re-emerged, typically as a three-shelf food "trolley".

Bugatti, Carlo (1856–1940) An Italian furniture designer and maker who founded workshops in 1888. His style is

Bugatti chair overlaid in beaten copper, 1902 [G]

unique: some pieces are inlaid with ebony, copper and pewter, and copper may be wrapped around uprights. He also used hand-painted vellum. Bugatti's inspiration came from nature and Moorish, Egyptian and Japanese art. The use of asymmetry and tassels are another feature of his work. He was the father of Rembrandt Bugatti, the sculptor, and Ettore, the car designer.

Buhl See BOULLE MARQUETRY.

Bulle clock A type of ELECTRIC CLOCK invented by the French clockmaker Favre-Bulle in the early 1920s. The movement is usually skeletonized and set on a mahogany base, covered by a glass dome. The battery is concealed within a vertical brass pillar or in the base.

Bullet mould A metal accessory into which molten lead was poured to manufacture bullets. Moulds were in use as early as 1375, but the development of the CARTRIDGE in the 19th century made them obsolete.

Bullet teapot A style first made during the 1730s from silver and porcelain and so named because its spherical shape resembles the round lead musket ball of the period.

English bullet teapot, c.1730 [D]

Bullock, George (c.1738–1819) An English furniture-maker, born in Liverpool. By 1814 he was working as a sculptor and furniture-maker in London, where he became one of the leading names during the Regency period and designed furniture for Napoleon when he was imprisoned on St Helena. The massive size and quality of his oak furniture was made even more impressive

Bullock rosewood and brass-inlaid side cabinet, c.1815 [C]

by decoration in the form of marquetry, often in EBONY, or native woods such as HOLLY, ELM and LARCH, and brass inlay in a variety of classical motifs.

Bun foot A round turned foot, flattened at the top and bottom, introduced in furniture of the late 17th century and revived in the early 19th.

Bunzlau potteries Grey STONEWARE (known as *gres*) was made here in Silesia, Germany, in the 16th and 17th centuries, but it is difficult to attribute accurately. In the 19th century there was a resurgence of grey stoneware – applied with flowers or coats of arms – and a big trade in coffee and chocolate pots. A 4.5-m (15-ft) high, 19th-century coffeepot was preserved in Bunzlau town hall. Various factories operated into the early 20th century including Lepper & Kuttner, Julius Paul & Son and Reinhold & Co.

Burano See LACE.

Burato (Italian: "canvas") A coarse woven fabric with a single warp thread and double twisted weft. It was produced to form the base for embroidered LACE in Italy from the 15th century.

Bureau A French term, used from the mid-17th century, for a writing desk or table with a flat top (BUREAU PLAT), a sloping front that folds down to form a writing surface, or a cylinder top that rolls up to reveal a flat writing surface.

British marquetry mahogany bureau, c.1900 [N]

Bureau plat A writing desk with a flat surface, often covered with leather, and with drawers in the FRIEZE, popular in France in the early 1700s.

Burgau porcelain factory Founded at Burgau-Goschwitz, Thuringia, Germany in 1900 by Ferdinand Solle, this factory produced utility, luxury and ART NOUVEAU items. It is no longer operating.

Burges, William (1827–81) An English architect and designer working in GOTHIC REVIVAL style. Cardiff Castle and Coch Castell, in Wales, both of which were built for his patron the Marquis of Bute, show a medieval influence. His work is rich in imagery, colour and texture. He also designed elaborately painted furniture and metalwork encrusted with precious stones.

Burgonet A light steel HELMET worn by infantry and light cavalry in Europe from c.1520 to c.1600. They are generally open-faced with a peak, hinged cheekpieces – usually pierced with ventilation holes – and a high comb.

Burl A type of growth on a tree trunk, also known as a burr, that when cut through reveals elaborate figuring that makes it useful for decorative veneering, as seen in particular on burr walnut pieces.

Burmantoft pottery An English pottery established in 1858 in Yorkshire by Wilcock & Co. to make architectural ceramics and bricks. In 1889 it was taken over by the Leeds Fireclay Company and the range was extended to include decorative EARTHENWARE fired at high temperatures. The company also produced single-glazed pieces in yellow, red and turquoise and colourful "Isnic" pieces inspired by William DE MORGAN. The factory closed in the 1950s.

Burmese glass A type of opaque coloured ART GLASS, shading from yellow to pink with a satin finish, that was patented in 1885 by the US MOUNT WASHINGTON GLASS CO. and used for table glass and small, ornamental vases and dressing table articles. It found favour with Queen Victoria, and from 1886, the British company of Thomas WEBB & Sons was licensed to produce their own version known as "Queen's Burmese", which was used for tableware and decorative glass, often with painted decoration.

Webb's Burmese glass posy vase, c.1890 [O]

Burne-Jones, Sir Edward C. (1833–98) An influential pre-Raphaelite artist, who became a partner in the leading ARTS AND CRAFTS firm of MORRIS & CO. for whom he designed stained glass, embroideries and tapestries. Among his best known and most successful designs are those for the tapestry-weaving workshops at Merton Abbey in London.

Burr See BURL and DRYPOINT.

Burse A stiffened square pocket or bag which has two common usages. The first is to carry the Lord Chancellor's great seal. In this case it is heavily embroidered with the monarch's coat of arms in metallic threads on a red velvet ground. A burse is also used to carry ecclesiastical vestments, in particular the corporal (linen cloth) used at Holy Communion.

Burt, John (1690–1745) An American colonial silversmith active in Boston, from c.1700. Burt's products, which are rare and highly prized, include simple HOLLOWWARE and CANDLESTICKS, which were made by very few early American silversmiths. He was succeeded by his sons Benjamin, Samuel and William.

Busby A tall fur hat used as part of British military uniform, sometimes with a plume. The name originated from the military supplier W. Busby of the Strand, London, and originally only applied to the fur caps of the Hussars and Horse Artillery in the 18th century. It is now applied to the full ceremonial headdress worn by Royal Engineers and the Corps of Signals.

Bustelli, Franz Anton (1723–63) A fine and distinctive porcelain modeller who was born in Locarno, Switzerland, and died in Munich. Bustelli began his career as a sculptor at the

Two-tile panel designed by Burne-Jones, 1861 [M]

NYMPHENBURG PORCELAIN factory, from 1754 until 1763. Although little is known of his early life, it is thought that he moved to Munich from Vienna. His numerous figures and groups – and especially his COMMEDIA DELL'ARTE FIGURES – exhibit great sophistication and sensitivity. They represent the pinnacle of modelling of the ROCOCO period, and are rivalled only by the work of J.J. KÄNDLER at MEISSEN.

Bustelli egg-seller figure, c.1755 [B]

Butler's tray A portable table, developed in Britain in the 18th century and popular throughout the 19th, consisting of a wooden or silver tray, often with a solid GALLERY and pierced handles, mounted on a folding stand or legs.

Butterfly table

Butterfly table An American 18th-century DROP-LEAF TABLE with supports resembling a butterfly with outspread wings (or the rudder of a rowing boat). They usually have outward slanting legs and one drawer. The term can also refer to a PEMBROKE table.

Button The button probably originated in Europe in the late 12th century and is made from a variety of materials, including wood, ivory, horn, silver and plastics

Buttoning An upholstery technique in which buttons are used to secure the layers of padding inside the covering. It produces a decorative pattern of indentations on sofas and chairs.

Byzantine style

Byzantine gold bracelet, c.500 [G]

A term used to describe a style of art and architecture that flourished in the Byzantine Empire from the foundation of Constantinople (Istanbul) as the capital of the eastern Roman Empire in AD 330 until its fall to the Ottoman Empire in 1453. The term "Byzantine" is employed in a more general sense to refer to works produced in this period in parts of western Europe, especially Italy, Spain and France, as well as those made before and after the 15th century in eastern Europe and Russia, where the Orthodox church was the dominant form of Christianity.

Art of the Byzantine Empire is characterized by an overall effect of rich decoration, combining elements of late imperial Roman Classicism with ornament from Islamic art, for example in the silks woven in Constantinople from the 8th century decorated with lions, elephants and other motifs derived from Persian art. Silver dishes, chalices and other ecclesiastical objects such as IVORY carvings, CLOISONNÉ ENAMELS and MOSAICS were also produced. Typical motifs include geometric patterns, vines, peacocks, PALMETTES and stylized figures of emperors, saints and angels. In the 19th century, the style was revived but was not as widely adopted as the GOTHIC or RENAISSANCE REVIVALS. Byzantine influence is found mainly in jewellery, particularly in the use of cloisonné enamel and GILDING, and in some furniture by the Italian ART NOUVEAU designer Carlo BUGATTI.

¹Cabaret A term used to describe a sofa for two people, especially one of an S-shape so that the two people are nearly face to face when seated. See also CONFIDANTE.

²Cabaret (or *tête-a-tête*) A term used for a tea or coffee service, usually comprising two cups and saucers, a small teapot, a sucrier, a cream jug and a tray, especially from the French porcelain factories.

Sèvres cabaret service, c.1880 [H]

Cabinet A type of CASE FURNITURE with drawers, pigeonholes and shelves used for writing and for storing valuables. Early examples, known in Italy and France in the 16th century and in Britain in the 17th, were often designed to sit on a stand or low piece of furniture. They were often highly decorative, made of exotic woods with elaborate inlays.

Cabinet on stand, lacquered, c.1700 [C]

Cabinet ware Richly decorated small pieces, such as plates, cups and saucers, that were intended not for use but to be shown off in a display cabinet. This was a 19th-century concept, popular throughout Europe and the US.

Cable moulding

Cable moulding Carved ornament resembling twisted rope, sometimes called ropework. A typical ROMANESQUE form used on arches and ARCADING, it was used in the 18th century as an edging on silver and ceramics and also as imitation ropework legs and stretchers on furniture. The motif was favoured for ironwork in the 19th and 20th century, as it was particularly well suited to being cast.

Cabochon decoration A French term for a smooth domed gem. As a raised oval or circular ornament, the cabochon was a popular motif for carving and stonework in GOTHIC and GOTHIC REVIVAL architecture. It was also favoured for jewelled STRAPWORK on ELIZABETHAN and JACOBEAN woodwork and metalwork, occasionally alternating with the LOZENGE. In ROCOCO furniture, it may also refer to a small convex CARTOUCHE form with a carved surround on the knee of a cabriole leg. It was revived during the ARTS AND CRAFTS period as a decoration on metalware.

Cabriole leg

Caboose The rear wagon on North American goods trains which carries the guard and workers, known as the guard's van in the UK.

Cabriole leg A leg used on chairs and CASE FURNITURE that consists of two curves, convex above blending into concave below to form an attenuated S-shape. It was introduced from France into English and US furniture in the first half of the 18th century. The cabriole underwent several stylistic evolutions, ranging from simple carving on the knee to elaborate carved decoration down its length, which was often gilded during the ROCOCO period. The cabriole leg was combined with different types of FOOT until it was superseded by the straight leg around the mid-18th century.

Cachepot (French: "hide the pot") A decorative receptacle to contain a flower pot, a smaller form of JARDINIÈRE. The term was coined in the 19th century although the items were made by many factories, including in stoneware by WEDGWOOD from the late 18th century, and are still made today.

Cachou box A small box of gold or silver often with enamel or lacquerwork and a close-fitting cover, made to contain breath-freshening tablets or cachous. They were usually circular and found favour in 18th-century continental Europe. Plain silver examples were common in Holland and known as peppermint boxes.

Caddy See TEA CADDY.

English caddy spoon, c.1809 [R]

Caddy spoon A small spoon, often fancifully shaped, for transferring tea from a caddy to a teapot, made from the 1770s. They are usually stamped from a thin sheet of silver, so they are light and fragile. Handles are sometimes made from bone, ivory or mother-of-pearl. Silver spoons, popular in the 19th century, are often die-stamped.

Cadogan teapot A teapot in the peach shape of a Chinese wine pot, named after an Earl of Cadogan. It was filled through a hole in the base. The tea was poured when the pot was held upside down. They were made by the ROCKINGHAM factory in the early 19th century. The moulds were bought by SPODE after Rockingham closed in 1842.

English Cadogan teapot, 1820 [P]

Caduceus See AARON'S ROD.

Caen porcelain A porcelain factory from 1793 at Calvados, Normandy, run by d'Aigmont-Desmares and Ducheval. The name of the town was used as the mark. It made tablewares with landscapes in black in panels suspended from green and gold wreaths, until closure in 1806.

Cafaggiolo maiolica, early 16th century [E]

Cafaggiolo In 1506 Piero and Stefano Cafaggiolo started to make MAIOLICA near Florence, Italy. For nearly 100 years the same family (later known as Fattorini) ran the workshop. From 1506–26 they made maiolica of great distinction, boldly painted against a bright blue background and including the arms of the Medici family. The best examples are influenced by the work of Florentine artists such as Botticelli. The factory's most outstanding painter was Jacopo Fattorini. From *c*.1535 the workshop made simpler wares decorated with ARABESQUES and PUTTI. It seems to have closed in the mid-18th century but later wares are undated.

Caffiéri, Jacques (*c*.1673–1755) A French metalworker and sculptor. He trained as a sculptor and became a master metalworker of gilt-bronze in 1715. From 1736 he worked at Versailles and other royal palaces of Louis XV of France, producing elaborate gilt-bronze ROCOCO clock cases, chandeliers and other furnishings, often in collaboration with his son Philippe Caffiéri (1714–74).

Cagework (French: *à cage*) A type of decoration most usually found in silver cups of the 17th century, in which the background of the design of the cup was cut away like fretwork leaving the silver CHASING or REPOUSSÉ work. The cup then had a plain liner, often gilt for contrast.

Caillouté (French *caillou*: "pebble") A type of ceramic decoration, usually in gilding, of oval "pebble" shapes on a dark ground, especially popular at SÈVRES and copied by some English factories.

Cairngorm A variety of Scottish quartz ranging from grey and pale yellow (citrine) to brown and with a smoky appearance. Found in the Cairngorm mountains of north-east Scotland, it has been used from the 19th century for mounting in decorative jewellery and silver, particularly for the Scottish market, e.g. QUAICHS and plaid brooches, but was also exported.

Cake basket A receptacle for cakes, similar to those used for bread or fruit, most usually in openwork silver with a handle that could swing to one side, although similar items were

made in porcelain. These first appeared in the mid-18th century and continued in use throughout the 19th century.

Calamander See EBONY.

Calcite glass A smooth-surfaced, plated glass simulating ivory, used at the US STEUBEN GLASSWORKS on decorative wares and lampshades in the early 20th century.

Caldwell, J.E. & Company A US jeweller and silversmiths founded in Philadelphia in 1839. Throughout the later 19th century Caldwell specialized in high quality, elaborately CHASED or REPOUSSÉ silver HOLLOWWARE in revivalist style. It is clearly marked. Caldwell also produced elaborate French-influenced clocks, mantel GARNITURES and other bronze work. The most highly regarded examples feature enamel decoration.

Calendar aperture A small window on a clock or watch dial displaying the day, month or year, or all of these. Calendar apertures are found on domestic clocks from the 16th century onward.

Calico (Also known as Calicut, after the Indian city on the Malabar Coast) In the 17th century calico became a general name for cotton cloths of all kinds imported from the East, and subsequently also for various cotton fabrics made in Europe. Nowadays the name is chiefly applied to plain white unprinted cotton cloth, either bleached or unbleached.

Calotype of a pagoda, c.1860 [P]

English George III silver cake basket, 1772 [D]

Calotype The first practical photographic process to produce a negative from which identical positives could be printed. The English pioneer of photography William Henry Fox Talbot (1780-1877) patented it in 1840. Sometimes known as a talbotype, it was never as popular as the DAGUERREOTYPE. Both processes were used until about 1851 when they were superseded by the collodion wet-plate process.

Caltagirone potteries See SICILIAN POTTERIES.

Camaïeu, en A French term used to describe painting in different tones of the same colour.

Italian cameo brooch of Cupid and Psyche, 1750 [H]

Cameo A gem, hardstone or shell carved in relief to depict various subjects including classical groups, landscapes and mythological deities. The colour of the subject may contrast with the background. Purely decorative, cameos first appeared in Classical jewellery and furniture and were revived in the RENAISSANCE and in 18th century NEO-CLASSICAL ornament. Cameos were popular in 19th- and 20th-century jewellery.

Cameo glass
A type of decorated glass made from two or more layers of different colours, where the top layer(s) is carved or etched away to reveal a contrasting coloured background. Used on early Roman glass and revived in the 19th century.

Cameo glass plaque, English c.1885 [H]

Camera obscura An optical device invented in the 18th century in which light entering a room via a pinhole casts an image of the scene outside on the back wall of the room. These were constructed as panoramas in gardens or parks but were also used in box form by artists. The image is upside down but can be rectified with a mirror and then traced or sketched. The obscura was mainly used in the 18th century to make enlarged drawings of small objects and portraits.

Campaign furniture Furniture that could be easily assembled, dismantled and occasionally packed flat and transported

Campaign chest, Anglo-Indian c.1830 [I]

during military campaigns, often in special crates that could themselves be used as furniture. Made in woods native to the campaign area, furniture took the form of small case pieces such as chests with writing or storage drawers, inset handles and detachable feet. Chairs sometimes had folding seats, backs that dismantled and legs that unscrewed.

Campana vase (Italian: *campana* "bell") A Classical vessel, of silver or bronze, in the form of an inverted stylized bell.

Canabas The name by which the cabinet-maker Joseph Gegenbach (1712–97) was known. He was born in Baden, Germany, but by 1745 had settled in Paris where he produced austere but practical multi-functional furniture, often in mahogany, specializing in pieces that could be easily dismantled and reassembled for travelling, such as CAMPAIGN FURNITURE.

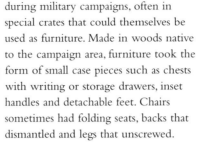

Walnut canapé, French Louis XV Revival c.1890 [G]

Canapé The French term for a SOFA or settee, a type of upholstered seat furniture with a back and arms and designed to seat two or more people. The term was first used in the late 17th century and, by the 18th century, variations on the canapé proliferated, including the CONFIDANTE.

Canary glass An American term for glass of a bright yellow colour, resembling VASELINE GLASS, and mostly of 19th-century origin.

Cancellation mark A term usually used of the crossed swords mark on MEISSEN porcelain, where two lines have been scratched across the swords to indicate that the piece was sold as being below the usual standard. These pieces were most probably decorated outside the factory.

Candelabrum A multibranched candlestick for use on a table. Candelabra commonly have three to nine lights. Although they are known throughout history, silver examples do not really pre-date the mid-17th century. They were also made in porcelain in the 18th century. They are similar in style to contemporary candlesticks.

Candleslide A small wooden support for a candlestick found on desks, work-tables and similar pieces of furniture primarily from the 18th and 19th centuries. When not in use, it slides out of sight into a built-in recess.

Candle snuffer A small scissor-like tool with a "box" section on the blades enabling a candle wick to be simultaneously extinguished, trimmed and safely retained. The better quality examples were made of silver and had a small tray on which they were kept. The earliest surviving pair dates from 1512. They were common throughout the 18th century but were then superseded by the cone-shaped snuffer of the type found on CHAMBERSTICKS.

Candle stand A small, portable round-topped table with a long central support ending in tripod legs and designed to hold a candlestick or lantern. Popular in the second half of the 17th century, they are typically made of oak or walnut with octagonal-shaped tops, sometimes elaborately inlaid. See also TORCHÈRE.

Candlestick A stable "column" for holding a candle vertically in a socket at a given height for the purpose intended e.g. library, altar, hand- or taper-candlestick. Athough made from most materials, silver is particularly suitable as it reflects light. Extant examples pre-1660 are extremely rare.

Silver candlestick, mid-18th century [H]

¹Cane The material obtained from the rattan palm and used to make furniture. Cane was imported into Europe from what is now Malaysia by the Dutch East India Company and from 1664 was used to make the backs and seats of chairs that were light, easy to clean and durable. Cane chairs remained popular until the early 18th century, and then enjoyed a revival in the late 18th/early 19th and again in the early 20th century.

²Cane A bundle of single monochrome glass RODS, or composite polychrome rods, that are fused together and used in the manufacture of MILLEFIORE glass or drinking-glass stems.

Canephorus An architectural MOTIF, often used on bronze furniture mounts, in the form of a female figure carrying a basket on her head. See also CARYATID.

Caneware A buff or cane-coloured stoneware made by Wedgwood and other contemporary Staffordshire potters, sometimes enriched with enamel decoration. Essentially it was a refinement of the ordinary buff body, which Wedgwood made in a lighter weight in 1770 and called "cane".

Cannelé (French: *chanel* "flute") A fabric displaying a textured stepped effect, created when an additional warp thread, often gold or silver, is fixed at intervals to the surface of a woven fabric, which is usually silk.

Cannetille A method of working gold, usually in the form of wire, into elaborate scrolls, spirals, flowers, coils and beads on a filigree core, used extensively in the early 19th century in English and French jewellery. Effective when combined with gems such as aquamarine, amethyst and topaz or hardstone and shell cameos. Cannetille-work PARURES regularly appear on the market today.

Canopic vase An earthenware and alabaster vase used in the Egyptian mummifying process. The liver, lungs, spleen and stomach were entrusted to the gods in four canopic vases and painted with heads of people, baboons, falcons and jackals. Made at Canopus in Egypt.

Canova, Antonio (1757–1822) An Italian sculptor who became famous in his day and was patronized by Englishmen on the GRAND TOUR. His marble group of *The Three Graces* is now in the Victoria & Albert Museum, London. Many of his works were copied in PARIAN WARE.

Cantagalli, Ulisse (1839–1901) An Italian potter who established a factory in Florence in 1877, making imitations of Italian maiolica wares of the 16th century. His mark is a crowing cockerel, a rebus on his name, and the pottery is still producing ware today. He also copied products of other potteries, including Iznik.

Canephorous

Cántaro The Spanish term for a closed jug, made in CATALAN GLASSHOUSES in the 17th and 18th centuries, with a fixed ring-shaped vertical handle and two spouts: a short wide one for filling and pouring and a longer one for drinking from.

Cántaro

Canted The surface produced by bevelling off a corner. Also known as a chamfered corner, this was common on Gothic and 18th-century furniture.

Canteen A service of matching silver or, later, plate flatware fitted in a piece of furniture such as a side table or box. The term can also apply to these fitted boxes or to a set of flatware and cutlery with 12 place settings or more. Late 17th-century canteens exist but most are of later date.

Canterbury A small stand, made from the late 18th century, with slatted racks or divisions, perhaps originally for an Archbishop of Canterbury, and produced in two versions. The music canterbury was generally rectangular, with racks to hold sheet music. The supper canterbury was a round tray set above racks to hold cutlery and stood beside a dining table.

Walnut canterbury, English c.1870 [K]

Cantilever chair A chair without back legs which is supported by a cantilevered frame in which the front legs curve round and under to form the base. It was particularly popular with Modernist designers of the 20th century who explored the technique in tubular steel (see also Marcel BREUER) and moulded plywood (see also Alvar AALTO).

Canton enamel Chinese painted enamel on copper, developed in the late 17th century with the aid of Europeans, produced mainly at Canton in south China for export. Decoration usually comprises figures, flowers and insects in the FAMILLE ROSE palette. Wares include dishes, tea kettles, boxes and, in the 20th century, such small items as matchboxes and ashtrays.

Canton enamel snuff-box, c.1750 [H]

Canton porcelain These wares, made for export in the 18th to 20th centuries, were made at JINGDEZHEN, but decorated at Canton in south China. Canton FAMILLE ROSE in the 19th century was typically decorated with alternate panels of figures and birds, flowers and insects, predominantly in pink and green. See also MANDARIN PALETTE, CHINESE EXPORT PORCELAIN and CANTON ENAMEL.

Canton famille rose vase, c.1850 [K, a pair]

Cap and ball A slang term for a PERCUSSION LOCK – particularly when used to describe a REVOLVER – derived from a combination of the cap or primer and the spherical lead bullet or ball.

Cape Cod This peninsula off the eastern coast of Massachusetts was an important centre of the American glass industry in the 19th century, owing to the availability of silica-rich sand and reeds (used for packing). Cape Cod is known for the earliest PRESSED GLASS in the 1820s and the manufacture of inexpensive pattern glass and lamps for whale oil until the early 20th century.

Capital The top or crown of an architectural COLUMN or pillar supporting the entablature. Although most often based on flowers and foliage, the carved decoration of a capital can be varied to include animals, wicker patterns, cube and bell shapes.

Capitonné (French: *capiton* "tuft") A form of upholstery in which a padded surface is drawn in at intervals to produce an organized pattern. These indentations, held in place by decorative tufts stitched through the fabric and pulled tight, were fashionable in the 19th century.

Capodimonte porcelain factory Founded in 1743 in Naples when the "Porcelain Princess" Princess Marie Amalia of Saxony married King Charles III of Naples and Sicily. The factory copied the styles of Meissen. Giovanni Caselli was a fine painter working there and Guiseppe Gricci was a modeller from 1744. When King Charles succeeded to the Spanish throne in 1759, he moved his court and his factory to Madrid, and the factory was set up in the grounds of the

Capodimonte porcelain bowl, mid-18th century [L]

BUEN RETIRO palace. The factory returned to Naples in the late 18th century and reproductions of the true soft-paste Capodimonte figures have been made in the area ever since.

Cappiello, Leonetto (1875–1942) An Italian poster designer who settled in Paris. He made his name during the poster boom period, *c.*1900, with designs similar to those of Jules CHÉRET (1836–1933) but redesigned the *fin-de-siècle* pictures into images more relevant to the faster pace of the 20th century.

Capstan table See DRUM TABLE.

Carafe A container for wine or water, shaped rather like a rounded decanter but with a wider neck and no stopper. Used on the dinner table from the early 19th century, a carafe with an inverted tumbler was also used as a bedroom water-jug.

Carat The standard unit of weight for diamonds, gems and pearls. One carat is equivalent to one-fifth of a gram. The term carat is additionally used as a unit of fineness for gold where the pure metal is divided into 24 parts, thus "9 carat" is 9 parts pure gold and 15 parts metal.

Carbine A short, light RIFLE or MUSKET for cavalry troops. The term was first used in the late 16th century for French light horseman called *carabins* who were armed with short, light guns. Carbines were still in use in World War II.

Carboy A large bottle or flagon made of thick glass, used to transport or store dangerous liquids, such as ammonia, or for display in pharmacies. Most have a basketwork cover or string round the neck to provide grip. The term appears to date from the 18th century.

Carcass, carcase The structure or body of a piece of CASE FURNITURE before elements such as drawers, doors, shelves or feet are added. It acts as a foundation for VENEERS or other applied decoration.

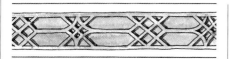

Card-cut ornament

Card-cut ornament A lattice-like unpierced, FRETWORK ornament for wood, cut in low relief. A popular motif for furniture in CHINOISERIE and GOTHIC taste, it was mainly applied in horizontal sections, e.g. along the top of a tallboy.

Carder, Frederick (1864–1963) An English-born American glassmaker, who began his career at STEVENS & WILLIAMS in 1881. He was artistic director of the STEUBEN GLASSWORKS in Corning, New York, from 1903 to 1933, and introduced several artistic lines, notably "Aurene", an iridescent gold or blue glass designed to rival the popular FAVRILE glass of TIFFANY. In later life, Carder worked independently in Corning, making advanced artistic glass including replicas of ancient vessels and CIRE-PERDUE work, most of which has an engraved signature.

Cardew, Michael (1901–83) An English studio potter who learned his craft at Fishley Holland, Devon, and with Bernard LEACH at St Ives, Cornwall. In 1926 he opened his own pottery, Winchcombe at Gleet, Gloucestershire, making slip- and sgraffito-decorated domestic pottery. Leaving Winchcombe under the direction of Ray Finch, he opened a new pottery at Wenford Bridge, Cornwall (joined by his son Seth in 1971). His enthusiasm for functional studio-made pottery led him to help set up potteries in several West African countries and in Northern Territories in Australia (1968).

Slipware jug by Cardew, c.1929 [L]

Card table A type of table specifically designed for playing card games, introduced at the end of the 17th century, usually with a folding baize-covered top (often green) that opens out.

Carette et Cie, Georges (1886–1917) A toy-making company founded in 1886 in Nuremberg by an exiled Frenchman, concentrating on tin/brass painted toys. From 1900–17 it made high quality painted and lithographed tin-plate trains, cars, steam engines, boats and scientific toys. Some items were made specifically for BASSETT-LOWKE. Carette had to flee Germany in 1917 and his tools and patterns were disseminated into other parts of the German toy industry.

Carillon A set of bells, or a tune played on a series of bells by manual or mechanical means.

Louis XVI tulipwood and marquetry commode à vantaux by Carlin [A]

Carlin, Martin (d.1785) A French furniture maker of German birth. By 1759, he had settled in Paris, where he may have worked in the workshop of Jean-François OEBEN, whose sister he married. He is known for his elegant small-scale furniture, in the LOUIS XVI style, often decorated with plaques by the SÈVRES porcelain factory.

Carlton House desk A type of writing table or desk that was first named in a cost book of GILLOWS in 1796 and is probably

named after the residence of the then Prince of Wales. It has a superstructure with a pierced brass GALLERY and drawers surrounding a leather or polished wood writing surface, with drawers in the frieze below. Desks of this type are still made as "reproduction" pieces.

Carlton ware A trade name used from the mid-1890s by Wiltshaw & Robinson Ltd of the Carlton Works, Stoke. They produced china and earthenware and crested souvenir type wares, on which the name Crown China may occur. The name became Carlton Ware Ltd in 1958 and various manufacturers now make limited edition pieces under license.

Carlton ware "Anenome" jug, 1930 [P]

Car mascot A metal or glass ornament that is attached to the top of a car radiator. Often a human or animal form, designs include Rolls Royce's Spirit of Ecstasy and the many beautiful forms made from glass by René LALIQUE.

Carnival glass Inexpensive, ornamental pressed glass, mostly iridescent and of deep amethyst colour, produced in the US and Britain from the late 19th century until the present, and sometimes used as a carnival prizes. Most US carnival glass was made during the depression years of the early 1930s.

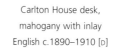

Carlton House desk, mahogany with inlay English c.1890–1910 [D]

Carolean style The decorative style popular in England during the reign of Charles II from 1660 to 1685, also known as the RESTORATION STYLE. It is characterized by a reaction against the austerity of the CROMWELLIAN STYLE and by the introduction of Dutch and, to some extent, French artistic influences brought back by the Court on its return from exile on the Continent.

Carolean walnut carved armchair, c.1690 [F]

New types of furniture appeared in this period: cabinets-on-stands, chests-of-drawers, armchairs, wing chairs, day beds and settees.

Walnut veneer replaced oak as the most fashionable wood, while the use of JAPANNING, imported LACQUER and cane for chair seats and backs reflected the craze for CHINOISERIE. Dutch influence appeared in the use of MARQUETRY and parquetry, while ornate carved and gilded supports were decorated with naturalistic fruits, foliage and arabesques. The overall effect of magnificence and opulence was enhanced by CREWELWORK bed hangings and tapestries and velvets and brocades for upholstery. Silver is characterized by embossing, especially of fruit and flowers, and flat-chased chinoiserie scenes of Oriental-style figures and landscapes; innovations included toilet sets for wealthy patrons and tea- and coffeepots, arising from the popularity of these new drinks. This period is also marked by the development of the English glass industry, especially after the invention of lead glass by George RAVENSCROFT, *c.*1676. The fashion for collecting Oriental blue and white porcelain is also evident in the production of BLUE-DASH CHARGERS. After the 1688 Revolution and the accession of William III and Mary II the Carolean style was superseded by the WILLIAM AND MARY STYLE.

Carpet A floor covering, machine- or handmade, in wool, cotton or silk. In handmade examples the term refers to larger-scale pieces, as opposed to rugs, which are of smaller proportions.

Carpet toy Also known as a floor toy. Originally of wood or CAST IRON but now of plastic, they include pull-along trains (without rails), large buses and trucks suitable for the smaller child.

Carrara A fine white marble that came from the quarries of the town of Carrara in Italy. In English ceramics the word is used to denote a dense white stoneware with a slight glaze that gave its surface a texture suggestive of marble.

Carriage clock A small, spring-driven clock, designed for travelling, developed in the early 19th century in France. The case, usually plain or gilt-brass, is rectangular with a carrying handle and often set with glass or more rarely enamel or porcelain panels. A feature of carriage clocks is the PLATFORM ESCAPEMENT, sometimes visible through a glazed aperture on the top of the case.

Length of Carrickmacross lace, 1880 [M]

Carrickmacross A centre for Irish lace that was first exhibited at the GREAT EXHIBITION of 1851 and was promoted by the Ladies' Industrial Society as employment after the mid-19th-century potato famine. It is typified by delicate muslin floral motifs hand-stitched to machine net then cut out, and was used for collars, veils and other clothing. Machine-made versions were also made.

Carrier-Belleuse, Albert-Ernest (1824–87) A French modeller and sculptor who worked in terracotta, marble and bronze. He also made models for LIMOGES porcelain factories and worked in England as a modeller at MINTON and other STAFFORDSHIRE factories. He went back to France in 1876 and worked at SÈVRES as artistic director until his death. His pieces may be signed "A Carrier".

French brass carriage clock, c.1890 [H]

Carriès, Jean (1855–94) A French sculptor and potter with kilns at Montriveau, near

Nevers. He made stoneware influenced by Japanese pottery, including figures, masks and animal models.

Carron ironworks
A foundry started in 1759 near Falkirk, Scotland. It was one of the most successful British firms producing cast-iron fire-backs, stoves, grates and other furnishings, often using the NEO-CLASSICAL designs of Robert ADAM. Such pieces were reproduced by the firm in the early 20th century.

Cartel clock An ornate spring-driven WALL CLOCK made mainly in France during the 18th and 19th centuries, also in Sweden. It features a white enamelled dial set in a carved and gilded wood or gilt-bronze frame. Early ROCOCO frames are characterized by exuberant scrollwork, flowers and shells, while later NEO-classical pieces feature laurel leaves, urns and masks.

Carter, Stabler & Adams See POOLE.

Cartier brooch, 1925 [C]

Cartier A jewellery company founded in 1847 in Paris by Louis-François Cartier (1819–1904), moving in 1899 to the prestigious Rue de la Paix. Famous for its jewellery created for the royal families of Europe and its innovative designs for pocket watches, using enamel and crystal to produce excellent decorative examples. From 1888 they were among the first to make WRISTWATCHES.

French cartel clock, late 19th century [H]

Cartonnier A piece of furniture, popular in France in the mid-18th century, fitted with pigeonholes or other types of compartments designed to hold paper. An early type of filing cabinet, small versions were designed to sit on a writing table such as a BUREAU PLAT; larger versions stood independently next to a desk.

¹Cartoon A design for a tapestry, sometimes coloured, sometimes monochrome. Many famous painters produced cartoons for tapestry-weaving. Two notable examples are Raphael's cartoons for the BRUSSELS TAPESTRY workshop during the early 16th century and Boucher's design for BEAUVAIS during the 18th century.

²Cartoon A humorous drawing, with an element of caricature and commenting on current affairs, usually first published in magazines, such as the 19th-century French *Charivari* or the English *Punch*. Famous cartoonists include George du Maurier, Phil May and Honoré Daumier.

Cartouche The French term for a scroll or an escutcheon. A framed ornamental panel in the form of a sheet of paper or a scroll with curling edges, the cartouche

Cartouche

may have a plain, elaborately decorated or inscribed centre. Widely used in RENAISSANCE decoration and promoted by pattern-book engravers, the device frequently appears in 16th- and 17th-century ornament, but enjoyed its greatest popularity during the ROCOCO period, when it was seen on carved boiseries, ceramics and silver.

Cartridge (Italian *carta*: "a roll of paper") A round of ammunition. Originally cartridges were made of paper, but from the mid-19th century they were mostly made of metal and contained their own means of ignition.

Carver chair An American open armchair first made in New England in the mid-17th century. Carvers differ from BREWSTER CHAIRS in having no spindles beneath the rush-woven seat. Plain examples, with little turning, may be called PILGRIM CHAIRS. Also refers to the chair with arms in a dining suite.

Cary, John (1754–1835) A pioneering English cartographer who produced many finely designed and engraved MAPS based on the latest available geographical data. His output included clear and highly accurate English county maps, town plans, world and regional maps, GLOBES and canal and road maps.

Caryatid A Greek term for an architectural column in the form of a full-length male or female figure. The same motif was also used on NEO-classical and EMPIRE-style 17th- and 18th-century furniture cast in bronze as brackets, furniture legs or small items such as desk handles. See also CANEPHORUS.

Caryatid

Cased glass A type of glass that consists of two or more layers of different colours – a thick outer layer and a second layer which is blown into it. Further layers can then be blown in. The layers are fused when the piece is reheated.

English mahogany chest-of-drawers, 1770 [C]

Case furniture A type of furniture designed to act as a receptacle or storage space. It generally consists of a box-like "case" structure or CARCASS into which drawers or shelves are fitted. The earliest example of case furniture, based on a hollowed-out log (hence the term "trunk" for a travelling case) is the medieval CHEST or coffer, usually made of oak in northern Europe and walnut in southern Europe.

As furniture-making grew more sophisticated, the chest evolved into the CHEST-OF-DRAWERS in the 17th century. It was usually made with joints secured by iron nails, later with DOVETAILING. Drawers were a 16th-century development, initially called "tills" or "drawing boxes" in Britain.

The chest-of-drawers branched out into all its many forms such as the COMMODE, LINEN PRESS, WARDROBE; the CUPBOARD or DRESSER; the DRESSING TABLE; the many different types of BUREAU and bookshelves. Each of these in turn developed more specialized forms.

Cash pattern An Oriental ceramic pattern based on a design of small, circular Chinese coins with a square central hole for stringing. Occasionally the beribboned coins are painted as decoration on porcelain, and as a symbol of the Chinese Immortal Liu Hai.

Cassapanca The Italian term for a wooden bench, often with an upright back, in which the seat lifts up to reveal a storage chest.

Cassolette A vase with a reversible lid on which a candle could be placed. The candle-holder was concealed when the lid was in the "normal" position. A cassolette could also be a vase or urn in metal, earthenware or porphyry with a pierced cover in which scented charcoal or perfume was heated to create aromatic fumes. See also ATHÉNIENNE.

Cassone The Italian name for a type of free-standing low chest, made in Italy from the 15th and 16th centuries, often with elaborate decoration in the form of carving, applied GESSO decoration or painting. Cassoni were often wedding chests and so made in pairs, decorated with heraldic devices and symbols associated with the two families and apt scenes from Classical mythology, such as the marriage of Peleus and Thetis.

Castel Durante
MAIOLICA was made here, near URBINO in central Italy, especially during the first 30 years of the 16th century. The town was renamed Urbania in 1635 after Pope Urban. The two great artists Giovanni Maria and Nicola Pellipario gave the decoration pre-eminence. Dishes with inner borders in BIANCO-SOPRA-BIANCO were a special feature, as were portraits of ladies and helmeted warriors. The workshops flourished in the 16th century but declined in the 17th.

Castellani, Fortunato Pio (1793–1865)
An Italian goldsmith who pioneered the fashion for Classical, and particularly Etruscan, revivalist gold jewellery inspired by the recent archeological finds. Frequently incorporating authentic ancient objects, including semi-precious stones and coins, Castellani mastered the technique of applying complex decoration such as filigree and granulation.

Gold ram's head Castellani brooch, 1870 [F]

Castelli potteries A group of MAIOLICA factories in the 17th and 18th centuries, near Teramo in the former kingdom of Naples. Earliest wares included BIANCO DI FAENZA but they were known for ISTORIATO wares from c.1650 to the late 18th century. The Grue and Gentili families were the best known exponents. Their distinctly local style used cooler and lighter colours than other Italian makers of maiolica, including a pale grey-blue, buffs, browns and olive-green. The scenes were usually inspired by prints after BAROQUE artists of religious and mythological scenes as well as picturesque landscapes. The scenes were often "pounced" on to the ceramic surface. The design was drawn on paper and holes

Castel Durante tondino (round dish), c.1540 [I]

Castelli maiolica plaque with conversion of Saul, c.1740 [H]

were made along the lines. When a fine powder was rubbed over the paper, it went through the holes, transferring the design, ready to be painted over.

Small dishes were popular wares, and the wide rims were usually decorated with figures of PUTTI and garlands of fruit and flowers, highlighted with gilding. The Castelli potteries also manufactured large numbers of plaques, as well as ALBARELLI, double-handed bottles and dragon-spouted syrup pots.

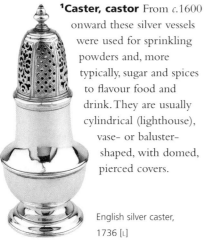

¹Caster, castor From *c.*1600 onward these silver vessels were used for sprinkling powders and, more typically, sugar and spices to flavour food and drink. They are usually cylindrical (lighthouse), vase- or baluster-shaped, with domed, pierced covers.

English silver caster, 1736 [L]

²Caster From the 16th century, small wheels used on the ends of furniture legs, particularly dining tables and heavy chairs, to make moving them easier.

Castiglioni, Achille (b.1918) An Italian architect and designer. Born in Milan, he set up a studio with his brother Pier Giacomo (1913–68) in 1944, and went on to produce a number of outstanding

designs for furniture (e.g. "Mezzadro" tractor stool, 1955) and lighting, including in 1962 the marble and steel "Arco" lamp, the cone-shaped "Taccia" and "Toio" lights, and in 1967 the "Snoopy" lamp, based on the famous cartoon character. He also designs silver, glass and ceramics.

Casting Forming a solid article from a liquid such as molten glass, silver or bronze, or from a semi-liquid such as wet clay, by pouring or forcing it into a pre-constructed mould. After the material has set or dried, the mould is dismantled. See also LOST WAX.

Cast iron One of the two main types of iron for items such as grilles, fireplace furnishings, furniture and railings (the other being wrought iron). It is produced by casting iron with a high carbon content in moulds of compressed sand. In the 19th century cast iron was popular for garden furniture, coat stands, plant stands and other items. It is more brittle than wrought iron.

Cast-iron toys Typically American, peak production was between the 1870s and 1930s. Toys may be single- or multipiece, usually transport-related, such as wagons, fire engines and trucks. Savings ("piggy") banks were also made, some with a mechanism triggered by the coin. Castings are riveted, bolted or held together by interlocking springs. Fakes are common.

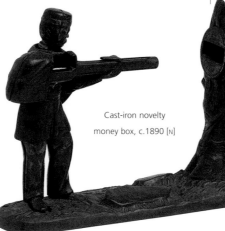

Cast-iron novelty money box, c.1890 [N]

Castle, Wendell (b.1932) A highly original American furniture-maker maintaining the craft tradition but with modern forms and interpretations. His furniture, often in exotic woods, sometimes uses *trompe l'oeil* effects. He also works in moulded plastic. He established a school in 1980.

Wendell Castle games table, 1975 [J]

Castleford pottery
A Yorkshire factory founded in 1790 by David Dunderdale that produced creamware, pearlware, whiteware, basaltes ware and a white semi-translucent body of porcelain appearance. The mark combined his initials and the word CASTLEFORD. Dunderdale published a pattern-book in 1796 including many creamware pieces. He died in 1799, and was succeeded by his son, also David. The factory closed in 1821.

Castleford ware The word Castleford covers a range of slip-cast tea wares that often have added relief decoration – usually semi-translucent – and look similar to the wares of the LEEDS POTTERIES in the 19th century. Typical are teapots with sliding and hinged lids, often with blue borders, which is usually the only glaze on the exterior. Some were made by David Dunderdale in Castleford, Yorkshire, from *c.*1790 but many are from Staffordshire.

Castle-top Embossed or engraved decoration on silver card cases, snuff-boxes and vinaigrettes, depicting a castle, historic house or landscape. Made from the 1830s, largely in Birmingham, UK, some were produced as souvenirs for tourists since their popularity coincided with the opening of passenger railways in Britain. The most prestigious maker was Nathaniel Mills.

Castle-top box with scene of Abbotsford, 1839 [J]

Castwork Usually decorative sections on silver items, which have been cast then soldered or applied to the main body of the article, e.g. a CARTOUCHE or a FINIAL.

Cat A stand comprising three wooden or metal rods joined in the centre, used in the 18th and 19th centuries for keeping plates warm in front of an open fire.

Catalan glasshouses The term used to denote the numerous glasshouses active from the Middle Ages in Catalonia, a region in north-east Spain famous for its long glass-making tradition and distinctive 17th- and 18th-century regional forms such as the CÁNTARO, often with elaborate trailed and combed decoration. Barcelona, the Catalan capital, was known in the 16th and 17th centuries for its transparent glass with an unusually "white" body. By the 20th century, Catalan glasshouses were the main suppliers of glass for the home market.

Caucasian carpet A carpet made in the region between the Caspian and Black seas. Carpets made here are woven by nomadic, semi-nomadic and village weavers. Little is known about the carpets that may have been made here before the

Caucasian Karabagh runner, c.1800 [E]

mid-17th century. The oldest identifiable group is the so-called KUBA dragon carpets. The name is, however, misleading as it is now thought they were woven in the KARABAGH district of the south-east Caucasus. These rugs display a naively geometrical rendering of Persian animal carpet designs from Tabriz, Kashan and Kerman during the Safavid period (1501–1732). Sometimes the design is so stylized that its origins are barely recognizable. By the mid-18th century, production weaving ceased but carpet-making revived in the 19th century.

The nomadic tradition of weaving, together with inspiration from earlier examples and carpets from Turkey, produced items with formal designs,

displaying intensive geometric stylized plant and animal forms in vibrant jewel-like colours.

Some districts/villages produce finer woven carpets with greater detail. Kuba, Shirvan and Dagestan represent this finer weaving tradition; Dagestan is particularly known for the production of PRAYER RUGS. They often have white MIHRAB and the design format is formal. In rugs from Karabagh and KAZAK, the designs are based on earlier Classical forms, both Persian and Anatolian. Designs from these two regions are considerably bolder, with more sparse decoration, although the colour combinations remain strong, powerful and jewel-like.

Rugs are mainly woven, carpets are rare and infrequently seen. Rugs made after 1880 often display one or several harsh chemical dyes – bright orange and purple are frequently seen. These colours tend to ruin the artistic quality of the rug. Earlier examples are considerably more attractive and highly individual.

Caudle cup A vessel in silver or pottery with a lift-off cover to take caudle – a hot, spiced wine drink made with gruel or porridge, thought to be medicinal. These two-handled cups were usually of baluster form with a flat base or low feet and often with a matching broad-rimmed stand. They were produced between c.1650 and c.1700. See also PORRINGER.

English silver caudle cup, 1676 [E]

Caughley porcelain factory
In 1772, Thomas Turner moved from WORCESTER to the   c.1775–90 Caughley pottery, near Broseley, Shropshire. He began to make

Caughley saucer, c.1780 [R]

transfer-printed porcelain called SALOPIAN ware that was similar to Worcester, although by transmitted light the Caughley body is more orange than Worcester. Early wares – mainly tea services – were painted or printed in underglaze blue in Chinese style. The Chamberlain factory of Worcester bought large quantities of Caughley porcelain from 1780–95 and much of the finest decorating was added by them. The blue printed patterns are generally marked with a crescent or with S for Salopian. The early wares also include many shapes made at Worcester, including leaf-moulded jugs with mask-moulded spouts. Other shapes were openwork baskets, salad bowls and butter dishes. When Thomas Turner sold off the Caughley works in 1799 he also sold the stock of unglazed goods, moulds and copper-plates. The factory continued for 15 years under Edward Blakeway and John ROSE of COALPORT.

Caughley miniature teapot, c.1785–90 [Q]

Cauliflower ware English pottery tea- and coffeepots and wares moulded to simulate cauliflowers (and pineapples) and coloured with fine semi-translucent glazes of green and yellow, made from the mid-18th century and into the 19th century.

Cauling A technique used in furniture in which a heated "caul", usually consisting of a slightly convex panel of wood (sometimes a sheet of zinc or aluminium), is heated and then clamped over the assembled veneer to ensure that the glue on the carcass is freely released and the veneer fixes closely to the carcass.

Cavetto moulding

Cavetto moulding (or hollow chamfer) A quarter-round hollow moulding, used in furniture-making from the 17th century, primarily for cornices on cabinets that were faced with veneer.

Cedar The comon name for several species of trees, mainly softwoods. The aromatic red cedar used from c.1750 as a moth-resistant lining for drawers, wardrobe trays, boxes and chests was from *Juniperus virginiana* or *Cedrela odorata*.

Celadon A glaze derived from iron with a distinctive grey-green or blue-green colour, used to imitate nephrite jade in China for over 2,000 years and almost as long in South Korea and Japan. Decoration is often moulded or carved in low relief. Wares include bowls, vases, EWERS, CENSERS and large dishes. Much celadon ware was exported from the 12th century, finding particular favour in the Middle East. The technique was much revived in the 19th century.

Cellaret A receptacle for holding wine bottles or decanters, either a free-standing square, round or octagonal chest, often lead-lined. The term can also refer to a drawer in a sideboard fitted out for the same purpose.

Cellini, Benvenuto (1500–71) An Italian sculptor and goldsmith. From 1519 he worked as a medallist and goldsmith in Rome under the patronage of Pope Clement VI, but from 1540 to 1545 was employed at the court of Francis I of France, where he produced his only surviving definitely attributed work: an ornate gold and enamel salt cellar (1540) with MANNERIST figures, seahorses and dolphins. His autobiography (1558) describes his workshop methods.

Celluloid A flammable, brittle and glossy PLASTIC used for the manufacture of dolls' heads and bodies. It was invented by the Hyatt Brothers, Newark, NJ, in 1869 and is the trade name for pyroxylin. It is often marked with a turtle in a diamond shape, the mark of the Rheinische Gummi und Celluloid Fabrik in Bavaria. It was widely replaced by vinyl before 1950.

Celtic Revival The late 19th- and early 20th-century revival of Celtic ornament, particularly in Britain and Ireland. It is found in silverwork and jewellery produced by members of the ARTS AND CRAFTS movement and in CYMRIC and TUDRIC wares produced by LIBERTY & Co. It is characterized by interlaced designs, coloured enamels and CABOCHON semi-precious stones.

Cellaret, English, late 18th-century [H]

Celtic style The arts and crafts of the Celts, a race who originally inhabited an area comprising eastern France, Holland, West Germany and Austria. In *c*.250 BC they invaded the British Isles. They were renowned for fine GOLD and BRONZE metalwork, including mirrors, weaponry, ARMOUR and jewellery, buried in the graves of chiefs and intended for their use in the afterlife. With the arrival of Christianity in Ireland in 435 and in Britain in 635, Celtic art also included CHALICES and other ecclesiastical SILVER, sculptural stone crosses and illuminated manuscripts.

Celtic art is characterized by decoration of stylized, curvilinear ornament, especially INTERLACING, knot work, LOZENGES and spirals, and sinuous animals and figures. Metalwork is often embellished with CLOISONNÉ and CHAMPLEVÉ enamels, and SEMI-PRECIOUS or PRECIOUS STONES. Among the most notable works of Celtic art are the bronze Battersea Shield (1st century AD), gold jewellery found at Sutton Hoo (mid-7th century) and, in Ireland, the Tara Brooch and the *Book of Kells* (both 8th century). Celtic art had died out in England by the late 9th century, but survived until the 12th century in Ireland. Interest in Celtic art was revived following excavations in the late 19th century and the emergence of nationalist movements in Ireland and Scotland. Like all medieval art, it had a particular influence on British ARTS AND CRAFTS and ART NOUVEAU designers, manifested especially in designs for silver and jewellery with interlacing motifs and ENAMEL decoration.

Celtic style copy of the Tara Brooch in parcel gilt, c.1910 [R]

Censer A Chinese incense burner usually made in BRONZE, JADE, POTTERY or PORCELAIN. They are often shaped like a cauldron on three feet, but can also be formed as a fabulous animal or bird. The Japanese equivalent is a KORO.

Centennial A term used in the US when America celebrated the 100th anniversary of signing the Declaration of Independence (4 July 1776). Centennial furniture is typically an authentic reproduction of high quality COLONIAL or AMERICAN CHIPPENDALE furniture.

Centennial style: American Chippendale double chair back settee, c.1880 [G]

COLONIAL REVIVAL pieces tend to be in oak. American Chippendale reproductions, which were more popular and have remained in production by some manufacturers, are in mahogany. By the year of the Centennial, furniture-makers were well established in several American cities, notably New York, Chicago and Philadelphia. The style was popularized by American furniture-makers at the Centennial Exposition, an international trade show in Philadelphia in the summer of 1876 modelled on London's GREAT EXHIBITION of 1851. Here, historical furniture of high quality, representing America's colonial past, was shown to a wide public and proved appealing to a newly unified US infused with patriotism.

The term may also describe items made specifically for the 1876 centennial celebrations, including historical documents that were reproduced in large editions. It is also applied to American folk art of *c*.1876 featuring patriotic imagery, particularly the Stars and Stripes, EAGLES, images of historic buildings and notable former presidents, including George Washington and Abraham Lincoln.

Ceramics (Greek: *Keramikos*; *Keramos* "potter's clay"; "pottery") The word is used to describe a hard brittle material made by firing clay or an object made from it. It includes POTTERY, PORCELAIN, STONEWARE and EARTHENWARE.

Chad Valley A leading British toy manufacturer, formed in 1919 at Harborne, Birmingham, from a printing firm originally in the nearby Chad Valley area. From the 1920s the company made toys, games, dolls and TEDDY BEARS, noted for their large, golden MOHAIR PLUSH bodies, large ears and small feet, inspiring other teddy bear makers such as MERRYTHOUGHT LTD. Typical Chad Valley lines include the 1927 novelty stuffed toy "Bonzo" (a bull terrier based on a

Chad Valley: selection of games, c.1930 [R]

newspaper cartoon) and his girlfriend "Oolo" (1930s) and the "Great Western Railway" series of jigsaw puzzles (1930s). After World War II, Chad Valley cooperated with the Metal Box Company to produce a range of tinplate "toy" biscuit tins, then tinplate toys such as humming tops, money boxes and train sets, vehicles and dolls' tea sets. In 1967, Chad Valley took over CHILTERN and the whole became part of Palitoy in 1972. Chad Valley's records were destroyed in 1978, so dating is not easy.

Chafing dish (French: *chauffer* "to heat") A serving dish with a heating apparatus below, either used for cooking or keeping food warm at the table, made from SILVER or PLATED wares in various forms during the 18th, 19th and early 20th centuries. Heated by burning charcoal, the chafing dish is the forerunner of the electric hotplate.

Chain stitch A series of looped stitches that are interlinked. Worked either with a needle or a hook and sometimes referred to as TAMBOUR stitch, it was a comparatively simple stitch and therefore suited to large-scale furnishings such as curtains, wall- and bed-hangings.

Chair A type of free-standing seat furniture with a back and with or without arms, designed for one person. With evidence of examples in ancient Egypt from the third millennium BC, the chair is one of the earliest types of furniture. Early forms such as the Greek KLISMOS, the portable Roman folding X-CHAIR and the medieval post seat with posts at each corner of the seat, evolved over the centuries into a huge variety of armless SIDE CHAIRS and dining chairs, armchairs (see CARVER CHAIR), upholstered armchairs (see BERGÈRE and CONFIDANTE) and contemporary styles such as the CANTILEVER CHAIR.

Chaise-longue (French: "long chair") A type of day-bed with an upholstered back, allowing the occupant to recline along its length. Introduced in France *c.*1625, it arrived in Britain with the restoration of Charles II (1660). Jacques-Louis David's portrait of

Chaise-longue, English
c.1840 [H]

Madame Récamier reclining on a chaise-longue (1800) made it fashionable once again and it was often known as a *récamier* in France. It was popular in late 19th-century Britain and the US in florid versions.

Chalice A wine cup or goblet used by the Catholic church during Mass, made in SILVER, SILVER GILT or GOLD. Usually with a paten (a matching plate) to hold the offering of bread.

Chalkware Decorative ornaments made from plaster of Paris and decorated with bright colours, popular from the 18th to the mid-20th centuries in the US and Britain. Made to imitate pottery and porcelain, forms were taken from STAFFORDSHIRE moulds and porcelain figures and sold as cheaper examples of authentic pieces.

Chamberlain family A family of English ceramicists connected with the WORCESTER PORCELAIN FACTORY. Robert Chamberlain (1737–98) was apprenticed as a porcelain decorator at Worcester but left in 1786 to set up independently. By 1791 his establishment was producing its own porcelain, a hybrid HARD-PASTE type, used for high quality tea, dessert and ornamental wares. After his death, his two sons and his nephew, Walter, carried on the business, which continued to operate successfully in competition with Worcester. In 1840 Walter Chamberlain and his brother-in-law John Lilly guided the company to a merger with BARR, FLIGHT & BARR, after which it became Chamberlain & Co. until 1852.

Chair backs

Queen Anne period (1702–14) chair backs are found into the 1730s. In the mid-18th century, makers incorporated chinoiserie and Neo-classical designs. Rope-twists were inspired by the British victory of Trafalgar in 1805. In the US the shield-back was common in the Federal period. French influence was stronger in the American Empire period.

Fiddle-back, c.1720s–30s

Cockpen, c.1755

Shield-back, c.1780

Rope-twist, c.1810

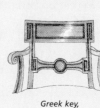
Greek key, c.1815

Button-back, c.1850

Chamber pot A toilet receptacle for use in the bedchamber. Made in metal and pottery and then in porcelain – both simple and luxurious, from small sizes for children to adult sizes and from early times until the 20th century. In late Victorian times they were included in bedroom sets with a jug and basin.

Mason's Ironstone chamber pot, 1830 [M]

Chambers, Sir William (1723–96) An English architect, born in Sweden of Scottish parents. He travelled widely and trained as an architect in Paris and Rome before settling in London in 1755, where he was tutor in architecture to George, Prince of Wales, later George III. A highly distinguished architect, he also designed some furniture in a sober NEO-CLASSICAL style for Blenheim Palace (made by INCE & MAYHEW), seat furniture for the artist Sir Joshua Reynolds and clock cases.

Chamberstick A saucer-like dish with a central candleholder and a detachable conical snuffer or a slot to take scissor snuffers. A handle enabled the bearer to carry the lighted candle about safely. Chambersticks are generally made from non-combustible materials, particularly silver and plate. Although 17th-century silver examples are scarce, this type of candlestick is known to have pre-dated the Reformation.

Chamfer The surface produced by bevelling off an angle. Used as a finish on stone, wood or metal, in which

Chamfer

right-angled edges are flattened, chamfering can be used as a purely decorative device or to protect a corner from damage.

Champagne glass There are two styles: a FLUTE with a deep, narrow-mouthed bowl that retains the bubbles and, from c.1830, the "saucer" glass, with a wide, shallow bowl, supposedly modelled on the breasts of Madame de Pompadour, Louis XV's mistress.

Champagne saucer glass c.1890 [s]

Champion, Richard (1743–91) A shareholder in the PLYMOUTH factory making hard-paste porcelain. Champion took part in the management of the works and the original patent was transferred to him when William COOKWORTHY retired in 1774. The patent was due to expire in 1782 and Champion tried to extend it for 14 years, but the Staffordshire potters opposed it. Champion carried on but the factory closed in 1781 and the remaining stock was sold in 1782.

Champlevé An enamelling technique in which the background of an object is hollowed out into individual cavities with thin metal walls, filled with enamel in its powder state and then fired in a kiln. See also CLOISONNÉ.

Chandelier A lighting device designed to hang from the ceiling, consisting of a central frame with branches fitted with candle-nozzles. Early examples were hung with cut glass ornaments, from the early 18th century, chandeliers became more elaborate, with drops and festoons,

and the metal frame was concealed with glass. The popularity of candle chandeliers waned with the advent of gas lighting.

Chanel, Gabrielle "Coco" (1883–1971) French fashion designer active in Paris in the 1930s and 1940s, remembered for the "little black dress", formal suits, handbags, perfume and, most important to collectors, costume jewellery, especially pearls. The fashion house survives today.

Chang ware Produced at ROYAL DOULTON from the early 20th century, after experiments by C.J. Noke with transmutation glazes. Inspired by the Chinese ceramics of the Sung dynasty, thick, brightly coloured and crackled glazes creep down the sides. No two pieces of Chang are alike because of the glaze. Production ended in the 1940s.

Chantilly A French centre for BOBBIN LACE, producing BLONDE in the early 19th century and then a high quality heavier black or blonde lace made with grenadine silk. Black Chantilly lace was exported to Spain for mantillas.

French bronze champlevé Tartar warrior, 1840 [c]

Chantilly porcelain factory Founded by Louis Henri de Bourbon, Prince de Condé, in Chantilly, Oise, France

1725–1800

*c.*1725. The factory had large buildings outside the city, and started making soft-paste porcelain in the 1730s. At first the porcelain had a white tin glaze, later a lead glaze. Ciquaire Cirou was the first director from *c.*1725–51 and worked with the modeller Louis Fournier. Many of the workers either came from SÈVRES or went there from Chantilly, including the painter Charles Buteux who went to work at the Sèvres factory in 1756.

The Prince de Condé was a great collector of Oriental porcelain and much Chantilly ware was in the style of the KAKIEMON potters of Japan – also copied at MEISSEN on hard paste. Most wares are under 25cm (10in) tall. The painting at Chantilly was done with great care although much of the ware was for modest households. Chantilly produced table services, CACHE-POTS, jugs, bowls and wine bottle coolers. It also made charming SNUFF BOXES, ÉTUIS, cane handles and figures. In 1792 it was bought by an Englishman, Christopher Potter, who also owned the Paris factory in the Rue de Crussol. The mark was a hunting horn (usually in red), sometimes with the word Chantilly. The factory closed *c.*1800. The ware was copied in hard paste by SAMSON, the great French "faker".

Chantilly sprig Sketchy sprays of flowers, twigs, grasses or ears of corn, usually in blue on CHANTILLY porcelain, but sometimes in crimson, manganese or purple. It became popular at MENNECY, ARRAS and TOURNAI and was copied in England at DERBY and CAUGHLEY.

Chantilly figure of seated Chinese girl with nodding head, c.1730 [C]

Chapter ring The ring on a clock dial on which hour and/or minute numbers are painted, engraved or attached. Roman numerals are used on most chapter rings, although Arabic numerals were popular in the late 19th and early 20th centuries.

Character doll A doll resembling a real child rather than an idealized one. The first character doll called "Kaiser Baby" was produced by KÄMMER & REINHARDT in 1909 and was apparently modelled on the German emperor's son. Further moulds soon followed with character dolls from other makers such as HEUBACH, Armand MARSEILLE and the SOCIÉTÉ FRANÇAISE DE FABRICATION DE BÉBÉS ET JOUETS.

Chantilly Kakiemon jug, c.1735 [F]

Charcoal blue A technique where polished steel is heated in a bed of burning charcoal to produce a brilliant blue surface finish that is decorative and prevents corrosion.

Chareau, Pierre (1883–1950) A French designer and architect of ART DECO and the MODERN MOVEMENT. He began as a draughtsman in the furniture department of WARING & GILLOW in their Paris office but in 1919 he set up his own practice. He designed the famous Maison de Verre in Paris, which was built between 1928 and 1931. He designed for private commissions, not mass production, and his work is clean and sophisticated, sometimes incorporating some form of movement or movable part.

Charger A large, often ornate, dish, principally for display but also for serving at the table. The term is generally restricted to 16th and 17th century ceramic, enamel, silver and gold dishes.

Chase, Martha Jenks (active 1880s to 1925) An American doll-maker who set up the Chase Hospital Doll Company in Pawtucket, Rhode Island, during the 1880s. Her stockinet dolls can be distinguished by oil-painted hair and facial features and cotton-wool stuffed white sateen or later cotton bodies. Her company ceased trading in 1925.

Chasing Surface decoration on metals, especially silver (often in conjunction with EMBOSSING). The design is drawn on the piece then the decorator hammers it with a blunt ball-point chisel to displace, distort and texture the metal's surface, achieving the desired effect without removing any metal.

Chased silver porringer c.1880 [M]

Chassis The main frame of a vehicle carrying all the mechanical components, surmounted by the coachwork. In toy vehicles used to indicate the base unit carrying wheels, fender and bumpers.

Chelsea porcelain factory

The Chelsea Porcelain factory (*c*.1744–69), thought to be the first in England, made soft-paste porcelain with a glassy glaze that was aimed at the aristocratic market. The first director, Charles Gouyn, was replaced by Nicholas Sprimont, a young Huguenot silversmith from Liège in 1749. The factory's history can be divided according to the four different marks that it used on its wares.

Triangle period c.1744–49

These early products bore an incised triangle mark. Most of the wares were white and were strongly influenced by silver designs – the most notable products of the period were white saltcellars in the shape of crayfish. Perhaps the most famous pieces are the "Goat and Bee" jugs with the date 1747, also based on a silver model. Copies of these were made at COALPORT in the next century.

Raised anchor period 1749–52

In this period, the paste and glaze were modified to produce a clear, white, slightly opaque surface on which to paint. The influence of MEISSEN is evident in the classical figures among Italianate ruins and harbour scenes and adaptations from Francis Barlow's edition of *Aesop's Fables*. In 1751, copies were made of two Meissen services. Chelsea also made figures, birds and animals inspired by Meissen originals. Flowers and landscapes were copied from VINCENNES.

Red anchor period 1752–56

KAKIEMON subjects were popular from the late 1740s until *c*.1758, inspired by the original Japanese and then by Meissen and CHANTILLY. Some English-inspired tableware decorated with botanically accurate plants, copied from *The Gardener's Dictionary* (*1752*) was also produced in this period.

Gold anchor period 1756–69

The influence of SÈVRES was very strong and French taste was in the ascendancy. The gold anchor period saw rich coloured grounds, lavish gilding and the nervous energy of the ROCOCO style. In the 1750s and 1760s, Chelsea was also famous for its TOYS, which included BONBONNIÈRES, scent bottles, ÉTUIS, THIMBLES and small SEALS, many with inscriptions in French. The failing factory was bought in 1769 by William DUESBURY of Derby who ran it until 1784.

Peach-shaped bowl, red anchor period, c.1753 [G]

Rococo-style dish, gold anchor period, c.1760 [J]

Gilded coffee cup, gold anchor period c.1768 [O]

Factory marks

The Chelsea factory had four factory marks over a period of 24 years, during which time, the style of artifacts altered with changing fashions. After 1769, it became very similar to Derby ware and was sometimes known as Chelsea Derby.

Triangle

Raised anchor

Red anchor

Gold anchor, Chelsea Derby

Chasuble An ecclesiastical vestment worn by the officiating priest. Originally almost circular in shape, the shape changed in the 16th century and became elongated allowing the arms to hang freely. These vestments are normally elaborately embroidered, frequently using expensive gold and silver threads.

Chatelaine A decorative belt hook or clasp worn at the waist with a series of chains suspended from it, each mounted with a useful household appendage such as scissors, THIMBLE, WATCH, key or NÉCESSAIRE. Chatelaines were worn by many housekeepers in the 19th century.

Cut steel chatelaine, French early 19th century [L]

Chatönes A type of decorative nailhead used on Spanish furniture.

Checkerwork A pattern of alternating squares or lozenges of contrasting colours or textures, similar to the pattern on a chess board. A favourite motif in the 16th and 17th centuries for textiles and tiled floors, checkerwork was also favoured by cabinet-makers for inlay decoration. A checker pattern was frequently adopted as a decorative motif on metal and ceramics, following the introduction of engine-turned decoration in the late 18th century.

Chelsea Keramic Art Works A US factory producing ART POTTERY glazed wares in Massachusetts in the late 19th century. Its Scottish

immigrant owner Hugh Robertson (1844–1908) was concerned with replicating Oriental high-fired CRACKLE glazes on original designs, which served to give a feeling of age to pieces. The distinctive crackle was achieved by exposing twice-fired pieces quickly to cold air while still hot. Black colouring was then often added to accentuate the CRAZING. The Works relocated to Dedham, Massachusetts, in 1896 and pieces from then are known as DEDHAM POTTERY until they closed in 1943. Hallmarks of the style include crackle glazes, blue and white colour schemes and decorative motif borders. Rabbits were the company's most popular motif.

Chenet The French term for an ANDIRON or FIREDOG.

Chenghua porcelain CHINESE PORCELAIN made during the reign of the MING DYNASTY emperor Chenghua (1465–1487). The wares tend to be small, decorated in UNDERGLAZE blue, a monochrome glaze or in the DOUCAI palette. The Chenghua reign mark was extensively copied in the 19th and 20th centuries.

Chenille (French: "caterpillar") A velvety cord, usually silk but sometimes wool or cotton. It has the appearance of being "hairy", having short fibres that stick out from the central thread. Introduced during the 17th century as a decorative embroidery thread, it was

Chelsea Keramic "Volcanic" vase by Hugh Robertson for Dedham Pottery, c.1910 [N]

Chéret poster advertising bicycles, 1891 [N]

particularly popular in the 19th century and continues in use to the present day, frequently in fringing.

Chequerwork See CHECKERWORK.

Chéret, Jules (1836–1933) A French artist and poster designer. In 1866 he produced the first colour LITHOGRAPHIC posters in Paris, designing over 1,000 during his lifetime. Recognized as the father of the modern poster his designs were hugely popular, particularly for the theatre and circus, and influenced TOULOUSE-LAUTREC and other artists.

Cherry (*Prunus spp.*) A tree found in Europe, North America and the Far East that provides a FRUITWOOD varying in colour from pinkish yellow to brown. It was used both for INLAY and small pieces of furniture in the 17th century and extensively for 18th-century French provincial furniture. It was also widely used in the ARTS AND CRAFTS furniture of the late 19th/early 20th century.

Cherub The first hierarchy of angels in Christian iconography. Later, it came to designate a beautiful winged child or head. Cherubs are often indistinguishable from the CUPIDS, or PUTTI, in secular schemes. The motif appears frequently from the 15th century on architectural ornament, spoons and clock-faces.

Chesapeake Pottery Founded by Henry & Isaac Broughman in Baltimore, US, in 1880. Sold to David F. Haynes (1882) and then to Edwin Bennett (1887). The factory made PARIAN WARE, MAJOLICA and Calvert ware: a blue or green-glazed ware with bands of decoration. It closed in 1924.

George III mahogany bow-front chest-of-drawers, c.1780 [G]

Chest (chest-of-drawers, chest-on-chest, chest-on-stand) The chest, in the form of a wooden box with a lid, was one of the earliest types of furniture and is found in almost all cultures. Primitive examples were simply hollowed-out logs, fitted with a lid, and known as "dug outs". BOARDED CHESTS developed in the 13th century and were gradually superseded by panelled chests (see CASSONE). Various types of CASE FURNITURE developed from the chest: from the mid-16th century, the bases of travelling chests or coffers were sometimes fitted with small drawers, and by the mid-17th century an early form of the chest-of-drawers had evolved. Subsequently, it was to undergo several refinements and different styles and names such as the BACHELOR'S CHEST, the CHIFFONIER, the COMMODE, the tallboy and its US variant the HIGHBOY, and the LOWBOY.

Chesterfield A term used from the late 19th century to designate a large overstuffed sofa with a straight back and often with buttoned leather upholstery.

Chestnut There are two species of chestnut tree found in Europe – the horse chestnut (*Aesculus hippocastanum*) and the Spanish or sweet chestnut (*Castanea vesca*). *Castanea dentata* was native to the eastern US but has largely succumbed to disease. The wood from these trees is often confused and they were all employed as substitutes for SATINWOOD in the second half of the 18th century. Horse chestnut wood is soft, yellowish and not very durable but was used for some turned work and inlay; Spanish or sweet chestnut is light brown, more durable and was widely used in the manufacture of most types of furniture.

American chest-on-stand or highboy, 1760–80 [A]

Cheval glass (French *cheval*: "horse") A type of standing mirror, supported by a four-legged frame from which the name derives, that can be tilted to allow a full-length reflection. First developed in the last quarter of the 18th century, they remained popular until the early 20th.

Chevalier de Béthune The term for an ESCAPEMENT invented *c.*1720 and used by some French clockmakers throughout the 18th century, distinguished by having a double ARBOR. The Chevalier may have been an amateur horologist.

Cheveret A small writing or worktable, often with a detachable top for carrying books and usually made in SATINWOOD or MAHOGANY. It was common in the late 18th century. It is supported on long tapering legs, and has a drawer in the frieze and shelves or pigeonholes to the rear of the work surface.

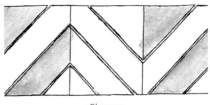

Chevron

Chevron One of the simplest geometric forms, composed of a linked zigzag motif or used singly in a vertical arrangement. An early symbol used on woven textiles and incised ceramics, the chevron was an important feature of the 19th-century neo-Norman style. In furniture, chevrons appear in chip-carved ornament, and GOTHIC REVIVAL pieces frequently incorporate inlaid chevron bands. The chevron motif was one of the most popular geometric patterns adopted for ART DECO ornament in the 1930s.

Chiffonier A term generally used for a type of display cupboard, introduced in the late 18th century, having an open shelf on top, with a cupboard and sometimes a drawer beneath. It is the anglicized version of CHIFFONIÈRE.

Chiffonière The French term for the CHIFFONIER. Also a term used in the 18th century for a small set of shallow drawers for storing fabrics and sewing accessories.

Child & Child A firm of London silversmiths and goldsmiths active at the end of the 19th century specializing in distinctive enamel, silver and gold gem-set jewellery such as buckles and naturalistic brooches. Often lodged in green leather cases, their jewellery was invariably signed with a sunflower motif between the initials "CC".

Children's ware Ceramic items produced specifically for children including plates, cups and saucers and, later, figures of animals. Originating in the late 19th century and often produced by the Staffordshire factories, these wares were made especially for the nursery and bore TRANSFER-PRINTED moral and educational MOTTOES and images. The child could thus be educated and improved even while eating. Scenes of nature were also popular and the first half of the 20th century saw the start of a more relaxed and whimsical choice of subjects based around children's stories and popular culture, including the characters of Beatrix Potter and ROYAL DOULTON's Bunnykins figures.

Children's ware pottery plate, c.1835 [Q]

Chiltern (1908–67) A toy works in Chesham, Buckinghamshire, founded in 1908 by Joseph Eisenmann. Chiltern's first bear, the Master Teddy, with a flat face and googly eyes, was produced from 1915. The well-known "Hugmee" range was introduced in 1923 and continued until the company's takeover by CHAD VALLEY in 1967.

Chimera A fire-breathing beast originating in Classical mythology, with the head, mane and legs of a lion, the tail of a dragon, body of a goat and frequently the wings of an eagle. The RENAISSANCE borrowed it from Classical sources such as Pompeian wall paintings, and often featured it as part of grotesque ornament. A popular motif on 18th-century NEO-CLASSICAL ornament, it was employed in the EMPIRE and REGENCY periods as supports for console tables or as the sides of armchairs.

Chimera

Chiming See STRIKING SYSTEMS.

Chimney board See DUMMY BOARD FIGURES.

Chimney-piece A marble, stone, brick or wood frame that surrounds a fireplace comprising two verticals, a horizontal shelf and sometimes incorporating an overmantel mirror or panel. Also known as a mantelpiece.

China A word used to denote porcelain, from the name of the country of origin of "real" porcelain. It was exported by the Chinese along the Silk Route to Istanbul (Constantinople) and thence to Europe. It was later shipped by the various East India companies in their ships bringing tea and silk to Europe in the 17th and 18th centuries, and termed "china ware". See also BONE CHINA.

China cabinet A type of cabinet, also known as a china case, which was introduced in the late 17th century to display the newly fashionable Oriental china, with interior shelves and either glazed or solid doors.

China clay See KAOLIN.

China head doll A doll with a glazed porcelain head. "China" (i.e. hard-paste porcelain) was commonly used to produce dolls between c.1840 and c.1900, the moulds reflecting the rapidly changing hairstyles and accessories of the 19th century. Once moulded the heads were fired at a high temperature, painted with facial details, glazed and fired again. China SHOULDER HEADS were attached to the fabric bodies by means of first two, later three, pierced holes in the SHOULDER PLATE.

German china head doll, c.1860 [O]

China stone The English name for PETUNTSE, the essential ingredient for making hard-paste porcelain. It is also known as "Cornish stone". "China stone" refers to the feldspar (a silicate of potassium and aluminium) with which KAOLIN is mixed. The BODY is fired at a high temperature and the feldspar fuses to form a kind of natural glass, which gives the porcelain its hardness and TRANSLUCENCY. The Chinese meaning of petuntse is "little white bricks" (pai-tun-tsu), which reflects the process in China whereby the stone was pulverized and sent to the porcelain makers in the form of small bricks.

Chinese export porcelain

From the 16th to the 20th centuries, a wide range of porcelain was made and decorated in China exclusively for export to Europe. The styles and decoration contrasted with those intended for the domestic market.

Soup plate with coat of arms in a grisaille Chinese landscape, Yongzheng period, c.1730 [E]

Early China trade

Wares from the 16th century include Kraak porcelain, Yixing stonewares, blanc-de-Chine, blue and white, famille verte, noire, jaune and rose, Chinese Imari, armorial wares and Canton porcelain. Chinese export porcelain is generally decorative, but without the symbolic significance of wares produced for the home market. With the exception of the rare *huashi* (Chinese SOFT PASTE) wares, Chinese porcelain is hard paste. While rim chips and hairline cracks are common, pieces tend not to stain. Chinese wares are usually thinner than Japanese and do not have the Japanese stilt marks.

In the 16th century, Portuguese traders began importing late MING DYNASTY BLUE AND WHITE porcelains to Europe, resulting in the growth of the KRAAK PORCELAIN trade (named after the Portuguese ships called carracks in which it was transported). In 1602 and 1604, two Portuguese carracks, the *San Yago* and *Santa Catarina*, were captured by the Dutch and their contents, which included thousands of items of porcelain, were auctioned, igniting a European mania for porcelain. Buyers included the kings of England and France. Many European nations then established trading companies in the East, the most important being the Dutch East India Company or VOC. The trade continued until the mid-17th century when civil wars caused by the fall of the MING DYNASTY in 1644 disrupted supplies and the European traders turned to Japan.

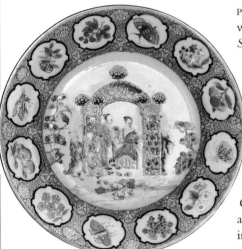

Famille rose dinner plate, after design by Cornelis Pronk, c.1735 [F]

Under the KANGXI Emperor (1662–1722) the Chinese porcelain industry at JINGDEZHEN was re-organized and the export trade was soon flourishing again. Chinese export porcelain from the late 17th century includes BLUE AND WHITE and FAMILLE VERTE wares (and occasionally FAMILLE NOIRE and JAUNE). Ware included garnitures of vases, dishes, tewares, ewers and other useful wares, figure models, animals and birds. BLANC-DE-CHINE porcelains and YIXING stonewares arrived in Europe giving inspiration to many of the European potters.

Shipwrecked cargoes

Knowledge of Chinese export porcelain has been greatly enhanced by the recovery of the cargoes of several sunken trading vessels. The "Nanking Cargo" was the contents of the *Geldermalsen*, a huge Dutch East Indiaman (sank 3 January 1752), from which over 100,000 pieces of porcelain were salvaged in 1986 and sold at auction. The "Hatcher Junk" (named after the Captain Hatcher who recovered it) sank *c.*1643–46 and over 25,000 pieces of unbroken Jingdezhen blue and white and celadon porcelain were rescued for sale. These cargoes regularly come onto the market through auction.

Vegetable tureen and cover from the "Diana" cargo, c.1817 [J]

Wares and figures

Although European crests on Chinese porcelain can be found as early as the 16th century, around 1700 the demand for ARMORIAL porcelain dramatically increased. Thousands of services were ordered with drawings of individuals' coats of arms being sent out to China to be copied and shipped back to Europe and, from the late 18th century, to North America. Some were lavishly painted in polychrome enamels and gilding, while others, particularly later, might just incorporate a small crest or monogram in blue and white. Chinese potters copied the popular Japanese IMARI porcelains. Chinese Imari continued to be made for export into the second half of the 18th century, examples being recovered as part of the "Nanking" cargo from the wreck of the *Geldermalsen*.

Famille rose from Jingdezhen factory, Qianlong period, c.1750 [M]

A wide variety of shapes, some of Chinese or Islamic origin, others copying FAIENCE or metalwork were made. Oriental figures included Chinese gods and goddesses such as Guanyin (the goddess of mercy) and BUDAI (the god of contentment), figures with nodding heads, seated monks and laughing boys, as well as figures of Dutch men and women. From the mid-18th century, even copies of Meissen figures such as Tyrolean dancers were made for export to Europe. Birds and animals, including cows, cranes, dogs, eagles, elephants, pheasants, monkeys and puppies, were popular throughout the 18th century.

Dinner plate with "tobacco leaf" design, Qianlong period, c.1770 [H]

From *c*.1720, the new FAMILLE ROSE palette was adopted and quickly supplanted the earlier FAMILLE VERTE porcelains of the KANGXI period. Famille rose enamels for the export market included the MANDARIN PALETTE. Specific patterns such as "tobacco leaf" and "faux tobacco leaf" were popular as were, from *c*.1800, CANTON decorated porcelain with its figures and birds, flowers and insects. Many other types of decoration such as *encre de Chine* or JESUIT WARES, made for Christian missionaries, pieces with European subjects like the Judgment of Paris, or Adam and Eve, and wares copying European print sources, most notably those of Cornelis Pronk, were made for the European markets.

Blue and white custard cup and cover, c.1800 [S]

Later trade

As trade developed, finer quality wares were shipped by private traders who rented space on the East India Company ships. The bulk export wares of the 18th century were typically teawares and dinner services, often BLUE AND WHITE decorated with flowers, pine, prunus, bamboo or with pagoda landscapes, a style that inspired the ubiquitous WILLOW PATTERN. They were sometimes CLOBBERED in Holland and England to enhance their decorative appeal. By the late 18th century, imports of Chinese porcelain were in decline. Tastes were changing and competition from new European factories with mass-production brought about by industrialization took its toll.

Highly decorative CANTON PORCELAIN was produced throughout the 19th century but the quality of wares was in decline. By the end of the century BLUE AND WHITE wares in the KANGXI style (often with Kangxi and CHENGHUA reign marks) were produced in large quantities and almost every earlier style and type of ware was copied into the 20th century.

Blue and white Chinese export mug, c.1800 [Q]

Chinese furniture

Although Chinese furniture was made as early as the 14th century BC, most of the earliest surviving wooden pieces were made in the Ming dynasty (1368–1644), several hundred years after the fundamental change to chair-level living from around the 10th century AD.

Folding and reclining
armchair, made in Huang huali
17th century [J]

A revolution in furniture design

The practice of sitting on chairs rather than on mats or low platforms encouraged the development of new furniture types to supplement the previously narrow range of the screen (*ping*), altar or ritual tables, and the *kang* – originally a heated brick platform used in northern China. In the "Golden Age" of Chinese furniture during the Ming and early Qing dynasties (1368–1735), the *kang* developed into associated furniture types such as a low platform on legs used for sleeping, *kang* tables and the X-frame chair from the Sung dynasty (960–1279). During the late Qing (1735–1911), a flourishing export trade developed. Chinese furniture-makers adopted European forms and motifs. They cut down the legs of tables and chairs to suit European taste and produced 19th-century furniture that imitated older styles but generally lacked the high quality joinery and subtle decoration of the originals.

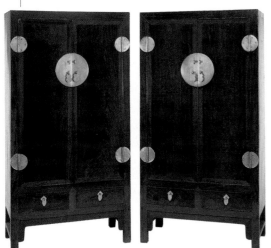

Hardwood square corner cabinets,
Fanghiaogui 17th century [D]

There were two basic types of furniture: waisted and waistless. In waisted furniture, a recessed panel was inserted between the top and the apron of tables, legs were set at the corners of the piece and were often square, with *mati* (horsehoof) upturned feet that faced inward or outward. By contrast, on waistless furniture, the top rested directly on the legs, which were usually round, set back, with high stretchers and splayed slightly outward. Common furniture types included: chairs (armchairs, side chairs, folding chairs and thrones), benches, stools (folding, drum, square, rectangular, round), tables (square dining tables, "zither" tables with legs at the corners, "wine" tables with recessed legs and mouldings to prevent liquid escaping, large wide tables for calligraphy or painting), incense stands, cabinets, coffers and chests, beds (day beds and canopy beds).

Construction

Chinese furniture is constructed using joinery alone, partly to accommodate extremes of temperature, usually the pure MORTISE AND TENON system without the use of DOWELS or nails, and with only the occasional use of glue. Woods are described by appearance and smell rather than species. One of the most highly prized woods was *zitan* (a type that includes rosewood) – a dark purple-brown timber with a very dense straight grain that was reserved largely for small pieces. More commonly used was *Huang huali* – a honey-coloured hardwood, often with a highly prized eccentric figuring. From *c.*1644 onward much Chinese furniture was made from a purplish-brown wood known as *jichi* ("chicken-wings") after its grain that resembled the feathers on chicken wings. In China, hardwood was not necessarily prized above softwood. Many of the finest pieces destined for the royal households were made of softwood covered with LACQUER, which was decorated and also served as protection against insects. Wooden furniture was rarely marked or dated and basic furniture forms were often made for centuries with few changes. By contrast, the bamboo furniture made in the south of China was essentially expendable and used outdoors.

Bamboo veneered wood armchair
(one of a pair),
Meiguiyi 18th century [H]

Chinese pillar rug, early 20th century [H]

Chinese carpets First produced in the 17th century and associated until the mid-19th century with Ninghsia, on the silk route in north-west China. Symbols include lions of Fo, dragons, bats, cranes, peony blossom and lotus, woven in a harmonious mix of geometric and curvilinear designs. Colours include yellow, ivory and blue. Carpets made in the 1920s are often called "Nichols" after the company they were made for, using non-traditional colours often in 19th-century French SAVONNERIE styles.

Chinese Chippendale A modern term for mid-18th-century furniture with CHINOISERIE lattice-work decoration, as illustrated in the *Gentleman and Cabinet-Maker's Director* by Thomas CHIPPENDALE and made by his workshop and other contemporary furniture-makers.

Chinese dynasty Chinese history is divided into dynasties of ruling families and, within these, reigns of emperors. The most important dynasties artistically are SHANG (*c*.1500–1028 BC), Han (206 BC–AD 220), TANG (618–906), SONG (960–1279), YUAN (1260–1368), MING (1368–1644) and QING (1644–1912).

Chinese export porcelain
See pp.102–103.

Chinese glass Made in China from *c*.300 BC, but most is from *c*.1662, when the Peking (Beijing) Imperial Glassworks was set up, imitating precious materials such as blue and white, "Imperial" yellow porcelain and lapis lazuli.

Chinese Imari See IMARI PORCELAIN.

Chinese pottery and porcelain
Dominating world ceramics, "CHINA" has influenced nearby Korea and Japan, the Islamic world and, from the 16th century, Europe. Neolithic Chinese pottery (*c*.5000–2000 BC) includes coiled pots and funerary urns. The use of FELDSPATHIC GLAZE was developed during the SHANG DYNASTY (*c*.1500–1028 BC). Soft absorbent pottery became important for burial wares. The famous terracotta army of over 7,000 life-size warriors and horses was made to guard the burial site of Qin Shihuang, the "First Emperor" in the Qin dynasty (221–206 BC). Pottery burial wares flourished in the Han dynasty (206 BC–220 AD) and include figures, horses, houses, tables, chairs and fruit. Green and brown lustrous lead glazes were developed at this time. While many examples are painted with flaky earth pigments, some fine large horses, camels, figures and earth spirits are partially glazed, usually in green, yellow, brown and sometimes blue from the TANG DYNASTY (618–906). The pure forms and subtle naturalistic decoration of SONG DYNASTY (960–1279) ceramics include

DING WARE, RU WARE, JUN WARE, Guan ware, Ge ware and slip-decorated CHIZOU WARES. Ceramics were exported to the Middle East from the YUAN DYNASTY (1260–1368), using Islamic shapes and designs, and often with CELADON glazes.

In the early MING DYNASTY (1368–1644), the use of Imperial REIGN MARKS became widespread and BLUE AND WHITE wares mainstream, including bowls, cups, dishes and ewers. Monochrome, CELADON or polychrome wares were also produced. Popular subjects include chrysanthemums, peony and lotus, pine, prunus and bamboo, dragons and phoenix. The most important early MING reigns are Yong Lo (1403–24), XUANDE (1426–35) and CHENGHUA (1465–87). See also DOUCAI and WUCAI.

Chinese bottle-shaped vase, *c*.1800 [O]

The CHINESE EXPORT trade with Europe began *c*.1570, first with the Portuguese, then the Dutch, English and other countries.

The most important reigns of the QING DYNASTY (1644–1912) are KANGXI (1662–1722), YONGZHENG (1723–35) and QIANLONG (1736–95). Enamelled porcelain replaced blue and white as the technically most advanced ware of the time and the FAMILLE VERTE colours were introduced in the late 17th century. The imperial wares of the time were in extremely fine quality monochrome. CANTON PORCELAIN of the 19th and 20th centuries tended to revive shapes, glazes and styles of earlier centuries.

Famille rose charger, 18th century [L, a pair]

Ch'ing dynasty
See QING DYNASTY.

Meissen silver-mounted tankard
with chinoiserie scene, c.1730 [D]

Giltwood chinoiserie mirror with
pagoda motif, c.1755 [E]

Etched chinoiserie wallpaper
showing figures in a stylized lanscape
with exotic blooms, English c.1770

Chinoiserie

European fascination with Oriental culture dates back to the 13th century but reached its heyday in the 18th century. Its motifs and forms, adapted to Western taste, translated well into the decorative arts.

The fashion for things oriental

When trade burgeoned between China and the West in the 17th century, so did the popularity of Oriental wares. Thanks to the foundation of the EAST INDIA COMPANIES and increased imports of luxury goods into Europe and America, Chinese BLUE AND WHITE export porcelain was hugely influential. It was avidly collected by the wealthy in the late 17th century and displayed on furniture and mantelpieces. It was imitated in TIN-GLAZED earthenware at DELFT and NEVERS; typical products included tiles, dishes, ewers and tulip vases, decorated with Chinese motifs and also with landscapes in the Netherlands. At Delft the fashion for blue and white was replaced in the early 1680s by the polychrome palette, influenced by Chinese FAMILLE ROSE and FAMILLE VERTE export porcelains, and Japanese IMARI and KAKIEMON porcelain.

During the early 18th century, CHINOISERIE was popular as a variant on the Rococo style, often combined with Rococo and Gothick motifs in fanciful designs. The 18th-century evolution of chinoiserie began in France, in the paintings of Antoine Watteau and François BOUCHER, but soon spread throughout Europe and America. In European porcelain there was continuing taste for decoration inspired by Japanese and Chinese originals, for example in figures of Chinese men in flowing robes and paintings of Chinese-style landscapes in wares made at MEISSEN, FRANKENTHAL, HÖCHST, NYMPHENBURG and many English factories. Tapestries and silks, mirror frames, ORMOLU mounts and silver were also vehicles for chinoiserie. Silver épergnes and centrepieces featured pagoda-like frames and Thomas Chippendale's *The Gentleman and Cabinet-Maker's Director*, first published in 1754, inspired a vogue for chinoiserie designs in furniture. The fashion continued throughout the Regency period – for example at the Royal Pavilion in Brighton, England and at the Palacio Real de Aranjuez in southern Spain, where the Porcelain Room was decorated in chinoiserie style in 1763. Its popularity declined in the late 19th century.

Recognizing the style

Chinese motifs were used in silk designs from the 14th century. By the late 17th century, Oriental landscapes, pagodas, figures, exotic birds, flowers and dragons were appearing on ceramics and silver. Thanks to Chippendale, many items of furniture were decorated with carved latticework and fretwork, pagoda-style motifs and dragons from the second half of the 18th century.

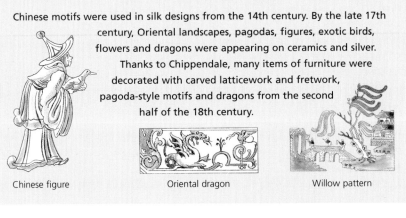

Chinese figure   Oriental dragon   Willow pattern

Chinkinbori A Japanese term that describes a type of decoration used on LACQUER, which involves incising or carving lines into the lacquer surface and filling them with gold foil or powder. Often associated with MAKI-E techniques.

Chintz (Hindi *Chint* or *Chitta*: "variegated") Chintz was originally the name given to high quality floral patterned glazed cottons imported from India. Chintz is described in early Greek literature, but it first appeared in the West during the late 16th and early 17th centuries. Used primarily for household furnishings such as curtains and bed covers, the term now describes both floral and plain glazed cloths.

Chintzware cheese
dish, English c.1935 [o]

Chintzware The name given to an all-over floral pattern, mostly on tea services, and now much collected. It was much used by ROYAL WINTON.

Chiparus, Dimitri
(1888–1950) A Romanian-born sculptor, who worked in Paris and was renowned for his strong ART DECO figures in BRONZE and IVORY. He also produced theatrical, religious and sentimental sculptural subjects and ceramic busts and figures. These are not as sought after as his Art Deco bronzes and ivories.

Chiparus figure
"The Squall", c.1925 [G]

Chip carving A simple decoration used on early (13th to early 17th century) wooden furniture, in which geometric motifs were chipped out with knives, gouges and chisels.

Chippendale, Thomas
See pp.108–109.

Chocolate pot A rare pot for preparing drinking chocolate, made of heavy-gauge silver with handles of FRUITWOOD or IVORY. They resemble COFFEEPOTS of the 1700s, but have two important differences. An aperture in the cover of the pot has a cover of its own, through which a *molinet* or stirring stick can be inserted to stir up the chocolate sediment, and the handle is set at right angles to the spout to facilitate pouring. Chocolate was introduced into Britain as a drink c.1657 and was highly fashionable until c.1740. The earliest hallmarked chocolate pot dates from 1685. Some examples were converted from coffeepots.

Silver chocolate pot,
George II period [G]

Choreutoscope A lantern slide, popular in the mid-19th century. Choreutoscopes carry six images and the slide can be moved along intermittently by turning a handle, so projecting the six images in turn. These images can be shown in such rapid succession that they appear to be moving, exploiting the phenomenon of persistence of vision. This instrument was invented in 1832 independently by Stampfer in Austria, who called it the "Stroboscope" and by Plateau in Belgium, who called his version the "Phenakistoscope". It was the first device to present the illusion of true moving pictures and it embodies the basic principles of modern cinema.

Christmas tree lights See FAIRY LAMPS.

Christofle, Charles (1805–63)
A Parisian jeweller who began making domestic silverware in the 1830s. He pioneered ELECTROPLATING in France, acquiring patents for it in the early 1840s and thus effectively ended the far more labour-intensive and costly fused plate industry in France as ELKINGTON and Co. had done with SHEFFIELD PLATE in England. As Christofle's business grew he relinquished his jewellery interests to concentrate on plating and then, late in the 1850s, began manufacturing silver articles. A second factory was opened, and noted sculptors and designers such as Mathurin Moreau (1821–1912) were employed. They began producing articles in a variety of styles including RENAISSANCE REVIVAL, Greco-Roman and Classical architectural styles. On Christofle's death, his sons, nephew and grandson continued the business. In the 1860s and 70s they experimented with Eastern Oriental and JAPANESQUE forms, possibly in response to market trends and competition, particularly from TIFFANY & CO. who employed Japanese metalworkers. In the 1880s the business changed direction stylistically, moving toward ROCOCO REVIVAL and the flowing forms and sculpture of ART NOUVEAU. The company is still in production today.

Christofle
silver-plated
teapot,
c.1900 [D]

George III Ormolu-mounted
satinwood and rosewood commode
made for Harewood House [A]

George III glass-fronted
satinwood bookcase [A]

Thomas Chippendale (1718–79)

This famous English cabinet-maker and furniture designer was born in Otley, Yorkshire, where his father was a joiner. He may have had an early training with his father, which he probably continued in York, under the cabinet-maker Richard Wood (*c*.1707–72).

First publication of furniture designs

Chippendale set up in business in London *c*.1747. By 1753 he had a cabinet-making workshop in St Martin's Lane, but he first attracted national attention with the publication in April 1754 of *The Gentleman and Cabinet-Maker's Director*. It was the first book of furniture designs to be published in England and, according to the title-page, illustrated in 161 engraved plates, a "large collection of the most elegant and useful designs of household furniture in the Gothic, Chinese and modern [i.e. Rococo] tastes". It was dedicated to the 2nd Earl of Northumberland and subscribers included several influential and aristocratic patrons of the arts as well as many craftsmen working in a variety of media.

Champion of Rococo style

The *Director* became the most influential ROCOCO pattern book. Such was its success that Chippendale moved to larger premises in St Martin's Lane and a second edition was published in 1755; in October 1759 a significantly revised and enlarged third edition with over 100 new plates appeared in three parts, followed by a collected volume in 1762, which was also issued in French. The new edition was dedicated to His Royal Highness Prince William Henry (later William IV), and in the preface Chippendale stoutly defended the viability of his designs. However, among the new plates were designs for the RIBBON-BACK or "ribband-back" chair that represented the apogee of the carver's skill and was so expensive and technically demanding that few were ever made. This edition also reflected Chippendale's interest in the newly fashionable NEO-CLASSICAL style, which is evident in the use of motifs such as AEGRICANES (rams' heads) and CARYATIDS. This interest in Neo-classicism deepened and was finally realized in some of his finest furniture – a series of elegant designs for the great country houses of his native Yorkshire, with interiors designed by Robert ADAM. For Harewood House, Chippendale designed exceptionally fine MARQUETRY PIER TABLES and many

Chinese Chippendale

Some 60 of the 161 plates in Chippendale's *The Gentleman and Cabinet-Maker's Directory* were devoted to Chinese-style furniture with latticework, blind fretwork, pagoda-shaped mouldings, pierced stretchers and dragon-shaped finials that became known as "Chinese Chippendale". Some of his pieces are japanned and feature gilded decoration in imitation of the expensive and highly desirable lacquer furniture that was being imported from the East at the time. For some of his most prestigious commissions he would supply wallpapers and fabrics hand-painted in the Chinese taste to complement his furniture.

Chinese Chippendale upholstered chair with carved latticework arms and back and faux bamboo legs, 1770 [A]

items of cabinet furniture; for Nostell Priory he produced, among other pieces, a LIBRARY TABLE and richly carved library chairs (1767–68) in the "antique" taste.

A far-reaching influence

Thomas Chippendale's status as the best-known British furniture-maker was due partly to his talent as a designer but largely to his publications, which disseminated his style worldwide. *The Gentleman and Cabinet-Maker's Director* became the "bible" for English furniture-makers in Britain and North America. By the mid-1760s copies of the book had arrived in Philadelphia and they gave impetus to the AMERICAN CHIPPENDALE style. Copies of the French version of the third edition were held in the libraries of royal patrons such as Catherine the Great and Louis XVI of France. The Chippendale style became a worldwide phenomenon, and MAHOGANY chairs in particular were produced in the hundreds of designs that focused on intricately carved SPLATS and serpentine TOP RAILS. Chippendale's eldest son, Thomas Chippendale the Younger (1749–1822), joined the company *c.*1767 and became director when his father retired *c.*1777. He shared his father's talent for design. In 1799 he published *Sketches of Ornament* and also designed furniture in the Neo-classical style.

Chippendale revival

In the mid- and late 1800s the Victorians looked back to many earlier styles, including Gothic and Rococo, so Chippendale was a natural candidate for revival. Some Victorian pieces are of high quality, faithfully copied from the *Directory*, but other examples are much more ornate than earlier pieces, with overblown Rococo swirls and Gothic tracery encrusted with decoration. The Chippendale revival continued into Edwardian times, in the first decade of the 20th century.

A George III mahogany torchère, its fluid design typical of Chippendale [A, a pair].

An early George III giltwood mirror by Thomas Chippendale, made for Harewood House [A]

George III mahogany open armchair, by Thomas Chippendale, with Neo-classical Apollo-lyre splat [A]

George III mahogany pedestal desk designed by Thomas Chippendale [A]

Chrome dye One of a group of synthetic dyes produced from 1887 that use chromic salts as their mordant (colour fixative). Chrome dyes display excellent fastness to light and washing but do not mellow as natural mordant dyes do.

Chromium A silvery metal obtained by smelting lead chromates and usually plated on a base metal over nickel. Although discovered *c*.1797 in France, it was not introduced commercially until the 1920s, when it was favoured by progressive designers (e.g. Marcel BREUER) for tubular steel furniture because of its high resistance to corrosion and brilliant sheen.

Chromolithography Commercially produced colour LITHOGRAPHY from the second half of the 19th century. Similar to lithography, the outline of the image would be chalked onto the printer's stone and then the colours applied by any of the lithographic techniques, normally grease crayon, and printed. A separate stone is necessary for each colour.

FA cup cigarette cards issued by John Player, English, c.1920 [S]

Gold Waltham chronograph, American c.1890 [J]

Chronograph Any watch that both tells the time and has a facility to measure elapsed time in seconds or fractions of a second, and used particularly to record timed events and speed records in sport. The most familiar type of chronograph is the stopwatch, with a small knob for starting and stopping a seconds mechanism, which was first patented in 1862.

Chronometer A portable precision timekeeper developed by John HARRISON in the 18th century to enable mariners to calculate longitude, so as to determine their position at sea. It usually incorporates an extremely accurate spring DETENT ESCAPEMENT and is mounted on brass gimbals, to keep the mechanism level at sea, beneath a glazed cover in a square mahogany case. Most chronometers are of one, two or eight-day duration, with a subsidiary up/down dial to indicate the length of time before the instrument needs rewinding.

Chrysoberyl A precious gemstone with three varieties, all visually distinct from one another. These include cat's eye (a valuable honey-yellow to greenish gem polished *en cabochon* to display a singular iridescent optical effect known as chatoyancy), alexandrite (green) and chrysoberyl (a yellowish green gem used extensively in the 19th century and commercially known as chrysolite).

Cigar case From the 1830s, cases were made from various materials including silver and leather, of rounded oblong

Mid-19th century silver case for a single cigar [R]

form, curved to fit the pocket and large enough to take a small number of cigars, or tubular to take one. Early versions were known as cheroot cases.

Cigarette card A device to boost brand loyalty, developed from the cardboard stiffener placed inside every paper pack of cigarettes produced from the 19th century. Cards were issued in sets. Among the earliest known are a set of US Presidential Candidates from 1880. Tobacco companies Allen & Ginter in America and Wills in Britain made the largest number of cards by CHROMOLITHOGRAPHY, the peak period being between the World Wars. In the 1930s, penny albums were produced for collectors to stick in their ready-gummed cards. Since 1945 the fashion has moved toward tea and bubble-gum card issues.

Cigar-store Indians Near life-size carved wooden models of Native Americans holding tobacco leaves and standing on a plinth advertising the merits of a brand of cigar. Popular in the late 19th century, they often stood outside cigar retailers.

Life-size wooden cigar-store Indian, late 19th century [E]

Cinquefoil The five-lobed form of Gothic tracery. The cinquefoil was occasionally used in an arch, when the central foil might be pointed. It was widely adopted as a motif, as its leaf-like shape was a stylized version of the natural foliage favoured in GOTHIC ornament. The cinquefoil was also a common device in heraldry, where it was known as a fraise, frase, frasier, quint or quintfoil.

Circumferentor A surveying instrument with a central magnetic compass with a scale divided 0–360°, fitted with fixed and movable sights, for taking horizontal angles in the field. Later adapted in the 19th century to the miner's dial.

Ciré (French: "waxed") Term used to describe a smooth surface that has the appearance of having been polished, normally applied to silk.

Cire-perdue (French: "lost wax".) See LOST WAX TECHNIQUE.

Cistern barometer See STICK BAROMETER.

Chinese carved oviform Cizhou jar, Song Dynasty (960–1279) [E]

Cizhou ware Heavily potted Chinese stoneware produced from the SONG DYNASTY (960–1279) to the present, with a coarse buff or greyish white body. Often decorated with a coating of slip and painted or glazed in black or brown. Carved decoration and SGRAFFITO

techniques were popular, where the designs were incised through layers of different coloured SLIPS. Another type of decoration uses slip in conjunction with enamel colours. Bold designs of flowers and foliage or bamboo were used. Wares include ceramic pillows, brush pots, MEIPING vases and wine jars.

Clair de lune (French: "moonlight") A term used to describe a glaze of a soft, pale or lavender blue colour used on Chinese porcelain from the KANGXI period (1662–1722). Produced by adding tiny amounts of COBALT to the clear FELDSPATHIC GLAZE. The term is seldom used today, as the glaze is usually just referred to as pale blue.

Claret jug A silver or glass jug with a long, narrow, decanter-like neck and pouring lip for serving claret. Before the 1850s, most claret jugs were made entirely of silver; after that they were usually of glass, with silver mounts forming the neckpiece, lid and handle. Early glass versions with neither a stopper nor cover do occur from the late 18th century. Many Georgian and Victorian claret jugs have distinctive looped handles that are taller than the pouring lip.

Clark, Christopher (1875–1942) An English artist, known for historical and military paintings. He illustrated early British railway and travel posters of the 1920s and 30s in a highly colourful and optimistic style. He was elected in 1905 to the Royal Institute of Painters in Watercolours.

Clark & Co., David P. Based in Ohio, in 1897 Clark patented a rotating flywheel system, the first US mechanism to challenge the European CLOCKWORK used to

Clark & Co. tinplate toy, American c.1900 [G]

power toy road vehicles. The Dayton Friction Toy Works produced Hill Climber FRICTION Power Toys with TINPLATE bodywork and CAST IRON CHASSIS and mechanism until the Depression in the early 1930s.

Classicism See NEO-CLASSICAL STYLE.

Claw-and-ball foot See BALL-AND-CLAW FOOT.

Claw setting A method of mounting a gemstone whereby metal prongs extend from the base of the setting and are bent

Emeralds and diamonds claw-set in platinum, French, c.1905 [C]

around the girdle of the stone, securing it firmly. A circular arrangement of claws is often called a "coronet".

Claymore (Gaelic: "great sword") Originally, a large Scottish cross-hilted, double-handed BROADSWORD used from the 15th to 17th centuries, particularly by Scottish mercenaries in Ireland and on the Continent. From the mid-18th century onward, used to describe the characteristic Scottish basket-hilted broadsword that is still carried by officers in Highland Regiments today.

Clichy Glassworks

One of the three great French glassworks. The early history of the factory is unclear, but it was founded in 1837 and had relocated to Clichy-la-Garenne, Paris, by 1846, the year in which it probably began production of the PAPERWEIGHTS for which it remains best known today. Although largely unsigned and undated, Clichy paperweights have several distinctive characteristics, such as the "Clichy rose", a usually pink glass CANE, cut across to resemble an open rose. This may be a central motif or may be found in the concentric ring patterns or garland patterns used in the company's MILLEFIORI weights. A glass cane with the letter "C" may be included in the pattern. Some rare paperweights have a green moss background, miniature weights and OVERLAY weights, made of several layers of coloured glass, typically a soft turquoise or dark pink. Clichy weights are commonly almost completely globular, with only a small flat base. Unlike most French paperweights, they are not made of lead glass and are therefore lighter.

Clichy paperweight, mid-19th century [G]

In spite of their success at the GREAT EXHIBITION in 1851, by the end of the 1850s hardly any paperweights were being produced and in 1885 the glassworks closed down.

Cliff, Clarice (1899–1972) An English ceramic designer and decorator renowned for her colourful ART DECO designs. She left school at 13 and became an apprentice painter at the Lingard Webster Pottery in Tunstall, Staffordshire. In 1916

Clarice Cliff mark

she went to work at the factory of A.J. WILKINSON, near Burslem, and in 1922 she was apprenticed as a modeller. She later married the factory owner, Colley Shorter. Cliff excelled both as a painter and a modeller. She visited the Paris Exposition in 1925 and was influenced by Art Deco and Cubism. Her "Bizarre" decorated pieces went on sale in 1928/1929, inspired by her idea of using discarded stock at the firm's Newport factory. She transformed these blanks with bold patterns and colours. With the help of Gladys Scarlett, also from the Wilkinson factory, the original "Bizarre" ware was created with triangular shapes and patterns outlined and filled with coloured enamels. It was so successful that new designs were created and a new product range, "Fantasque", was brought out in September 1928. These pieces were marked under the Newport pottery for tax reasons.

From then on more brightly coloured, stylized landscape designs were produced. Clarice Cliff became Art Director of Wilkinson's in 1931. World War II made a break in the production of art pottery and, although Cliff continued to design in the 1940s and 1950s, the main period of innovative designs was pre-war.

Clobbered ware A type of pottery or porcelain with OVERGLAZE, ENAMEL COLOURS added at a later date to enhance the decorative appeal. It is typically seen on 18th-century blue and white CHINESE EXPORT PORCELAIN, which was clobbered in Holland or England in the 19th century. Clobbering reduces the value of a piece.

Clichy glass and ormolu chamberstick, c.1860 [O]

Clarice Cliff Bizarre range lotus jug, c.1929 [H]

Clarice Cliff "crocus" pattern honey pot, c.1933 [M]

Clock (medieval Latin: *clocca* "bell") The earliest daytime device, used in ancient Egypt, was the SUNDIAL. Water clocks and HOURGLASSES could be used during day and night. Mechanical clocks, powered by a weight falling under the force of gravity, first appeared in Europe in the late 13th century. Smaller weight-driven domestic clocks (with dials) were introduced in the 15th century; during this period, lighter portable clocks (and eventually watches) were developed, powered by a coiled spring in a barrel.

From the late Middle Ages domestic clocks were produced. The ESCAPEMENT enabled the power of weights or a spring to be transferred evenly to the movement; early clocks were fitted with a VERGE ESCAPEMENT then, in the late 17th century, with the more accurate ANCHOR ESCAPEMENT. The PENDULUM also appeared at this time. Accuracy improved and in the mid- to late 17th century minute hands were introduced. LONGCASE clocks developed, possibly to protect the pendulum, and the combination of a short pendulum and spring-driven mechanism inspired the portable BRACKET CLOCK. In the 18th century, scientists produced many precision devices, such as the DEADBEAT escapement, the COMPENSATED pendulum, REGULATORS and CHRONOMETERS.

In the 19th-century, clocks had increasingly elaborate cases and striking systems, especially on novelty types such as PICTURE, SKELETON, MYSTERY and BLACK FOREST clocks

From the mid-19th century electric mechanisms were introduced, superseded in the 20th century by the quartz crystal timepiece, first invented in 1929, and then by the caesium atomic clock in 1955.

Clocks

Clocks vary in their shapes and sizes according to where they were kept, from the mantelshelf to the floor. They varied also in the materials used, from the indigenous timber of the Black Forest clock to expensive imported timbers and boulle work. The details of their mechanisms and hands also changed through centuries of clockmaking.

Wall clock,
1600s–

Mantel clock,
1650s–

Bell-top clock,
18th century

Lantern clock,
1620s–

Longcase clock,
1650s–

Skeleton clock,
c.1750–

Regulator clock,
18th century

Carriage clock,
c.1796–

Banjo clock,
1802–

Clock hands

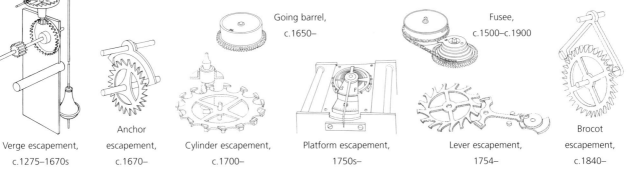

Spade,
c.1660–75

Early lantern,
c.1660–1800

Late Stuart,
c.1675–1700

Queen Anne
style, c.1700–20

Late Georgian,
c.1760–1820

1810–70

Clock escapements

Going barrel,
c.1650–

Fusee,
c.1500–c.1900

Verge escapement,
c.1275–1670s

Anchor
escapement,
c.1670–

Cylinder escapement,
c.1700–

Platform escapement,
1750s–

Lever escapement,
1754–

Brocot
escapement,
c.1840–

Clockwork mechanism A key-wound spiral spring motor that provides power for a toy. The key may be fixed or removable. The spring may be of flat or round section; round is cheaper. On more complicated toys the motor can power additional features, e.g. mystery steering or opening doors.

Cloisonné A method of enamelling in which thin strips of metal are soldered onto the surface of an object to form individual decorative cells. These are filled with powdered enamel and then fired in a kiln. See also CHAMPLEVÉ.

Cloisonné vase and cover,
Chinese Qianlong reign (1736–95) [F]

Closed-back setting Commonly used in 17th- and 18th-century jewellery, these settings involve securing a gem in a solid metal back so that only the crown of the stone is visible. An open-back setting secures the gem in a sleeve without a back, enabling all the available light to pass through. See COLLET and FOILING.

Close-plating A method of plating steel or iron with silver leaf, patented in 1779 by the London goldsmith Richard Ellis. Much stronger than plated copper or nickel, it was used for such implements as knives and scissors. The process involves dipping the object into a sal ammoniac

solution then into molten tin. It is then coated with silver leaf and rubbed with a hot soldering iron to fuse the silver with the tin. It was adopted largely by the Sheffield cutlery industry from the late 18th to the mid-19th century and was the precursor of plating methods such as SHEFFIELD PLATE.

Close stool A movable latrine consisting of an enclosed box or trunk, often richly upholstered and decorated, holding a metal or earthenware receptacle. They were used from the 15th until the early 18th century, by which time they were often incorporated in a chair. Close stools were superseded by night tables and pot cupboards.

Cloth doll See RAG DOLL.

Club foot In furniture, a type of foot shaped like a club, often resting on a turned circular PAD FOOT, that was used throughout the 18th century in conjunction with straight or CABRIOLE legs.

Cluny lace See FLEMISH LACE.

Clutha glass (Old Scottish: "cloudy") A type of glass in pale green, amber and yellow with cloudy streaks and sometimes AVENTURINE inclusions, made by the firm of James Couper & Sons in Glasgow from c.1885 to 1905. Vessels often reflect ART NOUVEAU plant forms. The company produced designs by Christopher DRESSER and George Walton.

Clutha glass bowl, c.1900 [G]

Cluthra glass An American term for heavily made artistic glass of mottled colouring and with bubble inclusions, comparable to the Scottish CLUTHA. Cluthra was used as a trademark by STEUBEN GLASSWORKS on a line introduced in 1920. The bubbles in Steuben Cluthra were made by rolling the hot glass over tapioca.

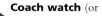

Gilt-metal double-dialled coach watch, c.1800 [K]

Coach watch (or chaise watch) A large watch made in the 1770s for travelling. They were similar to contemporary pocket watches but about double the size to accommodate features such as alarms or STRIKING or REPEATING mechanisms.

Coade stone A vitreous ware used for architectural ornament, made in London by a firm of the same name run by Mrs Coade from 1771 until her death in 1796. It consisted of a kaolinitic clay, finely ground quartz and flint and a flux, possibly ground glass.

Coalbrookdale Co. An iron foundry in Shropshire, England, founded in 1708. A large maker of CAST-IRON furniture in the 19th century, producing decorative grates, railings, stoves, wall plaques and garden furniture. Some was exported to the US and Europe. It produced some designs by Christopher DRESSER. The firm is still in existence.

Coalport and Coalbrookdale porcelain factory Founded at Coalport, Shropshire, by the River Severn c.1796 by John ROSE, believed to have been apprenticed to Thomas Turner at CAUGHLEY. Rose and his partners bought the Caughley factory in 1799 and made mainly blue-printed tewares. Some Caughley ware was decorated at Coalport.

Coalport inkstand,
c.1805 [M]

Another factory at Coalport (1800–14) belonged to John Rose's brother Thomas with his partners Robert Anstice and Robert Horton. It produced similar wares with patterns like those of John Rose. In 1814 John Rose bought his brother's factory, dismantled the Caughley works and put all his efforts into Coalport.

Early Coalport porcelains were unmarked and often confused with those of Chamberlain WORCESTER. Distinguishing features of the early wares are the six slight indentations around the rim on plates. Inexpensive enamelled copies of Chinese patterns on teawares sold well and from 1801 the much imitated "Indian Tree" pattern was used. The use of independent decorators such as Thomas BAXTER accounts for much of the great variety of decoration.

After 1810 Coalport achieved the soft white translucency and smooth surface for which it is celebrated. In 1820 John Rose was awarded the Society of Arts Gold Medal for a leadless feldspathic glaze. After 1820 wares with this glaze had large circular printed marks.

Coalport's influences were varied. From Neo-classical and brightly coloured "Japan" patterns, they turned to French-style floral wares, and from c.1820–50 the factory specialized in painted flowers as well as ROCOCO REVIVAL applied flowers in high relief. These encrusted wares were known as "English Dresden" and gave rise to the term "Coalbrookdale" (the name of the neighbouring town) which describes similar productions by other factories. Marks include "C.D.", "C. Dale", "Coalport" and "Coalbrookdale" in underglaze blue.

Coalport wares after 1835 became more sophisticated – rich ground colours were introduced in imitation of CHELSEA and SÈVRES and marks too were often copied. Coalport also copied SWANSEA bone china with fake marks. Much Victorian Coalport was unmarked until 1881 when all examples were marked.

The Coalport factory changed hands several times. In 1924 it was sold to the Staffordshire firm of Cauldon Potteries Ltd, and in 1926 the works were transferred to the Cauldon Works at Shelton. In 1936 they moved to the Crescent Pottery at Stoke, formerly the works of George JONES & Co. In 1951 the name of Coalport China Ltd was adopted. This closed in 1958 when E. Brain & Co. (makers of FOLEY china) took it over and moved it to Fenton, Stoke on Trent, where production continues today. In 1967 Coalport joined the WEDGWOOD group; the main production is high quality bone china tableware.

Coalport vase and cover painted by F.H. Chivers, 1900 [L]

Coal scuttle A receptacle for coal kept by a fireplace. Introduced in the early 18th century when coal was first used for domestic heating, they are generally made of copper, brass, japanned tin or wood. Most pieces date from the mid-19th century, when helmet, vase or box shapes were especially popular.

Coaster A term originally describing a circular stand with a wooden base and pierced, engraved or embossed silver GALLERY, made in pairs or sets. They were used from c.1760 for passing wine bottles or decanters round the dining-table, the undersides covered with baize to protect the table. The term later came to include stands made in a variety of materials and used under drinking glasses.

Set of papier-mâché coasters, c.1810 [M]

Cobalt The black pigment cobalt oxide, which turns blue on firing; see also CHINESE POTTERY AND PORCELAIN and BLUE AND WHITE.

Cobb, John (c.1715–78) An English furniture-maker. His partnership with William Vile (see VILE & COBB) was one of the most successful in London. He supplied upholstery to George III and, after Vile's retirement in 1765, took on furniture production, notably fine pieces with marquetry in Robert ADAM style.

Coburg pottery and porcelain A German factory producing TIN-GLAZED EARTHENWARE from 1738, marked "CB" and often painted by BAYREUTH decorators. It closed in 1789. In 1860 Albert Riemann founded a factory in Upper Franconia, making porcelain figures. The mark was "AR" and "Coburg".

Cock beading A small, curved strip of semicircular BEAD MOULDING used on furniture. It was applied as a finish to the edges of drawer fronts from the mid-18th to the early 19th centuries. Several strips of cock beading applied together create the effect of REEDING.

Colonial style

The term "Colonial" describes the period, the decorative arts and the architecture of the North American colonies under Dutch and (mainly) English rule, from *c*.1600 to *c*.1780. It is largely reserved for furniture, silver, metalware, textiles and paintings that compare to the style and manufacture of contemporary English or Dutch provincial work.

Home from home – early furniture

Few decorative arts were produced by European settlers before the third quarter of the 17th century because the population was low. New Amsterdam, later New York City, was a town of 300 inhabitants in 1625; Jamestown, Virginia, was among the largest settlements with 900. Demand was also limited, with a largely puritanical, self-sufficient lifestyle, and early settlers tended to bring many everyday items with them. Such pieces may be described as "Colonial", but those made in America are of greatest value to modern collectors and museums. The most sought after today are in original condition. Examples are very rare and reproductions and fakes have been made since the CENTENNIAL, the best of which are highly deceptive. Functional items, including chests and simple seating, are among the earliest recorded American Colonial furniture.

The oldest surviving items include furniture made in New England coastal communities by joiners, who were specialized carpenters and predecessors of the modern professional furniture-maker. Most is of jointed and panelled construction, held together with MORTISE AND TENON joints and pegging. Hinges may be of leather or (usually imported) metal. Oak and other indigenous woods were plentiful in New England and blanket chests were made from wide boards, particularly in Connecticut where many were carved and even painted. "Presses", from the Dutch word for linen cupboard, were also made by the mid-17th century. They are normally of simple, panelled construction with an upper and lower level and little applied or carved ornament, resembling simplified versions of the ELIZABETHAN COURT CUPBOARD. Few pieces from this period can be attributed, but some early makers have been identified, including Thomas DENNIS of the Massachusetts colony and Nicholas DISBROWE of Connecticut. Regional variety makes geographical attribution relatively easy, however. The CONNECTICUT CHEST is an early example of evolved, characteristic form. Other

New England Wainscot chair in oak and maple, modified from the English version, 17th century [A]

Massachusetts maple side chair, with turned decoration and scroll-carving on the back c.1710–20 [A]

Recognizing the style

Early furniture used turned wood decoration such as balusters and spindles, like its Elizabethan counterparts, and carving. Ornament included heraldic emblems such as unicorns and eagles and motifs taken from the natural world. Textiles were often geometrically patterned.

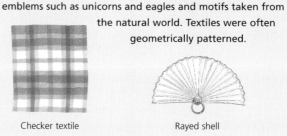

Checker textile   Rayed shell   Stylized bird

modified English forms include BREWSTER and WAINSCOT CHAIRS, identified with Massachusetts and there are also styles associated with Long Island, New York State and Williamsburg, Virginia. Virginia and the other southern colonies relied heavily on imported goods, although there were cabinet-makers active there as well. Chests-of-drawers and more ambitious furniture, including bedsteads, gateleg tables and chairs with turned elements, some upholstered in English fabric, start to appear in northern colonies by the mid-17th century.

Skilled immigrants bring smaller crafts

The diverse population of early eastern America included significant Dutch and French immigrant communities, all of which produced their own distinctive decorative arts in Colonial times. Most of the ceramics and glass used by early colonists was imported and few items are now described as Colonial. But by the late 17th century craftspeople were making silver, pewter and other metalwork. Surviving examples are rare, typically plain and unmarked, making them hard to distinguish from imported items.

Silver quart can in plain style by Paul Revere, c.1770 [A]

HUGUENOTS from France and the Netherlands, who sought political and religious freedom in the New World from about 1675, pursued the silver trade in particular. Among the best known was second-generation Paul REVERE (1734–1818), a silversmith and romantic hero of the War of Independence (1775–81). French Colonial furniture is scarce and most French influence is seen in Huguenot work of later immigrants during the FEDERAL period.

American Chippendale mahogany high chest-of-drawers, c.1760–80 [A]

Most Dutch decorative arts of the 17th century are comparable to those made by English colonists, mirroring the cross-fertilization between the two cultures in Europe. However, one distinctively Dutch colonial furniture form is the kas (storage cupboard, plural kasten), made mainly in the Dutch settlements of northern New York State, New Jersey and Connecticut in the first half of the 18th century. Kasten are typically massive, tall cupboards with two doors opening to shelves and raised on BUN FEET. Woods include cherry, pine and walnut and a few show original paint.

Other European influences

German Lutheran immigrants, many of whom settled in Pennsylvania, continued the colonial lifestyle well into the 20th century (and even to the present day in some communities). Their particular style and culture is generically referred to as PENNSYLVANIA DUTCH, a misspelling of *Deutsch* ("German"). American decorative arts and architecture produced mainly in the western and southern states under Spanish influence are referred to as SPANISH COLONIAL.

About 1780 the Colonial style gave way to FEDERAL. Colonial furniture made in a fashionable or formal 18th-century style is often referred to as QUEEN ANNE (before *c.*1750) or AMERICAN CHIPPENDALE, because the English furniture-maker was much admired and copied in the US. Similiarly, American 18th-century items made in informal style but not commercially produced may be referred to as "folk art" rather than Colonial.

Female settlers passed on needlecraft skills to their daughters as on this silk on linen needlework sampler, Newport, Rhode Island c.1773 [K]

Cock motif A motif in Christian, Oriental, Scandinavian and Celtic art. In Classical ornament the cock is occasionally depicted pulling the chariot of the god Mercury and may also symbolize lust. Associated with the dawn and rising sun, it often figures in designs featuring Apollo and as a symbol of day sometimes decorates timepieces. Long a national symbol of France, the cock was embraced as an emblem of the Revolution.

Coconut cup A goblet formed from the shell of a coconut, sometimes plain and polished, sometimes carved, often mounted in silver. These exotic nuts were brought into Britain in quantity during the Tudor period and were not only a novelty but suspected to have mystical properties. Tudor examples are now extremely scarce but the cups enjoyed a revival in the late 18th century.

Paris porcelain coffee can, c.1820 [Q]

Coffee can A cup for coffee, but of cylindrical shape, made from the end of the 18th century and early 19th century. Previously the shape had been a tall, narrow U-shape.

Coffeepot After the spread of coffee-drinking in Europe in the early 18th century, pots of silver, ceramic and other metals were produced. The earliest extant HALLMARKED silver example dates from 1681. Although they changed with fashion, their simple form is usually a tapering cylinder or baluster with a hinged domed cover and a scroll handle. With the advent of chocolate, some were converted into CHOCOLATE-POTS.

Coffer A portable strong box, storage box or trunk, the simplest form of CHEST, and known from ancient times until superseded by the chest of drawers. It was usually made of wood and could be covered with leather and banding.

Oak coffer, English c.1680 [J]

Cogswell, John (active 1769–82) An American cabinet-maker working in Boston, making fashionable carved mahogany furniture in the AMERICAN CHIPPENDALE style. Cogswell's work can be compared to that of Benjamin FROTHINGHAM, and includes chests-of-drawers of the BLOCK-FRONT type.

Coif A type of close-fitting cap often finely embroidered and worn by both men and women until the 17th century.

Coiffeuse (French *coiffer*: "to dress the hair") A 19th-century French term for a DRESSING TABLE.

Coiling A term denoting a pot hand-formed by "snakes" of clay coiled to the desired shape. The snake may vary from a thin strip to a large "sausage". Pre-Columbian American and West African pottery are examples of

Coffeepot, silver, English c.1767 [H]

this method. Neolithic and Bronze Age people used the technique, which is still employed today for the decorative effect.

Coin glass A term used for glassware displaying an embedded coin (or coins). Almost always refers to stemmed drinking glasses, tankards or jugs, where a coin has been embedded in the KNOP or foot. Examples are known from the 18th century and coin glass is still made.

Coin moulding See EYE-AND-SCALE MOTIF.

Cold painting Painting in coloured enamels on ceramics, glass and bronze, but without firing, so the colours and gilding are not permanent. The technique was used on some early MEISSEN pieces.

Cold stamping A decorative technique used in leatherwork and one of the earliest bookbinding decorations. Metal dies are stamped into the dampened leather, impressing a pattern which is fixed once dry. Gilding or colour is not applied to the design.

Cole, Sir Henry (1808–82) An English designer and arts administrator. Under the pseudonym Felix Summerly he opened Summerly's Art Manufacturers (1847) in an attempt to produce good designs, for household wares, particularly pottery. A great reformer, he organized the South Kensington Museum (now the Victoria & Albert Museum) and was involved in the 1851 GREAT EXHIBITION.

Cole, James Ferguson (1798–1880) **and Thomas** (1800–64) English clock- and watchmaker brothers, business partners until 1829. James made one of the earliest CARRIAGE CLOCKS in England.

From 1845 Thomas worked independently as a maker of watches and extremely high quality mantel and other ornamental clocks.

Calendar and moon phase strut clock by Thomas Cole, c.1850 [E]

Collar An applied glass ring on a wineglass stem covering the joins between the bowl and the stem, the stem and the foot, and between the KNOPS.

Collet setting A sleeve or "dish" of metal holding a gemstone in signet rings and necklaces. Particularly associated with diamonds, a collet necklace has a line of stones in settings of tightly enclosing bands. A millegrain collet is a band decorated with tiny beads.

Collinson & Lock English furniture-makers established in London in 1870 and known for their ART FURNITURE. They were taken over by GILLOWS in 1897. Designers

Collet setting

who were associated with them include E.W. GODWIN, John Moyr Smith and Bruce Talbert.

Cologne potteries There were three main 16th-century stoneware factories in Cologne, in Germany's Rhineland: Maximinenstrasse flourished from 1520 to 1540 making religious figures, antique busts and designs after engravings; Komödiengasse made "Greybeards", also called BELLARMINES, with leaf decoration and inscribed bands; and Eigelstein made ornamental tankards (*schnellen*) with religious and allegorical subjects. Though production of Rhenish stoneware was disrupted by the outbreak of the Thirty Years War in 1618, works continued throughout the 17th century.

Colonial See pp.116–117.

Colonial Revival See CENTENNIAL.

Colour hardening

A technique in which a steel item is heated in an iron box with high carbon material such as bone dust or old leather. This makes the surface of the steel hard and durable. It also produces a decorative finish of swirling browns, blues and greys.

Colt, Samuel (1814–62) An American firearms designer and entrepreneur, often referred to as the first tycoon. Colt obtained his first patent for a REVOLVER in 1836. His factory at Hartford, Connecticut, was among the first to use machinery to make firearms with interchangeable parts. Colt firearms were widely used in the American Civil War (1861–65) and in both World Wars; the factory is still in production today.

Colt revolver, US c.1855 [J]

Column See box below.

Combed decoration A pattern of feathered lines, also called "feathering" or "combing", used in ceramic-making. One colour, usually white, is trailed across a ground slip of contrasting colour and a bristle, bulrush or feather is then "combed" across the lines, to give the feathering pattern. John DWIGHT developed the technique in the 17th century and it then spread to the STAFFORDSHIRE POTTERIES.

Column

The Classical column varied in its mouldings on the bases and capitals, the shaft and the carved decoration of anthemions and volutes. They returned to popularity in the Renaissance and were used on furniture in the Neo-classical style either as structural supports or as decoration.

Tuscan · Doric · Ionic · Composite · Corinthian

Comedy and tragedy masks

Traditional symbols of drama. Masks are among the attributes of the Muses of Comedy and Tragedy – Thalia and Melpomene – and appear in Classical Greek drama to express the spirit or type of character being performed. From the Renaissance, the motif has frequently been linked with ancient instruments, such as pipes and cymbals, and widely applied to decorative ornament of a theatrical nature.

Staffordshire comforter dogs, c.1880 [P]

Comforter dog A large earthenware figure of a spaniel made mainly in the 19th century in Staffordshire, as a fireplace ornament. They were supposed to comfort lonely people and were also purchased by errant husbands to comfort their irate wives.

Commedia dell'Arte

figures A genre of improvised comedy from 16th-century Italy that tended to be lively and ribald. Characters were Harlequin, Brighella, Pantalone and the Doctor, the Captain, who had a huge nose, Pulcinella with a hump-back (the Punch of "Punch and Judy") and Columbine and Pierrot – the lovers. Italian actors played in Germany in the 18th century and were the inspiration for MEISSEN figures.

Commedia dell'Arte Harlequin figure by Meissen, c.1750 [D]

These were then much copied in the 18th century by factories such as BOW and CHELSEA and their manufacture continued into the 19th century.

Commemorative ware

Articles in pottery, porcelain and many other materials commemorating incidents of royal, historical, sociological, political, theatrical and topographical interest. The event being commemorated could be painted or occasionally printed or moulded in the body of ceramic ware. It is also found as figures or busts of people or animals and even models of infamous houses. The ware was made over a wide geographical area and over long periods of time.

Commode A French term for a low chest of drawers with deep drawers, first used in France in the late 17th century. The term was then adopted in Britain in the mid-18th century, when French furniture became fashionable, to describe highly decorative, low chests of drawers with SERPENTINE fronts and other curving forms that evolved in the ROCOCO style. In 19th-century England, the term was also adopted to describe a CLOSE STOOL.

Compass A case, usually made of brass, holding a magnetized wire or needle that indicates the direction of magnetic north. The needle may be placed over a "rose" or "card" marked with compass points or a scale of degrees to ascertain the direction of north and therefore of any other bearing or direction. An essential instrument for navigation at sea as well as for surveying. Compasses were developed in the 12th century by mariners in Europe and China.

Commemorative jug for 60th anniversary of Queen Victoria's accession to the throne, Doulton, 1897 [O]

Compendium

A rectangular box, usually late 19th century, and often made of mahogany, used to store games such as chess, draughts and cards. Many have a hinged top, and an upright front fitted with small drawers.

Compensation Treatment of a PENDULUM to ensure that it remains a constant length in spite of temperature changes, so that the timekeeping of the clock remains accurate. Various types of compensated pendulum were developed in the 18th century, especially the gridiron and mercury types, though some compensated pendulums simply incorporated a wooden rather than a metal rod (as wood hardly expands or contracts when heated or cooled). Compensated pendulums were used principally in precision clocks, for example, REGULATORS and CHRONOMETERS.

Comport A dish, usually on a foot or stem, to hold fruit for the dessert course. Part of a service with a centrepiece, sauce tureens, covers and stands, ice pails and plates.

"Three Graces", Meissen comport, c.1880 [J]

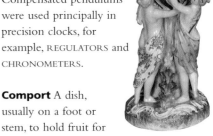

Ship's compass, English, 1920 [M]

Composition
A combination of moulded plaster, woodpulp, glue and other ingredients, used from 1850 to 1950 for items, such as dolls' bodies, that were made of composite artificial materials that imitated natural substances, such as ivory. From 1900 onward, it was used as a cheaper alternative to BISQUE for the production of dolls' heads. It was superseded in the 1950s by plastic.

Compound twist stems A rare type of wineglass stem in which several types of twists – air, coloured and opaque – are combined.

Comtoise clocks A type of LONGCASE CLOCK produced in the French Franche-Comté region, especially at Morbier and Morez, from the 18th century. It has a bulbous-shaped wooden case, sometimes inlaid or painted, fitted with a glazed aperture revealing an ornate pressed-brass pendulum.

Comyns, William & Sons English silver makers, founded in 1848 in London by William Comyns to make hand-crafted silver. They made good quality Victorian pieces and also worked in the ARTS AND CRAFTS style. Comyns produced a vast amount of small silver pieces and continues trading.

Concertina action A method for extending hinged-top card and tea tables using a sliding device hinged to movable legs that straightened when the legs were pulled out and folded back when they were pushed back in.

Confidante A French term for a type of chair or sofa, known also as a companion, conversation or *tête à tête*, popular in France and Britain in the mid- and late-19th century, consisting of two or three seats joined by an S-shaped curve so that the seated people half faced each other.

Wineglass with compound twist stem, English c.1750 [K]

Congreve clock A type of SKELETON CLOCK, also known as a rolling ball clock, in which the ESCAPEMENT is impulsed by a ball rolling back and forth across a pivoted plate. Such clocks were first developed in the 17th century, but the best-known version was invented by the English scientist and clockmaker Sir William Congreve (1772–1828) in the early 19th century. The top of the clock is pediment-shaped and set with three dials. Original 19th-century pieces are rare and most examples found today are 20th-century reproductions.

Connecticut chest A generic term given to blanket chests made in the Connecticut River Valley area in America, c.1680 to c.1770. Most specimens are of oak and resemble contemporary English forms, including MULE CHESTS. Distinctive varieties include those carved with panels of stylized tulips or florettes and applied with ebonized stiles, identified with the area of Hartford or Wethersfield, and plainer chests with extensive shallow carving, which are termed "Hadley" chests after an area of the upper Connecticut River Valley.

Console table A side table fixed or joined to a wall and supported at the front by either two legs or a decorative central bracket.

Cookworthy, William
An English apothecary who used KAOLIN found in Cornwall in 1745 to try to make porcelain firstly in PLYMOUTH, Devon, then later in Bristol. He had great difficulty in mixing and firing the BODY and made a rather poor hard-paste porcelain. In the 1760s he patented several formulas which he assigned to Richard CHAMPION.

Cooper, Susie (1902–95) A ceramic and textile designer who studied and worked in the STAFFORDSHIRE POTTERIES. A prolific designer from the mid-1920s to the 1970s. She started as a decorator and later as a designer for A.E. Gray & Co. Ltd, then opened her own decorating firm, Crown Works, and bought blanks from local firms before having her own shapes made. One of her most popular streamlined shapes was "Kestrel"-shape teaware. In 1940 she became a "Royal Designer for Industry". She bought the Bone China factory in London and exhibited at the Festival of Britain (1951). In the 1960s, the factory merged first with R.H. & S.L. Plant and was then later taken over by the Wedgwood Group.

Susie Cooper cup and saucer, 1928 [R]

Cope An ecclesiastical cloak worn on important occasions by Christian priests. Frequently heavily embroidered, and made of fine materials, for example brocades.

Copeland and Garrett The SPODE factory was taken over by W.T. Copeland and T. Garrett in 1833 and used various marks incorporating their names until 1847.

Copeland and Garrett sauce tureen, c.1840. Whole dessert service [C]

Copenhagen porcelain factory Although FAIENCE was produced in Copenhagen from the early 18th century, the production of PORCELAIN proved elusive. Between 1759 and 1766, the Frenchman Louis Fournier produced a limited amount of soft-paste porcelain, but discontinued owing to its prohibitive expense. In 1774, chemist Franz Heinrich Müller began to produce hard-paste porcelain, using KAOLIN from the island of Bornholm, which had been discovered in 1755. In 1779, the factory was taken over by King Christian VII and named the Royal Danish Porcelain Factory. The earliest Copenhagen porcelain was greyish in colour, decorated in UNDERGLAZE blue, notably the "Immortell" pattern, inspired by MEISSEN designs. Other products included severe NEO-CLASSICAL products influenced by other European factories, such as Berlin, Vienna and SÈVRES, and flower patterns, including the famous "Flora Danica" service (1789–1802), created as a gift for Catherine the Great of Russia, who died during its production. The service of 1,602 items was intended to display every

1775 onward

Copenhagen tureen, 19th century [I]

Royal Copenhagen Christmas plate, 1929 [R]

wild plant in the kingdom, and was painted by the flower-painter Johann Christoph Bayer, who worked in Copenhagen from 1776. In 1801, the King pensioned off Müller and production declined. In 1824, Gustav Hetsch became director and the factory produced some richly decorated wares From 1835 it began production of figures after the sculptor Bertel Thorvaldsen (1768–1844). The factory was sold in 1868 and became the Royal Copenhagen. The architect and painter Arnold Krog (1856–1931), director from 1885–1916, revived the factory's fortunes with underglaze blue decoration and products decorated with Japanese and ART NOUVEAU motifs. The factory retains its artistic reputation still making figures and the "Immortell" and "Flora Danica" patterns.

Coper, Hans (1920–81) A German studio potter who worked in England. Coper first trained as an engineer before becoming a studio potter. He came to England in 1939 and became an assistant to Lucie RIE after his war service. He established a studio in 1956. His work is often characterized by strong sculptural shapes.

Copland, Henry (1720–c.53) An English engraver. In spite of the important role he played in introducing and developing the ROCOCO STYLE in England, little is known about him, other than his involvement in two important pattern-books for the new style: his own *A New Book of Ornaments* (1746), and another book with the same title, in collaboration with Matthias Lock (d.1765), which was published in 1752.

Copper A dense and soft red metallic element. Known since prehistoric times, copper is one of the most widely used metals both in its pure state and, alloyed with tin and zinc, as BRONZE and BRASS. Owing to its high conductivity of heat and electricity, its ductility and resistance to corrosion, it has been used for many things including cooking vessels, jewellery, wire and coins. Copper is also plated with silver to produce SHEFFIELD PLATE. Inexpensive and easily worked, hand-hammered sheet copper was popular with ARTS AND CRAFTS designers for small items such as vases, bowls and frames, especially in the US, in the late 19th century.

Coper stoneware vase, c.23cm (9") c.1963 [E]

Coquillage (French: "shell") One of the strongest themes in ROCOCO ornament, the shell form was adopted in ceramics and silver for sauceboats, tureens, salt cellars and plates.

Coral The tree-like skeleton of *Corallium rubrum*, a marine organism. There are many species of coral but only this one, otherwise known as Precious Coral, found in the Mediterranean and Pacific regions is suitable for carving and has been used as a versatile decorative material in objects and jewellery for centuries. The principal centre of manufacture in the 19th century was Naples; some of the more popular colours include Pelle d'Angelo (angel's skin), Rosso (red) and Carbonetto (ox blood).

Coralene A type of applied glass decoration named after the sprays of coral that it imitated. Developed by the MOUNT WASHINGTON GLASS CO. and subsequently used by other American and

European factories, the technique involved fusing small glass beads to enamelled lines painted on the surface of the glass.

Corbel A bracket or block of stone or wood projecting from a vertical member, used to support a beam or horizontal feature from below.

Corbel

Cordial glass A drinking glass, made and used from the second half of the 17th century to the last quarter of the 19th century, in the form of a small wineglass with a tall stem and bowl with a capacity of some 25–38g (1–1.5oz) and used for liqueurs and cordials.

Core forming One of the earliest glass-making processes, used from c.1500–c.1200 BC in ancient Egypt and Rome, in which molten trails of glass were wound round a core of mud, clay or straw on a metal rod to make small bottles and flasks.

Corgi toys Introduced in 1956 by METTOY under the slogan "The Ones With Windows", these mainly 1:43 scale DIECAST toy road vehicles were in direct competition with

Cordial glass, English c.1760 [κ]

DINKY TOYS. Corgis had windows, independent suspension and openable hoods. The famous 1965 "James Bond Aston Martin" sold approximately four million in four years. Since the 1980s, after a few changes of ownership, the company is now producing collector's models.

Cork Glass Company An Irish glasshouse founded in Cork in 1783 (and known until 1818). The company produced decanters, jugs and other tableware in a medium quality glass with a slight blue tinge, often with engraved or shallow-cut decoration and marked on the base with the factory name.

Cork pictures Carving cork in relief was a popular hobby in the middle years of the 19th century. Subjects range from Classical scenes, particularly ruins, to castles and landscapes. Most pictures were sold as kits with black velvet backgrounds and maple frames. The material does not wear well and good examples are rare.

Corncob motif A standard motif in 19th-century American ornament. A popular decorative theme for ironwork, ceramics, furniture details and wallpaper, the corncob was first used with tobacco leaves for the Corinthian-style capitals devised by Benjamin Latrobe for the rebuilding of the Capitol in Washington, DC. In England, breadknives with corncob handles were first made by Summerly's Art Manufactures (an experiment by Henry COLE) in the 1850s, and remained a popular design well into the 20th century.

Cornelius and Company A metalworks in Philadelphia, founded by Christian Cornelius in 1812 for the manufacture of silver and cast metalwork. The company specialized throughout the American Empire period in making elements for and assembling ARGAND LAMPS, which were extremely popular decorations in American homes throughout the 19th century.

Corner chair A chair designed to stand in the corner of a room. Developed in England in the first half of the 18th century, they typically have a bowed top rail and back splats on two sides.

Cornice A projecting moulding or a horizontal member at the top of a piece of furniture, typically a tall cupboard.

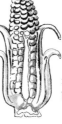

Corncob motif

Corning, New York A large and important American glass-making centre. Since the mid-19th century, Corning – about 315 km (250 miles) north of New York City – has been home to many glassworks, most specializing in cutting. Since 1903, the main firm has been STEUBEN, which still operates in Corning from a large complex also housing America's largest Museum of Glass.

Cornucopia (or "horn of plenty") A symbol of fertility and abundance since Classical times. A goat's horn overflowing with ears of wheat and fruit, the cornucopia was popular from the RENAISSANCE for architectural ornament, including VOLUTES and BRACKETS. On French Empire and American Federal furniture, it was an emblem of peace and fortune; with Cupid's arrows and quivers it is a symbol of fecundity. In ceramics, cornucopias were popular from c.1750–c.1870 hung on walls with ribbons to hold flowers.

Corgi toys, English, 1966–67 [R, per car]

Cornucopia

Joseff of Hollywood camel pin, one of many pieces
produced echoing the popular movie
The Thief of Baghdad, 1940s [Q]

Chanel collar necklace in gold plate
and glass emeralds and rubies, designed by
Robert Goossens, 1950s [H]

Necklace and earrings by Stanley Hagler,
New York, designed by Ian St Gielar, and showing
skilful use of Venetian glass, 1970s [M]

Costume jewellery

In the last hundred years, with changes in culture, materials and manufacturing processes, the wearing of jewellery has crossed social divides and costume jewellery has become an art form in its own right.

Jewellery for all

The 20th century saw a radical change in jewellery fashions, as designers and manufacturers freed themselves from the constraints of using gems and precious metals. Costume jewellery has seen a new wave of design with radically different criteria. It has become associated with innovative creations comprising inexpensive materials and, in many cases, high quality craftsmanship. Instead of gold and diamonds, stylish jewellery could be manufactured from brass, chromium, bakelite, wood and glass. Pieces were often inspired by events such as the discovery of Tutankhamen's tomb in 1922–23 or movements such as ART NOUVEAU and the designs of the WIENER WERKSTÄTTE and BAUHAUS. Original examples by designers such as Joseph HOFFMANN and Koloman MOSER are now very sought after, but die-stamped silver jewellery of the period with enamelled decoration and inspired by such designers can still be found in a wide range of prices.

Trifari blueberry pin, late
1950 [S] and bug pin
designed by Alfred
Philippe, 1940s/50s [O]

Paris in the 1920s and 30s was the centre of world fashion and costume jewellery developed rapidly into incredible flights of fancy with designers such as René LALIQUE and Jean DUNAND. The Americans, too, developed an insatiable appetite for costume jewellery. An increasing number of women in the US could afford jewellery made from high-quality imitation stones, or revolutionary plastics and alloys. It was this period that saw the rise of the best-known designers and manufacturers such as Marcel Boucher, Hattie Carnegie, Coro, Inc. (Corocraft), Miriam Haskell, Hobé, Mazer & Co. and Trifari. Hollywood jewellers such as Joseff designed for the most spectacular movies as well as ranges for mass-production.

During World War II, the manufacture of costume jewellery continued on a large scale in the US, while in the UK austerity jewellery in the form of bakelite Scottie dogs and patriotic symbols was more characteristic. However, the couture houses of Chanel and Schiaparelli, who moved to the US during the war, proved a foil to this bleakness, producing some of the finest and most sought-after examples of costume jewellery ever made.

Post-war prosperity increased demand. Through the 1940s, 50s and 60s, Dior, Yves St Laurent, Paco Rabanne, Lanvin and Pucci have produced an ever-diverse selection of designs. American designers such as Kenneth Jay Lane and Stanley Hagler were also highly influential. Trifari retained its popularity, aided by Mamie Eisenhower who commissioned parures from them for the presidential inaugurations of the 1950s. In Britain, Butler & Wilson, originally antique dealers, used their stock of Art Nouveau, Art Deco and antique pieces to inspire a new decorative range of costume jewellery. Giorgio Armani commissioned a collection from them in 1984, thus establishing their worldwide reputation.

Coromandel lacquer
A LACQUER technique used most commonly on folding screens. A wooden screen is coated with a layer of white chalk and then lacquered. The lacquer is cut away in a pattern to reveal the underlying layer, which is then painted or coloured. These screens were popular in Europe from the 17th century, when they were imported from India's Coromandel coast, and are still being produced today.

Coromandel tree
(*Diospyros melanoxylon*)
A tree native to the Coromandel coast of India. Produces a timber known also as "Bombay" EBONY. The fine-grained jet-black hardwood has distinctive yellow stripes and was used on high-quality furniture, especially during the Regency period, for BANDING, STRINGING and VENEERING.

Corona A type of 19th-century metal lighting fixture, similar to a chandelier, of one or more hoops with sockets for lamps or candles.

Corsage Worn extensively in the 18th and 19th centuries, a corsage jewel was usually a bold and imposing BROOCH set with diamonds and gems, with clasps, chains and tassels.

Cotswold School A term used for furniture that cannot be ascribed to a known maker, but that is handmade and in keeping with ARTS AND CRAFTS principles, in particular the work of Ernest GIMSON and Sydney and Ernest BARNSLEY, who originally had workshops in the Cotswolds, Gloucestershire, England. The term can also be applied to second-generation makers of the style.

Coromandel lacquer screen, early 18th century [C]

Cottage A pottery or porcelain model, mostly English, made in large quantities in the 19th and 20th centuries. They may be in two sections for use as a PASTILLE BURNER, or in one with a slit in the roof, for use as a money box. Some were models of notorious houses.

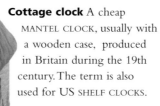

Earthenware Art Cottage, 1930s [R]

Cottage clock A cheap MANTEL CLOCK, usually with a wooden case, produced in Britain during the 19th century. The term is also used for US SHELF CLOCKS.

Couch A much extended chair, also known as a DAY BED or CHAISE LONGUE.

Couched work An embroidery technique, common from the 16th century, in which a decorative thread is sewn onto a ground fabric by another thread.

Counter box A 17th-century silver box, sometimes pierced, made to hold a set of gaming counters. In the late 18th century, they were also made of turned ivory.

Count wheel A metal wheel with a segmented edge or with pins on one side, used to control the striking TRAIN in early clocks. Replaced from the late 17th century by the "rack and snail" device.

Coup perdu (French: "lost stroke")
A type of clock, usually French, that has a pendulum beating half-seconds but which registers full seconds with its seconds hand. The ESCAPEMENT allows the escape wheel to advance once for each alternate, rather than full, swing of the pendulum.

Courtauld, Augustus (*c.*1686–1751)
An English silversmith who learned his trade in a Huguenot workshop. His best-known work is the Swordbearer's Salt in London's Mansion House. His son Samuel (1720–65) worked in the Rococo style.

Court cupboard (French *court*: "short")
A low or short cupboard, consisting initially of open tiers used to display plates. Such cupboards were first made in England in the late 16th century, usually in oak, and in Britain and America in the 17th centuries. They were widely imitated in the 19th century.

Court cupboard, English c.1670 [E]

Courting mirror An early American style of mirror, in which the frame was made of strips of glass held in a metal surround and painted.

Cow creamer A milk or cream jug in the form of a cow, with the mouth as the spout and the tail looped over the back as a handle, made from the mid-18th century. One of the most famous makers of creamers in silver was John Schuppe. Numerous Staffordshire potters created them in ceramics.

Cozzi porcelain factory Established in 1764 by Geminiano Cozzi in the San Giobbe district of Venice, with support from the Venetian Senate. Cozzi learned the art of porcelain-making from the German Nathaniel Hewelke (who had a factory in Udine) and from some workers from the Le NOVE porcelain factory. He made HARD-PASTE PORCELAIN and produced tablewares, snuff-boxes, cane handles and figures. The mark was a large red anchor. The factory closed in 1812.

Crabstock The handle of a tea- or coffeepot modelled as a branch of a crab apple tree, usually on pottery with the body of the pot in the form of a fruit.

Crace, John Gregory (1809–89) An English designer of interiors and furniture. His grandfather John Crace (1754–1819) worked on the NEO-CLASSICAL interior of Carlton House for the Prince Regent, and his father, Frederick Crace (1779–1859), was responsible for the interior of the Royal Pavilion, Brighton. His son, John Diblee Crace (1838–1917), specialized in interiors in Italian Renaissance style. John Gregory joined the family firm in 1826 and was associated with A.W.N. PUGIN and the GOTHIC REVIVAL interiors of the new Palace of Westminster and with the Medieval Court at the GREAT EXHIBITION.

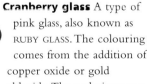

Cranberry drinking glass, English c.1880 [R]

Cracked ice A term used of Chinese porcelain to describe a blue ground that represents the frozen water of rivers with white lines indicating cracking ice. This decoration symbolizes the end of winter and the coming of spring.

Crackle (crackling) The deliberate crazing of ceramics for decorative effect. First discovered in the SONG DYNASTY (960–1279) in Kuan wares, it was exploited by later Chinese potters and imitated in Western ceramics from the late 19th century onward, especially in STUDIO POTTERY. The similar term "craquelure" describes age cracks in the varnish of oil paintings.

Crackle on a Christopher Dresser bowl, 1890s [P]

Crackled glass See ICE GLASS.

Craftsman style A term used to describe US ARTS AND CRAFTS architecture, interior decoration, furniture and ceramics, from the 1890s until the end of World War I. The term is taken from Gustav STICKLEY's trademark "Craftsman Furniture" introduced c.1900. In 1901 Stickley founded a periodical called *The Craftsman*, published until 1916, which helped spread his concepts of "simplicity, honesty and integrity" in design and so promoted the Craftsman style. The style was taken up at the same time by potters such as Adelaide ROBINEAU and tilemakers such as Ernest Batchelder who had been in touch with the ARTS AND CRAFTS movement in Europe.

Cranberry glass A type of pink glass, also known as RUBY GLASS. The colouring comes from the addition of copper oxide or gold chloride. The technique was known to the ancient Romans but was at its most popular in Victorian England. Most was made at STOURBRIDGE. American cranberry glass was made at various glassworks including SANDWICH.

Cranbrook Academy A US school of design founded in Bloomfield Hills, Michigan, by the newspaper magnate George G. Booth in 1925, under the directorship of the Finnish architect Eliel Saarinen, who also designed the campus buildings. Cranbrook was at the hub of American Modernism, particularly the "Organic" style. Graduates include Harry BERTOIA, Charles EAMES, Florence Knoll and Eero SAARINEN, son of the director.

Crane, Walter (1845–1915) An influential British painter and designer in the ARTS AND CRAFTS MOVEMENT. He was the ART WORKERS GUILD's first president and became principal of the Royal College of Art. Well known for his paintings and book illustrations, he also designed furniture, ceramics and textiles.

Tile by Walter Crane, late 19th century [Q]

Crane motif A motif appearing in both Roman ornament and medieval church decoration as a symbol of vigilance. The crane also features in Oriental art, as a messenger of the gods in China, and as an emblem of happiness and prosperity in Japan. In the 18th century, the crane played a leading role in CHINOISERIE decorative schemes, frequently paired with the HO HO BIRD.

Crafts Revival

This 20th-century movement in applied arts advocated a return to high quality hand craftsmanship, the use of natural materials and the production of unique objects or limited series.

Crafts in the US

The movement began in the US in the late 1950s, mainly as a reaction against the standardization and poor quality of many mass-produced goods and the perceived austerity of the MODERN MOVEMENT. Though influenced by the organic forms and materials of Scandinavian design after World War II, it is more of a survival than a revival of craft traditions, following on from the CRAFTSMAN STYLE of the early 20th century.

The development of the Crafts Revival movement in the US was reinforced by the influx of refugee artists from Europe, some of whom had trained at the BAUHAUS, for example Margarete Friedlander (1896–1985), a ceramicist who worked in California from the 1940s. The STUDIO GLASS and STUDIO POTTERY movements, which emphasized form, colour and technique rather than applied ornament, also contributed to the Crafts Revival.

Studio potters such as Gertrud (1908–71) and Otto Natzler (b.1908), who emigrated from Austria to the US in 1938, produced earthenware with rough-textured glazes. From the mid-1950s, the studio pottery movement was also influenced by current fine art movements, particularly in the work of Peter Voulkos (b.1924), who produced sculptural, wheel-thrown and modelled ware assembled from apparently disparate pieces of clay and with random colouring. Studio glass-makers such as Dale Chihuly (b.1941) also experimented with various techniques, especially hot glass. Crafts Revival furniture, for example by Wendell CASTLE, continued to be influenced by ARTS AND CRAFTS traditions. Castle emphasized the aesthetic qualities of materials by hand-carving rare and expensive woods.

The British tradition

In Britain, the craft tradition was strengthened in the post-World War II period by the emergence of the new profession of the designer-maker and by the establishment of the Crafts Council in 1975. The work of the furniture-maker Gordon RUSSELL combined traditional construction with a limited use of luxury materials such as ivory and of ART DECO motifs such as sunbursts. HEAL & SON produced limed oak furniture in limited editions, featuring simple rectilinear designs with minimal ornament. The studio ceramics movement flourished from the 1920s, under the influence of Bernard LEACH and his apprentice Michael CARDEW. As in the US, significant artist-potters included refugees from mainland Europe, notably Lucie RIE and Hans COPER. In furniture-making, John MAKEPEACE and his followers created pieces in organic shapes and different woods showing great respect for the nature and figure of the wood itself.

Dwarf chest-of-drawers in satin birch by Gordon Russell, 1930s [H]

Large covered stoneware container by Peter Voulkos, c.1955 [Q]

"Seaform" piece by the American art glassworker Dale Chihuly, 1980s [C]

Hand-carved hickory seat by John Makepeace, 1983 [G]

Crazing A fine network of cracks in a ceramic GLAZE, caused by the accidental unequal shrinkage of the body and the glaze during the cooling after firing.

Creamware A refined cream-coloured EARTHENWARE that was the potter's answer to the rival PORCELAIN. Early in the 18th century, Staffordshire potters had created a white ware of light weight and thin gauge with a smooth LEAD GLAZE, which had ousted tin-glazed DELFTWARE. When the white body was fired to a high temperature it produced a STONEWARE. But, fired to a medium temperature and combined with a lead glaze, a new cream-coloured ware evolved. Introduced *c*.1740 this became popular with Staffordshire, Yorkshire

Creamware coffeepot, English c.1780 [Q]

and other potters. WEDGWOOD called it QUEENSWARE in 1767, but the usual term was "cream colour", the abbreviation for which is "cc". Creamware soon superseded other bodies and Wedgwood and others built up a flourishing export trade. It was decorated with RELIEF moulding, painting and OVERGLAZE printing. Apart from creamware made at Wedgwood, LEEDS and a few other potteries, it is mostly unmarked and therefore difficult to attribute.

Credence table A type of semicircular domestic SIDE TABLE with a hinged top that folds out and is supported on a gate-leg underframe. Credence tables of oak or walnut were made in Britain from the second half of the 17th century. In the 19th century such space-saving tables were often used to prepare the sacrament in English churches and the name "credence table" now only refers to such church tables.

Credenza The Italian term for a serving table, CREDENCE table or sideboard. It was popularly used in the 19th century as a side cabinet with a central door flanked by display shelves.

Creil et Montereau A French FAIENCE factory founded *c*.1796. It also tried to produce porcelain but without success. The factory united with Montereau in the early 19th century and continued until 1895, producing cream-coloured and white EARTHENWARE, much of which was purchased and TRANSFER-PRINTED by Stone, Coquerel & Le Gros. The views of Paris, French châteaux and English country houses are very popular. Montereau continued using the name until 1955.

Cressent, Charles (1685–1768) A French furniture-maker. He trained as a sculptor in Amiens but later turned to furniture-making, becoming one of the leading exponents of the RÉGENCE and ROCOCO styles. His superb COMMODES and clock cases, decorated with elaborate ORMOLU mounts which he cast and gilded himself, were produced for many royal and aristocratic European clients.

Cresson, Louis (1706–71) An important French furniture-maker who was born into a respected dynasty of Parisian MENUISIERS. In 1738 he became a master joiner and built his reputation as the most talented of the Cresson family with a range of chairs and other elegant upholstered furniture for an aristocratic clientele that included the royal household of Louis XV.

Early Louis XV giltwood armchair by Louis Cresson, c.1740 [c, a pair]

Crested ware Ceramic souvenirs decorated with the coats of arms of various seaside resorts. Crested china was popular in the late 19th and early 20th centuries, when vast quantities were made in England and Germany. See also GOSS PORCELAIN FACTORY.

Cresting Carved wooden decoration along the top of a horizontal member, typically found on CASE FURNITURE, mirrors, picture frames and the TOP RAILS of chairs.

Crewelwork A technique in embroidery using a wool thread on a linen or linen-mix ground, usually worked in chain stitch to create free-

Oak credence table, English c.1680 [F]

flowing designs, often depicting foliage, but sometimes also incorporating animals and birds. Fashionable during the 17th and 18th centuries, it is found most commonly on large-scale bed- and wall-hangings, curtains and coverlets. Crewelwork was revived in the mid-19th century.

Crewelwork bed-hanging, English late 17th century [E]

Cricket gourd A vessel traditionally used in China to keep singing crickets. Made from a hard-rinded fleshy fruit of the cucumber family, and often embellished with Huo Hui (fire painting), a decorative technique in which lines are scorched on the surface with a hot metal needle. The lids are made from a diverse range of materials, such as sandalwood, jade, ivory, mother-of-pearl, tortoiseshell and coconut shell.

Cricket memorabilia Cricket began in England c.1744. The range of collectors' items is varied: autographed memorabilia, unusual patents, bats, balls, stumps (before 1776 only two stumps were used), team photographs, art work, books including the famous *Wisden Cricketers' Almanac*, table/parlour games (from the turn of the 20th century), trophies, lapel pins, medals, advertising cards and figurines.

Cricket table A type of small, plain table with three legs made throughout the 17th century, generally with a circular top with a triangular frieze below and a triangular shelf joining the three legs.

Cristallo The Italian name for colourless SODA GLASS, developed in Venice in the mid-15th century. It remained malleable for a long time after heating and so was particularly suited to elaborate shapes. Too hard for cut or carved decoration, cristallo glass was embellished with enamelled and gilded decoration or trailing.

Crizzling A defect in the body of glass made with an excess of lead alkali, which produces a network of internal cracks and may make the glass crumble and decompose. George RAVENSCROFT solved the defect in 1676 by adding lead oxide.

Crock In the United States, a SALT-GLAZED stoneware utilitarian or commercial vessel, made throughout the eastern states during most of the 19th and early 20th centuries. The most valuable crocks are early and attributable to, for example, Hubbell & Chesebro, New York or William E. Warner, New York, with unusual folk art decoration in cobalt blue.

Cromwellian style The decorative arts, particularly relating to furniture and silver, produced during the English Commonwealth (1649–60), the government established by Oliver Cromwell. Owing to the influence of the Puritans and the absence of royal patronage, production of the decorative arts decreased dramatically, and those items that were made at this time are distinguished by austere forms with little or no applied ornament.

Cros, Henri (1840–1907) French sculptor, glass and ceramic artist, who rediscovered PÂTE-DE-VERRE (a process long favoured by the ancient Egyptians) after many years of research. From 1893, he worked for SÈVRES.

Crossbanding

Crossbanding A line of decorative VENEER in which the veneer runs at right angles to the main veneer or timber on the drawer, panel, door or table top of which it forms the edge.

Crossbow A projectile weapon consisting of a bow mounted crosswise on a wooden shaft called a tiller. Crossbows were used in China from 400 BC onward. Their first use in European warfare dates from c.AD 1000 and they were obsolete by the mid-16th century. They continue to be used for hunting and sport shooting to the present day.

Cross-stitch A simple stitch in which two diagonal stitches are placed across a ground thread at right angles to each other. forming an X. Used throughout the world it became so popular in 19th-century sampler-making that it is occasionally referred to as "sampler stitch".

Cross-stitched bed curtains, French 18th century [B]

Crouch ware English stoneware made of common clay and sand-glazed with salt – usually of a greenish tint. Most crouch ware was made in Staffordshire in the late 17th and 18th century.

Crown Derby A porcelain factory established in 1876 in Derby, England, by William Litherland and Edward Phillips

Royal Crown Derby dish, c.1888 [o]

and called Derby Crown Porcelain Co. until 1890 when it became Royal Crown Derby Porcelain, following the award of a Royal Warrant. They made, and still make, richly decorated pieces of a very thin porcelain, painted by excellent artists such as Albert Gregory and Cuthbert Gresley. The finest all-round decorator was Désiré Leroy who did painting, jewelling, gilding and burnishing. He died in 1908 – his work is now keenly collected, very expensive and almost always signed.

Crown Devon Pottery made by the Staffordshire firm of S. Fielding & Co., founded in 1870. Originally called Railway Pottery, then Devon Pottery from 1911. The printed mark of Crown Devon was used from 1930 onward. They produced a wide range of good quality majolica wares and earthenwares, including figurines,

Crown Devon
figurine, 1930s [k]

TOBY JUGS, wall plaques and novelty wares. The pottery closed in 1982.

Crown Ducal
A trade name used by A.G. Richardson & Co., of the Gordon Pottery, Tunstall, Staffordshire, founded in 1915, then at the Britannia Pottery in Cobridge (1924–1974). Crown Ducal specialized in decal-decorated ware; their most famous designer was Charlotte RHEAD.

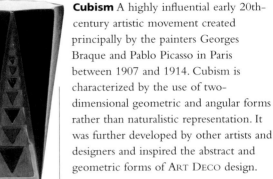

Crown Ducal
Art Deco
vase, 1930s [Q]

Crown glass Blown sheet-glass made in a large flat disc with a central bull's eye and concentric wavy lines that produce a slight rippling effect.

Cruet A small glass bottle or jug with a stopper, to hold condiments such as oil or vinegar. They were made in various shapes and types of glass, as single items or in sets.

Cruet set, English c.1849 [o]

Crystal See LEAD CRYSTAL.

Crystalline glaze A glaze with crystals of zinc or calcium suspended in it, creating patches of colour. The effect is produced by cooling the kiln in which the ware has been fired extremely slowly.

C-scroll A variation on Classical scrolled ornament developed in the ROCOCO period when the curved forms of C- and S-SCROLLS were used to create a fancy framework for other motifs.

Cubism A highly influential early 20th-century artistic movement created principally by the painters Georges Braque and Pablo Picasso in Paris between 1907 and 1914. Cubism is characterized by the use of two-dimensional geometric and angular forms rather than naturalistic representation. It was further developed by other artists and designers and inspired the abstract and geometric forms of ART DECO design.

Cuckoo clock A type of BLACK FOREST CLOCK with an elaborate carved wooden case (sometimes in the form of a chalet) from which a wooden cuckoo emerges when activated by the striking mechanism. Some also include two small organ pipes emitting simulated birdsong. Cuckoo clocks were mass-produced from the mid-19th century onward, and are still being made today, mainly as souvenirs of the Black Forest region.

Cufflinks Sleeve fasteners on men's shirts, made from various metals and materials, which gained popularity at the end of the 19th century. Cufflinks are often collected today, especially sporting, novelty or signed items by CARTIER or FABERGÉ.

Cuirass (French: "breastplate") A piece of ARMOUR that protects the torso and could be worn without other armour. They have been in use in warfare from early times to the present day.

Cuir bouilli (French: "boiled leather") A technique known in Europe from the 14th century. Leather was soaked or boiled to make it soft (although actual boiling is not necessary) after which it could be moulded into a shape such as a cup, flask or casket, then tooled or punched. Once dried, it would set in the desired shape, becoming rigid.

Cullet Fragments of scrap glass added to the ingredients of a new glass batch.

Cup and cover Turned decoration, frequently used on furniture legs and BALUSTERS from the mid-16th century. A bulbous shape resembling a deep-bowled cup is topped with a domed lid.

Cupboard A term now used to describe a piece of closed storage furniture with a door on the front. The earliest cupboards were open sets of shelves (see COURT CUPBOARD); the earliest type of small closed cupboard or AUMBRY with one door was soon adapted into new forms with two doors, two storeys with four doors, and from the 16th century became increasingly elaborate, with carved COLUMNS and CORNICES. See also ARMOIRE; LIVERY CUPBOARD.

Cupid motif (Latin *cupido*: "desire") The Roman god of love (or Eros in Greece) was a favourite subject for Classical ornament. A popular theme in RENAISSANCE decoration and emblem books, Cupid frequently appears in the company of his mother, Venus, with a bow, quiver and arrows. The Cupid motif became ubiquitous as an emblem of love during the 18th century, adorning bedroom furniture, decorative panelling and marriage gifts. Cupid also appears alongside a personification of Time symbolizing the popular theme of Love's triumph over Time, a favourite subject on 18th-century French clocks.

Cushion drawer A drawer with a front that is convex from top to bottom and runs the full width of the piece. Such drawers were usually found on walnut or oak secretaire-cabinets in the late 17th and early 18th centuries and may have been VENEERED or BANDED.

Cut-card work Relief decoration on silver articles of HUGUENOT origin that was popular in England and France in the late 17th and early 18th centuries. A pattern of swirls, leaves or flames, for example, is cut from a thin sheet of silver, and is then overlaid and soldered to the body or cover of a piece.

Cut glass A term used for glassware decorated with grooves and facets cut by hand or by a wheel. The technique was developed in Ancient Egypt *c*.700 BC and is the earliest form of glass decoration. It was widely used in BOHEMIA in the 16th and 17th centuries and in English and Irish LEAD CRYSTAL in the 18th century. The development of lead glass *c*.1676 was a major breakthrough as the thick, soft glass was ideally suited to cut decoration and allowed for deeper and more elaborate cutting. This started a fashion for cut glass in a wide range of styles that reached its peak in the late 19th-century with the highly polished American "brilliant" style cut glass.

Cutlass A sword with a short, broad single-edged blade, sometimes slightly curved, in use from the 15th century. During the 18th and 19th centuries, its size made the cutlass ideal for use on a ship and the name was then usually confined to naval swords.

Cutlery Traditionally, articles made by a cutler, who was responsible for edged weapons such as swords as well as some eating utensils, namely knives. The term is now often incorrectly used to include spoons and forks and services of FLATWARE but really only applies to pieces with a cutting edge.

Cut glass styles

The patterns in cut glass are formed by cutting with small disc tools, originally made of sandstone but now diamond, that rotate on a lathe. The diamonds or flutes can be either in relief or intaglio and the patterns are created by a process analogous to chip carving. Cutting leaves a matt surface which is then polished to produce a smooth reflective surface.

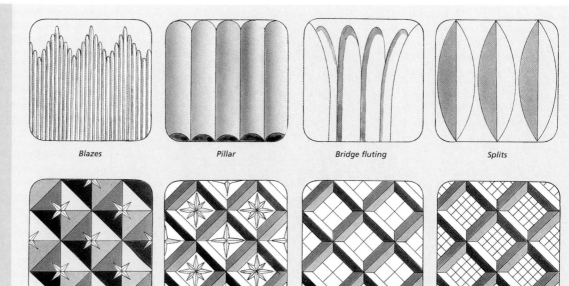

Blazes

Pillar

Bridge fluting

Splits

Cross-cut diamond

Hobnail

Chequered diamond

Strawberry diamond

Cutlery urn A KNIFE BOX in the form of a lidded urn, usually in mahogany or satinwood. The vase-shaped form was introduced in the 1780s and made in pairs to stand at either end of a sideboard. It remained popular until the early 19th century, when the fitted cutlery drawer superseded the knife box.

Cymric style enamel and silver brooch from Liberty, c.1900 [L]

Cut steel Jewellery made by riveting faceted steel studs onto plates to imitate gems, used extensively in 18th- and 19th-century England. The best known maker was Matthew BOULTON, who produced jewellery and accessories such as shoe buckles and CHATELAINES. The main areas of manufacture were Woodstock in Oxfordshire, London and Birmingham.

Cylinder escapement Perfected by the clock and watch maker George Graham in the early 1700s, the cylinder escapement was a vast improvement in timekeeping over its predecessor the VERGE ESCAPEMENT. The escape wheel comes into direct contact with the balance wheel and is also known as a frictional rest escapement.

Cylinder fall A type of BUREAU or DESK with a curving or TAMBOUR roll top made up of horizontal slats or a single curved section of wood, often elaborately inlaid, that slides up and back to reveal the writing surface. First introduced in the 18th century, possibly by one of its most famous exponents, Jean-François OEBEN, the cylinder fall front is still in use today.

Cymric style A range of ART NOUVEAU silver jewellery and other small wares made by LIBERTY & CO. in conjunction with W.H. Haseler, silversmiths in Birmingham. Designers such as Archibald KNOX and Oliver Baker were commissioned by Liberty's. The name reflects the fact that the style was heavily influenced by CELTIC motifs.

Cyphers (or ciphers) A method of secret writing using substitution or transposition of letters, or a design consisting of interwoven letters, used as a monogram or on a seal, or on porcelain forming part of the decoration.

Cypress (*Cupressus sempervirens*) A conifer native to Iran and the Middle East. Its wood is aromatic, with a close reddish grain that is highly resistant to worm and moth. Cypress was widely used for small storage boxes and linen chests from the end of the 16th century.

Satinwood cylinder fall desk, English c.1900 [H]

D

Dagger A general term for a short-bladed stabbing weapon. The dagger is one of humanity's oldest weapons and is encountered globally. It has been made from a variety of materials – flint, bone, wood, copper, bronze, iron and even plastic. Major types of dagger include the Baselard, DIRK, stiletto, eared dagger, rondel and Swiss dagger. The *main-gauche* dagger was carried in the left hand, as the name suggests, and used in conjunction with the RAPIER.

Russian dagger and sheath, c.1880 [J]

Daguerreotype The first practical photographic process, invented by L.J.M. Daguerre in 1839. The Daguerreotype is a direct positive image on a metal plate and was the main means of processing until the 1850s. Daguerreotype images are sometimes hand-tinted and slotted into special cases, or fitted in lockets or other jewellery. A daguerreotype cannot be duplicated and so each image is unique.

Daisho (Japanese: "long and short"; "pair of swords".) The long and short swords carried by Japanese samurai (warriors). Both swords had identical guards, hilt mounts and scabbard decoration.

Damascening A method of decorating metal, usually steel, in which silver or gold wire is inlaid into a pattern of fine grooves and hammered flush with the surface. Developed by metalworkers in the Near East, the technique was first used in Europe in Italy in the late 16th century on swords and armour. It was popular in the mid-19th century for presentation pieces. The term also refers to the method of creating a watered pattern on steel, especially sword blades.

Damascus twist A technique for making gun barrels. Iron and steel wire is beaten into a ribbon, which is wound around a mandrel. The whole is hammer-welded at white heat to form the barrel tube.

Damascus twist on English 12-bore, 1897 [D]

Damask A rich woven fabric usually of silk, linen or cotton, based on a satin weave. Damask relies for its effect on the different way light is reflected from the warp and weft threads. Originally deriving its name from Damascus, in Syria, damasks were imported into Europe from the 15th century. From the 16th century heavy damask was used for furnishing fabric and linen damask started to appear in household table inventories.

Darning sampler Popular from the late 18th century until *c.*1830, darning samplers were usually worked at school or under the instruction of a governess. They demonstrated a girl's ability to work darns that simulated a variety of woven cloths. They often included floral motifs infilled with darning techniques.

Date aperture A small opening on a clock or watch dial displaying the date. See also CALENDAR aperture.

Date letter First instituted in 1478, a letter of the alphabet stamped with a punch in conjunction with HALLMARKS on British silver. Each letter represents a specific year, so recording officially the exact date of manufacture of an article.

Daumenglas The German term for a cylindrical or barrel-shaped beaker made in Germany and the Low Countries in the 16th and 17th centuries that tapers inwards towards the mouth, with circular "thumb" and "finger" grips to the sides.

Daum Frères A French glassworks in Nancy, France, taken over by Jean Daum (1825–85) as a bad debt (1878). His sons joined the firm: Auguste (1853–1909) in 1879 and Antonin (1864–1931) in 1887. It was the two brothers who transformed the works into an artistic force to be reckoned with. Inspired by the work of GALLÉ and others, they employed specialist decorators. They made cameo and wheel carved glass, later ART DECO and post-war sculptural pieces. Salvador Dali designed for them in the 1970s. The glassworks still exist today.

Davenport pottery and porcelain factory A large firm trading for some 90 years from 1795. After working in Dublin and Liverpool, John Davenport (b.1765), took over a pottery in Longport in Staffordshire, at first producing EARTHENWARE, but about 1800 he started to make PORCELAIN tablewares and well-decorated REGENCY vases. The firm also made plaques (with the impressed mark of Davenport). It closed in 1887.

Davenport porcelain tazza, *c.*1840 [Q]

Davenport writing desk A narrow chest-of-drawers with a sloping writing surface and a flat ledge behind it, usually fitted with small drawers. First made in the last decade of the 18th century, reputedly for a Captain Davenport. Usually made from mahogany, rosewood or burr-walnut, the davenport remained popular as a ladies' writing desk until the end of the 19th century.

In American furniture terminology, a davenport is a large parlour sofa, normally mid- to late 19th century, which may include a mechanically extending bed.

Dawes library chair A type of mahogany library chair, the back of which reclined at the press of a lever. It often also incorporated a retractable GOUT STOOL. Such chairs were made from *c.*1825–40 by Dawes, an English furniture manufacturing company.

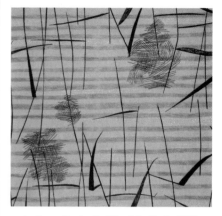

Lucienne Day textile "Tarn" for Heals, 1958 [N, for double bedspread size]

Day, Lucienne (b.1917) A textile designer important in post-war British design. Her designs for HEAL'S and Edinburgh Weavers embody simplicity of form, fitness for function and appropriate ornament. In 1951, her "Calyx" design for a screen printed linen won a gold medal in the Milan Triennale.

Davenport, English *c.*1815 [H]

Day, Robin (b.1915) An English furniture designer. In 1948 he opened a design studio in London with his wife, the textile designer Lucienne DAY, and became particularly well known for an innovative range of furniture designs for Hille Ltd, in particular the Hillestak chair (1950) and the moulded plastic Polyprop chair (Mark I, 1962; Mark II, 1963), which were all designed to be stacked and enjoyed a revival in the 1990s.

Day bed A term used virtually interchangeably with CHAISE LONGUE and COUCH to describe an elongated chair, usually without side-supports, sometimes in two parts with a separate footstool.

Deadbeat escapement A type of ANCHOR ESCAPEMENT used in precision timekeepers such as REGULATORS and supposedly first developed by the British clockmaker George GRAHAM in the early 18th century. It is more accurate than the ordinary anchor escapement because of the design of its pallets.

Deal The trade term for various softwoods including species of pine, spruce and hemlock used for inexpensive furniture. The white or pale yellow wood was a popular choice for cheap CARCASSES and was often veneered, or stained or coloured to imitate more expensive hardwoods such as EBONY or MAHOGANY, or enhanced with painted decoration in the 19th century.

Dean's Rag Book Co. One of Britain's oldest surviving toy manufacturers founded in 1903 by Henry Samuel Dean. Already well known for its children's rag books, Dean's started selling bears in 1915. One of Dean's most unusual bears is the "true to life" designed in the 1950s.

Decanter A decorative, typically handle-less, glass container with a matching stopper, used for serving wine, sherry and spirits that have been emptied from the bottle (decanted). First made in the mid-17th century, the shapes and designs are plainer than those of the 19th century, which are more elaborate. Sizes and shapes are dependent upon which type of drink they held and also upon contemporary fashions.

Deck, Theodore (1823–91) A French ceramicist. He began by making ceramic stoves before establishing his own pottery in Paris producing ceramics in the Persian style and later Chinese- and Japanese-influenced designs. He commissioned

Theodore Deck plate,
c.1880 [M]

talented artists to decorate wall plaques for him including Felix BRACQUEMOND. The rich, turquoise glaze that he often used became known as *bleu de Deck*. In his last years, he was head of the SÈVRES factory and later director of HAVILAND at Auteuil.

Decorative motif See MOTIFS.

Décor bois A decoration simulating wood, painted on porcelain, sometimes with panels of pictures for a TROMPE L'OEIL effect. Usually European, from the French factory of NIDERVILLER, in particular.

Décorchemont, François-Emile (1880–1917) A French glass-maker. He trained as a painter and potter, but in 1902 set up a glass workshop in Conches, where he produced thick-walled PÂTE DE VERRE vases and bowls with textured exteriors and smooth interiors coloured with metallic oxides and *pâte-de-cristal* pieces. Art deco and Neo-classical designs are typical.

Decanters

The decanter shape stemmed from the jug, with the neck being made narrower for a stopper. Some, like the claret decanter shown right, retained their handles. Others were enamelled or engraved or, in the 19th century, made of cut lead crystal. Rings round the neck improved the grip for pouring. The "ship's decanter" was made with an especially squat shape for stability. The stoppers too varied in shape, from lozenge and mushroom, to flat or cut in facets.

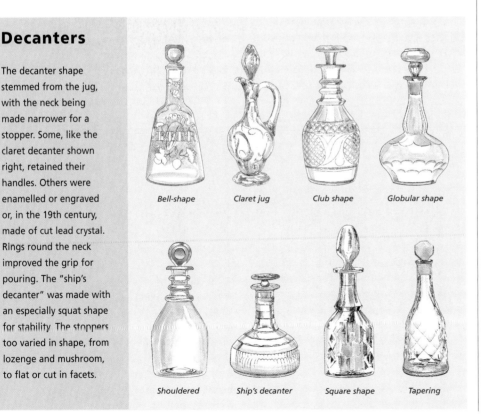

Bell-shape   Claret jug   Club shape   Globular shape

Shouldered   Ship's decanter   Square shape   Tapering

Découpage The art of decorating household objects and furniture with images made from colourful paper cut-outs glued onto surfaces. Originating in 12th century China, it flourished in Europe from the 18th century to the Victorian era, when collages were created with a bold, sentimental feel.

Dedham Pottery (1896–1943) See CHELSEA KERAMIC ART WORKS.

Dehua porcelain factories These factories at Dehua, near Foochow in the Fujian province of south-east China, have produced BLANC-DE-CHINE, from the MING DYNASTY (1368–1644) to the present day. Large quantities arrived in Europe as CHINESE EXPORT PORCELAIN in the early 18th century and it was copied at MEISSEN and elsewhere. Crisply modelled figures with a smooth white glaze were popular as were joss-stick holders, brush pots, DOGS OF FO, libation cups and boxes.

Delaherche, Auguste (1857–1940) A French art potter who opened his own studio in 1887 making stoneware inspired by the Orient, using the thick running glazes of Japan and with floral or figured decoration. In the 1890s, he increasingly used porcelain with various experimental oxidized, reduced copper flambé and crystalline glazes. From 1904 one-off white pieces featured stylized flowers.

De Lamerie See LAMERIE, PAUL DE.

Delft ware The town of Delft in Holland became important in the 17th century for the manufacture of tin-enamelled earthenware. Delft ware was originally inspired by the BLUE AND WHITE porcelain brought to Europe from

Delft mantel clock, early 19th century [H]

the Orient by the ships of the Dutch East India Company. In 1659 there were 23 workshops in the area; by 1680 there were about 30.

During the 18th century, manufacturing steadily declined – due firstly to the competition from porcelain and later from the creamware producers. By 1850, almost all the Delft manufactories had gone out of business but the industry was revived and Dutch Delft is still made as reproductions.

Among the many factories in Delft were: *De Drie Klokken* (Three Bells) 1671–1845, first owned by Barbara Rottewel, followed by her son and finally from 1830–40 by Van Putten & Co.; *De Drie Porseleyne Flessies* (Three Porcelain Bottles) 1679–1764, owned until 1720 by the Kam family, bought then by Zacharias Dextra who introduced enamel colours; *De Dubbele Schenkken* (Double Jug) c.1648–second half of the 18th century; *De Grieksche A* (The Greek A) 1658–1820, made excellent products such as tulip vases, milk pans, pagoda urns – some for Hampton Court and Chatsworth in England; *De Paeuw* (The Peacock) 1651–1779 and *De Porseleyne Klaeuw* (The Porcelain Claw) 1662–1840.

Delft polychrome plate, 18th century [R]

Delftware (English delft, Dublin delft) A term used to describe a British-made TIN-GLAZED EARTHENWARE that emulates the wares from Delft in the Netherlands. This delftware is usually more thinly potted and has a shiny, slightly bluish glaze. Rarely marked, it was made in many places including London, Norwich, Bristol, Liverpool, Wincanton and Glasgow. The early wares were inspired by Chinese patterns in blue, sometimes with the addition of yellow and manganese. Wares included large dishes (chargers), smaller plates, tankards, mugs and more unusual objects such as bulb bowls, puzzle jugs, punch-bowls, barber's bowls, jugs and commemorative wares. Some early figures were made, but these are rare.

Delftware plate, English c.1750 [M]

British delftware was challenged and vanquished in the second half of the 18th century by creamware and porcelain.

Della Robbia Pottery An English ART POTTERY company begun in 1893 by H.B. Rathbone and Conrad Dressler at Birkenhead, Cheshire. Mostly made in red clay decorated with coloured slips and SGRAFFITO decoration. Pieces are marked with a galleon and D R, sgraffito and painters' monograms. Designers included Robert Anning Bell, Ford Maddox Brown and Conrad Dressler. Closed in 1906.

Della Robbia, Lucca See ROBBIA, DELLA LUCCA.

De Morgan, William Frend (1839–1917)
An English ceramicist, designer of stained glass windows and novelist, married to the artist Evelyn De Morgan. One of the finest 19th-century ART POTTERS, his designs, use of colour and mastery of glazes were outstanding. He is known for his LUSTRE glazes based on HISPANO-MORESQUE ceramics and those showing a Persian influence in turquoise, green, blue, yellow and red. He made a variety of decorative items and tiles, some featuring in William MORRIS and Philip WEBB interiors. He worked for various potteries: CHELSEA (1872), Merton Abbey (1882) and Sands End, Fulham (1889). He stopped working as a potter in 1906 and became a successful novelist instead.

De Morgan earthenware charger, c.1870 [F]

Denby Pottery Based at Denby, Derbyshire, UK, the pottery began producing Staffordshire-type STONEWARE in 1809 and is still working today. In its early days, it specialized in GIN FLASKS, later in kitchen wares, notably the fireproof ranges and other utilitarian ware such as the "Nevva-drip" teapot in the 1920s. Ornamental pieces were also made, including "Butterfly Ware" vases at the beginning of the 20th century.

Dennis, Thomas (active c.1660–1700) An English-born American carpenter and furniture-maker, active in Colonial Massachusetts and specializing in WAINSCOT CHAIRS. His style can be compared to that of his lesser-known mentor William Searle and follows the richly carved, BAROQUE taste popular at the time in the English West Country, the birthplace of both men.

Dent, Edward (1790–1853)
A prominent English maker of carriage clocks, watches and chronometers. He worked with the clockmaker John R. Arnold from 1830, but in 1840 he set up his own business. In 1851, he was awarded the commission to build the clock for the tower of the Houses of Parliament ("Big Ben"). After his death, it was completed by his stepson Frederick.

Dent Hardware Co. A leading American manufacturer of CAST IRON toy vehicles, founded in 1895 at Fullerton, Pennsylvania. The castings are particularly fine, with details such as running boards from 1910, making them easy to identify even though they are unmarked. In the 1920s they modelled planes and airships. The company still manufactures hardware but stopped making toys in the 1950s.

Dent iron horse and carriage, c.1910 [K]

Dentils, dentil rim (Latin *dens:* "tooth") An ornamental device from Classical architecture, dentils consist of a series of small rectangular blocks resembling teeth running beneath a CORNICE. In ceramics, a border painted with notches under a cornice is known as a dentil rim.

Dentil rim

Derbyshire Potteries A group of potteries in Derbyshire, including CHESTERFIELD and DENBY producing similar wares to the STAFFORDSHIRE potteries, from medieval times to the present day.

Derringer The general name for a small pocket pistol. It takes its name from Henry Derringer of Philadelphia (1786–1869) who popularized small but powerful PERCUSSION pocket pistols in the 1840s. Most major American gun-making firms produced derringers, including COLT and REMINGTON.

Colt No. 1 derringer, US c.1870 [K]

Deruta An important pottery in Umbria, central Italy, from the Middle Ages. During the Renaissance, Deruta made MAIOLICA, reaching a peak of production after 1500 with wares that were technically accomplished and painted in a warm palette of yellow, ochre and green. Some designs were influenced by the Umbrian school of painting, sometimes copying frescoes by Perugino. Deruta was also known for the technique of LUSTRE glazing, giving a subtle iridescent sheen to wares of softer colouring, typically decorated with overlapping scales and zigzag patterns. Deruta declined after 1530, but continued during the 17th century to produce much peasant-type maiolica. Today it makes popular reproductions of its traditional designs.

Derby porcelain factories

Inspired by European models, the factories at Derby in the English Midlands produced what are considered today to be some of the finest English porcelain figures. In the late 18th century it excelled in "cabinet wares" intended for display, such as painted, highly gilded dishes and vases.

Huguenot craftsmanship

Derby already had a tradition of pottery manufacture by the time that porcelain was made there. The story of its porcelain manufacture probably began with the arrival in 1748 of the modeller Andrew Planché. One of a circle of HUGUENOT craftsmen, Planché had trained as a jeweller in London, but had also probably gained experience visiting French porcelain factories. CHINOISERIE figure groups are among the first porcelain made at Derby, considered finest when left undecorated. Derby's wares of 1750–56 are sometimes known as "dry edge", as the characteristic creamy, glass-like glaze dribbled slightly and had to be wiped before firing to prevent adhesion to the kiln shelves. Towards the end of this time, some figures are decorated in pale pink, blue, yellow and green, known as the "Pale Family". Planché left Derby soon after 1756, when the factory was acquired by William DUESBURY and his business partner, the banker John Heath.

Duesbury and Heath's wares included shepherds and shepherdesses, blackamoors and leading actors of the day, all displaying the MEISSEN influence that led the factory to describe itself as the "second Dresden". TRANSFER-PRINTED wares included mugs with coronation portraits of George III and Queen Charlotte in 1761, and in 1788 the Prince of Wales ordered a dessert service with his crest.

Duesbury died in 1786 and his son, also William, guided the Derby factory through a particularly fine period in which "display wares" for a richer market were decorated by artists such as Zachariah BOREMAN (1738–1810) who painted landscapes, George Complin (active *c*.1755–95) who painted fruit and flowers, and William BILLINGSLEY (1758–1828), the greatest of all English flower-painters. William Duesbury II died in 1797. In 1811, Robert Bloor, the company clerk, bought the factory, remaining in control until 1825. In the 1830s the factory again copied contemporary Meissen designs and some from SÈVRES, but they could not compete with them or with the Staffordshire factories. It closed in 1848 but other factories in the town carried on the name, including the Derby Crown Porcelain Co. in 1870, which in 1890 became Royal CROWN DERBY and continues today.

Porcelain marks

The earliest Derby wares, are mostly unmarked. From c.1780 until the present day nearly 30 marks were used, the three illustrated being the most common. As the early marks (until c.1825) were hand-painted by different artists, many slight variations occur. Some early pieces are marked only by a model number.

c.1782–1825

c.1820–40

1862–1935

Sauce tureen decorated with naturalistic flowers, c.1785–1800 [I]

Rococo Revival shepherd candelabrum with bocage, c.1830 [M]

The fresh, naturalistic flowers on this lozenge-shaped dish are typical of this period, c.1820 [O, a pair]

Design registration

A mark printed, impressed or incised on some British ceramics, glass, metalwork and textiles from 1842 onward, indicating that the design of the object has been registered with the Patent Office. Until 1883 the mark – a form of copyright – consisted of a lozenge incorporating various numerals and letters indicating the day, month and year of registration and the class of the article (e.g. Class I for metalwork). This was replaced after 1883 by a serial number with the prefix "Rd No", "Regd." or "Regd. No.".

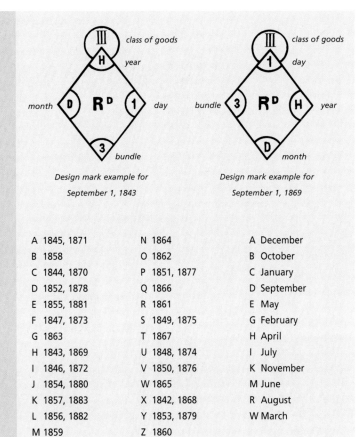

Design mark example for September 1, 1843

Design mark example for September 1, 1869

A 1845, 1871	N 1864	A December
B 1858	O 1862	B October
C 1844, 1870	P 1851, 1877	C January
D 1852, 1878	Q 1866	D September
E 1855, 1881	R 1861	E May
F 1847, 1873	S 1849, 1875	G February
G 1863	T 1867	H April
H 1843, 1869	U 1848, 1874	I July
I 1846, 1872	V 1850, 1876	K November
J 1854, 1880	W 1865	M June
K 1857, 1883	X 1842, 1868	R August
L 1856, 1882	Y 1853, 1879	W March
M 1859	Z 1860	

Desk A piece of furniture that combines a flat writing surface and drawers or other storage space for stationery. Before the late 16th century, the desk took the form of a small portable box, with a sloping lid that acted both as a book support and a writing surface and lifted up to reveal a storage space. By the end of the century, such boxes were supported on stands. Most of the different types of desk (BONHEUR DU JOUR; BUREAU; CARLTON HOUSE DESK; DAVENPORT; ESCRITOIRE; FALL FRONT) are variations on this theme.

Steel and leather stool by Deskey, 20th century [K]

Deskey, Donald (1894–1989) A US industrial designer responsible for the interior of Radio City Music Hall, New York (1932). He worked in many fields, including packaging, metal furniture, lighting, fabrics, wallpaper and interiors. In 1925 he visited the Paris Exposition and his work shows affinities to CUBISM and ART DECO. Donald Deskey Associates became one of the leading design practices in the US after World War II, designing interiors of houses, restaurants, clubs and hotels throughout the US.

Dessert service Wares used for the dessert course of a meal, which from the end of the 18th century was served after the main part of the meal (prior to that, all the food was put on the table at the same time). Sometimes dessert was served in a different room. The many confections such as ices, jellies, fruit and nuts were served on the dishes of the dessert service, which comprised ice pails, sauce tureens, COMPORTS and plates.

Detent escapement A type of ESCAPEMENT used in precision clocks, especially CHRONOMETERS. Developed in Britain in the 18th century, it incorporates a DETENT or steel catch controlling the movement of the escape wheel.

Deutsche Blumen (German: "German flowers") Naturalistic flower motifs, fashionable from c.1740. They were first used at MEISSEN and then throughout Europe as porcelain became widely used. One of the principal sources was the eight-volume florilegium, *Phytanthiza Iconographia*, 1735–45, by J.W. Weinmann which contained over 1,000 hand-coloured engravings after drawings by G.D. Ehret, J.E. Riedinger and B. Seuter.

Deutsche blumen in gilt cartouches on a Meissen tureen and cover, c.1750 [F, with stand]

Devon lace See HONITON.

Devonshire potteries Several small factories in north Devon, England, notably at Barnstaple, Bideford and Fremington, making SLIPWARE from the 17th century to the present day. The wares are similar to the products of other English slipware factories, apart from some large jugs decorated with nautical motifs, such as mariners, compasses and ships, which were made at Bideford.

Dhurri A tapestry-woven cotton carpet, rug or wall hanging made in India. Traditionally they are of a rectangular shape with fringing at either end.

Diagonal barometer
See ANGLE BAROMETER.

Dial The part of a clock or watch that displays the time. The dial consists principally of a metal or wooden plate – the DIAL PLATE – with a CHAPTER RING and hour and minute hands. Minute hands were only introduced in the late 17th century when the invention of the PENDULUM increased the accuracy of timekeeping.
See also CLOCKS.

Dial clock A circular English WALL CLOCK comprising a large round dial in a simple wooden case, with a brass bezel and glass cover. It was used in stations, shops and offices until the introduction of electric clocks in the early 20th century.

Dial plate A shaped metal or wooden plate attached to the front plate of a clock or watch movement. On clocks the dial plate is usually square, circular or arched, with the latter sometimes incorporating a STRIKE/SILENT LEVER, calendar work, automata or musical work in the arch.

Diamond Carbon in its purest state, which occurs naturally in many areas of the world in alluvial deposits and deep volcanic pipes. Diamonds are assessed according to the so-called "four Cs":
(i) Colour is the dominant factor. A "D"-colour stone is completely colourless and letters of the alphabet from D to Z define an increasing intensity of yellow.
(ii) Clarity describes the presence or lack of inclusions and imperfections where "flawless" is the top grade.
(iii) Carat defines size.
(iv) Cut describes the facetting and shape and finish of the polished stone.
Because of the complexity of diamond grading and the increasing number of convincing synthetics, many diamonds are routinely certificated. Fancy colour diamonds, notably reds, greens, blues and pinks, are among the most rare and costly of all gemstones.

Diamond-point engraving on a goblet, c.1890 [J]

Diamond-point engraving A type of glass decoration made by scratching the design onto the surface with a diamond-point stylus. This type of light decoration was mostly used on 17th-century Dutch and Italian glass, in particular wineglasses.

Diaper A decorative motif consisting of repeated diamonds, lozenges, squares or other geometrical shapes. It was used on early Tudor brickwork and later was commonly used for woven textiles and in CHINOISERIE and JAPONAISERIE decoration. The pattern was particularly favoured in the 19th century for furniture, floor tiles, ceramics, many types of textiles and wallcoverings.

Diaper

Diecast The method of making an item by injecting molten metal, usually mazak (an alloy consisting mainly of

Diecast toy truck by Corgi, c.1968 [R]

zinc), into a closed metal die or mould. The casting is removed from the die after a short cooling period.

Die-stamping A method of forming the body or part of an article, developed in the late 18th century and used in the SHEFFIELD PLATE industry. Metal sheet was sandwiched under pressure between two shaped, steel blocks or dies by machine and therefore more economically than by traditional methods.

Dimity A tough cotton fabric woven using a double warp thread for strength. It has a slightly ribbed pattern of stripes or checks and was used in household furnishings, especially bed and wall hangings from the 17th century.

Dinanderie Brassware such as candlesticks and drinking and cooking vessels, made in and around Dinant, in Belgium, in the early Middle Ages. Used in a wider sense to describe any decorative ware made in non-precious metals, especially INLAID, PATINATED or LACQUERED COPPER.

Ding (ting) ware A type of Chinese porcelain made in the TANG DYNASTY (618–906) and throughout the SONG DYNASTY (960–1279). It has an ivory white glaze, orange translucency and characteristic unglazed rims often bound with copper alloy or, more rarely, silver or gold. Conical bowls with carved, INCISED or moulded decoration are most common (formerly called "ting" ware).

Dolls

Toys in the shape of a human figure have existed in most civilizations. Evidence of them has been found in Egyptian and Roman tombs, although the earliest surviving dolls tend to date from the 18th century.

Eighteenth century

Some dolls of this date were made of wax, but most surviving English examples are of wood, usually with pine heads and torsos carved out of one piece of wood to which jointed legs and nailed or tied arms are attached. In the latter half of the century, the quality of English wooden dolls declined. Four established continental wood-carving centres gained strength with a greater output of more coarsely carved dolls: GRÖDNERTAL in Austria, and SONNEBERG, Oberammergau and Berchtesgarten in Germany. In these centres toy- and doll-making became a large industry, whose products were exported all over the Western world.

Nineteenth century

Wood was gradually replaced by other materials, while the Industrial Revolution brought changes in the manufacturing process. The wooden Grödnertal doll, popular between 1800 and 1830, captured the Empire spirit with its simple painted hairstyle. Its torso was elegantly carved, ideal for modelling the high-waisted muslin gowns *en vogue*. The Grödnertal was superseded by the Biedermeier doll, a papier-mâché creation popular between 1820 and 1850. Papier-mâché had been used as a cheaper substitute for wood since the 18th century and was suitable for moulding the elaborate hairstyles of the Biedermeier period. Although most mass-produced papier-mâché dolls were made in Germany, some, often wrongly referred to as "Pauline" types, with inset black eyes, were produced in France.

German Parian doll, c.1880, the white unglazed porcelain head resembles marble from Paros in Greece [O]

German character "Piano Baby" doll, c.1905, so called because it was intended for display on a piano [M]

German painted wooden Grödnertal doll, 1840 [M]

Bisque and how it developed

The charm and sophistication of the dolls of the last half of the 19th-century are due to the development of bisque as a raw material. At first, bisque was a stiff clay paste pressed into moulds. Later, a pourable semi-liquid clay slip was perfected, which produced a smoother surface and finer details. Bisque doll heads, and later bodies and limbs, were fired twice. After the first firing, the head was removed from the mould, cleaned, sanded and painted all over to give a skin colour. When dried, the facial details were painted on and the head fired again at a lower temperature. The most important centre of bisque doll manufacture was Thuringia, in eastern Germany.

German bisque-headed doll, c.1910, an appealing toddler doll typical of German dolls produced in this period [N]

Another commonly used material for the production of dolls' heads in the first half of the century was wax. Initially, a solid block of wax was carved and black glass bead eyes and strands of real hair were inserted. From around 1840, hollow poured wax heads took over, made by a technique perfected by two London-based Italian families, MONTANARI and PIEROTTI.

Soon, a cheaper alternative was developed known as WAX OVER COMPOSITION. This technique was used all over Europe. From about 1840, dolls made of "china" (see CHINA HEAD DOLL) were produced by porcelain factories in Germany and the rest of Europe. A continuation of the type of earlier papier-mâché dolls, they were more durable and provided the ideal ground for the newly developed dyes. The FROZEN CHARLOTTE "china" doll was made entirely of porcelain.

Bisque appeared in the second half of the century, a material that dominated the doll market until the 1920s. Up to 1875, bisque FASHION DOLLS, showing the season's latest fashions, were popular, made by such companies as the French BRU JEUNE ET CIE. By the 1880s, these were supplanted by BÉBÉS, which were produced by German factories such as JUMEAU, STEINER and Schmitt. Toward the end of the 19th century, competition from German imports forced French makers to found the SOCIÉTÉ FRANÇAISE DE FABRICATION DE BÉBÉS ET JOUETS (SFBJ).

French character doll, c.1910, with bisque head and wood and composition body, in a popular style made up to c.1930 [o]

Twentieth century

The first quarter of the century was dominated by German manufacturers of bisque-headed dolls such as Armand MARSEILLE, KESTNER and SIMON & HALBIG. From 1890 these companies made cheaper dolls in direct competition with French makers, their most innovative designs being CHARACTER DOLLS.

The beginning of the century also saw the emergence of commercially produced fabric dolls. These had been made earlier but early examples have often become torn or dirty and been thrown away. In Germany Käthe KRUSE made fabric dolls, and in the US the fabric doll tradition, represented by Izannah Walker and Martha CHASE, was continued by companies such as Sheppard & Co. of Philadelphia. At the same time LENCI produced felt dolls in Italy and Norah WELLINGS in England.

Set of five composition dolls by Alexander of New York, 1937, made to commemorate the birth of quins [Q]

English Chad Valley rag dolls were made from the 1920s and had a "Hygienic" label [o]

Another popular material was celluloid. Although a 19th-century invention, it was used in the 1920s and 1930s by factories such as the Rheinische Gummi-und Celluloid-Fabrik of Bavaria. Composition, a substance made from wood or paper pulp mixed with various reinforcing ingredients, had been used for the manufacture of dolls' bodies since the mid-19th century, and was a popular alternative to bisque for dolls' heads until 1950. A huge variety of composition dolls was produced until first plastic, then vinyl, took over. Vinyl's most famous product is undoubtedly BARBIE, introduced in 1959 and still coveted by girls today. The early models are increasingly a popular collector's item.

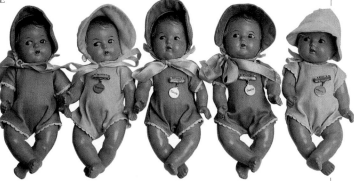

American Barbie doll with various outfits, by Mattel International, 1960s [Q]

Dinky toys This famous range of DIECAST toy vehicles was first made in December 1933. They were designed originally as accessories for the HORNBY "0"-gauge trains, and sold as "Modelled Miniatures". Early examples were cast in lead, but mazak (an alloy) was used from

Dinky toys,
Foden truck
c.1948–64 [o]

late 1934. Road vehicles form the majority of production but planes and ships were also made, both pre- and post-war. Competition from the mid-1950s from CORGI and European factories caused Dinky to update their designs. A series of changes of ownership followed and the brand ceased production in 1979. The most collectable Dinkies are pre-war examples, which are now scarce and liable to fatigue (disintegration caused by impurities in the metal) and post-war re-issues and new issues up to about 1964, particularly vans with advertising. Most of the later items were supplied in individual yellow boxes and are much more desirable when in the original box. From 1988–92, MATCHBOX, who owned the name, produced a new range under the Dinky brand to sell to collectors.

Diorama A scenic painting in which changes in colour and direction are lit to simulate movement, originating from Germany in the 19th century and later made in France and England. Typically, a small representation of a scene such as a garden or battle with three-dimensional figures viewed through a window.

Directoire style A variant of the NEO-CLASSICAL style found in French decorative arts, especially furniture, from c.1790 to c.1804. The style reached its peak of popularity during the Directoire political period (1795–99) and is characterized by austere classical forms such as tripods, X-framed stools and chairs, with minimal ornament. Some Directoire furniture, textiles and ceramics are decorated with revolutionary symbols such as the cap of liberty. It was superseded by the EMPIRE style.

Dirk A Scottish DAGGER carried by Highlanders from the mid-17th century onward. Its HILT was of dark wood, e.g. ivy root, and carved with Celtic basketweave patterns. It was carried in a leather sheath often with compartments for a small knife and fork.

Disbrowe, Nicholas (c.1612–c.1680) An English-born American Colonial "joiner" active in Hartford, Connecticut, from c.1639. Disbrowe is one of the earliest recorded furniture-makers in the US, associated with CONNECTICUT CHESTS of Hartford type, carved with formalized florette panels.

Disc joint A joint in soft toys consisting of two cardboard or metal discs connected by metal wire. It was first used by STEIFF in 1905 as an improvement on earlier rod jointing.

Dished tabletop A wooden circular tabletop, with slightly hollowed centre to create a concave surface with raised edges.

American table with dished top, c.1770–80 [F]

Dish ring A spool-shaped stand made of pierced and/or chased silver and Old Sheffield plate, designed to support a dish of hot food but also serving as a decorative adjunct. Silver examples were produced largely in Ireland from 1740, but decorative reproductions were made in Victorian and Edwardian England.

Distressed A term used to describe either genuine furniture in a poor state, or furniture which has been deliberately treated to make it appear older or more worn. Among the techniques used are sanding, scratching, burning, scorching, acid-dipping and various decorative finishes.

Dixon, James, & Son Ltd Originally founded by James Dixon and a Mr Smith in Sheffield c.1806. The mainstay of the business was wholesaling silver and plated wares to customers worldwide; they also produced trade catalogues. James Dixon retired in 1842. The company opened its first London premises in 1873; it became a limited company in 1920, and is still a going concern.

James Dixon silver candlestick, c.1900–10 [K, a pair]

Doccia porcelain factory Founded in 1737 by the Marchese Carlo Ginori on his estate in Florence. Johann Karl Wendelin Anreiter von Zirnfeld, a HAUSMALER from Vienna, arrived in 1737 and the early productions, c.1740, show strong links with Du Paquier's VIENNA PORCELAIN. Workers were also bribed to join from MEISSEN and this shows in the chinoiserie decorations. Doccia made figures in the style of Meissen but the modelling is heavier and clumsier. As renowned Italian

Late 18th century

Doccia soup tureen and cover, c.1780 [E]

artists were recruited it created a character of its own. Doccia's *masso bastardo* body (a rather grey hard paste) was used for statues and vases in sizes not seen before. The figures were influenced by RENAISSANCE sculpture.

At the beginning of the 19th century Doccia bought moulds and models from CAPODIMONTE and made copies of cups and saucers moulded with battle scenes, on which they used the crowned N of NAPLES. Essentially a family business, the firm still exists today, although in 1896 it was incorporated with the Richard factory of Milan to become Richard-Ginori. In 1897 the company was incorporated with the ceramic factory in Mondovi, and in 1906 it bought the Rifredi factory in Florence to make electrical insulators. With eight factories in Lombardy, Piedmont and Tuscany, Doccia now produces artistic porcelain and runs the "Sesto Fiorentino", which deals with industrial production.

Dog of Fo
A mythical animal used in Chinese art. The figures are made in pairs;

Chinese blanc-de-Chine dog of Fo joss-stick holder, 18th century [O]

the male usually has one paw on a brocade ball, while the female is depicted with a cub. Originally used as temple guardians, they are also known as Buddhist lion dogs; "Fo" means Buddha. The Japanese equivalent is "Shi Shi".

Dogtooth motif An early English ornament developed from the nailhead pattern and consisting of a series of four-cornered stars diagonally arranged as a repeating embellishment for mouldings. Carved in low relief, it remained popular for decorative brickwork and woodwork throughout the 15th and 16th centuries.

Doily A small napkin or mat, made of cotton, linen, lace or paper, used to decorate plates before food is added.

Doll See pp.140–41.

Doll mark on a German Handwerk doll, c.1910, 53.3cm (21in) high [O]

Doll mark Indicating the manufacturer, mould number, patent or size of a doll, marks are usually impressed or stamped on the back of moulded heads. They sometimes appear as stamps or labels on kid leather, fabric or composition bodies.

Dolls' house See pp.144–45.

Dolphin motif A decorative motif with origins in Classical art and a powerful symbol in

Christian iconography. From the Renaissance, dolphins have featured in architectural ornament, as furniture and lamp supports, or adopted as grotesques. It is a natural component of marine ornament, and remains popular for fountains, wellheads and waterspouts.

Dominick and Haff American silversmiths, established in New York City in 1872 by Blanchard Dominick and Leroy Haff. The firm made small items such as VINAIGRETTES as well as silver-plated ware of high quality, including chased HOLLOWWARE in Japanese taste, until it was sold in 1928 to become part of REED & Barton.

Don Pottery Founded *c.*1790, at Swinton, in Yorkshire, near the Rockingham factory, Don Pottery was acquired by John Green of the Leeds Pottery *c.*1800 and taken over by Samuel Baker of Mexborough in late 1830s. The factory made creamware, earthenware, transfer-printed ware and also black stoneware, using an impressed mark of DON POTTERY. It closed in 1893.

Dorflinger, Christian (1828–1915) A German (Alsace)-born American glass-maker, founder of the Greenpoint Glassworks in Brooklyn, New York, in 1860, and two further glassworks including C. Dorflinger & Sons at White Mills, Pennsylvania (1873–1921). Dorflinger introduced advanced European techniques of cutting and making lead glass, mostly in a heavy style comparable to the best Bohemian work.

Dolphin motif on Georg Jensen silver box ◄ c.1915–20 [K]

Dolls' houses

Evoking a magical world of childhood, dolls' houses as we know them today span a period of more than four centuries, originating in Germany in the 16th century. Made with painstaking craftsmanship, they reflect the styles of their time and offer us a world in miniature.

Cupboards and cabinets

Early forms of miniature "room settings" from Egyptian, Greek and Roman civilizations still exist today and they probably continued to be made and used, some as funerary offerings. In northern Europe, from the 15th century onward, the first dolls' houses took the form of "dolls' cupboards", used by adults for storing and displaying collections of miniature porcelain and silver. The first recorded acquisition of a dolls' house was in 1558, when Albrecht V of Bavaria commissioned a miniature house for his daughter: an elaborate four-storey building, with furnishings including silver and tapestries, it was sadly destroyed by fire in 1674. The earliest known surviving dolls' house in existence is dated 1611, and is in the Germanisches Nationalmuseum, Nuremberg, a heavy wooden "cabinet house", of three storeys, with original, ornately carved, wooden furniture. This is one of several historic early dolls' houses in the museum, showing the origins of the dolls' house in Germany and, toward the end of the 17th century, in the neighbouring Low Countries.

In 1688 William of Orange became William III of Great Britain and he and his wife Queen Mary brought with them Dutch influence in taste and interior decoration. The first English dolls' houses ("baby houses") were made, including a surviving one for Ann Sharp, daughter of the Archbishop of York. Still in cabinet form, and quite roughly constructed, it was intended as a plaything, rather than for an adult's amusement. Furniture is of the period, and it contains a household of named dolls, including "Lord Rochette", "Mrs Lemon", "Fanny Long, ye chambermaid" and "Roger, ye butler". This dolls' house is still in private ownership in England and is often loaned for exhibitions.

In America, the first dolls' houses date from the 18th century and show a Dutch influence. The "Van Cortlandt Mansion" of 1744 can be seen in the museum of that name in New York.

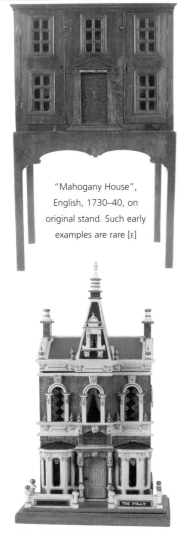

"Mahogany House", English, 1730–40, on original stand. Such early examples are rare [E]

"The Folly" by Moritz Göttschalk, a fine example of a "blue roof" house, sold with original furnishings, German c.1885 [E]

English wood and paper dolls' house, c.1900. A typical favourite in the Victorian and Edwardian nursery [M]

The American doll house

The first American doll houses are based on Dutch models and date from the mid-18th century. From c.1860 they were mass-produced by manufacturers such as Rufus Bliss of Pawtucket, Rhode Island, who, from the 1890s onward, made typical papered wooden houses and the McLoughlin Brothers of New York.

Bliss doll house, c.1920 [J]

Design for living

Throughout the 18th century and the early part of the 19th century, dolls' houses in Britain, Europe and the US reflected the architectural styles of the period and were individually crafted. From the mid-19th century, the introduction of CHROMOLITHOGRAPHY meant that manufacturers could easily decorate wooden or cardboard houses, and dolls' houses were produced in much greater quantities. A dolls' house became part of the furnishings of the English Victorian nursery, elaborately equipped with servants, dinner sets and even tiny plaster "food". From *c*.1895, G. & J. LINES in London produced wooden houses with brick-printed paper, continuing to keep pace with fashion until the 1920s, when the company was renamed TRIANG, a trade name now eagerly sought after by collectors. Germany still monopolized the international dolls' house market, producing houses in different styles to suit the tastes of their export market. Two of the best-known post-World War I firms are Christian Hacker in Nuremberg, and Moritz Göttschalk in Saxony, who specialized in colourful villa-style houses, some equipped with lifts.

Gee Bee dolls' house in the style
of a Swiss chalet, c.1968 [s]

The number of American dolls' houses increased steadily after 1850. Many early American examples can be traced to their particular region by their architectural styles and are usually quite primitive, with simple structures and furnishings. Later, around 1890, more decorative houses came into vogue, such as those produced by Rufus Bliss, quite small in size, with wooden structures and colourful chromolithographed exteriors, often with the intricately carved porches, balconies, cupolas and balustrades associated with the American houses of the time. Bliss also manufactured good-quality miniature furniture to go inside the houses.

Dolls' house figures,
French and German,
late 19th century [o]

Handmade dolls' houses

At the top end of the market, handmade dolls' houses were based on the real homes of the wealthy and aristocratic. A dolls' house made for Queen Mary, consort of George V of England, was designed by the architect Sir Edwin Lutyens. It took four years to complete and was first shown to an admiring public at the British Empire Exhibition in 1924. Inspired by Buckingham Palace, it had a garden by the famous garden designer Gertrude Jekyll and modern conveniences such as electric light and piped hot and cold water. In America, too, there were many showpiece dolls' houses. The "Fairy Castle" of Colleen Moore, built in the late 1920s, is 3m (9ft) square and was dreamed up by Hollywood set designers as a mixture of legend, fairy tale and glitz. "Early Fairy" in style, it contains jewelled furniture made from pieces in Miss Moore's own collection and is now in the Museum of Science and Industry, Chicago.

Late 19th century
American doll's house furniture
in 1840s style [L]

From *c*.1930 DINKY TOYS in Britain launched the "Dolly Varden" range for girls, including dolls' houses fitted with scaled-down furniture. Other well-known manufacturers include CHAD VALLEY, who manufactured TINPLATE houses. From the 1950s, dolls' houses were smaller than earlier versions and equipped with modern domestic appliances. This type of miniaturized appliance was manufactured by specialists such as MECCANO and BRITAINS. Today, enthusiasts appreciate such novelties as the dolls' house inspired by the children's television programme *Sesame Street*, manufactured by the leading American toy company Fisher Price, as well as good-quality reproductions of the favourites of past times.

Dolls' house food, English
1880s–1950s [o]

Doulton pottery and porcelain factory

In 1815 John Doulton (1793–1873) bought into a pottery in Lambeth, south London. It made stoneware chimney pots and products for the chemical industry and was known as Doulton & Watts until the death of John's partner John Watts in 1858. Doulton's son Henry (1820–97) then steered the company to success as Henry Doulton & Co.

Sanitation pipes to art pottery

Early stoneware products included hunting jugs, mugs, bowls, tobacco jars and tea and coffee pots. In 1820 jugs were made in the images of Napoleon, Wellington and Nelson, followed in 1832 by flasks commemorating the First Reform Act. From then on, commemorative wares featured strongly, including pieces for Queen Victoria, the Crimean War and Gladstone. Henry Doulton's foresight transformed Doulton's fortunes. Success with stoneware sanitation pipes enabled him to open a studio devoted to ART POTTERY. The project began with students from the Lambeth School of Art, e.g. George Tinworth and the BARLOW family. Their small output was seen in 1867 at the Paris Exhibition and in 1871 at the International Exhibition in London. By the 1880s it was employing more than 200 workers. Doulton's art stoneware varied from stylized patterns in the Victorian taste to the high quality ART NOUVEAU designs of Eliza Simmance. "Carrara" ware was named after the Italian marble quarry, "Silicon" ware had a stoneware body, and "Chine" ware was made to John Slater's patent. Doulton Faience was introduced for naturalistic hand-painted decoration, as were fine porcelain pieces. Doulton's hand-painted tiles can still be seen in Harrods' food hall in London.

Doulton stoneware jug commemorating General Gordon, 1885 [Q]

Pair of Doulton stoneware candlesticks, c.1890 [N]

Royal Doulton bone china teapot, c.1935 [R]

In 1877 Henry Doulton bought a large stake in Pinder Bourne & Co., Burslem, which he later took over. Here he produced EARTHENWARE and later BONE CHINA. The International Exhibition in Chicago in 1893 brought world acclaim for Doulton's art wares. Charles Noke (1858–1941) became art director, introducing decorative figures that developed into the HN series, followed by Series Ware in 1901. Then came Rembrandt and Holbein wares, Kingsware, and character and TOBY JUGS in 1934. Doulton figures such as the "Old Balloon Seller" were made throughout the 20th century. Decorative bone china figures designed by Lesley Harradine in the 1920s and 30s are keenly collected today. Highly individual ceramics resulted from transmutation glazes such as Flambé, Titanian and Crystalline. Production ended at Lambeth in 1956 but continues at Burslem under the name of Royal Doulton Fine China to this day.

Character jug "The Angler" by David Biggs, 1997 [R]

Doulton marks

Variations of the marks below were used from 1858. Production at Lambeth ceased in 1956. Burslem wares started in about 1877 and continue to this day.

Impressed mark 1891–1902

Standard impressed mark 1902–27 and 1927–36

Doucai ("Contrasting" or "dovetailing") A technique of painting on Chinese PORCELAIN where the design is first outlined in soft UNDERGLAZE blue then filled in using OVERGLAZE enamels. It was introduced during the CHENGHUA reign (1465–87) for small, high quality wares and revived from the early 18th century.

Dovetail A type of JOINT, first used in furniture-making at the end of the 17th century, in which two pieces of wood are joined at right angles by "dovetailed" triangular-shaped "teeth" at the end of one piece that lock into corresponding recesses on the edge of the other piece.

Dowel A small headless wooden pin that is used in furniture construction to join two pieces of wood. It was first used in the 16th century as a peg to strengthen MORTISE AND TENON joints. However, such pegged or joined construction was gradually abandoned by the mid-18th century when stronger glues were developed.

Dragon's blood A red, resinous substance extracted from trees and traditionally used by painters and decorators to tint LACQUERS and VARNISHES. There have been many sources, notably the *Dracaena cinnabari* of Socrota (described in the writings of Pliny); the *Dracaena draco* of the Canary Islands (in use by the 15th century); and various *Daemonorhops* species of palm growing in the East Indies and Malaya. Depending on the source, colours range from bright red to a dark, reddish brown.

Dragon style A style of late 19th- and early 20th-century Scandinavian, particularly Norwegian, silver, furniture and treen, with forms and ornament

Dragon style

inspired by Norse and Viking art. Silver vessels were made in the form of ships and drinking horns, often decorated with colourful enamelling and figures from medieval myths and sagas.

Dram glass A small glass with a short or rudimentary stem, usually with a conical foot, made with a variety of bowl shapes and used in 18th century taverns to serve spirits.

Dram glass with annulated foot, c.1775 [Q]

Drapery A popular decorative device derived from antiquity. SWAGS of drapery sometimes appear in place of flower garlands in Classical and RENAISSANCE decorative schemes and 16th-century STRAPWORK designs often feature masks swathed in drapery. A fitting accessory for the theatrical BAROQUE STYLE, drapery was enthusiastically embraced across Europe for painted and carved decoration, for mirrors, windows and chimney pieces. A favourite ornament on American FEDERAL and English NEO-CLASSICAL furniture, lavish swags of real drapery decorated fashionable interiors in the early 19th century.

Drapery

Draw-leaf table A type of dining table fitted with an extra leaf at either end beneath the main top. The leaves could be pulled or drawn out to double the length of the table. The device, which was first introduced in Britain, Germany and the Netherlands in the mid-16th century, is still used today.

Drawn stem A stem, also known as a drawn shank, formed by drawing glass from the bottom of the bowl of a drinking glass.

Drawn thread work A decorative embroidery technique on linen produced by pulling threads apart and drawing

them together using a variety of stitches in different combinations to form open patterns. Used for decorating clothing and household linen, it was particularly fashionable in the 16th and 17th centuries and was revived in the latter part of the 19th century.

Dream baby by Armand Marseille, c.1925 [P]

Dream baby A doll modelled on a newly born baby, with domed head, narrow eyes, chubby cheeks and bent limbs and a fabric body. Dream babies are variations on Grace Putnam's "Bye-Lo" baby, designed in 1922. Overwhelming demand soon spawned imitations, the most common dream baby being mould number 341/351, first produced by Armand MARSEILLE in 1924.

Dredger A vessel, usually in cut glass or silver and with a perforated top, used for sprinkling powdery substances such as sugar, salt and pepper on food, or for sprinkling sand on wet ink.

Dresden faience factory Founded by J.F. BÖTTGER in 1708, just before he discovered PORCELAIN. The best FAIENCE dates from 1710–38, under the management of Peter Eggerbrecht from the BERLIN faience factory, and includes drug pots, COMMEDIA DELL'ARTE FIGURES and large CHINOISERIE vases. The factory closed in 1784.

Dresden lace Refers to DRAWN THREAD WORK on muslin, rather than true LACE.

Dresden porcelain A generic term for German porcelain wares and figures from in and around Dresden, Saxony, that were made in the style of MEISSEN (not far away up the River Elbe) from the second half of the 19th century. It includes factories making porcelain, as well as decorating establishments – many of whom tried to copy the mark of Meissen. There were 40 decorating establishments at the end of the 19th century and some of the best known factories are Dresden Porcelain Factory, Donath & Co., Helena WOLFSOHN, Carl THIEME of Potschappel, and the factory at Plaue on Havel in Thuringia. Dresden porcelain is still made. So-called Dresden ware was and is made even further afield, including in English factories, from the 19th century to today.

Dresden pot pourri vase and cover, c.1900 [O, a pair]

Dresden work The general name for exceptional 18th-century WHITEWORK embroidery produced in Germany, Denmark and England to decorate fine linen handkerchiefs, lappets and sleeve ruffles. Typically drawn, pulled and stitched in dense, flat elaborate patterns, it is reversible, and intended to rival fine BOBBIN LACE.

Dresser (US HUTCH) A piece of case furniture consisting of a rack of shelves to display or store pewter or ceramics on a base of drawers and a cupboard, or an open base with a pot board. It evolved from the side table in the late 17th century and is still popular as kitchen furniture. Regional types developed, especially in Wales: BREAK-FRONT dressers with closed racks above drawers and cupboards in North Wales; dressers with open racks and bases in South Wales.

Dresser, Christopher (1834–1904) An English designer, botanist and teacher. A radical pioneer, he may be considered one of the first modern industrial designers. He had the ability to distil the best of other cultures' design with his appreciation of form, based on his studies from nature, while embracing the machine and mass production. Many of his designs of the 1870s to 1880s are still "modern" today. He won a prize for the design of a clothing fabric in 1854 as well as submitting botanical drawings to the Department of Science and Art. He wrote an article "Botany as adapted to the Arts and Art Manufacturers" for the *Art Journal*. In 1861 became a fellow of the Linnean Society and in 1862 published his first book *The Art of Decorative Design*. Dresser was impressed by Japanese design and spent four months there in 1876–77. He visited cultural and manufacturing sites, being

Silver-plated tea set by Dresser, 1880 [I]

commissioned by TIFFANY & Co. to bring back items. He also became involved in importing Japanese artifacts. His designs were used by Elkington (silversmiths), COALBROOKDALE (iron foundry), Hukin & Heath (silver and plate makers), J. Couper & Sons (glass, notably the CLUTHA range) and LINTHORPE (pottery) to name but a few.

Dressing case A lockable, portable wooden box, often in MAHOGANY or COROMANDEL WOOD, with a fitted interior holding glass bottles and grooming accessories as well as compartments for jewellery. Popular in the 18th and 19th centuries, enabling gentlemen and ladies to transport vanity items together while travelling.

Dressing table A small table fitted with drawers designed to hold the accessories for a lady or gentleman's toilet. The term was in use from the 17th century. From the 18th century such tables usually included a free-standing looking glass.

Dressoir The French term for a medieval multi-purpose sideboard with storage cupboards, the top of which was used to display plate or serve food.

Dreyfuss, Henry (1904–72) An American industrial designer working from the late 1920s who observed how the manufacturing process affected design and believed that the practicality of a design was of primary importance over other concerns. His designs consider the consumer and user of the product foremost and include telephones and the interiors of aircraft.

Drinking glass See GLASS, DRINKING.

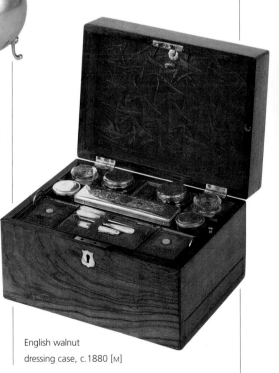

English walnut dressing case, c.1880 [M]

Silver drinking horn, Danish c.1900 [H]

Drinking horn

A hollowed-out animal horn is one of the earliest known natural drinking vessels. From the first millennium AD they have been mounted in gold or silver, on a foot or feet often with a detachable cover and decorated with enamel or jewels, perhaps for ceremonial use. They may be made in other materials such as rock crystal, ivory, wood or silver. Drinking horns are still made as ceremonial items.

Drop handle (or tear or swing drop) A handle shaped in the form of a single tear drop, used on good quality chests of drawers in the late 17th and early 18th centuries and copied later.

Drop-in seat The term used for a removable chair seat, usually upholstered, that is made separately and then "dropped in", or inserted into the seat rail. Drop-in seats were introduced in the early 18th century.

Dropleaf table The term used for a type of table introduced in the early 18th century, which has two hinged leaves that drop or fold down and are supported by pivoting legs.

Drug jar See APOTHECARY JAR.

Drum clock An early type of portable TABLE CLOCK with a cylindrical case on which the dial is mounted horizontally rather than vertically. Most drum clocks were made in Germany and central Europe in the 16th century and often had finely decorated metal cases. A type of drum clock with a glass-fronted brass case was popular in the 19th century.

Drum stool A Chinese stool in the form of an up-ended barrel with pierced sides, known to have been made in hardwood in the MING period (1368–1644).

Drum table, rent table A type of late 18th/early 19th century writing table with a round drum-shaped leather-covered top and drawers in the frieze below, which is supported on a central column on a tripod or pedestal base.

William IV mahogany drum table, 1830 [D]

Drypoint A technique in which a metal printing plate has an image directly scored into the surface with a sharp needle-like point. It produces a shallow groove, which fills with ink and gives a velvety black tone on the print. Rembrandt was a great exponent of the medium.

Dubreuil, André (b.1951) A French designer particularly known for his sophisticated and imaginative furniture, some in the style known as New Baroque. His furniture is good quality, often produced as limited editions and made in metal.

English duelling pistol by Durrs Egg, c.1810 [I]

Duelling pistols A pair of FLINTLOCK or PERCUSSION pistols made for formalized personal combat. Pistols superseded swords for duelling from c.1780. English makers such as Robert Wogden and John Rigby excelled in making duelling pistols that were technically advanced, but usually without decoration. The pistols are invariably contained in a wooden case with accessories for loading and maintenance. Duelling was made illegal and eventually fell out of favour in different countries at different times during the 19th century.

Duesbury, William (1725–86) A great entrepreneur in English porcelain, starting as a decorator of porcelain in London 1751–53. He went to DERBY and owned the factory there in 1756, then bought the failing factory of CHELSEA in 1770 and ran it for 14 years.

Dumb waiter A wooden stand with a tripod base and a central shaft supporting two or three revolving tiers, graduating in size. An English invention of the mid-18th century that remained popular in that form until the early 19th, the dumb waiter stood by the dining table and let diners help themselves to condiments.

George III mahogany dumb waiter, c.1800 [G]

Dummer, Jeremiah (1645–1718)
An English-born American silversmith.
Dummer was one of the first silversmiths
recorded in Boston, Massachusetts, where
he was apprenticed to English silversmith
John Hull. Examples, which, typically of
American Colonial silver, may bear a
maker's mark only, are plain.

Dummy board figure A thin flat
wooden panel that was painted and cut
in the shape of a person (housemaids
were particularly popular) or an
animal (usually a dog or a cat) and
either fixed to the wall or placed
about the room. They were
thought to have originated in
the Netherlands, were used
as firescreens in Britain
from the late 17th-century
and were popular as
decorations in the
mid–18th century.

Dummy board figure, 155cm
(5ft) high, English c.1630 [K]

Dunand, Jean (1877–1942)
A Swiss-born French designer and
LACQUER artist. His skill and artistry in
traditional lacquer techniques made it a
popular medium in the ART DECO
period, although few could match him in
ability. He is responsible for some of the
best French Art Deco lacquerwork.

Jean Dunand lacquer and mother-of-pearl
inlaid box, c.1925 [L]

Dunlap, John (1746–92) An American
furniture-maker active in Goffstown,
New Hampshire, from 1768. Dunlap and
his brother Samuel (1752–1830), made
furniture of relatively plain type, mostly in
local maple. Ambitious Dunlap pieces,
including HIGHBOYS, are distinct from

other contemporary examples by being
embellished with exaggerated scrolls,
cabriole legs and carved aprons. New
Hampshire furniture of this type is
referred to as "Dunlap School" if
it is otherwise unattributable.

Du Paquier See VIENNA
PORCELAIN FACTORY.

Duplex escapement
A type of ESCAPEMENT used
principally in watches but also
in some 19th-century clocks,
in which there are two escape
wheels rather than one. One
wheel is for locking and the
other for impulsing.

Durlach pottery A faience
factory started in 1723 near
Baden, in south-west
Germany, with a privilege
granted by the Margrave Carl
Wilhelm to Johann Heinrich
Wachenfeld who had previously been in
STRASBOURG and ANSBACH. From 1723 to
1749 the blue-decorated ware was in the
style of ROUEN. Cream-coloured
earthenware was also made, impressed
"Durlach" after c.1818. Many of the
painters signed with their
names and included Heim,
Keim, Lower and Pfalzgraf.
The factory closed in 1840.

Dutch Colonial furniture
Furniture made in Dutch
types and hybrid styles in the
Dutch East Indies colonies
(present-day Indonesia) from
the early 17th until the mid-
20th century. Case furniture, beds, chairs,
tables and other pieces were made in
indigenous woods such as EBONY,
CALAMANDER, SATINWOOD and TEAK both
for officials of the Dutch East India
Company and for export to Europe.
CANE was often used both in the early
seating furniture and in the distinctive
reclining veranda chairs developed in
the 19th century.

Dutch Delft ware There were a few
factories in towns in Holland other than
DELFT that made both Delft wares and
tiles. These include Amsterdam, Bolsward,
Delftshaven, Dordrecht, Gorinchem,
Gouda, Haarlem, Hoorn, Reiden,
Makkum and Middelburg.

Dutch peg doll See PENNY WOODEN.

Dutch strike A type of STRIKING
SYSTEM in which the hours are sounded
on a large, low-pitched bell and at the
half-hour the succeeding hour is struck
on a smaller, high-pitched bell. Dutch
striking could be used only with the
COUNT WHEEL and so is found mainly on
clocks from before the late 17th century.

Dux See ROYAL DUX.

Dwight, John (1635–1703) An English
potter who took out a patent for
"Transparent Earthenware" in 1671. He
founded a pottery at FULHAM and made
BELLARMINES in Rhenish stone style. He
also made REDWARE teapots similar to
those of YIXING (China). These
innovations paved the way for the
development of English pottery in

Dutch Colonial
chest-on-stand,
late 17th century [F]

Salt-glazed stoneware mug
by John Dwight c.1680 [H]

Staffordshire. Dwight made excellent salt-glazed stoneware figures, from small figures of ancient gods to a life-size bust of Prince Rupert.

Dye A compound that, when applied to textiles or other materials, will effect a more or less permanent colour change. The degree of permanence of the colour is defined as its "fastness". A colour-fast dye is capable of resisting washing, wear and exposure to light without fading.

Dyes can be classified, according to the chemical process involved, into "direct", "mordant" and "vat" dyes. Direct dyes are frequently unstable; mordant dyes are more "fast" and vat dyes are firmly chemically attached to the fibre, although they tend to be weaker in shade.

Until the 18th century all dyes were derived from animal, mineral or vegetable sources. The first reference to a synthetic dye, "essence of indigo", dates from 1740 but it was not until 1856 that the first fully synthetic dyes appeared. Although these first synthetic or "aniline" dyes were not very colour-fast, by the end of the 19th century thousands of good synthetic dyes in all colours were widely available.

Dyottville Glassworks A US glass works founded in 1831 by Dr T.W. Dyott in Kensington, Pennsylvania. Typical production included flasks, moulded with portraits or historical images, and inexpensive tableware of all types in clear and coloured glass. It closed c.1840.

E

Eagle A symbol of power and victory from ancient times. The eagle was associated with Jove, celestial king of the Olympian gods, and hence stood for pre-eminence and regality. The double-headed eagle symbolizes watchful power. The Roman army featured the noble bird on its standards and it has been used ever since by many kingdoms and nations, from the Hapsburgs to the American republic. The American eagle is often portrayed clutching a sheaf of thunderbolts. It was a key motif of the Napoleonic EMPIRE style and, more generally, tends to appear wherever a heavy classical style of ornament is being used, e.g. in gateways, console supports or mirrors.

Eagle

Eames, Charles See p.152.

Earnshaw, Thomas (1749–1829) An English clock- and watch-maker. He began his career as a finisher of verge and cylinder watches but is best known for developing the spring DETENT ESCAPEMENT for marine CHRONOMETERS and was one of the first clock-makers to produce chronometers on a commercial basis.

Earrings Worn since ancient times and in general use since the 18th century, earrings have undergone many transformations in the past 300 years. Late 18th and early 19th-century forms tended towards an elongated, GIRANDOLE or simple NEO-CLASSICAL style or closely-set clusters of diamonds. Many gems were backed with coloured tinfoil to enhance their colour. Earrings of the 1860s and 1870s took their inspiration from Revivalist and novelty themes and, by the end of the century, a discreet floral cluster or single-stone stud was commonplace. The delicate garland themes of the early 20th century were replaced by strong linear forms of the ART DECO period and, by the 1940s, large gold earclips of ribbon, scroll and flowerhead design were set with large semi-precious gems such as aquamarine.

Earthenware Pottery made of a porous clay body, that has to be waterproofed by a coating glaze. Pottery can be divided into two main types – earthenware and STONEWARE. A criterion for this division is the porosity of the BODY after firing. Earthenware has a porosity of more than 5 per cent. See also MAJOLICA, FAIENCE and SLIPWARE.

East India Company An imperialistic trading company formed to exploit trade links with south-east and east Asia and India initially to break the spice trade monopoly. Companies were formed by England in 1600 and later by the Netherlands, France and Denmark. Goods imported into Europe included tea, spices, timber and porcelain. See also CHINESE EXPORT PORCELAIN.

Arita plate with the Dutch East India Company's initials VOC, Japanese late 17th century [C]

Moulded fibreglass Shell armchair
designed by Charles & Ray Eames,
c.1948–50 [o]

Charles Eames (1907–78)

An American architect, furniture designer and film maker. In 1930 he became a fellow of the Cranbrook Art Institute, where he met his future wife, Ray Kaiser, a painter. The couple formed a lifelong partnership, collaborating on many designs, and were pioneers of the American Modern Movement. Their chair designs were particularly influential.

Pioneer in plywood

In 1941, Eames and his wife moved to Southern California, where they accepted a commission from the US Navy to make lightweight plywood splints. Eames had first started experimenting with PLYWOOD with Eero SAARINEN, making moulded shells for chairs. They had submitted a shell chair of bent and laminated wood to the Museum of Modern Art's "Organic Design in the Home" Exhibition in 1940, where they won first prize. Eames and Saarinen's plywood pieces were simple, practical and pleasing. They produced a variety of chairs, as well as a screen made of six panels of undulating section, united by long canvas hinges. Because each panel was identical it was cheap to produce and easy to store.

In 1944, Charles and Ray Eames set up their own design practice, which remained active until Charles's death in 1978. In 1946 the designer George Nelson, with whom Charles had collaborated on a number of projects, introduced them to the progressive furniture manufacturer, Herman Miller. This led to a lasting business relationship. While Charles was responsible for structure and production concerns, Ray managed the aesthetic side of the business. This teamwork, coupled with their inventiveness, versatility and artistic integrity, was the driving force behind their success.

Eames lounge chair with ottoman,
designed in 1956 [H]

Eames chairs – modern classics

Most Eames chairs produced after World War II were made by the Herman Miller Company and may bear this mark. Early examples in plywood show the influence of Finnish design. Later designs are typically of fibreglass or plastic shell type. Many models are still in production. Today the early, experimental pieces not intended for commercial production are the most sought after.

In 1950 Zenith Plastics made an Eames chair for Herman Miller in fibreglass reinforced plastic, the moulded seat supported on metal rod legs. It was the first chair of its type to leave the plastic shell exposed. Although Eero Saarinen had used the material first for his "Womb" armchair, the shell had been upholstered. The Eames chair was inexpensive to make and many imitations followed.

Eames rosewood lounge chair,
designed in 1945–46 [H]

One of their most famous and popular designs is the lounge chair with ottoman (above left), which won a gold medal in the 1960 Milan XII Triennale. The shell is moulded plywood with a rosewood veneer (after 1990 this changed to walnut and cherry). Structural support is provided by cast aluminium and the chair swivels and rocks. Although it was one of their more expensive designs (they usually aimed to produce good, low-cost design) and was never intended to be mass produced, over 100,000 have been produced since it first appeared.

Eastlake, Charles Locke (1836–1906)
An English writer, journalist and designer who trained as an architect. He was at his most powerful and influential as a promoter and writer on design. In 1868 his book *Hints on Household Taste* was published. It was hugely popular and was responsible for taking the design debate beyond the realm of artists and architects to a wider audience. It was particularly popular in the US where it was reprinted eight times.

Charles Eastlake was an exponent of ART FURNITURE, rather than mass production, and he advocated discussion and dialogue between the buyer and the maker. He promoted the use of traditional methods of joinery, particularly pegged joints, which proved popular with the ARTS AND CRAFTS Movement. Although he was in favour of MARQUETRY decoration, gilt highlights and linear fluting, he was against FRENCH POLISH, preferring wood to have a natural finish "… simply rubbed with boiled oil or if they must be stained at all let them be stained black". The book included many of Eastlake's own designs for furniture and wallpaper, which inspired copies and variations – in the US they are referred to as the "Eastlake Style".

He designed for various British firms: metalwork for Benham & Froud, wallpaper for Jeffrey & Company and fabrics for Cowlshaw and Nicol & Co. His jewellery was retailed through Howell, James & Co. and his furniture was made by the Art Furniture Company, Jackson & Graham and Heaton, Butler & Bayne.

Charles Eastlake
oak day bed, c.1875 [H]

Eastman, George (1854–1932) An American industrialist, who founded the Eastman Kodak Company in 1892. He conceived his first camera in 1885 and it went on sale about two years later. The camera had a revolutionary shutter design, but manufacture was plagued by problems and it eventually proved too costly to produce. Evidence suggests that only 75 were made and it is believed that just one example survives, which is now in the Smithsonian Institute. Eastman obviously learned from his previous experience and he launched a new model later that same year. This was received with great enthusiasm. (See also BOX BROWNIE.)

The camera was simple in appearance but represents a major technological advance in photographic history. It ushered in the era of the amateur photographer and the end of the time-consuming and complicated processes involved in using heavy glass negative plates and plateholders. Its commercial success was based on the fact that it was compatible with the recently invented celluloid rollfilm developed by Thomas Edison. The camera was also lightweight, small, cheap to manufacture, simple to operate and could take 100 exposures on one roll of film.

By 1927, the Eastman Kodak Company virtually monopolized the United States photographic industry, and it remains one of the biggest American names in its field.

Eastman 6 Series camera, c.1930–35 [R]

Easy chair Originally a contemporary term for the comfortable, upholstered WING armchair, designed primarily for the elderly and infirm. Introduced in the late 17th century, it has since come to be used for many types of upholstered armchair.

Ebéniste A French term for a cabinet-maker, introduced in the 17th century. The fashion for EBONY in Europe demanded a revival of veneering that was largely the province of skilled cabinet-makers. They then became known by the name of the luxury hardwood with which they worked. (See also MENUISIER.)

Eberlein, Johann Friedrich (1696–1749) A German sculptor who worked at MEISSEN under KÄNDLER from 1735 until 1749. He assisted with the Monkey Band figures for the Japanese Palace and in 1742 he designed the ROCOCO decoration for the Swan Service. His work also includes figures of Classical deities and allegorical characters.

Meissen figure of Harlequin modelled by Eberlein, c.1745–50 [F]

Ebonized Wood or furniture whose surface has been stained or polished to resemble EBONY. The process was known in the late 17th century and was revived during the 19th-century fashion for the AESTHETIC style and JAPONISME.

Ebony (*Diospyros spp*) A heavy, black hardwood with a smooth, close grain from trees (see also COROMANDEL) native to the Indian subcontinent and Sri Lanka. Used as veneer in Ancient Greece, Egypt and Rome, ebony was reintroduced into Europe in the late 17th century.

Eclecticism The combination of motifs and forms from different styles in a single object. Eclecticism was evident in the decorative arts in the 18th century, when the development of the picturesque movement encouraged the combination of ROCOCO, GOTHICK and CHINOISERIE motifs for aesthetic effect. However, it became one of the distinguishing features of the VICTORIAN STYLE from the 1830s as a result of several factors: the widespread interest in historical styles; the emergence of the tourist industry leading to a fashion for exotic motifs and ornament derived from Byzantine, Indian Egyptian, Persian, Turkish and other non-European arts; the introduction of new methods of manufacturing that enabled exact reproductions of historical objects; the establishment of museums of the decorative arts and schools of design; and the display of products from around the world at the numerous 19th-century international exhibitions.

Meissen écuelle and stand, c.1740 [J]

Similarly, pattern-books such as the *Grammar of Ornament* (1856) by Owen JONES, featuring motifs from a great range of styles, allowed designers to appropriate a huge variety of ornament for every type of object. In high-quality pieces decoration remained restrained and finely executed, but in less expensive items, motifs were often indiscriminately combined with little regard for scale or proportion or for the form or function of the object. Eclectic attitudes toward design also led to the development of styles such as the JACOBETHAN, which combined Tudor, Elizabethan Jacobean and sometimes Gothic motifs. In the late 19th century the ARTS AND CRAFTS MOVEMENT challenged eclecticism, advocating a simpler approach in which ornament should be appropriate to function.

Ecuelle (French: "bowl".) A shallow circular silver or ceramic dish, used for individual soup servings. It had a flat handle on each side and a cover with a finial. Ecuelles were popular in France during the late 17th and 18th centuries. They were less common in the rest of Europe, although silver examples were made in England by refugee HUGUENOT craftsmen.

Edo period The Japanese period, named after Edo (the former name of Tokyo), extending from 1615 to the beginning of the Meiji period in 1868. During this time the production of PORCELAIN, LACQUER and IVORY-carving flourished.

Edwards, John (1671–1746) An American silversmith active in Boston, Massachusetts, making domestic and church plate of simple design, similar to the work of Jeremiah DUMMER. His pieces are extremely rare and may be marked with an IE or IE and IA in QUATREFOIL (during his association with the silversmith John Allen). Edwards began a dynasty of Boston silversmiths, that included his sons Samuel (1705–62) and Thomas (1701–50) and grandson Joseph.

Egermann, Friedrich (1777–1864) A Bohemian glassmaker born in Blottendorf, Austria, where he set up a glass factory and experimented with new types of coloured glass. He created a yellow STAIN c.1820 and a ruby red stain c.1830, as well as LITHYALIN glass in 1828.

Glass beaker by Friedrich Egermann, c.1830 [J]

Egg and dart

Egg and dart Also called egg and tongue, an OVOLO moulding consisting of a repeating pattern of alternating egg and arrowhead shapes. One of the most commonly used Classical mouldings, egg and dart featured on woodwork from the 16th century and was popular in the 18th century on NEO-CLASSICAL furniture, and for mouldings on classical-style buildings.

Eggshell porcelain Thinly potted porcelain first produced in the MING DYNASTY reign of Yongle (1403–24), sometimes with ANHUA decoration. Later produced in the QING DYNASTY (1644–1912) and from c.1900 mass

Eggshell porcelain saucer, Chinese c.1730 [J, with teabowl]

produced in Japan for export to the West. It was also made in Europe, notably at the BELLEEK PORCELAIN FACTORY, Ireland.

Egyptian pottery The ceramics made in Egypt since antiquity. The Egyptian ceramics industry dates back some 8,000 years, when various regional wares were produced. Among these were the fine, burnished brown or red Badarian wares from the late 5th millennium BC, with simple ripple decoration and a black upper body. More lively decoration appeared soon after this period, including

Amratian pottery, a red ware painted in white with trees and animals. From *c*.4000 BC a light-coloured ground stone ware known as "Gerzean" or "Naqada II" was produced. This was decorated in red and imitated pottery tomb vessels. These elegant ground stone vessels made of basalt, ALABASTER or granite are unique to ancient Egypt. Highly polished red-brown Meydum bowls represent the best pottery of the Old Kingdom (2700–2200 BC). In Roman Egypt, the "Egyptian faience" technique was used for wares known as "glazed quartz FRITWARE", coloured with an intense turquoise blue. Fritware was revived by Islamic potters throughout the Near East from the 12th century AD.

Egyptian style

Forms and motifs inspired by ancient Egyptian art and architecture. Motifs such as SPHINXES and OBELISKS were used in applied arts from the 16th century, but the vogue for Egyptian ornament reached its peak in the late 18th and early 19th centuries, as part of the REGENCY, EMPIRE and FEDERAL styles, inspired by Napoleon's campaigns in Egypt of the 1790s and the publications of Baron Vivant Denon. Typical motifs include hieroglyphs, winged griffins, PALMETTES and lotus leaves. The fashion for Egyptian style continued as a strand of HISTORICISM throughout the 19th century. The discovery of the tomb of Tutankhamen in 1922 led to another surge in popularity, which is especially evident in ART DECO jewellery.

Egyptian-style stand by Wedgwood, c.1800 [o]

Elbow chair
A 17th-century term initially used to identify the CARVER, armchair or armchairs in a set of dining chairs. By the second half of the century the term had come to describe any type of chair with arms.

Electric clock A type of clock using electricity rather than a spring or weight to power the movement. Pioneered by Alexander BAIN in the 1840s, electric clocks were originally developed as precision timekeepers, but in the early 20th century they were also produced for domestic use, one of the earliest being the BULLE CLOCK. Today, the quartz-crystal clock is one of the most common electrically powered clocks.

Electric motor mechanism
A means of providing automated action to a toy, using an electric motor, sometimes with a gearbox and/or cam-driven links. In electric model TRAINS the power is supplied through the rails from a central transformer and controller linked to the mains supply. Electric racing cars use a similar system. See also BATTERY MECHANISM.

Electroplate A layer of metal (usually gold or silver) chemically deposited by electrolysis onto any object (usually base metal) that will conduct electricity. For example, a copper pot can be placed in a solution of silver salts then a current passed through the pot and the liquid. The pot acts as the cathode and positively charged ions of silver in the solution migrate toward and adhere to it. The longer the process continues, the heavier the deposit of silver becomes. Electroplating, pioneered by George

German electroplated silver fruit bowl, c.1900 [L]

ELKINGTON, became commercially viable *c*.1840 and effectively put an end to the SHEFFIELD PLATE industry.

Electrotype A metal article, often copper (but can be other base metals or silver) reproduced from an original of which a mould is made. The mould is then used as a pattern and by the action of prolonged electroplating a replica metal object is built up or formed within the mould, faithfully reproducing the form and shape of the original article. The process was developed by several different people in the 1830s and improved in the 1840s by George ELKINGTON.

Elephant motif
A motif that has been used as a symbol of sovereignty, wisdom and moral and spiritual strength since ancient times. The

Elephant motif

elephant enjoyed an illustrious reputation in the cultures of Greece, India, Persia and China, and is widely represented in the Hindu and Buddhist religions. The elephant features prominently in medieval decorative schemes and, along with other motifs with roots in the East, was adopted for Italian silk designs as early as the 13th century. The elephant's alternative role as a beast of burden is echoed in its decorative function as a support for furniture, clocks, and vases.

Elers Brothers, John and David
Dutch potters who settled in Vauxhall, London, in 1688. They made a red STONEWARE, in London until 1693 then in Staffordshire, using a red clay that they sifted to make a fine body. SPRIGS of foliage and birds were made in engraved brass and copper moulds and then applied to the body – in imitation of the Yi Hsing stoneware from China. Their workshop closed in 1698.

Elizabethan Revival A style of architecture and decorative arts popular in England from the 1820s to the 1850s, reviving elements of the ELIZABETHAN style, often combined with TUDOR and JACOBEAN styles. Its popularity was reinforced by the association of Queen Victoria's reign with that of Elizabeth I, especially in its economic prosperity and the expansion of maritime trade. Motifs such as STRAPWORK, GROTESQUES and heraldry, as well as needlework upholstery and spiral TURNINGS are characteristic of the Elizabethan style. A later revival took place in the 1920s and 30s, with furniture and fabrics made by LIBERTY'S.

Elizabethan style The architecture and decorative arts dominant in England during the reign of Elizabeth I from 1558 to 1603. It was essentially the last phase of the TUDOR style, although the Italian Renaissance style prevalent in the mid-16th century was to some extent supplanted by MANNERISM. Elizabethan style first appeared in the great country houses built during the late 16th century by the English nobility and gentry, featuring symmetrical façades and elaborate chimneys, friezes and relief sculpture. In the decorative arts, typical motifs include cherub heads, STRAPWORK, GROTESQUES and ARABESQUES.

Elizabethan silver communion cup by John Jones of Exeter, c.1572 [E]

Derived from French, Flemish and German pattern-books, including those by Virgil Solis (1514–62), Hans Vredeman de Vries (1527–1604), Hans Brosamer (active 1535–50) and Jacques Androuet du Cerceau (c.1520–84), such motifs were also introduced by Protestant refugee craftsmen fleeing religious persecution on the Continent.

Elizabethan furniture is characterized by the use of oak and massive, heavy forms with ornate carving and large bulbous shapes modelled on silver cups and covers for bed posts, table legs and supports for cupboards. Some pieces feature MARQUETRY and INLAY of architectural perspectives and naturalistic ornament. All-over patterns of arabesques, fruit and flowers appear on needlework hangings, table covers and other textiles. Similarly, silver, of which mainly ceremonial pieces such as ewers, cups and covers and salt cellars have survived, was decorated with strapwork, animal heads and masks, naturalistic snails, fruits and flowers, arabesques and grotesques. The Elizabethan style evolved into the JACOBEAN style at the start of the 17th century during the reign of James I.

Elkington, George Richard (1801–65) The founder of Elkington & Co. Ltd, an English silversmithing and plating company. He pioneered ELECTROPLATING

in Britain and patented the process in the 1830s, also licensing it out to other manufacturers, such as Charles CHRISTOFLE. After various partnerships, George Elkington built two large factories in Birmingham to handle the production of his silver and plated wares with the help and financial support of his partner Josiah Mason. The firm adopted the name of Elkington, Mason & Co. in 1842. It had a London showroom and further expanded the business by making ornaments and perfecting its GILDING processes, with premises in London, Dublin, Liverpool and Birmingham.

The partnership with Mason ended in 1858, George died in 1865 and the firm continued as Elkington & Co. with his

Elkington & Co. electrotype casket, c.1850 [M]

co-partners and sons Frederick, James Barclay, Alfred John and Howard at the helm. The company was a great retailer but also produced trade catalogues and vast quantities of silver and plated wares from domestic flatware to ceremonial and display pieces, bronzes, enamels and ornaments and supplied hotels and steamships as well as individuals.

Elkington's employed numerous artists and designers, notably Léonard Morel-Ladeuil (1820–88), Edward Welby PUGIN and Christopher DRESSER. The firm was represented at most of the major exhibitions from 1840 to 1914 including the GREAT EXHIBITION of 1851 in London and that of 1855 in Paris. The company became limited in 1887 and continued until 1963 when it became a division of British Silverware Ltd.

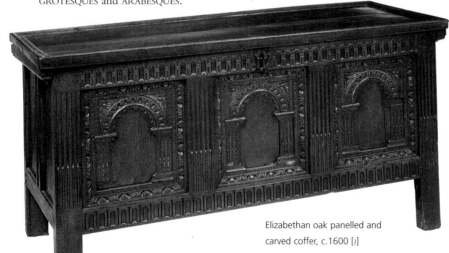

Elizabethan oak panelled and carved coffer, c.1600 [J]

Embroidery

A method of decorating a fabric ground with various stitching techniques, often incorporating the use of other fabrics, beads, precious stones and a variety of threads, including gold and silver.

Crossing cultures and centuries

Embroidery has varied through the ages depending on the materials available and on the demands of royal courts, the Church and wealthy households. From archaeological and anecdotal evidence it is known that embroidered goods were traded at least as early as biblical times. However, early examples are rare. A group of Chinese chain-stitched embroideries, discovered in the tombs of Noin Ula in Mongolia, are believed to date back 2,000 years. In Europe, a gold-embroidered border probably from the 6th century, found in a tomb in France, is one of the first known examples. In England, some Anglo-Saxon ecclesiastical vestments survive, notably the stole of St Cuthbert of Durham (c. 909–916).

Of the early medieval period perhaps the most famous embroidery is the Bayeux tapestry (despite its name, not a tapestry at all), made c.1066–1082 at either Canterbury or Winchester. From the late 12th until the 14th century fine linens and silks were entirely worked with gold, silver and exotic silk threads in all the major European centres. Some of the best work came from professional English workshops. "OPUS ANGLICANUM" (English work) was so prized that Pope Innocent IV personally asked the English church to send him embroidered orphreys (the borders of ecclesiastical vestments) in 1246.

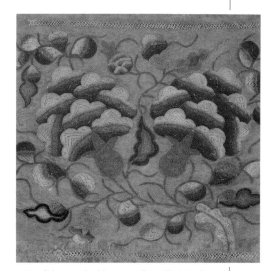

Needleloop embroidery on yellow silk damask, late Yuan Ming dynasty (14th century), much imitated in later European embroidery

A fine embroidery in coloured silks in tent stitch, depicting the Adoration of the Magi and the Flight into Egypt, c.1600 [E]

By the 14th century embroidery on velvet grounds appeared. At the same time, fine silk needle painting became fashionable in the Italian Renaissance centres. From the mid-16th century, some secular embroidery survives, most of it professionally made. Increasing trade with the East, availability of materials and the invention of printing contributed to changes in Western embroidery. As the merchant class demanded more household furnishings, pictures and embroidered costume and accessories, embroidery as a pastime flourished. Home embroidery evolved from 17th-century STUMPWORK in silk and metal thread and CREWELWORK in wool to 18th-century canvaswork, where the designs were embroidered in silk or wool onto open-weave canvas. BERLIN WOOLWORK became hugely popular in the 19th century.

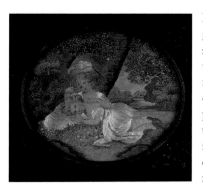

Picture in silk and chenille threads using long and short stitch, English c.1800 [M]

Many of these home crafts arrived in the US via immigrants and often remained current there after they had died out in Europe. Needlework SAMPLERS and pictures were worked from the 17th century on and many surviving examples are the work of young girls being trained in domestic skills. Samplers may incorporate the maker's name, a motto or a religious theme. Embroidered pictures were sometimes based on an actual painting or a historical personage or event.

Chasuble embroidered with silver thread and silk floral patterns, European 18th century [L]

Ellicott, John (1706–72) Son of John Ellicott the elder, a maker of mirrors and clocks in London. He produced high quality clocks and watches and became clockmaker to George III (reigned 1760–1820). He is best known today for his invention of a COMPENSATED PENDULUM in the mid-1750s, featuring a brass rod attached to an iron rod and incorporating a system of levers. When the brass expands under heat, the levers are raised; when it contracts they are lowered to compensate for the differing rate of expansion and contraction of iron. Expensive and complex to make, it was never as popular as other types.

Elm (*Ulmus spp.*) Various species native to Europe and North America (now largely destroyed by Dutch elm disease in the UK) that provides a fibrous, coarse-grained, light gingery-brown hardwood. It was used for country furniture such as chairs and table tops. BURR elm was a popular veneer in the late 18th and early 19th centuries.

Elm veneer

Elmslie, George Grant (1871–1952) A Scottish-born US architect and designer who worked in partnership with the architects William Grey Purcell (1880–1952) and George Feick Jnr (1881–1945). It is thought that Elmslie was responsible for the decorative detail and interiors of their commissions, which included furniture, fixtures and fittings.

Elton, Sir Edmund Harry (1846–1920) An English ART POTTER who set up a pottery and kilns in Clevedon, Somerset. He is known for his

Terracotta vase by Sir Edmund Harry Elton, c.1900 [P]

vases decorated in relief with flowering branches, covered with streaky gold, platinum, silver and copper glazes.

Embossing The decoration of metals (or leather) using hammers to bulge or force the material to one side. Popular from the late 1660s onward, embossing produces a raised (relief) or hollowed (incuse) three-dimensional pattern. The pattern is usually further enhanced by CHASING. As well as decoration, embossing adds strength and rigidity to what might otherwise be a plain, flimsy article. See also REPOUSSÉ WORK.

Embroidery See p.157.

Emerald The green gem variety of beryl. It is found in several locations but the most valuable deposits are the Muzo and Chivor mines of Colombia. The rarest stones are vibrant bluish-green and the scarcity of INCLUSIONS increases the value considerably. Many modern emeralds are enhanced with artificial oils and resins.

Enamel Often erroneously used to mean the opaque glaze applied to EARTHENWARE, the word correctly describes coloured glass fused by heating in a furnace to create a design or decorative finish on a metallic surface. Enamel can be produced in a broad spectrum of translucent or opaque colours and may take the place of gemstones without diminishing the appearance. There are many distinct enamelling techniques; some, such as CLOISONNÉ, date back to 1400 BC.

GUILLOCHÉ ENAMEL was used extensively by FABERGÉ and CARTIER. PLIQUE À JOUR was much used by ART NOUVEAU goldsmiths. *En ronde bosse* (the opaque enamelling of miniature objects or figures in high relief) was used in the Middle Ages. GRISAILLE is enamelling in black and white. Enamel *en resaille* is a rare type of enamelling inlaid in glass. Painted enamel is a method of creating a picture similar to painting on canvas but is usually executed on copper. In counter enamel a coating of plain enamel on the reverse of a decorated enamel plaque was used to strengthen it during firing. This is often seen in Swiss enamel jewellery. (See also CHAMPLEVÉ and BASSE TAILLE.)

Enamel colours A vitreous onglaze ceramic pigment that fuses when fired at a relatively low temperature (700–900°C). They are also known as *petit feu* colours, as opposed to *grand feu* (see HIGH-TEMPERATURE COLOURS). The technique derives from China and the Near East and was used in Europe by Venetian glassworkers in the 16th century. A full palette of colours was in use by the end of the 17th century.

Enamel twist decoration Decoration used in wineglass stems, where coloured enamels are incorporated in a twisted pattern in a DRAWN STEM. The enamels are usually white, but can include red or green, rarely blue and yellow.

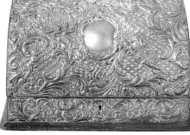
Silver embossed box, English c.1850 [K]

Choker clasp enamelled on gold with a Bacchic scene, Italian c.1600 [E]

Staffordshire enamelled wine label, early 19th century [R]

Empire style

The Empire style spans Napoleon I's reign as consul (1799–1804) and emperor (1804–15) of France. It influenced the REGENCY style in England and dominated those countries of Europe where members of the Bonaparte family were the occupying rulers. It also spread to the US, where there was a strong sympathy with the French.

The trappings of a Roman emperor

The Empire style can be seen as the last phase of NEO-CLASSICISM, but it was more opulent and historically accurate. Napoleon modelled his vast empire on that of ancient Rome, and the style was inspired by archaeological excavations in Greece, Italy and Egypt. The architects Charles PERCIER and Pierre-François-Léonard FONTAINE, who refurbished interiors for Napoleon and the Empress Josephine at Fontainebleau, Malmaison and Compiègne, established the style. Their designs were popularized in *Recueil de décorations intérieurs* (1812), and Roman ornament was used in bronzework, carpets, furniture, silver and ceramics. There was also a vogue for EGYPTIAN STYLE motifs inspired by Napoleon's campaigns in Egypt (1797–98). Furniture by François-Honoré-Georges JACOB-DESMALTER was based on Classical forms: X-CHAIRS, LITS-EN-BÂTEAU and TRIPOD TABLES, with SABRE LEGS, lion monopodia and CARYATIDS as supports. Mahogany was the most popular wood but some cabinet-makers used maple, ash and other native woods when the British blockaded French ports during the Napoleonic Wars (1799–1815). Porcelain produced by SÈVRES was based on Neo-classical urns and vases but was heavier, with rich colours ornamented with gilt bands of palm, acanthus and Egyptian motifs. Despite Napoleon's fall from power in 1815, the Empire style persisted in Europe and was taken up by many Federal cabinet-makers such as Duncan PHYFE in the US.

In the SECOND EMPIRE (1852–70), Napoleon III tried to resurrect the greatness of the Bonapartes. The decorative styles used during his reign were even more eclectic than under Napoleon I and even more opulently executed.

Empire chair with lion and serpent forms,
based on a Pharaoh's throne,
c.1810 [c]

Siena marble and
bronze candelabrum,
French c.1815 [c]

Second Empire silver bowl with glass inset,
decorated with heavy swags,
French c.1860 [D]

Recognizing the style

Motifs from imperial Rome, such as laurel wreaths and eagles, combined with Neo-classical palmettes, paterae, anthemions, guilloches, acanthus and swags, were the most commonly found decoration. Egyptian sphinxes, pyramids, hieroglyphs, lotus leaves, obelisks, lions and winged discs were popular, along with bees (Napoleon's personal emblem) and swans (Josephine's own symbol).

Swans

Sphinx

Lion

Gilded porcelain cup and saucer,
Second Empire period
French c.1870 [R]

Encaustic tile A tile with coloured clay inlaid in a pattern within the body clay. The decoration is permanent even when the covering glaze has worn. The Cistercian monks produced them as paving tiles but they are better known today from the mid-19th-century revival for use in fire-surrounds and floors.

Encoignure (French *coin*: "corner") A type of 18th-century corner cupboard on legs with graduated shelves. They evolved from triangular-shaped free-standing or hanging cupboards that fitted into the corner of a room. Probably first introduced in the early 17th century, they were common by the late 17th century.

End board The solid board forming the end of a chest or, often shaped, the support for a bench or early (pre-17th century) stool made without legs.

End-of-the-day glass A small item made by a glassworker in his own time from the molten glass that was left in the pot at the end of work. These pieces – rolling pins, bells, witches' balls and walking sticks – often designed to show off the maker's skills. See also FRIGGER.

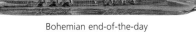

Bohemian end-of-the-day lavender or "tear" glasses, c.1869 [S]

End grain The grain that is revealed when a piece of wood is cut across rather than along the grain.

End support A general term used by furniture-makers to refer to an upright post or support.

Engine-turning A curving or geometric decorative pattern incised in metal or clay by turning on a lathe. Developed in the late 18th century, designs included chevrons, fluting, chequer and basket-

weave patterns. French goldsmiths first practised the technique in the 1760s and it was adopted in England for pottery by the ELERS brothers and Josiah WEDGWOOD. It was also used on silver in England into the 19th century.

English engine-turned silver snuffbox, c.1820 [L]

English cottage style A term used in the US to describe a style of interior design and architecture contemporary with Edwardian England (1901–10). A revival of WILLIAM AND MARY style.

English needle lace Followed the VENETIAN lead with such styles as RETICELLA and PUNTO IN ARIA then adopted the French forms of needle lace such as *point de France*. HOLLIE POINT was an English 18th-century form.

¹Engraving A process for decorating glass and metal in which the design is cut with a sharp instrument such as a DIAMOND POINT or WHEEL to create an image in small dots (see STIPPLE) or INTAGLIO or relief (see HOCHSCHNITT).

²Engraving A PRINT made by cutting a picture into wood or metal (copper or steel), inking the plate and pressing paper onto it. On wood, the print is in relief; on metal, in intaglio.

Entrée dish (French: "first course") A term now normally applied to silver and plated vegetable dishes with domed covers and handles. They were made in pairs or sets of four or more and could be square, circular or oval. Late 18th-century dishes are far less common than 19th- and early 20th-century examples.

Entrelac (French *entrelacer*: "to interlace") Interlaced tendril ornament of Celtic origin, primarily used in jewellery

making and revived by Arts and Crafts designers including Walter CRANE and William MORRIS. Entrelac decoration also featured in ART NOUVEAU stone and metalwork designs at the end of the 19th century, and in CELTIC REVIVAL designs.

Epergne A table centrepiece made of silver gilt-metal, glass or ceramic and known from the early 18th century. Early examples, used during the main course, were large, flat structures on feet with sockets or brackets to take saucers or casters for condiments or spices. Later examples were used for dessert courses and were larger, tiered structures with many branches, detachable dishes, sweetmeat-baskets and candleholders. The term is also used of copper, electroplate and silver hot-water or tea urns.

English silver épergne, c.1755 [A]

Ephemera (Greek: "lasting only a day") A term applied to all kinds of printed matter intended for immediate use and disposal. In packaging, the design and style can indicate the attitudes and tastes of a bygone age. Other ephemera include tickets, matchbox labels, wine labels, trade cards, cigar labels and shop window advertisements. Some collectors specialize in one area, such as postage stamps, CIGARETTE CARDS, GREETINGS CARDS and POSTCARDS. Some of the earliest wrappers and labels were fairly austere in design

BLICK GEGEN VIERWALDSTÄTTERSEE VON
STANSERHORN
VIEW OVER THE LAKE OF LUCERNE
VUE SUR LE LAC DES QUATRE CANTONS
GEZICHT OF HET VIERWALDSTÄTTERMEER

Ephemera: Swiss holiday brochure, c.1953 [s]

but soon became broadly pictorial with the advent of colour printing. Collecting tends to be concentrated on items from the late 19th and the 20th centuries.

EPNS An abbreviation for electroplated nickel silver and referring to any article made of a nickel base that is electroplated with a silver deposit. The initials EPNS are often stamped on such 20th-century articles. See ELECTROPLATING.

Equation dial See MEAN TIME.

Equinoctial dial A horizontal SUNDIAL usable in all latitudes, made largely during the 18th century before being superseded by the CHRONOMETER. Usually octagonal, with a central compass and a hinged, curved arm rising up one side marked with degrees of latitude. A hinged ring, bearing the GNOMON, is marked with the hours and slides up and down the curved arm, depending on the latitude of the user.

Escutcheon

Espagnolette

Escapement A mechanical device regulating the motive power from the weights, spring, electric current or other power source to the movement in a clock or watch. The simplest form of escapement comprises a toothed wheel and an arm with a pallet (a catch) at either end; the wheel is positioned so that only one tooth "escapes" at a time. Early clocks were fitted with a VERGE escapement, but the introduction of the ANCHOR ESCAPEMENT in the late 17th century, used in conjunction with the PENDULUM, dramatically improved the accuracy of timekeeping.

Escritoire A French term for a type of writing desk or SECRÉTAIRE made from the 16th century. A vertical FALL FRONT writing surface is hinged at the bottom, opens to provide the writing surface and folds up when not in use. The earliest portable writing boxes were called escritoires, but the closest relative is the 16th-century Spanish VARGUEÑO.

Escutcheon A term borrowed from heraldry to describe the often very decorative metal or ivory keyhole plates used on furniture to surround and protect the keyhole, and carved shield-shaped decoration incorporating monograms.

Esherick, Wharton (1887–1980) An American craftsman and sculptor, working in Paoli, Pennsylvania, who kept the craft tradition alive in post-war America. He made furniture in modern styles and with a sculptor's eye for space and form, using traditional techniques and skills.

Espagnolette The term for a female mask surrounded by a large, stiff, lace collar, which may have been of Mexican origin. A popular French decorative motif in the 18th century, the espagnolette was widely used by furniture designers during the RÉGENCE and the Louis XV period, featuring in

the designs of Daniel MAROT, Claude AUDRAN, Jean BÉRAIN and Jean-Antoine Watteau, as well as in BOULLE work.

Estampille The French term for the mark struck with a cold iron stamp on French furniture. The intaglio impression carried the maker's name, initials or monogram and was compulsory on furniture made by Parisian MENUISIERS-ÉBÉNISTES from 1751–91, except for pieces made for the Royal household.

Este pottery Founded in Este, near Venice, Italy, c.1779 by a French modeller, Jean-Pierre Varion, who had worked at VINCENNES, with Gerolamo Francini. The partnership was later dissolved. Varion began to manufacture porcelain, but he died in 1780 and the business was continued by his widow. No tablewares have been identified, but the figures are of fine quality. These were modelled by Varion and made after his death. Francini went on to make creamwares.

French kingwood étagère, c.1880 [G]

Etagère A French 19th century term describing free-standing shelves in two or three tiers, either square or rectangular, supported by corner posts or upright members. Similar to the English and American whatnot, the étagère was also used to serve food.

Etching See ACID ETCHING.

Etruria pottery See WEDGWOOD.

Etruscan maiolica See MAIOLICA.

Etruscan style The decorative arts and interior decoration inspired by the discovery of ancient Etruscan and Greek artifacts in the late 18th century. Part of the NEO-CLASSICAL STYLE, it is characterized by the use of a palette of terracotta and black and white and motifs such as PALMETTES and ANTHEMIONS found on late Classical Greek figure vases, which at the time were thought to be Etruscan. The most notable example of the style is the Etruscan Room (1775) at Osterley Park in Middlesex, by Robert ADAM. In the 1870s, there was a vogue for historically accurate adaptations of Etruscan gold jewellery featuring GRANULATION and wirework decoration.

Etui A pocket-sized case dating from the 18th to the 19th century made of silver, gold, enamel, gilt metal, tortoiseshell or lacquer. They were usually of tapering form with a hinged cover and a button catch, fitted to contain various small useful articles, such as lancets, writing sets, scent bottles, sewing accessories or knife, fork and spoon sets. They could be carried hung by a chain from a CHÂTELAINE.

Enamel étui, English
late 18th/early 19th century [K]

Everted A term designating an outwardly turned or flaring shape. It is most frequently used to describe the lip of a jug, pitcher or sauceboat, or the rim of a vessel made from ceramic or glass.

Ewer A large jug or pitcher with a wide mouth, the word originating from the French 14th-century word *évier*. They were made in many materials including metal, glass, earthenware and porcelain. Originally for carrying water for washing the hands – hence the occupation of "ewerer", a servant who supplied guests with water for that purpose.

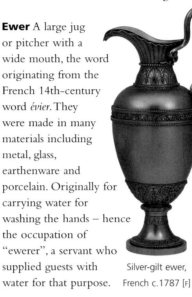

Silver-gilt ewer,
French c.1787 [F]

Excelsior A material made of wood shavings that look like straw, used as a stuffing in teddy bears.

Export porcelain See CHINESE EXPORT PORCELAIN.

Eye-and-scale motif A US term for coin moulding – a repeating pattern of overlapping discs, used horizontally or vertically, primarily on massive Classical styles. Coin moulding is known as eye-and-scale when used to describe mould-blown or pressed glass.

Eye motif A decorative device originating in ancient Egypt, as a symbol of protection. For the ancient Greeks, the eye was a good luck charm. In Christian iconography, it features in emblem books representing the eye of God and it is often depicted as the focus of a triangle symbolizing the Holy Trinity. In both American and French Revolutionary ornament, the eye symbolizes enlightenment. It was also an 18th-century term designating the centre of a volute scroll in the Ionic Order.

F

Fabergé menthol-
holder brooch,
c.1900 [L]

Fabergé, Peter Carl (1846–1920) Son of Gustav Fabergé, a St Petersburg goldsmith of Huguenot descent. After serving an apprenticeship in Frankfurt, Germany, he returned to Russia and took over the family business in 1870. He won the Gold Medal at the Pan-Russian Exhibition of 1882 and swiftly gained a reputation for his jewellery and objets d'art, combining the very highest artistic flair with minute attention to detail. He came to the notice of the Imperial Court and was commissioned to make the first Easter Egg by Tsar Alexander III in 1884. Over the next 30 years, he won the patronage of several royal houses and established shops in several Russian cities as well as in London. In 1917, the Revolution ended the Romanov dynasty and Fabergé's decline paralleled that of his patron, the Tsar. He fled Russia in 1918 and died in Lausanne, Switzerland.

Fabergé's incomparable skill as a master craftsman was matched by the progressive methods he adopted to run his business. He had a team of workmasters, each with his or her own individual speciality and responsibility. Although best known for the 57 Imperial eggs, they created hardstone carvings, flower studies, silver and jewellery as well as functional boxes, bellpushes and frames. Fabergé achieved a level of competence in enamelling and goldsmithing unlikely ever to be surpassed.

Fabergé gold
and pearl tie pin,
1900 [H]

Facet A type of decoration used on glass and jewellery, consisting of a series of shallow cuts creating sharp edges that reflect the light. Facet-cut stems were first used on English wineglasses from *c.*1750 and remained popular until the end of the century.

Façon de Venise

(French: "Venetian style") A term applied to glassware made in Europe from the mid-16th century and throughout the 17th, often by emigrant Venetian glassmakers, usually in a grey-toned soda glass and often with elaborate FILIGRANA decoration or with ornate applied decoration, as found on serpent-stemmed glasses.

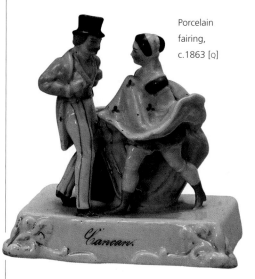

Façon de Venise glass, English *c.*1680 [I]

Faenza potteries

This influential Italian centre of maiolica production probably started in the 13th century with the manufacture of lead-glazed pottery but by 1450 the maiolica industry was well established. The early wares were in the "green and purple" styles as used at Orvieto with figures, animals and heraldic monsters against hatched backgrounds. This style was followed by one dominated by blue and many motifs of Near Eastern origin were used. They also used "Gothic" foliage – bold leaves in manganese, orange and a strong blue

Faenza albarello with strapwork, *c.*1520 [C, a pair]

and peacock feathers – to form borders and all-over diapers. After 1500, the products became more distinctive: one workshop was called Casa Pirota, having a motif of a *pyros rota* (fire bomb), a rebus on the family name. Early in the 16th century pictorial painting was introduced and gave rise to the ISTORIATO style.

Large dishes and ALBARELLI were made, the latter with borders of foliage and the labels in Gothic letters. Some wares directly copied Chinese MING porcelain, called *a porcellana*. The Casa Pirota painted wares in opaque white on a pale blue ground, called *berettino*. The artists of early Faenza are mostly unknown but, from about 1530, when the ISTORIATO style was copied from URBINO, the artists Baldassare Manara, Giovanni B. dale Palle and Francisco Mezzarisa are known. From 1600–75 the industry was in decline but revived in 1693 when Count Annibale Ferniani bought the main workshop. The Ferniani factory survived into the 20th century.

Faience "horn of plenty", French 1880 [I]

Faience

The French name for tin-glazed earthenware popular in Europe in 16th and 17th centuries. Used as a general term from *c.*1610 and probably derived from the town of Faenza in Italy. The German form is fayence. Faience was lightly baked earthenware of a buff or pale red colour covered with white enamel or glaze, which gives it the appearance of porcelain. There are two kinds:
(i) faience blanche, which was only lightly decorated if at all.
(ii) *grand feu*, painted in high temperature colours from metallic oxides, blue, purple, yellow, orange-red, green and sometimes red. *Grand feu* colours are painted onto

the unfired glaze, the colours melting into the glaze in the firing. Around 1750, *petit feu* colours were developed in France. They were brighter and included pink, crimson and vermilion. With *petit feu*, the glaze was fired and painted on, then fired again at a lower temperature.

Faience was used for making table services but also for garden pots. The industry was widespread in France, the chief centres being Aprey, Lyons, Luneville, Marseilles, Montpellier, Moustiers, Nevers, Rouen, Sceaux and Strasbourg. The industry reached its peak in France in the first three-quarters of the 18th century and then declined due to porcelain and creamware imports, although it has survived in many provincial areas, particularly QUIMPER.

Fairing A small porcelain figure or, more often, a group, made in eastern Germany mostly by Conta & Bohne of Pössneck. Fairings were given as prizes or bought cheaply at fairs. They are usually amusing, often in a saucy seaside style, and may have some sexual innuendo.

Porcelain fairing, *c.*1863 [Q]

Fairy lamp A small glass porcelain or coloured glass 19th-century night light holding a slow-burning candle. The term comes from the trademark of Samuel Clarke, the most prolific UK maker. Also refers to the small electric Christmas tree lights descended from votive candles.

Fairyland lustre
The designs by Daisy Makeig Jones when she was working at WEDGWOOD in the 1920s. Painted and printed in gold, they portrayed fairies, goblins and pixies in magical landscapes. The patterns are numbered and prefixed with a Z. Rarely, they bear the initials of Miss Jones.

One of a pair of famille rose dishes, c.1720s [I]

Falize, Alexis (1811–98) and his son **Lucien** (1838–97) Parisian jewellers specializing in colourful cloisonné enamelling with a strong Japanese influence. Lucien Falize entered into partnership with Germain Bapst from 1880 to 1892 and favoured jewels of neo-Renaissance or Persian design.

Fall front

Fall front (or drop front) The straight front flap of a bureau, cabinet or desk that is hinged at the bottom and opens or falls to form a horizontal writing surface.

False plate A sheet or cast-iron plate set between the dial and movement on some LONGCASE CLOCKS with painted iron dials. They were introduced with mass-produced painted iron dials in the 19th century and had holes for attaching the dial to the movement.

Famille jaune, noire, rose, verte
Terms used to classify Chinese porcelain by its colour palette. Famille verte, adopted in the KANGXI reign (1662–1722), uses green and iron red with other overglaze colours. It developed from the WUCAI style. Famille jaune is a variation using famille verte enamels on a yellow ground and famille noire uses a black ground (although some CLOBBERED WARES had the black added in the 19th century). Famille rose, introduced c.1720, used mainly pink or purple and remained popular throughout the 18th and 19th centuries (see also CHINESE EXPORT PORCELAIN and CANTON PORCELAIN).

Fans Fans were used in China and Japan for centuries before they permeated Western culture through trade. By the 17th century fans were made in Europe as well as imported. They were status symbols and combined function (cooling) with aesthetics. The earliest fans were fixed open, usually with a central stick. Sticks were made from luxury materials such as ivory and tortoiseshell, carved and decorated with precious metals or stones. Leaves were made from silk or paper, often printed or painted with pastoral or social scenes.

French silk fan, c.1890 [L]

Farnell & Co. An English toy and doll manufacturer founded by John Farnell in Notting Hill, London, in 1840. Farnell was producing rabbitskin-covered soft toys by 1897 and claimed to be the first English firm to have made MOHAIR PLUSH TEDDY BEARS. In 1921 Farnell took up the "Alpha" trademark. It is said that A.A. Milne's character Winnie the Pooh was based on a Farnell bear given to his son Christopher Robin. Farnell bears had robust bodies and rather long arms. The factory closed in 1968.

Farnell & Co. teddy bear, c.1920 [K]

Fasces (Latin: "bundles") A bound bundle of rods, often incorporating the head of an axe, the emblem of authority of the magistrates in ancient Rome. The fasces was an important motif in furniture decoration in the EMPIRE style and reappeared in the first decade of the 20th century.

Fashion doll (or Parisienne) A bisque or occasionally CHINA HEAD DOLL, mainly produced in France between 1860 and 1880, easily distinguishable from BÉBÉS by their smaller heads and accentuated waists. They evolved from miniature fashion mannequins and represent fashionably dressed young ladies.

Fauteuil A French term for a formal, often richly covered, open armchair with generous proportions, introduced in the early 18th century at the court of Louis XIV.

Faux bois (French: "false wood") Softwood painted with a marked grain.

Favrile glass IRIDESCENT glass developed by TIFFANY, patented in 1894 and used for a range of ART NOUVEAU glassware, most notably decorative vases in organic plant and flower-like shapes.

"Favrile" sprinkler by Tiffany, c.1900 [C]

Fazackerley A style of floral painting on English delft, the name probably deriving from two LIVERPOOL ware mugs painted with the names of Thomas and Catherine Fazackerley that were destroyed during World War II. However, "Fazackerley colours" came to mean several bright enamel colours – purple, green, blue and

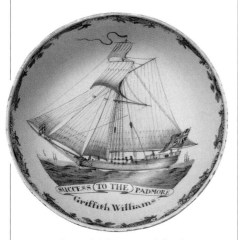

Liverpool delftware punch bowl
painted in Fazackerley colours, c.1768 [I]

yellow – that were used to decorate plates, punch bowls, flower bricks and bowls with flowers and foliage.

Feather banding See HERRINGBONE BANDING.

Feather-edge A silver and plated FLATWARE pattern (also used on porcelain knife handles). This variant of the Old English pattern is distinguished by an engraved narrow border of diagonal feather-like cuts. First made in England c.1765, this pattern is still produced today.

Feathers motif The emblem adopted for the Prince of Wales in England from the 14th century. By the early 18th century, it was widely used without any heraldic significance, as an ornamental cresting on mirrors and featuring in the designs of Daniel MAROT and Jean BÉRAIN. During the Adam period, feathers appear on capitals in Classical-style interiors. In the

Feathers motif

19th century the feather emblem was fashionable for chairs, tables, pediments, bookcases and beds.

Featherwork The use of coloured feathers as decoration originated in Oceania and Pre-Columbian America where exotic bird feathers adorned clothes and textiles. It was also used in the 18th and 19th centuries in Europe for textiles and domestic pieces; some feathers used were dyed to add colour.

Federal style See pp.166–67.

Feilner, Simon (1726–98) A German porcelain modeller, born in Weiden. He worked as a stuccoist and painter at Schloss Saarbrucken and then at HÖCHST as a flower painter, decorator and modeller. In 1753 he went to FÜRSTENBERG and in 1770 to FRANKENTHAL as a modeller and ARCANIST, later becoming a director. He is known for his COMMEDIA DELL'ARTE and Classical figures and miners.

Feldspar A crystalline mineral derived from granite, used as one of the fusible ingredients of porcelain or as a FLUX. Europe's purest deposits are in Norway, Sweden and Russia.

Feldspathic glaze A glaze containing a high (50–100) percentage of FELDSPAR. The term is also used for a glaze that, while containing less then 50 per cent of feldspar, is compounded of minerals that create an artificial feldspar.

Fell, Isaac (1758–1818) An American furniture-maker, active in Savannah, from c.1780. Fell worked mainly in mahogany, making furniture in the English taste, but his work is considered more provincial than contemporary pieces from the north-eastern states.

Felt A non-woven textile usually made from sheep's wool, used extensively in Central Asia and South America for rugs, tents, wall hangings and clothing. Its use in Europe is thought to date back to the 5th century. It was used for clothing until the 17th century when it started to be used in embroidery.

Felt doll A type of doll mainly produced between 1920 and 1940 by manufacturers such as LENCI, STEIFF, CHAD VALLEY and Norah WELLINGS. The felt used for a doll's face tends to be moulded over a buckram base to enhance longevity. Fingers could be delineated by stitching.

Felt Snow White and the Seven Dwarfs
by Chad Valley, late 1930s [K]

Fender A low metal screen used since the 17th century to prevent coals from rolling from the hearth into the room.

Fern A popular motif in the late 19th century when ferns were keenly collected and used to decorate cast-iron garden furniture and architectural features such as column capitals. In keeping with the contemporary fancy for heavy and extravagant forms drawn from nature, fern patterns were also favoured as decoration for glass, textiles and ceramics.

Ferronnerie The French term for wrought ironwork. Scrolling patterns of arabesques and volutes, which derived from *ferronneries*, decorated 16th-century tin-glazed ceramics from Antwerp, and faience from Moustiers, Strasbourg and Rouen dating to the 17th and early 18th centuries. A number of designs by Jean BÉRAIN include ferronneries.

Neo-classical coffee-pot in the form of an urn
by James Musgrave of Philadelphia, c.1795 [D]

The influence of English furniture design
is seen in this Hepplewhite-style
mahogany settee, c.1800 [F]

Recognizing the style

The Federal age was one of great
national pride. Patriotic American
motifs, carved shells and Classical
elements such as fluting and scrolls
are commonly found.

American eagle

Stars and Stripes

Federal style

This period and style of American Neo-classical architecture and artifacts began in the 1780s and lasted until the dwindling of Neo-classical taste in the 1830s. The best Federal style captures the elements of confidence and prosperity felt in the newly formed United States.

Energy and optimism in a new country

In political history, America's Federal period began with the establishment of the first Federal government under President George Washington in New York City in 1789. The importance of NEO-CLASSICAL style to the dignity of the recently united country can be seen in the government buildings of the day, notably the White House in Washington DC.

Federal style emerged with independence from Great Britain, but was nevertheless heavily inspired by British taste, particularly in the realm of furniture design. The architectural concepts of Robert ADAM are the foundation of most Neo-classical design of this period, particularly neo-Grecian taste. However, it was the popularizers of Adam who were widely read and interpreted in the US. The publications of the English designers George HEPPLEWHITE, Thomas Shearer and Thomas SHERATON were the most influential works and some Federal cabinet-makers copied designs from them closely.

American designers were also inspired by contemporary discoveries of the ancient world, particularly Pompeii. Culturally the new American republic identified closely with ancient Rome and with post-revolutionary France. This fascination and admiration was reflected in the lifestyle of enlightened Americans who surrounded themselves with artifacts and libraries, in the manner of European dilettanti. This led to new demands for furniture, particularly bookcases, writing desks and chairs of every description. A great deal of formal furniture continued to be imported from England and France, but American cabinet-makers also kept pace with innovative, high quality work.

Federal cabinet-makers also developed new forms. Bookcases and desks were combined into one piece, called a SECRETARY, which replaced the earlier slant-front desk or bureau bookcase form. Most secretaries are of mahogany with satinwood stringing or inlay in the Hepplewhite taste and have elegant, slender proportions. Other new forms were WORK TABLES, SOFA TABLES, SOFAS, chairs of all description including "lolling" or high-back, upholstered open-armchairs, SIDEBOARDS, CELLARETS and KNIFEBOXES. Federal furniture can be distinguished from British by the scale (usually a little grander), regional stylistic variety and details such as carving or inlay, construction techniques (which are not as uniform as British) and materials. Of the common timbers employed, MAPLE, a pale wood indigenous to North America, was also used as an alternative to satinwood as inlay or contrast, for example on drawer-fronts. Maplewood Federal furniture is normally of New England origin and may be formal or provincial. It often has interesting figuring to the grain, including striped "tiger maple", knotted "birds-eye maple" or richly figured "curly maple". Gilding was used sparingly, except for mirror frames.

Mirrors of the age

A classic Federal mirror form is the circular wall mirror with wide, OGEE-moulded frame holding a convex "bulls-eye" glass. Such mirrors often have patriotic, heraldic eagle mounts. Some examples are fitted with twin candle arms and are termed GIRANDOLES. Another common mirror form is the rectangular, vertical wall mirror with a moulded cornice and divided glass. Many of these are quite small and may feature an ÉGLOMISÉ upper panel. Mirrors of this type remained popular throughout the 19th century and are relatively common today. Among the best known and most sought-after Federal cabinet-makers in the British tradition are Benjamin Randolph of Philadelphia, John and Thomas Seymour of Boston and Duncan PHYFE of New York City, who later also adopted the French style.

Flame-cut mahogany sideboard
inlaid with maple banding,
c.1800 [E]

Mahogany Federal side chair with elaborately
carved back rails, c.1815 [O]

American Empire style

From about 1800 the French Empire style became popular in the eastern states, due in part to the emigration of wealthy and fashionable French revolutionary exiles, including cabinet-makers and other craftspeople. New York City, Baltimore and, especially, Philadelphia, were the main centres of French settlement in the Federal period. Federal furniture made in this style, which remained popular into the early 1840s, is known as American Empire. The most ornate treatment appears on this type of furniture, which also saw an increase in gilding and the introduction of stencilled decoration, usually applied in black onto pale wood such as maple. The French immigrant cabinet-maker Charles-Honoré LANNUIER is considered the best exponent of this style.

American Empire style draws influence from contemporary French furniture, publications documenting archaeological discovery in the ancient world (including Egypt), and design journals, notably that of Thomas HOPE. New and popular forms included tables and chairs with SABRE LEGS, including the KLISMOS chair of Greco-Roman inspiration. PIER TABLES were CONSOLE TABLES designed to stand between windows. They were usually made in mahogany with marble tops and (sometimes) marble column supports flanking a mirrored back. Card tables with flip-tops (typically made in pairs) in the French taste are distinctive examples of American Empire furniture. The best examples display the virtuosity of the cabinet-maker in the supports. DOLPHINS, winged GRIFFINS and SPHINXES adorn tables made by the best French immigrant and American makers. Many are richly decorated with PARCEL GILDING, stencilling and paint.

Sheraton-style mirror with the
American eagle, c.1815 [A]

Mahogany card table
showing Empire influence,
c.1820 [G]

Festoon of flowers and fruit

Festoon Ornament in the form of a garland of fruit and flowers, tied with ribbons and leaves and suspended in a loop from both ends. Originating in the temple decorations of Classical Rome, festoons spread during the Renaissance, sometimes embellished with rings, rosettes, lion masks and putti. Festoons were frequently also enriched with vegetables and shells in the 16th and 17th centuries. The taste for lavishly chased and embossed SWAGS on silver vessels complemented the extravagant BAROQUE festoons carved for furniture and interiors in the 17th century. Although the festoon fell from favour early in the 18th century as the fashion for elaborate, heavily carved decoration waned, it re-emerged in the lighter style in the NEO-CLASSICAL period in the designs of Robert ADAM and remained a popular decorative motif well into the 19th century.

Fiddle pattern Silver and plated FLATWARE so named because the stems of spoons and forks resemble the shape of a violin or fiddle. Popular in 18th-century France, this pattern appeared in England c.1740 and became one of the most well-known, with a popular variant called fiddle, thread and shell.

Field, fielded panel A framed or enclosed raised wooden panel with bevelled edges and a flat central field.

Figures, toy A scale replica of a person or animal, usually made of lead, sometimes a resin mixture and, later, plastic. Soldiers and farm and zoo animals are the most common. Wood was used for animals for Noah's Ark toys.

Figuring The natural markings and graining found on wood that make a decorative pattern.

Filet See LACIS.

Filigrana An Italian term for glass decorated with embedded threads of white or coloured glass in various patterns. The technique was first used in Murano, Italy, in the second quarter of the 16th century, flourished there until the 18th and was revived by MURANO GLASSHOUSES in the 20th century.

Gold and gemstone filigree, English c.1830 [D]

Filigree Ornamental work of twisted gold and silver wire, soldered into openwork forms or two-dimensional panels and used as decoration or in articles like small caskets, trays, frames and objects of vertu. This extremely delicate art form was most popular throughout Europe in the late 17th century and enjoyed sporadic comebacks during the 19th and 20th centuries.

Filigree glass The English term for FILIGRANA – clear glass pieces decorated with a fine network of white or coloured threads in a variety of complex patterns.

Fillet A narrow BAND or strip of wood, found between mouldings or used as an inlaid STRING, where it may have the grain at right angles to the piece inlaid.

Finial A decorative turned or carved ornament surmounting a prominent terminal. Generally taking the form of an acorn, pinecone or urn, although frequently much more elaborate finials appear on furniture from the 15th century – on the uprights of chairs, bed testers and cabinet cornices – and on the covers of silver, pottery, porcelain or glass vessels, where they often double as handles. See also KNOP.

Firangi (Northern India: "foreigner") An Indian sword using either an imported European blade or one made in the European style. These swords were principally used in the Maharatta empire from the late 16th century.

Firearms Although gunpowder was probably invented by the Chinese in the 7th century AD, it was the Europeans who harnessed its explosive force to project missiles from tubes. Guns were known in England from the early 14th century. The first practical hand-held firearms appeared in the 1470s and were ignited by lengths of glowing cord. These developed into the MATCHLOCK, which survived until the 1680s. The WHEEL LOCK was probably invented in Germany c.1500, but was complicated and expensive to make. The SNAPHAUNCE lock mimicked human hands using flint and steel to make sparks. This was later refined, c.1590, to become the FLINTLOCK or the French lock as it was sometimes known. Experiments by the Reverend Alexander Forsyth in the first decade of the 19th century with fulminate of mercury led to the development of the PERCUSSION LOCK. This used a copper cap containing a tiny amount of explosive that exploded violently when struck. The

Wheel lock pistol, German c.1630 [F]

flash from this set off the gunpowder. The percussion cap paved the way for both repeating and BREECHLOADING firearms. In 1835, LeFaucheux invented the PINFIRE system, which used a self-contained CARTRIDGE. Flobert modified the percussion cap to produce the rimfire cartridge. In 1861, the centrefire cartridge was introduced in Britain, based on designs by Pottet & Schneider and Edward Boxer. This cartridge type is still in use today and there have been few real advances in firearms technology since 1871. Thereafter, designers concentrated on perfecting repeating guns and ultimately on self-loading and fully automatic firearms.

Fire-back A heavy arched cast- or wrought-iron panel set at the back of a fireplace, partly for decoration, partly as an aid to retain and radiate the heat of the fire but also to shield the wall from excess heat damage. Made from the 16th century, fire-backs are often decorated with heraldic devices, foliage, figures or mythological scenes in low relief. Late 16th- and early 17th-century examples are particularly decorative; often cast in relief with figures, coats of arms and dates. They were superseded in the early 18th century by one-piece fireplace grates.

Fire-dog See ANDIRON.

Fire gilding See MERCURY GILDING.

Fire polishing The process of reheating a piece of worked glass to give it a bright finish. Glass worked with tools, cast pieces and sculpted pieces may be reintroduced into the glory hole (a simple reheating drum) or into a kiln before annealing.

Firescreen A portable device used to screen people from the excessive heat of an open fire. Known from the Middle Ages and used consistently until the demise of the open fire as the main form of heating, fire screens were made in a variety of forms, most of which consisted of a portable wooden support and frame, sometimes carved, or painted and gilded, with either a fixed or adjustable panel made of needlework, tapestry, leather or scrapwork. (See also POLE SCREEN and BACK SCREEN.)

Firing The process of heat treatment of ceramic ware in a kiln or oven, to develop a vitreous or crystalline bond. The temperature required may be from *c.*800°C for earthenware to *c.*1450°C for porcelain. The achievement of sufficiently high temperatures for firing was one of the major factors in the development of true porcelain.

Firing glass A short-stemmed sturdy DRAM glass with a thick foot and sometimes engraved with Masonic symbols. Made from the 18th century onward, such glasses were traditionally rapped on the table after a toast and sounded like muskets firing.

Firing glass, English 1768 [P]

Fish slice A silver or plated serving trowel or slice, usually with a single blade on one side, designed during the 18th century for serving fish, later becoming a common serving piece in most CANTEENS.

Fitzhugh pattern An elaborate border pattern on CHINESE EXPORT PORCELAIN of butterflies, finger citron (an Oriental fruit resembling a hand), flowers, foliage and cell DIAPER, popular with the American market *c.*1790–1810. Usually underglaze blue, but also in bright green, brown and orange. Named after Thomas Fitzhugh, a director of the East India Company, who ordered a service *c.*1780. The pattern was taken up by the CAUGHLEY and COALPORT factories.

Tapestry and mahogany fire screen, English c.1840 [M]

Qianlong Fitzhugh pattern platter, c.1750 [K]

Fitzroy barometer,
c.1890 [L]

Fitzroy barometer
Designed by and named
after Admiral Robert
Fitzroy (1805–65), a British
meteorologist. It has two
pointers that record
atmospheric pressure on
successive days. It is usually
set in a carved and glazed
rectangular wooden case.

Fixed eyes Enamelled or
glass eyes set in a doll's head
and held in a rigid position
with plaster.

Flagg, James Montgomery
(1877–1960) An American
illustrator, poster artist and
portrait painter, famous
for his World War I
recruitment poster of
Uncle Sam with the caption "I Want
You". He designed many film posters,
including *Lost Horizon* (1937), and covers
for *Life* magazine.

Flagon A tall,
often narrow
cylindrical vessel
used from the
16th century for
serving wine,
usually with a
moulded foot, flat
or domed lid, a
lip, a large curving
handle and
thumbpiece. Flagons were generally made
of pewter, stoneware or faience, although
silver examples – often former
ecclesiastical ones – also survive.

Flambé glaze A high-fired glaze
(1200°C/2190°F), which may flow in the
kiln, giving rise to flame-like streaks of
purple or blue in Chinese wares e.g. SANG
DE BOEUF, and in some modern pottery.

Flagg recruitment poster,
c.1917 [S]

Flamboyant Gothic A variant of the
Gothic style in medieval architecture and
the decorative arts, characterized by
elaborate flame-like branching tracery. It
is found mainly in 15th-century metalwork, decorated with detailed naturalistic
foliage, arches, crockets, frets and bosses.

Flame stitch See BARGELLO.

Flame veneer A technique in which a
veneer is cut at an angle to produce a
swirling flame-like FIGURING.

Flanders See FLEMISH LACE.

Flange A collar or rim applied to an
object to strengthen it, or for attaching it
to another object.

Flange neck See SOCKET HEAD.

Flatback A Staffordshire pottery figure
or group made by various potters in the
19th century. They were
painted in bright colours
on the front but, for
reasons of economy,
left white on the back
and also flat
so that they
could stand
against the wall
on the
mantelshelf.

Staffordshire flatback "Dick Turpin",
c.1850–60 [N]

Flat chasing
A form of CHASING on
the flat surfaces of silver
articles, e.g. the centre of a salver, that was
used to great decorative effect in the late
17th century, mid-18th century and early
19th century.

Flat toy A thin cast lead figure with one
or both sides in relief. Flats originated in
Germany and became generally popular
in the 19th century. Usually hand-painted
with alcohol-based paints, flats continued
to be made until the 1920s and were
again produced in plastic by several
companies in the 1960s.

Flatware The term for all flat articles of
tableware such as plates, spoons and forks
but excluding those with a cutting edge
(cutlery). However, it may also mean
forks, spoons and cutlery as opposed to
other wares, such as HOLLOWWARE vases.

Flatweave A pile-less rug or carpet,
e.g. KILIMS, SOUMAKS, Verneh, SILEH and
Indian DHURRIES, woven with a tapestry
technique. Their name depends on where
and how they are made.

Flaxman, John (1755–1826) The
leading English Neo-classical modeller
and sculptor. His father worked for
WEDGWOOD and John also worked for
them as a modeller from 1775. He
modelled friezes of Classical scenes such
as *The Muses* (1777) and *Hercules in the
Garden of the Hesperides* (1787), as well as
relief portraits of many contemporary
notables. Wedgwood sponsored Flaxman
to study fine art in Rome from 1787–94
although, while there, he
continued to supply
Wedgwood with designs, for
JASPER WARE and BASALTES
WARE. Later, he worked
mostly as a marble
sculptor and also
made models for
the silversmith
Paul STORR.

Flecked glass
Glass with flecks of
opaque glass embedded
in its surface. First
made in Roman times, the best-known
examples were made in England in the
early 19th century (see NAILSEA), when
the technique was used to make a range of
inexpensive novelties. Interesting variations
were also made in Europe and the US.

Flemish lace A general term for needle
and bobbin LACE made in Flanders,
notably Antwerp, BINCHE, Brabant, Cluny,
Bruges, BRUSSELS and MECHLIN. Flemish
flax produced an exceptionally fine
thread, ensuring the highest quality lace.

Flemish scroll A type of double scroll that was used on the front legs and stretchers of late 17th-century chairs in which the foot scrolled inward and the "knee" scrolled outward.

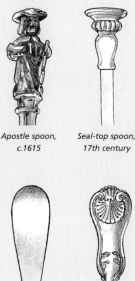

Fleur-de-lis (French: "lily flower") A stylized lily, this heraldic flower with three petals appears in Christian iconography as an emblem reflecting the purity of the Virgin Mary. A central device in the royal arms of France

Fleur-de-lis

from the 12th century, the fleur-de-lis was a popular motif in late Gothic tracery designs, and was taken up by the Gothic Revival style, featuring as an ornament for screens, tiles and ironwork.

Flint glass An archaic term often used for English LEAD GLASS. It refers to glass made from around the mid-17th century in which ground flint, rather than the Venetian pebbles previously used, was the source of the silica. The resulting glass is known as LEAD CRYSTAL.

Flintlock gun, Belgian c.1760 [K]

Flintlock
A mechanism for striking sparks from flint and steel. Its earliest form was the SNAPHAUNCE, which appeared in the mid-16th century. This was refined c.1600 by LeBourgeois. The flintlock was easy and cheap to make and remained in use until the middle of the 19th century.

Flirty eyes SLEEPING EYES in dolls, which can move from side to side.

Florence potteries A group of factories around Florence from the late 14th century until c.1475 when FAENZA took the lead. Maiolica was made in Florence itself from c.1300. Technical and decorative devices originated from Hispano-Moresque wares imported into Italy in quantities. Their forms included jugs, ALBARELLI and OAK LEAF JARS. Human figures and animals in stylized foliage appear before the end of the 15th century on tiles and large dishes, most of which seem to have been made for use rather than decoration. The pottery in Florence seems to have closed after 1530.

Florence tapestry factory Founded in 1545 by Duke Cosimo de Medici, the Arrazzeria Medicea was intended to turn Florence into a major tapestry-weaving centre. With cartoons by major Florentine artists and heavy subsidies from the Medicis, the factory flourished. From 1554 all production was for the Medici household. The factory closed in 1737.

Florentine carving A general term for elaborate scroll and leaf carving, used on picture and mirror frames from the 17th century. May also refer to the carving used in Florence during the BAROQUE period of the late 17th and early 18th century in which sculptors created carved and often gilt armchairs, decorated with putti, mythological figures and masks.

Flatware handles

Services of matching flatware became known from the early 18th century. Flatware can often be approximately dated from the pattern of its handles, as different patterns became popular in certain periods. In Europe many makers would use the same pattern but, in the US, patterns were often patented and can therefore be assigned to a particular maker and a particular date.

Apostle spoon, c.1615

Seal-top spoon, 17th century

Puritan spoon, 1649–60

Trefid pattern, late 17th century

Dog-nose spoon, c.1700

Hanoverian pattern, c.1710–1770

Onslow fork handle, c.1760

Old English, c.1765

Queen's, early 19th century

King's, early 19th century

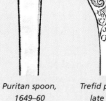

Fiddle, with crest, early 19th century

Fiddle, thread and shell, c.1840

Albert pattern, 1875

Albany spoon, c.1860

Florentine mosaic An English term used to describe PIETRE DURE panels made in Florence from the mid-16th century and also later variations in the technique in countries as far afield as England and India. Coloured semi-precious stones were inlaid in marble in designs that included landscapes, flowers and fruit and birds. The resulting panels were used to decorate interiors and, from the late 17th century into the 19th, the tops of tables.

Florentine stitch See BARGELLO.

Floss silk A silk thread that has been reeled onto BOBBINS direct from the cocoon, sometimes with a slight twist, rather than spun. Only the highest quality silk from the centre of cocoons is used to make thread in this way and it has therefore always been expensive.

Flow blue A deep COBALT blue used for underglaze painting on ceramics. The colour, which tends to flow into the glaze, giving a blurred effect, is obtained by placing volatile chlorides in the SAGGER containing the ware. Chlorine is given off and combines with the cobalt making it slightly soluble in the glaze.

English delft flower brick, c.1740 [K]

Flower brick A ceramic holder for flowers, of 18th-century origin. Most were rectangular but some were square. The top was pierced with holes for the stems of the flowers and, usually, a central square hole to fill the brick with water.

Flute A tall drinking glass with an extremely narrow inverted conical bowl resting on a very short stem. Early examples were used for wine in Germany and Holland in the 17th centuries. Later, in the late 18th and early 19th centuries, the flute spread to other countries and shorter flutes were used as CHAMPAGNE GLASSES.

Fluting A pattern of shallow, rounded, parallel channels running vertically along the shaft of a COLUMN, PILASTER or other surface. A favourite ornament for furniture from the 16th century, fluting has been used to decorate ceramics and silver vessels and for the bowls and stems of 18th-century wine glasses. It is the opposite of REEDING or GADROONING.

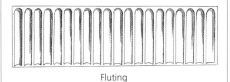

Fluting

Flux A material, commonly sodium oxide, added to the ingredients (the batch) in glass-making to reduce the temperature at which they fuse together.

Flywheel A heavy wheel designed to improve the smooth running of steam engines but also used to maintain balance in some toys, e.g. tops, gyroscopes and motor cycles. See also FRICTION MOTOR MECHANISM.

Fob chain See POCKET WATCH.

Foiling A technique of jewellery-making in use since the Renaissance, foiling is a way of enhancing the colour and lustre of a gemstone or paste imitation by inserting plain or coloured tinfoil behind the stone, and securing it in a CLOSED-BACK SETTING. The practice of foiling has inevitably resulted in deliberate deception, for instance, colourless rock crystal being passed off as sapphire by the insertion of blue tinfoil.

Folded foot A type of foot used on drinking glasses and other glass items in which the rim of the foot is folded under to give extra stability. Popular in the 18th century.

▲ Folded foot on a wine glass

Foley pottery See SHELLEY.

Fondporzellan See GROUND COLOURS.

Fontaine, Pierre-François-Léonard (1762–1853) A French architect and designer of furniture, textiles, silver and interiors. Born in Pontoise, he studied architecture at the Ecole des Beaux-Arts in Paris, where in 1779 he met a fellow student, Charles PERCIER. Together they set up in partnership after studying Classical and Renaissance architecture in Rome. In 1799 they were commissioned to redecorate the interior of Malmaison, the residence just outside Paris of Josephine de Beauharnais, the consort of Napoleon I, and later the Tuileries Palace and the Louvre. They created the EMPIRE style, which was illustrated in their *Receuil des décorations intérieurs* (published 1801).

Fontange A lady's wired headdress of linen and lace fashionable *c.*1700; see POINT DE NEIGE.

Football (English) memorabilia Football's roots can be traced back to the Chinese Han dynasty, but the team game as we know it today was developed along the rules drawn up by the UK Football Association, founded in 1863. Caps, shirts, balls, programmes, commemorative ceramics, books, art, bronzes, medals and other autographed memorabilia are now collected.

Football: crested china vase, English, 1898 [S]

American football memorabilia: jersey
worn by Larry Csonka, 1975 [N]

Football (American) memorabilia
Items relating to American football, an
eleven-player team game that can be
traced back to early 19th-century English
rugby. They include autographed
footballs, helmets, books, magazines,
posters, jerseys and bubble-gum cards.

Footman
A four-legged stand, made of
iron or brass, that stood in front of the
fire and was used as a stand for hot dishes.
Known from the late 18th century.

Foot-rim
The projecting circular support
on the bottom of a plate, utensil or vessel.
Sometimes called a basal rim or foot ring.

Foot warmer
A portable metal or
ceramic container for hot water or
burning coals, used for keeping the feet
warm. Metal examples usually have a
pierced metal or wooden outer cover.
They were used by travellers in carriages
from the 17th to the 19th centuries;
earthenware examples survived in use
into the 20th century.

Fork
Originating in Europe in the 6th or
7th century, eating forks were introduced
into Britain at the Restoration in 1660
and have been commonly used since
then. Meat and dessert forks became
separate items during the 17th century.
Meat forks were at first made with two
or three prongs, but the four-pronged
type became common in the later 17th
century. See also FLATWARE.

Fornasetti, Piero
(1913–88) An Italian
designer, engraver, manufacturer and
painter known for his witty designs of
ceramics, furniture and textiles. He was
employed by Gio PONTI on decorative
work for interiors. His style commonly
combines images from antique
engravings and surrealistic
and TROMPE L'OEIL effects.

Fortuny, Mariano
(1871–1949) Born in
Granada, Spain, Fortuny
settled in Venice in 1889.
Initially a photographer
and theatre designer, by 1906
his attention had turned to
textile and fashion design. In
1909 he patented a technique for
undulating and pleating silk, as
used for his famous Delphes dresses.
In 1921 he opened a factory that
recreated historic woven fabric designs on
cotton, using an industrial printing
process that he developed himself. The
factory still operates today.

Fornasetti plate,
1950s [P]

Foxing
A term applied to antique books
and prints, indicating circular spots of
brownish discoloration on paper. It is
caused by particles of iron or copper
present in the paper from mill machinery
or, more commonly, by biological activity
in the form of tiny mould growths.

Frankenthal porcelain factory
One of the leading German 18th-
century porcelain
factories, known
for its wares in
high ROCOCO
style. It was
founded at
Frankenthal, near   1762–
Mannheim in   1790s
Palatinate
Germany, in 1755 by Paul-
Antoine Hannong (see
STRASBOURG POTTERY

Frankenthal couple,
c.1778 [I]

AND PORCELAIN FACTORIES) with J.J.
RINGLER. Hannong's two sons, Charles
François Paul and Joseph-Anton, took
over the factory in 1759. Their output
was considerable but they were financially
unsuccessful, and the factory was
acquired by the Elector Palatine
in 1762. Adam Bergdoll was
director until 1775, then
Simon FEILNER until
1797. The factory made
tablewares, vases and
clocks – sometimes finely
painted by Jakob Osterspei
with mythological scenes,
highly prized today. But
figure production (often BISCUIT
porcelain) was predominant. The
modellers were the court
sculptor, Konrad Linck
(1730–93), who made ambitious
theatrical figures, J. W. Lanz, Johann F.
Luck, and Karl G. Luck. In 1795, the
factory was occupied by the French and,
after operating briefly under their
ownership, closed in 1799 or 1800. Some
moulds went to NYMPHENBURG and
were used to reproduce figures.

Friedrich Augustus I,
Elector of
Saxony and King of Poland (1670–1733)
Popularly known as AUGUSTUS THE
STRONG, from the number of his amours
and illegitimate children. He converted to
Catholicism in order to claim the
throne of Poland. Augustus had
a considerable effect on the
history of ceramics and was
an obsessive collector
of Oriental porcelain
and the founder,
patron and eventual
owner of the
MEISSEN porcelain
factory. He is notorious
for having bartered an
entire regiment of
600 dragoons for 48
Chinese blue and
white vases from
Frederick the
Great of Prussia.

Free blowing One of the earliest techniques for making glass in which the glass-maker collects a GATHER of molten glass from the furnace on the end of a blowing rod and then inflates it with his breath, manipulating the rod to create the desired shape.

French knot A knot created by winding the thread around the needle twice before securing the stitch, creating a knot-like bobble. Particularly fashionable in late 18th-century silk work embroidery.

French needle lace in
point de France, 1720s [K]

French needle lace From the 1660s France imported VENETIAN NEEDLE LACE until Louis XIV appointed Jean Baptiste Colbert minister for French lace. The French then developed their own *point de France* lace for elaborate flounces, some with Bérainesque designs on a hexagonal ground. Lace-making centres were established in ALENÇON and ARGENTAN.

French polish A process introduced *c.*1820 for creating a highly polished surface on wooden furniture. It involves applying a series of very even layers of clear SHELLAC dissolved in spirit, each of which is sanded down before the next is applied, to build up a high gloss.

Fretwork A carved geometric decoration of intersecting lines in which the spaces may be pierced through or not

Fretwork

(in the latter case, it is called "blind" fretwork). A common decoration of ancient origin, fretwork became popular in the mid-18th century in ROCOCO items, particularly in the GOTHIC and Chinese taste. In furniture, fretwork was used on bookcases, tables, cabinets and chairs, frequently as a border, or to form a GALLERY. Fanciful Rococo fretwork was toned down in the NEO-CLASSICAL period, replaced by the GREEK KEY pattern and confined to border decoration on furniture, silver and ceramics. In the late 19th century, the term was chiefly applied to ornamental openwork patterns carved from wood with a fretsaw.

Friction motor mechanism
Also known as "push and go", this method of driving toy vehicles uses a FLYWHEEL geared to an axle as an energy store to propel the toy. When the toy is pushed hard, the flywheel speeds up and absorbs the necessary power to drive it. This method is used mainly on tinplate vehicles, but there are diecast examples, e.g. some 1956 CORGI toys.

Frieze Originally an architectural term that describes the section between the ARCHITRAVE and CORNICE on the upper part of a Classical order, it is also used to describe a horizontal piece of wood that supports the top of a table, or a cornice on a piece of CASE FURNITURE.

Frigger A more elaborate END-OF-THE-DAY GLASS, using up leftover coloured glass to make small decorative objects.

Fringe The loose strands of wool, cotton or silk at each end of a rug or carpet. In handmade examples they are an integral part of the rug, formed by the warp threads. They often enhance the visual appearance of a piece and are sometimes plaited and braided.

Frit A mixture of powdered or ground ingredients added at the end of the glass-making process. The term also describes impurities such as sand that are found in old glass.

Fritware A low-fired artificial porcelain body of ground quartz, white clay and glaze, introduced by 12th-century Islamic potters in imitation of Chinese Ding porcelains, then reaching the Near East from China. Resembles later, more highly fired, European soft-paste porcelain bodies, being white and translucent when thinly potted, and covered with a translucent alkaline glaze.

Blue printed frog mug,
c.1830 [N]

Frog mug An English mainly 19th-century ceramic mug of cylindrical shape with a frog modelled and attached to the inside of the mug about two-thirds of the way down, which would become visible to the drinker as the level fell.

Fromanteel family An English family of clockmakers of Dutch or Flemish origin. Ahasuerus Fromanteel I worked as a clockmaker in Smithfield, London, from *c.*1620–*c.*1690 and was probably one of the earliest makers of pendulum clocks in England; one John Fromanteel, possibly Ahasuerus's son, studied the manufacture of such clocks in the Netherlands in 1657–58. Other clockmakers with the Fromanteel name were recorded in the late 17th century as members of the Clockmakers' Company in London.

Frosted glass A type of glass with a matt or "frosted" finish. The technique was introduced in the mid-19th century for coarse frosting. From 1880 a silkier finish was achieved using acid and was particularly popular in the ART DECO period, when it was used on decorative glass by such masters as René LALIQUE and also on pressed decorative glass.

Frosted glass claret jug with clear twist handle, c.1860 [Q]

Frosted silver A textured or matt finish on the surface of silver giving the effect or look of a layer of frost. This surface finish is achieved either by hand with the use of fine chasing tools or by immersion in acid to cause etching.

Frothingham, Benjamin (1734–1809) An American cabinet-maker. Frothingham was active in Charlestown, near Boston, Massachusetts, making high quality, fashionable case furniture in the American CHIPPENDALE style. Labelled examples are extremely rare.

Frozen Charlotte (also Frozen Charlie and Bathing Baby) An all-in-one porcelain doll with moulded hair and painted features, stretched limbs and bent arms with clenched fists. They were made in the late 19th century by various German factories.

Fruitwood Country furniture was often constructed from the wood of fruit trees. Pearwood, strong and heavy with a fine, red-tinged grain, was stained black and polished or varnished to imitate ebony. It was used as an inlay on Elizabethan and Jacobean furniture. In the 17th and 18th centuries, it was used for picture frames and bracket clocks.

Applewood, a light warm-toned fruitwood, was also used for decorative veneer, inlay, carving and small decorative boxes. Plum and cherry also provide a similar dense-grained wood.

Fubako A Japanese box for storing letters and correspondence. The exterior of these boxes are often decorated with LACQUER.

Fuddling cup A tavern joke known from the 16th to the 18th century. Formed of three or more conjoined cups with an interconnecting pipe, the drinker was "befuddled" as to which to drink from. They are particularly sought after in 17th- and 18th-century English delft.

Fulda pottery and porcelain factory Founded in Hesse, Germany, in 1741 by the Prince-Bishop of Fulda, Heinrich von Bibra, with Nikolaus Paul from Berlin and the painter J.P. Schick. The factory burned down in 1767, was rebuilt and continued until 1790. They made tablewares influenced by MEISSEN, painted with landscapes featuring ruins and shipping, blue and manganese wares and well-modelled figures.

Fulham pottery John DWIGHT founded a pottery at Fulham in London in the 17th century, making BELLARMINE and brown stoneware. It carried on production through the 19th century.

Fuller A groove cut into the sides of a sword blade to reduce its weight without loss of strength. Often referred to (wrongly) as a "blood groove".

Fruitwood tea caddies, English, c.1790 [H, each]

Fulper pottery An American pottery established at Flemington, New Jersey, in 1805. Fulper produced simple, utilitarian wares in its early period, which are unmarked. From about 1910, Fulper made artistic wares under Martin Stangl and Willam H. Fulper II. It specialized in matt- or crystalline-glazed vessels in Japanese or ARTS AND CRAFTS form. Most were marked with a vertical printed or impressed FULPER. The most valuable examples are large table-lamps with shades that have inset glass panels and artist-signed lustreware. The pottery closed c.1935.

Fulper pottery vessel with flambé glaze, c.1909 [K]

Fumed oak A type of oak furniture, popular in the ART DECO period, with a distinctive powdery grey surface. It was achieved either by painting the piece with ammonia or by exposing it to ammonia fumes in a fuming box until the desired colour was reached.

Furniture – styles and dates

Looking at details such as the legs, handles, feet and mounts used on a piece of furniture can help to date it. The dates shown here record when particular styles were first used, but it is important to remember that they have been reproduced through the centuries and so should not be relied upon as the only means of dating an item of furniture.

Legs

Spiral twist leg,
1700–20

Block and spindle leg,
1720–40

Cabriole leg,
1720–40

Cabriole leg,
1740–60

Husk carved leg,
1760–80

Square tapered leg,
1780–1800

Rope-twist leg,
1800–20

Sabre leg,
1820–40

Baluster leg,
1820–40

Ring-turned leg,
1840–60

Bobbin-turned leg,
1840–60

Turned leg,
1860–80

Block and leaf leg,
1880–1900

Handles

Drop handle,
1700–20

Ring handle,
1700–20

Swan-neck handle,
1720–40

Rococo handle,
1740–60

Louis XV1 handle,
1780–1800

Knob,
1780–1800

Federal handle,
1800–20

Lion's mask handle,
1800–20

Wooden knob,
1840–60

Second Empire handle,
1860–80

Aesthetic style,
1860–80

Arts and Crafts handle,
1880–1900

Feet

Ball foot,
1700–20

Bracket foot,
1700–20

Pad foot,
1740–60

Ball and claw foot,
1760–80

Scroll foot,
1760–80

Spade foot,
1780–1800

Bobbin turned foot,
1800–20

Winged paw,
1820–1840

Turned foot,
1840–60

Gadrooned foot,
1840–60

Leaf-carved foot,
1860–80

Scroll foot,
1880–90

Mounts

Gothic wrought iron strap hinge,
medieval

Empire-style escutcheon plate, c.1800–20

Boulle leaf hinge, c.1700–20

Baroque barrel hinge,
c.1700–40

Biedermeier steel escutcheon plate,
c.1820–40

Hinges by
Josef Hoffmann,
Viennese school

Functionalism A movement in architecture and the applied arts advocating the theory that the form of an object should be determined solely by its function. Its earliest proponent is considered to be the American architect Louis Sullivan, who contended in the late 19th century that "form follows function". In practice, the term refers to the international modernist style of the 1920s and 1930s, characterized by austere, geometric forms devoid of ornament. It is associated particularly with designers of the BAUHAUS, for example Marcel BREUER, who aimed to create good-quality, efficient and standardized design for all, particularly through new materials such as tubular steel.

Furniture See pp.176–7.

Fürstenberg One of the leading German manufacturers of hard-paste porcelain, producing high-quality wares from 1753 to c.1800. Founded in 1747 by Charles I, Duke of Brunswick, its attempts to manufacture porcelain were unsuccessful until the arrival of Johann Benckgraff from HÖCHST in 1753. Early wares suffered from defective colours and firing specks. Many figures produced at Fürstenberg imitated those produced at MEISSEN, HÖCHST and BERLIN. The most important modeller was Simon Feilner (1726-98) from Höchst, who became chief modeller in 1754. His work included a fine series of characters from the *commedia dell'arte*. WEDGWOOD became a dominant influence at the end of the 18th century. Crude copies of the earlier models were reproduced at the factory in the 19th century.

Fürstenberg Commedia dell'Arte figure, c.1755 [B]

Fusee A grooved, cone-shaped device used in spring-driven clocks to offset the force of the spring as it runs down.

G

Gabbeh A type of tribal rug made in south and west Persia, with a thick wool pile and bold abstract coloured designs. Originally for domestic use, now commercially produced for the export market. Examples from the 19th and 20th centuries are common, but earlier examples are rare.

Gadrooning A decorative border of convex flutes or lobes, usually applied as an edging on a curved surface. It developed during the Renaissance from Classical reeding and was popular on furniture and woodwork from the 16th century, particularly for bulbous supports and mouldings. It was also widely adopted for ornament around the bases of silver and ceramic vessels. Throughout the 18th century it was widely used on chests, highboys, tables and chairs, as well as on Neo-classical silver and ceramic urns and vases.

Gainsborough chair An armchair made from the mid-18th century onward, so-called from its appearance in the portraits of Thomas Gainsborough. It has an upholstered seat and back, and concave arm supports. The legs and arms are often carved with GOTHIC, CHINOISERIE or ROCOCO motifs.

English mahogany Gainsborough chair, 1860 [E]

Galleon motif A motif based on a traditional ship of war, widely adopted by the ARTS AND CRAFTS movement as a decorative pattern for ironwork, tiles, ceramics, textiles and glass.

Gallery An ornamental miniature railing, of wood or metal, set round the edge of a tray, table or cabinet from the mid-18th century onward.

Fitted games compendium box, c.1870 [J]

Games compendium A decorative or plain wooden or cardboard box or case, containing a selection of games such as chess, draughts, backgammon, cards, cribbage and roulette. A popular domestic item from the 1860s.

Gardner porcelain factory The most successful private porcelain factory in pre-Revolutionary Russia, founded c.1765 by an Englishman, Francis Gardner, at Verbilki, near Moscow. Its most famous wares are the four services that were made for the imperial orders of St George, St Andrew, St Alexander Nevsky and St Vladimir between 1777 and 1785. From the early 19th century until its closure in 1891 the factory made brightly coloured, picturesque models of tradespeople and craftworkers.

Garnet An abundant gemstone occurring in various shades of red (almandine and pyrope), brown (spessartite), orange (hessonite) and the rarer and far more valuable green variety (demantoid, uvarovite and andradite). Garnet was used extensively throughout the 19th century, either faceted or polished *en* CABOCHON. Bohemian garnets are the pyrope variety, used in PAVÉ SETTINGS in decorative costume jewellery.

Emile Gallé (1846–1904)

Technical skill and artistic inspiration reached its height in the work of this supreme French glass-maker of the ART NOUVEAU period. As well as glassware, Gallé designed furniture and ceramics.

Early influences

Born in 1846, Emile Gallé was the son of a prosperous glass and faience factory owner in Nancy, the chief town of Lorraine, where there had been a strong tradition of fine glass-making since the 16th century. While he was growing up he used to visit the factories and so became conversant with his father's business from an early age. He continued his studies after school with courses in botany, drawing and landscape painting. Between 1862 and 1864 Gallé studied in Weimar, Germany, where he met Franz Liszt and mixed in artistic circles. He also visited London to round off his education, spending time at the Royal Botanical Gardens in Kew and studying the ancient glass collections in the British Museum, including the Roman PORTLAND VASE.

After working in the glass industry at the firm of Burgun, Schwerer & Co. in Miesenthal, Germany, Gallé set up his own glass workshop in Nancy. He joined forces with his father, who stepped down as head of the business in 1874.

International renown

Initially, the factory produced clear coloured glass with enamelled decoration, drawing on Gallé's love of plants and animals for inspiration. However, the International Exhibition in Paris in 1878 opened his eyes to other possibilities. There he saw the work of other inspired glass-makers who each had a different perspective on this malleable material. Gallé himself won four gold medals but what was to come would be more inspired: CAMEO GLASS with naturalistic relief decoration; subtle detailing with wheel-carving; applications of glass cabochons; vases made to simulate various hardstones; mould-blown pieces; internal decoration from mica and foil inclusions to crackle and bubbles; and sculpted pieces. His range of vases included the *Verres Parlantes* ("Talking Glasses"), which were inscribed with lines from the work of contemporary poets such as Stéphane Mallarmé and Charles Baudelaire.

By 1890, Gallé's factory was employing over 300 workmen, producing series after series of spectacular pieces, similar though not identical in style, which were highly sought after by contemporary collectors and museums. He opened several of his own retail outlets, and from 1896 onward his work was exhibited at La Maison de l'Art Nouveau, the Paris shop opened by the art dealer Samuel (Siegfried) BING to show the most innovative styles of the day.

Gallé also opened a carpentry shop employing cabinet-makers to produce furniture. His speciality was MARQUETRY. As with his glass, nature was the major source of inspiration for the decoration. Gallé gave his workers artistic freedom (except for pieces designed by him), with the proviso that when nature was represented it was done so accurately. His work earned him many prizes and he was made a Commander of the French Legion of Honour. After his death the factory's work was marked with a star beside the word "Gallé". The factory closed in 1914 but re-opened after World War I until the early 1930s.

Gallé faience model of a French bulldog dressed as an 18th-century beau, 1885 [H]

Gallé table showing the sinuous lines and fine marquetry of Art Nouveau, c.1900 [H]

The dark colours on this acid-etched and wheel-engraved cameo vase are typical of later Gallé workshop pieces, c.1920 [H]

Blue and white garniture de cheminée, Chinese, 18th century [E]

Garniture de cheminée A set of five vases, comprising three baluster-shaped items with covers and two trumpet-shaped beakers, designed to stand on a mantelshelf. First produced in China in the 17th century for the European market, they were soon being made in Europe, especially in DELFT. A smaller set would have one covered jar and two bottles.

Garrard, Robert (I) (1760–1818) A respected London silversmith who became a freeman at the firm of Wakelin & Co., Panton Street, and went into partnership with John Wakelin in 1792, gaining a reputation for quality and workmanship. He had three sons, Robert, James and Sebastian. Robert (II) (1793–1881) entered his first mark in 1818 after his father died and developed the business, gaining many commissions. He became Royal Goldsmith and Jeweller to King William IV in 1830. Garrards still retains the royal warrant. The company amalgamated with ASPREY in 1999.

Gasolier A lighting fixture, resembling a chandelier, used for gas lighting in domestic and public buildings from the mid-19th century until the advent of electric lighting from 1880. Generally made of brass, with plain or coloured glass shades at the end of each branch, it comprises a central shaft through which gas is distributed to each burner.

Gastaldi, Giacomo (c.1500–c.1565) Cosmographer to the Venetian Republic and the foremost Italian cartographer of the 16th century. Works include the landmark 1548 Venetian edition of PTOLEMY's *Geographia*, which was the first to be translated into Italian, the first pocket-sized ATLAS and the first to contain regional maps of the New World, including the first of North America's east coast and of South America by itself.

Gateleg table A table with a hinged folding top of one or two leaves that open out and are supported on pivoting legs that are joined at the top and bottom by stretchers. Introduced in the late 16th century, gateleg tables are still being made today.

Oak gateleg table, British, late 17th century [J]

Gather The blob of molten glass "gathered" on the end of the blowing iron.

Gaudi y Cornet, Antonio (1852–1926) A Spanish architect and one of the most original ART NOUVEAU designers. Floral embellishment and asymmetry typified his furniture, the majority of which was produced to accompany his eccentric buildings. His organic style was strongly influenced by his Catalonian heritage, the GOTHIC REVIVAL, John Ruskin and Hispano-Moresque art and architecture.

Gaudy Dutch Staffordshire pottery decorated for the American market (c.1810–30), especially the Pennsylvania Dutch. They were usually "cottage" wares painted in underglaze blue and then thick, bright overglaze enamels, often imitating IMARI-pattern wares.

Genoa A centre for heavy 17th-century BOBBIN LACE, typically scalloped borders for collars incorporating wheatear motif.

Georgian style See p.182.

Germain, Thomas (1673–1748) France's greatest Rococo gold- and silversmith. Born into a family of goldsmiths, he worked as an apprentice in

Germain silver burner and stand, c.1725 [F]

Italy and returned to France in 1706. He became a master goldsmith in 1720 and Goldsmith to the King, Louis XV, in 1723. In contrast to earlier silver, his work is asymmetrical and naturalistic, with movement and realism. His hunting table centrepiece of c.1730, for instance, is modelled and cast in high relief with game, shells, scrolls and reptiles. He made many objects for the French royal family and European nobility, but most were lost in the Lisbon earthquake of 1755 or melted to finance the Seven Years War (1756–63).

German silver See NICKEL SILVER.

Carved padouk chair by Gaudi, c.1902 [C]

Gems

The term "precious gem" refers to commercial value rather than aesthetic and applies to diamonds, emeralds, rubies, sapphires and pearls. "Semi-precious" describes gems of a lower value such as aquamarine, amethyst, peridot and tourmaline, while "ornamental" usually refers to hardstones such as agate, lapis lazuli and onyx. Factors affecting the value of a gemstone include its cut, colour, clarity and size.

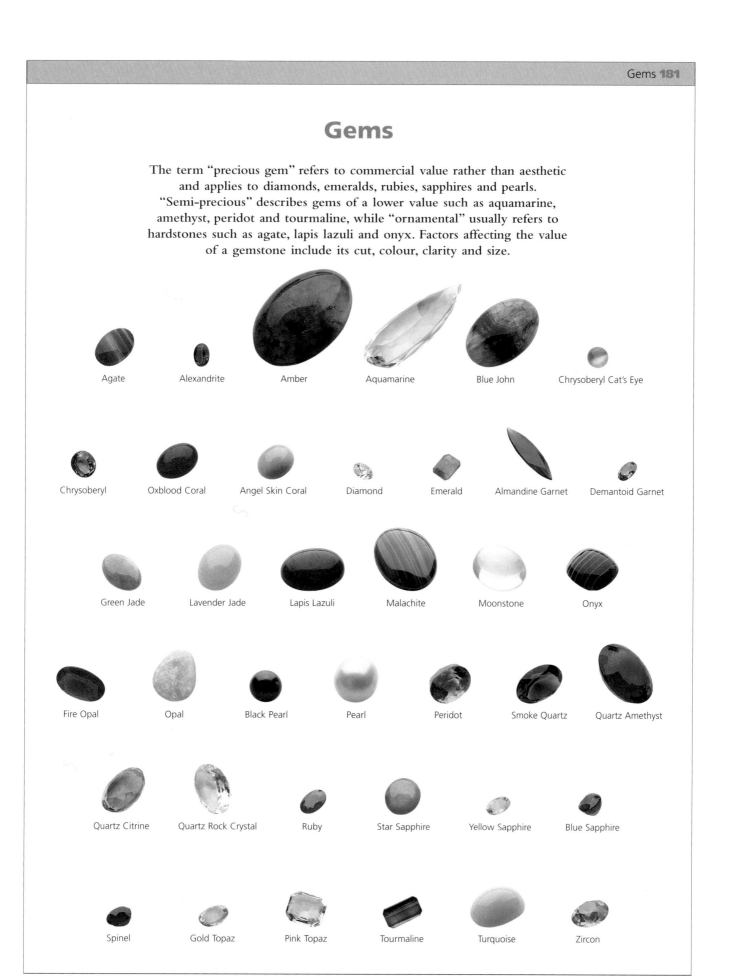

Agate   Alexandrite   Amber   Aquamarine   Blue John   Chrysoberyl Cat's Eye

Chrysoberyl   Oxblood Coral   Angel Skin Coral   Diamond   Emerald   Almandine Garnet   Demantoid Garnet

Green Jade   Lavender Jade   Lapis Lazuli   Malachite   Moonstone   Onyx

Fire Opal   Opal   Black Pearl   Pearl   Peridot   Smoke Quartz   Quartz Amethyst

Quartz Citrine   Quartz Rock Crystal   Ruby   Star Sapphire   Yellow Sapphire   Blue Sapphire

Spinel   Gold Topaz   Pink Topaz   Tourmaline   Turquoise   Zircon

Georgian style

For just over a century, architecture and the decorative arts in Great Britain reached a peak of elegance and refinement, unmatched since that time and still widely imitated. The Georgian style includes varying elements but was broadly inspired by the proportions and ornament of Classical architecture.

The age of elegance

The early Georgian period, from the accession of George I in 1714 to the 1730s, was dominated by the PALLADIAN style. On his return from the GRAND TOUR, Richard Boyle, 3rd Earl of Burlington, designed Chiswick House, near London, and built it from *c*.1725 to hold his collection of Greek and Roman art and sculpture. The Classical theme was continued in furniture by William KENT, a protégé of Burlington's. From *c*.1740 the lighter ROCOCO style reached Britain. Its impact on design was evident by the middle of the century, in the work of the HUGUENOT silversmiths, for example, and in CHIPPENDALE furniture and porcelain from Chelsea and Derby.

George III silver egg cruet made by the leading silversmith Matthew Boulton, 1788 [K]

When, in 1760, George III ascended the throne, the main source of inspiration in architecture and the decorative arts was still the Classical world. Further discoveries had been made, however, particularly at Herculaneum and Pompeii. Designers were entranced by the delicate decorative motifs they revealed, which resulted in the NEO-CLASSICAL style, led by Robert ADAM. Silverware, porcelain and glass also took up the theme. During the 1780s there was a move to a further refinement of form, especially in furniture, where newly-imported timbers from all over the world were used for sophisticated VENEERS and MARQUETRY. This style was associated particularly with Thomas SHERATON and George HEPPLEWHITE. Elegant classical lines were still the basis of the REGENCY style, from 1811, but in accordance with the tastes of the Prince Regent, embellished with lavish French-inspired decoration. During the late Georgian and Regency period, the popularity of Turkish, Indian, Chinese Rococo and Gothic motifs anticipated the eclecticism of the VICTORIAN style.

Georgian walnut chest-on-stand, typical of the architectural style of the early Georgian period, c.1730 [E]

Georgian decanter with mushroom stopper, decorated with fine hand-cutting, 1810 [P]

Recognizing the style

Typical motifs of the Palladian included triumphal arcs or temple fronts. Interiors of this period were commonly adorned with herms and heavily sculpted eagles and dolphins. Rococo serpentine lines and asymmetrical scroll- and shellwork, combined with Gothick and chinoiserie, gave way to the motifs that characterized Neo-classical style – paterae, palmettes, husks, rosettes, garlands, urns and cameos.

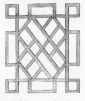

Herm   Dolphin   "Chinese" lattice

Gesso A paste-like mixture of chalk or plaster of Paris and size, used as a base for carved and gilded decoration on wooden picture frames and furniture from the Middle Ages. It was especially popular on carved and GILTWOOD furniture in the late 17th and 18th centuries.

Ghashghai An important tribal group from the Fars district of south-west Iran, weavers of fine and coarse rugs, KILIMS and functional artifacts. Examples from the 19th century are particularly fine, with jewel-like colours employed in designs of stylized flora and fauna. Later examples tend to be coarse and lack the individuality of earlier ones.

Gilding on porcelain

Ghiordes knot See TURKISH KNOT.

Ghom An important centre of rug and carpet production in central Iran, where weaving began c.1930. Wool and silk are used for the pile, while warps and wefts are of cotton or silk. Curvilinear designs in subtle colours are used on a white ground, the BOTEH motif appears frequently as do geometric designs inspired from the Caucasus.

Gibbons, Grinling (1648–1721) The leading woodcarver and sculptor of the English BAROQUE style. He probably trained in Amsterdam but had returned to England by 1667. He attracted the attention of Sir Christopher Wren, and by 1693 he was appointed Master Carver to the Crown and produced outstanding ornamental carved wood decoration for such royal residences as Kensington Palace, Hampton Court and the Royal Apartments at Windsor Castle.

Gien pottery A FAIENCE factory is recorded in this town on the river Loire, north-west France, from c.1822. It made cream-coloured EARTHENWARE, which was plain or marbled, sponged, simply painted or printed. After 1860, various

decorative techniques were exploited such as LUSTRE and FLAMBÉ, and large vessels, sometimes painted in Renaissance style, became a speciality. The town still produces high-quality FAIENCE.

Gilding A decorative finish in which gold is applied to wood, leather, silver, ceramics or glass. Known from ancient Egypt, the process involves laying gold leaf or powdered gold (or silver) onto a base – of GESSO, for example. Wood-gilding may be either water-gilding, which takes a high burnish, or the cheaper and more durable oil-gilding. In Europe, gilding was extensively used on furniture from the 17th century. Types include HONEY GILDING; MERCURY GILDING; ORMOLU; PARCEL GILT; SIZE GILDING.

Giles, James (1718–80) An English OUTSIDE DECORATOR of porcelain and glass. He is recorded from 1749 as a "Chinaman" (i.e. vendor or importer of porcelain) and from 1763 as a painter. He decorated white porcelain from WORCESTER and probably also from BOW and LONGTON HALL. He seems to have gone bankrupt in 1776. His work is not signed but the fuchsia flower is characteristic of his decoration.

Gillinder, James and Sons An American glassworks established in 1860 in Philadelphia by William Gillinder. He also operated as the Franklin Flint Glass Company, making clear, robust, pressed table glass popular in North America after the Civil War. One favourite pattern, made until the company closed in the 1930s and also reproduced by other companies today, was "Westward Ho", featuring images of buffalo, elk and native Americans.

Gillows An English family firm of furniture manufacturers founded

in Lancaster, c.1727, by Robert Gillow (1704–72). By 1769, Robert Gillow II (1745–95) was managing a showroom in London's Oxford Street and Richard Gillow (1734–1811) the Lancaster factory.

Gillows bonheur du jour, c.1795 [D]

Gillows became the leading furniture manufacturers outside the capital. Their success was largely due to good quality and workmanship, and a shrewd choice of middle-of-the-road designs that appealed to the provincial middle classes. From c.1780 some of the furniture was stamped GILLOWS LANCASTER, and by the end of the century, Gillows launched several new furniture types, including the DAVENPORT. In 1900, Gillows merged with S. J. Waring & Sons to become WARING & GILLOW.

Gilt bronze See ORMOLU.

Giltwood Wood that has been gilded, usually through the application of gold leaf onto a layer of GESSO.

Giltwood Louis XVI chair, c.1780 [L]

Gimmal, gemel A type of flask, made from the 17th century, consisting of two separately blown bottles that are then fused together to form a double container with two separate necks and mouths that sometimes face in opposite directions. Most often used for oil and vinegar.

Gimson, Ernest William (1864–1919) An English architect and designer, renowned for his furniture designs and metalware. He was a leading figure in the ARTS AND CRAFTS movement and in what became known as the COTSWOLD SCHOOL. With Sydney and Ernest BARNSLEY he revived the best traditions of English cabinet-making to produce beautifully hand-crafted pieces. He employed the Dutch cabinet-maker Peter van der Waals to run his workshops.

Gin flask A salt-glazed stoneware flask produced from the 1820s to the 1850s to commemorate important events, people or royalty, particularly associated with the Reform Act in 1832. Main producers are Stephen Green, Lambeth, and Oldfield & Co., Chesterfield. Some have an impressed mark of the wine and spirit merchant or public house for which they were made.

Stoneware spirit flask, c.1840 [L]

Ginger jar A small squat jar with a fitted cover made in China but also copied by European factories in the 17th century, usually decorated in underglaze blue. They originally held Chinese stem ginger.

¹Girandole An Italian term used in the 18th-century to describe elaborate giltwood SCONCES. They were made in both NEO-CLASSICAL and ROCOCO styles and featured strongly in Thomas CHIPPENDALE's *Director*.

Girandole earrings, Spanish c.1760 [E]

²Girandole Earrings or pendants of chandelier design fashioned as a circular cluster of stones above a bow or foliate centrepiece with three pear-shaped cluster drops suspended below. Popular in 18th-century France and Spain.

Girl in a swing A porcelain factory that ran from 1749 to 1759 in the house of Charles Gouyn, in Bennet Street, London. Gouyn was a jeweller and specialized in "toys" – porcelain scent bottles, *bonbonnières* and seals, with gold mounts. The term "Girl in a Swing" is derived from a figure group once attributed to Gouyn's factory, in the Victoria and Albert Museum.

Giuliano, Carlo (*c*.1831–95) A Neapolitan goldsmith, initially employed by CASTELLANI, who settled in London *c*.1860 and established an "art jewellery" business. Making technically superb enamelled gold work, he selected gems for colour rather than value as did his sons Carlo (b.1860) and Arthur (1864–1919). The business closed in 1914.

Girl in a swing perfume bottle, 18th century [I]

Glasgow potteries A factory at Delftfield (1748–1810) made tin-glazed earthenware decorated with Chinese-style flowers in manganese, yellow, blue, bluish-green and dark violet. From 1770 they made cream-coloured earthenware. John & Matthew P. Bell founded a second factory (1842–1940), which made Parian and a wide range of earthenware.

Glasgow School A Scottish group of designers active from the 1890s up to World War I. Central figures were Charles Rennie MACKINTOSH, his wife Margaret Macdonald, her sister Frances and her husband Herbert McNair. They developed their own version of ART NOUVEAU with some CELTIC influences.

Glass A hard brittle material, usually translucent, made by fusing together ingredients by heat. The basic component is silica, found in sand and quartz, to which an alkaline flux is added and other components that determine the glass type.

Glastonbury chair A 19th-century term for a late 16th-century wooden folding chair, usually of oak, possibly based on a chair made for the last Abbot of Glastonbury, England. It was devised for use in churches before pews became common.

Glaze A layer of glass fused into place on a ceramic body, which provides a hygienic covering because it is non-porous and also increases the strength of the ware. It is applied to the body in the form of a layer of powder, composed of fluxes, stabilizers and glass-forming material, which fuse during firing and make a compact layer of molten material. The fluxes are alkaline oxides, usually soda, potash, magnesia or lead oxide. Alumina is the most commonly used stabilizer.
  Glazes may be either transparent, as in LEAD GLAZE, or opaque as in TIN and CELADON glazes. Lead glaze was used in China as early as 200 BC and celadon glaze from the time of the SONG DYNASTY. The practice of glazing spread slowly across Europe from the east, probably transmitted by the Moors, and was standard by the 18th century.

Glazing bars See ASTRAGAL.

Glasses

Drinking glasses with a bowl, stem and foot were made in a variety of styles and decoration, which help both to date the piece and to identify the drink it was designed to hold. Early glasses were all blown, not moulded, and mostly the bowl and stem were drawn from one gather of glass with the foot added last. Later glasses were made in separate gathers of glass, with visible joins, and inexpensive examples were moulded.

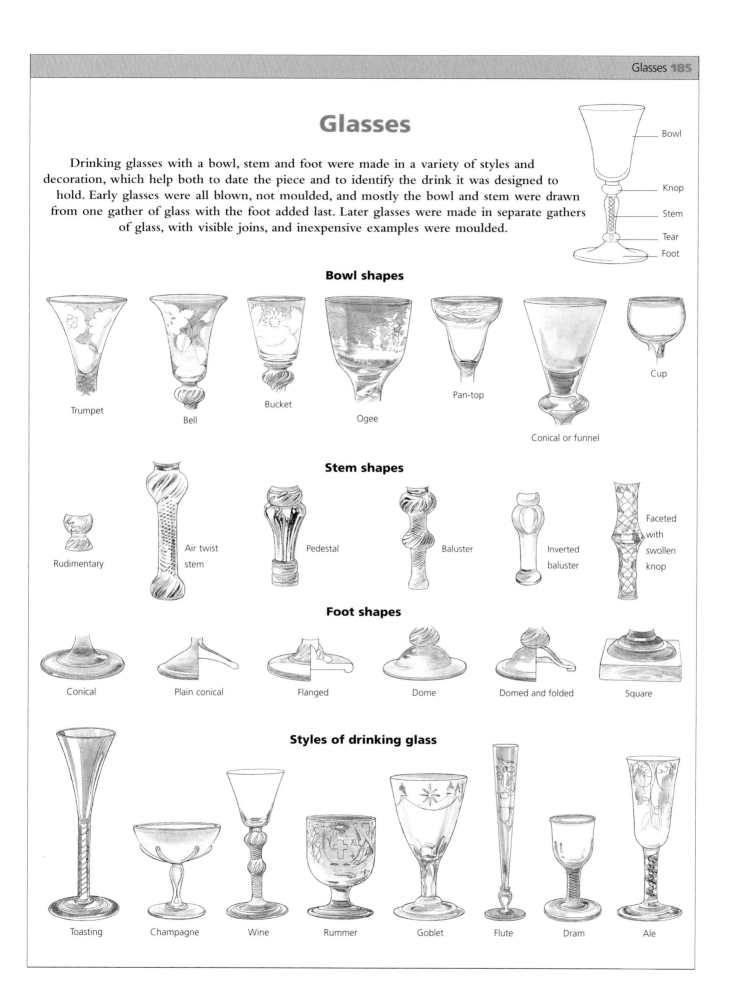

Bowl
Knop
Stem
Tear
Foot

Bowl shapes

Trumpet

Bell

Bucket

Ogee

Pan-top

Conical or funnel

Cup

Stem shapes

Rudimentary

Air twist stem

Pedestal

Baluster

Inverted baluster

Faceted with swollen knop

Foot shapes

Conical

Plain conical

Flanged

Dome

Domed and folded

Square

Styles of drinking glass

Toasting

Champagne

Wine

Rummer

Goblet

Flute

Dram

Ale

Gobelins tapestry factory

Set up in Paris in 1662–63 to make furnishings for Louis XIV, the factory at the Hôtel des Gobelins was the brainchild of the minister of finance Jean-Baptiste Colbert (1619–83) and the court painter Charles Le Brun (1619–90), who became the artistic director.

Louis XIV visiting the Gobelins factory, a design by Le Brun, c.1667 [A]

Gobelins tapestry with a figure of Time in the arch, after a design by Claude Audran, early 18th century [C]

Pastoral scene with Jupiter and Mercury seated on a cloud and *enfants jardiniers* in the foreground, early 18th century [B]

The rise of an industry

Colbert employed over 800 artists, weavers, dyers and apprentices at the Gobelins factory. The weavers were divided into five workshops, three weaving on high-warp looms and two on low-warp looms. A dyeing workshop was run separately. Most tapestries were commissioned by the crown, which supplied the materials – including silk, gold or silver threads – but some were made for private customers.

Le Brun oversaw the Gobelins factory with great success. In 1664 the first tapestries entitled "The Fames and Mars" were completed. A new series of "Acts of the Apostles" after Raphael, and a series entitled "History of Alexander" from cartoons by Le Brun himself soon followed. In the late 1660s the *Histoire du Roi* series, also designed by Le Brun, was completed and were considered to be amongst the greatest work produced at Gobelins.

After the deaths of Colbert and Le Brun and with royal spending curtailed because of the war with the Netherlands, artistic originality stagnated at the Gobelins factory. In April 1694, the factory almost closed completely, workers were dismissed, some weavers returning to Flanders, others going to work at BEAUVAIS. One low-warp workshop remained active and in January 1699, under the direction of Robert de Cotte, the workshops re-opened. Renowned artists were called upon to provide cartoons and the Gobelins flourished once again.

Rococo influence

After 1699 the tapestries gradually began to reflect the evolution of a lighter style. By the early 18th century tapestries *à alentours* (simulating a panel with elaborate floral surrounds) became popular. Cartoons by the artists Jean Baptiste Oudry and François Boucher maintained the traditions of large wall hangings, while at the same time reinforcing the importance of the artist. Increasingly, tapestries imitated paintings.

After the French Revolution (1789–99), production recovered during the Empire period (1804–15), with tapestries commissioned for the Imperial palaces. After the fall of the SECOND EMPIRE (1852–70) an unsettled period followed. The Gobelins was renamed the Manufacture Nationale des Gobelins and produced several large hangings for public buildings such as the Opéra, the Palais du Luxembourg and the Bibliothèque Nationale in Paris. Interest in tapestries was further revived by the painter and designer Jean Lurçat (1892–1966) who advocated a return to Gobelins' original traditions. In 1939, Gobelins was moved to Aubusson where artists like Gromaire, Picasso and Miró, under Lurçat's influence, produced cartoons for monumental hangings for state buildings, continuing the tradition for which Gobelins was famed. Today, the Gobelins factory is still producing tapestries and continues its tradition of basing tapestries on paintings by selecting those of 20th-century artists such as Matisse.

Globe A spherical map of the Earth (a terrestrial globe) or the heavens (a celestial or astronomical globe), ranging in size from novelty pocket globes to larger library globes. First used to aid navigation, the oldest known terrestrial globe was made in 1492 by the German Martin Behaim but globes were made in ancient times. Islamic globes were mostly constructed from copper, brass or silver. In Europe, they were made from a papier mâché sphere and plaster that was covered with printed strips of paper "gores". In the 20th century, cartographical images can be printed directly onto spheres without using gores. Important makers include John Moxon, Dudley Adams, Charles Schmalcalder and John Senex. Globes were part of the furnishings of private libraries and are still universal schoolroom equipment. Pocket globes can be dated from the geographical knowledge of the time – for example, new tracks and coastlines were defined by Cook's three voyages 1768–74.

Paper and wood globe, Scottish 1930s [L]

Gnomon Often of triangular form and cut out of pierced metal such as copper or brass, the gnomon is the part of the SUNDIAL that projects a shadow from the sun to give a reading from the dial.

Gobelins The Manufacture Royale des Meubles de la Couronne was established in 1663 in Paris to provide furnishings, including pieces in bronze, gold and silver, for King Louis XIV. It also provided training for craftsmen but closed in 1694 and was then subsumed into the GOBELINS TAPESTRY FACTORY.

Goblet, English mid-19th century [S]

Goblet A drinking glass with a large bowl, sometimes with a detachable cover, supported by a stemmed foot.

Goddard, John (1723–85) An American cabinet-maker active in Newport, Rhode Island, from c.1745. He and his brother were apprenticed to Job Townshend. The "Goddard Townshend" school of furniture is considered the earliest and possibly finest exponent of AMERICAN CHIPPENDALE, a style John Goddard is credited with developing. Features include richly coloured mahogany with bold shell carving, often centred within a BLOCK FRONT. Examples are rare and valuable. Goddard's sons carried on the firm until the mid-19th century.

Godwin, Edward William (1833–86) An English architect and designer. His first important commission was Northampton town hall, in which he was influenced by John Ruskin's studies of Venetian architecture. In Ireland, he built Dromore and Glenbeigh Towers. He was one of the first to study Japanese art and use it to produce original work in the context of western culture. His furniture designs were made by William Watt, Art Furniture Co. and COLLINSON & LOCK, but he also designed wallpaper, metalwork and dresses for LIBERTY & Co. He patented his furniture designs because they were often copied.

Going barrel See BARREL.

Gold A soft, dense yellow metal, regarded since ancient times as one of the most valuable metals and used mainly for coins

Gold Fabergé cigarette case, c.1900 [K]

and jewellery. Resistant to corrosion, gold is the most malleable and ductile of all metals, capable of being hammered or drawn into wafer-thin sheets or fine wire. The purity of gold is measured in CARATS, the purest being 24cts. But, most gold is alloyed with silver, copper or other metals to make it harder. See also GILDING.

Gold glass An early form of ZWISCHENGOLDGLAS, known in Ancient Greece and Rome, in which glass was decorated with designs cut or engraved in a layer of applied gold leaf that was protected by being sandwiched between a further layer of glass.

Gold-ruby glass (*Goldrubinglas*) Glass with a deep red ruby colour created by adding gold chloride to the batch. The technique was perfected by Johann KUNCKEL c.1679 in Potsdam and was then used in both in Nuremberg and Augsburg to make luxury pieces, many of which were decorated with engraving and gilding.

Gold-ruby beaker, German c.1700 [C]

Goldscheider earthenware and porcelain factory Founded by Friedrich Goldscheider in Vienna in 1885 and continued by his widow and then his sons until it closed in 1954. At the turn of the 19th century, they specialized in figurative subjects and ART NOUVEAU terracotta figures of maidens and then, in the 1920s and 30s, Art Deco figures and masks.

Goldscheider "Butterfly girl", c.1930 [H]

Gold tooling Decorative embossing or tooled work on leather, particularly book bindings, which is picked out or heightened by gold leaf. The term is also used for gold motifs or borderwork inset into channels or inlaid into another metal usually steel (see DAMASCENING) and to the CHASING or tooled work on gold items.

Golfing memorabilia Golf is a sport played since the 15th century in Scotland. While the equipment needed has changed very little from the early beginnings, it has improved and developed and the traditional crafts passed on for many generations are unlikely to survive into the 21st century. The most valued items today those made by early clubmakers and ballmakers. Wooden shafted clubs, balls, tees, bags, books, unusual patents, ephemera, score cards, photographs, autographs, programmes, invoices, catalogues, artwork, prints and even early golfing shoes are collected.

Leather and goose feather golf ball, Scottish c.1840 [E]

Gong A coil of steel wire attached at one end to a clock's MOVEMENT, emitting a bell-like sound when struck. Smaller than a bell, it was popular in STRIKING SYSTEMS from the early 19th century.

Goode & Co., Thomas A famed retailer of fine china and glass established in 1827 in central London. They moved to a custom re-designed building in South Audley St in 1845 are still there to this day. Goode & Co. are retailers of WEDGWOOD, Royal DOULTON and Royal WORCESTER, among others. Two large MINTON elephants bought from the 1878 Paris Exhibition have become their trademark.

Googly eyes A term used for the round, sidewards-glancing, glass dolls' eyes generally associated with CHARACTER DOLLS which were first marketed in 1911.

Gorham Manufacturing Co. The largest American silversmiths and one of the biggest in the world. It was founded c.1815 in Providence, Rhode Island, by Jabez Gorham (1792–1869) and became the Gorham Manufacturing Co. in 1865. In 1848 Gorham's son John (1820–98) introduced the impressed anchor trademark still used today. The firm converted to steam power in the 1850s and introduced electroplating techniques pioneered by ELKINGTON & Co.

The sterling standard of silver, not previously required of American silversmiths, was adopted in 1868. For the next 30 years, the firm produced high quality silver and silver-plated wares, specializing in HOLLOWWARE in RENAISSANCE REVIVAL or NEO-CLASSICAL taste, much of it by European craftsmen including the Englishmen George Wilkinson (1819–94), chief designer from 1860–91, and Thomas J. Pairpoint (1847–1902). The firm also made mixed metal and enamelled pieces in AESTHETIC or Japanese taste. The best examples of Gorham JAPANESQUE silver are comparable to TIFFANY & CO. A line of ARTS AND CRAFTS style ecclesiastical ware, e.g. chalices in silver, wood, stone and bronze, was made from 1885. From 1894 the firm was run by Edward Holbrook, who with the English artistic director William Christmas Codman (1839–1921), introduced the MARTELÉ range, with its distinctive marks and French ART NOUVEAU forms. Only c.5000 martelé pieces were made. During the early 20th

century, Gorham was a foundry for bronzes by modern US sculptors (including Harriet Whitney Frishmuth), rivalling the Roman Bronze Works of New York City. The firm was sold to Textron Inc. in 1967, to Dansk International in 1989, and then to Brown-Forman in 1991.

Goss, William Henry (1833–1906) An English maker of glazed PARIAN wares, terracotta and "ivory" and EGGSHELL porcelain at the Falcon Pottery, Stoke-on-Trent, from 1858. The factory used the impressed or printed mark of "W.H. Goss" from 1862 on. From c.1880 Goss made vast quantities of cheap mass-produced trinkets with the coats of arms or crests of nearly every town in the British Isles. These sold widely at the time. The firm even issued a *Goss Collectors* magazine and by 1912 the "League of Goss Collectors" had over 1,000 members. Other firms tried to cash in on their success, but the genuine examples have a printed mark of a goshawk. It was re-named Goss China Ltd c.1931 when taken over by Cauldon Potteries Ltd. In the 1980s DOULTON – who possess a number of the original Goss pattern books – re-started production of some Goss porcelains.

Jug with flags of the Allies by Goss, 1914 [S]

Iron Japanesque tea set by Gorham Manufacturing Co., 1883 [L]

Gothic styles

The Gothic was the dominant style in European ecclesiastical architecture from the 12th to the 15th centuries, replacing the earlier ROMANESQUE. It inspired later architecture and decorative arts in two main flowerings, one in the 18th and one in the 19th century.

A source of inspiration

The characteristics of medieval Gothic architecture were also applied to contemporary furniture such as COFFERS and tables, and metalwork, in particular ecclesiastical silver such as CHALICES, patens, monstrances and reliquaries. The manufacture of STAINED GLASS reached its peak during the Gothic period, while IVORY carving, mainly of religious and courtly themes, is also of exceptional quality. The Gothic style was superseded by the RENAISSANCE in southern Europe in the 15th century, but it continued to flourish in northern Europe well into the 16th century, especially in metalwork.

Interest in the Gothic style was revived c.1750–70 as part of the picturesque movement, providing a romanticized view of the Middle Ages. Although first used for garden buildings, the style was employed for interior decoration and furnishings at the writer Horace Walpole's house at Strawberry Hill, Twickenham, Middlesex (1750s), and at Fonthill Abbey, Wiltshire (begun 1796), built for the collector William Beckford. However, Gothic architectural motifs were simply applied to 18th-century forms and sometimes fancifully combined with ROCOCO or CHINOISERIE motifs; little attempt was made to replicate authentic medieval furnishings. See also GOTHICK.

This romantic approach to the Gothic style was challenged in the 1830s by A.W.N. PUGIN as part of a wider religious revival. In his *True Principles of Pointed or Christian Architecture* (1843), he advocated a more archeologically exact approach in which furniture, silver and other applied arts were based accurately on medieval precedents. He designed furniture, ecclesiastical silver, jewellery, tiles and other ceramics and wallpapers, following closely the forms and ornament of historical examples, and was responsible for the furnishings of the new Houses of Parliament in London and the design of the Medieval Court at the GREAT EXHIBITION of 1851. In this way, the GOTHIC REVIVAL came to be considered as the national style of British art and architecture, and was emulated by later 19th-century designers such as William BURGES and Bruce TALBERT.

Gothic Revival Minton Intarsia ware plate by A.W.N. Pugin, c.1870 [K]

Gothic Revival "York Minster" Parian ware jug attributed to Charles Meigh, c.1845 [Q]

Oak cupboard with linenfold panelling, carved overall with Gothic fretwork, English 15th/16th century [A]

Recognizing the style

The Gothic style is characterized by the use of architectural forms: the pointed or ogee arch, pinnacle, cluster column, rib vault and crocket, and by tracery forms such as trefoils, quatrefoils and cinquefoils (three-, four- and five-lobed shapes).

Crocket

Quatrefoil

Gothic Revival This style rebirth began in the 18th century (see GOTHICK) but grew in the 19th century, promoted by designers such as A.W.N. PUGIN and W. BURGES. It was a revival of the art of the 12th–15th centuries and employed arches, tracery, flying buttresses, quatrefoils and trefoils, carving, grotesque imagery, heraldic motifs, cornices and inlaid motifs. Used chiefly in church architecture, it also affected applied arts, e.g. furniture became heavy, decorated with architectural details. The Gothic Revival influenced the growth of the English ARTS AND CRAFTS movement. It was also popular in France – where its chief advocate was Eugène-Emmanuel Viollet-le-Duc (1814–79) – and in the US where Alexander Jackson Davis (1803–92) designed Gothic-style furniture and buildings in the 1840s.

Gothic Revival armchair, English, c.1860 [H]

Gothic styles See p.189.

Gothick A style of 18th-century architecture and decorative arts inspired by medieval GOTHIC architecture. It was principally a strand of the ROCOCO style, often combined with CHINOISERIE; unlike the more historically accurate 19th-

century GOTHIC REVIVAL, it was essentially decorative and fanciful. Arches, pinnacles, crockets, tracery, frets, quatrefoils and other architectural motifs are characteristically added to standard 18th-century forms.

Gouda potteries An early factory was set up in Gouda, Holland, in 1621 by Willem Jansz who made tin-enamelled earthenware but was not successful. The later factory, "Zuid Holland", was founded in 1898 and was one of the leading Dutch potteries until it closed in 1965. Gouda pottery was particularly important in the early 20th century, producing many pieces in ART NOUVEAU and ART DECO styles. There are three modern factories in Gouda.

Gouge carving Shallow carved decoration, often fluted or architectural, scooped out with a gouge and most commonly found on late 16th- and 17th-century oak furniture.

Gouthière, Pierre (1732–1813) A French bronzeworker and gilder. He became a master gilder in 1758 and in the 1760s and 1770s was the pre-eminent gilder and bronzeworker at the court of Louis XVI. He produced a wide variety of furnishings in the Neo-classical style, including candlesticks, chandeliers, mirror frames, furniture mounts and clock cases, characterized by high-quality CHASING and modelling. He executed models by leading sculptors, including Louis-Simon Boizot, who designed his most famous work, the Avignon Clock (1771). His work is rare and fakes are common.

Gout stool A stool with an adjustable seat, the height and angle of which could be altered by a ratchet to suit the gout sufferer; alternatively a fixed stool with generous upholstery. Gout stools were especially common in late 18th- and 19th-century England.

Gouda double-handled earthenware vase, 1920s [o]

Graffito See SGRAFFITO.

Graham, George (c.1673–1751) An English clock- and watchmaker. He began as assistant to Thomas TOMPION but set up his own business in London after Tompion's death. He made various types of clock, watches and scientific instruments, but is best known for two inventions designed to improve the accuracy of clocks: the DEADBEAT escapement, in 1715, and the mercury COMPENSATED pendulum, in 1726.

Graining The painting of woodwork or wooden furniture with a counterfeit grain in imitation of more expensive timber. The technique was used from as early as the 16th century, largely to imitate oak and walnut, and remained in use into the 20th century.

Gramophone A machine using discs, a stylus and a diaphragm to reproduce sound that is amplified through a horn. The US inventor Thomas Edison pioneered the use of discs to reproduce sound but the gramophone was developed by Emile Berliner in 1888. They may have external or built-in horns or horns mounted in decorative cabinets. The gramophone evolved into the record player with an electric turntable.

Mahogany wind-up gramophone, HMV model 109, British, 1920s [o]

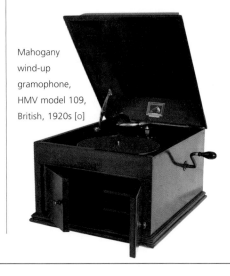

Grande sonnerie A STRIKING SYSTEM in which the quarter hours strike one, two and three times with a different tone from that of the hour bell. The preceding hour may also be struck at each quarter.

Grandfather clock See LONGCASE CLOCK.

Grand-feu See HIGH-TEMPERATURE COLOUR.

Grand Rapids oak dressing chest, c.1880 [K]

Grand Rapids Furniture Grand Rapids was a US centre for furniture production from the mid-19th century. The Grand Rapids Fair was a place for manufacturers to attract retailers. Gustav STICKLEY chose to launch his furniture at the 1900 show in an attempt to attract more support for his furniture among the middle classes. By 1908 there were 49 furniture factories here. Many closed in the Depression of the 1920s but revived in the late 1930s with mass-produced modern designs.

Grand Tour The journey undertaken by young European gentlemen, especially British, to complete their education. In a tour usually lasting one or two years, they visited major cities in France, the Low Countries, and sometimes Germany and eastern Europe. It always culminated in Italy, regarded as the centre of art, architecture and learning. It developed in the late 16th and early 17th centuries but was most popular during the 18th, when visitors to Italy went to admire ancient Roman sculpture and architecture, and Renaissance and Baroque painting.

Pratt pot lid depicting Grand Tourists halting near Italian ruins, English, 1865 [R]

Collecting art and antiquities eventually became one of the main functions of the tour and the formation of collections by British visitors had a powerful impact on the development of Classically inspired architecture and design in 18th-century Britain. One of the earliest travellers making the Grand Tour was Thomas Howard, 2nd Earl of Arundel, who made several tours, most notably one in 1613 in the company of architect Inigo Jones (1573–1652), and who formed the first collections of Classical sculpture and Old Master drawings in England.

In the following century the development of the PALLADIAN STYLE was largely a result of the enthusiasm of Richard Boyle, 3rd Earl of Burlington (1694–1753), for the work of the Italian architect Andrea Palladio (1508–80) which he saw on his second Grand Tour in 1719. Artists and architects also made the tour, in particular Robert ADAM, James Wyatt and William CHAMBERS, renowned exponents of the NEO-CLASSICAL style in Britain. The popularity of the Grand Tour reached a peak in the later 18th century, following the discovery of Herculaneum and Pompeii. It declined during the Napoleonic Wars and in the 19th century with the development of modern tourism.

Granite ware The term used for several types of English 18th and 19th-century pottery. (i) Wares made by mingling segments of differently coloured clays (solid AGATE WARE) or given a surface coating of differently coloured slips or glazes. (ii) Earthenware or stone china sprayed with lead glaze to give a speckled appearance, made by WEDGWOOD and several Staffordshire potteries in the 18th century. (iii) Durable white ironstone-type services and functional ware produced by DAVENPORT and others from c.1850.

Granulation The creation of decorative patterns or texture on gold or silver, usually by the application of granules, beads or particles of the metal to the surface of the piece.

Grapevine motif

Grapevine motif A decorative motif with ancient origins, sacred to Bacchus and Apollo in Classical mythology. The grapevine also plays a symbolic role in Judaic and Christian iconography. An important element of Renaissance ornament, grapevines decorated vessels associated with the serving and drinking of wine and the handles of 19th-century flatware. The motif appears in decorative schemes of the seasons as a symbol of autumn, in the 17th and 18th centuries.

Grate A raised container in a fireplace, usually an iron or steel basket, introduced in the 16th century to hold coal, which required an updraft to burn. Grates became more elaborate and designs were included in cabinet-makers' pattern-books.

Gravity clock A clock in which the power source is the weight of the clock itself. See also RACK CLOCK.

Gravity escapement A type of ESCAPEMENT developed in the mid-19th century in TURRET CLOCKS, e.g. Big Ben at the Houses of Parliament, London. The impulse from the escapement to the pendulum is independent of the power applied to the TRAIN and also of the action of wind and weather.

Gravyboat See SAUCEBOAT.

Gray, Eileen (1879–1976) An Irish architect and furniture designer, born in Enniscorthy, County Wexford. She trained at the Slade School of Art, London, then moved to Paris in 1902 to train with a Japanese LACQUER master. Her early designs were largely for lacquer furniture: screens, tables and some larger pieces. Her all-white lacquer bedroom suite shown at the Salon des Artistes Decorateurs, Paris, in 1923 was equally admired and criticized. From 1925 she made increasing use of tubular steel, glass and aluminium.

Lacquered wood sofa by Gray, 1920–25 [A]

Greatbach, William (1735–1813) A modeller, potter and maker of transfer-printed creamware at Lane Delph in Fenton, Staffordshire; best known for teapots depicting the Prodigal Son. An extant bill for modelling designs for WEDGWOOD (with whom he was closely associated) includes "a leaf candlestick, 1 pineapple teapot". Early wares are not normally marked, but waste pieces have been found with impressed W.G. monogram.

Engraving of the India section from Dickinson's *Picture of the Great Exhibition*, 1851 [R]

Great Exhibition, The The "Great Exhibition of the Works of Industry of All Nations" was held in the Crystal Palace in Hyde Park, London, from May to October 1851. It featured manufactured objects from all over the world, with an emphasis on technological innovations. Profits contributed to the new South Kensington (later Victoria & Albert) Museum.

Greek key See KEY PATTERN.

Greek pottery Greek civilization began *c*.1700 BC, when Hellenic people from the north settled in the mainland and islands of what is now Greece, the first extensive civilization being the Mycenean in Crete. Greek pottery is mostly utilitarian, wheel-made, painted, unglazed and low-fired. Large vessels were made in sections and LUTED, then smoothed on the potter's wheel. Most became distorted in the firing process. Shapes used over the centuries include the AMPHORA (storage jar), KRATER (mixing bowl), kyathos (jug for wine), kylix (shallow stem cup), hydria (three-handled water pot), oenochoe (jug for wine), kantharos (small drinking goblet), lekythos (oil jug), ARYBALLOS (small vase for oil or ointment), pyx (toilet box) and psykter (cooler for iced water). Greek pottery is classified by style:

(i) Geometric style 1000–700 BC. Shapes include amphoras and hydrias decorated with bands of geometric motifs and animals and figures in silhouette. Some were large egg-shaped vases with trumpet necks and tall stems for tomb monuments, painted with funeral processions.

(ii) Oriental influence 750–550 BC. The Geometric style declined and became just narrow bands. Shapes were more interesting: lion-mouthed jugs, owl perfume bottles and later human – and gorgon-head – scent bottles. Silhouette painting was gradually reduced to outline, while animals, birds and plants became naturalistic.

(iii) Black Figure style 600–530 BC. Developed by Corinthian potters who painted human figures and built up an extensive export trade, it was improved by Athenian potters. Some wares are signed. Greeks travelled to many areas of the Mediterranean and pottery has been found wherever they settled, for example, in Italy and Egypt.

Nikosthenic amphora, *c*.530 BC [B]

Greek Red Figure kylix, c.500 BC [C]

(iv) Red Figure style 530–470 BC. Figures were drawn in a fine line against a black ground, showing anatomical details and flowing draperies.

(v) Mixed style from 450 BC. The defeat of Athens in the Peloponnesian war brought an end to painted pottery vases and metal (bronze) vases became more commonly used.

Greek Revival A style of architecture and decorative arts inspired by ancient Greek art, popular in Europe and the US from c.1750 to c.1850. Interest in Greek art emerged as part of the NEO-CLASSICAL style, through the publication of such Greek studies as *The Antiquities of Athens* (1762) by James STUART and Nicholas Revett. An early strand of this, known in France as the *goût grec* ("Greek taste"), was characterized by well-proportioned forms decorated with architectural motifs – VITRUVIAN scrolls, urns, Greek KEY PATTERN – and was much heavier than the later style popularized by Robert ADAM. The Greek Revival reached its peak of popularity during the Regency period, perhaps stimulated by the arrival of the Parthenon (Elgin) Marbles in England in 1806. Dominated by austere, monumental forms, it was adopted by leading architects such as Sir John Soane and Benjamin Latrobe, while Thomas HOPE pioneered a more archeologically accurate approach to furniture, copying designs from ancient GREEK POTTERY. Massive urn and krater forms, sparingly decorated with PALMETTES, ANTHEMIONS and beading were

Victorian Valentine greetings card [S]

popular in silver (e.g. Benjamin SMITH) and ceramics (WEDGWOOD vases). John FLAXMAN popularized flat, linear depictions of Greek mythology through his illustrations of Homer's works. The style declined from the 1850s, but Greek motifs continued to be used throughout the 19th and into the 20th century.

Green glazed wares Green has been one of the most common colours used in pottery decoration and glazes from early times. Copper in a lead glaze gives a leaf or sea green, in an alkaline glaze it is blue-green. Copper was used to produce the greens of early tin-enamelled pottery and the overglaze pigments popular from the 18th century.

Greene & Greene An architectural practice of brothers, Charles Sumner Greene (1868–1957) and Henry Mather Greene (1870–1954), in Pasadena, California. They designed the furniture and furnishings for their characteristically long and low bungalows. Their work shows the influence of Japan and the English ARTS AND CRAFTS movement. Pieces are jointed with screws concealed in slots, and pegs used to decorative effect; edges are rounded and softened. The Peter Hall Manufacturing Co. made their designs to a high standard.

Greetings card Originating from 18th-century European visiting cards, greetings cards were popular in the mid-19th century. Sir Henry COLE designed the first Christmas card in 1843 and this was followed by cards produced for all manner of occasions. Raphael Tuck & Sons and Thomas De La Rue were the principal makers of British Victorian cards. In the 19th century elaborate cards were made for Valentine's Day, Easter and Christmas.

Grendey, Giles (1693–1780) An important mid-18th century English cabinet-maker. Born in Wootton-under-Edge, Gloucestershire, he was apprenticed in London in 1709. By 1716 he was a freeman of the Joiners' Company. His clients included Spanish and English nobility, for whom he made high quality walnut, mahogany and JAPANNED pieces.

"Begonia leaf" bread plates by Griffen, Smith & Hill, c.1880 [K]

Griffen, Smith & Hill A pottery founded in 1880 in Phoenixville, Pennsylvania, by a partnership headed by John Griffen, an ironmaker, as a successor to the Phoenix Pottery (est. 1872). It is best known as the producer of "Etruscan majolica", America's most successful majolica glazed ware. Most Etruscan majolica, which resembles English majolica, is marked with a GSH monogram, sometimes including the word ETRUSCAN or a design number with the prefix E.

Griffin (griffon, gryphon) A mythological creature with the body of a lion and the head, claws and wings of an eagle, with origins in the ancient East. It was a popular decorative motif for Renaissance furniture. An emblem of courage and watchfulness, it often appears without wings in heraldry designs. Its association with Apollo, god of the sun, rendered it appropriate for candlesticks, torchères, candelabra and perfume burners during the NEO-CLASSICAL period. The motif was used in the REGENCY and EMPIRE styles.

Griffin

Grisaille The French term for decorative patterns painted on wood, GLASS, CERAMICS, plaster or stone in a palette of grey, black and white, which imitate marble or stone figure sculptures or RELIEF ornament. Favoured especially during the Renaissance period, grisaille was adopted in the 16th century by LIMOGES enamellers. The technique was sometimes used to imitate CAMEO decoration and it was taken up by NEO-CLASSICAL designers in the late 18th century, stimulating interest in original Classical sculpture and stone engraving.

Teapot with grisaille decoration, English c.1810 [R]

Grödnertal A valley in Tirol, Austria, that has become a generic term for early 19th-century wooden dolls. Grödnertals can be distinguished from ordinary PEG DOLLS by their finely painted features and hair, often with an accentuated comb on the crown and kiss-curls on the forehead. They are slender, often with double-jointed limbs and gessoed hands and feet.

Gropius, Walter (1883–1969) A German architect and teacher. He founded the BAUHAUS in 1919 and was its director until 1929. Gropius was a Modernist whose modular furniture greatly influenced post-war designers. He moved to London in 1934 where he practised architecture. In 1937 he emigrated to the US and became a professor at Harvard.

Gros bleu An intense UNDERGLAZE blue, introduced at VINCENNES in 1749. When copied by English porcelain factories it was called MAZARIN.

Gros point An embroidery stitch in which the embroidery thread usually crosses two threads of the coarse canvas foundation on which it was worked. Gros point was particularly fashionable for seat covers during the 18th and 19th centuries.

Grotesque

Grotesque

Ornament consisting of linked motifs such as animal and human figures, masks, panels, sphinxes and flowers, often combined in fantastical compositions. Grotesques first appeared in European decorative arts during the Renaissance of the early 16th century. They were derived from the discovery of painted and sculpted wall decoration with such motifs in the ruins of subterranean Roman buildings (known as "grotte"), such as the Golden House of Nero, excavated c.1500. This Classical ornament was adapted for interior decoration by Raphael in his designs for the interiors of the Vatican Loggie, executed largely by his assistant Giovanni di Udine (1517–19). Thereafter, grotesque motifs were introduced throughout Europe in every medium of applied art, especially textiles, murals, tapestries and ceramics. The style of grotesques evolved over the centuries –

Gropius tea service, c.1958 [K]

Mannerist designers of the 16th century including Jacques Androuet du Cerceau (c.1520–84), Cornelis Floris (1514–75) and Cornelis Bos (d.1556) incorporated scrolls and broad bands of STRAPWORK. In the late 17th and early 18th centuries, the individual elements of grotesques became lighter and more attenuated, in keeping with the RÉGENCE and ROCOCO styles, for example in designs by Jean BÉRAIN. Grotesques remained a popular motif throughout the NEO-CLASSICAL period and in the 19th century, but fantastical elements were more restrained and the ornament was often arranged within panels rather than as loose structures.

Grotto ornament Decorative ornament inspired by artificial grottoes, particularly irregular rockwork, exotic shells, and creatures such as frogs and snails. This type of ornament originated in the 16th century, particularly in ceramics by Bernard PALISSY, but was also a feature of the 18th-century ROCOCO style, especially in the silver of Juste-Aurele Meissonnier, Nicholas SPRIMONT, and Paul Crespin.

Groult, André (1884–1967) A French furniture designer. A member of the Société des Artistes Décorateurs, he contributed to several pavilions at the Exposition des Arts Décoratifs et Industrielles Modernes in Paris, in 1925. He is best known for his ART DECO furniture, often in oak, which incorporated luxurious decoration such as SHAGREEN mosaic and rosewood inlaid with ivory.

Ground colour The surface colour of ceramics, onto which painted decoration is often applied. Originating in China during the MING DYNASTY, ground colours were used in Europe from the early 18th century, first at MEISSEN, and later at almost all porcelain factories

Growler (or "voice box") A sound-producing mechanism used in TEDDY BEARS from the early 20th century until the 1950s. It usually consisted of a weight in a cardboard tube with air holes.

Grueby, William Henry (1867–1925)
An American art potter and founder of
the GRUEBY FAIENCE COMPANY, Boston.
Grueby is thought to have been
influenced by the work of French potters,
Chaplet and DELAHERCHE, who had
exhibited in the US. He is best known for
his hand-thrown vases which have relief
or carved decoration, particularly leaves
and flowers, and distinctive matt glazes in
browns, greens and ochres. Today, the
most desirable examples of Grueby's work
include large, signed vases with
decoration in contrasting colours (usually
yellow petals on a green background)
and lamp bases that were
made for TIFFANY.
In the late 20th century,
inexpensive decorative
Grueby copies became
common in America.

Grueby Faience Company

An American art
pottery founded in
1894 by William H.
GRUEBY in Boston.
Throughout its history
the company specialized
in handmade tiles and
slip-cast vessels with thick,
matt glazes in organic
tones, mostly shades of
green, yellow and ochre.
Although the pottery it
produced was much admired, the
company was never prosperous. In 1908 it
went bankrupt and in 1910 William
opened the Grueby Faience and Tile
Company, which made architectural
wares. In 1920 this was bought out by
the C. Pardee Works of Perth Amboy,
New Jersey.

Grueby vase, c.1900 [M]

Guard chain A long gold, silver or gilt
metal chain usually composed of a series
of small, uniform, repeated links. Guard
chains were frequently used to suspend a
fob watch, locket, keys or accessories and
were in common use from the early 19th
century to the early 20th century.

Gubbio potteries A centre of maiolica
manufacture in Urbino, Italy, famous for
lustre decoration. This was introduced by
Giorgio Andreoli in 1490; wares bearing
his signature survive. He produced a gold
lustre that is much finer than that made
by the DERUTA POTTERIES and a brilliant
ruby lustre. From c.1530
wares from
Urbino and
Faenza were sent
to Gubbio to be
enriched with lustre.
In the 19th century,
lustre decoration was
revived in Gubbio by
Giovannni Spinacci
(c.1853–76). The town
still produces pottery.

Guéridon table, French 1815 [C]

Guéridon A small
ornamental
wooden stand
originally designed
to hold a CANDELABRUM. Introduced in
France in the mid-17th century, the
pedestal base of Louis XIV guéridons
often took the form of a carved African
carrying a round tray. By the end of the
18th century, the term
guéridon was used for round
tables with a splayed support
and waisted legs, often with
elaborate inlaid tops.

Worcester guglet, c.1760 [M]

Guglet A water bottle
with a KNOP at the top
of a tall neck, which
causes the water to
make a gurgling
sound as it is poured.

Guild of Handicraft Ltd

A guild founded by
C.R. ASHBEE in London in 1888 as a
School of Handicraft, which later became
a guild of artist craftsmen. Ashbee designed
for them and some early work appears
with his initials, CRA. When the Guild
was registered as a limited company in
1898, the marks became G of H Ltd. The

company moved to Chipping Campden,
Gloucestershire, in 1902. Although it
closed in 1908, it continued loosely as a
guild with the remaining silversmiths,
metalworkers and furniture-makers
working as individuals until 1921. The
silversmith George Hart continued to
make silverware and the work
continued through his
son Henry, grandson
David and his great-
grandsons. The Hart
silversmiths have used the
mark, G of H, since 1912.

Guilloche A continuous
scroll pattern of interlacing
bands twisted to form a
plait, the gaps occasionally
filled with rosettes or other
floral motifs. Originally a FRIEZE
ornament derived from Classical
architecture, the guilloche was revived in
the Renaissance. Adopted as a decorative
motif for metalwork and for carved, inlaid
and painted furniture from the middle of
the 16th century, the pattern enjoyed
renewed popularity during the NEO-
CLASSICAL period. Guilloche is often
produced by mechanical methods for
gold and silver items.

Guilloche

Guilloché enamel A technique that
involves firing several layers of translucent
enamel onto a surface that has previously
been engraved with a distinctive pattern,
such as a sunburst. FABERGÉ made
extensive use of this form of decoration.

Guimard, Hector (1867–1942) A major
French ART NOUVEAU architect, decorator
and designer, best known for his designs
for the entrances to the Paris Métro. The
creator of wonderfully fluid, organic and
often asymmetric designs, he was highly
regarded for his furniture and metalware.

Gul A Persian term meaning flower. It refers to a stylized flowerhead motif seen particularly in central Asian Turkoman rugs. Its shape and form often give an indication as to the tribal origin of a rug.

Gunmetal A bronze-like alloy used mainly in the manufacture of gun barrels, but also for some furnishings.

Gustavsberg pottery A factory founded near Bredsjö, Sweden, in 1786, initially producing FAIENCE in the style of MARIEBERG. From about 1820 the factory made STAFFORDSHIRE-type pottery, and also copied Wedgwood's JASPER WARE. In the 1840s and 1860s they used self-coloured prints in underglaze blue or black, with scenic centres and elaborate borders, in the English manner of the period. A modern revival took place around 1900 when Gunnar Wennerberg was appointed as the artistic director, followed by Wilhelm Kåge in 1917, whose famous "Argenta" range was produced from 1929 to 1952. The factory is still in production.

Guttae Small drop-like projections beneath the triglyph on the ARCHITRAVE of a Doric column. Decorative ornament symbolising guttae, known in the 18th century as "bells", "drops" or "Doric drops", appears on NEO-CLASSICAL furniture. Occasionally guttae formed the feet of tables and chairs, as seen in the designs of Thomas CHIPPENDALE.

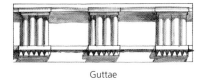

Guttae

Gutta-percha A resinous, oil-based material, the product of the Malaysian *Palaquium* tree. Used from the mid-19th century for various items including dolls and, from c.1850, golf balls ("gutties").

H

Haffner, Johann A German toy manufacturer, based near Nuremberg, that produced hand-painted lead soldiers and figures. Active from 1863 to 1893.

Haig, Thomas (d.1803) An English businessman, now best known as the partner and bookkeeper of Thomas CHIPPENDALE, with whom he worked following the death of Chippendale's first partner, James Rannie, in 1766. After Chippendale's death, Haig carried on the business with Chippendale's son, Thomas Chippendale the younger, (1749–1822), retiring in 1796.

Gustavsberg gourd vase and cover, early 20th century [o]

Haircloth A hard-wearing furniture covering made from a woven combination of hair from horses' manes and tails, or camel hair and linen or cotton. A popular choice for upholstery for library and dining chairs from the last quarter of the 18th century, when it was mentioned in George HEPPLEWHITE's *Guide*. It was also used for stiffening in garments.

Hairwork picture An embroidered picture worked with hair and occasionally some fine SILK onto a silk satin ground. They were fashionable in the late 18th and early 19th centuries, especially for mourning pictures.

Hairy paw foot A foot carved in the form of an animal's – usually a lion's – paw, complete with hair. This type of ornament originated in Classical Greece and was commonly used on 18th-century and REGENCY furniture.

Half hour strike See STRIKING SYSTEMS.

Half hunter See HUNTER.

Half-tester See TESTER.

Hallmarking The practice of stamping on a GOLD or SILVER item to attest to its purity and also to enable it to be traced to its source, in the event of its proving to be below standard. In most European countries hallmarking dates back to the Middle Ages. Usually, gold- and silversmiths belonged to guilds, who administered their own standards. In the UK, silversmiths were obliged from the year 1300 to have silver items ASSAYED. In 1327, Edward III granted a charter to the Worshipful Company of Goldsmiths to enforce the assaying system. Silversmiths thereafter took their wares to the Goldsmiths' Hall in London for testing. The Goldsmiths' Company ensured that a standard of purity for metals was maintained and also kept records of all silversmiths and their maker's marks. If a piece passed the tests, the hallmark would be stamped on it.

French silver was marked from c.1272 and a royal decree introduced a standard in 1378. From the 16th century, French silver was stamped by the silversmiths' guild. But the silver was still of varying levels of purity. It was not until after the Revolution, in 1797, when control passed from the guilds to the state, that two standards were established, of 95 per cent and 80 per cent purity, denoted by the numerals 1 and 2 respectively.

German silver standards were also controlled by the guilds until Germany became a state at the end of the 19th century. Items were struck with a town and a maker's mark. Some larger towns also had a date letter system. A crown and crescent mark was introduced in 1888 to denote purity of at least 80 per cent.

From the 16th century, Spanish silver had town and maker's marks, with the assay master also adding his own mark. A number denotes the year of testing.

Assay offices were set up in Moscow and St Petersburg in the 17th century. Russian silver was struck with a city mark, assay mark and the maker's mark.

In the US, a standard for purity and marking was not established until 1869, when the sterling standard was adopted.

Hallmarks

A hallmark usually consists of a collection of stamps on items of silver or gold, which give a brief history of the piece. They may denote such things as purity, the maker's name, the place of origin and the date of assay.

National variations

Most countries eventually established more than one assaying centre. In the UK, centres were established in centres such as London, Birmingham, Sheffield and Edinburgh and later in other provincial towns, such as Chester and Exeter. These centres all had their own marks: Birmingham, for example, had an anchor and Edinburgh a castle. Major cities also had their own marks in other European countries but the significance of the marks varied from country to country. In France, a piece might have a "community mark", confirming the purity of the metal, a maker's mark, a city mark, a "juranda mark" (the date) and a "charge mark", denoting that tax had been paid on the item. Before the unification of Germany, the separate states and cities had their own marks, with a maker's mark and a year mark, but the silver purity was not standardized until 1888. In 1972, an international standard was agreed by several European countries.

In Russia, silversmithing was at first often practised in monasteries and in the 17th century all silver was marked with the blessing hand. However, Peter the Great standardized the purity of gold and silver in 1700 and assay offices were then established in various cities.

In the US, there was no standard system of assaying and hallmarking until 1869, marks being confined to makers' names (except briefly in Baltimore from 1814 to 1830). Some makers stamped their pieces with imitations of the British lion mark, others used an eagle, but none of these marks meant anything consistent about the purity of the metal. Some goods, however, from the mid–1800s, were marked with indications of quality from "standard" to "premium". In 1869, sterling silver was adopted throughout the US.

British Isles

London Assay Office, 18th century

Chester Assay Office, (closed 1954)

Glasgow Assay Office, (1819–1964)

Dublin Assay Office, from 1730

Europe and Russia

Guild mark for Paris, 1724–25

Strasbourg, Germany, 1725

Copenhagen, Denmark, 1725

Amsterdam, Netherlands, c.1606

Turin, Italy, 18th century

St Petersburg, Russia, Guild mark 1775

United States

Paul Revere, 1725

Myer Myers, 1745

Tiffany & Co, since 1902

How to read a British hallmark

The hallmark on a silver item made in the British Isles after 1544 consists of four statutory items and other possible optional ones. The maker's mark gives the initials of the maker; the sterling mark indicates that it is the required standard of silver; the assay mark indicates in which town the piece was tested; the date letter gives a letter for the year of assay, which varies from town to town; finally, the maker may add special commemorative marks.

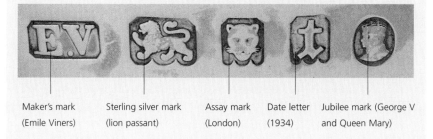

| Maker's mark (Emile Viners) | Sterling silver mark (lion passant) | Assay mark (London) | Date letter (1934) | Jubilee mark (George V and Queen Mary) |

Hall chair A formal high-backed wooden chair, with or without arms and with a hard seat, that was introduced in the 18th century and placed in the halls or corridors of grand houses where it was used as a waiting chair. Usually made of OAK or MAHOGANY, the backs were often carved with Classical motifs, family crests or coats of arms.

Hall chair, c.1840 [K]

Hall stand

A term now used to describe a combined stand for hats and umbrellas, with rows of hooks for hats above an open umbrella stand. First introduced in the early 19th century, these stands, made of wood or metal –

Bamboo hall stand, French c.1870 [L]

elaborate cast-iron examples were common – came in a variety of styles and often included a wooden or marble shelf, drawers and a mirror.

Hamada, Shoji (1894–1978) A Japanese STUDIO POTTER, born in Tokyo, who was influential in Britain, Japan and the US. He was a lifelong friend and supporter of Bernard LEACH and helped him to establish his own pottery in St Ives, Cornwall. Hamada worked at ST IVES from 1920 to 1923, and exhibited in London in 1923, 1929, and 1931. He established his own pottery at Mashiko, Japan, in 1930, and was declared "A National Living Treasure" in 1955.

Hamada tea bowl, 1950s [N]

Hamadan carpets Carpets made in Hamadan, a city in West Persia, and the surrounding villages, in the 19th and 20th centuries. Hamadan carpets have a coarse, open weave and a geometric or stylized floral design in shades of pink and blue. Characteristically, pieces are woven with wool pile on a single-wefted cotton foundation.

Hammered A term used to describe metal that has been fashioned into shape by repeated hammer blows after it has first been softened by heating until red hot. Though the hammered finish is often polished smooth, during the ARTS AND CRAFTS period in particular, the numerous small hammer dents were often left or even added as surface decoration, to give a textured, mottled effect.

Hanau Pottery A German FAIENCE factory started by two Dutch potters Daniel Behaghel and his son-in-law Jacobus van der Walle in 1661, which continued under several changes of ownership until 1806. It had Dutch owners and employed

Dutch workers until 1726, when it was taken over by Heinrich von Alpen. Although the early wares are imitative of Dutch BLUE AND WHITE ceramics, they did not use the lead OVERGLAZE (kwaart) that gave the Dutch ware a shiny surface. The Dutch/Chinese influence lasted until the middle of the 18th century, when it gave way to DEUTSCHE BLUMEN and some use of enamel colours and gold. The quality of the wares declined from 1787 and in 1806 the factory closed.

Hancock, Robert (1731–1817) An engraver who made prints for transfer-printing on to porcelain. He worked at BOW from 1753, then at WORCESTER, CAUGHLEY and other factories. His best-known subjects are The Tea Party, L'Amour and The Fortune Teller. Some examples on Worcester porcelain are marked with the letters RH – probably his initials – and an anchor, which is a rebus on the name of Holdship, a director of the factory.

Hancock, William (1794–c.1860) An American furniture-maker active in Boston from 1820 to c.1850. Hancock's early designs in the fashionable English Regency style compare to Duncan PHYFE. After c.1830 Hancock made parlour furniture and is credited with introducing the spring-seated ROCKING CHAIR with buttoned upholstery, known generically as the "American rocker".

Robert Hancock print on Worcester mug, c.1770 [L]

Hand cooler A solid egg-shaped piece of glass, marble or hardstone that was used to cool the hands. Originating in ancient Rome, hand coolers were made in France and England in the 18th century. Examples with MILLEFIORI decoration were made by the SAINT-LOUIS GLASSWORKS.

Handel Company An American glass manufacturer founded in Meriden, Connecticut, in 1885 by Philip J. Handel (1867–1914). Handel specialized in reverse-painted glass lampshades. These are typically hemispherical and painted with scenic views or flora on the interior and finished on the exterior with frosting resembling chipped ice. Most are signed on the shade border and metalwork. Rare designs rival many TIFFANY lamps in value. Production ceased in 1936.

Hand warmer A small receptacle containing hot water or charcoal embers, for warming the hands in cold weather. Hand warmers were made from the late Middle Ages in COPPER, BRASS or SILVER, often with a pierced, spherical outer cover, sometimes in the shape of a book. DELFTWARE examples were also produced in the 17th century.

Handkerchief table A type of 18th-century American table, with a single drop leaf. Both the leaf and top are triangular in shape, and when raised the leaf and top form a square. The table fits neatly in a corner when the leaf is closed.

Mahogany handkerchief table, c.1750 [G]

Hanger A short SWORD often used for hunting. Sometimes called a "cuttoe", from the French for hunting knife, *couteau de chasse*. The term also describes the device used to suspend a SWORD from a waistbelt.

Hanoverian pattern A pattern of FLATWARE and cutlery that first appeared c.1710 just before the reign of the first Hanoverian King, George I (1714–27) and has been in production ever since. The handles have a raised rib or ridge down the front and back and a rounded terminal or end; the forks generally have two or three prongs. Early spoons (c.1710–30) have a decorative RAT TAIL running down the length of the back of the bowls.

Hanoverian pattern spoon and fork, c.1730 [P]

Hardoy chair A chair consisting of a leather seat suspended by corner pockets from a rigid frame made from a continuous strip of metal. A post-World War II design, it was inspired by a folding chair used by Italian forces in the North Africa campaign and was named after the Argentinian designer Jorge Ferrari-Hardoy.

Hard-paste porcelain A hard, dense ceramic made from a compound of the feldspathic rock PETUNTSE and KAOLIN fired at a very high temperature. First made in China c.AD 800, the secret of its manufacture was not known in Europe until 1709, when J. BÖTTGER of MEISSEN discovered the formula. Despite attempts to keep it secret, the process spread to other German factories and eventually became known throughout the West.

Hardstone A term describing decorative opaque gemstones such as ONYX, cornelian, jasper and AGATE. Hardstones may be carved into CAMEOS and INTAGLIOS or mounted in a variety of media including architectural or floral patterns known as PIETRA DURA.

Harewood A term for SYCAMORE or MAPLE wood that has been dyed silvery grey with iron oxide. It was used for VENEERING and BANDING, small items such as TEA CADDIES and high quality furniture.

Harigaki A Japanese term for a decorative lacquerwork technique that involves scratching or incising into the surface of the lacquer before it is dry with a needle.

Harlequin set A term used to describe a set of furniture or ceramics, popular in the 18th century, in which the various pieces are similar rather than identical. Today the term is also used to describe items of the same pattern or design that have been put together to make a set.

Harlequin table A variation on the sofa or PEMBROKE table, introduced at the end of the 18th century. It included a set of small drawers and pigeonholes concealed within the body of the table, which rose up by means of a system of weights.

Harrison, John (1693–1776) An English clockmaker who trained as a carpenter and land surveyor, but took up clockmaking c.1715. In c.1725 he invented the gridiron pendulum, a form of temperature-COMPENSATED PENDULUM. However, he is best known for his lengthy but eventually successful experiments to develop a marine CHRONOMETER that would enable sailors to calculate longitude accurately and thus determine their position at sea. The British government offered a prize of £20,000 for anyone who could develop such a device, and Harrison was belatedly awarded it after his fourth version successfully completed sea trials in 1761 and 1764.

Hausmaler (German: "home painter") A term for a freelance painter who decorated porcelain bought "in the white" from a factory or sold as defective. *Hausmalerei* of the 18th century is not classed as forgery – indeed, some artists' work is highly prized. These include pieces by both Johann and Sabina AUFFENWERTH of Augsburg; Ignaz Bottengruber of Breslau; F.J. Ferner; and Bartholomäus Seuter of Augsburg.

Meissen hausmalerei beaker by Ferner, c.1730 [L]

Haviland & Co. A French pottery and porcelain factory founded in 1842 in Limoges (with the advantage of KAOLIN at nearby St Yrieix) by the American David Haviland (1814–79). The factory made porcelain mainly for the US market and achieved great commercial success. It used industrial techniques and cheap methods of decoration such as CHROMOLITHOGRAPHY, as well as overglaze and underglaze painting. In 1873 a design studio was established in Paris, directed by David Haviland's son Charles, which made ART POTTERY. In 1890 David Haviland's son Theodore built a new factory in Limoges, which is still in production as Haviland SA. Haviland's grandson Charles Field Haviland took over the Alluaud porcelain factory in LIMOGES and also founded the firm which bears his name in New York.

Heal & Son A firm of furniture-makers and retailers founded in 1810 by John Harris Heal. Under his great grandson Sir Ambrose Heal (1872–1959), the company established its place in 20th-century design history, with his own designs for furniture (from ARTS AND CRAFTS to ART DECO). New premises were built in 1913 in Tottenham Court Road, London. The top floor gallery showed work by designers such as Alvar AALTO and Marcel Lajos BREUER in the 1920s and 30s. The shop still exists but the Heal family are not involved.

Heal & Son Arts and Crafts oak dining chair, c.1920 [O]

Heaped and piled effect

Heaped and piled effect An accidental effect on Chinese BLUE AND WHITE porcelain of the early MING DYNASTY where cobalt oxide was unevenly applied producing dark spots. The effect was copied in the 18th century by painting in dark dots.

Heartwood The dense timber from the inner core of the tree. It is usually harder and often darker in colour than the SAPWOOD, the contrast between the two being used to decorative effect with such woods as yew and laburnum.

Hellenistic The period of Greek civilization from the death of Alexander the Great (323 BC) to the defeat of Antony and Cleopatra (30 BC) and following the Classical Hellenic period.

Helmet An item of defensive armour for the head, used from the earliest times to the present. Helmets were made from various materials including metals – iron, steel and bronze – padded textiles, leather, horn, wickerwork, plastics and ceramics. In Europe, helmets fell out of use from c.1650 although they were revived during World War I as a defence against shrapnel. (See also ARMOUR and MORION.)

Helmet ewer A EWER with either the whole or the upper body, rim and spout resembling an inverted helmet. They were made in silver and bronze, ceramics, glass, hardstone and enamel from the early 16th to the early 18th century.

Henri Deux See SAINT-PORCHAIRE.

Hepplewhite, George (d.1786) An English furniture-maker. Little is known of his life except for his PATTERN-BOOK, the *Cabinet-maker and Upholsterer's Guide*, that was influential both in Europe and North America. It was published posthumously in 1788, with revised editions in 1789 and 1794, and contains Hepplewhite's designs for slender elegant furniture, with inlaid and painted rather than carved decoration of such motifs as SUNBURSTS, HUSKS, scrolls and PATERAE, and for chairs with distinctive shield-shaped backs or square backs incorporating Prince of Wales feathers.

Shield-backed Hepplewhite chair, c.1790 [G]

Heraldic decoration A variety of emblems representing the bearer and his status in society. Developed during the 12th century, heraldic ornament was applied to architecture and on precious possessions such as silver and gold objects, porcelain and books. From medieval times, the arms of the wife's family were added to those of her husband upon marriage and may be incorporated into the decoration of a house interior, in tapestries or the marriage bed. In the 16th century, cities, towns and guilds in

Commemorative jug from the Paris Exhibition with heraldic decoration, English, 1855 [J]

Germany and in the Low Countries began incorporating heraldic motifs on stoneware and glass as national emblems. Heraldic coats of arms were used on dinner services in Europe and America from the turn of the 18th century and also on CHINESE EXPORT PORCELAIN. They are still widely used on commemorative pieces of all kinds.

Herat An important carpet-producing town in the KHORASSAN district of north-east Persia during the 16th century. Carpets were very fine with floral curvilinear patterns in jewel-like colours. Carpet production had effectively finished here by the mid-18th century.

Herati A frequently seen repeat design on Oriental carpets. The motif is formed by a central diamond lozenge with four serrated leaves, often resembling fish, forming the corners. It is seen in both urban and tribal rugs, carpets and also in KILIMS from Kurdistan.

Hereke An important Turkish carpet-manufacturing town. Carpet-weaving started at the end of the 19th century and is still prolific today. The town is renowned for fine silk rugs, many of PRAYER design, with delicate floral patterns, others with overall repeat designs. Woollen carpets are also made there today.

Herend porcelain factory Founded in Hungary in 1839 by Moritz Fischer, this factory made (and still makes, although nationalized in 1948) copies of all kinds of European and Oriental porcelain. They may be marked with the name Herend and the coat of arms of Hungary.

Herat carpet, north-east Persia, 18th century [E]

Heriz A town in north-west Persia producing carpets and some rugs in the 19th and 20th centuries. The designs have an overall repeat format or a central medallion. Older colours include ivory, terracotta and pale blues; stronger colours were used in the 20th century. They were usually wool on cotton although some were of silk in the late 19th century.

Herman Miller Inc. A firm of US furniture-manufacturers founded in 1905 by Herman Miller in Zeeland, Michigan. Under Gilbert Rohde in the 1930s the company become one of the most progressive makers of post-war furniture, a reputation that survives today. Designers who have worked for them include Charles and Ray EAMES, Isamu Noguchi, Poul Kajaerholm and Verner Panton.

Hermann The Hermann dynasty of German toy-makers was founded by Johann Hermann in 1896 near Sonneberg, Thuringia. The first PLUSH bears were produced in 1907. Most can be distinguished by their inset snouts of shorter plush and three claws. Gebrüder Hermann introduced their "Zotty" bears in the 1950s to compete with STEIFF. Hermann are still producing toys today.

Herringbone banding A banding of veneer formed of two narrow strips laid together, with the grain of each running diagonally to produce a herringbone or feather effect. Herringboning was adopted for drawer fronts on walnut furniture of the late 17th and early 18th centuries, and was also used in early brickwork.

Helmet styles

The weight and shape of helmets varied with the type of soldier (cavalry or infantry) and which weapons he was expected to encounter.

Closed-face tournament helmet, 15th century

Spanish morion, 16th century

Open-faced burgonet with cheek plates, 16th century

Cromwellian pot helmet, early 17th century

Herter Brothers German-born Gustav (1830–98) and his half-brother Christian (1840–83) were leading furniture-makers and interior decorators in New York. Gustav established his interior decorating firm in the 1850s, having previously designed silver for TIFFANY & CO. He was joined by Christian in 1860; when Gustav returned to Germany in 1870 Christian continued running Herter Brothers until around 1880. Until its closure in 1905 the firm produced some of the finest American Aesthetic and Renaissance Revival furniture, specializing in intricate inlaid work in exotic woods, and also embraced Japanese influences and the EASTLAKE style. Most examples are signed or well documented.

Heubach, Gebrüder This porcelain factory in Lichte, Thuringia, was founded *c.*1820 by the Heubach brothers. After 1909 it specialized in CHARACTER DOLLS, often with INTAGLIO eyes and moulded hair. Gebrüder Heubach dolls can be distinguished by their exaggerated facial expression; the "petulant boy" is the most sought after. The factory also produced FAIRINGS and other biscuit porcelain. It closed in 1940. The company's mark was a square or a rising sun. Gebrüder Heubach is not to be confused with the unrelated dollmaker Ernst Heubach of Koppelsdorf.

Heyde, Georg Established a toy soldier company in Dresden in 1872, manufacturing metal solid-cast painted figures. By *c.*1900 he was the world leading exporter of toy soldiers, producing armies of the world, figures of the Wild West and the Ancient World, and knights. Heyde continued production up to World War II. The factory was bombed during the war and production ceased in the late 1940s.

Highboy A double CHEST-OF-DRAWERS or chest-on-chest, the American form of the English TALLBOY. Highboys were made throughout the north-eastern states from about 1710. The most valuable are formal, carved mahogany examples with important family provenance and a known maker. Plain examples, typically of maple, cherry or walnut, are more common.

High-temperature colours The colours – shades of green (copper oxide), blue (cobalt), purple (manganese), yellow (antimony) and orange (iron) – used to decorate tin-glazed earthenware until the 18th century (after which *petit feu*, or ENAMEL COLOURS were more common). They are known in French as *grand feu* due to the high temperature used to unite them with a tin glaze.

High-warp A tapestry-weaving technique, used at the GOBELINS factory in Paris. The loom holds the warp threads vertically, tensioned between two horizontal rollers. The bulk of the warp is rolled onto the upper roller and completed work is rolled at intervals onto the bottom one.

Hille Co. Ltd Manufacturers of quality reproduction furniture founded by the emigré Salomon Hille (1875–1940) in London in 1906. In the early years they supplied Waring & Gillow and Maples. In the 1920s and 1930s, Ray Hille, Salomon's daughter, created ART DECO designs and Chinese lacqueur work pieces after CHIPPENDALE. Robin DAY became Design Director at Hille Co. Ltd in 1950.

American Chippendale mahogany highboy, Philadelphia, 1770–80 [A]

Heubach shoulder head doll, c.1912 [N]

Hilt The handle of a SWORD, BAYONET, DAGGER or knife, composed of the grip, the pommel (a counterweight for the blade) and the guard, which protects the hand. Hilts, made from metal and a variety of materials, were often the most decorated part of the weapon.

Hinge A folding metal joint between two pieces of wood, such as a door and frame, or chest and lid, allowing them to open and close. In the early 17th century, coffer lid hinges were made from wire loops; by the end of the century wrought-iron butterfly and strap hinges were used. Subsequently, hinges became more refined, e.g. the pierced, decorative light brass hinges used in 18th-century cabinet-work and early 19th-century lacquer cabinets on stands.

Hipped knee A type of CABRIOLE chair leg used from the early 18th century, which has carved decoration from the the top outward curve ("knee") to the seat rail. It was used in the early 19th century (*c.*1810–40) on the sabre legs found on CARD and PEMBROKE tables.

Hipped knee

Hirado ware Japanese porcelain made at Mikawachi near ARITA and exported from the port of Hirado. The main period of production was *c.*1750–*c.*1830. Wares, e.g. vases, ewers, CENSERS and animal

Hirado okimono, Meiji period [H]

models, have a fine quality white body, are crisply modelled and are sometimes decorated in a soft, slightly purple underglaze blue or iron brown.

Hiramé A process in which pieces of gold or silver sheet are applied under a clear LACQUER. (See also NASHIJI.)

Hispano-Moresque ware The Moors invaded Spain in AD 711 and the ceramics they produced introduced two techniques to Europe: glazing with an opaque white tin glaze, and painting in metallic lustres. Malaga in southern Spain was particularly celebrated for its gold lustrewares in the 14th century; Valencia and its suburbs Manises and Paterna also became important centres. Albarelli and lustre dishes with coats of arms were made for rich Italians and Spanish. The Moors were expelled from Spain in 1492, but the Hispano-Moresque style survived in the province of Valencia. Later wares usually have a coarse reddish-buff body, dark blue decoration and lustre.

Hispano-Moresque lustre vase, c.1500 [D]

Historicism The 19th-century revival of historical styles. While the 18th century saw revivals of the Gothic and Classical styles, in the 19th century there was more concern for accurate representations of Gothic and Classical art. There was also interest in Renaissance, Byzantine, Islamic, Egyptian, Elizabethan and Oriental art inspired by archeological discoveries, scholarly publications and the foundation of decorative arts museums. Technical advances and mechanized manufacture allowed exact replicas of historical pieces, although styles were often bizarrely combined (see ECLECTICISM).

Historismus glass Largely German 19th-century glass made in styles from earlier centuries. It was particularly popular following the reunification of Germany in 1871, when, in an attempt to create a national identity, traditional drinking glasses such as HUMPEN and RÖMER were produced, with enamelled decoration of fictional coats of arms.

Hitchcock, Lambert (1795–1856) An American chair-maker active from about 1818 in Hitchcockville (now Riverton), Connecticut. The "Hitchcock chair", was introduced in the mid-1820s and is still made in Riverton. Made in birch or maple, it is japanned with a layer of black over red and decorated in gilt stencilling. Most have rush seats and a lightweight design showing the influence of SHERATON. Early Hitchcock chairs are often signed and are popular with collectors if in original condition. Similar American chairs are termed "Hitchcock type".

Ho A Chinese bronze kettle with a cover and three or four legs, made from the SHANG (c.1500–1028 BC) to the Han dynasties (206 BC–220 AD). The earliest form has a bulbous body, cylindrical spout and loop handle. A later version has an oblong body, short cabriole legs and animal mask spout.

Hobbs, Brockunier & Co. An American glass manufacturer established in 1863 in Wheeling, West Virginia, by former employees of the NEW ENGLAND GLASS CO. to make flint glass. By the time it closed in 1891 the firm was one of the largest glassworks in the US. It specialized in PEACHBLOW and AMBERINA colour pressed glass, both introduced in 1886.

Hochschnitt (German: "high cut") A form of relief decoration on glass where the background is cut away to leave the design standing proud of the surface. Used on early Roman glass, it is now most closely identified with superb pieces made by Bohemian and German glass-makers in the late 17th century.

Hochschnitt cup and cover, c.1700 [F]

Höchst pottery and porcelain factory A faience factory was run in Höchst by Adam von LÖWENFINCK 1746–58, producing tureens and dishes modelled as turkeys, boar's heads, pheasants, fruit and vegetables, in bold Rococo form.

After the arrival of Joseph RINGLER and Johann Benckgraff in 1750 the factory began to produce porcelain. It made charming Rococo wares and figures, with a creamy white paste. The modellers G.F. Riedel, Laurentius Russinger, J.P. MELCHIOR and Simon FEILNER produced figures in Meissen style, including Italian comedy and conversation groups often inspired by French engravings. Melchior modelled many groups of children. Late figures are NEO-CLASSICAL in style. They used an underglaze blue wheel mark from c.1750, and production ceased in 1796. The old Höchst moulds were passed to Damm (est. 1827) who produced the designs in faience. Other factories also made copies, e.g. Dressel, Kister & Co. at Passau (from 1840) and Mehlem of Bonn (from 1836).

Höchst porcelain soup tureen and cover, c.1760 [G]

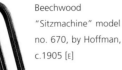

Beechwood "Sitzmachine" model no. 670, by Hoffman, c.1905 [E]

Hoffmann, Josef (1870–1956) An Austrian architect and a leading 20th-century designer. He was associated with the VIENNA SECESSION with Koloman MOSER, was a founding member of the WIENER WERKSTÄTTE (1903) and designed metalwork, jewellery and furniture. Hoffman favoured a more geometric approach within the ART NOUVEAU style and was influenced by the work of Charles Rennie MACKINTOSH.

Hogarth chair A mid-19th-century term for a type of chair in the QUEEN ANNE style with cabriole legs and a splat back. It was named after the artist William Hogarth, in whose paintings such chairs are often depicted.

Hogenberg, Frans See BRAUN, Georg and HOGENBERG, Frans.

Hohlwein, Ludwig (1874–1949) A German artist and poster designer. He was a pioneer in the use of large flat areas of colour and compositions of extreme simplicity. His work was evocative of the 1920s and 30s and his designs are found on travel and other advertising posters.

Ho ho bird (Japanese: "phoenix") A mythical bird symbolizing fire, the ho ho bird emerges in Italian grotesque ornament of the 16th century. With a long beak and curving neck, flowing tail, claws and crest, it was a spirited component of 18th-century CHINOISERIE decoration for ceramics, woodwork and plasterwork. Frequently it is portrayed as an amalgam of several birds, including the phoenix, pheasant, stork, heron and bird of paradise.

Ho ho bird

Holbeinesque The term given to 19th-century gold and enamel jewellery inspired by the designs of Hans Holbein, 16th-century court artist to Henry VIII. Holbeinesque jewels are invariably enamelled in several primary colours and are set with correspondingly vivid gemstones such as garnets cut en CABOCHON, chrysolite and diamond.

Hollie point Distinctive 18th-century ENGLISH NEEDLE LACE used on linen christening caps and shirts; finely worked rows of buttonhole stitching giving the baby's name and date of birth, as well as flowers and birds, in series of small holes.

Hollow-cast figures A process invented by BRITAINS LTD in 1895 to reduce the weight and production cost of their lead figures. The mould was filled with molten lead and left for a short while for the outside surface to cool after which the liquid centre of the figure was poured out. The method was soon copied by other makers.

English lead hollow-cast figures, 1920s [P]

Hollowware A term used most commonly in relation to silver or plated wares, but also used for articles made in other metals and ceramics. It describes domestic articles such as jugs, coffeepots and baskets that are hollow or hollowed as receptacles for food and drink. (See also FLATWARE.)

Holly (*Ilex aquifolium*) A tree native to Britain and Europe with a hard, fine grain and a distinctive ivory or greenish-white colour. It was used for inlay and marquetry from the 16th century.

Holster A container, usually made of leather, for a pistol or REVOLVER. Originally mounted on the front of a saddle, but from the mid-19th century onward worn on a waistbelt.

Honey gilding The process of fixing gold leaf to ceramics using honey. After the piece is lightly fired it shows a good colour and a soft dull tone. The technique was developed at SÈVRES in the mid-18th century and much used at CHELSEA. It was superseded by MERCURY GILDING.

Honiton lace BOBBIN LACE made in rural Devon in the 17th and 18th centuries was despatched to centres such as London from the town of Honiton and became known as Honiton lace. Designs used naturalistic motifs, including roses, birds and wild flowers. In the 19th century, the lace motifs were occasionally appliqued onto machine-made net.

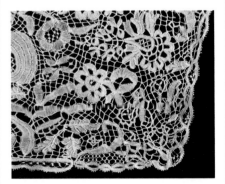

Honiton lace, 48 x 40.5cm (19 x 16in), 1870 [S]

Hood The part of the case on a LONGCASE CLOCK enclosing the dial and movement, set above the trunk housing the pendulum and weights. Hoods on early longcases, before *c*.1700, were generally square and decorated with architectural-style pediments and twist columns. Later hoods were made in a variety of styles, for example with PAGODA TOPS.

Hoof foot (cloven foot) The hoof of the goat or ram employed as a terminal to the legs of furniture. A motif first used by the ancient Egyptians, it was introduced in Europe in the late 17th century. Found on the legs of early CABRIOLE chairs, the hoof foot – also known by the French term *pied de biche* – remained a popular device throughout the 18th century.

Hooked rug A type of piled rug where the pile tufts, which may be lengths of wool or strips of material, are tied to the foundation of canvas or burlap using a hooked tool. This was a common domestic craft in Europe and the US in the 18th and 19th centuries and survives in rural areas today.

Hope, Thomas (1769–1831) An English collector and furniture designer who travelled widely in the Mediterranean and in the Middle East before settling in London, where he designed his house in

Carved giltwood stool designed by Hope, c.1810 [E]

Duchess Street round his collection of pictures and furnished rooms in different styles. He collected Greek and Roman Classical sculpture and objets d'art but he

also took up the Egyptian style promoted by the French designer Dominique Denon. Hope's book, *Household Furniture and Decoration* (1807), was one of the most influential collections of archeologically accurate NEO-CLASSICAL and REGENCY furniture designs, including his well-known Grecian chairs.

Hope chest An American term for a carved or painted wooden blanket chest of a type also called a marriage or dowry chest. The most desirable hope chests are of PENNSYLVANIA DUTCH origin.

Hornby "0"-gauge train set, 1940s [P]

Hornby, Frank (1863–1936) The most significant figure in the British toy industry. He invented the construction set called Mechanics Made Easy in 1901, which became MECCANO in 1907. Hornby trains, in "0"-gauge lithographed TINPLATE, were introduced in 1920. The early examples, up to 1925, were bolted together as in Meccano. They were powered by CLOCKWORK until electric train sets were made in 1926. (A short-lived 240-volt set was sold from 1925.) The first versions used 4- or 6-volt accumulators but a 20-volt system was added in 1932. The range expanded into train types, rolling stock, stations and lineside effects like DINKY TOYS, mostly made of lithographed tinplate. When production restarted after World War II, only the small 4-wheel locomotives

reappeared but they ceased production in 1957. However, the Hornby-Dublo, the "00"-gauge system produced from 1938 to compete with BASSETT-LOWKE's Trix, was successful. Hornby was taken over by TRIANG in 1964 but became Hornby Railways again in 1971 and production continues today.

Höroldt (Herold), Johann Gregor (1696–1775)

Meissen tankard by Höroldt, c.1728 [D]

A German miniature and enamel painter, Höroldt went to MEISSEN in 1720, became court painter in 1723 and director in 1731. During his time, a new source of clay was discovered that produced a creamy-white body. Höroldt was a colour chemist and rediscovered the "secret" of the underglaze blue used earlier by David Köhler and various other enamel colours including those for KAKIEMON patterns. He produced a book of etchings of CHINOISERIES for use on porcelain and also a book of his colour researches. He fled at the outbreak of the Seven Years' War in 1756, returned to Meissen in 1763 and was pensioned off in 1765.

Horse brass A decorative brass plaque attached to a horse's harness, probably of medieval origin. They were produced mainly in the 19th century in a range of often symbolic or commemorative designs, such as trees, animals, flowers, diamonds and stars. Early cast brasses are heavier than later machine-stamped ones.

Horse hair Curled horse hair has been widely used for upholstery since the 17th century because its "springy" nature retains its shape after constant use. During the 19th century, it was also used to make a hard-wearing woven cloth which was used for upholstering seat furniture.

Horseshoe table A small LIBRARY, WRITING, or WORK TABLE shaped like a horseshoe. The term also refers to a Hunt table, associated with the drinking of STIRRUP CUPS. The shape was introduced in the 18th century and was extant throughout the 19th century.

Horta, Victor (1861–1947) A leading Belgian architect and ART NOUVEAU designer. He designed integrated interiors including metalwork fixtures, door frames and panelling. His style was sinuous and organic and he was at the forefront of establishing the Art Nouveau style.

Hot-water plate, English, c.1800 [L]

Hot-water plate A dinner plate or dish popular in the REGENCY and VICTORIAN periods, made of silver, plated ware, pewter, tinned metals or ceramics. It has a container underneath and an aperture through which it is filled with hot water to keep the plate and its contents warm.

Hourglass (or sand glass) An instrument for measuring time, widely used since the Middle Ages. Early ones have two clear blown glass bulbs mounted one above the other and bound together at the necks; from the mid-18th century they were blown in one piece. Set in a metal, wood or ivory frame with a quantity of sand flowing from the upper container into the lower at a known speed, its uses included measuring a ship's speed.

Hour striking A clock that strikes on every hour, invented in the 16th century. The hour-and-half hour strike that strikes both on the hour and every half-hour, is a derivative of the hour striking.

Howard & Sons One of the best-known furniture-manufacturers of its day, founded in London in 1820 by John Howard. From the 1860s the company made pieces by ARTS AND CRAFTS designers, as well as its own range of high quality upholstered furniture, in particular armchairs. The stamp is found on the castors or mounts.

Hu An ancient Chinese bronze vessel, originally used for storing wine for ritual use. The body of the vessel, often with two handles near the mouth, is usually pear-, gourd- or flask-shaped.

Hubbard, Elbert Green (1856–1915) A leading exponent of the ARTS AND CRAFTS movement in the US. In 1895 he founded a community of craftsmen, the Roycrofters, at East Aurora, New York, based on the principles of William MORRIS, whom he had met on a visit to England in 1894. The Roycrofters produced metalwork, leatherwork and simple MISSION furniture, marked with a cross with two horizontal bars and an R in a circle. Hubbard's son, Elbert Hubbard Jnr, took over the Roycrofters when Hubbard and his wife went down on the *Lusitania* in 1915. The Roycrofters workshops closed in 1938.

Hubley Manufacturing Co. One of the leading US manufacturers of early CAST IRON toys, founded by John E. Hubley in 1894 in Lancaster, Pennsylvania. Successful lines included

Fire-engine by Hubley Manufacturing Co., c.1905 [M]

wagons, fire-engines and circus trains, and by the 1920s included cars and motorbikes. They were marked "Hubley" and noted for their complexity. The company survived into the 1940s by turning to DIECAST production.

Huguenot The term for Protestant refugees who fled France and settled in England and other Protestant countries, such as Germany, Holland and Switzerland, following the Revocation of the Edict of Nantes in 1685. After the accession of William III in England in 1688, many Huguenot craftsmen arrived in London, bringing with them the French BAROQUE style in the influential furniture designs of Daniel MAROT. Engraved decoration and new forms – including soup tureens, sauceboats and wine coolers – were introduced by leading Huguenot silversmiths such as Paul de LAMERIE. Silk textiles were produced in SPITALFIELDS by Huguenot weavers. The silversmith and porcelain maker Nicholas SPRIMONT was of Huguenot origin.

Hummel figure A small porcelain figurine depicting a rural child, made from 1935 at William Goebel's factory in Bavaria from the designs of a Franciscan nun Sister Maria Innocentia (Berta Hummel). Many of the original designs are still in production.

Hubbard Roycrofters bookstand, c.1910 [H]

Humpen A German drinking glass in the form of a tall, straight-sided beaker, used for beer and wine. They were made in Germany and Bohemia from the mid-16th to the 18th century, usually of WALDGLAS, with enamelled coats of arms.

Hunter A watch made from *c.*1800 to the early 19th century with a protective cover over the dial, often engraved or enamelled. A half-hunter, used from *c.*1860, has an aperture in the cover through which the time can be read.

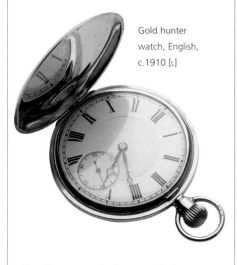

Gold hunter watch, English, c.1910 [L]

Hunting carpets A carpet design created by Persian artists of the early Safavid period (1501–1732) depicting huntsmen on horseback armed with lances and bows, tracking down their prey or fighting wild beasts. These motifs originate from Safavid manuscripts. Countless variations on this theme can be found on carpets produced since the 19th century from Persia, Turkey and India.

Husk motif A stylized motif based on a husk of corn or the BELLFLOWER and composed of three short, flat leaves, typically in swags or bands, sometimes graduated in size or alternated with beads. It was a popular decoration on furniture, ceramics and metalwork in the late 18th century, particularly in England and the US, where it replaced the heavy, florid FESTOON. Husk swags were also adopted for marble and STUCCO work.

Hutch An English term derived from the French *huche* which denoted both a roughly constructed chest and a more sophisticated storage piece with legs, one or more doors and carved decoration. Both were used for storing food and clothes from the Middle Ages and into the 16th century.

Hyalith glass An opaque sealing-wax red or jet-black glass created *c.*1818 in Bohemia at the glasshouses of Jiri, Count von Buquoy (1781–1851). Hyalith glass was thought to have been inspired by the BASALTES WARE and ROSSO ANTICO wares of Josiah WEDGWOOD and was used to make similar ornament forms, often with CHINOISERIE designs. See also LITHYALIN GLASS.

Hyalith glass, Bohemian, 1850 [N]

Hybrid paste A porcelain formula developed *c.*1782 at the English factory of New Hall, Staffordshire, UK, that combines ingredients of HARD-PASTE and SOFT-PASTE porcelain in an attempt to produce a more workable body.

Hydrofluoric acid A colourless corrosive acid that attacks silica and silicates, used by glass-makers. First discovered in 1771, from the mid-19th century it was used for ACID-ETCHING, ACID POLISHING and in the making of FROSTED GLASS.

Hygrometer A device for indicating the level of humidity, set on the cases of many 18th and 19th-century WHEEL BAROMETERS. It usually consists of a beard (tiny spiral) of oats that furls and unfurls with variations in air moisture.

Ice glass A type of glass with a rough surface resembling cracked ice, first made in Venice in the 16th century and revived in Britain in the 19th century. The effect is created by plunging partially blown molten glass into cold water to create fissures on the surface that then expand when the glass is gently reheated.

Ideal Novelty & Toy Co. A toy company founded in 1903 in New York by Rose and Morris Michtom. They claimed to have made the first teddy bear in 1903 based on a cartoon depicting "Teddy" Roosevelt refusing to shoot a bear cub. Early Ideal bears are rarely marked, but can be recognized by their long triangular snout and pointy toes. Ideal was taken over by CBS Inc. in 1982.

Imari porcelain A type of Japanese porcelain made at ARITA from the late 17th century and shipped from the port of Imari. It has a characteristic palette of underglaze blue, decorated with iron red and gilt. Chinese copies (Chinese Imari) were produced in the 18th century as CHINESE EXPORT PORCELAIN. The style was adapted by many of Europe's major porcelain-making factories from the 19th century, including those at MEISSEN, DELFT and DERBY. See also JAPANESE POTTERY AND PORCELAIN.

Japanese Imari bowl, c.1900 [S]

Imperial yellow A clear strong yellow glaze based on iron or antimony, used on Chinese monochrome porcelain from the mid-15th century, applied as an overglaze. From the 16th century, it was also applied to biscuit porcelain. Particularly fine examples with incised or moulded decoration were produced in the KANGXI period (1662–1722).

Ince & Mayhew An English cabinet-making and upholstery firm. William Ince (d.1804) and John Mayhew (c.1736–1811) set up business in Soho, London, in 1759 and in 1762 they had a joint wedding to two sisters. They were also jointly responsible for *The Universal System of Household Furniture* – a collection of over 300 engraved furniture and metalwork ROCOCO designs issued between 1759 and 1762. Their later designs were NEO-CLASSICAL and Grecian in inspiration. The firm is thought to have closed in 1803.

Ince & Mayhew chest-of-drawers, c.1765 [D]

Incised decoration A pattern scratched into the body of a ceramic or glass vessel with a sharp instrument, such as a metal point, as decoration or to record an inscription, date or name.

Inclined plane clock See RACK CLOCK.

Inclusions A term used to cover all types of small particles of decorative material that are embedded in the body of a glass piece, for example the copper added to AVENTURINE GLASS.

Indianische blumen (German: "Indian flowers") A decoration commonly used on MEISSEN and other porcelain from c.1720. Based on Japanese KAKIEMON styles, derived from the large quantities of Oriental porcelain brought to Europe in the ships of the East India companies.

Meissen bottle vase with Indianische blumen, 1725–30 [B]

Indian style Architecture and decorative arts inspired by the culture of the Indian subcontinent. Indian artifacts had been imported into Europe, and particularly England, from the 17th century, but it was only after the British consolidated their power in the subcontinent in the late 18th century that Indian influence emerged in British art. Features such as OGEE arches, pointed onion domes and LATTICEWORK were used to create a picturesque, exotic style in such buildings as the façade of the Guildhall, London, (1788) by George Dance, and the remodelled Royal Pavilion, Brighton, (completed 1822) by John Nash. As India became more significant within the British Empire, the popularity of the style grew, especially when the title Empress of India was created for Queen Victoria in 1877. The Durbar Room at Osborne House, one of the queen's residences, is one of the best examples of Indian-style interior decor, with elaborate projecting cornices and ornate plasterwork.

In the decorative arts, Indian influence is evident in the use of richly patterned cottons and other fabrics, motifs such as elephants and designs of temple buildings in landscapes on TRANSFER-PRINTED ceramics. It was often combined with ARABIAN or ISLAMIC STYLE elements.

Indo-Portuguese furniture European furniture made from the early 16th to the mid-17th century in the Portuguese colonies of Cochin, Ceylon (now Sri Lanka), Goa, Malacca (west coast of the Malaysian peninsula) and also in Bombay and near Calcutta. Chairs, tables, bedsteads and case furniture were made from indigenous TEAK and EBONY, first for local European workers and later for export. Dutch occupation from the mid-17th century resulted in the development of DUTCH COLONIAL FURNITURE in most previously Portuguese colonies, except Goa.

Inkstand A tray or box on feet, in silver, papier mâché, wood and other materials with a hinged cover or covers either fitted with or containing writing equipment. Early 17th-century examples usually had a compartment for quills, an ink vessel and a CASTER for POUNCE. Eighteenth-century inkstands often had a bell; 19th-century examples usually have two inkpots and a sealing wax container.

Inkwell A small container used to hold liquid writing ink. Glass inkwells had the advantage of being both acid-resistant and transparent. They were made in huge quantities throughout the 19th century, ranging from simple glass inserts to cylindrical bottles with inverted conc-shaped centres to square inkwells. Some had cut decoration and cut glass tops.

Inlaid decoration This ceramic technique, done by impressing the body with a design and filling in with a different coloured clay, was used on the so-called Henri Deux ware made at SAINT-PORCHAIRE c.1525–26. Also used in tiles. See also ENCAUSTIC TILES.

Inlay A type of furniture decoration first used on OAK and WALNUT furniture in the 16th and 17th centuries. Patterns made up of different-coloured woods or other materials such as bone, horn, IVORY and MOTHER-OF-PEARL are sunk into the solid wood surface, rather than covering the entire surface as with MARQUETRY.

Lacquered inros, Japanese 1780–1850 [L, each]

Inro A small rectangular box made up of sections, usually decorated with lacquer and used to hold herbs or tobacco. It hung from the OBI (sash) of a kimono (which had no pockets) using a NETSUKE as a toggle. In use in Japan from the mid-16th century, inros are still made today.

Intaglio The Italian term for a type of cut or engraved decoration on glass where the design is incised into the glass and lies below the surface. The German term is *tiefschnitt* – "deep cut". This type of decoration was a German and Bohemian speciality from the 17th century, perfected in the 18th century. The term is also used to describe a method of PRINT-making.

Intaglio eyes Moulded and painted dolls' eyes with a raised white dot on the concave pupils. They are usually found on CHARACTER DOLLS.

Intarsia The Italian term for a type of INLAY decoration using different woods to make realistic pictures in upright panels such as doors. Known also as tarsia, it was developed in Siena in the 14th century and remained popular, especially for church furniture, until the mid-16th century. The technique used indigenous woods – including walnut, oak and pear – that were polished and often stained various colours.

Interlacing See ENTRELAC.

Iribe, Paul (1883–1935) A French commercial artist and designer of wallpaper, furniture, jewellery and textiles. He was an early exponent of what was to be called ART DECO; his work between 1910 and 1914, particularly for the couturier Jacques Doucet, was influential in setting the style. He spent the next 16 years in the US designing film sets in Hollywood before returning to France, where he designed jewellery for CHANEL.

Iridescent glass Glass with a lustrous, rainbow-like surface that changes colour depending on how the light hits it. The natural iridescence found on excavated Roman glass as a result of burial in damp earth was imitated in the 19th century by exposing glass to metal oxide fumes or by spraying or painting it with metal oxides. See also FAVRILE and TIFFANY.

Iridescent gold glass bowl, US c.1900 [P]

Irish glass Glass made in Ireland from the 18th centuries to the present day, initially in English styles but subsequently

Irish glass bowl, c.1800 [L]

in distinctive Irish forms, such as bowls with turn-over rims or canoe-shaped bowls with scalloped edges and heavy, square "lemon-squeezer" feet. Bowls, decanters, butter dishes and salt cellars were made in clear, heavily cut lead glass at glasshouses in BELFAST, Cork, Dublin and Waterford. The heyday of Irish glass was from c.1780, when the ban on exporting glass was abolished, until c.1825, when excise duty was imposed on Irish glass, but the industry still continues.

Iron A durable and malleable metal, one of the most abundant and widely used round the world. It was used from c.3500 BC for tools and weapons, but large-scale production of wrought and CAST IRON began only with technological advances in the late Middle Ages. Iron has been and is used for fireplace furnishings, candlesticks, jewellery and cooking utensils.

Ironstone china See MASON'S PATENT IRONSTONE CHINA.

Isfahan An important Persian city renowned for the production of fine carpets during the 16th and 17th centuries under the Safavid dynasty and also important for 20th-century production. Fine wool and silk is used to create highly detailed intense curvilinear designs in subtle complementary colours. Rugs, carpets, and prayer rugs are made. See also PERSIAN CARPETS.

Islamic ewer, late
13th century [D]

Islamic pottery The Islamic era started
in 622, the date of the prophet
Mohammed's journey to Mecca. From
633 Muslim armies moved rapidly,
subsuming first the Byzantine and
Sassanian empires, then Syria, Palestine,
Mesopotamia, Anatolia, Persia, Afghanistan
and Egypt. Spain was conquered by 711.
At the height of its power the Empire
comprised a great number of quite
disparate traditions, as a result little
aesthetic or stylistic unity is evident in
Islamic decorative arts from its early years.
By the late 8th century, however, a style
of pottery that became recognized as
unmistakeably Islamic had emerged, as is
evident in the continuity of motif styles
employed across the Empire.

Ceramics from the Islamic era are
often divided into three sections:
i) Early Medieval (622–1200)
Trade links with
China were well
established by this
era and the influence
of ceramics from the Tang
dynasty can be seen on
LUSTREWARES,
produced by
Mesopotamian
potters, and on some
early white wares
excavated at Samarra
in the Persian Gulf.
Ceramics from this
period were excavated

Bronze mortar and
pestle, inlaid with
silver and copper,
Islamic 13th century [E]

at Nishapur (in modern-day Iran) and
Samarkand (Uzbekistan). The HISPANO-
MORESQUE style emerged in Spain in the
8th century, under the Fatimids.
ii) Middle (1200–1400) Ceramic
decoration from SONG China, particularly
white porcelain of Dingyao and
Yingquin, and green
CELADONS, notably of
Zhejiang, all impacted on
the style of pottery of
this era. Wares,
however, were not
merely imitative. In
striving to perfect their
craft, Islamic potters
developed wares of their
own, such as FRITWARE, as
well as many techniques that are
still used by modern potters.
iii) Late/Post-medieval (1400
onward) The influence of blue
and white porcelain of the Yuan and
Ming dynasties is evident in ceramics
made by Near and Middle Eastern
potters. Wares made in IZNIK and Kütahya
in Anatolia are particularly notable and
had a major influence on European
decorative arts, for example on 19th-
century MAIOLICA from Padua.

Islamic style A central principle of
Islamic art is the ruling in the Koran that
no human or animal form should be
represented. Ornament
on Islamic art,
including metalwork,
glass, ceramics and textiles,
is, therefore, dominated by flat,
dense, repeating abstract
patterns, pierced fretwork and
interlacing and calligraphic KUFIC
script, which in turn influenced the
arts of countries to which Islam
spread in the Middle Ages,
especially Spain and Turkey. It
was also popular in the 19th
century, e.g. on DAMASCENED
metalwork and enamelled glass, as part of
the European interest in non-Western arts
and flourished in the 19th-century
adoption of ARABIAN STYLE.

Isleworth Pottery An English
earthenware factory established c.1760 by
Joseph Shore and Richard and William
Goulding. Until c.1825 they made various
useful wares of Staffordshire type, including
combed SLIPWARE, using the mark
"S. & G". German 19th-century wares
made at Bodenbach in Bohemia
and at Aschach in Bavaria
have been erroneously
attributed to Isleworth.

Istoriato (Italian:
"story-painted")
A painting telling a
story and found on
Italian MAIOLICA, especially
at URBINO in the early 16th
century. At first it was confined
to the centre of the plate, but
was later used across the entire
surface. Copied from engravings
by Marcantonio Raimondi among others,
istoriato covered historical, mythological,
allegorical, genre and biblical scenes.

Istoriato maiolica plate,
Italian 16th century [E]

Ivory glass cameo vase, English c.1870 [L]

Ivory glass Glass designed to resemble
old carved ivory. The technique, patented
in Britain by Thomas WEBB & SONS in
1887, was used to produce opaque white
glass with etched and engraved designs
that were similar to CAMEO and
heightened with coloured stains.

Ivrene Ivory-coloured translucent ART
GLASS with a slightly iridescent surface.
Developed at the STEUBEN GLASSWORKS
by Frederick Carder in the 1920s, it was
initially used for light-fittings and
subsequently for ornamental glass.

Ivory

Ivory is primarily obtained from elephant tusks, but can also be from walrus, sperm whale and narwhal tusks and, to a lesser degree, from wild boar tusks and hippopotamus teeth.

The qualities of the material

Mainly taken from the African elephant, there are two forms of elephant ivory: soft ivory from the east of Africa, and harder darker ivory from the west. Ivory is durable and smooth, with a creamy lustre when polished, and is ideal for carving. For these qualities it has been considered a precious material from ancient times. Before the introduction of mechanical carving machines at the turn of the 20th century, all ivory was worked by hand using chisels and gouges.

Carved ivory figure of a man kneeling, with traces of original pigment, Chinese Ming dynasty [G]

Ivory carving has a long history in China, with examples found in tombs dating from the SHANG DYNASTY (18th–12th century BC). Ivory writing tablets known as *hu* were used by high-ranking officials from the 12th century BC until the late 17th century AD. Ivory was also used for decorative objects and was sometimes coloured with dyes. From the late 17th century, Peking and Canton had the greatest concentration of ivory-carvers. By the early 20th century, the industry devoted itself to supplying tourists with increasingly roughly carved, novelty and souvenir pieces.

The Japanese came to ivory-carving relatively late, but by the early 17th century were great exponents of the art. Its major use was for carving NETSUKE, but it was also used for other items including boxes. As in China, the late 19th and early 20th century saw a decline in quality with the production of items for an export and tourist market, e.g. chess pieces, card cases, boxes, OKIMONO and brooches.

Figure of an egg-seller carved from one piece of ivory, Japanese c.1900 [H]

Ivory bangle in the form of a coiled serpent, English 1920s [R]

Ivory has been used in the Middle East for centuries, primarily as an inlay or for carved panels on boxes, doors and furniture. In the West, ivory was used for religious panels known as "ivories" until the 15th century, which were commissioned by pious laymen or the clergy. In the 18th century seamen and whale-hunters carved ivory into ship models and SCRIMSHAW. Perhaps its most widespread Western use, apart from chess pieces and inlay or banding on furniture, was for piano keys.

The late 19th century saw an increase in awareness of the declining numbers of African elephants. Replacement materials were sought, such as a plastic developed by Alexander Parkes in the late 19th century known as "ivorine" or "Parkesine". It resembled ivory in colour and surface texture, but the fine striations were more regular. Today, in some parts of Africa, elephants have been hunted almost to extinction in the quest for ivory. The production of ivory pieces is now strictly monitored and discouraged; worldwide trade in elephant ivory has been effectively banned since 1990. The illicit trade continues, however, and purchasers should check the origin of ivory articles offered as "antique".

Ebonized wood frame inlaid with ivory, Anglo-Indian 1920s [S]

Ivy motif

Ivy motif A popular motif in Greek and Roman ornament, particularly for ceramics. Sacred to Bacchus, ivy plays an integral role in the decoration of Classical objects such as drinking vessels. Because of its tenacious tendrils, it also symbolizes fidelity, friendship, marriage and, being evergreen, immortality. It appears in much GOTHIC ornament with other TREFOIL-shaped leaves. In the 18th century it appealed to the GOTHICK taste for images of rustic decay, when associated with ruins. The 19th century favoured ivy as a motif for jewellery, as well as for cast-iron balconies and garden furniture, catering to the Victorian taste for lush evergreen foliage. In the US ivy was a favourite ornament of the GOTHIC REVIVAL.

Iznik potteries Potteries existed since the 15th century at the town of Iznik, south-west of Istanbul, where the finest Ottoman Turkish ceramics were produced. The ancient Nicaea of biblical times, Iznik flourished due to its position on one of the main trade routes across Anatolia from the East and its wares show the influences of China and Central Asia.

Production at Iznik falls into three phases. The first one of c.1490–c.1525 produced mostly blue and white wares, with shapes derived from metal prototypes and showing a strong Chinese influence. From c.1525 to c.1535, more varied colours were introduced, such as shades of turquoise and sage-green, and flower motifs including tulips, carnations and bluebells were used. From the second quarter of the 16th century, coinciding with the reign of Süleyman the Magnificent (1520-66), there was a leap forward in artistic achievement, with the use of more brilliant blues, and a characteristic "sealing-wax" red, standing out in relief from the surface. A wide variety of wares was produced, including dishes, jugs and mosque lamps.

Iznik also produced TILES for the mosques and palaces of Istanbul, including the mosque of Rüstem Pasha (1550) and the Sultan's palace of Topkapi Saray (1571–2). The provision of over 20,000 tiles for the Blue Mosque, completed in 1617, marks the end of Iznik as a major supplier of tiles to the court. At the peak of production over 300 workers were employed, but the weakening of Ottoman power and patronage meant that by c.1700 the industry was nearly extinct. Thereafter, the main centre moved to Kütahya, south of Iznik.

Iznik pottery was exported to Europe in the 16th century, often acquiring European silver-gilt mounts.

Through the trading links between Turkey and Venice, it influenced the design of Italian MAIOLICA. Interest faded until the mid-19th century, when the revival of interest in the Near East led to imitations in France.

William DE MORGAN and other art potters in Britain were also inspired to produce Iznik-style designs.

Iznik also describes ceramic decoration characterized by long, curling, serrated *saz* leaves on thin spiralling stems, with flowers based on roses, tulips and carnations.

Iznik water bottle, 1565 [C]

J

Jackfield pottery A type of English red earthenware with a glossy black glaze, first made at the factory of Maurice Thursfield, in Jackfield, near Coalport in Shropshire c.1750–75. The name "Jackfield" has since become a generic term used to describe the similar ware that was produced by many potters in Shropshire and Staffordshire in the mid- to late 19th century. This type of pottery, also known as "japanned ware", is often embellished with gilded decoration. Jackfield pottery encompasses well-made tea and coffee pots, as well as ornamental pieces, such as vases, animal figures and souvenir ware.

Jacob, Georges (1739–1814) A French cabinet-maker whose career and designs spanned totally different political and artistic styles – LOUIS XV, LOUIS XVI and EMPIRE. Born in Cheny, Burgundy, he arrived in Paris in 1755, was a *maître ÉBÉNISTE* by 1765, and by the 1780s had established a reputation as one of the most important cabinet-makers in Paris.

Louis XVI armchair by Jacob, c.1780 [D]

He produced COMMODES with EBONY, SATINWOOD and PEWTER MARQUETRY, and elaborate beds for aristocratic patrons, but is probably best known as an innovative chair designer. He lightened and simplified chair design, introducing such features as the tapering fluted leg topped by a ROSETTE, and SPLATS carved and PIERCED with NEO-CLASSICAL motifs. He was the first French maker to use MAHOGANY, probably under the influence of Thomas CHIPPENDALE. An established cabinet-maker of the *ancien régime*, he

Jacobean oak buffet, early 17th century [E]

survived the French Revolution thanks to the protection of the artist Jacques-Louis David (1748–1825), for whom he made the earliest examples of furniture directly based on Greek and Roman prototypes, in what was to become known as the EMPIRE style.

Jacob-Desmalter, François-Honoré-Georges (1770–1841) A French furniture-maker, the son of Georges JACOB, under whom he trained. He ran the family business with his brother Georges Jacob II (1768–1803) as Jacob Frères when his father retired in 1796. Following the death of Georges Jacob II, his father became his business partner.

The company, now known as Jacob-Desmalter et Cie, produced mainly EMPIRE style furniture, for both the imperial residences of Napoleon and the royal palaces of Europe.

Jacobean A term applied to decorative arts produced in the UK during the reign of James I (1603–25) and more loosely to those from the first half of the 17th century. The style is characterized by the prevalence of OAK for furniture and the use of rich velvet, silk and needlework UPHOLSTERY, as well as the emergence of new furniture forms such as GATELEG tables, DAY BEDS, SETTEES, trestle benches, and WAINSCOT and X-frame chairs. It is similar to the ELIZABETHAN style, but features RENAISSANCE ornament such as STRAPWORK, geometric motifs and GADROONING.

Jacobean Revival A style of 19th-century architecture and decorative arts in the UK, principally furniture, inspired by early 17th-century JACOBEAN originals. Characteristic elements are spiral turned legs and STRETCHERS, tall crested chair backs and rich CHINTZ UPHOLSTERY.

Jacobethan A revivalist style popular in the late 19th and early 20th centuries, combining elements of the ELIZABETHAN and JACOBEAN REVIVALS, such as bulbous legs on tables, carved FRIEZES and spiral TURNINGS. Motifs such as PALMETTES and PATERAE from other styles such as the NEO-CLASSICAL were also incorporated.

Jacobite glass See AMEN GLASS.

Jacobsen Series 7 chair, 1950s [Q]

Jacobsen, Arne (1902–71) A Danish architect and designer credited with introducing Modernism to Denmark. His two most famous buildings – for which he also designed the interior decoration and furnishings – were the SAS Air Terminal and the Royal Hotel in Copenhagen (1956–60). He designed furniture for the maker Fritz Hansen.

Jacquard loom A loom invented *c.*1805 by the French inventor Joseph-Marie Jacquard. It used a perforated card system rather than manual lifting of the warp threads, so initiating MASS PRODUCTION.

Jade A term used to describe two minerals, jadeite and nephrite. Jadeite, the more valuable of the two, is found in a range of colours; emerald-green known as "Imperial Jade", is the most highly prized. Nephrite is dark green and is widely used as an ornamental HARDSTONE.

Jade brush pot, Chinese 18th century [D]

The Dutch East India Company supplied Japan with wooden versions of European pots to copy in porcelain as in this Arita gallipot, c.1680 [c]

Arita dish in Chinese wucai (literally "five colours") style, showing the influence of Chinese design, c.1700 [o]

The factory of Hirado near Arita produced pierced wares with botanical subjects, such as this Hirado bowl with irises, 1880–1900 [i]

Japanese pottery and porcelain

From earliest times the craft of ceramic-making was practised in Japan. The tranquil rituals of Buddhism and traditional artistic skills produced high-quality wares, increasingly popular in the West.

Time for tea

Jomon ware, named after the rope impressions sometimes used as decoration, is the earliest Japanese pottery. It was made throughout the Neolithic period using unrefined clays and coiling techniques. In the 4th to the 7th centuries AD terracotta tomb figures called "Haniwa figures" similar to those made in China were produced. In the 12th to the 14th centuries the introduction of oxidation firing advanced the industry, while by the early 16th century the Buddhist tea ceremony or "cha no yu" became increasingly important, developing its own complex protocol that required specific utensils deliberately humble in appearance.

The Japanese craze

In the 16th century Japan invaded Korea and the returning Japanese forces were accompanied by Korean stoneware potters who settled around the town of ARITA, in the southern province of Kyushu. The immigrants produced the first Japanese porcelains c.1620–40, with designs following Korean stonewares. In competition with the Chinese porcelain industry, the Arita potters continued to expand and supply the growing European demand for porcelain, producing IMARI, KAKIEMON and BLUE AND WHITE wares. Both IMARI and KAKIEMON designs were extensively copied and adapted in Europe. Apart from porcelain exports, Japan closed trading links with the West for fear of the corrupting influence of foreigners.

Porcelain plate with segmented floral patterns, c.1900 [Q, a pair]

However, in 1853 the United States navy entered Japanese territorial waters, opening up a new era of trading relations with the West after over 200 years of self-imposed Japanese isolation. The Japanese porcelain industry responded by increasing production and making brilliant showpieces for international exhibitions and trade fairs, held in London in the 1860s, in Paris (1867) and in Philadelphia (1876). Vast quantities of Japanese ceramics saturated the markets of Europe and the US. The most sophisticated, with the finest decoration, enthralled the public and inspired the Impressionists, the designers of the AESTHETIC MOVEMENT and porcelain factories such as ROYAL WORCESTER.

Japanese ceramic marks, in the form of impressed seals or painted characters, are both numerous and inconsistent. In addition to the family name and, sometimes, a place-name wares are often inscribed with an "art-name", granted to the potter by a patron or adopted as a workshop name. Cyclical dates and Japanese period-names (*nengo*) occasionally appeared on porcelain dated to the 18th century and earlier. Otherwise, wares from this period were seldom marked.

Jalousie (literally: "jealousy") A blind or shutter with an openwork pattern. Perhaps so called because one can look through it without being seen.

Jambiyah (Arabic) A type of knife found throughout the Arab world. Its blade is always curved and double-edged, but there are regional distinctions in its HILT and scabbard.

Jambiyah, c.1880 [K]

Japanesque Referring to 19th-century European interpretation of Japanese design, particularly popular from the 1860s to 1900. See JAPONAISERIE.

Japanning The process of coating objects with layers of coloured varnish in imitation of true Chinese and Japanese LACQUER. The varnish was made up of gum-lac, seed-lac or SHELLAC dissolved in alcohol; the lac being a secretion of the *Coccus lacca* insect. Each layer was allowed to dry, then sanded down and another applied. Japanning, usually in black, scarlet or green, was used on a wide variety of pieces, from small wooden boxes and trays to larger items of cased furniture. Relief decoration was built up

Japanned armchair, c.1710 [G]

from sawdust and gum arabic and many pieces were also decorated with CHINOISERIE decoration. Japanning was first introduced in the mid-17th century, and the first accurate account of the process was *A Treatise of Japanning and Varnishing* by John STALKER and George Parker published in 1688; a French patent for VERNIS MARTIN followed in 1730. Japanning was practised extensively in Europe in the 18th and 19th centuries on wooden objects including CHESTS-ON-STANDS, BUREAU CABINETS and SECRETAIRE CABINETS. It was used in North America, where it is known as TOLEWARE from *c.*1740 onwards.

Japonaiserie (or Japonisme) A style of European and American decorative arts inspired by Japanese art and design. Western interest in Japan was stimulated by the re-opening of trade between Japan and West in 1850s and subsequent displays of Japanese art in international exhibitions. Japanese design had a particular influence on designers of the AESTHETIC MOVEMENT, for example E.W. GODWIN, who designed ebonized furniture in simple, rectilinear forms. Many European and American potters also experimented with lustre and iridescent glazes as found in Japanese ceramics, and TIFFANY & CO. produced silverware featuring mixed metal decoration of

copper and brass. Popular motifs in Japonaiserie included chrysanthemums, birds and flowers, and stylized branches.

Japy Frères A firm of clock- and watchmakers, founded *c.*1770 at Beaucourt in the Jura region of France by Frédéric Japy (1749–1812). The firm, later taken over by his three sons, specialized in the mass production of brass movements and watches, but from the late 1880s began to produce complete clocks, such as MANTEL CLOCKS. The company ceased making clocks in 1936.

Japonaiserie: Royal Worcester part set, 1883 [L]

Jardinière A large ornamental vessel, usually ceramic, for holding cut flowers or for growing plants. Popular in Europe from the 17th century onward.

Jasper ware A fine-grained, unglazed, sometimes slightly translucent ware, introduced by Josiah WEDGWOOD in 1774. It was regarded by Wedgwood as a biscuit porcelain and was sometimes fired to the point of vitrification. It contained a new ingredient, sulphate of barium, which was known as "cawk". The jasper ware BODY can be white or stained with metallic oxides, producing coloured bodies, including the well-known blue. The coloured ground was often decorated with white relief classical-style figures. "Jasper dip" refers to a piece with a surface layer of colour over a white body.

Ornate decoration and unplanished bodies characterized Jensen's early designs, such as this Jensen oilburner, produced post-1945 [I]

Georg Jensen (1866–1935)

This leading Danish silversmith and designer set up a studio in Copenhagen in 1904, founding a firm that developed a modern style that combined simple, elegant forms with ornamentation. Jensen's firm enjoys continued success and still produces many of his designs today.

Sculptural simplicity

When Georg Jensen was a child he and his family moved to Copenhagen and Georg was apprenticed to a goldsmith. Throughout his apprenticeship Georg furthered his education with art classes, followed by studies in modelling and engraving. While supporting himself as a goldsmith he enrolled at the Royal Danish Academy of Fine Arts in 1887, his ambition being to become a sculptor. Having completed his studies he briefly worked as a modeller for the porcelain factory of BING & GRØNDAHL before a period of study in Paris.

Eventually, Jensen decided to settle as an independent silversmith. Back in Copenhagen, he met the metalworker Mogens Ballin, who encouraged him to reappraise himself and the medium of silver and gold. However, he always referred to himself as an *orfèvre sculpteur* (goldsmith sculptor) in the same way as a French court goldsmith. He opened his first workshop in 1904 producing a small selection of silver jewellery that was exhibited in the Danish Museum of Decorative Art. His jewellery was influenced by the ideals of the ARTS AND CRAFTS movement and was aimed at an artistically enlightened middle class. His designs were inspired by nature and sometimes incorporated SEMI-PRECIOUS STONES, such as opal, moonstone and amber.

His early silverware is reminiscent of French 18th-century silver, with rounded forms and decorated with fruit, roses and tendril forms for handles and FINIALS and animal forms such as claws for feet.

The ivory handle is a feature used by Jensen to provide decorative contrast, as on this "Blossom" sugar basin and teapot, produced post-1945 [G]

The tradition of jewellery still continues with the firm today, although Jensen's international reputation is based on silverware, especially FLATWARE, teapots, coffeepots and other domestic wares, with their characteristic clean outlines, sense of balance and satiny finish. The firm commissions work from the best contemporary designers. One of the first was Johan Rohde (1856–1935), who in 1915 designed the "Acorn" pattern flatware, still popular today. Others who have continued to offer excellence in design are Harald Nielsen, and Sigvard Bernadotte before World War II; and, in the post-war period, HENNING KOPPEL (1918–81) and Jensen's son Søren George Jensen (1917–82), chief designer from 1962 to 1974. Today, the firm has branches worldwide, notably in New York and London.

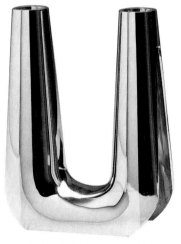

By the 1940s the company had become noted for its minimalist style, typified by this candelabrum designed by Søren George Jensen, 1960 [F]

Jensen marks

Marks on Georg Jensen silver are well-documented and provide a good means of identifying an authentic piece. These are three of the most commonly found. Pieces can also be marked with a design number or the initials of the designer.

GI 925 S

1915–30

1933–44

GEORG JENSEN

1945 onward

Jewel cuts

Gemstones are cut to increase the refraction of light from the facets and thus the brilliance of the stone. Most cuts are associated with cutting diamonds, such as the 58-facet modern brilliant, the old European cut, the cushion, the rose cut of 24 triangular facets, the simple eight cut (single cut) and the baton-shaped baguette. Other cuts include calibré, square, emerald, step, marquise (boat-shaped) and cabochon (polished dome shape, used if a stone is flawed).

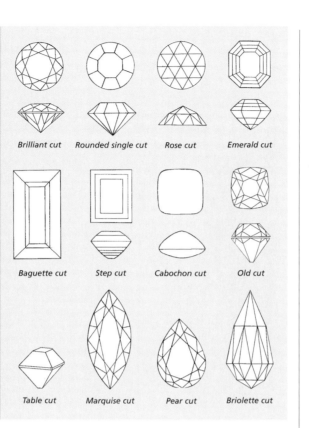

Brilliant cut   Rounded single cut   Rose cut   Emerald cut

Baguette cut   Step cut   Cabochon cut   Old cut

Table cut   Marquise cut   Pear cut   Briolette cut

from the 17th century. It was decorated with Christian subjects from European prints, typically, the Crucifixion, Resurrection and Ascension, usually in black or sepia monochrome with gilding.

Jet A type of black lignite, used especially in Victorian MOURNING JEWELLERY. Most jet comes from Whitby in Yorkshire, England, and by the 1860s scores of workshops there were producing carved and polished jet jewellery and *objets d'art*. Its popularity waned by the end of the 19th century, but the jet industry of Whitby still survives today.

Jewel cuts See box left.

Jewelled decoration A decoration on ceramics and glass simulating precious and semi-precious stones and pearls set on the surface. Coloured drops of enamel backed by gold foil were used at SÈVRES in the 1780s. It was also used in the 19th century in England, particularly at WORCESTER and COALPORT.

Jaune jonquille (French: "daffodil yellow") A light yellow ground colour, also known as *jaune clair*, used at SÈVRES in the 1750s, although rarely because the critical firing temperature resulted in many wasters in the kiln.

Jefferys, Thomas (*c.*1695–1771) An English cartographer best known for his maps of North America and the West Indies. Many were published after his death by his successor, William Faden, or by the firm of Sayer and Bennet.

Jelly glass A small glass vessel used to serve savoury or sweet jellies, made in Britain in the 18th and 19th centuries. The bowls are usually of an inverted conical or bell-like shape, supported by a short stem.

Jennens & Bettridge An English manufacturer who specialized in PAPIER-MÂCHÉ wares. Based in Birmingham and active between 1816 and 1864, the company made a wide range of JAPANNED papier-mâché items, many with an impressed signature, from small boxes and trays to larger pieces such as chairs, work tables and cabinets, some inlaid with mother-of-pearl.

Jennens and Bettridge inkstand, mid-19th century [M]

Jersey City Porcelain and Earthenware Company A US ceramics factory founded in 1825 in Jersey City that won a prize the following year for the quality of its china, none of which survives. It was sold in 1828 to the Scottish-born brothers David and James Henderson, who mechanized production to make moulded stoneware and in 1833 changed the company name to the AMERICAN POTTERY CO. Production ceased in 1854.

Jesuit ware A type of 18th-century CHINESE EXPORT PORCELAIN, named after the French Jesuit missionaries in China

Jewelling A term used to describe the presence of jewels in a watch movement, to reduce friction and wear on the PIVOTS. In modern watches synthetic jewels are used. Most modern watches are "fully jewelled", i.e. fitted with a minimum of 15 jewels. The technique was the invention of a Swiss watchmaker, Nicholas Facio, who patented it in England in 1704 and it was first used extensively by Abraham-Louis BREGUET.

Jewel setting The various methods of securing a gemstone into the mount (often referred to as the gallery) include CLAW SETTING, closed and open back setting, COLLET SETTING, PAVÉ SETTING, gipsy setting (sunk into the metal surround) and star setting (gipsy setting with engraved lines radiating from the stone itself).

Jiajing (Chia Ching) porcelain Chinese porcelain made in the reign of the MING DYNASTY emperor Jiajing (1522–66). BLUE AND WHITE wares were popular, often with Daoist themes, such as children at play. Monochrome and polychrome wares were also produced. European export trade began at this time.

Jiajing porcelain jar, c.1522–66 [C]

Jingdezhen A centre of the Chinese ceramic industry, in the Jiangxi province, which produced much of the MING and QING dynasty porcelains (except BLANC-DE-CHINE and YIXING stonewares). The kilns gained Imperial patronage from the reign of Emperor Hongwu (1368–98). It was destroyed by fire in 1675 and rebuilt in 1683. Jingdezhen is still a major ceramics centre.

Jingdezhen vase, late 19th century [M]

Joel, Betty (1896–1984) A Scottish furniture designer who worked in England. One of the few British designers to produce ART DECO designs. She opened her own factory, the Token Works, with the support of her husband, David Joel. She often used exotic woods and most pieces bear a label with the names of the designer and the cabinet-maker and the date.

Joint A method of joining two pieces of wood together with or without the additional use of wedges or glue. Early forms of jointing include halving and housing joints, the MORTISE-AND-TENON, in which the tenon may protrude right through the mortise and be pegged or wedged, and the DOVETAIL, introduced in the late 17th century.

Jointing The way a doll's limbs are attached to its torso in an attempt to simulate natural movement.

Joint stool ("joined" stool) A 16th- or 17th-century wooden stool of MORTISE-AND-TENON construction with turned legs connected by stretchers below and rails or a frieze above.

Jones, George & Sons An English pottery founded in 1861 at Trent Potteries, Stoke-on-Trent. It produced earthenwares, including MAJOLICA and PÂTE-SUR-PÂTE, and tinted PARIAN. The firm started making BONE CHINA in 1872 and good quality porcelain tablewares in the 20th century. The first mark was a monogram of the initials GJ with "& Sons" added from December 1873 and a crescent shape from 1874. George Jones himself died in 1893 but the factory continued until 1951.

George Jones majolica partridge tureen, c.1870 [D]

Jones, Owen (1809–74) An English architect and designer. His furniture is often inlaid with floral and foliate decoration. He designed some furniture

for the 19th-century furniture-makers Jackson & Graham but is best known for his theories on decoration, published in his *Grammar of Ornament* in 1856.

Joubert, Gilles (1689–1775) A French furniture-maker. A highly skilled craftsman, he was employed by the Royal household of Louis XV, for whom he produced pieces with elaborate inlay and heavy ormolu mounts, although few of them were stamped.

Judaic decoration Decoration relating to Judaism, usually found on ritual objects of the religion, such as the menorah, torah ornaments, wine cups and Passover and Seder plates. It includes representations of these ritual objects as well as Hebrew inscriptions, naturalistic birds, fruit, flowers, and scenes from the Old Testament.

Jufti knot A type of Persian knot used in carpet-weaving, which instead of covering two warp threads, covers four, making the knot density 50 per cent less than usual. The carpets produced tend to be less durable. The knot is frequently used in carpets from KHORASSAN.

Jufti knot

Jugendstil The German name for ART NOUVEAU, literally "youth style". It was derived from the name of the contemporary art magazine *Jugend* (first published in 1896). The German interpretation of Art Nouveau was, with one or two exceptions, more restrained than the French equivalent as it

Jugendstil copper and brass pitcher, German c.1903 [O]

was also influenced by the English ARTS AND CRAFTS movement. Jugendstil also influenced and was affected by the VIENNA SECESSION.

Jumeau A French doll-making company established in 1842, one of the largest of the 19th century. The Jumeau factory was founded in Paris by Pierre François Jumeau in 1842 and continued under the direction of his son Emile until it became one of the founding members of the SOCIÉTÉ FRANÇAISE DE FABRICATION DE BÉBÉS ET JOUETS in 1899. Jumeau made exquisite fashion dolls and BÉBÉS including the *Jumeau triste* with its wistful expression, modelled by Henri Carrier-Belleuse. The generally high quality of the BISQUE deteriorated in the company's last ten years. Jumeau dolls can be recognised by their typical facial expression, their bulging PAPERWEIGHT eyes and their finely painted features. Many of the products are stamped or labelled. The company closed in 1899.

Jumeau doll c.1890 [L]

Jun ware (Chun ware) Chinese stoneware made in the Henan province during the SONG DYNASTY (960–1279). The glaze can be green, lavender blue or blue splashed or streaked with purple. It is always thick, opaque and suffused with tiny bubbles. Wares include bulb pots, flower pots and vases.

Juval A pile-woven artifact made by the Turkoman tribes of West Turkestan. Juvals are large storage bags in which nomadic tribes keep their belongings and which are decorated with the same colours and motifs as their rugs.

Ju ware See RU WARE.

K

Ka'aba An Islamic concept of the place where heaven and earth meet, enshrined in a cuboid building in Mecca. Used in decorative devices, often with a notional pilgrim path encircling the cube.

Kabistan A name referring to the rug-producing area around KUBA, in the north CAUCASUS.

Kaendler See KÄNDLER, J.J.

Kaga ware Ceramics made in Kaga, on the Japanese island of Honshu. Large quantities of stoneware were produced here from early times, but porcelain began to be made only in the 19th century and is known as KUTANI ware.

Kakiemon See p.220.

Kakihan A Japanese term for a small personalized seal often made up of kanji characters carved or written on objects to identify the artist in association with the impressed seal or signature.

Kaleidoscope An optical toy developed and patented by the Scottish physicist Sir David Brewster in 1817 and sold by many of the scientific instrument-makers in London in the 19th century. It usually consists of a tube made of tin or cardboard containing two mirrors running the length of the tube at 60 degrees to each other. The tube has a compartment at one end with a frosted glass cover holding pieces of coloured glass or other small objects. The viewer holds the toy up to the light and looks down the tube when multiple reflections in the mirrors are seen in symmetrical patterns, which change as the bottom compartment is rotated. The number of the reflections and the

complexity of the patterns depend on the angle between the mirrors. Kaleidoscopes are still sold by toy shops today.

Kamakura period The Japanese period AD 1185–1333 under the rule of the Minamoto and Hojo Shoguns who were based in Kamakura. It was a period of great literary and artistic activity, when many Buddhist temples and gardens were created. The "Six Old Kilns" were the most important ceramic centres. (See also JAPANESE POTTERY AND PORCELAIN.)

Kämmer & Reinhardt A German doll factory founded in 1886 by Ernst Kämmer & Franz Reinhardt in Waltershausen. Their trademark "KR" is often found with S & H, referring to SIMON & HALBIG, the factory that produced most of Kämmer & Reinhardt's BISQUE heads. The company's best known product is its 100 series of bisque CHARACTER dolls, the first of which was the "Kaiser Baby", mould 100, first produced in 1909. Character children came in girl or boy forms with painted features and mohair hair. Another of Kämmer & Reinhardt's popular lines was the *Mein Liebling* ("My darling") doll, which had a closed mouth and sleeping glass eyes. The factory closed in 1940.

Kämmer & Reinhardt doll and mark (above), c.1900–1920s [P]

Kakiemon

From the mid-17th century, Kakiemon wares were produced at the factories of Arita in Japan. The superb quality of its enamel decoration was highly prized in the West and widely imitated by the major European porcelain manufacturers.

Dish finely decorated with geese and Buddhist symbols, 1650–1700 [C]

The art of enamelling

The Japanese potter Sakaida Kakiemon (1596–1666) is popularly credited with being the first in Japan to discover the secret of enamel decoration on porcelain. The name "Kakiemon" was bestowed by his overlord on Sakaida, who had perfected a design of twin persimmons (*kaki*: persimmon) and who then developed the distinctive palette of soft red, yellow, blue and turquoise green. Kakiemon has become a generic term describing wares made in the ARITA factories using the characteristic Kakiemon overglaze enamels and decorative styles. However, shards from the Kakiemon kiln site at Nangawara show that blue and white and celadon wares were also produced.

Kakiemon decoration is usually of high quality, delicate and with asymmetric well-balanced designs. These were sparsely applied to emphasize the fine white porcelain body known in Japan as NIGOSHIDE (milky-white) which was used for the finest pieces. Kakiemon wares are usually painted with birds, flying squirrels, the "Quail and Millet" design, the "Three Friends of Winter" (pine, prunus and bamboo), flowers (especially the chrysanthemum, the national flower of Japan) and figural subjects such as the popular "Hob in the Well", illustrating a Chinese folk tale where a sage saves his friend who has fallen into a large fishbowl.

Figure in typical Kakiemon colours, late 17th century [B]

Prized by kings

Kakiemon porcelain was imported into Europe and prized even above Chinese porcelain. Augustus the Strong of Saxony and Mary II of England both owned examples. The earliest inventory to include Japanese porcelain in Europe was made at Burghley House, Lincolnshire, in 1688. These include a fabulous standing elephant with its trunk raised and a model of two wrestlers.

Wares include bowls, dishes and plates, often hexagonal, octagonal or fluted with scalloped edges. The famed white *nigoshide* body was only used with open forms, and not for closed shapes such as vases, bottles and teapots, or for figures and animals. The hexagonal Kakiemon vases and covers known as "Hampton Court" vases are named after a pair at Hampton Court Palace, London, recorded in an inventory of 1696. This shape was copied at MEISSEN *c.*1730, at CHELSEA and WORCESTER in the 1750s and by SAMSON in the 19th century.

Kakiemon porcelain proved a major influence on the new porcelain factories of 18th-century Europe. Meissen copies can be extremely close to the originals, alternatively the factory painters might just borrow designs and use them with other shapes and styles, Meissen's "INDIANISCHE BLUMEN" being a Kakiemon derivative. As well as at Meissen, the Kakiemon style was adapted in Germany and Austria by the DU PAQUIER and VIENNA factories, in France at CHANTILLY, MENNECY and SAINT-CLOUD, and in England by BOW, Chelsea and Worcester, and occasionally LONGTON HALL. Kakiemon was also an influence on DUTCH DELFT pottery and CHINESE EXPORT PORCELAIN.

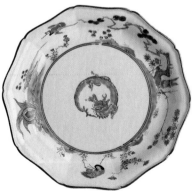

Dish showing the distinctive colours of soft red, blue and turquoise green, 1690 [E]

Kandler, Charles An important early 18th-century gold/silversmith of German extraction, working in London in partnership with James Murray (their first piece of dated work was recorded in 1727). Though little is known about his life, the sculptural quality of his work has led scholars to speculate that he may have had some family connection with Johann Joachim KÄNDLER of the MEISSEN porcelain factory. His partnership with Murray seems to have dissolved; he (alone) entered several marks at Goldsmiths' Hall and work of his appears bearing date letters for up to 1751. His most famous surviving work is a massive silver wine-cooler of 1734, now in the Hermitage Museum, St Petersburg.

J.J. Kändler, hen teapot, c.1740 [E, a pair]

Kändler, Johann Joachim (1706–75) The chief modeller at the MEISSEN factory between 1733 and 1775, responsible in the 1730s and 40s for some of the finest individual figures and groups ever made there. He was engaged at the factory in 1731, after an apprenticeship at Dresden with Benjamin Thomae, the leading sculptor at the Saxon Court. In spite of his lack of knowledge of porcelain, Kändler took to the new medium with ease, assisting KIRCHNER with a series of large white porcelain animals for the "Japanese" palace of Augustus the Strong, Elector of Saxony. The difficulties and the high cost of producing such works encouraged Kändler to experiment with the production of small-scale figures. From 1735 he modelled over 1,000 figures – including COMMEDIA DELL'ARTE actors and actresses, Paris street vendors, people from distant lands and crinoline groups – to adorn the tables of the rich. Collecting these enchanting figures became a great fashion for "high society". Many pieces were inspired by contemporary engravings and were widely copied by other European factories. In addition to figures, Kändler and his team of modellers created an extensive range of ARMORIAL dinner services and tea and coffee services for members of the aristocracy, among which the Swan Service for Count von Brühl, Augustus the Strong's chief minister, is particularly noted for its size (over 2,200 items) and exquisite modelling. The MONKEY BAND series of 1753, modelled by Kändler and Peter Reinicke after drawings by the French Rococo painter Huet, was widely imitated. Kändler stayed in Meissen during the Seven Years War (1756–63) when the occupation of Dresden by Frederick the Great halted porcelain production. When the war ended and the factory was reorganized in 1763, fashions had changed. Kändler was pushed aside for new talent. His health was failing and he died in 1775.

Kangxi porcelain Chinese porcelain made in the reign of the QING dynasty emperor Kangxi (1662–1722) at JINGDEZHEN in east China. During the Kangxi period the factory was reorganized, new colours and glazes were developed. Production increased for the domestic market, the Imperial court and the European EXPORT market. Wares include BLUE AND WHITE, the new FAMILLE VERTE, JAUNE AND NOIRE porcelains, fine monochromes, BLANC-DE-CHINE, YIXING stonewares, ARMORIAL wares, figures and animals and, toward the end of the period, CHINESE IMARI and FAMILLE ROSE wares.

J.J. Kändler, Scaramouche and Columbine, c.1740 [B]

Kaolin White china clay, a very pure aluminium silicate, is the main substance used in the production of porcelain. The name derives from the main place of discovery – the mountain Kao-Ling in China. In Europe it is found at Aue and Passau in Germany; Bornholm in Denmark; Vicenza in Italy; Limoges in France and St Austell, Cornwall, in England. Georgia is the largest producer in the US.

Kapok The cotton-wool-like fibre from the kapok tree (*Ceiba pentandra*), native to Java. From the 1890s it was used as a soft stuffing for TEDDY BEARS.

Karabagh A carpet-producing area of the Caucasus that borders north Persia, important for the production of rugs in the 17th to the 19th century. Rugs have long thick piles and use bold geometric designs with colours tending to be too bright or too sombre. Sometimes European floral/Rococo-inspired designs are seen, although crudely interpreted. FLATWEAVE products are also made.

Karakusa An octopus scrollwork pattern, originating from Chinese vine scrolls. A favourite pattern on Japanese ARITA porcelain.

Kangxi lidded vase, c.1700 [J]

Karatsu water stoop for a tea ceremony, 17th century [C]

Karatsu potteries Japanese potteries established in and around the town of Karatsu, near ARITA in the Hizen province, by Korean immigrant potters from the late 16th century. About 200 kilns made coarse-textured wares for daily use and occasionally for the TEA CEREMONY. Wares may be plain or decorated, often in the Korean style. Dark TEMMOKU and opaque white glazes are typical. It declined in the mid-17th century in favour of porcelain. See JAPANESE POTTERY AND PORCELAIN.

Kas (Dutch *kast*) A large Dutch provincial clothes cupboard or wardrobe originating in 17th-century Holland. The form was introduced to America by Dutch settlers, principally in New Jersey and New York state in the 18th and early 19th centuries.

Kashan An important Persian city, the centre of silk carpet-making during Safavid rule (1501–1732). Carpet-weaving was revived at the end of the 19th century producing fine wool rugs and carpets, with curvilinear designs in jewel-like colours and a high knot count. PRAYER RUGS are also a favoured product.

Kashgai See GHASHGHAI.

Kashgar A carpet-producing region in the Sinkiang province of China, East Turkestan, well known for 18th and 19th century production of rugs and carpets.

A mixture of geometric motifs and naturalistic flowerheads is seen in a formal format, with typical colours including shades of terracotta, light blue, yellow and brown; silk is sometimes used.

Kassel pottery and porcelain factories Two factories made faience at Kassel, Germany, from 1680–1788 and 1771–1862. A porcelain factory operated 1766–88, although not to a high artistic level. The ARCANIST was Nikolaus Paul, the REPAIRER Franz Joachim Hess, and the modeller Pahland from FÜRSTENBERG. The mark was a lion rampant and the initials H.C.

Katar (Indian) A distinctive Indian DAGGER used exclusively by Hindus. Instead of a conventional HILT, it features two crossbars which are gripped by the fist. The Katar is used with a punching action. The blade is straight, double edged and its point is often reinforced to pierce chain mail armour.

Kayser & Söhne A German firm of pewterers founded in 1885 by Engelbert Kayser (1840–1911) at Krefeld-Bochum, near Dusseldorf. From 1896 a range of

pewter was mass-produced including dishes, ashtrays, vases and lamps in ART NOUVEAU style, featuring curvilinear shapes and sinuous flower and plant decoration. These are marked "KAYSERZINN" with a number above and below, or with a number in a circle or oval. The firm closed *c*.1904.

Kazak An important and famous rug-producing district in the Caucasian republic of Armenia in the 18th and 19th centuries. Rugs display bold geometric designs of stylized floral and animal forms in strong harmonic jewel-like colours. The pile tends to be long with the use of quality wool.

Kazak wool rug, c.1920 [H]

Kelsterbach pottery and porcelain factory A German faience factory was founded near here in 1758 by Wilhelm Cron and Johann Christian Frede. In 1761 it was taken over by the Landgrave Ludwig VIII von Hessen-Darmstadt and began to make porcelain. C.D. Busch from MEISSEN was the director until 1764. In 1766 a new factory was built, but after the Landgrave's death in 1768 porcelain production ceased. For the next 20 years it made only faience. In 1789 the director J.J. Lay began to make porcelain again, but production was discontinued in 1802. Until the factory closed in *c*.1823 it made cream-coloured earthenware.

Kendi A Persian drinking vessel with a bulbous body, a side spout and a waisted cylindrical neck, which acts as a handle, made for the Persian market in China, Korea, Japan and the Middle East.

Blue and white kendi, Chinese c.1600 [K]

Kent, William (1685–1748) An English architect, interior decorator and designer of furniture and metalwork. Born in Bridlington, Yorkshire, a sponsored trip to Italy enabled him to absorb the ROMAN BAROQUE style and meet Richard Boyle, 3rd Earl of Burlington (1694–1753), under whose patronage he became a leading interior decorator through his designs for Burlington's Palladian villa, Chiswick House. His GILTWOOD, walnut and mahogany furniture reflects the influence of his Italian sojourn and is made on a grand scale, richly carved with PUTTI, MASKS and other Classical motifs.

Kenzan, Ogata Shinsei
A famous Japanese potter (1663–1743) working near Kyoto from c.1687 and later at Edo (Tokyo). He was the younger brother of Ogata Korin (1658–1716), a celebrated painter, with whom he sometimes worked making brown-glazed stonewares. Well educated, he was also a poet, painter, lacquerer and calligrapher. Kenzan took lessons from the master potter, Ninsei. His wares were usually made for the TEA CEREMONY in low-fired pottery using bold, beautiful and original designs in Japanese taste with flowers, pine and notably snowy landscapes in white slip. His palette includes greyish blue, green, brown and black. A copy of his notebooks (the *Edo Densho*) was published in English by Bernard LEACH.

Kerman An important carpet-producing city in south-east Persia from the Safavid era (1501–1732) to the present day. Rugs and carpets are made with a curvilinear formal design repertoire. Examples from the 19th century are particularly finely woven with soft colour combinations often on an ivory-coloured background.

Kerman was also famous in the 19th century for the production of pictorial rugs and carpets. Post-1930 pieces tend to be of poor quality.

Kestner & Co A German manufacturer of dolls and doll parts in Waltershausen, Thuringia, founded by Johannes Daniel Kestner in 1805. Previously unsuccessful in the production of papier-mâché buttons and slates, he tried his luck with papier-mâché dolls clad in swaddling (baptism) clothes, sold as "Täuflinge". From 1860 china and bisque heads were produced. Kestner's best known products are the Gibson Girl of 1910, the KEWPIE produced from 1913 onward and the "Bye-Lo" baby. Most of the company's products are marked JDK. Production stopped in 1930.

Kestner & Co.
"character child",
c.1910 [K]

Kettle shape See BOMBÉ.

Kettle stand A small stand or table designed to hold a hot-water urn or kettle. Introduced in the first half of the 18th century, following the fashion for specialized TEA TABLES, early examples usually took the form of small tripods supporting a round top, but later versions were made in a variety of shapes, with square, galleried tops and pull-out slides for the teapot or teacup.

Kew blas The trade mark used by the Union Glassworks of Somerville, Massachusetts, in the early 20th century on iridescent ART GLASS made as an inferior version of Louis Comfort TIFFANY glass with "pulled feather" decoration.

Kewpies An all-bisque doll designed by Rose O'Neil, first produced by KESTNER in 1913. Kewpies have since been copied

in various materials by a number of factories. They can be recognized by their moulded blonde locks, sidewards glancing INTAGLIO EYES, jointed arms with spread fingers and tiny blue wings.

Keyless watch The keyless mechanism was invented in 1822 by Thomas Prest, foreman to John ARNOLD. It allowed the watch to be wound by a winding crown instead of a separate key. It was initially used by many good makers but was not universally taken up until the 1880s. See also WINDING MECHANISM.

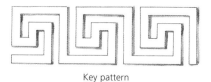

Gold cased keyless watch, early 19th century [L]

Key pattern An important Classical motif of interlocking vertical and right-angled lines. One of a number of variations on the fret pattern – including the well-known Greek key – the key pattern was widely used in Greek and Roman art and for much later Classically inspired ornament. It was usually applied as a continuous pattern and occasionally included ROSETTES or PATERAE within the squares of the design. In the medieval period the key pattern appealed to the taste for interlacing and labyrinth forms.

Key pattern

Khilim See KILIM.

Khiva A marketing town for rugs and carpets on the Uzbekistan and Turkmenistan border in central Asia. While carpets woven by the nomadic Turkoman tribes are erroneously classified under this name, few if any rugs were ever produced here.

Khmer pottery Wares made in Cambodia from the 9th to the 15th century, at Phnom Kulen. Bowls, jars and KENDI as well as architectural ceramics were produced from a poor quality clay and usually have either a green or a mottled brown glaze. Decoration includes zoomorphic forms and simple geometric designs.

Khorassan A carpet-weaving province in north-east Persia, prolific during the 16th and 17th centuries. The carpets have curvilinear floral designs in sombre shades of deep red and blue. The quality ranges from coarse to fine. In the 19th century, carpet-weaving was revived in the region, at Mashhad and neighbouring villages. Some pieces made in the 20th century are extremely fine and bear the signature of the master weaver, Amoghli and Sabir being the most famous.

Khotan A carpet-weaving town in east Turkestan that produced distinctive rugs and carpets in the 18th and 19th centuries. Wool and silk pile weavings sometimes with metal thread BROCADE were made with a repeating flower-head design in a typical colour palette of terracotta, shades of blue, yellow and brown. A particularly famous design includes a repeat pomegranate and foliate pattern, often seen on a blue background.

Kick A shallow or deep indentation in glass made when the PUNTY is applied to the base of the object and pushed up further to avoid a rough PONTIL MARK, also to add stability and reduce capacity.

Kidderminster An English town that housed several carpet factories, believed to have started in the early 17th century, although no examples of this age have been identified. The moquette carpet in the Brussels style, introduced in 1753, was popular through to the 18th century.

Kidney table A table with a kidney-shaped top. First introduced in the mid- to late 18th century and revived in the mid-19th, the kidney shape was most commonly used for WRITING TABLES, KNEEHOLE DESKS, DRESSING TABLES and small WORK TABLES for ladies.

French two-tier kidney-shaped table, c.1880 [J]

Kilim (also "kelim", "khilim" and "ghilim") A term used for a pile-less, smooth-surfaced weaving. The pattern is formed by the different coloured weft shoots which conceal the warp threads. Made of wool, cotton and sometimes of silk, by nomadic tribes and in villages but rarely in town workshops.

Anatolian part-cotton kilim, c.1890 [K]

Kimbel and Cabus An American furniture partnership of Anthony Kimbel and Joseph Cabus (a former employee of Alexandre ROUX), active in New York City from 1863 to 1882. The firm made innovative, modern furniture including neo-Gothic designs and aesthetic pieces influenced by Charles Locke EASTLAKE.

Kindjal A long knife commonly carried in the Caucasus. A dual-purpose artifact doubling as tool and weapon, it is characterized by a double-edged blade often with multiple FULLERS. THE HILT is usually of horn and is a simple "I" shape. The scabbard is often decorated with silver NIELLO work.

Kingsbury Manufacturing Co. A US toy-making firm established by Henry T. Kingsbury in Keane, New Hampshire, in 1919. It used medium-grade pressed steel to produce good, solid toys and was famed for the land-speed record cars made in the 1920s and 30s and versions of the Chrysler Airflow, painted in brilliant colours and fitted with sealed CLOCKWORK motors, which Kingsbury patented. It closed in 1942.

King's pattern An ornate silver and silver-plated FLATWARE pattern with a distinctive waisted or wavy stem decorated on the lower section with a thread border and two protruding "shoulders" and on the upper section with a stamped scallop SHELL MOTIF and a scroll border. King's is probably the most prolifically made pattern and dates from c.1810 to the present.

Kingwood (*Dalbergia cearensis*) A 19th-century name for a rich brownish-purple timber, known as "princewood" when first imported into Britain from Brazil in the late 17th century. Kingwood was particularly popular in France for MARQUETRY, BANDING and INLAY.

Kinji The Japanese term for bright finish gold or silver grounds in LACQUER decoration. Powdered gold or silver are sprinkled onto the surface and then lacquered over. The opposite term, *fundame,* denotes dull or matt gold or silver lacquer finishes.

Kinkozan A Japanese kiln founded in the 17th century at Kyoto. In the 19th and early 20th centuries the family pottery made ornate, cream-coloured pottery in Satsuma style for Western markets. It became one of the largest manufactories of Satsuma pottery with over 1,000 workers. The kiln closed in 1927.

Kinrande (Japanese: "gold brocade") Chinese porcelain with overglaze gold decoration, particularly popular in Japan. Kinrande was made in the 16th century, notably during the Jiajing reign (1522–1566). The most common wares are bowls and the decoration scrolls on a blue, overglaze iron red, green or white ground.

Kirchner, Johann Gottlob (b.1706) A German ceramics modeller, born at Merseburg. He worked in Meissen from 1730, becoming its first chief modeller in 1731. He worked on the life-size porcelain figures for the Japanese Palace in Dresden and made several animal models but these did not meet with the approval of the Elector, Augustus the Strong. With the arrival of J.J. Kändler, Kirchner found himself out-classed and resigned in 1733 to return to being a sculptor. He spent his last years in Berlin.

Kirchner Meissen satyr, mid-18th century [i]

Kirchner, Raphael (1876–1917) A Viennese portrait painter and illustrator who worked in the US and moved to Paris in 1905 where he was greatly influenced by Art Nouveau. He designed many

postcards in this style, often using his wife as a model. Some of these are similar in style to those of Alphonse Mucha.

Kirk, Samuel & Son A firm of American silversmiths established in Baltimore by Samuel Kirk (1793–1872) in 1815 and still active today. Throughout the late 19th century, Kirk specialized in flatware and hollowware with heavy repoussé work or chased decoration, often in neo-Rococo taste. Most products are signed.

Kirk & Son silver teapot, mid-19th century [i]

Kirman carpet See Kerman.

Kirman pottery A type of pottery made at Kirman in central southern Iran from the 12th to the 19th centuries. See also Persian pottery.

Kitsch A word used as a noun or adjective to describe inexpensive, commercial objects of the mid-20th century, made in a style that reflects no understanding of traditional aesthetics and designed to be eye-catching or whimsical.

Klismos A Greek term for a light, elegant chair with a broad curved top rail and distinctive concave sabre legs that splay outward, first developed in ancient Greece c.6th century BC. It strongly influenced Greek Revival furniture – often painted with motifs – designed in the late 18th and early 19th by, among others, Thomas Hope.

Klöster Veilsdorf
A porcelain factory founded in 1760 in Thuringia, Germany, by Prince F. von Hildburghausen. After his death in 1795 it was owned by Duke Friedrich von Sachsen-Altenberg. He sold it to the Greiner family who ran it until 1822 making good quality, early Rococo-style products. Services in the Meissen style and Italian comedy figures modelled by Wenzel Neu are highly valued today. It is now under private ownership.

Klöster Veilsdorf covered bowl, c.1770 [J]

Klösterle A ceramics factory founded in Bohemia in 1794 by Ignaz Prosse, which made porcelain from 1819. Its earliest production was in the style of Thuringian ware. It was taken over by Count Mathias Thun and was known as Graflich Thunsche Porzellan Fabrik Klösterle until the 20th century. Its best quality porcelain, often in the Meissen style, was produced between 1830 and 1850. Five other factories in the region joined forces to create the Porcelain Union but this dissolved in 1939. The factory at Klösterle (now Klásterac) ceased production in 1993.

Kneehole desk (or dressing table) A table with one or two drawers along its length, a central recess for the user's legs (often with a cupboard), and drawers down each side. It was introduced in France and the Netherlands in the late 17th century and gave rise to the pedestal desk in the mid-18th, but the basic design has been used ever since.

Mahogany Klismos chair, c.1810 [c]

Knibb family An English family of clock- and watchmakers, principally John Knibb (active *c*.1650) and his brother Joseph Knibb (d. *c*.1711). The family was originally from Oxford but moved to London. Joseph Knibb became a member of the Clockmakers' Company in 1670 and was one of the leading clockmakers in late 17th-century London. He produced LANTERN clocks, BRACKET clocks, walnut-veneered LONGCASE clocks and wall clocks. He also devised the Roman striking system for bracket clocks (see STRIKING SYSTEMS).

Knife box (or case) A case with a decorative exterior and an interior fitted with slots for storing cutlery; knives and forks handle up, and spoons bowl up. Introduced in the 18th century, they were often made in pairs, in a box shape with a slanting top and a BOW- or SERPENTINE-front, often in SHAGREEN or mahogany with silver or brass mounts. (See also CUTLERY URN.)

Mahogany knife box, English c.1790 [K]

Knife rest A small, low piece of glass (sometimes porcelain or metal) some 10–13cm (4–5in) long, that was placed on a dinner table to keep the carving knife off the surface. They were made in various decorative shapes from the 18th century, usually in pairs.

Knole settee An upholstered high-backed SETTEE with sides that can be lowered to form a DAY BED, popular in the 1920s and 30s. The prototype was made for Knole, a palace in Kent, *c*.1605–20, and had sides that were lowered using a ratchet. In the 20th century the sides were tied with loops to the back.

Knoll Associates A design group and maker of furniture founded in 1938 by Hans G. Knoll as Knoll Furniture Co., New York. He married Florence Schust, a designer with the company in 1946. The name changed to Knoll Associates as other designers joined them. From 1948 Knoll produced MIES VAN DER ROHE's Barcelona Chair and encouraged Harry BERTOIA to make his wire chairs. Other designers included Pierre Jeanneret, Eero SAARINEN, and Isamu Naguchi. Hans died in 1955 and the company was subsequently sold in 1959 and again in 1965. In 1968 it took over Gavina and its stable of designers. It was known in Europe from 1951 and in the US in 1969 as Knoll International.

Knop The decorative knob on lids and covers, or the cast finial at the end of a spoon handle. In metalwork and ceramics knops frequently serve as handles on the lids of tureens, in forms suggesting the contents of the vessel, such as vegetables or fruit. A knop is also the decorative bulge on the stem of a drinking glass, goblet or candlestick, usually halfway up the stem. A popular form of decoration in Britain after the development of lead glass in the 17th century, the knop appears in

Mason's tureen with knop, English c.1820 [Q] ▶

many shapes, including a tyre, egg, cylinder, acorn, mushroom, cone, drop, cushion or ball.

Knotted lace One of the original forms of lace-making, closely related to utilitarian products of knotting such as fishnets and hammocks. Its appearance depends on the weight of the thread and the precise technique, but designs are usually geometric.

Knowles, Taylor & Knowles Co. An American ceramic-maker founded in East Liverpool, Ohio, by John Taylor and Homer Knowles in 1870. The firm made ironstone, ROCKINGHAM ware and, from about 1889, American BELLEEK porcelain, sold under the trademark "Lotus Ware". Products may be signed with a mark resembling that of Royal WORCESTER. The factory closed in 1929.

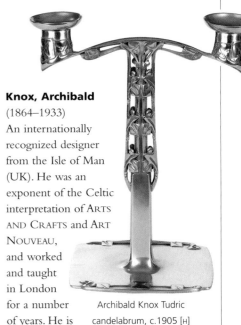

Knox, Archibald (1864–1933) An internationally recognized designer from the Isle of Man (UK). He was an exponent of the Celtic interpretation of ARTS AND CRAFTS and ART NOUVEAU, and worked and taught in London for a number of years. He is principally known now for his designs for LIBERTY & CO.: CYMRIC (silver, in the Celtic style), TUDRIC (pewter), jewellery, clocks, vases and carpets. He made use of the ENTRELAC motif, enamel and cabochons of turquoise. His jewellery was mostly in silver and could be enamelled or set with precious or semi-precious stones.

Archibald Knox Tudric candelabrum, c.1905 [H]

Knuckle joint A type of wooden, movable interlocking joint used in the 18th century for drop-leaf tables. It was the hinge for the strut and leg, which swung out to support the raised leaf. It was cut by hand in the wood of the rail and strut then a flat-topped iron pin was inserted through the centre.

Knulling A type of irregularly outlined GADROONING used to decorate silver wares. A popular technique in mid-18th century England, it was favoured mainly for the borders of trays and platters.

Knurling A series of fine ridges or serrations stamped or impressed on silver or metal articles enabling the piece to be gripped more easily, like the twist cap on a flask. It is also used as border decoration.

Kobako (Japanese: "small box") Made for general use rather than a specific purpose, they are usually rectangular, sometimes with lift-out compartments. Made in LACQUER, pottery or porcelain, they can be highly ornate, intricate works of art.

Kodansu Small Japanese lacquer cabinets that contain a chest-of-drawers. They often have engraved silver mounts, but the best

Lacquer Kodansu,
Japanese c.1890 [H]

examples are inlaid with mother-of-pearl and tortoiseshell. They were made for export in the 19th and 20th centuries.

Kogo (Japanese: "incense") A small box and cover, usually circular, to hold incense. Made in LACQUER, pottery or porcelain, they were used in the TEA CEREMONY. Lids may be modelled in relief, or the box formed as a bird, animal, fruit or flower.

Königsberg potteries Founded *c.*1772–75 by J.E.L. Ehrenreich in Königsberg, near Hamburg, these works produced good quality FAIENCE, making plates with pierced borders and painted flowers. Stoneware and earthenware were also made. (See also MARIEBERG.)

Koninklijke Nederlandse Glasfabrik See ROYAL DUTCH GLASSWORKS.

Koppel, Henning (1918–81) A prominent Scandinavian sculptor and designer who joined the Danish firm of silversmiths/retailers Georg JENSEN in the late 1940s. Koppel injected a fresh approach to post-war silver and jewellery design which won him various medals. He used the "free form" and asymmetry in contrast to the more regimented, geometric style which typified Jensen's later designs.

Silver pill box
by Koppel, 1950s [I]

Korean porcelain and pottery Although inspired by and resembling Chinese styles, Korean ceramics have their own character. The oldest pieces date from around AD 100 and are unglazed grey stoneware; porcelain was used from the 11th century onward. There are three groups, named after dynasties: the Silla (57 BC–AD 936), the Koryo (936–1392) and the Yi (1392–1910). The Koryo was the golden age of Korean ceramics with fine quality Chinese style

celadon glazes used on boxes, wine jars and vases. Motifs include plants, flowers, dragons, stars, lobed and reeded mouldings.

Koro A Japanese incense burner or CENSER often used for the TEA CEREMONY. Examples are usually of globular form with three feet, made in pottery, IMARI PORCELAIN, KAKIEMON, SATSUMA, enamel or bronze.

Kosta Glasbruk A Swedish glassworks founded in the Småland region in 1742. Early production consisted of window glass, chandeliers and drinking glasses, but the factory was later at the forefront of new trends and technical developments, producing PRESSED GLASS from the 1840s and setting up a new glass-cutting workshop in the 1880s. In 1903, the company merged with the Reijmyre glassworks (est. Ostergötland, 1810) but both retained their own names and Kosta went on to maintain its reputation as one of the leading Swedish manufacturers with a range of fine art glass and tableware by such distinguished designers as Monica Morales-Schildt (b.1908) and Vicke Lindstrand (1904–83), artistic director from 1950–73. It is still active today.

Kosta Glasbruk ornament
by Morales-Schildt, 1960s [P]

Kothgasser, Anton
(1769–1851) An Austrian glass and porcelain decorator. A painter at the Royal porcelain factory in VIENNA, he is today best known for the transparent enamelled decoration of landscapes, cityscapes and portraits that he applied to beakers and tumblers.

Kovsh A form of drinking vessel or ladle peculiar to Russia, with a shallow boat-shaped body and a rising handle at one end. Examples from the 18th and 19th centuries were often made from silver, gold, possibly enamelled, but kovsh were probably made from wood in early times, sometimes in hardwood like MAZERS.

Kraak porcelain A type of CHINESE EXPORT PORCELAIN produced from the WANLI reign (1573–1619) until c.1640 and named after the Portuguese ships (carracks), in which it was transported. Kraak was the first Chinese export ware to arrive in Europe in large quantities. It is BLUE AND WHITE, decorated with stylized flowers such as peonies and

Kothgasser Viennese gold-ground enamelled "Ranftbecher", c.1830 [E]

Kraak porcelain charger, Chinese Wanli period [J]

chrysanthemums, and with wide border panels. Wares include large dishes, bowls and vases. Pieces are often warped and fused and have tool "chatter marks" on the bases. Kraak was copied by ARITA and DELFT potters.

Krater (Greek: "mixing bowl") Used to mix wine and water before serving. A Greek krater could be VOLUTE-, column- or bell-shaped.

Kris The distinctive knife of the Malay archipelago. The blade incorporates meteoric iron and often has wavy edges. The HILT is sometimes made in the form of the god Vishnu.

Kruse, Käthe (1910–68) A German dollmaker whose dislike of mass-produced dolls inspired her to manufacture a virtually indestructible, realistic doll. After an unsuccessful joint venture with KÄMMER & REINHARDT in 1910, she set up her own workshop in Bad Kösen, Silesia. All Kruse dolls produced before 1950 are made of stockinet over buckram with oil-painted facial features. The company she founded is still in production today.

Character doll by Kruse, with stockinet body, German c.1928 [J]

Kuba A major rug-producing district in the eastern Caucasus. Village and nomadic rugs with geometric designs were made with a high density of knots and frequently with cotton for the foundation. Kubas have centralized designs, jewel-like colours and a great variety of motifs. The pile tends to be clipped short and braided fringes are characteristic. Carpets survive from the 16th century and they are still made today. (See also CAUCASIAN CARPETS.)

Kuchenreuter A large family of gunmakers from Regensburg, Bavaria, active from the early 18th to the end of the 19th centuries. Their guns were of the highest quality and it is not unusual to find earlier barrels remounted in later firearms. (See also TRANTER.)

Kufic script A type of Arabic calligraphy, frequently used in stylized form in early Islamic architecture, carpets and pottery. Widely adopted as a decorative motif by European craftsmen who were ignorant of its original function, kufic inscriptions appear in jumbled forms on Italian silk cloth, Hispano-Moresque architecture and pottery and less frequently on French and English ornament. In the 19th century, Kufic script was regarded as an integral part of the Turkish or Moorish ornamental styles.

Kulah A rug-weaving town between Izmir and Ushakin, Turkey, which is well known for the production of PRAYER RUGS with multiple borders. They have red or white wool warps, with the weft of cotton or wool. Often they have a charcoal field with meandering vine borders. Rugs have been made here from the 16th century to the present day. (See also TURKISH CARPETS.)

Kunckel, Johann F. (c.1630–1703) A German chemist and glassmaker. He was employed as a chemist and alchemist by various royal patrons, including a period in the secret laboratory of the Elector of Saxony in the 1670s. In 1678, the Prussian Elector Friedrich Wilhelm invited him to Potsdam to be the director of the Potsdam Glasshouse (est. 1674). Here he developed a clear crystal glass and a new type of red glass – GOLD-RUBY GLASS or *goldrubinglas* – used for luxury pieces such as vases and drinking glasses. The leading glass-technologist of his day, he published three treatises: *Chymische Anmerkung* (1677), *Ars Vitraria Experimentalis* (1679) and *Laboratorium chymicum* (1716).

Kungsholm Glasbruk A Swedish glasshouse, founded in Stockholm by an Italian glassmaker Giacomo Scapitti in the late 17th century, and later run by Swedish noblemen. From the early 18th century it produced fine goblets incorporating Venetian and German elements and with intricately wrought stems. The factory closed in 1815.

Kunstschrank (or *Kabinettschrank*) A type of German CABINET fitted with drawers and recesses and used for storing precious objects, derived from the Spanish VARGUEÑO. Designed as works of art rather than furniture, they were a collaboration between cabinet-makers, goldsmiths and sculptors and combined luxurious materials such as EBONY, TORTOISESHELL, hardstones, IVORY and LACQUER. Most were made in Augsburg in the 16th and 17th centuries.

Kurdistan (or Kurdish) One of the most prolific carpet-producing areas in Persia, including the city of Senneh where pile carpets were made from the 19th century and from where the term SENNEH KNOT derives. Weaving has been carried out in Kurdistan since the 16th century but was most active in town workshops, villages and nomadic tribes in the 19th century. Today, production is more centralized. The Souj-Bulak is a compact strong Kurdish carpet. (See also PERSIAN CARPETS.)

Kurk Very soft, lustrous wool, taken from the neck and belly area of sheep in winter, when it most oily, and especially associated with fine quality KASHANS.

Kutani wares The term Ko Kutani (old Kutani) refers to 17th-century Japanese porcelain made in a small factory at Kutani (Kaga province) and painted in

Kutani vase and cover with detail of mark, Meiji period, c.1880 [J, a pair]

brilliant enamels with bold designs often derived from textile patterns. The wares, which include large dishes and vases, were probably made for the south-east Asian markets. Recent kiln excavations indicate that a large proportion of "Ko Kutani" ware was actually made at ARITA in imitation of true Kutani. The term "Kutani" (as opposed to Ko Kutani) refers to the products of a factory (from 1823) that made imitations of old Kutani, decorated predominantly in gilt on an iron red ground.

Kuttrolf The German term for a flask, usually made of WALDGLAS, with a neck made up of two or more thin tubes that ensure that the liquid inside the flask pours very slowly. Made in Germany in the Middle Ages, it probably evolved from a Roman precedent.

Kuttrolf glass vase, 17th century [H]

Kuznetzoff family A family who ran a number of large porcelain factories in Russia in the 19th century. They made commercial wares, mainly imitating western European styles, and figures of

Russian peasants. They started with a factory in Novocharitonova, which existed until 1870. In 1832, they opened a factory in Duljewo. In 1842 a member of the family opened a factory in Riga and another built the Wolchow factory employing 1,100 workers. In 1887 the family business was converted into a company, absorbing other porcelain factories including the GARDNER factory near Moscow. The family still runs the business today.

Kwaart A lead overglaze applied to DELFT WARE after the decoration and firing, giving it a shiny appearance.

Kyoto flower vase, c.1830 [K]

Kyoto potteries Japanese potteries in and around the imperial city of Kyoto. In the Edo period (1600–1868) many small potteries flourished, mainly at Awata, a suburb of Kyoto, producing wares for the home market. The most important were Ninsei and Ogata KENZAN. In the MEIJI PERIOD (1868–1912), as Japan re-opened trade links with the West, commercial concerns around Kyoto began mass-producing pottery in the SATSUMA style for export. While most was of poor quality, a number of studios made Satsuma-style wares of exceptional quality such as KINKOZAN. See also JAPANESE POTTERY AND PORCELAIN; RAKU WARE; and TEA CEREMONY WARES.

L

Laburnum (*Laburnum spp.*) A tree native to Europe and the US with a hard, yellowish-brown streaked wood with a strongly contrasting HEART, that was used for INLAY, PARQUETRY and OYSTER VENEER from the late 17th century.

Lace point de gaze butterfly, Belgian 1890 [Q]

Lace A term that refers to a wide variety of decorative fabrics that have evolved from two main techniques developed in 16th-century Italy: cutwork and NEEDLELACE. A plain woven linen cloth was the basis of the first cutwork – various threads were pulled and the resulting geometric holes were overstitched with needle and thread to form a reserve for stylized designs, or a design was darned into the grid. This led to the development of RETICELLA lace; LACIS was made with a knotted grid in the form of a fishnet and BURATTO with a twisted ground. BOBBIN LACE first developed in Italy at the same time.

All these were restricted to geometric patterns and straight edges until the invention of parchment patterns by the Venetian Cesare Vecellio in 1592 and others, thus creating the world of free NEEDLELACE – PUNTO in ARIA. VENETIAN NEEDLELACE flourished and was widely copied. Isabella Parasole published *Specchio delle Virtuose Donne* in 1595 including patterns for bobbin lace-making. Most lace was made with linen, some with silk or metal threads. The invention of machine-made net at the end of the 18th century started a gradual decline in the standard of lace-making throughout the 19th century, although lace schools at Burano, near Venice, Ireland, and others still copied early techniques.

Lace box A type of small square or rectangular box, with a flat hinged lid and fitted interior compartments that was used for storing lace, gloves or other such items. Made in the late 17th and early 18th centuries, these boxes were often decorated with MARQUETRY or cut paper and are sometimes accompanied by walnut stands of a later date.

Lacework An imitation of lace made in porcelain – achieved by dipping fabric lace into porcelain slip, which is then dried and fired so that the textile is burned away. The technique was introduced in MEISSEN *c.*1770 and was used a great deal on continental porcelain in the 19th century – also at DERBY and MINTON in England.

Lacis A knotted net onto which patterns are embroidered with needle and thread for church and domestic linen. Also known as darned netting; later FILET; see also LACE.

La Cloche Frères
Art Deco jardinière
brooch, 1925 [B]

La Cloche Frères A firm of jewellery manufacturers, based in Paris and London, and founded by four brothers in 1897. They quickly established a reputation for elegant diamond garland jewels and vivid ART DECO jewellery such as Egyptian revivalist bracelets and pendants depicting scenes from the fables of La Fontaine. The firm is still open today.

Lacquer A resin produced from the sap of the *Rhus* tree that is native to China but has been introduced in Japan. Once processed and dried in air the resin forms a hard, impermeable, smooth and lustrous surface. Used from the sixth century and often known as *urushi* lacquer, it was popular in Asia and particularly Japan where lacquerwork rose to a fine art, with lacquered objects being expensive and highly prized. Lacquer not produced by the Japanese, the leading exponents, is sometimes known as bantam work (after a village in Java).

Lacquer can be applied to many items including furniture, boxes, cases and INRO. It is most commonly seen with naturalistic, figurative or emblematic designs picked out in gold against a *roiro* (black) background but may also have a red or a gold background. Gold backgrounds can consist of specks of gold dust giving a cloudy effect known as NASHIJI. Pieces can also be highlighted with *chinkin-bori* (engraved lacquer), crushed shell, known as *raden*, or small inset pieces of mother of pearl, known as *aogai*. Lacquerwork takes great skill on the part of the craftsperson. The lacquer is

Charles II lacquer cabinet, English *c.*1670 [D]

applied using a brush to a wood or composition base in very thin layers that are dried and polished to a lustrous finish. Techniques include MAKI-E where flat or raised designs are built up with gold or coloured lacquering. Some 18th and 19th century pieces that appear to be lacquered are in fact JAPANNED.

Lacquer gilding A method of applying gilt decoration to ceramics (used on BÖTTGER wares), by grinding up gold leaf with lacquer varnish and brushing it on. It was more permanent than the earlier method of SIZE-GILDING.

Lacroix, Roger Vandercruse (1728–99) A leading French furniture-maker. He was the brother-in-law of Jean-François OEBEN and became a *maître* in 1755. Lacroix supplied furniture to a number of aristocratic patrons and Parisian dealers, specializing in small elegant pieces decorated with floral MARQUETRY, SÈVRES porcelain plaques and VERNIS MARTIN.

Lacroix tulipwood and marquetry commode, 1772 [A]

Lacy glass A term used in the US for late 19th century PRESSED GLASS decorated with elaborate, symmetrical patterns resembling lace work. Typical examples include SANDWICH GLASS bowls and plates with scalloped, ruffled rims.

Ladder-back A modern term for a chair, often with a rush seat, with a number of horizontal "rung-like" rails linking the back uprights. Such chairs were first made as country furniture in ELM, OAK and BEECH in the 17th century. In the 18th century they became part of the urban cabinet-makers' repertoire and from *c*.1740 to 1790 were made in MAHOGANY.

Ladik A town in west Turkey particularly famous for the production of PRAYER RUGS in the 18th and 19th centuries. Colours are always strong and jewel-like with the MIHRAB invariably bright red with blue for the SPANDRELS. Stylised tulip motifs are often seen as decoration.

Elm ladderback chair, English late 18th century [Q]

La Farge, John (1835–1910) An American painter, stained glass designer, decorator and author of artistic treatises. La Farge studied in France and England and was influenced by Romanticism and the Pre-Raphaelite movement. From about 1875 he began designing stained glass windows and encouraged Louis Comfort TIFFANY in this field. By the 1890s La Farge had produced thousands of windows, many of figural design in Pre-Raphaelite style for wealthy American patrons, and also in Japanese style after a visit to Japan and the Pacific.

Lag and feather A popular banding pattern on English ceramics. Adopted as a decorative motif by a number of ceramic manufactories in the late 18th and early 19th centuries, particularly WEDGWOOD, lag and feather imitates in two-dimensional form the FLUTING and HUSKS favoured for metalwork in the Adam style.

La Granja de San Ildefonso glasshouse (1728–1886) A Spanish glasshouse founded with royal patronage near the palace of La Granja de San Ildefonso outside Madrid in 1728. Initial production of window and mirror glass for the royal residences was succeeded, from *c*.1746, by mostly clear glass wares such as tumblers, often decorated with enamelling or engraving of flowers in particular. From the end of the 18th entury, cut glass was also made.

Lalique, René See p.232.

Lalonde, Richard de (fl.1780–90) A French designer of furniture and metalwork. He is best known for his *Cahiers d'Ameublement* ("furniture exercise-books"), which included detailed technical designs for a range of furniture – chairs, tables, commodes, chimney-pieces – predominantly in the LOUIS XVI style, although some NEO-CLASSICAL designs were also included. Some 30 of the *cahiers* were eventually published (*c*.1780–85) as *Oeuvres diverses de Lalande*.

Large Lalique frosted moulded glass vase,
(37 cm/14.5in high) c.1920 [B]

Lalique acid-etched
glass clock "La jour et la nuit",
c.1925 [A]

Lalique brooch in the form of a bat
in plique-à-jour enamel,
1920s [F]

René Lalique (1860–1945)

It is rare for a designer to excel at the highest level in two different periods, styles and mediums, but Lalique – a leading French jeweller and glass-maker – was just such a man.

A multitalented designer

After the early death of his father, René Lalique was apprenticed to the Parisian jeweller Louis Aucoc in 1876 at the age of 16. Like most jewellers at the time across Europe, Aucoc made abundant use of the diamonds and other precious stones then available from Colonial Africa. Lalique was to present a stunning alternative to large cut gemstones, making use of plant and insect forms, *plique-à-jour* enamels, semi-precious stones, sculptural elements and glass.

Lalique studied for two years in London before returning to Paris in 1880. Back in France, he continued to study, taking classes in sculpture and modelling while earning a living as a jewellery designer, working for such firms as Boucheron and CARTIER. He also designed fabrics and wallpaper. He opened a small workshop in 1886, creating innovative jewellery in the ART NOUVEAU style. His reputation soon grew and he moved to larger workshops, employing up to 30 people. He designed jewellery for the actress Sarah Bernhardt and received the support of Samuel BING, followed by critical acclaim at the Paris Exposition Internationale in 1900.

Lalique pour homme
limited edition
scent bottle for the
millennium year [M]

In the mid-1890s, Lalique began experimenting with glass, looking for sculptural effects and materials that would add a different dimension to his work. He experimented with glass cast through the LOST WAX method, known as cire-perdue. He also cast faces and masks from opalescent glass and continued to experiment with the chemistry of glass and blowing into moulds at home. He still used glass on a small scale for jewellery but also increased the size to large panels, which he exhibited as early as 1900.

The turning point for Lalique's work with glass came with a commission from François Coty for scent bottles in mass-produced numbers. This led to commissions from other perfume houses – he famously designed for Nina Ricci's L'Air du Temps, for example. His wonderful designs transformed an industrial process into a vehicle for creating beautiful objects. Lalique's use of "demi-crystal" glass, which needed little finishing after it came out of the mould, coupled with not over-using the moulds, gave a high level of definition. Using his knowledge of the chemistry of glass, he could produce the now famous opalescent glass as well as a range of vibrant colours.

Lalique made all manner of objects in glass from ashtrays to car mascots and vases to glass lampshades. He received critical acclaim for his ART DECO glass at the Paris 1925 exposition in much the same way as he had for his Art Nouveau jewellery in 1900. He continued to expand his range of glassware until his death in 1945. The glass made in his lifetime is marked R. Lalique, after his death only the word Lalique appears. The firm continues today.

Lambart, (James) Alfred (1902–71)
An English portrait painter, poster artist
and illustrator. He was commissioned by
the British privatized railway companies
to produce many travel and tourism
posters during the 1920s and 30s. He
created simple, bold, colourful images of
popular seaside resorts and holiday places,
including notably Teignmouth, of the
post-World War I period.

Tourism poster by Alfred Lambart, c.1930 [I]

Lambeth potteries A group of potteries
in Lambeth, London. TIN-GLAZED wares
were made from the 1630s to the end of
the 18th century. STONEWARE was made
from the late 17th century and continued,
with relief and incised decoration, into
the 19th. Despite differences in glazes and
bodies, it is difficult to distinguish between
the wares of Lambeth,
SOUTHWARK and
BRISTOL.
Stoneware
continued to be
made in Lambeth
by DOULTON.

Lambeth stoneware mug
with silver rim, c.1727 [K]

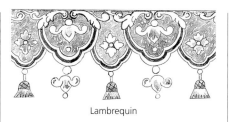

Lambrequin

Lambrequin Originally the decorative
covering over armour and the hangings at
jousting tournaments and in battle. The
term is now used for the shaped stiffened
surround placed above a door or window.
Often made of wood, lambrequins are set
in front of any curtaining. The word is
also used for decorative "fringes" on
furniture, silver and ceramics.

Lamé A woven fabric, often silk or a
synthetic equivalent, interwoven with
metallic threads, used extensively during
the 20th century in the production of
formal evening gowns.

Lamellé A leatherwork technique in
which thin slits are cut into the leather
and strips of coloured leather or foil are
threaded through to make patterns.

Lamerie, Paul de (1688–1751) The most
important English silversmith of the 18th
century. The son of French Protestant
parents who fled France,
Paul de Lamerie was
brought to London as a boy
and apprenticed to the
HUGUENOT silversmith Pierre
Platel in 1703. De Lamerie
entered his first mark at
Goldsmiths' Hall in 1713 and
became Goldsmith to King
George I in 1716 with premises in
Windmill Street, St James's.
He moved his premises to
Gerrard Street, Soho, in 1738.
    Although BRITANNIA STANDARD
silver was not obligatory after
1720, de Lamerie continued to
work in this purer and more costly metal
until 1739, when he entered his first
STERLING maker's mark at Goldsmiths'
Hall. Unusually, he made most of his

Paul de Lamerie
silver coffeepot,
c.1742 [A]

own moulds for casting handles, finials,
feet and other applied silver ornament.
De Lamerie saw the potential of the new
decorative style, English Rococo, when it
emerged in the late 1730s. With five or
six other Huguenots, he raised the
techniques and artistry of English
silversmithing to new heights. As some of
his original invoices and numerous pieces
survive, it is known that he supplied great
quantities of silver to many members of
the English aristocracy but he was able
to maintain high standards in his work,
in spite of a prodigious output.

Lamination A technique in which thin
layers (laminates) of wood are sandwiched
together with the grain at right angles for
strength and glued together. This
technique eventually led to the
production of PLYWOOD. The process was
described by Thomas SHERATON and
different types of lamination were used by
furniture-makers such as John Henry
BELTER. Designers such as Charles EAMES
and Alvar AALTO revolutionized chair
design by the use of plywood.

Lamp-blown glass A decorative glass
technique whereby RODS or tubes of glass
are heated in a flame until soft and then
manipulated into intricate shapes. It
was known in 15th-
century Venice, and
was used throughout
Europe in the 17th
century to produce
intricate glass figures.
In the 19th century it was
used to make PAPERWEIGHTS
and novelties sold at fairs, and
in the 20th century for
MURANO tourist glass.

Lance A spear for a horseman,
used for war, hunting and
tournaments. A lance comprises
a wooden shaft with a pointed
head at one end and a butt (counterweight)
at the other. Those lances intended for
tournaments usually have blunt or
rounded points to prevent injury.

Lannuier, Charles-Honoré (1779–1819)
A French-born cabinet-maker active in
New York City from 1803. He applied the
Louis XVI style of his native country to
American furniture types to create a
popular Franco-American style. His high
quality furniture uses extensive gilding and
Neo-classical motifs and luxurious
materials such as rosewood, marble and
ormolu. Lannuier became one of

Lannuier "American
Empire" games table,
c.1805 [c]

America's most fashionable furniture
suppliers and popularized the French
taste, in a style known as "American
Empire" or "New York Empire".

Lantern clock A type of
weight-driven wall clock,
shaped like a lantern.
Introduced in Britain
c.1620, it was made almost
completely in brass and
comprised a square case
on ball or urn feet, a large
circular dial (with a
chapter ring extending
beyond the width of the
case on early examples),
a single hour hand, and
a large bell and finial.
It usually had ornate
pierced fretwork on
top of the frame.

Brass lantern clock by
William Hanson, c.1690 [D]

Lapis lazuli A deep blue gemstone with
distinctive flecks of gold-coloured pyrites.
Lesser quality stones are paler blue with
veins or patches of white calcite. Deposits
are found in Afghanistan, Chile, Siberia
and the US. It has been used since ancient
times as a decorative hardstone and, when
powdered, as an artist's pigment.

Lappet A rectangular band of high-
quality lace used in pairs to hang from
the back of ladies' fashionable lace caps
c.1690 and throughout the 18th century,
often pinned in loops. See also Alençon;
Point de Neige; Valenciennes.

Lapping A method of concealing exposed
copper on the edge or rim of a Sheffield
plate object. From around 1758 it
involved cutting the edge of the plated
copper so that the layer of
silver extended over it could
be turned under to cover it. In
the 1770s this was superseded
by soldering a U-shaped
flattened tube of silver
along the exposed edge.

Larch (*Larix decidua*) A deciduous
conifer native to Northern Europe that
provides a straight-grained timber
ranging from yellowish-white to
reddish-brown. It was used for
country furniture and
carcasses in the late
18th and 19th century.

Latticework
A diamond-shaped
network of wood or
metal made from a
criss-cross of straight
members, used in the
mid-18th century on
Chinese Chippendale
furniture. It was also
popular on Regency
furniture, on the backs
of seat furniture and
in the form of brass
grilles on the silk-lined
doors of side cabinets.

Latticino, latticinio (Italian *latte*:
"milk") Clear glass decorated with
opaque white threads (see filigrana) in
a variety of patterns. It was first made in
16th-century Murano and spread
throughout Europe via façon de Venise.

Lattimo See milk glass.

Laub-und-bandelwerk (German:
"foliage and scrollwork") A late Baroque
decorative motif depicting formalized
interwoven leaves and intertwined bands.
Originating in late 17th-century France,
it was championed by Louis XIV's
leading decorators Charles Le Brun and
Jean Bérain. The foliate scrolls and
foliage framed by flat bands resemble
embroidery patterns and parterre garden
designs. In 18th-century Germany it
was used on room panelling,
furniture, metalwork, glass,
leather and textiles. At Meissen
it was applied to Böttger
stoneware and as a border
for chinoiserie ornament

Laub-und-bandelwerk   during the J.G. Höroldt period.

Laurel A Greek ornamental motif
composed of forms resembling bay leaves
(identified from Roman times as the
European or "true" laurel). In Classical
ornament, the laurel was an emblem of
renewal, glory and honour, presented in
the form of a wreath to herald
achievements or military victories.
The simple and distinctive shape of the
laurel leaf made it an appropriate choice
for garlands and festoons. A band or
frieze composed of laurel leaves
frequently incorporates laurel berries,
similar to the fashion of depicting
acorns with oak leaves.

Lava cameos The lava that spilled so
dramatically from Mt Vesuvius became a
popular curiosity after the excavation of
Pompeii in 1748. Italian glasscutters used
an ancient Roman technique to carve
cameos from the lava in matt shades of
brown, grey, white and black for travellers
doing the Grand Tour. Subjects include

Classical heads in profile as well as Italian portraits of prominent national figures, both of which were popular souvenirs.

Lava glass Iridescent gold ART GLASS, known also as volcanic glass, developed and patented by Louis Comfort TIFFANY in the late 19th century. Pieces usually have an irregular form, with a rough stone-like surface and "dripping" decoration that resembles the flow of molten lava.

Tiffany lava-glass vase, c.1910 [K]

Lava ware
A hard and coarse form of durable stoneware used for inexpensive tableware c.1850 to 1900. It was produced by mixing slag from iron foundries and clay and often has a blue or purplish colouring.

Lawn A fine, lightweight, white or cream-coloured fabric, either linen or cotton, used for handkerchiefs, children's clothes, and blouses.

Lazy Susan A US term from the 19th century, now used in Britain, for a revolving serving tray. They may have developed from "dumbwaiter" tables from which guests helped themselves when servants were not available late at night.

Leach, Bernard Howell
(1887–1979) An English studio potter, born in Hong Kong, who studied painting and etching at art school in London. On a teaching visit to Japan he became interested in ceramics and studied Japanese and Korean pottery (1916–19). He returned to England and opened the

Bernard Leach terracotta glazed vase, c.1920–30 [J]

ST IVES POTTERY, Cornwall, (1920) with the help of his friend and potter Shoji HAMADA. His work falls broadly into two areas: pieces showing an Oriental influence, and those inspired by the English slipware tradition. In his work, teaching and writing, Leach inspired his own generation and subsequent generations of studio potters.

Lead crystal Glass with a high (at least 20 per cent) red lead content that produces a heavy soft brilliant METAL ideally suited to CUT decoration. Perfected by George RAVENSCROFT in 1681, it is also popularly known as "crystal" or "quartz crystal" because of its brightness and light-reflecting quality.

Lead glaze A translucent glaze composed of silicaceous sand, salt and alkali such as potash and a mineral to colour it, fused with the acid of natural sulphide of lead (galena) or lead oxide. It is applied to pottery that has already been fired and is united to the surface by a subsequent firing at a lower temperature. It was used in the Middle Ages when the general colours were brown or green. The lead fumes, however, proved injurious and lead glazes have seldom been used since the early 19th centur, when a translucent FELDSPATHIC GLAZE was developed.

Leaf ornament
Foliate ornament widely used as a decorative motif, most frequently as a moulding or DIAPER pattern. From antiquity, leaf ornament (the Egyptian lotus leaf or Greco-Roman ACANTHUS foliage) was used to

Leaf ornament on Sheffield plate candelabrum, c.1830 [H, a pair]

embellish COLUMN capitals, which by the late Gothic period were more naturalistic. Leaf decoration for MOULDINGS and FRIEZES generally features as repeating ornament interspersed with other motifs, or it takes the form of a densely-packed Classical wreath or scrolling foliage. Leaves commonly adopted for ornament are the grapevine, oak, ivy, palm, LAUREL and thistle. In the 19th century, leaf shapes enjoyed popularity as ceramic or metalwork bowls and dishes. Leaf foliage played a key role in ART NOUVEAU and ART DECO ornament, frequently with flowers and fruit.

Leather The skins of animals, primarily cattle, horses and pigs, that have been treated and preserved to allow them to be used decoratively and practically. Practised for over 7,000 years, the skills of making leather were developed by the Egyptians and Hebrews and improved on greatly by the Arabs during the Middle Ages with Morocco and Cordovan leather being highly prized. Once treated and coloured, principally with tannins from minerals or plants (hence the term tanning), leather can be worked, punched, gilded and tooled, and is used to great aesthetic and practical effect on bookbindings, to cover boxes and cases and provide a writing surface on desks. Large skins have been worked and impressed to become highly decorative and now scarce wall coverings.

Le Corbusier (Charles Edouard Jeanneret, 1887–1965) The most important French architect-designer of his generation and a driving force in MODERNISM. He began to design furniture with Charlotte Perriand in the 1920s, inspired by industrial materials and shapes, producing classics such as the CHAISE LONGUE "cowboy chair".

Two-seater chair "Le Grand Confort" by Le Corbusier, 1928 [G]

Leech jar A large pottery jar used by pharmacists for storing leeches. English examples were either urn-shaped with handles or cylindrical, with a pierced lid, and were often made of glass or CREAMWARE c.1780 by LEEDS POTTERY.

Leeds pottery Founded at Hunslet, near Leeds, c.1760 and run by Humble, Greens & Co. from 1770–75. From 1775–1780 it was called Humble, Hartley Greens & Co. and Hartley Greens & Co. 1781–1820. Soon after 1770 they made CREAMWARE similar to that of WEDGWOOD but with a less even and yellow-tinged glaze. From the 1780s the factory made PEARLWARE and later added black BASALTES to its range of tablewares, which were decorated in ENAMEL COLOURS or with TRANSFER PRINTING in red or black. It also made models of large horses for saddlers. In the 19th century BATAVIAN WARE was made. The firm went bankrupt in 1820, then had various owners until 1878. The works closed a few years later. From 1888 Slee's "Modern Pottery" reproduced 18th-century style wares.

Leerdam See ROYAL DUTCH GLASSWORKS.

Lehmann, Ernst Paul (EPL) A German toymaker who established a factory called Lehmann in 1881 in Brandenburg. The factory made vast numbers of inexpensive light mass-market TINPLATE TOYS decorated with offset LITHO printing. The toys often featured figures or animals which moved in amusing ways. They exported to Europe and the US and survived just beyond World War II.

Lenci A Turin-based company established in 1908 by Enrico di Scavani that produced FELT DOLLS with expressive faces in colourful felt and muslin clothes. Most of Lenci's dolls were commissioned from leading Italian artists. Their dolls were sophisticated and intended for display, more for adults than for children. They had hand-painted pressed felt faces and wore detailed costumes. Lenci dolls are still being made today. From 1928 they introduced EARTHENWARE and PORCELAIN figures that offered distinctive style, fashion and their own brand of humour.

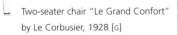

Lenci Art Deco fruit plate, 1930s [N]

Lenox porcelain company
A US porcelain manufacturer established in 1889 in Trenton, New Jersey, by Walter Scott Lenox (1859–1920), a former employee of the OTT & BREWER PORCELAIN FACTORY. The firm specialized in American BELLEEK from its inception, using a thinly potted, ivory-coloured porcelain with sparse decoration, which it still manufactures.

Lenticle A small, usually oval or round glazed aperture on the trunk of a LONGCASE CLOCK, revealing the pendulum inside. The lenticle is often fitted with a cast-metal surround.

Lesney Matchbox ambulance, c.1962 [S] and Yesteryear Mercer Raceabout, 1960s [S]

Lesney Products An English toymaker set up in 1947 in London by Leslie and Rodney Smith, who combined their first names in "Lesney". Rodney left the next year but Leslie teamed up with Jack Odell to make DIECAST items, including toys. A Royal Coach was produced in two sizes in the early 1950s. Over a million of the smaller size were sold in 1953, the year of Queen Elizabeth II's Coronation. That year, the MATCHBOX 1:75 Series of toy vehicles was begun, followed in 1959 by Models of Yesteryear. Lesney was taken over in 1982 by Universal Holdings of Hong Kong.

Lethaby, William Richard (1857–1913) An English architect-designer who founded a design group, Kenton & Co (1890–1920). He designed furniture for it in the ARTS AND CRAFTS style, using carved and inlaid indigenous woods.

Lever escapement (or detached escapement) Invented by Thomas Mudge in 1754, it was one of the first successful watch escapements to let the balance oscillate freely. A few early makers (Josiah Emery and A.L. Breguet) tried versions of the lever escapement, but it was only widely used from the 1880s and was the basis of watch mechanisms from then on.

Libbey Glass Company The largest modern American glassworks, founded in Toledo, Ohio, by William T. Libbey and his son, Edward, in 1888 as a successor to the NEW ENGLAND GLASS COMPANY. Libbey concentrated on clear, cut and pressed LEAD GLASS and coloured ART GLASS of BOHEMIAN type. Libbey changed direction in the 1940s away from art glass to table wares, which have remained their central products to this day.

Liberty "Melrose" Arts and Crafts reproduction fabric

Liberty & Co. A department store founded in Regent Street, London, in 1875 by Arthur Lasenby Liberty (1843–1917), at first called "East India House". Its fabrics attracted interest abroad and resulted in the Italians referring to ART NOUVEAU as *Stile Liberty*. Liberty started selling shawls and silks but soon added ARTS AND CRAFTS products, Japanese porcelain, screens and fans as well as imports from India, Persia, China, Morocco and Turkey.

In 1884, Liberty's opened a costume department, directed by E.W. GODWIN, and then Maison Liberty, for clothing, in Paris in 1889. Later, they commissioned from the British designers Christopher DRESSER, Walter CRANE, Rex Silver (who designed the "Peacock Feather"

pattern) and C.F.A. VOYSEY. In 1885 a wallpaper department was added, selling both imported papers and Liberty's own patterns. Carpets were also commissioned and made in Donegal, Ireland, from 1902. They introduced ART POTTERY from Britain and Europe in the 1880s, including ware from BRANNAM, MOORCROFT, DOULTON and the German firm Max Lauger. They also sold glass by James POWELL & SON, CLUTHA, and LOETZ from Austria. In 1894 they registered a Silver mark (LY & CO) at Goldsmiths Hall, although it was not until 1899 that their own silver, marketed as "Cymric", and jewellery appeared. "Tudric" pewter followed in 1901/1902. Designers for these included Archibald KNOX, Bernard Cuzner, Oliver Baker, the Silver Studio and Jessie M. King. The establishment of a Furnishing and Decoration Studio in 1883 saw a broad range of styles on offer. The ARTS AND CRAFTS pieces in oak designed by Leonard F. Wyburd and E.G. Punnett are the ones most usually recognized as Liberty designs. Liberty & Co. can still be found in Regent Street.

Library steps Folding or fixed ladders and steps for use in libraries. First introduced in the 17th century, they were in general use by *c.*1750 and took various forms, ranging from mobile miniature staircases in contemporary styles to ingenious folding steps that converted into stools or armchairs (see also METAMORPHIC FURNITURE).

Oak library steps, Gothic Revival, English c.1880 [H]

Rosewood library table, English 1830s [I]

Library table A large WRITING TABLE made to stand in the centre of a library in the late 18th and early 19th century. The open pedestal type, in mahogany, was popular. The pedestals were fitted with drawers and cupboards; 19th-century examples were often plain, veneered on all sides and without drawers.

Lignum vitae (*Guaiacum officinale*) A hard, dark brown, black-veined wood exported from South America and the West Indies to Europe in the 17th and 18th centuries. It was used for OYSTER VENEERS, PARQUETRY, small veneered pieces, turned bowls and other TREEN.

Lille pottery and porcelain factories Factories in this French town included a FAIENCE factory founded by Barthélemy Dorez in 1711. It also produced a SOFT-PASTE PORCELAIN similar to that of SAINT-CLOUD. It closed *c.*1820. In 1784 a HARD-PASTE PORCELAIN factory was established with royal support, called the Manufacture Royale de Monseigneur le Dauphin. Wares were marked with a dolphin. This factory closed in 1817.

Lily pad decoration A GATHER of glass applied to the lower part of a vessel and drawn up to resemble a lily pad. It is thought to have been introduced to the US by immigrant German glassworkers in the 18th century and was a popular American motif in the early 19th.

Lime (*Tilia vulgaris*) A tree native to northern Europe with soft, close-grained pale white or yellow wood well suited to carving. It was used for decorative picture and mirror frames and chimneypieces by Grinling GIBBONS and others of his era.

Limed oak Oak that has been treated with lime, which remains in the grain to produce a surface streaked and speckled with white. The process was introduced in the early 20th century and the resulting unpolished wood was used for "cottage style" furniture.

Limehouse porcelain factory

A short-lived but important factory established by Joseph Wilson & Co. in 1746 in Limehouse, London. Its products were influenced by the CHELSEA "Triangle" period – the shapes were imitative of contemporary ROCOCO silver and decorated in blue and white. The factory went bankrupt in 1748 and closed. The site was only discovered in 1989 – previously to that, many of the wares had been attributed to William Reid's factory in Liverpool.

Limoges enamel plaque, c.1530–40 [c]

Limoges enamel ware Enamelled objects produced in Limoges, France, during the 16th and 17th centuries are considered the best in Europe during that period. Produced primarily by a small number of families, early designs included Gothic-style religious scenes, Renaissance motifs and monochrome designs. Bright rather than harmonic colours dominated later production.

Limoges porcelain round box and cover, late 19th century [o]

Limoges porcelain Many factories sprang up in this area because of KAOLIN deposits at nearby St Yrieix in 1768 and Limoges became a generic name for wares produced locally. There were nearly 90 factories and decorating shops in and near the town through the 19th and 20th centuries, including François Allaud and the Grellet Bros. Porcelain is still produced. (See also HAVILAND & CO.)

Line inlay See BANDING.

Linen Obtained from the flax plant, linen thread has been valued for its strong, lustrous qualities since early history. By the medieval period, plain woven linen was produced throughout Europe, with patterned linens woven from the 14th century. Described as either "damasks" (large-scale figurative designs) or "diapers" (small repeat patterns, often geometric in form) they were used for towelling, tablecloths and napkins. From the end of the 17th century, a patent was granted to produce linen in Ireland. Thereafter, most linen used in England came from Ireland, which became a major producer of high-quality linens.

Linenfold Decoration of 15th-century Flemish origins representing in wood a piece of linen cloth hanging in vertical folds. Evolved by Tudor woodcarvers for panelling and furniture – especially chests and the doors of wardrobes – linenfold decoration was also widely adopted with regional variations in France and Germany. By the Renaissance its popularity had waned.

Linenfold

Linen press A device for pressing damp linen, consisting of two flat boards, the top one with a spiral screw that "pressed" the boards together. Known as early as the 16th century, they were sometimes mounted on stands, clamped to the top of chests-of-drawers or made as free-standing movable pieces. The term also describes a cabinet or cupboard for storing linen.

Linen smoother A piece of glass with a heavy flat or rounded bottom used as a pressing iron. Known from the Middle Ages, they were made in various styles until the 19th century.

Lines, G. & J. A rocking-horse firm established by George and Joseph Lines in King's Cross, London, in the 1870s. Joseph's four sons had joined the firm by the beginning of the 20th century. In 1918, three of Joseph Lines' sons set up Lines Bros Ltd. Joseph Lines continued with G. and J. Lines until his death in 1931, manufacturing mainly rocking-horses together with a large range of dolls' houses and wooden toys.

Lines Bros Ltd Based in south-east London from 1918, they produced high-quality wooden toys. In the 1920s, they made nursery furniture, dolls' houses, Pedigree prams and children's bicycles. In the 1930s, Lines produced FROG model planes and Penguin plastic kits. Other toys included Peddle cars, trucks, planes, trains, dolls' prams, scooters, pressed steel toy vehicles, construction sets, wooden soldiers, forts and theatres. MINIC (miniature clockwork) tinplate vehicles were introduced in 1935 until the 1950s. Soft toy production began in 1937, Pedigree dolls in 1938 and teddy bears in the 1940s. The factory closed in 1971.

François Linke
display cabinet,
c.1900 [C]

Linke, François (1855–1946) A French cabinet-maker of Czech birth. He became a leading cabinet-maker in Paris in the late 19th century, producing comparatively few, labour-intensive, superb quality COMMODES and cabinets, mostly in the Louis XV revival style, with curving shapes and decorated with ORMOLU mounts.

Linthorpe Pottery Set up by John Harrison in 1879, with the help of Christopher DRESSER until 1882, to make ART POTTERY and alleviate unemployment in Linthorpe, Middlesborough, UK. The factory was built on an old brickworks and red clay was used for the pottery. Dresser was art director and, although not directly involved, he provided distinctive designs, often covered with streaky glazes. The pottery closed in 1889.

Lionel Manufacturing Corporation Founded in New York in 1901 as the Lionel Manufacturing Company, they were America's most famous producer of electric toy trains, particularly noted for their working lineside features such as loading ramps, bridges and stations. All models were electrically powered and many had operating whistles and smoke units. The early sets were tinplate but used diecast locomotive bodies from 1936. The main era was the 1930s with the chief models being in "0" and "S" gauge. The models are exclusively of American outline. Only one set was made in "00" gauges in the late 1930s. In 1930 Lionel also gained control of their main rival, Ives. The company closed in 1969.

Lion mask A motif used from antiquity as an emblem of strength, courage and majesty. The lion mask holding a ring in its mouth for a handle derives from ancient Roman furniture and it continues to be popular as a doorknocker. Both Venetian and FAÇON DE VENISE goblets feature decorative PRUNTS moulded in the lion mask shapes alluding to the symbol of Venice, the lion of St Mark. From the early to mid–18th century, the lion mask enjoyed popularity as a favoured motif for furniture ornament, used as an arm rest support or to decorate a cabriole leg. Occasionally a lion's paw or pelt appears alongside the mask.

Linthorpe pottery
vase, c.1885 [R]

Lion's paw foot A foot carved to resemble the paw of a lion. A popular form for furniture legs – most often on chairs – from the late 17th to early 18th centuries, and again during the Empire and Regency periods.

Lit-en-bateau (French: "boat bed") A free-standing bed with deeply curving open sides that rose and curled over at the head and foot to form a boat shape. Introduced in France in the early 19th century, such beds were often designed to be set against a wall, with luxurious decoration on the exposed side, and elaborate canopies and drapes.

Empire burr-elm
lit-en-bateau,
c.1810 [F]

Lithography (Greek: *lithos* "stone") Developed in Germany by Aloys Senefelder in 1798. The process involves drawing an image with a grease crayon on a highly polished stone. Wherever the lithographic crayon has come into contact with stone, the ink will adhere and print so the printed line imitates a drawn line on paper. Different colours can be used. As a process for decorating ceramics, it was introduced in the late 1840s.

Lithophane A light screen of biscuit porcelain into which relief moulds are pressed creating the "picture". The thicker parts make shadows and the thinner parts the light. They can be framed and hung in windows or included in cup and plate bases. Some were erotic. First made in the 1820s by KPM BERLIN, then by MEISSEN, PARIS and factories in Thuringia and Bohemia, Japan and the UK.

Lithyalin glass Opaque marbled glass designed to resemble hardstones. Invented by Friedrich EGERMANN and patented in 1828, it was widely imitated and used for beakers and scent bottles, often with cut and gilded decoration, throughout the 19th century.

Lion's paw foot

Littler, William (1724–84) An English potter who was apprenticed at 14. At 21 he went into partnership with his brother-in-law Aaron Wedgwood, making STONEWARE. In 1750 Littler became manager of the LONGTON HALL factory, renowned for its brightly painted, moulded porcelain, characteristically adorned with fruit and vegetables. The variable quality of the factory's porcelain contributed to the firm's bankruptcy in 1760. Littler moved to Scotland in 1764, and later opened a porcelain works at West Pans nearly Musselburgh.

Littler's blue The deep cobalt glaze that William LITTLER is credited with having invented c.1750. He applied it to fine stoneware throughout his career.

Liverpool pottery and porcelain factories Throughout the 18th and 19th centuries Liverpool was one of the major centres of production of ceramics, from tin-glazed earthenware, also known as English DELFTWARE, to porcelain.

By 1760 there were 12 factories in Liverpool making blue and white delftware similar to that produced at BRISTOL and LAMBETH. From the early 19th century much of the Liverpool ware was exported to America. These were often adorned with transfer-prints of subjects to suit the American market, or decorated in an unusual range of ENAMEL COLOURS, known as FAZACKERLEY. Notable pottery factories in Liverpool include SADLER & GREEN, Pennington's, which made cream-coloured earthenware

Liverpool porcelain teabowl by Chaffers, c.1758 [N]

and delftware, and Herculaneum (1796–1841) which produced cream-coloured earthenware.

Among the porcelain factories that flourished from the mid-1750s were those of Samuel Gilbody and William Reid. The best known, however, was that

Liverpool pottery teapot by William Reid, c.1756 [G]

of Richard Chaffers, founded in 1756. He made both steatitic (soapstone) and bone ash porcelain to produce teawares in underglaze colours based on those of the FAMILLE ROSE. Upon his death he was succeeded by his partner Philip Christian.

Livery cupboard A free-standing or hanging cupboard, usually with perforated doors for ventilation, used for storing "liveries" (servants' night-time food). First designed after 1625, they were made until the 18th century.

Live steam mechanism The use of steam, generated by a spirit burner, to power a toy through a cylinder and crank linkage. It is mostly seen in replicas of steam-powered engines. Its popularity declined after 1939 with the increase in availability of electric power.

Lloyd Loom furniture Invented by the American Marshall Burns Lloyd, and patented in 1917, this furniture is made from twisted paper strengthened with lengths of metal wire, woven into a "fabric", which in turn is nailed onto a wooden frame. First made in Menominee, Michigan, it has the appearance of wicker because of the way it is woven, but no loom is involved in the process. The material was first marketed as "Art Fibre" because it was not thought anyone would buy furniture advertised as being made of paper. In fact, it is incredibly durable, does not warp or bend and, unlike cane or real wicker, it does not have sharp edges on which to catch your clothes.

The furniture's popularity was helped by a shortage of cane and rattan after World War I. It first became available in Europe in 1922 and was bought readily on both sides of the Atlantic until World War II. Companies attempted to copy Lloyd Loom, but the genuine items can be easily identified with the help of a

Lloyd Loom chair, c.1934 [R]

magnet – only Lloyd Loom used metal wires. Marshall Lloyd sold the rights to make Lloyd Loom furniture in the US to Heywood-Wakefield in 1921; abroad, he sold the rights to several companies including Lusty's in East London, the most successful. Lloyd Loom is a 20th-century success story with over 1,000 different designs produced (one of the most popular models was a pram) and still being made today.

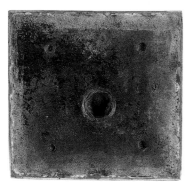

The loaded base of a candlestick

Loading The term for material, usually pitch, resin or plaster, and weights such as lead or iron discs, used to fill hollow, lightly constructed silver articles like candlesticks, which would be too delicate or unstable for practical use. Using silver as filling was expensive.

Lobmeyer, J. & L. A Viennese glassworks founded in 1822 by Josef Lobmeyer (1792–1855). His sons Josef and Ludwig continued the business, adding their initials to the company name in 1856. It produced high quality domestic glass in a variety of styles and techniques including engraved, cut, enamelled and painted. They received many accolades through the rest of the century. In 1902, the firm became a public company and was run by

"Islamic" vase by
J. & L. Lobmeyer, c.1880 [i]

their nephew, Stefan Roth. Under his directorship, they entered the new century, commissioning designs by the VIENNA SECESSION artists Josef HOFFMANN, Dagobert Peche, Otto Prutcher and other members of the WIENER WERKSTÄTTE. J. & L. Lobmeyer was taken over by a chandelier manufacturer in 1972.

Locke, Joseph (1846–1936) An English glass-maker. Born in Worcester, he worked for several English glasshouses. In 1882 he emigrated to the US to work for the NEW ENGLAND GLASS COMPANY in Massachusetts. Here he became a leading designer and developed new types of coloured ART GLASS such as AMBERINA, POMONA and a type of PEACHBLOW.

Locket An oval, circular or heart-shaped pendant opening to reveal compartments suitable for containing hair or miniature paintings or photographs. Often very sentimental, many Georgian examples could only be opened with a tiny key and were inscribed with messages of affection. Larger silver and gold lockets, pinned on broad collars, were popular at the end of the 19th century.

Silver and enamel locket, English c.1900 [s]

Loetz-Witwe Glass A Bohemian glassworks founded by Johann B. Eisner von Eisenstein at Klostermühle, in 1836. In 1851 it was bought by Susanna Gerstner (formerly Witwe), the widow of glass-maker Johann Loetz (1778–1844), and renamed Loetz-Witwe, which was, in

Loetz Art Nouveau vase, c.1900 [J]

time, shortened to Loetz (Lötz). Gerstner's grandson, Max Ritter von Spaun (d.1909), later took charge, leading the company to greater artistic heights. Around 1900, Von Sapun introduced organic-shaped, ART NOUVEAU style iridescent glass vessels in the manner of TIFFANY's FAVRILE glass. The glassworks closed in 1948.

Longcase clock A tall, narrow, free-standing weight-driven clock, introduced *c*.1660. The longcase is composed of a HOOD housing the dial and MOVEMENT, a trunk encasing the weights and pendulum and a plinth base. Cases were usually made by specialist cabinet-makers and thus reflect contemporary furniture styles. Ebony-veneered oak and walnut veneers were popular in the 17th and early 18th centuries, but these were later superseded by mahogany.

Early styles are relatively plain, with square dials and pediment-shaped hoods, but later longcase clocks often feature elaborate scrolled ornament, marquetry, fluting, ball-and-spire finials and arched dials, some of which feature AUTOMATA, and painted or engraved decorative dials. The American equivalent of the longcase clock is the TALLCASE clock. Longcase clocks are also known as GRANDFATHER clocks (and smaller examples as grandmother clocks).

Long Eliza (or *lange lyzen*) From a Dutch term describing tall Chinese ladies on Chinese porcelain, usually in UNDERGLAZE blue. They were copied on DUTCH DELFT and then on delft and English porcelain.

Longton Hall soft-paste porcelain figure of Spring, 1750s [K]

Longton Hall porcelain factory
Founded in 1750 in Staffordshire by William Jenkinson who engaged William LITTLER as manager. The site was excavated in 1955 and great quantities of kiln waste were found with signs of severe kiln failure, so they evidently had initial problems with porcelain-making. However, a wide range of useful wares was made – notably strawberry leaf dishes – with delicate polychrome painting. They also made figures first showing MEISSEN influence and later a strong affinity with BOW. The company went bankrupt and sold off its stock in 1760.

Looking glass See MIRROR.

Looping A type of glass decoration in which looped threads are attached to, and stand vertically proud of, the rim, instead of being applied to the surface, as in TRAILING. Looping was popular for such pieces as sweetmeat dishes.

Loos, Adolf (1870–1933) An Austrian architect and designer. Born in Brunn, Moravia (now Brno, Slovakia), he trained as a bricklayer and then as an architect in Dresden. After a trip to the US (1893–96), he set up his own practice in Vienna. He was opposed to the WIENER WERKSTÄTTE and reacted against the decorative excesses of ART NOUVEAU, both in his writings, such as the 1908 article *Ornament und Verbrechen* ("Ornament and Crime"), and in his simple, unadorned, rectilinear designs for furniture, metalwork and interiors. He created a range of equally minimalist glasses for the Austrian glass manufacturer LOBMEYER.

Adolf Loos clock, c.1902 [K]

Loo table A card table with a circular or oval top supported on a central pillar terminating in three or four feet. The name derives from a card game – called lanterloo or loo – which was first played in the 18th century. The game was highly popular in the mid-19th century when these tables were introduced.

Lopers The sliding rails or runners that are pulled forward to provide support for the opened flap of a BUREAU.

Lorenzl, Josef (fl. *c.*1918–*c.*1939) A prolific Austrian sculptor, who worked in ART DECO style in ivory, bronze and ceramics. His figures usually depict slender dancing girls adopting stylish poses without great detail. Lorenzl bronzes are instantly recognizable, with their long-limbed, slender and androgynous figures, acrobatic or athletic poses and fluid props such as cymbals, tambourines or scarves. They are generally COLD-PAINTED and some have additional coloured decoration to the dresses, signed

"Crejo". His work was issued through GOLDSCHEIDER, for whom he also designed ceramic figures, which are now keenly collected. Bronzes are signed in full or with shortened variations of "Lorenzl".

Lost wax A form of CASTING used for constructing objects of glass or metal such as silver and bronze. A pattern of the article to be reproduced is first made in wax. The wax pattern is encased in a mould, in which holes are left at the top and bottom. The molten glass or metal is poured in through the holes at the top of the mould, instantly melting the wax and forcing it out through the bottom holes. The molten glass or metal now takes the place of the wax in the mould. When the glass or metal sets solid, it forms the desired object.

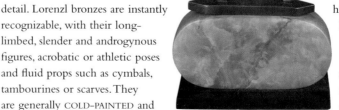

Josef Lorenzl bronze and ivory figure with onyx tambourine, c.1930 [H]

Lotto carpets The name given to a specific design in some Ottoman TURKISH CARPETS of the 16th and 17th century, so named as they appear in paintings by the late Renaissance Italian artist Lorenzo Lotto (*c.*1480–*c.*1556). The pattern is a development of Chinese brocade designs and features stylized yellow vines, leaves and palmettes on a bright red ground. Some may have kufic motifs. Portraits of Henry VIII (1491–1547) show him standing on Lotto carpets. In the 17th century, Spanish carpet-makers based designs on Lotto carpets, featuring a grid of arabesques.

Louis XIV style

The style of decorative arts and architecture fashionable in France during the reign (1643–1715) of Louis XIV, developed directly from the personal tastes and character of the king. Its emphasis on size, symmetry, formality, grandeur and luxury reflected the autocratic nature of his government and the magnificence of his court.

Massive display of strength

From 1661 when Louis began his personal rule, he ordered sumptuous furnishings for the royal palaces, especially Versailles, near Paris, in a unified decorative style from the Manufacture Royale des Meubles de la Couronne (Royal Manufactory of Furnishings) at GOBELINS. It was founded by the king's finance minister Jean-Baptiste Colbert and directed by the painter Charles Le Brun. Le Brun commissioned designs from leading French and foreign artists for furniture, silver, bronzework, HARDSTONES and especially TAPESTRIES, all made to exceptionally high standards. Among the most renowned craftsmen associated with Gobelins were the cabinet-makers Pierre Gole (c.1620-84) and Domenico Cucci (c.1630-1705) and the silversmith Claude Ballin I (c.1615-78).

The palace of Versailles was furnished with luxurious silver furniture and mirrors (as in the magnificent Galerie des Glaces). These furnishings, intended to display royal wealth and power, show the influence of the Italian BAROQUE STYLE with a distinctively French restrained classicism. Furniture was huge, with rich Italian velvet and brocaded upholstery, elaborately carved and gilded mounts and frames, and tall, rectangular padded backs on chairs. Luxury materials beside gilt-bronze mounts abounded, in particular hardstone MOSAICS on cabinets and tables, EBONY VENEER, and imported LACQUER panels. The cabinet-maker André-Charles BOULLE developed BOULLE MARQUETRY in elegant, symmetrical ARABESQUES influenced by the designs of Jean BÉRAIN. For propaganda the king required that symbolic motifs such as the sunburst and head of Apollo (Louis styled himself as the Sun King), the FLEUR-DE-LIS and the king's monogram of two interlaced Ls were liberally applied. Imports from East Asia inspired CHINOISERIE motifs, especially on ceramics.

The Louis XIV style spread through England, the Netherlands, Germany, Switzerland and the English colonies in America after the Revocation of the Edict of Nantes in 1685 forced HUGUENOT Protestant craftsmen to emigrate to avoid religious persecution. With the patronage of Huguenot artists by William III and Mary II in England, Louis XIV therefore had a strong influence on the WILLIAM AND MARY style. Toward the end of Louis XIV's reign, a reaction against the stiff and sombre formality of the style emerged, and the lighter and simpler RÉGENCE style became more popular.

Bureau Mazarin, named after Louis XIV's First Minister, late 17th century [B]

Bracket clock of Boulle marquetry on oak with gilt-bronze figures representing Love Triumphant over Time, c.1700 [E]

Ebony-veneered console table with Boulle marquetry, early 18th century [C]

Recognizing the style

Typical motifs, mainly inspired by Classical art, included large scrolling acanthus leaves, arabesques, putti, caryatids, masks, trophies and allegorical and mythological figures.

Scallop shell

Roman military trophy

Classical head

Louis XV style

This period in France covers the Régence (1715–23), when the king was a minor, and the years after he had attained his majority and ruled independently (1723–74). The Rococo style dominated the century, overlapping with the rather grander Régence at the beginning and the more restrained Neo-classical at the end.

Surface gaiety and liveliness

The fashions of the Louis XV period contrast strongly with the earlier Louis XIV style. Out went magnificence, gravitas and grandeur; in came informality, spontaneity and intimacy. These characteristics are evident in the use of smaller, lighter forms in furniture: tiny delicate feminine work tables replaced massive BUREAU PLATS. New furniture types were developed such as the *bergère*, with a deep seat and enveloping padded back; the *causeuse* and *marquise*, seats for two people; and the *duchesse*, a form of chaise longue with a rounded back, sometimes made in several parts (when it is termed a *duchesse brisée*). Furniture by leading cabinet-makers such as Charles CRESSENT and Jean-François OEBEN is characterized by the use of decorative gilt-bronze mounts, featuring elaborate C- and S-SCROLLS, curling tendril forms and boldly modelled PUTTI, birds and dragons; high legs, elaborate geometric PARQUETRY and MARQUETRY of flowers and ribbonwork; exotic woods such as amaranth and tulipwood; and BOMBÉ fronts and SERPENTINE lines. Some luxury furniture was also embellished with polychrome imitation LACQUER or VERNIS MARTIN panels, often featuring designs of flowers, Chinese-style figures and landscapes, or porcelain plaques. The latter were an expensive novelty, popular when porcelain production in France expanded during the period.

Kingwood work table with elegantly curved legs, c.1770 [H]

While porcelain was produced at MENNECY, CHANTILLY and SAINT-CLOUD, the most important factory was VINCENNES (later SÈVRES). In 1745 the king granted Sèvres a 20-year exclusive privilege to produce SOFT-PASTE PORCELAIN and it was the only French porcelain factory allowed to use gilding and yellow ground colour. The popularity of Sèvres porcelain among European aristocracy was partly the result of the patronage of Madame de Pompadour, the king's mistress. The factory's output included groups of lovers and children – favourite ROCOCO themes – as well as wares decorated with bouquets and sprigs of flowers. Flowers also feature on silks woven at Lyons, tapestries at BEAUVAIS and GOBELINS and carpets at SAVONNERIE. The Rococo emphasis on naturalism is found in silver, too, for example in the realistic fruit, vegetables, birds and animals on tureens and other wares by leading silversmiths Thomas GERMAIN and Juste-Aurèle MEISSONNIER. Mythological scenes and pastoral landscapes featuring idealized shepherds and shepherdesses were other popular Rococo decorative subjects. In the 1750s and 1760s, a reaction against the frivolous Rococo emerged. The NEO-CLASSICAL style was fully developed in France by the end of the king's reign but it is now more associated with the LOUIS XVI period.

Painted commode provincial chair in beech and cane with curved arms and legs and floral decoration, c.1760 [J]

Recognizing the style

Motifs of the Louis XV style were organic rather than classical. Shells, rocaille (resembling rock clefts in a grotto or sparkling splashes of water), scrolling arabesques, leafy tendrils and creepers and sprigs of frothy flowers abounded. Figures in porcelain plaques sometimes punctuated the restless curves of gilt mounts on furniture.

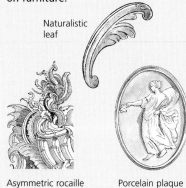

Naturalistic leaf

Asymmetric rocaille   Porcelain plaque

Louis XVI leather tub
armchair, c.1780 [J]

Louis XVI style The French
decorative arts associated with
the reign of Louis XVI (1774–93). The
period was dominated by the popularity
of the NEO-CLASSICAL style, which had
developed in the 1760s, toward the end of
the reign of Louis XV. This was
characterized by restraint and simplicity, as
opposed to the ROCOCO flourishes of the
LOUIS XV STYLE. Geometric forms were
widely employed, for example
ovals and squares for chair
backs and octagons in the
plates of the "Arabesque"
service (1783–87) made by the
SÈVRES porcelain factory.
Classically inspired shapes
such as urns and vases
were also popular in silver
and ceramics. In contrast to the
all-over decoration of the
Louis XV period, ornament
was compartmentalized
in panels, with motifs
derived from
classical art and
architecture, for
example FLUTING,
VITRUVIAN
SCROLLS,
PALMETTES, ANTHEMIONS,
frets, HUSKS and ARABESQUES.

Colours became more subdued and
GRISAILLE, inspired by ancient Roman
frescoes and CAMEOS, was especially
popular, while the light-hearted
decorative themes of the Rococo were
replaced by morally elevating classical
subjects. Nevertheless, the decorative arts
of the Louis XVI period remained
essentially luxury items, particularly
furniture by Martin CARLIN, Jean-Henri
RIESENER and Adam WEISWEILER,
featuring elaborate Neo-classical gilt-
bronze mounts, porcelain panels,
geometric MARQUETRY and a revival of
BOULLE marquetry and PIETRE DURE
INLAY. A more austere version of the style
developed in the 1770s and 1780s, with
simple wood VENEERS and refined forms.
Louis XVI fashions continued even after
the start of the French Revolution in
1789 and the execution of the king in
1793, but evolved into the much more
severe DIRECTOIRE style.

Louis Philippe style The style of
decorative arts dominant in France during
the reign of Louis Philippe (1830–48). It
encompassed a variety of revival styles, in
particular the RENAISSANCE, LOUIS XV
and LOUIS XVI. Their popularity was
largely due to the king's restoration of
French palaces such as Fontainebleau
and Versailles. It is characterized
by massive, solid forms with
profuse ornament, such
as GROTESQUES, foliage
and mythological figures.

Louis revivals Revivals in
the 19th century of the
decorative arts styles
current during the reigns
of LOUIS XV and
LOUIS XVI in the
18th century. The
Louis XV
revival, closely
related to the
ROCOCO style,
re-emerged
during the reign of Louis
Philippe. Some pieces were

Louis XV Revival mantel clock,
19th century [J]

copied directly from surviving 18th
century originals but were more often
loosely imitated to suit the requirements
of comfort and solidity as determined by
the growing middle classes. Forms are
therefore heavier and larger than the
originals, with deep-button upholstery on
furniture and lavish use of gilding,
piercing and carving. The Louis XVI
revival was popular during the SECOND
EMPIRE period and continued into the
early 20th century. While the Louis
revivals began in France, they also became
popular in other parts of Europe and in
the United States.

Love seat The modern term for a type
of wide chair or narrow SETTEE,
introduced in the 18th century. It could
just accommodate two people sitting side
by side. The French equivalent was a small
CANAPÉ known as a *causeuse*. The term
can also describe S-shaped sets
that accommodate two people.

Love spoon A wooden spoon
with a decoratively carved
handle. It originated in Wales
in the 17th century as a gift
from a young man to his
beloved as a token of his
affection. The handles are
commonly carved with
symbols or shapes in relief, or
may be PIERCED or have
FRETWORK ornament.

Love spoon

Low Art Tile Works An American
decorative tile manufacturer established in
Chelsea, Massachusetts, in 1879 by John
Gardner Low (1835–1907). Low
produced a wide range of high-quality,
award-winning glazed tiles, specializing in
dust-pressed, relief-moulded portrait and
scenic tiles with monochrome MAJOLICA
glazes. Most are clearly marked. The firm
operated until c.1902. William H. GRUEBY
worked at the factory and went on to
establish the Grueby Faience and Tile
Company in 1897.

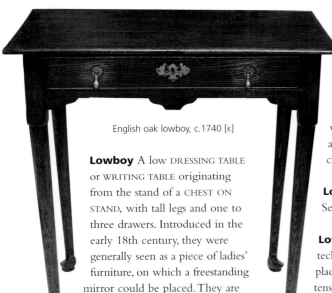

English oak lowboy, c.1740 [k]

Lowboy A low DRESSING TABLE or WRITING TABLE originating from the stand of a CHEST ON STAND, with tall legs and one to three drawers. Introduced in the early 18th century, they were generally seen as a piece of ladies' furniture, on which a freestanding mirror could be placed. They are mostly veneered with walnut, but later examples use mahogany and oak. In America they were often made to match a HIGHBOY.

Löwenfinck, Adam Friedrich von (1714–54). A much travelled porcelain and faience painter who specialized in KAKIEMON-style figures and flowers in a distinctive style. He worked at MEISSEN from 1727–36, then in Ansbach for a short period and from there moved to the BAYREUTH factory. In 1741 he was appointed Court enamel painter in Fulda. From 1746 to 1749 he was technical director at HÖCHST, where he may only have made faience. Later he was director of the faience factory of Hannong in Hagenau from 1749 until his death. His wife and two brothers were all porcelain painters.

Lowestoft porcelain factory Founded in Suffolk in 1757 by four partners, Philip Walker, Obed Aldred, John Richman and Robert Browne. They made a bone ash body resembling that of BOW. At first, they made simple underglaze blue wares in the style of Chinese porcelain; from c.1760 they used coloured decoration. Their blue and white copied WORCESTER. They had a good trade with Holland as well as a local trade for inscribed and dated pieces, including birth tablets, which are unique to Lowestoft. They also made a very few figures of animals and children. The factory closed in 1802.

Low temperature colours See ENAMEL COLOURS.

Low-warp A tapestry-weaving technique in which the loom is placed horizontally, with the tensioning rollers placed front and back. The warp thread is stored on the back roller and the finished tapestry is rolled onto the front roller. The cartoon is placed under the warp threads. This method was used at AUBUSSON and predominated in the Flemish workshops.

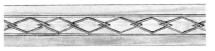

Lozenge

Lozenge A geometric motif most often used in jewelled STRAPWORK, as a DIAPER pattern, or forming the ground for other patterns. In Romanesque ornament its role is similar to the CHEVRON or zigzag, as a moulding enrichment. Heraldry decoration often features the lozenge surrounding the arms of a spinster or widow.

Lucca silk factories Lucca is capital of the Tuscan province of the same name. Although its exact origins are unknown the silk industry was firmly established here by the 12th century. Facilitated by the free trade treaties with Genoa in 1153 and 1166, raw silk, dyes

Lowestoft milk jug and cover, c.1785 [N]

and metal threads from the East were available to the Luccese silk workshops. Controlled by merchants, and sold through agents throughout Europe, Luccese silks appear in the accounts of royal wardrobes, church and papal inventories of 1295 and 1361. The area remained a notable centre of silk production until the late 18th century.

Luce, Jean (1895–1964) A French designer of glass and ceramics in ART DECO style. He exhibited ceramics at the 1925 Paris Exposition. His tableware for HAVILAND has stylized clouds and sunbursts in gold and platinum.

Lück (Lücke), Johann Christoph Ludwig von (c.1703–1780) He began as an ivory sculptor but was a modelling master at MEISSEN in 1728 (dismissed in 1729 because of unsatisfactory work). In 1751 he was in VIENNA as "first master modeller" but soon moved to FÜRSTENBERG. He founded the SCHLESWIG faience factory in 1755. He is recorded in England (1760), Dresden, Danzig and elsewhere.

Luckenbooth A heart-shaped brooch popular in 18th-century Scotland given as a love token or as a protection against the evil eye. Usually made of silver and occasionally gold or metal, they were so-called because they were sold in the small shops or "luckenbooths" clustered round the High Kirk of St Giles in Edinburgh.

Lucotte A Paris-based toy manufacturer that began making hand-painted solid-cast lead soldiers and figures c.1903, mainly depicting First Empire and Revolutionary toy figures. In 1928 the firm was sold to the rival toy soldier company Mignot.

Ludwigsburg pottery and porcelain factory Founded in Württemberg in 1758 by decree of the Duke Karl Eugen of Württemberg, as a "necessary attribute to splendour and dignity". The factory was first set up in a barracks, but was moved to a small castle in 1760. It was under the directorship of J.J. RINGLER until 1802 when he retired. The wares are in MEISSEN style, although the body is smoky and grey-brown in tint. The modellers Johann BEYER and Jean-Jacob Louis produced delightful figures, including a set of miniatures of the stalls and sideshows at the annual Württemberg "Venetian Fair" and figures of dancers of the Court Ballet and musicians. The business closed in 1824.

Ludwigsburg figure, c.1760 [H]

Lund's Bristol See BRISTOL PORCELAIN FACTORY.

Lunette In architecture, a semi-circular or crescent-shaped decorative area, left plain or occasionally ornamented. In 17th-century woodcarving, lunette-shaped ornament was applied in a series to form

Lunette

a band, occasionally filled with ACANTHUS foliage. This device re-emerged in the JACOBEAN REVIVAL. Lunette windows typically feature in architecture of the late 18th and early 19th centuries.

Lunéville A French faience factory founded by Jacques Chambrette (d.1758) in 1731, which produced faience similar to STRASBOURG, NIDERVILLER and SCEAUX. Wares are ROCOCO in style, but with less delicate painting and a less pure white tin glaze. They are indistinguishable from SAINT-CLÉMENT, which was also owned by Chambrette. Lunéville made large figures of lions and dogs to decorate doorways or gardens

and smaller figures in white-bodied earthenware after models by P.L. Cyfflé (1724–1806), who founded his own factory in Lunéville c.1766. When Chambrette died he left his factory to his son Gabriel and his son-in-law who started producing cream-coloured earthenware in the English style. They sold the moulds in the 1780s to Sebastian Keller. Throughout the 19th century earlier models such as the lions and dogs were repeated, with an impressed mark "Lunéville".

Lustre
A PRISMATIC cut glass drop used in candelabra and candlesticks both for decoration and to increase reflected light. It is also used as a general term for such types of candlestick.

Lunéville soup tureen and cover, c.1780 [M]

Lustreware Pottery with a shiny, metallic iridescent surface that is created by painting on a mixture of pigments of metallic oxides, such as gold, silver and copper suspended in oil, and then firing the piece so that the metals form a thin film on the surface (see FAVRILE glass). The metal is deposited on the glazed surface by reduction of the metal from a compound to the pure metal. Some of the metals used are gold, silver, platinum, copper, bismuth and tin. The temperature required is 750°C and good ventilation of the kiln is essential as the pigment is poisonous. Made in

Copper lustreware banded jug, c.1845 [R]

Mesopotamia and Persia as early as the 8th century, lustreware spread through the Near East (Sultanabad, Rayy, Kashan) and then into Spain, thence into Italy (see DERUTA and GUBBIO) in the 15th and 16th centuries. By the 19th century lustreware was being made at numerous potteries in Staffordshire and Sunderland. Production continues today.

Luting The process of joining two parts of a large clay vessel when it is "leather hard" by wetting the seam. Slip or slurry is used for fine clays; coarse clays are more effectively softened with water.

Lynn glass A mid-18th-century English drinking glass or decanter with distinctive bands of horizontal ribbing. The name, first used in the late 19th century, derives from King's Lynn in Norfolk, where such glassware was presumed to have been made.

Lyons potteries Faience was made here in France from c.1520 by Italian workers, to whom are attributed a group of late 16th-century dishes and ewers in ISTORIATO style in the manner of URBINO. Subjects were often derived from wood-block prints in books and bibles published in Lyons. Only one marked piece is known (in the British Museum, London), signed "GTVF/léon" and dated 1582. Known workers at Lyons include Jules Gambin who went on to start the first faience factory in NEVERS with the Conrade brothers in 1588. Later, in 1733, Joseph Combe revived the production of painted faience when he founded a factory with a royal privilege; his wares are similar to those of MOUSTIERS. Several other factories whose wares cannot easily be differentiated were operating in the city in the 18th century. Their specialty was *faiences patronymiques*, i.e. wares painted with saints and inscriptions of names and birth dates.

Lyre clock A SHELF or WALL clock developed in late 18th-century France, the most distinctive element of which is a gridiron PENDULUM with metal rods like the strings of a lyre. The marble or bronze frame, based on the LYRE MOTIF, is often set with GILT-BRONZE mounts, ENAMEL decoration, or paste gemstones. The term also refers to a variant of the BANJO CLOCK developed by Aaron Willard (1757–1844; brother of Simon Willard) in the US.

Lyre clock, French c.1900 [E]

Lyre motif This ancient musical instrument was adopted as a decorative motif for Grecian-style NEO-CLASSICAL ornament. Although the invention of the lyre is usually credited to the god Mercury, the motif mainly appears in decoration as an attribute of Apollo. As the god of song and music, Apollo's lyre frequently features – occasionally with an Apolline mask – in the decorative schemes and furniture of music rooms, e.g. on music stands. Decoration on French and American LYRE CLOCKS from the late 18th to 19th century often reflects Apollo's role as the god of the sun. The lyre was a popular ornamental device for chairbacks from c.1780 to c.1820 and was also used on WRITING TABLES where it alludes to Mercury as inventor of the alphabet.

Lyre motif

M

Macdonald, Margaret (1865–1933) **and Frances** (1874–1921) Scottish designers, sisters and leading members of the GLASGOW SCHOOL. They studied at the Glasgow School of Art, and worked separately and with their husbands, Charles Rennie MACKINTOSH and Herbert McNair. Both worked in various media and Frances taught at the Glasgow School of Art from 1907.

McGill, Donald (1875–1962) An English watercolourist who produced comic pictures for postcards from c.1905. They have been in use from Edwardian times to the present day. Popular subjects are children and the seaside.

Machine knotting Carpet-making by machine, which started at the end of the 18th century with the advent of steam power. This saw the rise of such companies as WILTON and AXMINSTER in England and many comparable firms in other countries for example, Belgium.

McGill postcard, 1920s–30s [S]

McIntire, Samuel (1757–1811) A US architect, woodcarver and sculptor, active in Salem, Massachusetts, from c.1782. He carved chair and sofa rails with baskets of fruit and other devices for Salem cabinet-makers, such as William Lemon, Jacob SANDERSON and Nehemiah Adams.

Macintyre, James & Co. (c.1847–1913) A pottery at Burslem, Staffordshire, producing mainly utility ware, and best known for its links with William MOORCROFT who made ART POTTERY there until setting up his own factory in 1913.

Mackmurdo, Arthur Heygate (1851–1942) An English architect, designer and co-founder of the Century Guild, which aimed to promote unity of design. He travelled to Italy with RUSKIN (1874) and is celebrated for a chair (1882) with a distinctive sinuous back and his title page to *Wren's City Churches* (1883), which both anticipate ART NOUVEAU.

McLaughlin, Mary Louise (1847–1939) A US pioneer of ART POTTERY who began as an amateur china painter in Cincinnatti in 1874. After seeing the CENTENNIAL exposition in 1876 she developed a type of earthenware painted in Barbotine style (underglaze painting in coloured slip). In 1898 she began to make porcelain comparable to LIMOGES. Her "Losanti" range (1900–04) is highly prized today. She also designed for the ROOKWOOD POTTERY.

Madrid tapestries The Real Fábrica de Tapices y Alfombras de S Bárbara, Madrid, was founded in 1720 by Philip V. The Spanish court had previously commissioned Flemish tapestries. Initially woven on LOW-WARP looms, in 1727 a HIGH-WARP weaver was recruited from GOBELINS to improve standards. At first copying earlier Flemish tapestries, the factory went on to commission cartoons from Spanish court painters, mainly scenes of contemporary life. The most notable were by Francesco de Goya, 1776–91. The factory continued into the 20th century, later returning to copying earlier tapestries.

Macintyre vase by William Moorcroft, c.1908 [O]

Charles Rennie Mackintosh (1868–1928)

A Scottish architect, furniture, graphic and textile designer and watercolour artist. He practised architecture at Honeyman and Keppie in Glasgow from 1889 to 1914, becoming a partner in 1901.

A modern designer

Mackintosh was one of the most talented architect/designers of his generation. He was a leader of the GLASGOW SCHOOL style which grew out of the need among some artists, designers and architects, as they approached the new century, to be the masters of their own creations, rather than repeating historical precedents. In this sense there is an allegiance to ART NOUVEAU. He had a unique eye and style, was appreciative of Japanese design and was influenced by the designers of the WIENER WERKSTÄTTE (who in turn were influenced by him).

His two most famous architectural commissions are the Glasgow School of Art, which he won in open competition in 1896/97, and Hill House, family home of publisher Walter Blackie in the prosperous town of Helensburgh, west of Glasgow. For each of these Mackintosh designed detailed integrated interiors.

Another of his patrons was Miss Kate Cranston (1849–1934) who commissioned him on numerous occasions between 1896 and 1917 to design her chain of tea rooms in Glasgow. The second tea room was in Argyle Street and for this he provided furniture: the first of his high-backed chairs with distinctive oval top rail was designed for this interior. Mackintosh went on to design a number of chairs with characteristic high backs. His next project for her was the Ingram Street tea room and for this he was in charge of the whole scheme. This was completed by the autumn of 1900, the same year that he and Margaret MACDONALD were married. The finest and perhaps the most famous tea room was The Willow in Sauchiehall Street. For this Mackintosh redesigned the façade of the mid-Victorian terrace as well as the interior. It also showed the "light-feminine" and "dark-masculine" code that Charles and Margaret had initiated in the design of their home. For example, the ladies' room at the front of the tea room was decorated in silver, white and rose, which contrasted with the main luncheon room decorated in grey and with oak panelling.

From 1905 Mackintosh's workload began to decline and this trend continued until his partnership within the practice ended in 1914. On holiday in Walberswick, Suffolk, he began painting again. From there, he and Margaret went to London and from 1915–23 they produced textile designs for various makers. After this, with one or two exceptions, he concentrated on painting. His watercolours are exceptionally good and show the influence of Post-Impressionism and Fauvism. He visited France several times from 1923 until his death in 1928 from cancer.

Chair for Miss Cranston's tea rooms, Glasgow 1896–97 [A]

Bureau for Miss Cranston's "Blue Bedroom", Nitshill, Glasgow, 1904 [B]

Silver casket commemorating the extension of the Glasgow School of Art by Mackintosh, c.1909 [A]

Magic lantern with slides, c.1880 [R]

Magic lantern Around 1660 the Dutch physicist Christian Huygens made what is regarded as the first magic lantern. The source of illumination for the very early lantern shows was either sunlight or candlelight; later, oil burners were used. The source of illumination was placed in front of a concave mirror that served to concentrate and reflect the light onto the lenses. Although the lanterns were used for educational purposes they were used in the 19th century for popular shows of ghostly apparitions and demons. The birth of moving pictures in 1896 signalled the end of the magic lantern for recreational purposes.

Magot (French: "dwarf") The name for a seated figure of a Chinese "buddha" – a Chinese man with a smiling face and long ear lobes, based on a Chinese figure of Pu-tai Ho-shang. Some were pierced so that the figure could be used as a PASTILLE BURNER; the smoke escaped through the eyes and ears. They were made in porcelain at MEISSEN, CHANTILLY and MENNECY.

Magot

Mahal An area of west Persia where loosely woven carpets were made in the 19th century and are still made today. Designs of various kinds are seen – bold all-over designs in pastel colours are particularly popular. Shades of red, blue and ivory are common background colours.

Mahogany (*Swietenia mahagoni*) A tree native to Central and South America and the West Indies that provides a heavy hardwearing deep reddish-brown timber with a close grain. From 1730, large quantities of mahogany were imported into Europe from Jamaica (Jamaica wood), then from Cuba, San Domingo (Spanish mahogany) and Honduras (known also as baywood). When supplies of WALNUT declined, mahogany became the preferred wood of cabinet-makers, used both in the solid and as a veneer. Its popularity was due to its inherent strength and the width of the boards, which were ideally suited to table leaves made in one piece.

Maiolica In Italy, tin-glazed earthenware was known as "maiolica" due to the importance in the trading network of the island of Majorca (Maiolica in medieval Italian). The term first applied to Hispano-Moresque LUSTREWARES from Spain, then to lustrewares made in Italy from factories including CASTEL DURANTE, FAENZA, FLORENCE, MONTELUPO and VENICE, and eventually included all tin-glazed pottery. Wares can be dated by their colours and motifs used in the decoration. Maiolica has been made from the 13th century and is still produced today.

Faenza maiolica albarello, 16th century [G]

Majolica A corrupted form of the word MAIOLICA, used in the 19th century for a type of earthenware elaborately modelled and covered with thick lead blue, purple-pink, turquoise and yellow glazes. It originated at

Minton majolica nut dish, c.1869 [L]

MINTON in Staffordshire and was first shown at the GREAT EXHIBITION of 1851. In the catalogue there is an illustration of "Messrs. Minton and their excellent Flower Vases coloured after the style of old majolica". It became popular especially for large objects such as jardinières, umbrella stands, garden seats, large fountains and birds and figures. Novelties included large cheese "bells" with grazing cow finials, oyster plates in the form of shells, pie dishes and tureens with quarries of the hunt modelled in relief. Majolica was occasionally termed DELLA ROBBIA ware, FAIENCE or PALISSY ware. From 1850–55 models were designed by CARRIER-BELLEUSE, who later returned to Sèvres. It was made by English factories such as WEDGWOOD, George JONES and T.G. Forester; in France, by Massier Choisy-le-Roi, SAINT-CLÉMENT, Sarreguemines, LUNÉVILLE, also in Germany, Czechoslovakia, Portugal (Caldas), Italy, Sweden and Russia. The American public discovered both English and American majolica at the 1876 Philadelphia CENTENNIAL Exposition and it became popular – and still is.

American majolica makers were Griffen, Smith & Hill of Phoenixville, Pennsylvania – there were eight other factories in the same town, an indication of the ware's high regard. Others making American majolica were James Carr of New York City, George Morley of East Liverpool and Trenton Potteries.

Majorelle, Louis (1859–1926) A French cabinet-maker who trained as a painter before taking over and industrializing his father's (Auguste Majorelle) cabinet-

Majorelle kingwood, mahogany and amaranth cabinet, c.1900 [D]

making business in Nancy in 1879. He was a master of Art Nouveau furniture and also designed metalware. His style is sinuous and fluid, Rococo with a contemporary twist. He was associated with Emile Gallé in the Ecole de Nancy, a society aimed at promoting art in the Lorraine region of France.

Makepeace, John (b.1939) An English furniture designer at the forefront of the British Craft Revival. He set up workshops at Parnham in Dorset, followed by a School for Furniture Craftsmen in 1977.

Maki-e (Japanese: "sprinkled picture") Japanese lacquerwork with a naturalistic, figurative or emblematic design in gold or coloured lacquer on a black, gold or red background. The three main types are the raised *takamaki-e*, the flat *hiramaki-e*, and *togidashi maki-e* where gold or silver dust is sprinkled onto the surface. Commonly found on boxes and inro.

Malachite An ornamental green hardstone with distinctive concentric bands of colour. Malachite was used extensively in the 19th century in items such as candelabra and desk ornaments or smaller pieces including cameos, beads and assorted jewellery.

Málaga potteries The Spanish centre producing lustred Hispano-Moresque ware from the mid-13th century, when they had a flourishing export trade with Egypt, Italy and Sicily, and from 1303 with England. The large "Alhambra" vases may have been made in Granada. Málaga stopped making lustrewares in the early 15th century although it made tin-glazed earthenware until the mid-16th century.

Mallet vase A Chinese vase with a cylindrical body and narrower cylindrical neck, possibly with two handles.

Malling jugs The name given to early delftware jugs from one found in the church of West Malling in Kent. They

have ovoid bodies and cylindrical necks and speckled brown, blue and turquoise glazes. Some have silver mounts. Malling jugs are the earliest tin-glazed earthenware thought to be made in England in the mid-16th century but may in fact come from the Netherlands.

Maltese lace Heavy silk bobbin lace first produced for the Great Exhibition and fashionable until early 20th century. It caan be black or blonde, usually with a Maltese cross and wheatear motif, and inspired by early Genoese laces and later copied in English Bedfordshire lace.

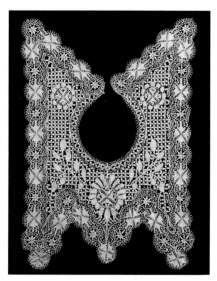

Silk Maltese lace collar, c.1900 [S]

Mamluk carpets Egyptian carpets made from 1250–1517 with dense overall geometric designs usually in green, crimson and white with yellow detailing.

Mamluk pottery The Mamluks were a dynasty in Egypt from 1250–1382 originating from Turkish slaves taken to Egypt. Much of the so-called Mamluk pottery was in fact made in Syria and pottery in the style of Raqqa (Syria) was copied in Egypt. They made lustreware and used sgraffito on a thick heavy body. Some wares were decorated in underglaze blue and black; imitations of Chinese celadon and blue and white ware were made in the 15th century.

Mandarin palette A decorative style on CHINESE EXPORT PORCELAIN in the second half of the 18th century, using FAMILLE ROSE enamels with iron red, gilding and other colours. The designs include Oriental figures in landscapes or gardens, usually set in panels on a Y-diaper, cell DIAPER or UNDERGLAZE blue ground. Staffordshire makers imitated the style in the first half of the 19th century. See also CANTON PORCELAIN.

Mandarin palette: Chinese jardinière, c.1780 [o]

Manganese A mineral used in making STEEL and ALLOYS and also in ceramic manufacture as a stain for GLAZES and BODIES since Egyptian times. In a lead glaze, it gives a rich purple-brown colour, in an alkaline glaze purple or violet manganese mixed with iron gives a rich near-black.

Manierblümen (German: "mannered flowers") A term meaning flowers in a mannered style, used to describe sharply-defined 18th-century flower painting on MEISSEN porcelain.

Mannerist A style of painting, sculpture, architecture and decorative arts developed in Rome and Florence from the 1520s. The style was introduced in painting, sculpture and architecture, for example in the work of Michelangelo (1475–1564) and Giulio Romano (c.1499–1546). It spread throughout Europe during the 16th century, especially after the Italian artists Rosso Fiorentino (1494–1540) and Francesco Primaticcio (1504–70) went to France to supervise the decoration of the chateau of Fontainebleau for Francis I. It was also disseminated through engraved ornament and pattern books. STRAPWORK is the most distinctive ornamental motif, combined with sinuous, exaggerated and twisted figures and three-dimensional representations of fantastical animals, birds

and sea creatures, often grouped in bizarre, and illusionistic compositions. Grotesques, GROTTO ornament such as shells, animal masks and realistic depictions of reptiles were also popular. Such ornament is found particularly in ceramics by Bernard PALISSY and silver by Benvenuto CELLINI and Wenzel Jamnitzer (1508–80). It also features in designs for silver, furniture and tapestries by Romano and other Italian artists, and by French and Flemish artists such as Jacques Androuet Du Cerceau (c.1520–84) and Hans Vredeman de Vries (1527–1604). Cups and ewers of semi-precious stones, NAUTILUS shells and other exotic items were set in elaborate silver-gilt mounts.

An original late version of the Mannerist style, known as the AURICULAR style, which originated with the VAN VIANEN family in the Netherlands in the early 17th century, continued the Mannerist preoccupation with fantastical forms derived from nature in the use of amorphous, fleshy, lobed shapes used to decorate silver and furniture.

Mantel clock A type of clock designed to stand on a shelf or mantelpiece. The term is used to refer to BRACKET CLOCKS, but also to describe some late 18th- and early 19th-century French clocks, often featuring gilt-bronze or marble cases richly embellished with figures, porcelain plaques, and NEO-CLASSICAL motifs. From the 1830s the French mantel clock was often part of a set, including matching urns,

Mantel clock, French c.1870 [L]

candelabra or candlesticks. Wooden and slate mantel clocks were in favour in the late 19th century and reproductions remain popular today.

Manton Bros (John 1752–1834; Joseph 1766–1835) Regarded as among the greatest English gunmakers. Born at Grantham in Lincolnshire, they set up business in London in 1781 and became Gunmakers-in-Ordinary to George III and to the Honourable East India Company. They were known for the manufacture of all types of firearms, but especially fine-quality sporting guns. The development of the English shotgun, decorated austerely but beautifully proportioned and superbly made, owes much to the Manton brothers.

Maple (*Acer campestris*) A species of sycamore that provides a hard, pale yellow-white wood used in furniture-making in Britain and Europe. Also used in MARQUETRY, often stained black to imitate EBONY in the 17th and 18th centuries, and occasionally as a VENEER. Several species of maple are also indigenous to North America and were used in American furniture from the end of the 17th century.

Marbled glass Glass with a swirling multi-coloured surface that resembles marble. Such glass was made in Venice in the 15th–17th centuries (see AGATE GLASS) and was also part of the development of coloured BOHEMIAN GLASS such as LITHYALIN.

Maps

The skills of cartography go back to pre-history and by the 2nd century AD the Greek astronomer Ptolemy was compiling accurate geographical data. As the great age of European exploration progressed, maps became vital tools of knowledge as well as works of art.

New worlds

Cartography – the art and science of making maps – is as old as civilization itself. The ancient Babylonians and Egyptians made maps on clay tablets and sheets of papyrus and the ancient Greeks, notably the 2nd-century astronomer Claudius Ptolemy, laid the foundations of Western cartography. His *Geographia*, published *c.*AD 150, was translated into Latin in the early 15th century, as the great age of European exploration began.

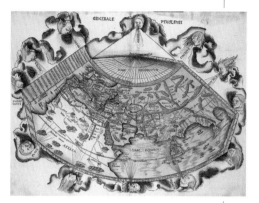

World map with the twelve winds
from Ptolemy's *Geographia*,
this edition 1513 [E]

The 1477 Bologna edition of the *Geographia* was the first printed edition to include maps – 26 of them, all based on Ptolemaic data. In later editions, maps based on the latest discoveries were added; the 1508 edition contained the earliest printed map to show a portion of the New World. This culminated in 1570, with the publication in Antwerp of the *Theatrum Orbis Terrarum* (Theatre of all the Countries of the World) by Abraham ORTELIUS. In 1585 MERCATOR published his landmark *Atlas,* with the projection that is still considered standard today. Perhaps the greatest expression of the Dutch mapmaker's art was the *Atlas Maior* (Grand Atlas) by Johannes BLAEU. Published in various editions between 1658 and 1672, it remains unsurpassed for the magnificence of its design.

Map of Italy from *Theatrum Orbis Terrarum*
by Abraham Ortelius,
1570 [K]

The newly discovered American territories appeared in Dutch maps from *c.*1530, also in the publications of John SPEED, the first Englishman to create a world atlas (in the 1627 edition California appears as an island, a miscalculation later rectified). By the end of the 17th century, the centre of the map world shifted to Paris, and French maps, also of America, were the most scientifically accurate of their day.

Classic maps are prized as historic documents and for the beauty of their engraving. In modern times, maps are still valued as records of changing political boundaries, or the rise and fall of different political regimes. As decorative objects, well-designed maps showing topographical scenes or the joys of tourism (such as a range of 1930s Swiss ski maps on linen) have a perennial appeal, though good condition is critical.

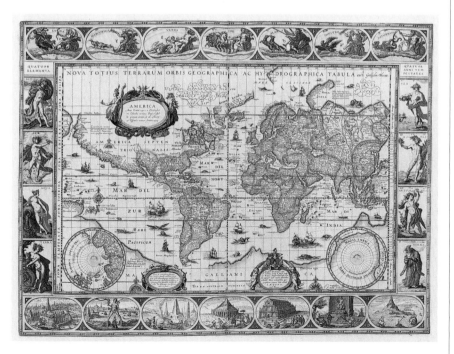

Blaeu's world map from the *Atlantis Appendix*,
incorporating the latest in maritime discoveries
and lavishly decorated, 1630 [D]

Marblehead Pottery A small American ART POTTERY founded in 1905 in Marblehead, Massachusetts, by Dr Herbert J. Hall, and owned by Arthur Eugene Baggs from 1915 until it closed in 1936. It specialized in matt-glazed ware including tiles, garden ornaments and bowls of simple form and decoration.

Marbled beech hall seat, English c.1800 [H]

Marbling A decorative painted colour and veining effect applied to wood in order to make it resemble marble. Used both on woodwork and furniture from the 17th century, it was a popular treatment for the tops of tables and commodes in particular, in the 18th, 19th and 20th centuries.

Marcotte, Leon (*c*.1825–85) A French-born American furniture-maker, interior designer and retailer, active in New York from 1854. His company specialized in the Renaissance and Louis XVI Revival styles manufactured in their New York workshops, but was particularly known for its furniture imported from France. He returned to Paris in 1869.

Marieberg pottery A Swedish FAIENCE and PORCELAIN factory founded in 1758 on an island near Stockholm by Johann Ehrenreich (see KÖNIGSBERG). After initial difficulties with porcelain production, it made faience, producing fine wares, including *trompe l'oeil* pieces, in the prevailing ROCOCO style. The soft-paste porcelain they made until 1777

shows strong French influence. The factory was bought by RÖRSTRAND in 1782 and closed in 1788.

Marinot, Maurice (1882–1960) A French artist who turned to glass-making in 1911, at the works of Viard Fils near Troyes. His sculptural, thick-walled glass with internal or impressed decoration, dates from *c*.1920 to 1937.

Mark, porcelain Marks – impressed, painted, modelled or printed – are applied to ceramics for a number of purposes: (i) factory marks, (ii) artists' signatures, (iii) marks of ownership, or dealer's marks, (iv) indications of date or quality, mould and pattern numbers, (v) workmen's signs. The drawing of the dome of Florence Cathedral, from 1575 to 1587 by the MEDICI factory, is the first use of a factory or maker's mark in modern times. The first regular use of a factory mark was at MEISSEN from 1723. Regular dating of wares was first used at SÈVRES. Adding the name of the country was made law by the US McKinley Act of 1891. See also HALL-MARKS; REIGN MARKS; TOUCH MARKS.

Marcotte ormolu ebonized rosewood sideboard, US, c.1880 [A]

Märklin The most important German factory producing TINPLATE TOYS during the late 19th and early 20th centuries. Gebrüder Märklin (Märklin Brothers) was founded in 1840 by Theodor Friedrich Wilhelm Märklin in Göppingen. In 1859 the company started manufacturing simple clockwork train sets.

Development and expansion made them the market leader by 1900. Model cars, boats and stationary steam engines were also in production by then, as were many smaller working toys designed to be driven by the steam engines. Trains were made in all gauges from "0" to "3", with clockwork and steam being used for the power. Although LITHO-GRAPHY was used by

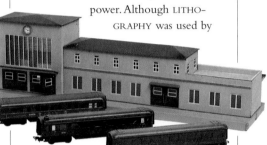

Marklin station and train carriages, 1930s [P]

Märklin, the high-quality finish was often painted onto the tinplate. By 1910 electric trains were also being made and sets were renowned for their wide range of lineside accessories. Stations, engine sheds and signals were all supplied, many being accurate representations of actual buildings, e.g. Stuttgart station.

Foreign lettering was used on the export models. With the build-up of naval power in the early 20th century, large battleships, torpedo boats and submarines were popular and are today some of the scarcest models, due to their frequent submersion in water and subsequent rusting. A wide range of DIECAST cars, buses and military vehicles was on sale by 1939. Production ceased during the war, but resumed afterward, with the company concentrating on a new range of diecast vehicles and extending their railway models. This has been the pattern since and Märklin is still the largest toy manufacturer in Europe.

Marlborough leg An English furniture term of uncertain derivation and used from the mid-18th century. It may have originated as a compliment to George Spencer, fourth Duke of Marlborough, the patron of INCE AND MAYHEW. It refers to a square, normally plain, leg with CHAMFERED edge, usually terminating in a block (square) foot. The Marlborough leg was common on English formal furniture in Chinese taste in the third quarter of the 18th century. In America, and Philadelphia in particular, it gained popularity over the CABRIOLE leg, especially in the work of Thomas AFFLECK.

Marot, Daniel (1663–1752) An influential French architect and designer, who worked for most of his life in Holland and England. The son of a well-known French architect, in 1685 he fled to Holland as a HUGUENOT refugee. Here he was appointed architect to William of Orange, for whom he designed interiors and furniture at Het Loo and Appeldorn. After William ascended the British throne in 1688, Marot also worked at Hampton Court Palace, near London. His distinctive style blended the European BAROQUE and WILLAM AND MARY. His engraved designs *Livres d'Appartements* (published *c*.1700) considerably influenced the design of furniture in the first decades of the 18th century.

Marotte A BISQUE doll's head mounted on a stick, usually in a multicoloured clown-like outfit, housing a music box triggered by turning the stick in rapidly changing clockwise and counter clockwise directions. They were made by Armand MARSEILLE and other leading 19th-century German manufacturers. Versions were also made in CELLULOID in the 1930s-40s.

Marquetry A type of decorative VENEER applied to furniture, made up of a sheet of small pieces of coloured woods and other materials, such as ivory, mother-of-pearl and bone, that were laid out in a pattern and then applied to the carcass. The technique was invented by Dutch cabinet-makers and was introduced to Britain in the 1660s. It took several forms, including floral marquetry (fashionable from *c*.1660–90) and SEAWEED or ARABESQUE (fashionable *c*.1690). It fell out of fashion briefly in the early 18th century in England, but was revived in the 1760s and 1770s. See also PARQUETRY.

Marriage, married A term for a piece of furniture composed of parts that were not originally made together but have been combined later. It is most common with two-piece cased furniture such as bureau-bookcases and dressers, where the upper part may have been lost or damaged and replaced with a contemporary or later equivalent; also common with replacement tops or bases for small tables.

Marriage of unrelated pieces of furniture

Marrow scoop A silver utensil, used for extracting the marrow from cooked bones, first known from the 1690s with a regular spoon bowl at one end and a channelled scoop at the other. This pattern was superseded by the scoop design, made from the early 18th to the 19th centuries, which had a scoop at each end of different sizes.

Marquetry detail on a cylinder fall bureau, c.1900

Marseille, Armand (1865–1940) A famous and prolific maker of BISQUE dolls and dolls' heads, with his son, also Armand Marseille. Marseille was born in Russia but founded a factory, in Thuringia, Germany, in 1885. Large numbers of dolls and dolls' heads were made from 1890 to 1920, with mould numbers 390 and 370 being the most common. In 1924 the DREAM BABY, the most popular doll made by Marseille, went into production, marked with mould numbers 341 and 351 for the OPEN MOUTH doll. These came in many versions, including black and Oriental, and were widely sold in Europe and America. Most of Marseille's wares are marked with the factory's initials or its full name, in conjunction with a mould number. The factory also made CHARACTER dolls and remained in production until the 1930s.

Armand Marseille doll, 1930s [M]

Marrow scoop, c.1765 [Q]

Marseilles green floral
faience plate, c.1760 [K]

Marseilles potteries Based around
Bouches-du-Rhône, France, an important
centre of faience manufacture with many
factories. Production started at St Jean du
Desert, which was worked from 1685 by
Joseph Clerissy. The factory remained in
Clerissy control until 1733 and continued
until 1743. During the next decades, with
the expansion of trade and also export
trade with the French colonies, the
number of factories multiplied. But by
1790 trade declined and in 1809 only one
factory survived. The most important
factories were Joseph Fauchier (1711–95),
Louis Leroy (1741–78), Claud Perrin
(1740–48, continued by his widow until
1793 and then by her son until 1803),
Honoré Savy (1764–82), Antoine
Bonnefoy (1762–93) and Joseph Gaspart
Robert (1750–95). Early products show
the influence of NEVERS and MOUSTIERS
and *style Bérain*.

Marshall, Mark Villars
(d.1912) An English potter,
renowned for his
distinctive, bold work
in stoneware for
DOULTON LAMBETH
and some ART NOUVEAU
pieces.

Martelé (French: "hammer-
wrought") A term used by
the GORHAM MANUFACTURING
CO. for a range of hand-finished

Martelé Art Deco
silver bowl, c.1930 [H]

silver introduced in 1897. Consisting of
HOLLOWWARE with a hammer-marked
surface, it was made from a high-grade
silver standard comparable to BRITANNIA.
See also PLANISHING.

Martin, Fernand France's biggest
manufacturer of tin toys. Martin founded
a factory in 1880 in Paris producing small
AUTOMATA – mechanical figures both
animals and people – from TINPLATE. For
approximately 20 years these amusing
pieces were painted but later were dressed
in "proper" clothes. Many of these items
were re-issued in the 1920s.

Martin, Thomas
(1786–1859) An English
potter and decorator who
served his apprenticeship
at COALPORT and also
worked at factories in
Derby and Pinxton.
Around 1825, he
founded a soft-paste
porcelain factory at
Madeley in
Shropshire.

Martin Brothers
An English family of
STUDIO POTTERS. Robert
Wallace Martin
(1843–1923) was the modeller,
having originally trained as a
stone carver. He opened a small
pottery in Fulham (1873),
moving to Southall (1877) in
partnership with his brothers. Walter
Frazer Martin (1857–1912) was
responsible for the throwing,
coloured glazes and some
of the incised
decoration. Edwin
Martin (1860–1915) was
the chief decorator and was
particularly good at aquatic
subjects and scenes. Charles
Martin (1846–1910) helped
out part-time with the business
affairs. They produced salt-
glazed pottery. The vases had

carved or incised decoration and the
grotesque birds were modelled with
separate heads and superb characterization.
The pottery closed in 1914.

Marvering The process in which
molten glass gathered on the end of an
iron rod is rolled on a polished iron or
marble table either to smooth and shape
it or to acquire or consolidate decoration.

Marx & Co, Louis An American toy
company founded c.1920 and lasting
around 50 years. The first factory in Erie,
Pennsylvania, was joined by ones in
Britain and Japan. By 1950, Marx
was the largest toy
manufacturer in the world.
This success was based on
well-priced TINPLATE
with offset LITHO-
printed (later plastic)
vehicles and other
toys often with
novelty action.
Their trade mark
was MAR on a
large X in a circle.
The company
continued until
1980 as Dunbee
Combex Marx.

Martin Brothers pot,
1906 [I]

Mary Gregory glass
The generic name given to
pieces of coloured glass painted
with white or pink-white
figural designs of Victorian
children, popularly made in the late 19th
century in England, Bohemia and the US.
The name derives from a (probably
fictional) glass decorator at the BOSTON
AND SANDWICH GLASS CO.

Mask A universal
decorative motif
originating in Classical
antiquity, variously
representing the heads of
humans, gods, goddesses,
animals birds or monsters.
Masks were revived

Classical mask

during the RENAISSANCE and feature as popular ornament on NEO-CLASSICAL silver and furniture, frequently with MONOPODIA.

In architecture, masks are either decorative – as ornament, for example, on capitals and keystones – or useful, such as a waterspout.

Mason's Ironstone mug, c.1830 [Q]

Mason, Miles and family See MASON'S PATENT IRONSTONE CHINA.

Masonic emblem A motif that originates from the symbolism and myths of masonic ritual, used for decorating objects belonging to freemasons, as well as to ornament their meeting places. Since the roots of freemasonry derived from the medieval craft guild of the stonemasons, many emblems represent their working tools, such as the drawing board or compass. Masonic emblems are most commonly found on glass and ceramic objects from the late 18th until the early 19th century, including German enamelled beakers, American flasks and English transfer-printed pottery, as well as on furniture used at masonic gatherings. Masonic emblems were often used to symbolize justice and equality.

Masonic emblem

Mason's Patent Ironstone China
Miles Mason (1752–1822) was a dealer in Chinese export porcelain but, when the East India Co. stopped importing Oriental china, he had to look for a new business. After a short but unsuccessful partnership with Thomas Wolfe in Liverpool, which ended in 1800, Mason moved to Staffordshire and in 1802 founded a major porcelain works making hybrid hard paste at Lane Delph. They used both Chinese and English designs and a neat impressed mark "M. MASON", as well as seal marks. In 1813, he passed the business on to his two sons, George and Charles James. It was Charles James who introduced in 1813 the famous "Patent Ironstone China", which is a hard earthenware made by adding ironstone slag to the porcelain mix.

It became popular for dinner services because it was strong and held heat well. It was usually decorated with bold "Oriental" patterns with flowers and birds. Production also included such items as fireplaces and large vases. Charles James was declared bankrupt in 1848 and subsequent Mason patterns and shapes have been produced under many company banners, including George ASHWORTH & BROS., and most recently as Mason's Ironstone under the WEDGWOOD Group since 1973.

Mass production
The manufacture of identical items in large quantities by mechanical methods. The introduction of machine methods, such as die-stamping in silver and press-moulding in glass, during the late 18th and early 19th centuries enabled

Mason's Ironstone vase, c.1820 [I]

manufacturers to meet a growing demand for standardized, inexpensive products, resulting from the increased prosperity of the urban middle classes. Mass production reached its high point with the introduction of the moving assembly line by Henry Ford for the Model T Ford in 1913. However, at the end of the 19th century the subordination of aesthetics to technology, which had become a distinguishing feature of mass-produced items, was challenged by the ARTS AND CRAFTS MOVEMENT, advocating return to hand craftsmanship, and continued in the 20th century by the CRAFTS REVIVAL movement.

Matchbox toys LESNEY registered their Matchbox 1:75 Series in 1953. The toys were small, accurate, sturdy, usually two-piece, castings of road and construction vehicles and were brightly enamelled and packed in boxes designed to look like match-boxes. The range was extremely successful and the range was kept at 75 models with one toy being dropped as a new one was introduced. The Models of Yesteryear range was introduced for collectors in 1956. The quality of the models declined in the 1960s and in 1982 Lesney was taken over by Universal Holdings.

Matchbox toy cars, c.1950–61 [R]

Match holder The part of the MATCHLOCK that held the glowing cord, known as a slow match, which ignited the powder charge. Also known as a serpentine from its curving, sinuous form.

Matchlock The earliest firearm mechanism that allowed a shooter to fire while taking an effective aim. It used a length of cord soaked in saltpetre (slow match), which burnt at a steady rate. The cord was gripped in the MATCH HOLDER, which was attached to the trigger. When the trigger was pressed, the glowing end was lowered into a small pan filled with gunpowder, firing the gun. The matchlock was simple to use and cheap to make. It survived in European warfare from *c*.1470 to *c*.1700.

Matchsafe See VESTA CASE.

Mathews, Arthur Frank (1860–1945) A US painter, architect, interior decorator and furniture designer in Oakland, California. Mathews is considered the founder of the California style of ARTS AND CRAFTS, characterized by a bold use of colour and Californian flora, on furniture and textiles. He founded "The Furniture Shop" (active 1906–1920), making and selling integrated elements of interior decoration.

Matryushka A nest of peasant dolls made in Russia. All the dolls are skilfully lathe-turned and neatly fit into each other. The set usually contains seven dolls, with a tiny solid one in the middle.

Matting A decorative technique producing a matt surface on silver. The effect is created by using small hammers or punches to form a pattern of densely packed dots or indentations. Matting is commonly found on drinking vessels as the textured surface make the drinker's grip more secure.

Mauchline ware Distinctive wooden SOUVENIR WARE including boxes and small household goods usually made from SYCAMORE with printed transfers, most often showing a view, decorating the surface. Taking its name from Mauchline in Ayrshire, Scotland, and made primarily by J. J. Smith from the 1820s, production was halted in 1933 when the box factory burned down.

Mazarin or mazareen blue An English name for an intense dark blue. Said to be inspired by Cardinal Mazarin (d.1661), the term was first used to denote a deep blue in 1686 and a material of the same colour in 1694. It was introduced at CHELSEA *c*.1755 and other factories later to imitate the *gros bleu* of VINCENNES and SÈVRES. It later described a blue garment worn by Common Councilmen in London.

Mazarine Generally refers to 18th-century pierced silver and Old SHEFFIELD stands. Oval in outline, mazarines sat within the border of silver serving dishes to support the fish or meat and allow the juices to strain through to the well below.

Mazer bowl A drinking bowl of turned hardwood, usually MAPLE, with gold, silver or SILVER-GILT mounts around the rim and base or foot and sometimes a decorative disc or boss in the centre of the bowl. Mazers survive in fairly large numbers from the 14th century but HALLMARKED silver ones are rare.

Maple mazer bowl, English 14th century [H]

Mean time Time as indicated on a clock running at an even rate throughout the year, divided into hours, minutes and seconds of equal length. Mean time is not equivalent to solar time – time as indicated by the movement of the sun's shadow on a sundial – because the apparent motion of the sun as seen from Earth varies, owing to the Earth's elliptical orbit around it and the inclination of its axis. The length of the mean day and solar day coincide only four times a year. In the late 17th and 18th centuries some clockmakers developed equation clocks, which recorded the variation between mean time and solar time.

Measham ware See BARGE WARE.

Meccano showman's engine with electric motor and steerable wheels, c.1934 [o]

Meccano "Mechanics Made Easy", a constructional toy invented by Frank HORNBY in 1901, changed its name to Meccano and was launched in 1907. Sets consisted mainly of metal strips and plates held together by nuts and bolts. Various special parts were introduced to enable more and more complicated models to be assembled. Clockwork, electric and even steam engines were also provided. The educational value of this toy was a strong marketing feature. Constructional sets for cars and aeroplanes were made in the 1930s. The British factory closed in 1979.

Mechanical bank An American SAVINGS BANK with moving parts and springs triggered by a coin to perform humorous feats, popular in the late 19th century.

Mechlin Fine quality 18th-century FLEMISH BOBBIN LACE having distinctive silk threads defining the designs.

mark of six circles with the initials FMMDE II for Francisco Medici magnus Dux, Etruriae II is known.

Meeks, Joseph and Sons A large and important American furniture-maker established in New York City in 1797 and active until 1868. The firm began making formal furniture in the FEDERAL period, but is best known for the exuberant and large-scale furniture produced in the second quarter of the century in late American EMPIRE STYLE. Parlour furniture comparable to the work of John Henry BELTER was made after 1850.

Gothic Revival mahogany marble-top centre table by Joseph Meeks, c.1830 [D]

Meerschaum (German "sea spray") A hard, white clay from Asia Minor and North America used primarily for making pipes for smoking tobacco. The raw clay was cleaned and dried and formed into pipes in a huge variety of novelty and figurative shapes, most commonly characterful heads. With use, the clay part of the pipe takes on tones ranging from gold to dark brown.

Meigh pottery (also called Old Hall) A family-run Staffordshire pottery, based at Hanley, which made good-quality EARTHENWARE. Founded in c.1770 by Job Meigh and joined by his sons 1805–34. One son, Charles, ran the factory 1835–49, adding

Stoneware Meigh vase with relief decoration, 1852 [R]

Medici glass Glassware made from the 16th to the 18th century at the various glasshouses established in and near Florence by the Medici family. In the 16th century, Cosimo I de' Medici (1519–74), a major patron of the arts, invited VENETIAN glass-makers and notable painters and engravers to develop glass designs. From the 17th century production included medical and scientific instruments as well as elaborate and ingenious drinking glasses, dishes, TAZZE and EWERS, often marked with the family or papal coat of arms.

Medici porcelain In the 16th century, the Grand Duke Francesco Maria I of Florence was the wealthy patron of a porcelain factory in the city (the first in Europe from which examples still survive). Production probably continued from c.1575 to c.1587. They produced a form of SOFT-PASTE PORCELAIN in which the BODY resembled glass in texture with a white tin glaze painted in UNDERGLAZE blue in Chinese style. But they experienced heavy kiln failures and, although work continued during the reigns of the next two Medici Grand Dukes, only 30 or so pieces have survived. Most are in museums round the world. They have as a mark the dome of the Cathedral of Florence with the initial F. One

Gothic Revival stoneware to the repertoire at the Old Hall Works. The firm was called C. Meigh & Son & Pankhurst 1850–51; Charles Meigh & Son 1851–61; Old Hall Earthenware Co Ltd 1861–86 and the Old Hall Porcelain Works Ltd 1886–1902, when it closed. Charles won a medal at the GREAT EXHIBITION for two stoneware gilt vases painted with royal portraits and views of Crystal Palace. Another branch, W. & R. Meigh, were at Stoke, 1894–99.

Meiji period (Japanese: "enlightened government") The historical period from 1868 to 1912. After world isolation during the Edo period (1600–1868), the Meiji emperor was restored to power and Japan was opened up to the Western world. The arts and crafts were encouraged. LACQUER wares, metalwares, ENAMELS and CERAMICS were shown to great acclaim and influence at international exhibitions. See also KINKOZAN; KUTANI and SATSUMA POTTERIES.

Imari-style baluster-form vase, Meiji period, c.1870 [J]

Meiping (Chinese: "prunus branch") A classic Chinese vase shape with a short narrow neck and bulbous shoulders tapering toward the base. Made from the SONG DYNASTY (960–1279 AD) onward and intended to hold a single branch of prunus blossom.

Chinese export Meiping vase depicting phoenix amid prunus and magnolia, c.1760 [C]

Plate from the "Swan Service", one of over 2,000 pieces made for the marriage of Meissen's director, Count von Brühl, 1738–41 [c]

Oval dish from the period under Count Camillo Marcolini, c.1790 [p]

A typical late 19th-century group, showing a vignette of pastoral life, c.1880 [j]

Meissen porcelain factory

The first European porcelain factory, unsurpassed throughout the 18th century in technical innovation and artistic skill. The Meissen designers and craftsmen were the originators of fashion and design which later factories copied extensively.

A model of style

Meissen was the first factory in Europe to make "real" or hard-paste porcelain. Many attempts had been made since Chinese porcelain had been exported to Europe, all unsuccessful. But on 23 January 1710 the first European porcelain factory was founded by royal decree in Dresden, Saxony, as a result of the work of the alchemist Johann Friedrich Böttger and the court chemist Count E. Tschirnhaus. Three months later, the factory was moved to the Albrechtsburg Castle in Meissen, near Dresden. There was a board of directors, but Böttger organized the workshop. During the 1710–1719 period they made a highfired red stoneware (cut by Bohemian glass cutters), imitating Oriental stoneware.

By 1719, when Böttger died, a slightly yellowish porcelain was produced. In that year J.G. HÖROLDT was appointed as director and he developed Meissen porcelain to hitherto undreamed of heights. The new source of KAOLIN at nearby Aue gave a pure white body and Höroldt's brilliance as a colour technician produced wonderful ground colours. Höroldt himself painted some pieces, as well as producing drawings for the other painters in the factory to copy. Augustus the Strong, Elector of Saxony, was an obsessive collector of oriental porcelain, so not only did the factory have a ready "reference library" but a knowledgeable and encouraging patron, a role that Augustus fulfilled until his death in 1733. In the early years, the main influence was oriental and the senior painters were Adam Friedrich von LÖWENFINCK, Johann Ehrenfried Stadler and Johann Gottfried Klinger, whose painting of insects and flowers included the popular DEUTSCHE BLUMEN or "German Flowers". Figure production started with the arrival of

Oval sugar box and cover, painted with marine scene, c.1725 [d]

Meissen's marks

Meissen's marks were much copied elsewhere, particularly the AR monogram intended only for wares made for Augustus the Strong. The crossed swords can be found on Derby and Minton as well as ware from Dresden factories.

Augustus Rex monogram

Dot period 1763–74

Marcolini period 1774–83

Biscuit ware after c.1780

Silver-mounted pot and cover painted in Kakiemon style, c.1735 [H]

Johann Joachim KÄNDLER in 1731, who was to be the most important single artist at the Meissen factory during his working life there of 44 years.

In order to understand the tremendous impact of the Meissen factory on fashion it is necessary to understand the customs of the 18th-century courts of Europe, with their rituals of dressing in rich and jewelled clothes, hunting, gossiping, gambling, and eating and drinking – all done to excess and with the purpose of outshining rivals. Since the 16th century it had been the custom of the aristocracy to decorate dining tables with silver and gold and also with elaborate "spun sugar" figures or animals in landscapes. When fine porcelain services were made, porcelain figures took the place of the spun sugar confections. So Count Brühl's famous "Swan Service" of over 2,000 pieces had, among that number, many models of swans, herons, and water nymphs, illustrating the theme of the service. Kändler modelled figures and groups of the most widely divergent styles – COMMEDIA DELL'ARTE and CHINOISERIE figures, figures in national dress, shepherds and shepherdesses, satirical groups, saints and other religious characters and the well-known MONKEY BAND. Such large-scale productions were often made as presents to the crowned heads of Europe; smaller items included SNUFF-BOXES, ETUIS, thimbles and cane handles.

Later history

The Meissen factory flourished up to 1756, opening up markets with Turkey and Russia. But by this time they were beginning to experience competition from other porcelain factories. During the Seven Years War (1756–63) Saxony was overrun by Prussia and the Meissen factory fell into the hands of Frederick the Great. Frederick had been jealous of Meissen for years and he took many of the best workmen to his own factory in BERLIN. However, Kändler remained at Meissen. When the war ended the factory was reorganized and production resumed. To adapt to changing fashion, a French sculptor, Michel-Victor ACIER, joined the factory in 1764 and an art school was set up within the factory – hence it became known as the Academic Period (1764–74). In 1774 Count Camillo Marcolini became director, and the factory began its so-called Marcolini Period (1774–83), with pieces marked with a six-pointed star placed between the hilts of the swords. By the 1814–33 period the factory was producing wares in the then popular NEO-CLASSICAL style. From 1833 to 1870 the director of the factory was Heinrich Gottlob Kühn and Meissen produced porcelain copies of famous paintings in the Dresden galleries and copied earlier figures and styles.

Export to America increased steadily in the late 19th century – the perfection of Meissen's PÂTE SUR PÂTE technique showed that the factory could still produce high-quality wares. ART NOUVEAU wares, produced from the 1890s, included plates by the Belgian designer Henry VAN DE VELDE, and figures of dancers and musicians by Paul Scheurich. Since 1945 the factory has been styled VEB (Staatliche Porzellan-Manufaktur Meissen) but it continues to use the famous crossed-swords mark. The modern Meissen factory still produces models of Kändler figures.

Modellers and painters

Decorative styles inspired by the Orient are seen in work of the 18th-century decorators such as Adam Friedrich von Löwenfinck and Johann Gregor Höroldt, who developed a new palette of bright enamel colours. The work of Johann Joachim Kändler brought figure making into a totally new dimension and was widely copied. Meissen produced some Art Nouveau ware by Julius Konrad Hentschel in the 1890s and by Henry van de Velde in the early 1900s. In the 1920s and 30s, Paul Scheurich produced mannered figure groups.

Plate from the Earl of Jersey service, painted with an oriental scene in the Löwenfinck style, c.1740 [E]

Plate by the Belgian Art Nouveau designer, Henry van de Velde, 1903 [M]

Melchior, Johann Peter (1742–1825) A German porcelain modeller, born in Lintorf near Düsseldorf and apprenticed to sculptors in Düsseldorf and Aachen. He became master modeller at the HÖCHST porcelain factory in 1767 where he was also court sculptor. He moved to the FRANKENTHAL factory in 1779 and stayed until 1793, and was then master modeller at NYMPHENBURG from 1797 to 1822.

Memento mori (Latin: "remember you must die") Memento mori jewellery was a reminder to make the best of your time on Earth and prepare yourself for the inevitability of death. From the 17th century through to the 19th, gold rings, brooches and lockets contained symbols of mortality such as skulls, urns and coffins, possibly with an inscription.

Diamond, enamel and gold memento mori ring with urn, 1810 [G]

Memorabilia An item that is linked to a famous person, event, place or activity, not necessarily of instrinsic value or interest itself, which becomes more desirable and valuable due to its links with that background. ROCK AND POP memorabilia is one of the most recognized forms, but SPORTING memorabilia is also highly regarded. Items of memorabilia can include paper EPHEMERA, photographs, personal items, COMMEMORATIVE WARES and autographs.

Memphis An Italian design group founded in 1981 by an international group of architects and designers led by Ettore SOTSASS, to design and make furniture, lighting and other domestic wares of a highly decorative and colourful nature. Their work and aims were in complete contrast to the sterility of MODERNISM, as they saw it, and are part of the POST-MODERN movement.

Mennecy porcelain factory François Barbin founded a factory in Paris in 1734 and was later given permission by the Duc de Villeroy to build a factory on his estate at Mennecy, c.1748. They made a creamy soft-paste porcelain, painted in enamel colours with bright floral designs. The early figures include some chaming groups of children, also some finely modelled biscuit porcelain COMMEDIA DELL'ARTE figures. The factory also produced domestic ware and small items such as knife-handles. The marks are a D.V., sometimes with a ducal coronet. In 1773 the factory transferred to Bourg-la-Reine and from 1780 largely made earthenware. The factory closed in 1806.

Mennecy snuff box, c.1750 [J]

Menu holder Sometimes known as place card holders, these small stands of silver and allied materials were made in sets to sit on tables either to indicate where each diner was to sit or to hold a menu card. Popular from c.1890 to c.1920, they were often decorated with enamel or engraved scenes depicting themes such as hunting or fishing.

Menuisier A French term for a joiner. Until the Revolution in 1789 there was a distinction in status between the *menuisier*, who specialized in small pieces of furniture constructed from plain wood and then carved, and the ÉBÉNISTE, who specialized in veneered pieces. The distinction was introduced in the mid-17th century, formalized in the mid-18th and lasted until the guild system was abolished with the Revolution.

Mercator, Gerard (1512–94) A major Flemish cartographer, second only to PTOLEMY, Mercator had a profound influence on both the art and science of map-making. Although he did not invent the projection (a way of representing a sphere on a flat surface) that bears his name, he applied it in navigational charts and in his 18-sheet world map of 1569. Mercator also produced maps of Europe and Britain (now extremely rare) and the maps for the 1578 Cologne edition of Ptolemy's *Geographia*. His best known work is his *Atlas* (the first compilation of maps to bear that title), published between 1585 and 1595, and revised and reissued many times by the Dutch cartographic firms of Hondius and later Jansson.

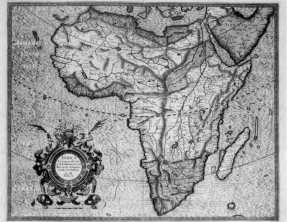

Mercator map of Africa [J]

Mercury gilding The technique of applying gilt to metals and later ceramics. An amalgam of gold and mercury is applied to the object, which is fired in a low-temperature kiln so that the mercury is driven off. The process usually has to be repeated several times until the layer of gold is thick enough. Mercury gilding was known in ancient China (4th century BC) and spread to the west from there, reaching its apogee in late 17th-century Paris with the work of such craftsmen as BOULLE and Jacques Caffieri (1673–1755). See also FIRE GILDING.

Mercury twist stem A type of mid-18th century drinking glass with a stem made with two skilfully-twisted TEARS that refract light and therefore have a silvery, mercury-like appearance.

Merryman plates A set of six DELFT plates, inspired by a Dutch potter, John van Hamme, made in both England and Holland. Each was painted in blue with one line of a verse: "What is a Merry Man/Let him do what he can/To entertain his guests/with wine and merry jests/But when his wife do frown/All merriment goes down". Made from the late 17th century to the early 18th, they were copied in the 19th and 20th centuries.

Merrythought An English toy factory founded in 1930 by W. G. Holmes and G. H. Laxton in Ironbridge, Shropshire, and still going. They made bears in fine MOHAIR and also unjointed "bear cubs". The company's best known products are the Bingie bear and the Cheeky bear with bells in its ears.

Merrythought mohair teddy bear, c.1930 [o]

Metal A term often used virtually interchangeably with glass to describe the molten or fused ingredients from which glass is made.

Mercury twist stem on cordial glass, English c.1745 [J]

Metal fatigue The breaking or weakening of any metal due to fluctuating stresses within it. For example, the repeated bending of a silver spoon may eventually cause it to break. Cast metals are particularly susceptible to fatigue.

Metal head dolls Popular from c.1880 to c.1920 as a lighter and stronger alternative to BISQUE. Most were made in Germany by companies such as Joseph Schön, Büschow and Beck, Minerva and Juno.

Metamorphic furniture Furniture that is designed to change in form and/or function, often incorporating space-saving features – for example, chairs and tables that convert into LIBRARY STEPS. Introduced in the early 18th century, such pieces have remained popular ever since.

Mettlach pottery A German glazed-earthenware factory founded in 1809 by Jean-François Boch, notable for its images of rural life in medieval and Renaissance Germany and its ART DECO wares. Boch also owned a second factory at Septfontaines in Luxembourg. The Boch factories were united in 1836 with those of the Villeroy family. The joint firm, VILLEROY & BOCH, acquired a number of other factories but lost those in East Germany after World War II. The factory at Mettlach is still in production.

Mettoy Co. Ltd An English toymaking company founded by Philip Ullmann in Northampton, in 1933. The main products were lithographed TINPLATE vehicles. Dolls' houses, stoves and more general toys followed by 1941. DIECAST models first appeared in 1948 followed by a brief run of some plastic vehicles. The company concentrated on their new CORGI range of diecast vehicles from 1956, all other production ceasing in 1958. The company closed in 1983.

Mezzotint (Italian: "half-tint") A technique, discovered c.1650, that enabled printmakers to achieve a greater tonal range. The metal printing plate is uniformly pitted with a tool called a roulette or rocker so that the rough parts hold the ink while lighter areas can be produced using a burnishing tool that smoothes parts of the plate.

Mezzotint from a painting by Van Huysum, English 1778 [J]

Micromosaic See MOSAIC JEWELLERY.

Microscope An instrument, made from the 17th century, for viewing tiny objects. Early examples were often constructed from wood, pasteboard and vellum. In the 18th century ivory and brass were used, and in the 19th century brass was the only material. The best lenses were Dutch. English makers include John Marshall (1663–1725), Edmund Culpeper (1660–1730), George ADAMS (1704–72) and John Cuff (1708–1772).

Microscope by Swift & Sons, English c.1900 [M]

Mies van der Rohe, Ludwig

(1886–1969) A German architect and designer of major importance to the MODERN MOVEMENT and the International Style of architecture. In his early years as an architect he worked for Peter BEHRENS and took over the directorship of the BAUHAUS in 1930. He is known for his tubular steel cantilevered furniture, especially chairs, made by the firm of Berliner Metallgewerbe from 1927 to 1931. These are considered modern classics, as are the BARCELONA CHAIR of 1929 and the Brno chair of 1930. He emigrated to America in 1937 and became head of the Chicago School of Architecture in 1938.

Mies van der Rohe tubular steel chair, c.1927 [K]

Mihrab In Islamic architecture, a niche, or an indication of a niche, in the wall of a mosque facing Mecca; a stylized version is the central motif on Oriental PRAYER RUGS. The design is also used on Islamic TILE decoration.

Milan pottery and porcelain factories

From the mid-18th century, three small potteries in Milan produced wares influenced by forms of silver, Chinese and Japanese porcelain and French FAIENCE. The last of these closed c.1830. In 1833 a porcelain and faience factory was founded by Luigi Tinelli. Among other wares they made copies of WEDGWOOD. In 1841, Luigi's brother

Carlo, who had taken over management of the factory, went into partnership with Giulio Richard from Turin. Under their management, wares with printed patterns and cream-coloured EARTHENWARE were made. In 1870 Richard became sole owner and in 1873 renamed the factory Società Ceramica Richard. In 1896 his son, August, expanded the factory and absorbed the Ginori factory at DOCCIA, becoming Richard-Ginori. It remains a leading manufacturer of Italian ceramics.

Milchglass See MILK GLASS.

Mildner glass Glass decorated with ZWISCHENGOLDGLAS medallion-shaped panels on the sides and sometimes the base. The name derives from Johann Joseph Mildner (1763–1808), the Austrian glassmaker who developed the technique and used it for beakers or tumblers from c.1787 until 1808.

Military furniture

See CAMPAIGN FURNITURE.

Milk glass An opaque white glass that resembles white porcelain. Developed in Venice in the late 15th century, it was popular during the 17th and 18th centuries, when it was made in France (as *blanc-de-lait*), Germany (*milchglas*) and Britain, and was often decorated with CHINOISERIE enamelling and gilding.

Millefiori (Italian: "thousand flowers") Glass decorated with slices of coloured CANES embedded in clear glass. Although used in Roman glass, the technique is now largely associated with decorative pieces such as HAND COOLERS and PERFUME BOTTLES and, since the mid-19th century, with PAPERWEIGHTS.

Early Ming bowl, 1426–35 [C]

Ming dynasty The imperial dynasty that ruled China from 1368 to the beginning of the Qing period in 1644. In this period, trade between China and Western Asia and Europe expanded significantly, as did the production of CHINESE EXPORT PORCELAIN and that of textiles, jade, ivory and lacquerware. The Ming dynasty is associated with the manufacture of porcelain of exceptional quality, particularly in JINGDEZHEN in the province of Jiangxi in southern China. The BLUE AND WHITE wares, characterized by a light, thin body and glassy glaze, produced during the CHENGHUA PERIOD (1465–87) are regarded as some of the finest ever made. Motifs such as dragons, phoenixes and landscape scenes are typical. The DOUCAI and WUCAI polychrome OVERGLAZE enamel techniques were also introduced in this period, as was KRAAK porcelain. These wares reached Europe in large quantities from the reign of the Ming emperor Wanli (1573-1619).

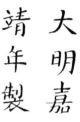

大明嘉靖年製

Ming (Jiajing) reign mark (1522–66)

Mint condition A term deriving from coinage, describing a piece in original condition, either unused or showing no signs of wear. Usually, a piece in "mint" condition is more valuable than a used one.

Millefiori vase, English c.1900 [S]

Miniatures

Finely made objects in miniature have exerted a fascination throughout history, both as replicas and works of art in their own right. Dolls' house and "apprentice" furniture record a bygone age. Portrait miniatures may depict a historic personage or a loved one.

Portrait miniature of a mother and child,
in watercolour on ivory,
Central European c.1780 [L]

Small worlds

The term "miniature" on its own usually refers to paintings up to a few inches across, developed from illuminated manuscript work and popular from the 16th century onwards. Usually painted on a vellum, metal or ivory support, these portraits, often of loved ones, were incorporated into jewellery, watches or other items carried on the person, such as SNUFF-BOXES, sometimes hidden underneath a false cover. Among the best known miniature painters, whose work is often characterized by exquisite detail and rich, jewel-like colours, were Hans Holbein and Jean and François Clouet in the early 16th century, Nicholas Hilliard – noted for his portraits of Elizabeth I – in the Elizabethan period, and Isaac Oliver and Samuel Cooper in the early 17th century. The period around 1790 is often regarded as the peak of British miniature painting, with many noted practitioners, including Richard Cosway and George Engleheart. Miniature painted portraits remained popular, especially on sentimental jewellery, in the late 18th and early 19th centuries, but were gradually replaced by photographs from the 1850s.

Bow miniature soft-paste porcelain service,
c.1765 (K), and miniature tip-top
tripod table, 1780–1810 (L)

Perhaps better known as "miniatures" today are the often minutely detailed items intended as toys for children. Among these are the furnishings produced for DOLLS' HOUSES, mass-produced in Germany, Britain and the United States from the mid-19th century. Well-known firms, such as ROCK & GRÄNER and SCHNEEGAS & SONS in Germany, J. Bubb and Evans & Cartwright in Britain, and Rufus Bliss and the McLoughlin Brothers in the US created houses with exact miniature furnishings in the most fashionable styles, often incorporating servants' quarters and tiny versions of the most desirable consumer goods and equipment. Sets of miniature furniture were also made to be sold separately. Other toys that can be classified as miniatures include TIN-PLATE figures, boats, TRAINS, racing cars, and airships made by such firms as MÄRKLIN.

By no means all miniaturized artifacts were made for children. Before the age of mass production, miniature furniture was made by apprentice cabinet-makers as part of their training. These "apprentice pieces", made from the 17th to the early 19th centuries, are now highly sought after, as is the miniature furniture made as samples or novelty gifts for travelling salesmen to advertise their full-size wares, or used in a shop front to attract custom. Other similar miniatures of note include musical instruments, such as violins, and sets of pottery and porcelain, the latter made in considerable quantities from the 17th to the 19th centuries, by factories such as CAUGHLEY, MASON'S and SPODE, as well as by Chinese potters for export to Europe. As small-scale portable versions of larger designs, CARRIAGE CLOCKS can also be classified as miniatures.

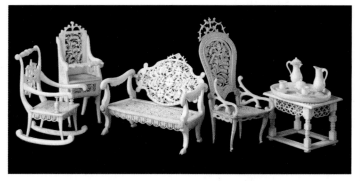

Miniature furniture, including a coffee service
on a tray, work table and rocking chair,
made of bone, English c.1800 [L]

Highly ornamental, elaborately modelled majolica candlestick, c.1859 [N]

Moon flask with imitation cloisonné decoration, typical of Minton's Oriental style from 1860 onward, c.1880 [O]

Secessionist ware jug designed by Wadsworth & Solon, typical of the tube-lined wares in Minton's Art Nouveau style, c.1900 [O]

Minton porcelain

Of all the English porcelain produced in the 18th and 19th centuries, that made by Minton is undoubtedly among the finest. Although many of Minton's products were inspired by other, earlier wares, they are not cheap imitations. The quality is extremely high, rivalling Sèvres or Meissen.

A great name in British ceramics

Thomas Minton (1765–1836) trained as an engraver at CAUGHLEY, where he developed the WILLOW PATTERN. He founded a ceramic factory in Stoke-on-Trent in 1796, initially producing EARTHENWARE in underglaze blue. From 1798 the factory also made SOFT-PASTE PORCELAIN tableware and elaborately decorated romantic figures, often copied directly from MEISSEN pieces. In the 1820s it started to produce useful wares and decorative pieces in BONE CHINA.

By the time Thomas Minton died, his firm had become one of the leading ceramics factories in England. Under the direction of his son, Herbert, Minton began to produce hard-paste porcelain of the very finest quality. No expense was spared to ensure that the porcelain was flawless, the glaze clear and smooth, and the decoration second to none. Their copies of fine pieces from the 18th century were particularly successful. Indeed, such was the quality of Minton's work, Sèvres were willing to supply them with casts from their own old moulds. In 1849, Léon Arnoux, a ceramicist from Sèvres, became art director at Minton, bringing other French artists with him. Among his innovations was the development of MAJOLICA in the RENAISSANCE style, for all kinds of objects from dishes to garden ornaments. Some of this was shown at the 1851 GREAT EXHIBITION in London, alongside large Sèvres-style vases. Around this time Minton were also making figures and busts in PARIAN, often copying work by the major sculptors of the day. After Herbert's death in 1858, the firm continued as Herbert Minton & Co. until 1883 and thereafter as Mintons Ltd. From the 1860s the company was greatly influenced by Oriental decoration, producing cloisonné-style vases and other wares. In 1870 Marc-Louis SOLON introduced the PÂTE-SUR-PÂTE technique from Sèvres, with stunning results. The quality of Minton's output has remained consistently high and their products, such as the ART NOUVEAU-style majolica vases, have reflected contemporary fashions. Today, Minton is part of the DOULTON group.

Minton's marks

Minton has used a wide variety of both printed and painted marks throughout its history. The early crossed swords mark is similar to the Sèvres double L device. From 1860 onward, the mark includes the factory name and a symbol denoting the date.

1800–30, early porcelain

1841–73, one of many

MINTONS
ENGLAND

1891–1912, basic mark

Miquelet lock rifle with ornate stock inlaid with
mother-of-pearl and brass, Persian c.1800 [H]

Miquelet lock A variant of the
FLINTLOCK, developed in Spain and also
found in other parts of the Mediterranean
and the Balkans. It differed from the true
flintlock by having the mainspring
mounted on the outside of the lockplate.
This lock first appeared *c.*1650 and
survived into the mid-19th century. It
was also adapted to PERCUSSION.

Mirror A polished surface designed to
reflect an image. Although mirrors made
of polished metal or glass backed with
metal were known in the Roman
Empire, it was the development of BROAD
GLASS in Venice in the 16th century and
plate glass in Paris in the late 17th
century that revolutionized mirror
production. From this time onward a
huge variety of shapes and sizes of mirror
was made, as well as decorative frames in
a variety of materials such as wood, silver
and GESSO. These tend to reflect
contemporary styles and range from
architectural mirrors such as PIER GLASSES,
to freestanding dressing and CHEVAL
mirrors, to mirrors mounted on furniture.

Mirror black A term used to describe a
lustrous black glaze occasionally with
slight iridescence, used on Chinese
porcelain from the KANGXI period
(1662–1722) onward. It is
derived from iron oxide and
manganese oxide and in
Chinese is known as "wu chin".
Some of the best examples of
mirror black porcelain are
embellished with delicate gilt
designs. It is distinct from the
FAMILLE NOIRE palette.

Mirror painting A decoration
painted in oils on the reverse
of mirror glass. The technique,
thought to have developed in
England at the end of the 17th

century, involved removing areas of
silvering from the back of the glass and
painting the decoration in reverse.

Mission style The term used in the US
to describe architecture, furniture and
decorative arts of the ARTS AND CRAFTS
period, made in a simple, honest style
comparable to the plain and frugal
designs of early American mission
churches and chapels. The term is used
less frequently today; most collectors and
professionals prefer the synonymous
"American Arts and Crafts". This
preference is due in part to the lack of
correspondence, beyond coincidental
stylistic similarities, between the
American Arts and Crafts designers and
designers of Mission buildings and
furnishings. Most so-called Mission style
was designed in the eastern or mid-
western states from about 1890 until the
1920s, by artists who were chiefly
influenced by contemporary movements
in Europe, as well as America's COLONIAL
past and Native American culture.
Mission buildings, which are mostly
found in the south-western states and
may date from the 17th or 18th
centuries, are of relatively insignificant
influence on this movement. The term is

Oak mission style table by Gustav Stickley,
early 20th-century [J]

most commonly
applied to practical and
robust oak furniture made in large
quantities, in various standards of quality
by scores of firms in numerous locations
from *c.*1890 to the 1940s. The best
known makers are members of the
STICKLEY family, who operated three
separate firms, the first headed by Gustav
Stickley. Mission
furniture of generic
type is common in the
United States, and is
typically found in
good condition.

Mitre-cutting A type of
cut decoration used on glass,
made with a V-shaped
grinding wheel to produce
a deep, angled groove.

Mixed stem (or mixed twist)
A decoration on the stem of a
glass that combines one or
more clear spirals of air
with opaque white or
coloured twisted
CANES. The technique
was invented in Venice in
the early 17th century
and revived in Europe,
especially England, from *c.*1760.

Mixed stem
wineglass,
English c.1770 [K]

Mocha ware A popular and inexpensive
type of pottery first produced in England
in the 1780s and also made on the
Continent and in the US
throughout the 19th
century. It is derived from
"mocha stone", a variety of
moss AGATE with feathery
markings. The decoration was
achieved by dripping an acid
colourant onto an alkaline
ground and the chemical
reaction formed a tree or leaf
motif. Mocha ware was made
by a number of firms. It is
not usually marked, although
some rare examples by SPODE
are known.

Mock pendulum A term describing the secondary pendulum bob attached to the actual PENDULUM of a clock and visible through an aperture on the DIAL, especially on 18th-century BRACKET CLOCKS.

Model A term used for a more or less accurate representation, depending on the maker's skill, of a specific prototype rather than a generic car, train or truck, which would more properly be called a toy.

Chromed metal and ponyskin chair by Le Corbusier, c.1920 [H]

Modern movement A term embracing diverse forms of decorative arts from c.1920 to the 1950s, which favoured clean lines and no decorative adornment. The technological changes occurring after World War I spurred a mood of change characterized by geometry, abstraction and mass-production. In art it manifested as Cubism, Fauvism, Futurism, De Stijl and Constructivism, while in design the machine was seen as a symbol of the new century and modern technology as the means to achieve good functional design. Teachers and students at the BAUHAUS came to dominate the style, advocating that form follow function. New materials had a great impact on the movement's expression and facilitated mass-production. There was for example no historical precedent for tubular steel furniture. The CANTILEVER CHAIR took advantage of the metal's strength, while chromium plating gave a clean, hygienic finish.

Mohair Fur from the Angora goat, with long, fine, lustrous fibres. It dyes easily and has long been used in woven cloths. It has been exported to the West from central Anatolia since the 17th century, and was used during the 19th century for dolls' hair and for the fur on early TEDDY BEARS.

Mohair plush Material from which most TEDDY BEARS' fur was made before 1930. It is used today as an alternative to nylon, artificial silk or cotton for good soft toys.

Monart An ART GLASS range made by the MONCRIEFF GLASSWORKS from 1924–61, a collaboration between Isobel, wife of John Moncrieff Jr, and Salvador YSART and his sons. Free-blown shapes were made using a technique in which coloured glass was sandwiched between two layers of clear glass. After World War II it was made by his son Paul Ysart, who specialized in PAPERWEIGHTS.

Moncrieff Glassworks A Scottish glassworks established in 1865 by John Moncrieff in Perth. The major production was industrial and laboratory glass, although the company is better known for its MONART range. It closed in 1996.

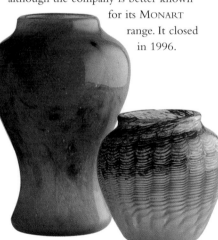

Monart glass vases by Moncrieff, c.1930 [I and J]

Money bank See SAVINGS BANK.

Monkey band (German: affenkappelle) An "orchestra" of porcelain monkeys dressed as humans in 18th-century court costume, modelled at MEISSEN by J.J. KÄNDLER. The full complement is 21 figures, including various instrumentalists, a singer and a conductor with a music stand. They are still being made and have also been copied by other European factories.

Montanari, Augusta (1818–1864) Together with Henry PIEROTTI, the most important maker of WAX DOLLS in the 19th century. Her workshop was in London, from where her blue-eyed dolls with their rooted hair and chubby limbs were exported to the rest of Europe and North America.

Monteith A large bowl with notched or crennelated rims (sometimes detachable) made in silver, ceramics or glass from

Silver monteith, English 1697 [B]

c.1680–c.1720. Named after a Scotsman called Monteith who "wore the bottome of his cloake or coate so notched", they were used to chill glasses which hung by their stems from the notches in the rim with their bowls in cold water. The earliest known hallmarked silver example dates from 1684.

Montelupo potteries A group of Italian MAIOLICA potteries founded in the 14th century near Pisa. By the 16th century high quality wares, depicting figures within a decorative band, were exported throughout Europe. Of a lesser quality are the brightly coloured peasant wares decorated with animals and soldiers which are typical of 17th century output. Montelupo still produces pottery today.

Moon A term applied to a small crescent mark or "tear" in the early porcelain body of CHELSEA, visible when held up to a strong light. Created from an imperfect mixture of ingredients and the expansion of the resulting air bubbles in the paste during the firing process, they also occur in porcelain from SÈVRES and TOURNAI.

Moonlight lustre A type of splashed or marbled pink or purple lustre developed by WEDGWOOD between 1805 and 1815.

Moonstone A bluish-white gemstone with a characteristic milky sheen known as adularescence. It was fashionable in late 19th-century brooches, pendants and fringe necklaces and was much admired by followers of the ARTS AND CRAFTS movement for its "spiritual" qualities. Compatible with silver settings, it was invariably cut *en cabochon*.

Moonstone glaze A trade name used by WEDGWOOD for a matt white glaze it developed in 1933. It has been used on wares designed by Keith MURRAY, animals designed by John Skeaping, NAUTILUS moulded ware, and many other objects. It is employed without decoration, to emphasize the object's form.

Moorcroft, William (1872–1945) An English ceramicist who worked as a designer for MACINTYRE's in Staffordshire, before leaving in 1913 to set up on his own. All his wares were handmade, with designs painted in raised slip (see TUBE-LINING). His patterns were largely floral with their roots in ART NOUVEAU. His son Walter Moorcroft took over on his father's death. The pottery is still active today, with designs that have become

Moorcroft vase, c.1925–35 [J]

more exotic but are still based on natural forms in characteristically rich colours.

Moquette A textile woven with a wool pile in coarse imitation of silk velvet, which has been made in Europe from the Middle Ages, particularly in the Low Countries.

Morbier striking system A STRIKING SYSTEM found on COMTOISE CLOCKS in which the clock strikes on the hour and again two minutes after. It is named after a town in the Franche-Comté area of France where such clocks were produced in the 18th century.

Morgan, William Frend De See DE MORGAN.

Morion A HELMET used in the 16th and early 17th centuries by light cavalry and infantry. They often feature a large comb, although those from Spain are pear-shaped with a small "stalk" on the top.

Morris chair A type of 19th-century EASY or armchair with an open wooden frame and loose seat and back cushions and a sloping adjustable back. Designed in 1883, it was manufactured by Morris, Marshall, Faulkner & Co. (see William MORRIS). As one of their most successful chair designs, it inspired many similar designs both in Britain and the US.

Morris, William (1834–96) An English designer, writer, romantic socialist and printer. A foundation stone of the ARTS AND CRAFTS movement, he was a major campaigner for the craft revival and was deeply opposed to factory production. In 1861 he co-founded Morris, Marshall, Faulkner & Co. (renamed Morris & Co. in 1875) which made furniture and furnishings for domestic interiors until 1940. Morris commissioned his friends, including Philip WEBB and E.C. BURNE-JONES, to design for him and incorporated

Dove and rose fabric by Morris, c.1879

ceramic tiles by William DE MORGAN and lighting by W.A.S. BENSON into his interiors. He set up a printing press and published over 50 books. His fame as a designer rests on his carpet, textile and wallpaper designs, which show a complete understanding of the nature of pattern and its creation.

Morse ivory Walrus tusk used for carving, most frequently by 19th-century sailors who created walking stick pommels, tools and other functional or decorative items from it during their long journeys. See also SCRIMSHAW.

¹Mortar A mixture of lime, sand and water laid between layers of bricks or stonework to aid adhesion.

²Mortar A small marble, hardstone or metal vessel used for pounding substances such as spices with a pestle.

Mortise and tenon One of the earliest types of JOINT used in furniture making, in which two pieces of wood are joined by the projecting tongue (tenon) at the end of one member fitting exactly into a corresponding cavity (mortise), usually rectangular, in the other.

Mortise and tenon

Mortlake tapestry factory Founded by King Charles I's secretary Sir Francis Crane in 1619 and directed by Phillippe de Maecht (d.1655), Mortlake initially produced copies of existing English court tapestries. In 1623 Charles purchased Raphael's original CARTOONS for the *Acts of the Apostles* from which tapestries were woven from 1625 to 1630. In 1629 Francis Cleyn became director, producing original cartoons. With an annual royal subsidy of £2,000, Mortlake flourished. The Civil War (1642–49) and Commonwealth period, however, led to its decline. Court patronage ceased, weavers left to set up their own workshops and only a limited production was maintained. Mortlake closed in 1703.

Mosaic A technique in which decorative designs made from small coloured glass cubes, known as tesserae, are embedded in the walls and floors of buildings. It was known in ancient Greece and developed by the ancient Romans but is particularly associated with BYZANTINE churches. Mosaic glass is made from, or decorated with, pieces of coloured glass that are heated until they fuse together without the colours mixing – a technique also known in ancient Greece. See also PIETRE DURE, MILLEFIORI.

Mosaic jewellery The fashion for MOSAIC jewellery centred on Rome and Florence encouraged by the popularity of the GRAND TOUR to Italy in the 18th and 19th centuries. Visitors to Rome collected "micromosaics" with colourful scenes of Classical ruins and wildlife. Florentine mosaics were predominantly flower studies in coloured hardstone on a black marble field (see also PIETRE DURE). Panels were brought home and made up into jewellery by London or Parisian craftsmen.

Moscow porcelain See GARDNER'S PORCELAIN FACTORY.

Moser, Koloman (1868–1918) An Austrian architect and designer associated with the VIENNA SECESSION and with

Ivory and lapis-mounted vase
by Moser, c.1905–11 [C]

establishing the WIENER WERKSTÄTTE in 1903. Moser was an influential designer and became a professor at the School of Decorative Arts, Vienna (1899).

Moser, Ludwig (1833–1916) The founder of a Bohemian glasshouse in 1857 at Meierhofen (now Nove Dvory, Czech Republic). A glass-engraver, his firm, Moser & Söhne, was known for the production of coloured glass with high-relief enamelled decoration.

Mote spoon A small silver spoon with pierced bowl and slender pointed stem, made from c.1690–1790. Mote spoons were probably used for straining tea leaves or fishing specks or "motes" from tea; the pointed end may have been for unclogging teapot spouts.

Mother-of-pearl A shiny, attractively coloured material from the interior of certain seashells, including the NAUTILUS shell. Also known as nacre and easily

carved, its uses include jewellery and inlay on objects of vertu and furniture. It is often used on items decorated with LACQUER and PAPIER-MÂCHÉ.

Motif See p.272.

Motschmann, Charles A doll manufacturer from SONNEBERG who patented the "Motschmann" body in 1857. His dolls' heads, pelvises and lower limbs are held together by strips of fabric, allowing movement between the parts. Motschmann was inspired by contemporary Japanese doll design.

Motto ware Table ceramics from the 19th and early 20th century, designed especially for children. It was made by the Staffordshire potteries among others. Often very decorative, the designs included moralistic mottos and religious quotes. See also CHILDREN'S WARE.

Mould blowing A glass-making technique, known from Roman times. The gather of molten glass is blown into either a full-size mould to create a regular shape or decoration, or a smaller "dip" mould to create a shape or decoration that can then be re-blown to the required size. From the early 19th century, the technique was widely used industrially.

Moulded glass See PRESSED GLASS.

Moulded pedestal stem Having a pronounced shoulder, this popular 18th-century decorative device for glass, ceramics and metalwork appears on a diverse range of objects, including drinking glasses, sweetmeat dishes and candlesticks.

Ebonized wood and mother-of-pearl box, c.1865 [O]

Moulding One or more thin strips of wood, stone, plaster or metal applied to a surface to make a uniform geometric profile either as decoration or to conceal a joint. Mouldings were used in ancient times on stone COLUMNS and FRIEZES. They became common on solid wood furniture in the 18th century and, in interiors, on door and window frames, fireplaces and cornices. Mouldings may take many forms: see ASTRAGAL; CAVETTO; CHAMFER; FILLET; OGEE and OVOLO.

Jet and hair mourning brooch, c.1880 [S]

Mould number A term commonly used in the manufacture of American toys. It is used to identify the casting or moulding and is usually cast into the surface of the toy. Different finishes would then be applied, e.g. Fire Dept, Police, Taxi.

Mount A term used to denote metal HINGES, LOCKS, ESCUTCHEONS and handles. It is used more specifically for the bronze, brass, gilt-bronze or ORMOLU decoration on late 17th- and 18th-century French furniture. Such mounts were introduced on French COMMODES in the late 17th century and were initially used for robustness by such cabinet-makers as BOULLE, as protection for vulnerable extremities, and subsequently for purely decorative purposes. In France they were designed and cast separately by specialist craftsmen and from 1745–55 were stamped with a crown and the letter C. Mounts were used by English, and later American, cabinet-makers on high quality 18th-century furniture.

Mount Washington Glassworks A large American glass manufacturer founded in New Bedford, Massachusetts, in 1837, best known for ART GLASS produced from c.1880 until the 20th century. The Mount Washington Glassworks specialized in satin-finished glass, with enamelled decoration and silver-plated mounts made at nearby Connecticut factories.

Mourning jewellery Jewellery of sentiment and remembrance particularly fashionable in the 18th and 19th centuries.

Georgian pieces tended toward the NEO-CLASSICAL ideal and were heavily romanticized, such as a lady weeping by a tomb in an enamel and pearl frame. Most 19th-century mourning jewellery was black enamelled, engraved with the deceased's name and contained a lock of their hair. The growth of the JET industry in England coincided with Queen Victoria's mourning after the death of Prince Albert in 1861.

Mouron, Adolphe (1901–68) A French graphic artist, stage designer and painter known by the pseudonym Cassandre. His poster designs influenced early 20th-century advertising enormously, notably his designs "Etoile du Nord" (1927) and "Dubo, Dubon, Dubonnet" (1934) – stylish images that reflected the fast-moving age. He saw the poster as "an announcing machine" rather than a decorative item.

Moustache cup Popular in European porcelain or pottery at the end of the 19th century when luxuriant moustaches were fashionable. The cup had an inner rim with a narrow slit through which liquid could flow so that the drinker's moustache could be kept dry and the wax from it did not flavour the tea.

Moustache cup, English c.1910 [S]

Moustiers potteries Now a popular tourist village in the *département* of Var, France, Moustiers-Ste-Marie has long been a leading pottery producer. From 1679 to the 19th century, it was one of the most important French FAIENCE towns, its wares copied in Spain and Italy. The first factory, founded by Antoine Clerissy (d.1679), began with earthenware but went on to make faience. It continued under Clerissy's son Antoine II and

grandson, Pierre II. Pierre founded the Moustiers faience industry, building a flourishing business with the help of François Viry and his sons. In 1783 it was sold to Joseph Fouque (1714–1800) whose descendents ran it until 1852. Earliest wares resemble ROUEN and NEVERS, decorated in UNDERGLAZE blue

Moustiers plate, c.1750 [L]

with figures, often after engravings by Tempesta, surrounded by finely painted LAMBREQUIN borders in "*style Bérain*".

The second factory was established in 1738 by Joseph Laugier and his brother-in-law Joseph Olerys who had worked at ALCORA in Spain; hence Moustiers ware can often resemble Alcora. The Laugier & Olerys factory used the "*style Bérain*" in early polychrome and had LO as a factory mark. They later painted MINIATURE mythological scenes in framed medallions and figures in a field of vegetation. Moustiers faience, still made today (the factory mark is an X), is usually light and finely potted. It can be difficult to differentiate from MARSEILLES.

Movement The complete timekeeping mechanism of a clock or watch, consisting of a set of wheels and PINIONS held between two brass or wooden plates (see BACKPLATE) and driven by the pull of weights, force of a coiled spring or by electrical power.

Motifs

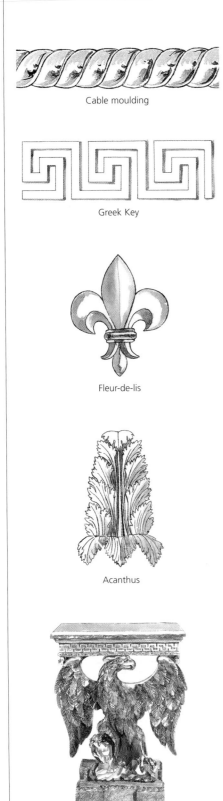

Cable moulding

Greek Key

Fleur-de-lis

Acanthus

Eagle

From the earliest civilizations onward, motifs have been a recurring feature of the decorative arts and have been inspired by sources as diverse as plant forms, human and animal figures and the patterns of geometry.

Early vocabularies of ornament

One of the oldest surviving catalogues of motifs dates to the Old Kingdom of ancient Egypt (2686–2181 BC). Archaeological excavations record wall-paintings, wooden furniture and other useful and decorative artifacts embellished with motifs such as palmettes, flowers, birds, and lions – the latter, usually combined with the head of the reigning pharaoh, also providing the model for the body of the SPHINX. Many of these motifs were absorbed into what has proved to be the most enduring vocabulary of ornament, the Classical Graeco-Roman. Gradually expanded from the 7th century BC (in ancient Greece) to the decline of the Roman Empire in AD c.300, this range of motifs was most eloquently expressed through the Classical Orders of architecture – on plinths, COLUMNS, capitals and entablatures – and was often closely echoed in the design of artifacts and the composition of wall-paintings. The principal categories of motif were naturalistic, notably indigenous plant forms such as ACANTHUS, anthemion, laurel and grapevine; mythological figures and beasts; symbols of war and religion and, under the Romans, emblems of imperial ambition, such as the EAGLE. In keeping with the inherent symmetry of Classical architecture, use was also made of linear patterns and mouldings, such as GREEK KEYS or fluting.

The enduring legacy of Classicism

Much of the subsequent history of motifs has been dominated by the recurring adaptation and development of Graeco-Roman prototypes. Influential in Byzantine, early Christian and Romanesque styles of architecture and ornament, they were also the stylistic driving force behind the Renaissance and underpinned the EMPIRE, FEDERAL, REGENCY and GREEK REVIVAL styles. However, Classical motifs have not completely dominated the last 2000 years of ornament. For example, heraldic emblems, such as achievements of arms and FLEUR-DE-LIS, were prominent in Medieval societies concerned with the code of chivalry and feudal status and enjoyed a revival during the 19th-century GOTHIC REVIVAL. Oriental imagery also became fashionable in the Western countries during the 18th century when trade with China flourished.

Decoration and symbolism

Ultimately, whether depicted in a naturalistic or a stylized manner, the primary appeal of motifs resides in their decorative qualities. Almost equally compelling, however, is the inherent symbolism of most motifs: the use of an eagle, for example, being not only a visually appealing "still life", but also an allusion, depending on the context, to sight (in Classical Greek mythology), imperial strength (in Classical Roman and Napoleonic Empire style decoration) and, in the United States, Classical aspirations, patriotism and Independence.

Sphinx

Mucha, Alphonse (Alfons Maria)
(1860–1939) A Czech painter, poster-
artist and designer who studied in
Munich, Vienna and Paris. He is popularly
known for his posters, often with a
flowing-haired woman as the focal point,
which are now regarded as the epitome
of the ART NOUVEAU style. He designed
jewellery for Georges Fouquet in
1898–1905, including some spectacular
theatrical pieces for Sarah Bernhardt. He
went to New York in 1904 and worked
with Louis Comfort TIFFANY.

Alphonse Mucha: poster for *Medée*,
starring Sarah Bernhardt, 1898 [E]

Muffineer A small CASTER, popular in
the 19th century, of glass, POTTERY,
SILVER or TREEN for sprinkling muffins
with cinnamon or salt. Also a round dish
with a cover used for serving hot muffins.

Mug A term used from the mid-
17th century for a drinking
vessel with a single handle on
one side. They are found
mainly in silver, pewter, glass
or ceramics and were used for
beer, wine or ale.

Mughal The Muslim dynasty
that ruled much of northern
India between 1526 and 1857.
Mughal decorative arts and
architecture display a strong Persian
influence, as the second ruler of the
dynasty, Humayan (reigned 1540–54)
spent some years as an exile in Persia at a
time when Islamic art reached a peak of
refinement. In the Mughal courts, the
decorative arts flourished from the mid-
16th to the mid-17th century, in
particular during the reigns of Akbar
(1556–1605), Jahangir (1605–28) and
Shah Jahan (1628–58), who built the Taj
Mahal. These enlightened rulers
encouraged the fusion of Persian and
native Indian artistic traditions, mainly
Hindu, especially in carpet-weaving,
hardstone carving, engraved and
enamelled metalwork, painted glassware,
and illuminated manuscripts. Features of
Mughal art include rich colours,
naturalistic animals and figures in intricate
patterns, and stylized flowers and leaves.

Mulberry (*Morus nigra* and *Morus alba*)
A tree native to Europe that gives a
heavy, hardwearing dark-streaked timber,
varying in colour from golden to reddish
brown. It was supposedly used in the
early 18th century as a VENEER for
cabinet work and small boxes. However, it
was often imitated and it is questionable
how much genuine mulberry furniture
was produced. Also, it is the tree used to
feed SILK-producing moths and hence is
grown in silk-producing areas.

Mule chest A term for a type of CHEST,
a hybrid of a COFFER and a CHEST-OF-
DRAWERS, made in England from the late
17th to the early 19th centuries. It has a
hinged top and drawers in the base.

Scottish mull,
c.1816 [M]

Mull An ornamental SNUFF-BOX,
often Scottish, made of a ram's or
sheep's horn, sometimes with a
cork hinged to the horn as a
stopper. As snuff-taking
became widespread during
the 18th century, snuff-boxes
were made in materials that
were less costly than the
traditional gold. However, some
horn mulls have tooled silver
mounts and use precious stones as
decoration or stopper mounts.

Müller Frères One of the leading
French makers of CAMEO GLASS, founded
in 1895 at Lunéville, near Nancy, by
Henri Müller and
associated with the
SCHOOL OF
NANCY. Müller
had worked for
GALLÉ and was
later joined by
his four
brothers and sister.
The factory was
known for its high-quality
landscape decoration on
vases and lampshades. It
made commercial glass and
ART DECO lamps
until *c.*1933.

Müller Frères table
lamp, 1900–10 [G]

Multi-face doll A novelty doll, made
from the 1860s onward, with two-, three-
or four-faced BISQUE or COMPOSITION
heads that rotate on horizontal or vertical
axles, enabling the doll to change moods
at the twist of a knop or other device.

Muntin A term in use since the 16th
century for the vertical dividers of
panelled frameworks that lie between the
STILES on the outside and connect the
top and bottom RAILS.

Murano glasshouses See VENETIAN
GLASSHOUSES.

Murray, Keith Day Pearce
(1892–1981) A New
Zealand-born architect,
glass and ceramic
designer, who designed
glass for STEVENS &
WILLIAMS and ceramics for
WEDGWOOD. His ceramics are
known for bold clean shapes,
often emphasized with
horizontal banding, and matt
and semi-matt glazes.

Earthenware vase by
Keith Murray for
Wedgwood, 1930s [K]

Murray, William Staite (1881–1962)
An English artist potter who set up his
own pottery in Rotherhithe (1919–24)
and then at Whickham Road, London.
Influenced by Chinese stoneware and
technically able, his work is skilfully
thrown and pieces are often large or tall.
He used rich glazes
fired in kilns he built
himself and
decoration was used
sparingly to
emphasize form.

William Staite
Murray vase,
c.1920 [L]

Mürrle, Bennett & Co. A London
jewellery wholesaler formed as a
partnership in 1884 between the German-
born Ernst Mürrle and an Englishman
called Bennett. They worked in various
styles and are well known for their ART
NOUVEAU pieces, some similar to LIBERTY
& CO.'S CYMRIC style. Some of the
production was done in Germany. Mürrle
was repatriated at the start of World War I
and the factory closed in 1914.

Musical box A cylinder musical box
employs a metal cylinder revolving at a
uniform rate with pins placed along it that
strike metal teeth on a comb. The
frequency of the sound produced is
governed by the length and width of the
teeth and sounds from the
succession of teeth
produce the tune.
Some musical boxes
employ bells and drums
and sometimes AUTOMATA
to produce and enhance the
tune. A second type uses
revolving discs with punched
slits and underhanging "pins"
that again strike teeth on a
horizontal comb. The first
musical box was made by the Swiss
watchmaker Antoine Favre in 1796, and
many fine examples of both types were
manufactured by companies including
NICOLE FRÈRES in Switzerland and
France from the early 19th century to
the early 20th century.

Musical clock A type of clock emitting
musical notes through bells, gongs or a
musical box. They were first introduced
in the late 16th century, but most of those
seen today date from the 18th, 19th
and 20th centuries; they often
combine musical work with
elaborate STRIKING SYSTEMS
or AUTOMATA such as figures
of musicians.

Musical watch Mechanical
music incorporated into watches.
The first musical watches (mid-
1700s) played on a nest of bells,
the hammers lifted by a pinned
barrel. With the invention of tuned
tines by Favre (see MUSICAL BOX),
the watch could be made thinner
and play more notes.

Music plate A type of dessert plate
first appearing in the late 17th
century with a song printed on it
so that diners could sing together
at the end of a meal. Made in many
factories including DELFT,
MOUSTIERS, ROUEN.

Music stool A small stool designed
for keyboard players. In the early
19th century it took the form of a
lyre-backed stool, or a stool with a
circular upholstered seat that could be
adjusted in height by means of a screw,
often concealed inside a central pillar. By
the mid-19th century these were largely
superseded by rectangular stools,
supported on four legs, with hinged,
padded seat lids that concealed a shallow
compartment for storing sheet music.

Musket The general term for infantry
shoulder firearms from the early 16th to
the mid-19th centuries. It generally
implies that the gun is smooth-bored.

Muzzle In firearms, the open front end
of a gun's barrel from which the shot or
bullet exits. Up to the 19th century, some
gun were loaded via the muzzle.

Myers, Myer (1723–95) An important
early American silversmith of the
COLONIAL period, active in New York
City. Most recorded examples, marked
with a single maker's mark only, are plain
but may feature ROCOCO CHASING.
Myers' work is extremely rare.

Mystery clock A type of
19th-century French clock
in which there is no
apparent connection
between the dial or
pendulum and
the movement.
One of the most
popular designs was
a brass or zinc figure
holding an apparently
free-swinging
pendulum: the
movement in the base
caused the figure to
rotate imperceptibly,
thereby swinging
the purely
decorative pendulum.

Mystery swinging clock,
French c.1910 [N]

N

Nabeshima Japanese porcelain made from the second half of the 17th century until *c*.1870 at Okawachi near ARITA for the Lords of Nabeshima. The wares are mostly curved dishes with high foot rims used for formal banquets or as gifts to the Shogun and other dignitaries. Designs were often derived from textiles using DOUCAI and WUCAI techniques or painted in underglaze blue sometimes in conjunction with a CELADON glaze. Fine Nabeshima of *c*.1720 is technically extremely high quality porcelain.

Nail-head decoration The ornamental use of dome-headed brass nails, used to secure upholstery to chairs or leather to chests or trunks. Sometimes called "close nail work".

Nails Early nails were made by hand, which is reflected in their slightly irregular form. Forged nails can be seen on iron hinges on early (for example, Jacobean) furniture. From the 19th century, nails were machine-made, with a regular form and a flat, even head. Nails come in a variety of forms from headless pins to decorative domed-head brass upholstery tacks used, from the 16th century, to fix leather to wooden understructures, such as bellows and chair seats.

Nailsea Glasshouse Founded at Nailsea, near Bristol, in 1788. The original production of window, sheet and BOTTLE GLASS is now less well known than the sideline of bottles, vases and jugs made from dark bottle glass with internal white flecked decoration that has become a general term for similar glassware made at other factories.

Nain A carpet-producing town in Central Persia. Weaving began *c*.1940 and continues today. Products are similar to carpets made in nearby ISFAHAN, with curvilinear floral designs, and details often outlined in white silk. Ivory and blue are typical colours. See also PERSIAN CARPETS.

Nancy School (Ecole de Nancy, Alliance Provinciale des Industries d'Art) An alliance of French artists working in and around the town of Nancy, Lorraine. Emile GALLÉ was president, with Louis MAJORELLE, Antonin DAUM and Eugène Vallin as vice-presidents. They organized courses to continue the tradition of craftsmanship in Lorraine. The main protagonists, all prominent ART NOUVEAU designers, were inspired by nature.

Nancy School bowl by Majorelle and Daum, 1920s [G]

Nanking ware (Nankeen, Nankin) Blue and white CHINESE EXPORT PORCELAIN made in the 18th and 19th centuries at JINGDEZHEN. It was carried by river to Nanking and thence to Canton by sea. Wares are often crude, decorated with Oriental landscapes and repetitive border designs. See also FITZHUGH PATTERN.

One of a pair of Nanking sauce tureens and covers, c.1770 [H]

Nantgarw porcelain factory Founded in South Wales in 1813 by William BILLINGSLEY and his son-in-law Samuel Walker. They moved to SWANSEA in 1814, but returned to Nantgarw in 1817. They made mostly plates, dishes, cabinet cups and saucers and some services. Billingsley was known for his high quality rose

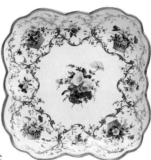

Nantgarw dish, c.1814–23 [K]

painting, but the richest decoration was done by decorators in London. Billingsley went to Coalport in 1819. The remaining stock was decorated by Thomas Pardoe until the factory closed in 1822.

Naples Royal porcelain The Fabbrica Reale Ferdinandea, founded by Ferdinand IV in 1771, began in the Royal Villa of Portici and in 1773 moved to the Royal Palace. It made Neo-classical style services with fine topographical scenes and some charming figures and groups. Under Napoleonic rule it became the property of a French firm in 1807, finally closing in 1834. Marks are a crowned N or FRF with a crown for Ferdinand IV REX. The crowned N has since been used by a number of other factories. Genuine Naples porcelain is rare.

Naples group, c.1790 [A]

Nashiji A Japanese lacquerwork technique where gold dust is sprinkled onto a slightly wet layer of LACQUER. Once dry, clear lacquer is applied on top and the whole polished to give a rich, cloudy "pear skin" appearance. It is often used as a background to designs on INRO, boxes and other ornaments.

Native American pottery A generic term for any pottery made by native cultures in North America from prehistoric relics to modern tourist ware. Most sought after examples are decorative, well-potted and in original condition, made for use by people in the south-west before Western intervention established a tourist trade.

Naturalistic style The naturalistic depiction of human figures, animals, birds and plants in art. It has featured in most fine and applied arts through the centuries but was particularly popular in the decorative arts during the mid- to late 19th century – especially on furniture c.1840–65 – when technical advances enabled the exact reproduction of natural forms through processes such as ELECTROTYPING and when scientific developments resulted in a widespread interest in the natural world.

Nautilus cup A standing cup, sometimes with a cover, of a type first imported into Europe from China in the 16th century. The bowl was made of a natural NAUTILUS SHELL held in place with silver-gilt or gold STRAPWORK mounts, often decorated with themes associated with the sea. Intended for display rather than use, they were fashionable in 16th- and 17th-century Europe, particularly in the Low Countries. The finest examples were made in late 16th- and early 17th-century Germany and were elaborately mounted in gold and silver.

Nautilus cup mounted in silver-gilt, made in Utrecht, 1613 [E]

Nautilus shell A large nacreous shell found in the Indian Ocean, used to

make NAUTILUS CUPS. Exotic shells were carried to Europe by 16th-century travellers to satisfy MANNERIST curiosity.

Navajo rug woven in wool, 19th century [G]

Navajo A significant group of native weavers in North America from the 16th to 20th centuries. The wool and dyes used are central to the bold geometric designs. Products are FLAT-WOVEN and are created from a continuous thread whose thickness is often subtly varied.

Nécessaire A French term for a small item of silver, leather-covered wood, porcelain or enamel, which carries everything necessary to accomplish a task. A *nécessaire à coudre,* for example, contains the needles, bodkin, thread, thimble, and scissors necessary for sewing.

Gold-mounted Bristol blue glass nécessaire, c.1760 [A]

Necklace Decorative hangings have been worn around the neck since earliest times, e.g. the Bronze Age and Ancient Egypt.

During the RENAISSANCE in Europe necklaces were used to hang PENDANTS. As the fashion for high collars and ruffs grew, they became longer. Toward the end of the 16th century open, square necklines allowed more delicate, shorter necklaces. Elaborate enamelled and gem-set examples continued into the 17th century, when decorative chains for men and knot motifs were also popular. In the 18th-century necklaces were often influenced by court fashions. NEO-CLASSICAL tastes such as MOSAIC emerged, as well as lines of graduated diamonds or gems known as *rivières*. In France, the Empress Josephine made CAMEO necklaces popular c.1805. The 1830s saw floral clusters of gems such as aquamarines and garnets and the taste for naturalism in the 1840s was typified by turquoise or enamelled gold serpents. The classical revivalist themes of the 1860s–70s progressed to repetitive necklaces of pearls, diamonds and gems in fringe formation. In the early 20th-century delicate diamond and platinum "garland" necklaces gave way to the heavy linear forms of the 1920s–30s. Designs of the 1940s–50s included collars of ribbon and scroll design and massive gold, gem-set "bibs".

Needlefire action A firearm whose mechanism incorporates a long needle that penetrates the base of a combustible CARTRIDGE to strike a priming pellet and fire the gun. It was perfected by the Prussian Nicholas von Dreyse in the 1830s.

Needlelace (or needlepoint) Lace made with a needle and single thread by working embroidered buttonhole stitches on a geometric grid (see RETICELLA). From the early 17th century it was made with a parchment pattern, releasing it from the geometric form. See also PUNTO IN ARIA; VENETIAN, FRENCH, SPANISH and ENGLISH NEEDLELACE.

Needlework See EMBROIDERY; STUMPWORK; CREWELWORK; SAMPLERS; and BERLIN WOOLWORK.

Needlework (or embroidered) carpets Made throughout Europe from the 16th to 19th centuries using a variety of NEEDLEWORK stitches. Designs reflect the styles of the day and are based upon patterns used in pile weavings. The technique allows for greater detail and definition of pattern than woven carpets.

Combined stereoscopic and postcard viewer by Negretti & Zambra, 1870 [Q]

Negretti & Zambra A London-based firm of scientific instrument makers founded in 1850 by the Italians Enrico Negretti (d.1879) and Joseph Warren Zambra (d.1877) and still operating today. They became Opticians and Meteorological Instrument Makers to Queen Victoria and gained a prize in the Great Exhibition in London in 1851.

Nelme, Anthony (*fl.*1672–1723) An English silversmith apprenticed to Richard Rowley and Isaac Deighton, who was granted the freedom of the Goldsmith's Company in 1679. He may have had foreigners and immigrants working in his workshop since the pieces he produced show HUGUENOT influence. By the end of 17th century he had one of the largest establishments in London, gaining many municipal orders and commissions for large items and services. His later works are in the QUEEN ANNE style. His son Francis (*fl.*1719–59) carried on the business, but his work was comparatively unremarkable.

Neo-classical style See p. 278.

Netsuke A small, often figurative, carving used from the 16th century as part of traditional Japanese dress. Netsuke are popularly thought of as made in IVORY, but as elephants are not native to Japan, other ivory tusks, teeth and stained and polished woods (such as CHERRY and BOXWOOD) were also used. Kimonos were worn in Japan until the mid-19th century and, as they lacked pockets, men hung boxes known as INRO, or pouches known collectively as *sagemono,* from their OBIS. To stop the cord from slipping through the obi, netsuke were used as a toggle. A sliding bead or OJIME was strung on the cord between the *sagemono* and the netsuke to loosen or tighten the opening. As inro became more popular from the late 16th century, so did netsuke.

Early netsuke are characterized by a simpler design, while later ones are more intricately carved. A wide variety exists, from the *manju* toggle formed as a simple rounded disc, to more complicated designs taking the forms of animals, people from Japanese legend or daily life, ghosts and masks. By the early 18th century renowned *netsukishi*, or netsuke carvers, existed whose signed works are highly prized, but many finely carved examples are not signed. Many reproductions exist, including late 19th- and early 20th-century examples, often with protruding parts that would not stand usage, made almost exclusively from ivory for export or tourist markets. More recently, they have been made in resin or plastic.

Japanese ivory netsuke in the form of a European gentleman, 18th century [K]

Nevers faience Italian potters working in the Italian MAIOLICA tradition arrived in Nevers, France, in the 16th century. The first to found their own factory (1588) were the three Conrade brothers from Albisola near Genoa who made strongly Italianate products, e.g. ISTORIATO dishes and ewers. It was only in the mid-17th century that native French potters imposed their own style upon the Conrade tradition.

New FAIENCE factories started from *c.*1632 and the French owners gradually moved from RENAISSANCE styles to FRENCH Baroque. On the baroque shapes the Nevers' decorators painted Chinese-style figures and landscapes, suggesting that they had Chinese porcelain originals to copy. Nevers also made large garden vases, much used in the Trianon de Porcelaine, the elaborate summerhouse at Versailles built in 1670. Wares were painted in attractive tones of a warm

Nevers faience dish with a hunting scene after Tempesta, c.1660 [F]

blue, soft orange and pale yellow, usually outlined in a soft purple. A style called BLEU PERSAN was also developed at Nevers in the 1670s. Nevers painters used engravings after Raphael, Nicolas Poussin and Simon Vouet and hunting scenes after Antonio Tempesta (1555–1630). In the 18th century they copied ROUEN and MOUSTIERS. They also made *faience patriotique* with Revolutionary sentiments, much collected in France. Pottery is still made in Nevers.

The Kimbolton cabinet with marquetry and
ormolu designed by Robert Adam
and made by Ince & Mayhew, c.1775 [A]

Federal Neo-classical
candlestick
with fluted stem,
1795 [E]

Paris Angoulème sprig tea wares,
c.1795 [N]

Neo-classical style

A style of architecture, painting, sculpture and decorative arts popular from
*c.*1750–*c.*1800, marked by a revival of interest in Greek and Roman antiquity.
It developed in France in the 1750s, partly as a reaction against what was
considered the excessive frivolity and sentimentality of the Rococo style.

Inspiration from the Antique

The development of Neo-classical style was prompted by the rediscovery in the
1740s of the ancient Roman cities of Herculaneum and Pompeii, which had
been buried by the eruption of Mount Vesuvius in AD 79. Domestic items such
as lamps, candelabra, small bronzes and frescoed wall decorations were found.

These discoveries were publicized throughout Europe in *Le antichita di Ercolano
esposti* (1757–96), *Recueil d'Antiquités* (1752–67) by the Comte de Caylus, and
Antiquities of Athens (1762) by James STUART and Nicholas Revett. Other factors
in the dominance of Neo-classicism were the popularity of the GRAND TOUR
and its association with the democracy of ancient Greece and republican Rome
in the newly established republics of France and the US (see FEDERAL style).

From the mid-18th century, furniture became rectilinear with architectural forms,
such as pediments on mirror frames. Classical urns and two-handled vases were
made in silver, e.g. by Matthew BOULTON, and ceramics at SÈVRES. A new tripod
form for candelabra and perfume-burners was copied from ATHÉNIENNES found at
Pompeii. Mythological themes dominated enamel painting and porcelain figures.

In the 1760s–70s a lighter style emerged, using GROTESQUES, FESTOONS, HUSKS,
ribbons and medallions, of which the leading exponent was Robert ADAM. He
also introduced the ETRUSCAN STYLE, which influenced WEDGWOOD's black
BASALTES and ROSSO ANTICO wares. Wedgwood's JASPER WARE was decorated to
imitate ancient Greek and Roman hardstone CAMEOS. The apparent flimsiness of
much Neo-classical silver in the 1770s and 1780s was emphasized by the
introduction of thin-gauge sheet silver, made by the new mechanical flatting
mills, for oval and cylindrical teapots. In the 1790s Neo-classical furniture
became more austere, especially in France during the DIRECTOIRE period. A
more archaeologically exact style developed in the early 19th century as part of
the REGENCY and EMPIRE styles. See also LOUIS XVI STYLE; GREEK REVIVAL.

Recognizing the style

Designers and craftsmen in all areas of the decorative arts
began to use motifs from Greek and Roman architecture,
e.g. Vitruvian scrolls, Greek key and guilloche patterns,
fluting, columns, anthemions and palmettes.

Classical urn   Greek key pattern   Athénienne

Newcastle glassware Glass made at the many glasshouses established in Newcastle upon Tyne, UK, since the city became a centre of glass production in the 17th century. The term also often describes the 18th-century Newcastle light BALUSTER drinking glasses, often with air-beaded KNOPS.

Newcomb Pottery A US ART POTTERY workshop established at Newcomb College, New Orleans, in 1895 as a women's venture under the direction of Ellsworth Woodward (1861–1939). Until its closure in 1930 the pottery specialized in matt-glazed vases with incised, floral decoration, the best examples of which are among the most highly prized of all US art pottery.

New England Glass Co. Amberina glass vase, c.1870 [R]

New England Glass Company A large, important American glassworks founded by Deming Jarves (1790–1863) in Cambridge, Massachusetts, in 1818. It developed the first glass-pressing machine and made useful and ornamental wares including PAPER-WEIGHTS, throughout the 19th century, much of it created by immigrant artisans from Europe. From the mid-19th century the company introduced numerous artistic lines, notably AMBERINA and Pomona, developed by Joseph Locke. The company moved to Toledo, Ohio, in 1888 and, as the LIBBEY GLASS COMPANY, is still in existence. Products are unmarked.

New Hall porcelain factory Founded in Staffordshire c.1781, this factory first made hybrid HARD-PASTE porcelain developed from Richard CHAMPION's patent. They did not achieve a white body, so c.1815 they turned instead to

New Hall bone china teapot and stand, c.1815 [M]

BONE CHINA and concentrated on saleable tea wares with simple Chinese-style floral patterns, some painted by Fidelle Duvivier. The factory closed in the 1830s.

Nickel silver A silvery coloured or white alloy of zinc, copper and nickel, which is well suited to the manufacture of FLATWARE and is also used as a good base for electroplating. See also EPNS and SILVER.

Nicole Frères A Swiss manufacturer of cylinder MUSICAL BOXes started by the brothers Raymond and Francis Nicole in Geneva in 1815, considered to be one of the finest makers of the 19th century. In 1881 they opened a retail branch in London. In 1906 they were taken over by the New Polyphon Company.

Niderviller pottery and porcelain factory A faience factory in Niderviller, Lorraine, France, founded by Jean-Louis, Baron de Beyerlé, in 1754. From 1754 until 1779 the director was a painter and chemist, François Antoine Anstett. In 1766 the production of ivory-toned delicately painted faience was abandoned. Porcelain with clay at first from Passau and then from St Yrieix was made on a large scale from 1768. In 1770 the factory was bought by Count

Philibert de Custine but, when Custine was guillotined in 1793, Claude-François Lanfrey, his manager, became owner until his death in 1827. The factory then made tableware with German-style decoration and figures with brightly coloured costumes. From 1827, porcelain-making was discontinued and the factory concentrated on cream-coloured earthenware and faience. From 1886 it became known as S.A. Fayencerie de Niderviller and produced copies from its 18th-century moulds. It is still active. Custine's mark is two intertwined Cs under a crown.

Niello A hard black alloy of lead, silver, sulphur and copper used to fill engraved designs on silver pieces thereby providing a decorative contrast. Although niello-work is known throughout Europe and Asia, the Russians were particularly fine exponents of the art from the 17th to the 19th centuries.

Nigoshide (Japanese: "milky white") In Japanese ceramics the famed pure white porcelain body used for the finest KAKIEMON wares. It seems only to have been used for open forms such as plates, dishes and bowls and was never used in conjunction with underglaze blue.

Niderviller armorial bough pot and cover by Joseph Deutsch, 1767–70 [I]

Nock, Henry (c.1741–1804) An English gunmaker whose patent BREECH designed in 1787 revolutionized firearms by improving ignition and ballistics. Nock was appointed Gunsmith-in-Ordinary to George III in 1789, and Master of the Gunmakers' Company in 1802. A maker of high quality firearms, Nock is mainly remembered for his seven-barrelled guns made for the Royal Navy.

Nocturnal A simple time-telling instrument used at night, usually made of BOXWOOD and occasionally of brass. It consists of two circular plates mounted one on top of the other, the larger outer disc having a long, shaped handle. To indicate the time, the pole star is viewed through the centre hole and the pointer turned to be in line with the Guards of the Bear. The earliest known dated English example is 1637.

Nonsuch chest A type of late 16th-century oak CHEST of German origin or made in London by immigrant craftsmen. The front panels were decorated with coloured wood inlay depicting a building that resembled Henry VIII's Palace of Nonsuch in Surrey.

Noritake A Japanese HARD-PASTE porcelain company established in 1904 near Nagoya, producing hand-painted tablewares for export as well as decorative teawares, vases, candlesticks and figures. It began by copying Victorian and Edwardian designs, but commissioned new patterns from eminent designers such as Frank Lloyd WRIGHT in the 1920s and 30s. Today, Noritake is a large international business.

Northwood, John (1836–1902) An English glassmaker who trained in several STOURBRIDGE glasshouses. In 1860 he and his brother Joseph founded J. & J. Northwood, a glass-decorating business specializing in ACID ETCHING and engraving. He also created many superb pieces of CAMEO GLASS, including a copy of the PORTLAND VASE, made in 1876.

Nottingham lace Machine-made LACE, the invention of which at the end of the 18th century hastened the decline of handmade lace. Machine-made copies of traditional designs were shown at the 1851 GREAT EXHIBITION, promoting cheaper laces for fashion and domestic use.

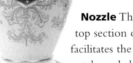

Noritake porcelain vase, 1910 [P]

Nove pottery and porcelain factories There were several FAIENCE factories at Le Nove, near Bassano, Italy. The first was founded by Giovanni Battista Antonibon (d.1738) in 1728, making dishes and tureens decorated in HIGH-TEMPERATURE COLOURS. In 1752 a porcelain kiln was added to this prosperous MAIOLICA factory by Pasquale Antonibon, assisted by a worker from DRESDEN. It was used to make delicate teawares and figures. Antonibon leased the maiolica business in 1774 for the next 30 years. From 1781–1802 the porcelain factory was leased to Francesco Parolin. The factory finally closed in 1832. The best porcelain was made from 1760–80 and was greyish, like COZZI. Le Nove is still an important centre for ceramics, producing TIN-GLAZED EARTHENWARE painted with flowers in soft colours.

Nozzle The detachable flanged top section of a candlestick which facilitates the removal of candle stubs and also serves as a drip pan.

Nuremberg potteries An important centre of German FAIENCE from the 16th century. Nuremberg is known for "Hafner" wares (lead-glazed stoves, stove tiles and vessels) attributed to Paul Preuning, and for a factory (1712–1840) managed by Johann Caspar Ripp (1681–1726), a potter from Ansbach. It made faience painted in blue (often on a greyish blue ground) and occasionally red, manganese and yellow. After c.1750 it used ENAMEL COLOURS. Specialities were jugs painted with tiny flowers and birds, jugs with pierced star-shaped rosettes and dishes with six heart-shaped

Nymphenburg plate painted by J. Zachenberger, c.1760 [D]

wells. Many HAUSMALER decorators also worked in Nuremberg, including Johann Ludwig Faber (fl.1678–93), Johann Heel (1637–1709) and Abraham Helmhack (1654–1724).

Nursing chair A chair, associated with the mid- to late 19th century, with a low seat and no arms, designed for women nursing babies.

Nutmeg grater In the 17th and 18th centuries nutmegs were used to flavour food and drinks. They were, however, expensive, and warranted special boxes, often silver or treen, to contain them. These were inset with a hardened steel grater. Late 17th-century examples may be cylindrical. From c.1750 egg- and other shaped forms appeared.

Nymphenburg porcelain A porcelain factory was founded at Neudeck in 1747 sponsored by Prince Maximilian Joseph of Bavaria. In 1761 it moved to premises in the Castle Rondell, Nymphenburg, Munich, where it continues to operate today. In 1753 J.J. RINGLER arrived and by 1757 the factory was making a fine white porcelain body but was in financial straits.

1753–present

When the FRANKENTHAL factory closed in 1799 some of its workers came to Nymphenburg. The factory began to flourish again, making good tea and dinner wares, but is most famous for the figures made by the Swiss modeller Franz Anton BUSTELLI. In 1862 the works were leased to a private company making utility wares, but from 1888 enjoyed new success. It continued the ROCOCO tradition using original moulds and also kept pace with modern forms. It still uses the 18th-century mark of the chequered shield of Bavaria.

O

Oak A hard, close-grained wood, generally pale honey-coloured. Throughout the Middle Ages oak was used to make fine furniture, giving way to walnut in the late 16th century in France and a century later in England. It is the typical timber for GOTHIC STYLES, Early Renaissance Flemish and German woodwork, and the Tudor and Jacobean periods in England. Simple oak furniture has continued to be widely made since the late 17th century.

Oak

Oak-leaf jar An APOTHECARY JAR decorated with stylized oak leaves in GOTHIC STYLE, often with heavily applied blue pigment, a pale buff body and a creamy white glaze. This rare early Italian MAIOLICA is of uncertain origin but most probably comes from mid-15th-century Florence. Decoration is usually drawn in purple manganese outline and includes heraldic lions, birds and human profiles.

Obelisk A tall tapering square or rectangular shaft of stone terminating in a pyramid. Originating in ancient Egypt, where its shadow was used to tell the time, the obelisk was brought to Europe during the Roman Empire. Admired during the Renaissance, it was adopted in Europe as FINIAL ornament from the late 16th century, when it also featured in Dutch and German architecture. During the 18th century, it was adopted in England for garden ornament and tomb decoration.

Object of vertu: a silver pill box, English 1901–02 [R]

Miniature decorative obelisks made from marble became popular in the early 19th century.

Obi (Japanese: "belt") A waist sash worn with a kimono.

Object of vertu (French: *objet de vertu*) A small accessory such as a SNUFF BOX, POMANDER, ÉTUI, or NÉCESSAIRE, made of luxury materials (e.g. porcelain, gold, silver, gemstones and enamel). They are valued for their workmanship and rarity rather than their function.

Occasional table A modern term for an all-purpose small table that can be easily moved from room to room. Occasional tables evolved in the 18th century to accommodate increasingly comfortable domestic interiors. Light and versatile, frequently with drawers, drop leaves and mounted on castors, it was used for a host of leisure activities from letter writing and reading, to serving tea and light meals, to playing cards and games.

Octant A navigational instrument in the form of an eighth of a circle usually constructed from ebony or mahogany. The arc, with a scale and VERNIER, can measure an angle of up to 90°; it also has an index arm, coloured filters, mirror and a pinhole sight. The octant was invented by John Hadley *c.*1731 as an advance on its predecessor, the BACKSTAFF, and the cross-staff. See also SEXTANT.

Oeben, Jean-François (*c.*1721–63) A German-born French *ébéniste*, designer and furniture-maker who settled in Paris in the 1740s. A skilled metalworker and mechanic, his furniture is distinguished by elaborate MARQUETRY and ingenious mechanical effects. Under the patronage of Madame de Pompadour, Oeben was promoted to the position of *ébéniste du roi* in 1754. In 1760, he made an elaborately decorated *bureau du roi Louis XV*, a large cylinder-top desk now at Versailles. Although he was responsible for the design as well as the complex mechanism of this masterpiece, the desk was completed and signed after his death by his equally renowned assistant Jean-Henri RIESENER. Among Oeben's specialities are the elaborately fitted multi-purpose pieces known as *meubles à secrets* and *meubles à surprises*, which became fashionable after 1750, along with the trend for smaller and more intimate rooms.

Oeben was appointed *maître ébéniste* in 1761 but died bankrupt a few years later. His workshop continued under the direction of Riesener, who married Oeben's widow in 1768.

Oeil de perdrix (French: "pheasant's eye") A circle motif (usually made up of a ring of tiny dots) with a bright dot in the centre, used repeatedly and close together as ground decoration on ceramics. Introduced at SÈVRES in 1760, then also used at DERBY and MINTON in Sèvres-style patterns.

"Off-hand" glass See FREE BLOWING.

Ogee A continuous shallow serpentine curve made up of convex and concave lines. From the 12th century the ogee form appeared in textiles, although it is most typical of GOTHIC STYLES. As an elaborate pointed arch, it was used as a MOULDING, for BRACKET FEET, or for the glazing bars of cabinets and bookcases from the mid-18th century. Ogee-headed panels occasionally feature as TRACERY on bookcase and cabinet doors, and on CASE FURNITURE in the GEORGIAN period.

Mahogany octant by Thomas Ripley, English 1788 [H]

Ogee clock See SHELF CLOCK.

Ohr, George E. (1857–1918) One of the foremost American ARTS AND CRAFTS studio potters, active at the Biloxi Pottery, Mississippi, c.1883–1906. He specialized in thinly potted vessels of irregular form and dark, iridescent glaze.

Ojime In traditional Japanese costume, the small bead by which the cords binding together an INRO and NETSUKE were loosened or tightened.

Okimono A small to medium-sized Japanese sculpture, often of ivory, made to stand inside an alcove or *tokonoma*. Made in the 19th century and later, their intricately carved figurative or animal designs and forms were often based on the smaller NETSUKE.

Old English pattern A silver FLATWARE pattern, very simple in form with the ends of the stems turning down. The Old English pattern succeeded the HANOVERIAN PATTERN and, although still popular today, was most extensively produced from c.1775 to c.1830.

Old Hall pottery See MEIGH POTTERY.

Old Sheffield See SHEFFIELD PLATE.

Olive A hard, close-grained greenish-yellow wood with dark, cloudy markings, originating in southern Europe. Used as a VENEER in PARQUETRY and for MOULDINGS from the late 17th century to the REGENCY period.

Omega Workshops A design company founded in 1913 in London by the art historian and influential art critic Roger Fry (1866–1934). He aimed to apply the aesthetic of post-Impressionism to British design, which he felt had become debased. The Omega workshop produced a broad range of painted furniture, textiles and decorative objects, as well as lively and colourful interior designs, employing artists such as Vanessa Bell (1879–1961)

and Duncan Grant (1885-1961). The workshop closed in 1919, because of declining sales during World War I, but it set the fashion for abstract and geometric patterns that was taken up in the 1920s. (See also STAINED GLASS.)

Meissen Onion pattern set, c.1890 [L]

Onion pattern (or *Zwiehelmuster*) A popular design of the MEISSEN porcelain factory. It was based on a Chinese blue and white original and produced from 1739. The rims of the plates were originally decorated with peaches, mistaken for onions by the Meissen painters. The design was copied by many other continental factories, in both the 18th and 19th centuries, and is still in production today.

Onslow pattern (or scroll) A silver FLATWARE pattern whose main distinguishing characteristic is the fanned out ends of the stems which terminate in a scroll motif. Produced from c.1750 and probably named after the Parliamentary speaker, Arthur Onslow (1691–1768). (See also ALBANY PATTERN.)

Onyx A mineral of the chalcedony family, onyx is predominantly jet black, black with lines of white (banded agate) or brown and white (sardonyx). Since antiquity it has been an important

medium for ornamental carving and jewellery. In the 19th-century it was widely used for MOURNING JEWELLERY.

Opal A gemstone celebrated for its unique play of rainbow colours. It was highly prized by the Romans and in the Middle Ages it was thought to have powers to predict disaster and to cure ophthalmia (inflammation of the eye). The largest source was traditionally Czechoslovakia, but today the most valuable variety is the black opal, mined in Australia since the 1870s, with its characteristic "harlequin" colours. Other varieties include the orange fire opal, mined in Mexico.

Opalescent glass An opal-like, milky-blue glass, with subtle gradations of colour in which opaque areas of thicker glass contrast with more translucent areas of thinner glass. It was first made by Venetian glassmakers in the 16th century, but is now closely identified with the luxury ART GLASS of the late 19th century and the ART DECO glass produced in France by celebrated glassmakers such as René LALIQUE and Marius Ernest SABINO. From the 1880s, inexpensive PRESS-MOULDED opalescent glass was also produced in quantity by British manufacturers. (See also PEARLINE GLASS.)

Opalescent glass dish, English 1930s [M]

Opal glass A translucent white glass resembling opal. It was made in Venice in the 17th and 18th centuries, and from the late 17th to the 19th centuries in Germany and Bohemia, where it was also known as BEINGLAS.

Opalina See MILK GLASS.

Opaline glass A semi-opaque glass, developed in France from *c.*1825 from a technique of adding bone ash to the glass mix. This results in the "fire" for which opaline is famed, where the colour of the glass changes when held to the light. Produced in Britain from *c.*1840 and subsequently made throughout Europe and in the United States at the BOSTON & SANDWICH GLASS COMPANY.

Opaque glass Glass that does not transmit light, generally the opposite of transparent or translucent glass, although in stained glass it refers to any glass that is not translucent. See also LITHYALIN.

Opaque twist stem A type of stem found in 18th-century English glasses consisting of a twisted rod embedded with threads of opaque white glass. See also AIR TWIST.

Opaque twist stem on ale glass, English 1755–75 [O]

Open back setting See CLOSED BACK SETTING

Open-closed mouth An early BISQUE doll, whose mouth has lips that appear parted but in fact has uncut plaster between the lips.

Open-faced watch The earliest type of watch, produced from the late 16th century, where the dial is protected by glass only, rather than a cover.

Open mouth A BISQUE doll made from *c.*1890 with parted lips and an opening between the lips, showing moulded or inserted teeth.

French opaline scent bottle, *c.*1845 [P]

Openwork One of the oldest techniques of metalworking, including methods such as piercing, saw cutting, or WIREWORK, that create openings in the body of an object, allowing light to shine through and its beauty to be appreciated. Openwork was functional on items such as tea strainers, but has also been used both in Western countries and in the Orient from the 18th century until the present day as a decoration on silver items such as breadbaskets and fruit bowls.

Opus Anglicanum (Latin: "English work") A term used in medieval continental Europe for English embroidery, whose characteristics include the use of intricately embroidered silver and gold threads. Considered some of the finest needlework ever made, it was mostly for ecclesiastical use.

Ormolu (English term from the French *or moulu*: "ground gold") Bronze gilded by the MERCURY or FIRE GILDING processes and used, especially in 18th- and early 19th-century France, as

Ormolu-mounted commode, Louis XIV period [A]

decorative mounts. The term is also used for a 19th-century gold-coloured alloy of copper, zinc and tin.

Orrefors Glassworks A glass factory founded in Orrefors, Småland, Sweden, in 1898. From 1916, Simon Gate was artistic director, joined in 1917 by Niels Hald. Hald had studied with Matisse and this period saw excellent quality glass produced. Two techniques in particular gained the company an international reputation: "Graal", developed in 1916 by Simon Gate, which is a type of engraved cased glass, and "Ariel", developed in 1937 by Vicke Lindstrand, where pieces are sandblasted with INTAGLIO patterns that are then CASED, thus trapping air in the cavities. Orrefors still produces high-quality glass and became part of the Royal Scandinavia group in 1997.

Orrefors "Graal" vase by Simon Gate *c.*1930 [L]

Orrery Originally a type of PLANETARIUM made in England in 1712 for the 4th Earl of Orrery, but now a table-top demonstrational instrument showing the motion of the earth around the sun and moon around the earth, made until the mid-19th century. Prolific makers include Benjamin Martin and W. & S. Jones.

Ortelius, Abraham (1527–98) A Dutch cartographer who produced several important maps before the publication in 1570 of his greatest work, the *Theatrum Orbis Terrarum* (Theatre of the Whole World). This was the first true modern ATLAS – a collection of uniformly sized and styled maps of the countries and regions of the world, based on the latest geographical data. The *Theatrum* continued to be revised and reissued in different languages until 1612.

Ottoman carpets

The Ottomans were originally a people from Central Asia, who established themselves in Turkey in the late 13th century. Ottoman carpets were made during the 16th and 17th centuries in the region that is modern Turkey.

The roots of a continuing tradition

The Turks seized control of Constantinople (now Istanbul) in 1453 and ruled until 1922. The art of weaving may have been brought to Turkey by the Seljuks, a Turkic people also from Central Asia who ruled Turkey from 1077 to 1307. Early carpets have geometric GUL medallion designs. Some of these have been given names derived from Western painters who portrayed carpets in their paintings. The "Memling gul" was named after the 15th-century German painter Hans Memling and consists of an octagon enclosing a stepped hooked medallion. Other carpets use the "Holbein" pattern, named after Hans Holbein the Younger, court painter to Henry VIII in England. These comprise rows of octagonal medallions framed by arabesques interspersed with smaller lozenge motifs. The LOTTO design, after Lorenzo Lotto, is also a favourite carpet.

In the mid-16th century, a development of the Ottoman court style of carpet-weaving appears to have derived from Cairo, which was colonized by the Ottomans in 1517. These rugs and carpets include such designs as the *cintamani* (three balls above a pair of wavy lines) – a design element that became one of the most popular devices in Ottoman art, found also in tiles, textiles and metalwork. Other patterns include bands of clouds, lotus PALMETTES from Chinese art, carnations, tulips, hyacinths, roses and large leaves.

A "Lotto" Ushak rug from West Anatolia, late 16th/early 17th century [C]

Star-shaped motifs alternate with smaller cruciform shapes in this "Star" Ushak rug from West Anatolia, late 16th century [B]

A "medallion" carpet with a central motif from West Anatolia, late 16th century [A]

In the late 16th and 17th centuries other designs evolved, typically, the large "medallion" and "star" carpets from USHAK. Both these types show an endless repeating design cut by the borders. The medallion format first seen in bindings of the Koran was probably borrowed from contemporary Persian carpets from Tabriz, since artists from here were employed by the Ottoman court. These carpets have either red or blue as the background shade with a decorative vine design in the other colour. Other motifs used are of Persian influence as in the use of flowerheads and ARABESQUE scrolls. The border designs were often interchangeable, such patterns include KUFIC SCRIPT, cloudbands, palmettes with floral sprays and floral CARTOUCHES. Most Turkish and a significant amount of Caucasian rug production from the 18th century to the present use designs developed or influenced by Ottoman carpet production of this time.

Osier pattern

Osier (ozier) A pattern simulating basket weave, moulded on the rims of porcelain plates, devised at MEISSEN in the 1730s. An early form was used on a service made for Count von Sulkowski designed by J.G. HÖROLDT in 1735. He also developed *Altozierrand* with radial rims, and *Neuozierran* (1742) with four sets of spiralling ribs.

.

Osler, F. & C. (1807–*c*.1940) An English glasshouse based in Birmingham that specialized in CUT-GLASS tablewares and in such large-scale projects as the huge *c*.8.5m (28ft) high glass fountain for the GREAT EXHIBITION in London in 1851.

Ostrich-egg cup The translucent cleaned egg of an ostrich set into a mount. Usually silver or gold, the mount is highly worked and decorated with figurative or floral and foliate motifs. An exotic curiosity made first in Europe in the 15th century, extensively in the 16th century and into the 17th century.

Ott & Brewer porcelain factory A US factory founded in 1863 as the Etruria Pottery in Trenton, New Jersey, by William Bloor, Thomas Booth and Joseph Ott. They were later joined by John Hart Brewer and in 1873 the factory was renamed Ott & Brewer. It initially made cream-coloured earthenware and white GRANITE WARE and in the late 1860s introduced PARIAN statuary and HOLLOW WARE, the best designed by Isaac Broome (1835–1922). In the 1880s, helped by William Bromley, the firm produced acclaimed American BELLEEK, some decorated by W.S. LENOX. The factory closed in 1893.

Ott & Brewer pitcher, c.1890 [N]

Ottoman A long, low, narrow upholstered sofa or bench without a back. A fashionable novelty in the late 18th century, it was designed in imitation of the Turkish mode of sitting. In the REGENCY period, it was synonymous with a divan, and in the 19th century it came to mean a coffer with tapering sides.

French mahogany ottoman, c.1850 [G]

Oude Loosdrecht porcelain factory A Dutch factory founded in 1771 by Johannes de Mol (d.1782) using the stock from WEESP. The arcanist L.V. Gerverot worked here *c*.1777. It made fine quality porcelain in the style of MEISSEN and SÈVRES. In 1784 the factory moved to Oude-Amstel but closed in 1820.

Outside decorator See HAUSMALER.

Overglaze A technique for decorating ceramics. After adding lavender oil and turpentine, enamels (colour-bound metals or oxides bound by a flux, usually finely ground quartz, firestone, red lead or bismuth oxide) are painted onto fired and glazed porcelain and fired in a muffle kiln at *c*.750°C (1380°F). See also ENAMEL COLOURS.

Overlay glass Glass made up of one or more layers of different coloured glass, as in CASED, FLASHED and CAMEO glass.

Overstuffed Seat furniture, such as chairs and sofas, with upholstery completely covering the wooden frame, leaving only minor decorative work exposed.

Ovolo A convex classical MOULDING, usually a quarter of a circle, often embellished with EGG AND DART or similar ornament. It was much used in RENAISSANCE decoration, on furniture cornices in the 16th and 17th centuries, and on JAPANNED and MARQUETRY mirror frames in the late 17th century.

Oxbow front A US term describing the undulating front surface of a CHEST-OF-DRAWERS or other type of CASE FURNITURE with two convex curves flanking a concave one. It is opposite to a SERPENTINE front.

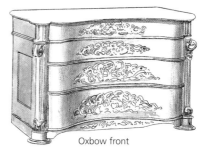

Oxbow front

Oxidized silver Silver whose surface colour has been changed by a chemical reaction creating a decorative layer of metal oxide, produced from *c*.1850–90 in France and England, particularly on figurative and statuary silver. Many colours can be created; in England dark staining and shades of red were popular.

Oyster veneer Wood sliced in a diagonal cross-section from the smaller branches of trees such as walnut and laburnum and laid together to resemble oyster shells. Originating in Holland, it was popular on cabinets, drawers and LONGCASE CLOCKS in the late 17th and early 18th centuries.

P

Paddington Bear A character invented by Michael Bond in 1958. Paddington Bear first featured in the book *A Bear Called Paddington* which was illustrated by Peggy Fortnum. In 1972 Shirley Clarkson of Gabrielle Designs made the first Paddington TEDDY BEAR based on Peggy Fortnum's illustrations. Although still produced by Gabrielle Designs in the UK, the Paddingtons sold outside Britain are made by the American company Eden Toys.

Paddington Bear, English c.1970 [S]

Pad foot A rounded foot resting on a circular base. Similar to the CLUB FOOT – but sometimes without the disc on the bottom – the pad foot was mainly used with the CABRIOLE LEG on furniture from the early 18th century onward.

Padouk A hard and heavy well-marked red wood (genus *Pterocarpus*), ranging from a golden brown colour to deep red or crimson. Originating in the Dutch and Portuguese East Indies, padouk was used extensively by French *ébénistes* in the 18th century and in England for fretwork and for solid pieces of furniture.

Pagoda top A motif representing a Chinese pagoda. Extensively featured in CHINOISERIE ornament, the pagoda roof was adopted by furniture-makers in 18th-century England and France to lend an Oriental flavour to such pieces as cabinets, clocks and mirrors.

Pair-cased watch The term for watches made with an outer protective case. Usually made of the same material as the inner case, some cases are covered with SHAGREEN or TORTOISESHELL.

Paisley pattern A decorative pattern evolved from stylized images of pinecones that have been embroidered with small, random motifs originating in the Indian BOTEH textile motif. A common decorative device symbolizing a broad variety of vegetation, resembling the palm, cypress, and almond plants, for example, can be found throughout the Orient, although its origins remain obscure. By the mid-19th century, fabric patterned with this motif had become fashionable in both France and England. Notably, it was produced in quantity at Paisley, a Scottish wool-weaving town, hence the name.

Paisley pattern from 19th-century French textile

Paktong A yellowish silvery-coloured, durable alloy of copper, zinc and nickel. Originating in China, possibly as early as the 1st century, it was not imported into Europe until the 17th century. A practical, inexpensive substitute for silver, it was used for fireplace furnishings, salvers, bowls and candlesticks. Its use was limited when the cheap nickel alloy, German silver, was created.

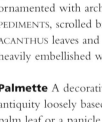

Palissy, Bernard (*c.*1510–90) A French Huguenot potter and glass-painter. In 1539 he settled at Saintes, Charente-Maritime, where he perfected various enamels and coloured glazes using tin, iron, lead, antimony, copper and Périgord stone. He made pottery with relief decoration copied closely from nature including lizards, snails and foliage, which became popular. His wares were imitated at Caldas da Rainha (1885–1908), Portugal's main FAIENCE factory, and he is accredited with being a source of inspiration for MAJOLICA. In 1575 he wrote a manual describing his potting techniques. He was arrested for heresy in 1586 and died in the Bastille.

Palladian A style of architecture and furniture popular in England during the first half of the 18th century and inspired by the work of the 16th-century Italian architect Andrea Palladio (1508–80). The furniture designed by William KENT, John Vardy (d.1765) and others for Palladian houses, is distinguished by solid, symmetrical and Classical forms, ornamented with architectural-style PEDIMENTS, scrolled brackets, garlands and ACANTHUS leaves and swags. It is often heavily embellished with GILDING.

Palmette A decorative motif from antiquity loosely based on the fan-shaped palm leaf or a panicle of flowers. Frequently used with the ANTHEMION, the two forms are hard to distinguish, especially when interpreted in a florid style. Revived during the Renaissance and Neo-classical periods, the Greek-style palmette – resembling honeysuckle flowers – was used on furniture, ceramics, and metalwork.

Palmette

Paktong chamberstick, English c.1770 [M]

Panel A flat surface sunk or raised within a framework, usually on furniture or as a wall covering. A FIELDED PANEL has a raised central flat surface often with bevelled edges. Panels could also be carved, with LINENFOLD, for example. Wall panelling developed in northern Europe from the 15th century to meet the need for draught-free rooms, reaching great sophistication in 18th-century France.

Panelled chest A CHEST, often oak, constructed with a framework of stiles and rails, held together by MORTISE-AND-TENON joints. One of the earliest types of furniture, the chest was usually decorated with simply carved designs.

Panton, Verner (1926–98) A Danish architect and designer of furniture, textiles, carpets and lighting. He designed the first all-in-one, plastic CANTILEVERED chair for the Swiss furniture company Herman Miller in 1967. He developed his own colour system for the interiors and textiles that he designed.

Pap boat A small flat invalid feeder, with a spout, for bread and milk (pap), usually 18th century, although found in the 19th. Often in earthenware with UNDERGLAZE blue printed patterns but also in silver.

Pap boat, c.1840 [S]

Paperweights Small, heavy, decorative glass objects used for holding down loose papers on a desk or table. Most have a circular base with a diameter of 5–10cm (2–4in) – glass weights with smaller or larger diameters are known as miniatures and magnums respectively – and a decorative ground that is magnified by a high dome of clear glass. The type of decoration varies enormously, from densely packed MILLEFIORI canes to

lampwork, fruit, flowers, vegetables, figures or snakes and insects, or cameo portraits made of glass-paste.

The idea of enclosing a cameo in a ball of glass probably originated from France in the early 19th century, but the golden era of production was not until 1845–50, when the French glassworks – BACCARAT, SAINT-LOUIS and CLICHY –

Paperweight from Clichy, French c.1845 [N]

made superb examples. As the fashion for paperweights declined in France in the 1850s, French makers took their skills to such companies as the BOSTON & SANDWICH and NEW ENGLAND glassworks. In this way the US became the centre of production, with British weights coming to the fore in the 20th century with the weights made by Paul YSART for the MONCRIEFF and the Caithness glassworks (est. Perth, Scotland, 1960).

Paperweight eyes Dolls' blown glass eyes with tiny threads running through the irises to create an illusion of depth.

Papier-mâché A lightweight material produced by moulding dampened and pulped paper into shapes that then harden as they dry. Usually gilded, JAPANNED or painted and varnished and often inlaid with MOTHER-OF-PEARL or decorated with DÉCOUPAGE, it was used for making trays and other small domestic objects as well as dolls. It may have originated in the Orient but became popular in Europe in the mid- to late 18th century. Its

popularity continued during the 19th century when gilt and inlaid decoration against a black background was popular. Papier-mâché furniture was made by Henry Clay in the 18th century and JENNENS & BETTRIDGE in the 19th.

Papier mâché doll A doll with its SHOULDER HEAD made of papier-mâché. Based on an established tradition in France, the German manufacturers rationalized the moulding process, allowing mass production of papier-mâché heads by c.1820. The shoulder heads are characterized by their black, moulded hair, reflecting changing fashion in style, and their painted features. The heads are attached to kid leather or cloth bodies and the lower limbs are carved from wood. Around 1870 PARIAN, china and BISQUE doll's heads became popular, but papier-mâché was still used for jointed dolls' bodies, which continued into the mid 20th century.

Papier-mâché doll, German c.1830 [N]

Parcel gilt An article that is only GILDED in part. Parcel gilding is used as a decorative effect and is applied, particularly to silverware and furniture, by a method known as FIRE GILDING.

Parian head doll PARIAN is a type of porcelain invented by COPELAND & GARRETT. Parian-headed dolls, however, are not made of Parian, but of a white untinted BISQUE. They were manufactured largely in Germany and were especially popular between c.1860 and c.1875.

Parianware A highly FELDSPATHIC porcelain named after the Greek island of Paros, which was famous for its white marble. It was made in England in the mid-19th century at a time of great interest in museums and art and a growing middle class that was aware of "antique sculpture". Parianware gave them the opportunity to have affordable copies of ancient sculpture and marble models by the sculptors of the day. MINTON and COPELAND were important manufacturers and sold vast quantities of these busts and figures.

Minton Parian group, c.1860 [o]

decorating establishments in Paris, including P.L. Dagoty in Boulevard Poissonnière, from the end of the 18th century; Darte Brothers, a porcelain factory from 1795 and also a decorating studio in the Palais Royal; Dastin, a factory from 1810; Deck, a workshop for artistic FAIENCES founded by Theodore DECK in 1859; Pierre Deruelle, a factory at Clignancourt in 1771 called Fabrique de Monsieur; Dihl, a factory founded in 1780 under the patronage of the Duc d'Angoulême, closed in 1829; SAMSON, the great copyists, Rue Béranger; a decorating studio owned by Feuillet in Rue de la Paix from 1820; Fleury in Rue de Faubourg St Lazare, 1803–47; La Courtille, founded by J.B. Locre in 1771; brothers Pouyts 1808–25; and Nast in Rue Popincourt.

Parisienne See FASHION DOLL.

Parquetry The INLAY of variously coloured small pieces of wood veneer on the carcass of a piece of furniture to produce a geometric pattern. A variation on MARQUETRY that was employed during the early period of walnut-veneered furniture in the 17th century,

parquetry mosaic was occasionally laid directly into the solid wood. By the mid-18th century, the technique was used with great virtuosity, particularly on commodes, in England and France.

Partners' desk A type of English pedestal desk or large library table but double-sized and double-sided to accommodate two people sitting opposite each other. Fashionable from the 1740s and throughout the 19th century, the desk was furnished with drawers and cupboards on both sides.

Partridge wood A close and heavy straight-grained wood in varying tones of brown and red, with streaks resembling the feathers of a bird. A tree native to Brazil, the wood was extensively used in small inlaid and parquetry work throughout the 17th century.

Parure A matching set of jewellery usually comprising a necklace, a pair of bracelets, earrings and a brooch. Parures were particularly common at the start of the 19th century, such as semi-precious stones in CANNETILLE frames. A demi-parure tends to comprise two components, e.g. necklace and earrings.

Seed pearl parure, English 1810 [F]

Paris porcelain plate, 1840 [R]

Paris potteries and porcelain factories An area of provenance for a vast amount of ceramics made and decorated in the city in the 19th century. Because SÈVRES, the Royal Factory, had been protected by a Royal Edict for so long (until 1784) there had been little room for other manufacturers. But, after the Napoleonic wars, there was a burgeoning of ceramic activity. With the discovery of KAOLIN near LIMOGES, hard-paste porcelain was made in great quantities. Some of the porcelain made in Limoges was decorated in the Parisian workshops and some factories produced their own porcelain and earthenware. French fashion influenced the taste of most of Europe in the 19th century. There were over 160 factories or

Pashmina (Kashmir *pashm*: "wool") A type of fine shawl made from the silky underbelly hair of a Himalayan mountain goat. Much prized throughout Mughal history, these shawls were supposed to be so fine that they could pass through a ring.

Enamel patchbox, English c.1820 [Q]

Passing strike A type of STRIKING SYSTEM in which a clock strikes only once on the passing of the hour, usually found in late 19th-century SKELETON CLOCKS.

¹Paste Paste is a compound of glass that was principally invented by Frédéric Strass, a French jeweller working in the 1730s. Strass discovered that a hard and versatile material is produced with many of the properties of real gemstones when selected oxides and minerals are added to FLINT GLASS. Paste jewellery in a wide variety of colours was worn in the 18th century, usually mounted in silver or gilt metal and FOILED to enhance colour and sparkle. Late 19th-century "French" paste lacked the quality of its 18th century-counterparts; much 20th-century paste was painted with a gold-coloured coating to intensify its appearance.

²Paste The "body" of porcelain, the mixture of clay and flux; it is used to describe "true" (or hard paste) and also soft-paste porcelain (*pâte tendre*).

Pastille burner A ceramic receptacle to hold a small perfumed tablet or pastille, which when lit gave off a fragrance in a room. These were a necessary accessory in the 18th and 19th centuries when houses were often damp, personal hygiene not of a high standard and the drains of poor quality.

Spode pastille burner, English c.1825 [L]

¹Patchbox A small box that originally held paper patches to cover smallpox scars. These patches became a fashion item in the 18th century and the boxes were decorated with enamelling or were engraved.

²Patchbox A small, lidded compartment in the stock of a muzzle-loading RIFLE for the greased cloth patches that were wrapped round rifle balls to improve the spin.

Patch mark A small round mark, larger than a SPUR MARK, on the underside of DERBY porcelain in the 18th and early 19th centuries, left from the small "pads" of clay on which the piece stood in the kiln.

Patchwork The decorative piecing together of different fabrics, most commonly applied to the coverlets made in Europe and North America. The first references to patchwork appear c.1700 but it was most popular in the 19th century.

Pate A rounded piece of either cork or PAPIER-MÂCHÉ that covers the WIG APERTURE of a DOLL and forms a base to which the wig can be attached.

Pâte-de-verre (French: "glass paste") An expensive and technically demanding glass-making technique in which a ground-glass paste is cast by the LOST-WAX technique. First used in ancient Egypt, the technique was revived in the 19th century by French glass-makers François-Emile DÉCORCHEMONT and Joseph-Gabriel ARGY-ROUSSEAU.

Patek Philippe Swiss watchmaker, founded in 1851, that produced and still produce some of the best and most complicated watches.

Patent furniture An early 19th century term for imaginatively designed types of "transformation furniture", such as adjustable chairs and expanding tables. Unlike the US, where most innovative furniture was patented, very little had officially granted patents in England.

Patera The Latin term for the dish or wine holder used in religious ceremonies. The oval or circular medallion ornament is generally decorated with a formalized flower, rosette or fluting. The patera was a popular motif in the NEO-CLASSICAL period for silver and furniture.

Patera

Pâte-sur-pâte (French: "paste on paste") A technique introduced in SÈVRES c.1849 by the head of the painting department. White clay or "slip" is built up in layers to give a striking effect of depth, on a dark background. The great exponent of *pâté-sur-pâté* was Marc Louis Solon who worked at Sèvres and MINTON.

Minton pâte-sur-pâte plate, c.1890 [J]

Patina (patination) A fine surface sheen and mellow appearance on silver and furniture. Years of handling, with an accumulation of polish and dirt, produce the attractive and desirable effect known as patination. A fine patina is a key ingredient looked for in a quality antique.

Pattern-book A book containing designs for furniture, such as the 18th-century examples by HEPPLEWHITE and SHERATON that were influential in establishing style, or issued by pottery factories as catalogues, or by fabric manufacturers or retailers to assist with sales or keeping records of designs. The pages in the book consisted of drawings, paintings or cut pieces of fabric – they were often known as swatch books.

Pattern number A system most usually used in English ceramics factories in the 19th century, although 18th century pattern numbers are known. Some factory PATTERN-BOOKS are still extant and give the year of the first introduction of a pattern and may also have drawings of the shapes, and give artists' names.

Pavé setting A method of mounting diamonds and gems where each individual stone is "paved" in side-by-side formation with its neighbour, so little or no setting is visible between. Pavé setting was often used in Georgian jewellery and in many post-war and contemporary diamond jewels.

Pavé-set brooch, Scandinavian 1940s [Q]

Paw Similar to the claw and hoof, the paw form usually decorates the base of a furniture leg. Originating in Classical antiquity, it was revived during the Renaissance. Grotesque supporting figures with paw feet feature in the designs of MANNERIST engravers. A favoured motif on the front of English and US chair legs from the early to mid-18th century, paws frequently embellish MONOPODIA.

Peach bloom A glaze derived from copper, ranging from red to green. First seen in Chinese KANGXI wares.

Peachblow Late 19th-century ART GLASS in shades of cream to pink or red, in imitation of PEACH BLOOM glaze. The majority were made in the US, notably by HOBBS, BROCKUNIER AND COMPANY and the NEW ENGLAND GLASS COMPANY.

Peacock motif A decorative motif since antiquity. In Classical ornament, the peacock was an emblem of immortality. In Christian iconography, it symbolizes

Peacock motif

immortality and Christ's resurrection. Peacock feathers were used on late 15th-century MAIOLICA from Faenza and often appeared on DELFTWARE apothecary jars of the mid-17th and 18th centuries. In the AESTHETIC MOVEMENT, the peacock symbolizing beauty appeared on William de Morgan ceramics, enamels, TIFFANY glass and LIBERTY fabrics.

Pear See FRUITWOOD.

Pearl Pearls are an accident of nature created by various species of bivalve molluscs. If an irritant lodges in the mollusc, it builds up a hard protective shell from an organic substance called conchiolin round the grain. This is called nacre and the thicker the layers, the larger and more valuable the pearl becomes. Pearls can occur in several colours, but those with a pinkish tint are most highly prized. Cultured pearls are formed when the irritant is introduced artificially. BAROQUE PEARLS are irregular in shape, freshwater pearls are found in mussels and have a rather dull lustre and seed pearls are very small pearls used in antique jewellery.

Pearline glass An opalescent PRESSED GLASS made by George Davidson & Co. in Gateshead, Northumberland. Introduced in 1889, Pearline pressed tableware was produced in various colours including blue made with the addition of cobalt, and yellow. See also PRIMROSE GLASS.

Pearlware English earthenware with a blue-tinted glaze, made from c.1770 to the first half of the 19th

Pearline sugar bowl by Davidson, c.1889 [S]

century. Often printed, but also painted in UNDERGLAZE blue and quite often dated. It was made in Staffordshire, Yorkshire, and Wales, but is unmarked and impossible to attribute.

Pearlware globular teapot and cover, English c.1786 [O]

Pedestal In Classical architecture, the base that supports a COLUMN. Since the Renaissance, decorative pedestals have been used to display vases, candelabra, lamps and sculpture. Eighteenth-century English SIDEBOARD pedestals were sometimes fitted with warming chambers and storage compartments.

Pedestal desk Derived from the pedestal LIBRARY or WRITING TABLE made in the mid-18th century by a number of London cabinet-makers, including Thomas CHIPPENDALE. The flat desk, often with a leather top, rests on two side pedestals with drawers or folio cupboards. Made originally in walnut, pedestal desks in various woods were popular from the 19th century to the present day.

Pedestal table A round or oval table supported on a single central pillar or column, usually with spreading feet or a tripod base. First made in

England in the 18th century – sometimes in pairs – pedestal library and dining tables have remained popular since.

Pediment A triangular gable above the portico of a Classical temple. The motif was adopted in Italy, France and England from the 16th century for the tops of windows and doors and for the CORNICES on tall CASE FURNITURE, such as bookcases, bureaux and LONGCASE clocks. A broken pediment has a central break for a FINIAL; a swan-neck pediment consists of two opposing S-scrolls.

Pediment

Pedometer An instrument for estimating distance travelled by measuring the paces of an individual. The first patent was in 1831. Often had a clip for attaching it to a belt and a single hand that moved each time a pace was taken.

Peepshow An enclosed box with a lit scene inside and a peep-hole for viewing. Some used a series of pictures to create a three-dimensional effect, while others had a lens that magnified the scene. They were often used by travelling showmen during the 17th and 18th centuries in Europe. Seaside peepshows with titillating subject matter were popular *c*.1900.

Peg doll See PENNY WOODEN.

Pegging See DOWEL.

Peg tankard A tankard, usually late 17th century, of Scandinavian origin but common in other European countries, in wood or silver with a row of applied pegs inside as a guide to the amount of liquid consumed.

Peking enamel Exquisitely painted enamel applied to copper-bodied items such as SNUFF BOTTLES and produced in the Imperial factories in Peking, China, from the 18th century. Often grouped into CANTON ENAMEL ware, these pieces are of far higher quality.

Pellatt, Apsley (1791–1863) A glass manufacturer who inherited the Falcon Glassworks, Southwark, London, which his father had founded *c*.1790. He specialized in decorative wares and experimented with new glassmaking techniques, including small decorative portraits known as sulphides, which he patented in 1831. He also revived ice glass and other Venetian glassmaking techniques, was a pioneer of PRESSED GLASS and exhibited at the Great Exhibition in London, 1851. In 1849 he published *Curiosities of Glass Making* – on the practice of glassmaking. The firm continued to make glass until the 1890s.

Pembroke table An elegant small OCCASIONAL TABLE with four legs, usually on castors, one or two frieze drawers and two drop leaves supported by wooden brackets on hinges (known as "elbows"). Believed to have been named after a Countess of Pembroke, the Pembroke table was produced in England from the mid-18th century. The tops were often elaborately inlaid with SATINWOOD, EBONY and BOXWOOD. In the 19th century, brass inlay became popular, and in the late 19th and early 20th centuries they were often painted in revival styles.

Pembroke table, c.1790 [D]

Pendants In the RENAISSANCE, gold, enamel and pearl pendants reflected status. By the 19th century, pendants were suspended from a necklace or long chain. Precious stones set in platinum and gold pendants of geometric form were fashionable in the 1920s and 1930s.

Pendelfin Handpainted stonecraft figures made by Pendelfin of Burnley, Lancashire, from 1953 to the present. The company name derives from Pendle – the infamous witch hill above the first workshop – and elfin – the look of the early models. Although now best known for rabbit figures, the rare earlier wares: myth and legend pieces, nursery rhyme characters and ducks, are in demand.

Pendulum A device controlling the timekeeping of a clock, developed in the mid-17th century by the Dutch scientist Christian Huygens. A brass, steel or wooden rod is made to swing in a regular arc by a flat or bulbous metal weight (bob) at the end. It is used with the ANCHOR ESCAPEMENT and VERGE ESCAPEMENT. The introduction of the pendulum in the mid-17th century dramatically improved accuracy, but the metal rod still expanded and contracted with changes in temperature. In the early 18th century, British clockmakers George Graham and John Harrison each developed a temperature-compensating pendulum, respectively the mercurial and gridiron pendulum. The mercurial pendulum has a mercury-filled glass jar as the bob: under heat, the expansion of the mercury counters that of the steel pendulum rod. The gridiron pendulum comprises alternating steel and brass rods: as they expand and contract at varying rates the pendulum length remains the same.

Pennsylvania Dutch style See p.292.

Pennsylvania tinware See TOLEWARE.

Painted pine "mule" dower chest
c.1800 [H]

Bird-tree of carved and painted pine,
wire and iron, c.1800–20 [K]

Pennsylvania Dutch style

Mainly German and Northern European immigrant communities developed this US style in Pennsylvania – chiefly Lancaster, Lebanon and Buckinghamshire (Bucks) counties – from Colonial times until the present.

A colourful folk art

The word "Dutch" is a corruption of *Deutsch*, or German. As a decorative style, Pennsylvania Dutch compares closely to provincial folk art of a type widely found in Germany, Scandinavia and neighbouring countries.

Furniture is typically brightly painted, practical and of simple construction from indigenous woods such as white or yellow pine, maple or cherry. Blanket chests of simple box type with a hinged lid were traditionally painted with panels of formalized folk imagery and may feature initials and dates (usually between *c.*1750 and *c.*1850) if they were originally presented as a marriage or dowry chest. Some furniture and other woodwork, including tool chests, bowls and small boxes, is also decorated with shallow carving and stippled surfaces and may be finished in thin "milk" paint of pastel colour. Some pieces are signed, or may be attributable stylistically to makers such as Joseph Long Lehn (1798–1892) of Lancaster County. Signatures on furniture include Seltzer-Rank, Jacob Schelli, John Drissel and John Maser.

Lead-glazed redware
pie dish, c.1820–40 [G]

Pottery is typically crudely made, useful RED WARE, produced from the second quarter of the 19th century. The best of it is SGRAFFITO-decorated through a yellow or green glaze. It is rarely signed but may be attributable or dated. Tinware is typically simply made, coffee pots being common. Painted examples are often decorated with "gaudy" tulips.

Textiles are typically bed QUILTS made in large numbers since the 18th century and often well preserved in blanket chests as heirlooms. The best quilts are dated and have strong colours and rich decoration of figural or folk images. Other textiles include hooked wool rugs and, rarely, needlework SAMPLERS. HOOKED RUGS are mostly 20th century and may have figural or geometric designs. Illuminated Pennsylvania Dutch manuscripts are known by the German word *Fractur* and typically record births or a family tree. They are valued as historical documents as well as works of folk art, although many are plain and may be in poor condition. The best examples feature vivid imagery and bold colours. Early (pre-1790) dates are not uncommon. Pennsylvania Dutch folk painting includes landscapes depicting farming, or daily pursuits of the late 18th or early 19th century.

Painted pine and maple chair,
mid-19th century [O]

Penny toy A small toy made in various materials from CAST METAL to wood, paper, TINPLATE and CELLULOID designed to be sold for a penny, usually by street vendors, between 1890 and 1935, mainly in France and Germany.

Penny wooden Also known as a DUTCH PEG DOLL, produced in Germany and Austria since the 19th century, it is a roughly carved doll with its head and torso in one piece, stick-like jointed arms and legs and crudely painted facial features and centre-parted black hair.

Penwork needlework casket, English c.1870 [K]

Penwork Decoration commonly applied to JAPANNED furniture such as tabletops, cabinet furniture and small items such as tea caddies, boxes and trays, produced mainly in England in the late 18th and early 19th centuries. Furniture embellished with penwork was japanned black before being painted with decorative patterns in white japan. Details and shading were achieved with black Indian ink using a fine quill pen.

Pepperbox A pistol with four or more barrels revolving around a central pin. Pepperboxes first came into use c.1825, but became obsolete with the introduction of the true REVOLVER in 1836.

Percier, Charles (1764–1838) A French architect, interior designer and decorator who trained in Paris under the architect A-F Peyre. In collaboration with Pierre-

François-Léonard FONTAINE, Percier formulated the EMPIRE style in books that were published in 1801. His studies of Classical and Renaissance architecture in Rome can be seen in his work. He became a set designer for the Paris Opéra, before joining Fontaine to create interiors and furniture for Napoléon I.

Percussion lock A system of ignition for firearms that uses a pressure-sensitive explosive compound e.g. mercury fulminate, to set off the gunpowder charge. Percussion ignition was pioneered by the Rev. Alexander Forsyth c.1800–05. Copper percussion caps were available from c.1819 onwards. The percussion cap revolutionized firearm design, paving the way for BREECHLOADING and repeating guns.

Perfume bottle A small glass or ceramic bottle, with either a glass or ceramic stopper or sealed with a cork or wood plug, used for storing perfumed oils and water. Scented oils were used in religious rituals and for cosmetic purposes in the ancient world: earthenware or terracotta perfume bottles in a wide variety of shapes were made in Ancient Egypt, Greece and the Roman Empire; small CORE-FORMED GLASS AMPHORAS were made in Egypt from as early as the 6th century BC and, with the development of glass BLOWING, numerous Roman perfume flasks in a variety of shapes were made from c.100 BC. Subsequently, ceramic and glass perfume bottles were made throughout Europe and East Asia and reflected the development of new techniques and contemporary styles and decoration. Ceramic perfume bottles were made by all the leading manufacturers – ROCOCO porcelain by CHELSEA and SÈVRES, NEO-CLASSICAL JASPER WARE by WEDGWOOD – and remained popular until the early 20th century. Glass perfume

Perfume bottle, English c.1880 [N]

bottles were made of MILLEFIORE, CASED GLASS and many different types of coloured glass (which protected the contents from deterioration), such as CUT, PRESSED, CAMEO and FROSTED glass. Size and shape also varied widely, including, from the end of the 18th century, double-ended bottles, dual-purpose bottles that included such features as PATCH BOXES or telescopes and novelties such as miniature bottles in the form of boots or shoes suspended from finger rings, or miniature fruit or cannons.

With the emergence of the true commercial perfume industry at the end of the 19th century, perfume came pre-packaged and the bottle was an integral part of the

Baccarat glass scent bottle, c.1930 [R]

manufacturers' identity and marketing strategy. French manufacturers commissioned sophisticated and elegant designs in the ART NOUVEAU and ART DECO styles from leading designers such as René LALIQUE and manufacturers such as the BACCARAT glassworks.

Peridot A yellowish-green gemstone with a slightly "oily" lustre found on St John Island in the Red Sea, Burma and Australia. Formerly known as "olivine", peridot was a popular gemstone in VICTORIAN and ARTS AND CRAFTS gold jewellery, where it was frequently set with pearls.

Period A term referring to a distinct historical style or fashion, or used in a more general sense to refer to decorative arts displaying authentic features of a particular historical style. The period room, in which all the furnishings belong to one historical period, developed as part of museum displays in the late 19th century.

An Isfahan carpet, central Persia,
17th century [A]

A Tabriz carpet, north-west Persia,
late 19th century [c]

Persian carpets

Persia (now Iran) is one of the most important countries for carpet making. The golden age of carpet weaving started in the 16th century under the Safavid dynasty (1501–1732). Persian carpet production continues today on a vast commercial scale.

City centres of production, villages and tribes

The earliest carpets are late 15th-century, from the city of Tabriz. These have a large medallion, often shaped as a lotus flower, with stylized cloudbands (derived from Chinese art) and ARABESQUES. Some, called hunting carpets, show animals in combat. Variations on these themes appear in later 19th- and 20th-century pieces. In the 17th century, the city of ISFAHAN was the Islamic cultural centre. Carpets displayed all-over designs of vine tendrils supporting large PALMETTES, and *saz* leaves (shaped like the blade of a scythe). The background colour was usually red, in varying tones.

Ghashghai tribal rug, south-west Persia,
c.1890 [H]

In the city of Kirman, in the 16th and 17th centuries, products included vase carpets, so-called from their use of Chinese-style vases, within an overall repeat of a vine lattice with palmettes and leaves. Another classic carpet is the "Polonaise" group, thought to have come from Poland, but in fact made in Isfahan. Bright green, blue, red and ivory are the distinctive colours, with lavish use of gilt or silver brocading.

Fewer and poorer quality carpets were made in the 18th and early 19th centuries. But, by the mid-19th century, the booming European market and vogue for things Eastern led to renewed interest. Two distinct types of carpet were produced, both rooted in tradition. Town workshop-type carpets use curvilinear designs, emphasizing floral forms, palmettes, flowering vines and leaves, and sometimes people and exotic beasts. The format is either an overall repeat pattern or a central medallion design. PRAYER RUGS were also made, often including a tree of life. The formal and intricate designs were first drawn by the *ustad* (designer) and anonymous weavers would then translate the pattern onto the loom. Sometimes the signature or distinguishing mark of the *ustad* is woven into the carpet. Tribal and village type production was quite different. Rugs were more often made than carpets because the looms were smaller (transportable for nomadic tribes). Technical quality can vary. The best-known Persian tribes are the Afshar, the Khamseh and the GHASHGHAI (Kashgai). Geometric designs were woven from memory, with stylized versions of the naturalistic town rugs.

Perry, Mary Chase See PEWABIC POTTERY.

Persian knot

(Also called senneh or asymmetric knot) A knot used extensively to create the pile in carpets from Central and Eastern Persia, India and Central Asia. The

Persian knot

yarn is wrapped around one warp strand. It is particularly effective when creating curvilinear designs.

Persian style Fascination for Persian art, particularly carpets, flourished in the West in the late 19th century and filtered into the decorative arts. The establishment of such firms as ZIEGLER & CO. exporting Persian goods to Europe and the US disseminated the style, as did the exotic motifs illustrated in well-known pattern-books such as Owen JONES'S *Grammar of Ornament* (1856). MOTIFS such as serrated leaves, palmettes, cypress trees, pomegranates, peacocks, roses, carnations and irises began to appear on Western carpets, textiles and wallpapers; a characteristic Persian-influenced design is a brightly coloured formalized pattern of leaves and flowers against a cream or white ground, sometimes also used on ceramics and glass. Ceramic artists such as William DE MORGAN and French potter Eugène-Victor Collinot (d.1882) produced wares with floral designs and colour schemes inspired by Persian or IZNIK ceramics.

Petit, Jacob (1796–1865) A French porcelain maker in Paris from *c*.1790. He copied MEISSEN but also had his own style. In the 1830s he acquired, with his brother, a factory at Belleville and bought the factory at Fontainebleau from Baruch Weil. He sold the latter in 1862. The mark "JP" was used at both factories on decorative wares, sculptural clock cases, vases and large figural scent bottles.

Petit feu See ENAMEL COLOURS.

Petit point Embroidery made up of short, finely worked stitches (normally 18 or more to the inch), which generally cross only one warp or weft thread. Used to create upholstery, pictures, cushions and polescreens.

Petite sonnerie See STRIKING SYSTEMS.

Petuntse See CHINA STONE.

Pewabic pottery An American ART POTTERY founded in Detroit, Michigan, in 1903 by Mary Chase Perry (1868–1961). The name is taken from a local native American word for a river and means "copper colour in clay". Pewabic specialized in matt-, iridescent- or crystalline-glazed, thrown vases of robust shape with little decoration, tiles and architectural ceramics. The pottery was active until the 1950s.

Pew group A primitive English STAFFORDSHIRE stoneware group, usually of three figures seated on a high-backed pew or bench and sometimes with an arched canopy overhead, made *c*.1730–1740s. The figures often wear "court" dress. Some examples are in white SALTGLAZE with details highlighted in dark brown; others have fine translucent green, ochre and brown glazes. Pew groups are associated with John ASTBURY and Aaron WOOD.

Jacob Petit teapot, c.1835 [Q]

Pewter An alloy of tin and lead, often with small amounts of copper and/or antimony. The production of pewter probably began in the 3rd century AD, but manufacture on a large scale only developed in Europe from the Middle Ages. Durable, and much less expensive than silver or ceramics, pewter was mainly used for utilitarian domestic wares such as chargers, flagons, plates, tankards and candlesticks. Little early pewter has survived. Most is plain, although some pieces are decorated with WRIGGLEWORK designs of flowers and leaves. In the 16th century the French pewterer François Briot (*c*.1550–*c*.1616) created

Pewter tankard, English c.1695 [I]

ornate ewers and dishes decorated with MANNERIST ornament in low relief. "Display pewter" was also made in Germany, particularly Nuremberg, at this time. Pewter was made in North America from the mid-17th century onward.

Production of pewter declined in the 19th century with the introduction of BRITANNIA METAL and ELECTROPLATE. However, it enjoyed a revival in the ART NOUVEAU period, e.g. in wares produced by WMF and KAYSER & SÖHNE in Germany, and the TUDRIC range of LIBERTY & CO. in England. Many pewter items are stamped with TOUCH MARKS.

Phenakistoscope See CHOREUTOSCOPE.

Duncan Phyfe (1768–1854)

This Scottish-born American furniture-maker was active in Brooklyn, New York City, from *c*.1792. He was one of the most prestigious and successful cabinet-makers of the Federal period, with over 100 employees operating from three premises at the height of his output around 1810.

Phyfe mahogany scroll-back chair with double-cross back, 1807 [i]

The epitome of Federal style

Most of the furniture attributable to Duncan Phyfe is stylistically derived from English pattern-books, particularly those of SHERATON and HEPPLEWHITE, which he typically rendered in the finest Honduras mahogany, using elegant proportions and high quality details, especially in the carving. Phyfe's furniture tends to have greater exuberance in form than the English prototypes, for example in the sweep of its SABRE LEGS or carved FINIALS. His success came at a time of rapid expansion in the United States, particularly in New York, which by 1820 was the nation's largest city. New York's affluence made it ideal for furniture-makers and over 100 were active there by 1805, notably Michael ALLISON, who occupied premises a few streets away from Phyfe. Many, like Allison, worked in the same style as Phyfe and it is difficult to attribute furniture directly to Phyfe's workshops, particularly as fewer than 20 labelled pieces exist, but his quality is outstanding. Phyfe was among the first US cabinet-makers to use factory "assembly-line" methods. He employed professional and apprentice carvers, turners and upholsterers, each performing a specific task.

Phyfe met the demands of the fashionable élite in New York and beyond with a wide range of furniture, particularly large and ambitious pieces for dining rooms. Among his clients were the wealthy merchant John Jacob Astor and the socialite Louisa Throop, for whom Phyfe made a well-documented suite of furniture in 1808. This included a Grecian style sofa with a carved, GREEK KEY frieze, a console table in the French taste with ORMOLU mounts, a bed in neo-Egyptian style and a lyre-back chair. The carved lyre, used as a chair back and support for work tables, is highly characteristic of Phyfe. Other typical carved features include ACANTHUS terminals and finials, extensive REEDING, sometimes overlaid with ribbons or drapery swags tied with tassels, pineapple finials and eagle splats. The Throop suite, with its wide range of influences, is representative of Phyfe's ability as an innovator. He was always at the forefront of developing trends and interpreted them in a restrained, elegant way. Much of his work is conservative, REGENCY-style mahogany furniture, distinguished mainly by high standards of craftsmanship. Phyfe's name and interpretation of the formal English Regency style have remained popular in the United States through extensive reproductions, which are generically referred to as "Duncan Phyfe style".

Upholstered mahogany sofa, by Duncan Phyfe, in which the toprail is finely carved with wheat sheaves, c.1800–15 [A]

Armchair *en gondole*, . with French-influenced lotus leaves on the arm supports, c.1830 [B]

Edison Gem phonograph, 1880s [N]

Phonograph A sound recording and reproducing machine, invented by the American Thomas Edison in 1877. It uses a revolving wax cylinder to record vibrations caused by noise via a stylus attached to a diaphragm. Later variations such as the popular "Gem" played pre-recorded cylinders, amplifying sound via a horn.

Phrenology head A representation of the head, usually ceramic, used in the 19th-century "science" of phrenology, an early form of psychology that linked the conformation of the skull to character. The most famous phrenological heads were made by the American Lorenzo Niles Fowler (1809–87). Nineteenth-century examples are relatively scarce but have been much reproduced.

Piano baby (or piano doll) A bisque figure of a baby with moulded hair and INTAGLIO eyes, intended for display on an upright piano. Most piano babies were produced by HEUBACH, between 1910 and 1920.

Phrenology head, c.1850 [J]

Picture back A die-stamped image in low relief on the backs of the bowls of some late 18th-century silver spoons. Images included squirrels, birds and flowers, or occasionally political or topical subjects.

Picture clock A type of clock in which the movement is concealed behind a painting, with a small aperture for the dial that appears as the clock on a tower, lighthouse or windmill. They were made by BLACK FOREST clockmakers in the mid-19th century and often incorporate automata or musical work.

Piecrust A popular motif in the mid-18th century, typified by a frilly decorative edging, commonly seen on English furniture, especially circular tea tables, as well as silver SALVERS and STRAWBERRY DISHES.

Piecrust ware Pie dishes and TUREENS made in CANEWARE or a light brown EARTHENWARE, with the cover moulded to simulate pastry. Popular in England during the Napoleonic wars when wheat was in short supply and made by various English factories, including WEDGWOOD. Piecrust borders also appeared on ceramic plates.

Pier A vertical solid, often load-bearing masonry support found between window and door frames and other openings.

Pierced decoration Intricate OPENWORK decoration. The piercing was initially done with a sharp hand-chisel, then with a fretsaw and finally by mechanical punches. The term also applies to the openwork carving of GOTHIC TRACERY and, in furniture, to the BAROQUE and ROCOCO detailing of chair backs, CRESTINGS and APRONS. A popular metalware technique, pierced decoration was frequently interspersed with engraved and chased designs on silver baskets. It also served a functional purpose for strainers, caster covers, mustard pots and salt cellars. Pottery and porcelain, especially potpourri vases and bouquetières, were also decorated with pierced designs from the 18th century onward.

Pier glass A tall, narrow mirror, popular in the 18th century, designed to hang on the wall between two windows (the pier), often above a PIER TABLE.

Pierotti Together with Augusta MONTANARI, the best-known manufacturer of poured WAX DOLLS in the middle of the 19th century. The family business was established in London around 1790 by the Italian Domenico Pierotti and was continued by successive generations until after 1925. The Pierottis were exceptionally skilled wax-modellers, and were particularly famous for their life-like portrait dolls. Pierotti dolls often have a slightly turned head and tend to have shorter hair and more slender limbs than their Montanari counterparts.

Pier table A small side table designed to stand against a pier – the wall between two windows. Fashionable from the 17th century, they were frequently surmounted by a PIER GLASS after the influential late 18th-century designs of the Scottish architect Robert ADAM, who believed that furniture should be an integral part of the overall decorative scheme of a room. The table and mirror, which were designed to stand together, featured common decorative elements.

Adam-style marble topped pier table, c.1780 [C]

Pietre dure An Italian term meaning HARDSTONES, such as jasper, lapis lazuli, agate and chalcedony. Pietre dure was an expensive form of inlay, using thin slivers from a variety of semi-precious stones and was initially reserved for small decorative objects. A highly developed technique in ancient Rome, it was revived during the Renaissance in Italy and perfected in the early 17th century. The most famous centre of production was the Ducal workshops in Florence under the patronage of the Medicis, but Italian craftsmen also spread the technique farther afield in Europe. Pietre dure was lavishly employed for large vases, ewers and bowls extravagantly mounted with gold, and for furniture, such as table tops and display cabinets.

Piggin A small cylindrical drinking vessel, made in glass, ceramic or silver in the shape of a half-barrel with a vertical stave for a handle. Glass versions were often used as dippers for milk and cream. The name may be related to "pipkin".

Pilaster An architectural term for a shallow pier or rectangular classical COLUMN, attached to a façade for decoration rather than structural support. Popular during periods of Classical revival, the pilaster generally appears along with other architectural MOTIFS, such as entablature and a flattened version of the appropriate column CAPITAL. Pilasters were carved on Tudor and Jacobean chests and bed heads, and in the 18th century they framed the doors of cabinets and cupboards, fluted with Corinthian or Composite capitals.

Pilaster

Pietre dure cabinet, Italian 17th century [G]

Pile The surface of a carpet when made with strands of wool, cotton or silk that are secured to a foundation, tufted and trimmed to the desired depth, which is determined by the fineness of the weave.

Pilgrim bottle A pottery gourd-shaped bottle with two loops at the sides for a strap to be threaded through to suspend the bottle. In primitive times they were made from goat-skin, but were later made in Italian maiolica and silver. Made all over Europe from the 16th century and sometimes decorated with a shell – the sign of a pilgrim.

Pilgrim chair A term used generically in the United States to describe a stick-constructed open armchair with rush-woven seat and turned elements, comparable to provincial English chairs of the 17th and 18th centuries. Indigenous woods such as maple, ash and hickory were used. The back pieces could be either turned or slats. The turned spindles and finials could be simple or elaborate and, generally, the more massive the turnings the earlier the chair.

Pilgrim furniture An American term for furniture made for the first Puritan settlers in New England in the 17th century. Simply and solidly constructed, pilgrim furniture typically mirrors English furniture styles. Pieces were made from white oak and American ash which were abundantly available.

Pilkington's Tile & Pottery Co. Known as Pilkington's and sometimes Royal Lancastrian (from 1913), the factory was founded near Manchester in 1891 by the Pilkington brothers to make architectural ceramics. They extended their range to include domestic vessels with distinctive glazes – Sunstone (1893), eggshell (1896), lustre (1906), mottled and matt, "Cunian" (1927/28) and Lapis wares (1928). They ceased making decorative ceramics in 1937 but continue to make tiles today.

Pillar-and-claw table See TRIPOD TABLE.

Pin box A porcelain box made in Europe during the late 19th and early 20th centuries. The covers often have FAIRING type figures or animals. They were inexpensive SOUVENIR WARES.

Pilkington lustre vase, c.1910 [J]

Pinchbeck An alloy of copper and zinc that closely resembles gold in appearance. It was invented in the early 18th century by Christopher Pinchbeck (1670–1732), a Fleet Street watchmaker and was widely used for making jewellery and small metal items such as snuff-boxes and shoe buckles until c.1854 when the sale of lower carat gold became legal.

Pine A straight-grained wood, coloured yellow or white, from species of *Pinus*. Widely grown, the term frequently designates other coniferous woods, including the fir, larch and cedar. Ranging from relatively hard to very soft, pine was widely used by English furniture-makers from the early 17th century, especially for the linings and sides of drawers, the backs of carcasses and as a foundation for gilding or veneers made of more expensive timbers. In the United States, Scandinavia and in Alpine areas, pine was the preferred wood for vernacular furniture and for cheaper furniture that was subsequently painted.

Pineapple motif An ancient motif symbolizing fertility. From the late 17th century, the pineapple motif appeared in both Europe and America, used primarily on entrance architecture, such as gate-posts, on guest beds and as a table centrepiece. Cultivated as an exotic fruit in the 17th century, after it was presented to

Pineapple motif

Charles II by his royal gardener John Rose, the pineapple is sometimes confused with pinecone ornament. Decorative silver cups for display were made in the form of pineapples in 17th-century Germany. During the ROCOCO period, the pineapple was typically appropriated for finials on furniture and silver. Josiah Wedgwood produced a tableware based on the pineapple form in the mid-18th century.

Pinfire action A BREECHLOADING firearm using a self-contained CARTRIDGE that incorporated a pin in its base. When this was struck by the hammer, it set off a percussion cap and fired the gun. The pinfire system was invented by Casimir LeFaucheaux in 1835 and, although obsolete by *c*.1870, it survived into the early 20th century.

Pinion A small, toothed wheel acting as a gear in a clock movement. The pinions, usually made of iron or steel but sometimes wood or brass, engage with larger wheels in the TRAIN.

Pinxton porcelain cup and saucer, c.1810 [R]

Pinxton porcelain factory An English factory founded near Derby, in 1796 by William BILLINGSLEY with the help, and on the estate, of John Coke. They made a fine soft paste, copied shapes from Derby and Worcester and sometimes decorated with flowers and landscapes, some by Billingsley himself. The partnership was dissolved in 1799. John Coke carried on, but closed the factory in 1813.

Pipe stopper (tamper) A pipe-smoker's tool with a flat, rounded end used for pressing tobacco into the bowl of a pipe. Made from the 17th century in various materials and forms.

Piqué (or piqué d'or) A decoration on tortoiseshell or ivory first developed in the mid-17th century by the Neapolitan jeweller Laurentini and used throughout the 19th century in jewellery, snuff-boxes and étuis. Small studs and strips of gold or silver were inlaid on the base material and secured in place by heating.

Pistol handle A style of knife haft or handle that tapers outward from the blade end and curves around at the other end

Pistol-handled knife, French c.1735 [R]

rather like the grip of a pistol. Pistol handles can be plain, or octagonal in section. They occur in silver, porcelain, ivory and wood from *c*.1715 through the 18th century. The grip was occasionally found on forks.

Pivot A small spindle or shaft, usually made of steel, on which a wheel or pinion of the TRAIN in a clock or watch movement rotates.

Plane A yellow-white, close-grained, durable wood. A variety of maple from eastern Europe, plane was primarily used as an inlay and veneer in the latter part of the 18th century. It was also used in country furniture for painted chairs and folding tables as a substitute for beech. A lacy FIGURE – known as lacewood – appears when it is quarter-sawn and this was popular in the ART DECO period.

Planetarium An expansion of the ORRERY, the planetarium is a complex instrument often made of brass, which

Planetarium by W&S Jones, English c.1800 [B]

demonstrates the motions of the sun, moon and planets. Ivory balls representing the planets are supported on wires with long rods to a central pivot and the instrument is cranked round by hand.

Planishing (French *planir*: "to smooth out") The action of giving a smooth or flat surface to a sheet of metal by using rollers or, more usually, beating it with a planishing hammer, i.e. one that has a broad smooth polished head, while the metal is supported on a stake.

Plank, Ernst One of the most important 19th-century German manufacturers of TINPLATE toys, founded in 1866 in Nuremberg. The company was possibly the first to make a TINPLATE electric train, in 1882. Steam trains, then clockwork, followed from 1890. Steam- and clockwork-driven boats were popular products, with steam cars produced from 1904. In 1914 an amphibious car/boat hybrid and a working lead diver were made. The company was taken over in the mid-1930s and toy production ceased.

Plastic (Greek: *plastikos*) A term applied to materials that can be moulded and shaped. Although natural plastics exist, such as tortoiseshell and shellac, plastics are primarily synthetic materials. The 19th century saw the birth of semi-synthetic and synthetic plastics with CELLULOID, xylonite and casein, but BAKELITE, invented in 1907 by the Belgian chemist Leo Baekland (1863–1944), is credited with being the first important completely synthetic plastic. Adaptable and often inexpensive, from the 1920s to the late 1940s plastics helped to free the world from the dominance of wood, ceramics and metal, and ushered in a new age of style. This was linked with an increasing interest in design, and many plastic objects display

Plastic record carrier, UK late 1950s [s]

Plastic: melamine tableware, late 1950s [s]

key elements from ART DECO and industrial design movements. Many famous 20th-century designers including René LALIQUE, Henry DREYFUSS, Walter Dorwin Teague, Raymond Loewy and Wells Coates designed plastic objects. One household object that benefited from the invention of plastic was the radio, whose simple wooden case changed to one of brightly coloured Catalin (a phenolic resin) or Bakelite, in a variety of modern and stylish designs. Domestic objects, as well as desk accessories and jewellery, were also made from an ever-increasing range of coloured plastics. The adaptability and low cost of plastics made them popular during the Depression years of the 1930s and later, but after World War II the nature of plastics changed with the introduction of injection moulding, acrylic, polythene and VINYL (used particularly in toymaking). But public taste also changed and the golden age of plastics was over.

[1]Plate An abbreviated form of SHEFFIELD PLATE.

[2]Plate A descriptive term corrupted from the Spanish *plata* to describe wrought gold and silver wares.

[3]Plate A shallow, usually circular dish of any material on which food is served.

Plate bucket A bucket-shaped wooden container with a brass handle, for carrying plates between kitchen and dining room in 18th-century houses. Also called plate pails, they sometimes had fretwork sides to facilitate warming, and a slot or open section for ready access to the plates.

Plate cameras The term for any camera that uses a fixed sensitized film or glass plate. Plate cameras date from *c.*1851, when the Englishman Frederick Scott

Plate camera, English 1940s [Q]

Archer invented a process that used a wooden box with a fixed brass-bound lens, the back of the box having a removable focusing screen and a wooden film plate. This held a glass plate coated with iodized collodion and sensitized with a solution of silver nitrate – the glass negative from which paper positives were printed before the coating dried and hardened. The process, called wet-plate photography, was practised for the next 40 years. Such cameras came in various formats and are highly prized today. Dry-plate cameras were used from 1871, when an English physician Richard Leach Maddox suggested gelatin emulsions be used instead of collodion which gave off harmful vapour. By 1880 gelatin dry plates were on sale and were used widely for the next 70 years. The roll-film camera, introduced by Kodak in 1888, gradually replaced plate cameras by the 20th century. See also BOX BROWNIE.

Platform lever escapement A type of ESCAPEMENT in clocks, similar to the LEVER ESCAPEMENT in watches, that incorporates an oscillating balance wheel instead of a pendulum. From the early 19th century it was commonly mounted on a platform on the top of a CARRIAGE

CLOCK. It enabled the clock to keep accurate time while in transit as it is not affected by movement.

Platinum A silvery-white and precious metal more valuable than silver and gold because of its rarity. Discovered in Mexico in the 16th century, it was only used in Europe from the 19th century when it was popular as a setting for diamonds. Malleable and ductile, with high tensile strength, it is usually alloyed with palladium, another metal of the platinum family.

Playing cards Thought to originate in ancient China, playing cards reached Europe via the Islamic Empire *c.*1380.

Playing cards, English 1930s–40s [s, each]

The now standard pack of 52 cards evolved from a 16th-century French design. They gradually became more decorative and many idiosyncratic packs were produced in England in the 17th and 18th centuries. Germany and Austria became the chief 19th-century producers.

Playworn (or "loved") A euphemism for poor condition when describing the appearance of a TEDDY BEAR.

Pleydell-Bouverie, Katherine
See STUDIO POTTERY.

Plique à jour A technique by which a translucent enamel is held in an unbacked framework to produce an effect similar to that of a stained glass window when light is shone through it. It was developed in

Plique à jour Art Nouveau pin, French 1905 [D]

Russia during the 17th century and used extensively by the jewellers of the ART NOUVEAU style.

Plum A FRUITWOOD of the *Prunus* genus, yielding a hard and heavy pinkish wood with a heart of deep brownish red. Plumwood was used from the 16th century for INLAY and turned work, and for country CABINET furniture, but fell from favour after the 17th century.

Plush A soft material with cut pile that resembles fur, used to make TEDDY BEARS from the early 20th century. It was also used for late 19th-century tablecloths.

Plymouth porcelain William COOKWORTHY, a chemist who first combined KAOLIN and CHINA STONE, produced England's first HARD-PASTE porcelain in 1768 at Plymouth. He was inexpert at firing and wares sometimes show distortion and a smoky, spotted glaze. In 1770 the factory moved to Castle Green, Bristol. In 1774 it was taken over by Richard CHAMPION and ceased to be called Plymouth.

Plymouth Pottery Co.
Founded by William Alsop, this pottery in Plymouth, England, made blue-printed earthenware, marked with the Queen's Arms from 1856 to 1863.

Plymouth porcelain mug, *c.*1770 [F]

Plywood A composition wood, of three or more layers, each alternate layer with the grain at right angles for strength. Used in furniture-making from the 18th century, it was appreciated by BIEDERMEIER craftsmen in Germany and Austria in the 19th century who developed it in BENTWOOD chair backs. It was popular into the 20th century, particularly in the US.

Pocket watch The first watch small enough to be carried in a pocket, made *c.*1550. Early watches were more decorative than useful. With the introduction of the balance spring in 1675, they became accurate enough to be used as timekeepers. Attached to a waistcoat with a FOB CHAIN from the early 19th century.

Pocket watch, English 1914 [P]

Point de neige (French: "stitch of snow") Late 17th-century VENETIAN NEEDLE LACE with small-scale design, used for items such as gentlemen's cravats, ladies' headdresses and LAPPETS.

Poker work The craft of creating formal patterns and pictorial scenes on light-coloured wood, such as holly, sycamore, chestnut or lime, by scorching the surface with hot metal rods or needles. A decorative technique practised from the 17th century in Italy, it was especially popular with artistic amateurs and ladies of leisure during the 19th century.

Polearm A weapon made up of a blade, head or spike (sometimes elaborately worked) mounted on a wooden shaft. In the late 17th century, polearms were superseded by firearms, but they were carried by officers as symbols of rank until the late 19th century.

Polescreen An adjustable FIRESCREEN on a pole, with a platform or tripod base. The screen may be moved vertically and locked at various heights. In general use from *c.*1730 to protect the user from the heat of a fire, versions were made by leading manufacturers of the day such as Robert ADAM and Thomas CHIPPENDALE.

Polyphon A German manufacturer of clocks and clockwork musical boxes, established in 1889 by Gustave Brachhausen. Polyphon Musikwerke produced clocks with disc movements that were often coin operated. Their musical boxes included tabletop 15-, 19⅝-, 22- and 24-inch disc models in upright cabinets, often with disc bins beneath for storage. The company is still in production.

Pomander (Old French *pomme d'ambre;* medieval Latin *pomum ambrae:* "apple of amber") A small container, usually spherical and made of silver gilt, gold, ceramic and metal from the 16th century to the present day. They are divided into compartments for holding scents and spices. Worn on a chain, they were thought to protect the wearer from disease.

Pomegranate motif A decorative Oriental and Classical device based on the fruit of the pomegranate tree, believed to symbolize fertility and plenty. Used in wood-carving and plasterwork, textiles and silver, the pomegranate was a favourite, naturally rendered motif in England during the JACOBEAN period and enjoyed a revival in the late 19th century.

Pomona glass A type of US ART GLASS stained amber and with etched, floral patterns. Pomona was a trademark at the NEW ENGLAND GLASS COMPANY, mostly for stemware, and was also used as a colour (known as Pomona green) by the STEUBEN GLASSWORKS.

Pompeiian style A variant of the NEO-CLASSICAL style popular from the late 18th to the mid-19th century, inspired by antiquities and frescoes excavated at the ancient Italian cities of Pompeii and Herculaneum in the 18th century. It is characterized by the use of a deep red colour, called Pompeiian red, and delicate Neo-classical motifs such as PATERAE, HUSKS and PALMETTES.

It is found on SÈVRES porcelain made in the 1840s and 1850s – not always on Classically inspired forms – as well as on textiles, wallpapers and painted furniture.

Ponti, Gio (1891–1979) An Italian architect and designer of ceramics (for Richard Ginori from 1923–30), furniture,

Cabinet by Gio Ponti, 1950s [I]

textiles, lighting and glass. He was also a professor of architecture and the editor of *Domus*, which he founded in 1928. As a designer he drew on Italy's Classical heritage but combined it with all the advantages that modern industrialization had to offer, managing to maintain the balance between both

Pontil mark An irregular or ring-shaped mark on the base of a blown glass made when the piece is taken off the pontil rod.

Pontil mark

Pontypool ware A type of JAPANNED tinplated iron produced at the Pontypool factory – founded by the Allgood family in Monmouthshire, Wales – from c.1680 to 1822. Wares typically include trays, boxes and urns japanned in black, brown or tortoiseshell colours and hand-painted or gilded with CHINOISERIE, flowers and, later, landscapes and sporting scenes. Pontypool gave its name to similar wares made elsewhere.

Poole Pottery An English pottery in Poole, Dorset, founded by Jesse Carter (1830–1927), a potter and tilemaker. It became known as Carters in 1901 and in 1921 a subsidiary was formed to make domestic artistic ceramics, hand-thrown and hand-decorated, often with stylized floral motifs in deep, subtle colours with predominant blue. The subsidiary company was known as Carter, Stabler and Adams after the principal designers. In 1962 it became Poole Potteries Ltd and is still active.

Poole Pottery vases, 1930s [Q (small); R (large)]

Poplar A yellowish-grey, fine-grained softwood, commonly chosen for inlay in the 16th and early 17th centuries. It was sometimes stained before use to create decorative marquetry for the veneers of cabinets, chests and chests-of-drawers.

Porcelain flowers See VINCENNES.

Porcellaneous A high quality porcelain-type stoneware made in China from the 6th century onward. It is like porcelain but less translucent. The Chinese do not distinguish between the two, calling both *ci* (*tz'u*). It was also made in Europe, particularly in the 19th century.

Porcelain

Porcelain was first produced in China and is recorded as early as the Sui (581–671) and T'ang (618–907) dynasties. The translucency of the ceramic material is noted as being the distinctive feature and was described in the 8th century by an Arab (Soliman or Saleyman).

What it is and how it is made

Efforts to imitate Chinese porcelain in Europe led first to the development of SOFT-PASTE PORCELAIN, made from white clay and ground glass, before the true, HARD-PASTE recipe was discovered in 1709 at MEISSEN. BONE CHINA, patented in 1748, is similar but with the addition of pure white bone ash. Not much porcelain was made in America before the 19th century. Porcelain is made from KAOLIN (china clay), QUARTZ and FELDSPAR. In European hard-paste porcelain the proportions are 40–65 per cent kaolin, 12–30 per cent quartz and 15–35 per cent feldspar. The feldspar and quartz act as a FLUX – they make the kaolin less plastic and reduce the firing and drying shrinkage. The kaolin, which is a brittle, earthy and easily crumbling clay, is scoured with water in a "churning" machine and coarse particles are sieved off. This well-stirred SLIP has the water removed in filter presses, leaving the kaolin to settle in small particles. The feldspar and quartz are broken down in stone crushers, crushing rollers and drum mills.

The prepared ingredients are mixed in precise proportions and stirred together in a large, vat-like container with a beater or agitator to form a stiff mixture. The mixture is pressed through filters to take out excess water. Although still containing some water the mass is now stored in a damp room. It has to be kneaded again before use, which also gets rid of any air bubbles. There are three ways to form a porcelain vessel from the kneaded body. Round, flat objects can be turned on the potter's wheel. The second method, moulding or casting, is used for figures and also for vases and tureens. The object is made in clay. A cast taken from this forms the mould, which is made in sections to enable it to be removed. The porcelain mass, which has been mixed with water and soda, is now poured into the plaster mould. The plaster draws out the water from the mass while it is drying, which causes shrinkage of a few millimetres from the sides of the mould. Any superfluous mass is poured off and the object is taken out. The third method is PRESS-MOULDING, used for mass production. The clay is placed in a container and a patterned metal mould is pressed onto it.

Drying, firing and glazing

The newly created porcelain items are dried out in specially aired rooms. This has to be done under carefully controlled conditions to stop cracks due to shrinking. Then the pieces are fired to 800°C (1470°F). The glaze is the next process (if left unglazed it is called BISCUIT porcelain). It is applied by immersing the piece into the liquid glaze, which is essentially of the same materials as the body, but containing more fluxing agents so that it is more glass-like and easier to melt. To be satisfactory a glaze must flow well at the relevant temperature. It must also have the same rate of expansion as the body, otherwise glaze cracks will develop. ENAMEL COLOURS can then be painted over the glaze. The glazed objects are put into "saggers" (round boxes of fireproof clay, so that the ware is protected from smoke). The saggers are stacked in the kiln and the second firing takes place at 1300–1400°C (2370–2550°F) to complete the process.

European porcelain was much influenced by Chinese blue and white as in this plate dating from the mid-18th century [s]

Rococo style perfectly suited the fragility and crisp moulding of this Meissen porcelain group with Cupid, by Kändler, c.1750–70 [F]

Bone china was the standard body for 19th-century English wares as in this sugar box designed by Miles Mason, c.1808–13 [P]

Porphyry (Greek *porphyros*: "purple") A hard volcanic rock varying in colour from green to red. Purple porphyry, found only at Mount Porphyrites in Egypt, was mined by the Romans from *c*.400 BC to *c*.AD 500. Many ancient pieces were reworked in the Renaissance, particularly in Florence. In the late 19th century the mines were re-opened and quantities of "Roman-style" porphyry came onto the market.

Silver porringer, English, 1836 [I]

¹Porringer (French *potager*: "soup bowl") A two-handled, cylindrical, slightly tapering cup with a curved base, with or without a cover. Made in silver, pewter or ceramics from *c*.1650–1750, for soup.

²Porringer In the US, a porringer is a shallow vessel with a flat, pierced handle, called a BLEEDING BOWL in Britain. See also CAUDLE CUP.

Portland Vase The finest CAMEO-GLASS vase surviving from antiquity, and an important influence on English glass and ceramics manufacturers from the late 18th century. Made between the 1st century BC and the 1st century AD, it was found in the late 16th century in a Classical tomb in Rome, passed into the ownership of the Barberini family and was brought to London in 1784 by Sir William Hamilton, ambassador to the Court of

Naples and a keen collector. He, in turn, sold the vase to the Dowager Duchess of Portland (hence its name). In 1810, her son, the 4th Duke of Portland, lent the vase to the British Museum, London, where it remains today. From 1790, it was copied in JASPER WARE by the WEDGWOOD factory. An exact copy in cameo glass was not made until 1876, after 20 years of experiment, by John NORTHWOOD; other copies followed.

Portrait doll A doll that portrays a person, either real or fictitious, made by leading manufacturers from *c*.1870. Perhaps the most sought-after 20th-century example is a doll depicting Queen Elizabeth II of Great Britain, aged 4, made in 1930 by Schönau and Hofmeister and later by CHAD VALLEY and others.

Posset pot A drinking vessel for posset (hot milk mixed with beer or wine and spices), of TIN-GLAZED EARTHENWARE, with double handles, a cover and spout from which the posset was drunk. Made in both England and Holland, from the 16th to the 18th centuries.

Postcards The world's first postcard was issued by the Austrian Post Office on 1 October 1869, and in 1872, when the German Post Office allowed privately printed cards, the first picture postcards were published. The golden age of postcards is considered to be from 1900 to World War 1, when the majority were printed by CHROMO-LITHOGRAPHY. Today, collectors seek vintage examples from that era, as well as more modern cards, particularly those featuring events and personalities that sum up the spirit of their time.

Wedgwood copy of the Portland Vase, c.1790 [E]

Post-Modernism A style initiated in the late 1970s/early 1980s in opposition to the stark surface content of Modernism. Generally, it aims to use ornament, past or present, to enhance furniture, furnishings and architecture, and create, in the words of Robert VENTURI, "messy vitality over obvious unity". Italy was the dominant producer of Post-Modernism, with the work of the Studio Alchimia and the MEMPHIS group leading the way.

Gold posy ring, 1680 [G]

Posy rings (or poesy rings) Originated in the 15th century and given as tokens of love. Early examples are simple gold bands with an engraved inscription such as "A loving wife, a happy life" or "God above increase our love".

Potash glass A type of glass in which potash has been used as the alkaline ingredient. The resulting glass, known as WALDGLAS in Germany and Bohemia and VERRE DE FOUGÈRE in France, was harder and more brilliant than SODA GLASS, and better suited to cutting and engraving. See also BOHEMIAN GLASS.

Staffordshire pot lid, Dale Hall Pottery, 1850 [Q]

Pot lid A cover of a shallow circular or oblong earthenware box, dating from the mid-19th and early 20th centuries. These boxes held substances such as hair grease and ointments. The covers were transfer-printed in colours or, rarely, in black and white, with a great variety of subjects (almost 300 have been estimated). The best lids were made by Felix Pratt.

Potschappel See THIEME, Carl.

Posters

War, peace and the lure of travel are some of the themes vividly conveyed by the vintage poster. This art form developed from the technique of lithography in the 1860s and proved an irresistible medium for some major 19th- and 20th-century designers.

The art of advertising

Although letterpress posters have existed since the 15th century, posters as we now know them date from the invention of LITHOGRAPHY in the 1860s. Brightly coloured images could be printed cheaply and easily, leading to the development of commercial poster production. The French artist Jules CHÉRET (1836–1932), produced over a thousand poster designs, while Henri de TOULOUSE-LAUTREC (1864–1901), whose posters have now achieved the status of fine art, designed only 31, creating a series of powerful images of Parisian night life in the 1890s. In the same period, Alphonse MUCHA developed a series of extravagant ART NOUVEAU designs, initially for the theatre, then for consumer products such as cigarettes and chocolate. Across Europe the style was adopted by such designers as T. Privat-Livemont (1861–1936) in Belgium, and Jan Toorop (1858–1928) in Austria. The advent of World War I in 1914 saw the poster evolve into a propaganda tool for the military. One of the most important from this date was the recruitment poster entitled "Your Country Needs You" by Alfred Leete (1882-1933), similar in patriotic appeal to James Montgomery FLAGG's version in the US.

Toulouse-Lautrec: "Divan Japonais", a classic image of a Parisian fin-de-siècle cafe with, in the foreground, the cabaret artist Jane Avril, 1892 [i]

After World War I, the great age of automotive travel arrived. Posters promoted cars, trains, planes and the latest routes offered by the great ocean liners such as the *Lusitania* and the ill-fated *Titanic* as well as immigrant shipping lines to Australia and New Zealand. Artists such as CASSANDRE and Ludwig HOHLWEIN created images that spoke volumes and the power of the poster as an effective means of mass-communication was realized in the way that we know it today.

The poster continues to be judged as a work of graphic art and such examples as Bernard Villemot's work for the Swiss shoe company Bally in the 1970s are considered outstanding. In the category of film posters, the impact of the film is what determines value as designers work "in house" and are consequently anonymous. Posters of classic films such as *The Mummy* (1932) and *Casablanca* (1942) grow in popularity. More recently, Clint Eastwood "cop" films such as *Magnum Force* (1973) have produced striking posters, which look set to become the antiques of the future.

Cunard Line poster depicting the "Aquitania" by the British designer Odin Rosenvinge, a prolific poster artist, c.1920 [i]

"The Tower of London" by Edward McKnight Kauffer (1890–1954), one of a series that Kauffer produced for London Underground, 1934 [o]

Pottery The craft of making wares from clay, developed from *c.*6000 BC in the ancient Near East. By *c.*3500 BC, the techniques of FIRING and using the wheel and turntable had been introduced, with LEAD GLAZES recorded in Mesopotamia from *c.*2000 BC. These spread to the Greek world, giving rise to Attic wares by 600 BC. In China, pottery enriched by Greek influences dates from the Han dynasty (206 BC–AD 220).

European pottery was comparatively primitive until the Middle Ages and the arrival of Oriental and Islamic influences. The process of adding tin oxide to the basic lead glaze led to a form of TIN-GLAZED EARTHENWARE, brought by the Moorish invaders to Spain and resulting in the production of HISPANO-MORESQUE wares; then Italian MAIOLICA, French FAIENCE, German fayence and, by the mid-16th century, Dutch and British DELFTWARE. In the mid-17th century European immigrants took their pottery skills to the New World. The craze for porcelain that swept the Western world from the early 18th century did not halt the development of the pottery industry, for instance in the STONEWARE and CREAMWARE factories of STAFFORDSHIRE. The simplicity of early forms has been rediscovered by ART and STUDIO POTTERS.

Pouffe A backless upholstered seat resembling a large round cushion, with a wooden frame. It first appeared in France *c.*1845 and remained popular throughout the late 19th and 20th centuries.

¹Pounce A fine powder of gum sandarach (pine resin) or cuttlefish bone, sprinkled on writing paper or parchment both before and after writing to prevent the ink from spreading, used from the Middle Ages until the end of the 18th century.

²Pounce A form of stippled decoration made by pricking or hammering with a sharp pointed instrument onto SILVER, PEWTER and other metals.

Pounce box (or pot) A box, made of silver or wood (TREEN) for POUNCE with a PIERCED cover, either produced singly or fitted to silver or pewter INKSTANDS in the 17th and 18th centuries.

Poupard (French: "baby doll") An all-in-one skittle-like doll, carved from a single piece of wood and painted to represent a baby in swaddling clothes. They were made throughout Europe, especially Germany, from the late 17th century onward. Present-day makers interpret traditional designs.

Powder-blue A traditional Chinese decorative technique for ceramics where, as an UNDERGLAZE decoration, powdered pigment is blown through a gauze onto an oiled surface giving a fine, grainy appearance or effect. It was imitated in Europe from the 18th century, especially at MEISSEN, SÈVRES, BOW and WORCESTER.

Powder-decorated glass A type of ART GLASS, patented in 1806 by the 19th-century Staffordshire earthenware and porcelain-maker John Davenport of Longport, and also known as Davenport's Patent Glass. A paste of powdered glass was applied to an object and a design incised on it, commonly of a sporting scene or coat of arms. This was then fused onto the glass. Powder-decorated glass was very fashionable: in 1806 and 1808 the Prince of Wales ordered extensive sets. It was made until the mid-19th century.

Powder flask A container used for loose gunpowder in MUZZLE-loading guns, from the early 18th century. Originally, leather bags were used, but it was soon found that cows' horns were safer. Flasks were later made in

Powder flask, English c.1840 [Q]

wood, metal, antler and ivory. Most incorporate a spout, which measures the correct gunpowder charge. From 1800–50, flasks were made from die-stamped metal, often incorporating decorative motifs. The metallic CARTRIDGE superseded powder flasks in the 1860s.

Powell, James & Sons
See WHITEFRIARS GLASSWORKS.

Powolny, Michael (1874–1954) An Austrian ceramicist and sculptor, one of the founders of the SECESSION and WIENER WERKSTÄTTE movements. He specialized in white FAIENCE figures painted in black in Secession style, and both as a teacher (Lucie RIE was a pupil) and craftsman influenced Austrian, British and US ceramics of the 1930s.

Prattware plate, 1850 [O]

Prattware A type of pottery made at Lane Delph in Staffordshire, at a factory founded *c.*1775 by William Pratt. It was copied by other factories such as BRISTOL. It is similar to PEARLWARE, but is characterized by a strong high-temperature palette of blue, green and yellow. In the mid-1840s, the same factory, styled F.R. Pratt & Co., excelled in multicoloured TRANSFER PRINTING, used to decorate tablewares and POT LIDS until the 1880s.

Praxinoscope An optical toy popular in the 19th century, patented by Reynaud in 1877, and a development of the MAGIC LANTERN. It consists of a cylindrical or polygonal box, open at the top, with a series of pictures arranged along the inside. Mirrors inside the box reflect the images of the pictures. When the box is rotated the reflections blend together, giving an illusion of movement. Subjects include galloping horses or somersaulting clowns. The praxinoscope is found in a variety of models, both hand- and steam-operated, or topped by either a candle or a spirit burner. They continued to be made up to the late 19th century.

Silk Feraghan prayer rug, west Persia
late 19th century [G]

Prayer rug A name that refers to both a functional artifact used by Muslims and to a decorative design on a carpet. The composition is always directional and asymmetrical. Prayer rugs are made in curvilinear form in cities and in rectilinear form by tribal groups. When the rug is used, the pointed end of the MIHRAB is aligned in the direction of Mecca.

Precious stones An arbitrary term for a group of gems notable for their beauty, rarity and value, which normally includes DIAMOND, EMERALD, RUBY, SAPPHIRE and PEARL. Other highly prized gemstones that could qualify, include Imperial JADE, black OPAL and ALEXANDRITE.

Preiss, Ferdinand
(1882–1943)
A Berlin-based ivory-carver and sculptor. In 1906 he formed the company Preiss-Kassler, which produced bronze and ivory figures in the classical style. It closed during World War I, but re-opened in 1919 and during the 1920s and 1930s produced bronze and ivory statuettes in the ART DECO style. Typical subjects are athletic young women, sometimes mistakenly identified with Nazism.

Preiss: "Bat Dance", c.1925 [E]

Press An archaic English term for a cupboard for storing clothes, linen and books. Now generally reserved for a type of cupboard from the 16th and 17th centuries, with doors enclosing a large compartment below, and two smaller compartments set side by side in the upper section. The term is also applied to a box for pressing linens in the 18th century. A type of Welsh press is known as a TRIDARN.

Pressed glass A form of glass made using a plunger to press molten glass into a mould. The technique was developed in the US from the 1820s and in Europe, particularly France and Bohemia, from the 1830s. By the mid-19th century most inexpensive mass-produced glassware was pressed.

Press-moulding A technique of ceramic-making, where clay is pressed into or over a single mould and then removed. Used from the early 18th century onward in England, especially at the STAFFORDSHIRE POTTERIES. In glass-making, it refers to the process by which PRESSED GLASS is made.

Pricket An early form of candlestick made of bronze, brass, copper or LIMOGES enamel. It had a sharp metal spike set in the capital or top section and secured a candle by spearing it through the base. Found from the 12th to the 16th centuries, when it was replaced by the CANDLESTICK, the pricket was used in great houses, churches and monasteries.

Prie-dieu A low-seated armless chair, introduced from France to Britain in the 19th century. It has a tall, narrow back and often also a wide toprail shelf to hold a prayer book. Ostensibly designed for kneeling in prayer, it was a popular occasional drawing-room chair. UPHOLSTERY was either plain, or upholstered with BERLIN WOOLWORK, embroidered with religious motifs. The cushioned seat is occasionally hinged to create storage for books.

Primrose glass A yellow version of Davidson's opalescent PEARLINE GLASS, made by the addition of uranium.

Print room A room used for displaying prints, fashionable in Britain from the 1760s to the early 19th century. It was influenced by Roman decorations discovered in Pompeii.

Walnut prie-dieu, English c.1870 [K]

Print The oldest printed images are thought to be of Chinese Buddhist scriptures and it was from China that the WOODCUT reached Japan by the 8th century. Printing methods fall into two categories, intaglio (ETCHINGS, LITHOGRAPHS, AQUATINTS and ENGRAVINGS), when an image is transferred from an indented surface, and relief (wood engravings and woodcuts), in which the printing surface is raised. Book printing, developed in Germany from the 15th century, has evolved into modern typography. Artists such as Rembrandt van Rijn (1606–69) Pablo Picasso (1881–1973) and David Hockney (b.1937) have all used the same methods.

Central band of printies on ▶ a decanter, c.1825 [Q]

Printie A shallow concave circular or oval cut lens-like decoration used on glass from the early 18th century.

Prismatic cutting Cut glass decoration in the form of abutting horizontal mitred grooves that catch light. It was popular in the early 19th century, when it was used on the necks of decanters in particular.

Prisoner of war work Domestic and decorative items such as COMPENDIUMS, ship models and jewellery boxes carved from bone by predominantly French prisoners of war in England during the Napoleonic wars. Straw was also used,

Prisoner of war ship, early 19th century [B]

being coloured and woven into pictorial panels and laid onto boxes. Imprisoned in "hulks" off the coast of Plymouth, Portsmouth and other places, the sailors would often combine their skills to make models from the limited materials available to pass the time or to sell.

Prouvé, Jean (1901–84) A French architect, engineer and metalworker, perhaps best known as the designer of some of the most innovative French modern furniture. He was the son of Victor Prouvé, co-founder of the ECOLE DE NANCY, studied metalwork in Paris from 1916–21, and opened his own metalworks in Nancy in 1923. As an architect he experimented with new materials, which influenced his bent and welded steel furniture designs.

Provenance A verifiable account or documentation accompanying a piece that identifies either its origins or history, or both. An interesting provenance or one connected to a renowned maker, owner, location or event can add value to a piece.

◀ Prunts on a römer, c.1830 [R]

Prunt A blob of molten glass applied to a piece of glass as decoration, particularly associated with drinking vessels such as the RÖMER, where they were applied to the stem, often modelled as raspberries.

Ptolemy (Ptolomaeus Claudius) (AD *c*.87–*c*.150) The most influential of the ancient astronomers and geographers, Ptolemy dominated cartographic thinking for more than 1,400 years. His eight-volume *Geographia*, published *c*.AD 150, was a monumental summation of existing

cartographic knowledge. Whether Ptolemy made maps himself is unknown. If he did, none have survived. His text, however, did survive through Byzantine and Arabic copies, many of which included maps reconstructed on the basis of his projections and latitude and longitude coordinates. The reintroduction of Ptolemy's *Geographia* to Western Europe in the 15th century helped to set the stage for European exploration.

Pugin, Augustus Welby Northmore (1812–52) An architect and designer, and leader of the GOTHIC REVIVAL in England. Following in the footsteps of his

Pugin oak clothes-press, 1830s [F]

French émigré father, Pugin designed furniture and silver until the 1830s when he turned to creating furniture that mirrored authentic medieval styles, rather than simply decorating contemporary designs with Gothic ornament, as had been the prevailing fashion. Pugin also designed Gothic-style church plate, tiles, ceramics and jewellery. He is perhaps best known for the furniture he created for the Houses of Parliament in 1836–37.

Puiforcat, Jean (1897–1945) The most important French ART DECO silversmith, who learned his craft in his father's workshops and joined the family firm after World War I. From the 1920s he produced solid silver tea sets, dishes and bowls in cylindrical or rectangular designs, giving way in the 1930s to purer, sleeker shapes which displayed his use of contrasting materials with silver. These textural and colour contrasts included exotic woods, ivory, amber and jade.

Pumpkin head
A type of WAX OVER COMPOSITION, SHOULDER HEAD doll, popular in the third quarter of the 19th century, produced by dipping a papier mâché shoulder head in heated wax. Pumpkin heads are named after their large round faces and usually have moulded blonde hair.

Puiforcat silver jug, c.1930 [F, the set]

Punch bowl A large, often circular, bowl of silver, ceramic, or glass, used for mixing and brewing punch – an alcoholic beverage of water, spirits, spices, sugar and citrus fruit, popular in England from the second half of the 17th century onward. Silver examples tend to be plain but some have engraved or embossed decoration, commonly of bunches of grapes.

Punched work Decoration by a technique of using shaped steel punches and hammer blows on the surface or borders of metal objects, particularly of more malleable metals such as silver.

Punch glass A type of small drinking glass with a handle that forms part of a punch set – a bowl with matching cups that were sometimes hung from the edge of the bowl.

Punto in aria (Italian: "stitch in the air") NEEDLELACE made with rows of buttonhole stitching and the aid of parchment patterns, published by Cesare Vecellio in 1592, Bartolomeo Danieli in 1610 and others. Used for dress decoration, ruffs, and scalloped borders in the early 17th century.

Punty See PONTIL MARK.

Purdonium A type of 19th-century coal-scuttle, named after a Mr Purdon, either its inventor or first owner. Made in a variety of materials, including wood and JAPANNED metal, and usually painted with elaborate scenes and shapes. Its popularity was enhanced with the later addition of a removable metal container. There are also versions with wheels, fitted shovels and padded tops.

Puritan spoon (Also called a slip-top spoon) A type of spoon with a slip-top handle – a hexagonal stem ending in a simple bevel, so-called because it resembles an APOSTLE SPOON, without the figure of an Apostle. Made from the early 16th century.

Purl A metal thread, sometimes bound in coloured silk, used extensively in 17th-century embroidery. Sometimes the term is used to describe the embroidery itself, hence "purl work".

Purple heart A dense hardwood from the Caribbean, of the genus *Peltogyne*, so-called because of the violet or purplish colour it becomes when freshly cut. In the 18th century, it was used for INLAY and veneer border bandings on furniture.

Push along/pull along mechanism Used in toys, usually for small children, when a movement within the toy is required to be activated by the moving of the toy along the ground, e.g. the nodding head of a dog on wheels.

Putto on Copenhagen dish cover, 19th century

Putto (Italian: "cherub" or "boy") A chubby infant boy, widely used in ornament, deriving from angelic spirits. Used from the RENAISSANCE, and particularly popular in the BAROQUE period, the putto is typically depicted playing among scrolling foliage, carrying festoons and swags and in panels of GROTESQUE ornament. Also widely used in RENAISSANCE REVIVAL ornament.

Puzzle jug A jug with a pierced cylindrical neck and a hollow handle which connects the lower part with a tube around the top, from which there are two or more "spouts". It is only possible to drink if one sucks at one of the spouts while blocking the others and a hole hidden under the top of the handle with one's fingers. Meant to be a joke or a challenge to a drinker. The earliest dated example in DELFTWARE is 1653; it is also known in DELFT of the 17th and 18th centuries.

Puzzle jug, late 19th century [Q]

Pyrex A trade name for a type of heat-resistant glassware patented in 1915 by the CORNING GLASSWORKS, New York, and subsequently produced under licence by manufacturers in Britain and elsewhere. It rapidly became the largest selling type of domestic glass.

Pyrography A decorative and ornamental technique used to apply a pattern to leather or wood using a hot poker to build up the design by burning the surface. Also known as pyrogravure and pokerwork, pyrography was used in the 19th century and earlier.

Q

Qianlong porcelain (Ch'ien Lung) Chinese porcelain made in the reign of the Qing dynasty emperor, Qianlong (1736–95). The JINGDEZHEN kilns produced vast quantities of CHINESE EXPORT PORCELAIN and fine Imperial wares often in the MING or SONG dynasty style. See also ARMORIAL WARE; CHINESE POTTERY AND PORCELAIN; FAMILLE ROSE; MANDARIN PALETTE.

Qianlong Chinese export soup plate, c.1745 [D, a pair]

Qing (Ch'ing) The Chinese dynasty (1644–1912) under the rule of the Manchu following the native MING dynasty (1368–1644). The early years were marked by civil war and the Imperial kilns at JINGDEZHEN, destroyed in 1673, were not rebuilt until the 1680s. Artistically, the three most important periods were under the emperors Kangxi (1662–1722), Yongzheng (1723–35) and Qianlong (1736–95) and under their patronage Jingdezhen underwent a renaissance. New glazes were perfected including peach bloom, ROBIN'S EGG, MIRROR BLACK, TEA DUST and CLAIR DE LUNE. Classic shapes and styles from the SONG and Ming dynasties were revived. Production for the CHINESE EXPORT market increased greatly as Chinese goods and tea drinking became fashionable in Europe. Export wares include FAMILLE VERTE, NOIRE, JAUNE AND ROSE porcelains, ARMORIAL WARES, BLANC DE CHINE, YIXING stonewares, CHINESE IMARI, and large quantities of BLUE AND WHITE. Other goods exported during the Qing period include JADE, LACQUERWORK, IVORY and furniture in BAMBOO and eastern hardwoods.

Quadrant An instrument used for measuring altitudes – of stars or the sun for navigation or mountains in surveying. Its name derives from its shape, a quarter of a circle, on which is marked a scale of degrees from 0° to 90° so that the angle of elevation can be read. Quadrants were invented in the Middle Ages and were superseded by the sextant c.1770. Gunter's quadrant was invented by the English astronomy professor Edmund Gunter and pocket-sized brass or boxwood instruments of his design date from 1650–1750.

Qing Imperial plate, c.1750 [H]

Quaich A shallow silver, pewter or wooden drinking bowl with two flat handles. It originated in medieval Scotland, probably in wood, and as such is an example of TREEN. Early surviving examples date from the 17th and 18th centuries.

Quail pattern A decorative scheme painted on PORCELAIN showing a pair of quails among rocks and foliage. This popular motif originated on KAKIEMON porcelain in Japan and was widely imitated in Europe on porcelain and TIN-GLAZED EARTHENWARE from the 18th to the 20th centuries.

Quare, Daniel (1648–1724) An English clock and watchmaker. He became master of the Clockmakers' Company in 1708 and produced longcase and BRACKET CLOCKS and watches, often with extremely fine piercing and ENGRAVING on the BACKPLATES. He invented the REPEATER watch in the late 17th century.

Quarter striking A clock that strikes on the quarter hours as well as the hour. See also STRIKING SYSTEMS.

Quarter veneer A technique whereby two matching sheets of veneer are sliced into two pairs. These are reversed and the pairs juxtaposed on the carcass of the furniture to form a decorative pattern.

Qing reign marks

These marks cover the three most important artistic eras of the Qing dynasty from 1662 to 1795.

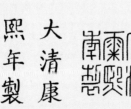

Kangxi 1662–1722

Yongzheng 1723–35

Qianlong 1736–95

Often used in walnut on table-tops, chests-of-drawers or desks in early 18th-century English furniture. It was revived in the mid-VICTORIAN period.

Quartetto tables A set of four small tables of graduated size that nest together, made primarily in MAHOGANY, ROSEWOOD, and SATINWOOD. The design originated in the early 19th century.

Quartz A family of gemstones and HARDSTONES common throughout the world. Crystalline quartz includes colourless (rock crystal), purple (amethyst), yellow to brown (citrine), deep brown (smokey quartz), pink (rose quartz) and aventurine (green with mica inclusions). Cryptocrystalline quartz, commonly known as chalcedony, incorporates chrysoprase (apple green), cornelian (reddish brown), bloodstone (green with red flecks) as well as agate, jasper and onyx.

Quartz glass An American term for opaque glass with marbling simulating QUARTZ or HARDSTONE. The term was used as a trademark by the STEUBEN GLASSWORKS for a line of CLUTHRA glass with matt finish, including a pink-coloured glass termed "Rose quartz".

Quatrefoil Four-lobed GOTHIC tracery form resembling a four-leaved clover. Perhaps originating in architectural features found in Moorish and Oriental mosques, the quatrefoil was used in the Gothic architecture of Venice. It survived into the RENAISSANCE in Italy, and enjoyed renewed popularity as a decorative motif on GOTHIC REVIVAL furniture of the 19th century.

Quatrefoil

Queen Anne The style of architecture and decorative arts, especially silver and furniture, dominant in England during Queen Anne's reign (1702–14) and

Queen Anne walnut chest-of-drawers, early 18th century [H]

adopted in the US *c.*1725 with strong regional characteristics. The style favoured restraint and limited ornament in contrast to the earlier BAROQUE style. Domestic silver by silversmiths including Anthony NELME, is devoid of decoration except for fine engraved ARMORIALS on some pieces. Walnut was the most fashionable wood, figuring, for example, in the use of burr walnut, and colouring was considered more important than applied ornament. Other characteristic features of Queen Anne furniture are the CABRIOLE LEG and chairs with vase or FIDDLE-SHAPED slats forming their backs.

Queen Anne Revival A style of architecture and decorative arts popular in the late 19th and early 20th centuries in England, based on the QUEEN ANNE style. It was popularized by architects such as Richard Norman Shaw (1831–1912) and Philip WEBB in their designs for red-brick town and country houses. The simplicity of Queen Anne furnishings appealed particularly to designers of the AESTHETIC MOVEMENT such as E.W. GODWIN. Direct reproductions of early 18th-century

items were also popular during this period but their craftsmanship is rarely as fine as that of the originals.

Queen's Burmese See BURMESE GLASS.

Queen's pattern An ornate silver (and plated) FLATWARE design similar to KING'S PATTERN. The main differences are the heavier decoration on Queen's and the SHELL MOTIF on the top of the stem, which stands proud in RELIEF and is much flatter or concave on King's.

Queensware CREAMWARE made by Josiah WEDGWOOD from *c.*1765. It was named after Queen Charlotte after she visited the factory.

Quervelle, Anthony G. (1789–1856). Born Antoine-Gabriel Quervelle in France, this top-quality American cabinet-maker was active in Philadelphia, US, from 1817. Typical products include MAHOGANY and GILTWOOD PIER TABLES comparable to contemporary FRENCH EMPIRE and English REGENCY examples.

Wedgwood Queensware vase, *c.*1765 [I]

Quezal glass (1901–1925) A glassworks that produced iridescent glass in the TIFFANY style. Founded by former Tiffany employees in New York, the company derived its name from its use of feather patterns similar to the brilliant green, red and white plumage of the "quetzal" bird.

Amish pieced wool and cotton quilt in cranberry, navy and purple star pattern, c.1850 [o]

Pieced and appliquéd cotton quilt with the American flag in the centre and pinwheels and sunflowers in the surround, c.1865 [J]

Cotton patchwork pinwheel quilt, US 19th century [K]

Quilts

Textiles formed by joining together two layers of fabric with a third layer of wadding secured between them. Simple quilting methods have been used since the earliest times for clothing and furnishings. It is believed that quilting first came to Europe from the East, with the earliest references being to quilted garments in the 12th century.

The art of quilting

Decorative quilting is recorded with increasing frequency from the 14th century. One of the earliest examples of European decorative quilting is a large cover dating from c.1400 which features scenes from the Story of Tristan, floral motifs and inscriptions in a Sicilian dialect. Typical of early European work, this quilt is not pieced but worked through two pieces of heavy linen. Parallel lines worked in backstitch create the design into which cord and braid have been inserted. Known as a "whole-cloth" quilt, most early surviving quilting is of this type.

In the 16th and 17th centuries, as trade between Europe and India increased, the ideas and fabrics of the East greatly influenced European quilt-making. Double-sided silk quilts from Portuguese India were imported for the first time, together with thinly wadded cotton quilts and painted and printed cotton chintzes. By the late 17th century these were being copied in Europe. Colourful chain stitch designs against flat quilted backgrounds were becoming popular, whilst the traditional heavy linen and wools were losing favour.

By the 18th century quilted bed covers or "quilts" were fairly widespread. Carefully planned quilts with centre panels and surrounding borders, known as "medallion quilts" were particularly favoured. Some incorporated APPLIQUÉD detail and imported printed cotton into their designs, others were whole-cloth quilts in plain cottons. Complex decorative quilting started to decline in popularity toward the end of the 18th century. In the 19th century PATCHWORK became more popular, although the two techniques were often combined.

In the 19th century decorative patchwork quilts became most closely associated with North America. Bed quilts served both a decorative and practical purpose and became an integral part of the social life of the women who worked them. Quilting "bees" were formed to make quilts in a sociable environment. Initially, patterns were based on English and Welsh designs but gradually American forms emerged, the "block" pattern and its endless variations being a good example. In this method the quilt is divided into blocks, usually 30.5cm (12in) in size. It lent itself to a multitude of geometric patterns, some based on American motifs, and enabled members of a quilting bee to work together more easily on the same quilt. ALBUM, autograph or friendship quilts were worked extensively in America; some of the most famous quilts known are mid-19th century "Baltimore album" quilts.

Although quilts are essentially utilitarian objects created by women with no artistic training, they now have a wide appeal as art works in their own right. Precipitated by exhibitions such as the 1971 Abstract Design in American Quilts, held at the Whitney Museum in New York, they are now seriously collected in many European countries as well as North America and Japan.

Quimper A factory in Finistère, France, making peasant-type pottery painted in bright colours with figures in Breton costume. FAIENCE had been made here since the end of the 17th century, but little of note was produced until the arrival of Pierre-Paul Causey, who ran the factory from 1743 to 1782, producing wares in the style of ROUEN. In 1853 Antoine de la Hubaudière took over the factory and Quimper from this time is marked with the monogram HB. Other faience factories in the area making similar wares include Eloury-Porquier-Beau and Dumaine-Tanqueray-Henriot, the latter established in 1778. By the beginning of the 19th century, faience production in France had nearly ceased as creamware had taken over. However, because of its isolated Breton position, Quimper persisted. Today the factory is still producing traditional-style faience.

Quimper faience dish from the factory of Antoine de la Hubaudière, c.1900 [M]

Quizzical bird A comical STONEWARE bird with a long beak and heavy-lidded eyes, made by the MARTIN BROTHERS at the end of the 19th and beginning of the 20th century.

Race, Ernest (1913–64) An English furniture and textile designer who founded Ernest Race Inc. with Noel Jordan in 1945. Early designs were governed by rationing restrictions after World War II – the BA chair (1946) was made from aluminium from scrapped war planes. In 1951 he designed the "Antelope" chair.

"Neptune" deck chair designed by Ernest Race for the P&O line, c.1953 [I]

Racinage A 19th-century technique for marbling leather with acid. It was not widely used as it damaged the leather.

Rack clock A clock in which the power source is the weight of the clock itself. The clock gradually descends a toothed vertical rack and is then pushed back up to the top. Rack clocks were popular from the 17th century in Germany and Austria and were reproduced in England in the mid-20th century.

Racquet sports memorabilia Items such as racquets, autographs, ceramics and books. Tennis dates from the 15th century, in a form now known as "real tennis". The modern game was developed in the 1870s. Badminton evolved from the ancient sport of battledore and shuttlecock. Squash, adapted from the game of "rackets", was founded at Harrow School, England.

"Real tennis" racquet by Brouaye, French c.1862 [N]

Radiogram A combined radio receiver, gramophone and loudspeaker. Often housed in a wooden cabinet, radiograms were popular from 1950 to the early 1970s.

Raeren potteries An important German centre of STONEWARE production near Aachen from c.1560 to the 17th century. At first they made COLOGNE-style brown-glazed wares and later grey stoneware with blue reliefs similar to WESTERWALD ware. Less notable wares were produced throughout the 19th century.

Rag doll Originally a home-made fabric toy. From the second half of the 19th century rag dolls were also mass-produced in kit form, as printed fabric patterns to be cut out, sewn and stuffed. They are made out of cotton, linen, felt or stockinet.

Raggedy Ann The trademark registered in 1915 in the US by John B. Gruelle for a RAG DOLL based on one his mother had. Raggedy Ann and her male companion Raggedy Andy have flat faces with a wide smile, round eyes with first six, later four, lower lashes and a shock of red woollen hair. First produced by Volland and Co. and later by the Georgene Novelty Company, they are currently made by Hasbro.

Rail The horizontal member in the framework or CARCASS of furniture, such as the seat rail of a chair, intended to support the vertical members.

Raising A technique used by silversmiths to create HOLLOWWARES out of sheet metal by hitting the metal with a round-headed hammer over an anvil or stake.

Raku ware A type of Japanese pottery made for TEA CEREMONY use. Raku is named after a seal mark meaning "enjoyment" which is found on early examples. It was first made *c.*1580 by Chojino, a Korean potter living near Kyoto. Chojino took the name Raku which has been passed down through generations. Many other small-scale potters also worked in the Raku tradition. Wares were modelled by hand (rather than thrown), asymmetric and uneven, with a thick LEAD GLAZE, usually black or brown but occasionally reddish, green, white or yellow. Raku is particular to the Japanese taste with the finest pieces held in high regard.

Omar Ramsden silver covered bowl, c.1920 [G]

Ramsden, Omar (1873–1939) An English ARTS AND CRAFTS metalworker, silversmith and artist craftsman who began in partnership with Alwyn Carr, running a small workshop, until he registered his own mark in 1918. Ramsden's workshops produced a large quantity of work, much of it ecclesiastical, civic and corporate. He produced numerous presentation pieces and held many private commissions. Many of his silver, metalwork and jewellery designs were re-interpreted from Tudor styles, often featuring coloured enamels and with an emphasis on quality and applied decorative detail. He is also well known for his ART NOUVEAU pieces. His works often feature the engraved inscription OMAR RAMSDEN ME FECIT – Omar Ramsden made me.

Randall, John (1810–1910) An English porcelain decorator who began as an apprentice to his uncle, Thomas MARTIN, at his china works at Madeley, Shropshire. He left in 1833 and in 1835 went to the COALPORT factory where he decorated plates, vases and other items. He specialized in finely painted exotic birds, first in imitation of SÈVRES and later in his own highly naturalistic style. In 1851, Coalport displayed Randall's French-style vases at the GREAT EXHIBITION in London, where they were much admired. Randall remained at Coalport for 40 years and retired in 1881.

Randolph, Benjamin (*c.*1745–*c.*1805) A celebrated American furniture-maker who was active in Philadelphia, Pennsylvania, from 1770. Randolph was a superb exponent of the AMERICAN CHIPPENDALE style (it is known that he owned a copy of Chippendale's *The Gentleman and Cabinet-maker's Director*). His flamboyant solid mahogany furniture, featuring ROCOCO details such as intricate openwork, acanthus carved knees and ball-and-claw feet, is comparable in quality and value to pieces by his contemporaries Thomas AFFLECK, William SAVERY, Hercules Courtenay and Thomas Johnson.

Rapier (Spanish: "dress sword") A thrusting sword with a straight double-edged blade up to 122cm (48in) long and often incorporating an elaborate hilt to protect the hand. Originating at the end of the 15th century, rapiers were everyday wear for gentlemen. At the height of its popularity the use of the rapier in swordplay was raised to an art form. They survived until the end of the 17th century, when they were replaced by the SMALLSWORD.

Ratafia glass, English 1760 [I]

Ratafia glass A type of slender drinking glass with a tall, narrow funnel-shaped bowl blending into the stem. Developed in the mid-18th century for drinking ratafia, an almond-flavoured liqueur.

Rat-tail spoon A type of spoon common in the late 17th to early 18th century with a tapering rib (resembling a rat's tail) from the handle to the back of the bowl to reinforce the joint.

Rattan See CANE.

Ravenscroft, George (1632–83) An English glassmaker who developed FLINT GLASS (or LEAD CRYSTAL). In 1676, during experiments to counter CRIZZLING, he added lead to the batch and created a new glass that was softer and easier to cut and more brilliant than any that had previously been available.

Ravilious, Eric William (1903–42) An English artist, designer, ceramic decorator engraver and war artist (he was killed flying with Coastal Command). His work for WEDGWOOD (1936–1940) included a dinner service decorated with the "Travel" pattern (1937) and a limited edition (200) "Boat Race" Bowl (1938).

Wedgwood coronation mug,1953, from a design by Ravilious in 1937 [Q]

Reading chair An armchair with a padded leather saddle-shaped seat and an adjustable platform to hold a book projecting from the back. Also known as a "library chair", it enabled the occupant to

Spanish cup-hilted rapier with pierced cup guard, 1630 [G]

either sit on it or to straddle the seat facing the back. It was a popular form in mid-18th century England.

Realism In painting, sculpture, architecture and applied arts, the naturalistic representation of humans, animals, birds or plants. Attempts at realism have been a feature of all arts throughout history, but were especially evident in applied arts in the 19th century, when new technical advances enabled more accurate depictions of the natural world. See also NATURALISTIC STYLE.

Slip-decorated red ware jug, 1774 [B]

Rebate (or rabbet) A rectangular recess cut into the edge of a piece of wood, in order to insert another piece. The meeting STILES of cabinet doors were often rebated together to form a dustproof joint and the bottom edge of drawer fronts were generally rebated to provide secure lodging for the bottom boards.

Recessed carving A method of decorating woodwork used in the 17th century on simple types of English furniture. A pattern was drawn onto the surface and the surrounding areas were carved away and then stippled or punched to create a rough background.

Réchampi A decorative technique in which ornamentation is picked out in gold or a colour that contrasts with the ground colour, such as chairs with carved decoration gilded against a white ground.

Red stoneware Wares made in China at Yi-Hsing in the 17th century and exported to Europe. Red stoneware was copied at MEISSEN and known as "BÖTTGER stoneware". In England, it was made by David and John ELERS at Fulham in London c.1693 and at Bradwell in

Staffordshire in 1698. It was also made in Holland by Ary-de-Milde and at Plaue-an-der-Havel in Prussia, but these examples tend to have softer "bodies" than the hard Böttger stoneware.

Red ware Term used in the US to describe RED STONEWARE and, generally, provincial pottery with a porous red body, typically decorated with coloured LEAD GLAZE and trailed SLIP or SGRAFITTO work. Most red ware was made during the 17th and 18th centuries.

Reed, Henry Gooding (1810–1901) An American silversmith and pioneer of ELECTROPLATING in the US. He was active in Taunton, Massachusetts, from 1834. His firm became Reed & Barton in 1840 and is still active as a prolific maker of silver and plated ware.

Reed-and-tie moulding

Reed-and-tie moulding REEDING loosely bound together with criss-crossed straps or ribbons, lending it the appearance of rods that have been tied together. An elaborate variation on the popular reed moulding, reed-and-tie – or reed-and-ribbon – was used to ornament silver from the 1770s and on furniture was applied as cast brass edging or to decorate the legs of chairs.

Reeding Fine parallel convex moulding derived from the decoration on Classical columns. The opposite of FLUTING, reeding was popular from the late 18th century, used to decorate fireplace and door surrounds, silver and parts of furniture such as chair and table legs.

Refectory table A long narrow rectangular hall or dining table, usually made of oak. The term was coined in the 19th century after the dining room used by monks during the Middle Ages. Early versions were constructed from planks of wood joined with pegs to a frame, with legs connected by a framework of rails and joined at the bottom by heavy stretchers. Found chiefly in prosperous households, by the late 17th century the refectory table had been largely superseded by the gateleg table, although they are still being made today.

Reform ware Ceramic jugs, bowls and flasks made in England around the time of the 1832 Reform Bill. Made from salt-glazed stoneware or Staffordshire pottery, they were decorated with moulded or transfer printed portraits of the leaders of Parliamentary reform, including Earl Grey and Lord John Russell. They also often bore relevant inscriptions.

Regard jewellery Sentimental and romantic jewellery popular in the first quarter of the 19th century in which the first letter of a line of gemstones spells a message such as REGARD (Ruby, Emerald, Garnet, Amethyst, Ruby, Diamond) and DEAREST (Diamond, Emerald, Amethyst, Ruby, Emerald, Sapphire, Topaz).

Régence style The French decorative arts and interior design named after the regency of Philippe, Duc d'Orléans (1715–23), though popular until the introduction of the ROCOCO style c.1730. Representing the transition between the BAROQUE and Rococo, Régence forms are still symmetrical and rectilinear but with curving and serpentine lines and lighter, more fantastical ornament such as ARABESQUES and GROTESQUES derived from the designs of Jean BERAIN. In furniture the style is epitomized by the work of the ÉBÉNISTE and sculptor, Charles CRESSENT, whose pieces feature light-coloured woods and elegant gilt-bronze mounts.

George III mahogany
dining-chair with
serpentine seat and
turned tapering legs,
based on a Sheraton
design of 1793 [o]

Regency style

This opulent style of architecture and decorative arts was popular in England from *c.*1790 to *c.*1830. It was named after the Regency (1811–20) of George, Prince of Wales (the Prince Regent), later George IV (1820–30). He commissioned magnificent interiors at Carlton House, London, and the Royal Pavilion, Brighton.

Ancient Greece and Rome with exotic overtones

A late development of the NEO-CLASSICAL STYLE, Regency forms were larger and more solid, curvaceous and richly ornamented than those of the late 18th century. Luxurious materials were much used such as brass inlay and figured woods on furniture and ivory and ebony handles and finials on silver. The style was influenced by the EMPIRE STYLE in France, which favoured historically accurate copies of Greek and Roman furniture prototypes rather than just applying Classical motifs to contemporary designs. In England this archeologically exact approach was adopted by Thomas HOPE, who filled his London house with antique reproduction furniture to complement his collection of Greek, Roman and Egyptian statuary and artifacts. Views of the rooms were published in his *Household Furniture and Interior Decoration* (1807), inspiring a vogue for the Greek KLISMOS chair, and X-framed stools and thrones with SABRE LEGS, SPHINXES, CARYATIDS, herms (armless male or female busts) or GRIFFINS. Cabinet-makers George SMITH and George BULLOCK imitated Hope's style.

The simple, rectilinear forms in Thomas SHERATON'S *The Cabinet-Maker and Upholsterer's Drawing Book* (1793–94) were also influential. Mahogany remained the most popular wood but ROSEWOOD, SATINWOOD, ZEBRAWOOD and AMBOYNA were also used. Silversmiths such as Paul STORR and Benjamin SMITH created copies of, for example, the WARWICK VASE, in silver or silver-gilt. The trend for massive, ornate forms also appeared in English and IRISH GLASS. Regency pieces can be distinguished from their French Empire counterparts by the absence of Napoleonic emblems, such as BEES and Ns, and of heavy GILT-BRONZE mounts. Exotic fashions such as TURKISH, INDIAN and CHINOISERIE motifs in the early 19th century anticipated Victorian ECLECTICISM. The EGYPTIAN STYLE was popular after Nelson's victory at the Battle of the Nile (1798), leading to a fashion for hieroglyphics, scarabs (winged beetles), winged discs and stylized lotus flowers.

Urn-shaped silver Argyle (gravy-warmer)
with mushroom finial, c.1812 [E]

Regency rummer with fluted cutting
simulating feathers on the bowl,
c.1815 [s]

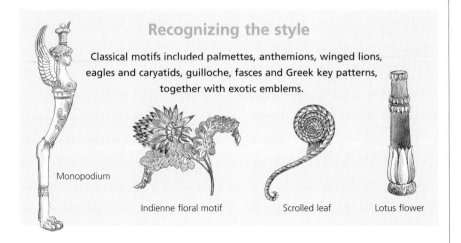

Recognizing the style

Classical motifs included palmettes, anthemions, winged lions, eagles and caryatids, guilloche, fasces and Greek key patterns, together with exotic emblems.

Monopodium

Indienne floral motif

Scrolled leaf

Lotus flower

Registry marks
See DESIGN REGISTRATION.

Regulator A precise timekeeper made from the 18th century and used to regulate other clocks. Produced in Britain, France, the US and especially Austria (see VIENNA REGULATOR), such clocks were of both LONGCASE and wall type, generally with extremely plain cases (although French types often feature ORMOLU mounts). To ensure extreme precision, regulators were fitted with a gridiron, wood-rod or mercurial compensated PENDULUM and DEADBEAT ESCAPEMENT with JEWELLED bearings to reduce friction. The chapter ring usually displays minutes, with subsidiary dials for hours and seconds.

Reign mark An Imperial Chinese mark used on ceramics and other works of art regularly from the beginning of the MING DYNASTY (1368–1644). They are written either as six or four characters, in regular script (*kaishu*) or seal form (*zhuanshu*), which became popular from the YONGZHENG reign (1723–35).

Reijmre glasshouse A Swedish glasshouse established in Östergötland in 1810. In the 19th century it was one of the major producers of tableware, including pressed glass and cut-glass dinner services. In the early 20th century it merged with KOSTA glassworks and began to produce decorative coloured glass. The factory is still active.

Relief A type of moulded, carved or stamped decoration raised above the background of a surface. Various styles of carving can be identified by the type of relief – high, low or medium – which depends upon the amount of background that has been

Relief-moulded stoneware jug by Jones and Walley c.1850 [Q]

removed to allow the design to emerge. The carving may be further modelled by UNDERCUTTING. In Europe the refinement of the early RENAISSANCE gave way to the robust, high relief of the late period, paving the way for the flamboyant BAROQUE STYLE. Relief carving later becomes more subtle (lower) ranging from foliage in the ROCOCO period to the delicate relief ornament by Robert ADAM in the NEO-CLASSICAL period. The Victorian taste for excess led to more ornate relief decoration, followed by a return to lower relief, in general, in the 20th century.

Reliquary A receptacle designed to hold sacred objects or relics of a saint or a holy person, often made of precious materials, such as silver or gold, mounted with rock crystal or gemstones. Few English examples have survived the Reformation but they were, and still are, an important part of the Catholic Church throughout Europe.

Remington, Eliphalet (1793–1861) An American firearms manufacturer. He first made firearms in 1816, built his factory on the Erie Canal, New York State, in 1828 and became a major competitor of COLT. Remington is best known for a series of simple and robust revolvers and an archetypal double-barrelled DERRINGER. Another major success was the rolling-block rifle, which was produced from 1864 to 1933.

Remontoire A device in a precision timekeeper, such as a CHRONOMETER, to supply constant force to the ESCAPEMENT despite changes in the power source. It consists of a small weight or a spring wound at intervals by the mainspring.

Renaissance (Italian: "rebirth") The revival of interest in the culture of ancient Greece and Rome that began in Florence, Italy, in the 15th century and, in the following century, spread throughout Europe. Significant developments included the European exploration of the Americas and Asia, the expansion of trade, advances in science, mathematics, medicine and law and the increasing power of the urban merchant classes.

Renaissance maiolica istoriato dish depicting Hydra and Hercules, c.1530 [E]

Painting, architecture and sculpture were dominated by the introduction of linear perspective and greater naturalism. The Renaissance style was also stimulated by the court patronage of the Medicis in Florence, the papacy in Rome, Francis I of France and Henry VIII of England.

The decorative arts are characterized by symmetry and strongly architectural and sculptural forms, decorated with motifs derived from Classical buildings and sculpture. These include architectural orders, COLUMNS, capitals, ACANTHUS leaves, TROPHIES and human and mythological figures. The discovery of ancient Roman wall paintings in buried ruins, for example the Golden House of Nero in Rome in 1488, resulted in the introduction of GROTESQUES, combined with masks, ARABESQUES, scrollwork, swags and wreaths. This wealth of ornament was circulated throughout Europe in engravings, made possible after the invention of the printing press in the 15th century, and adapted on Italian MAIOLICA at Urbino and Faenza, LIMOGES enamels, metalwork and textiles.

Renaissance Revival The 19th-century revival of forms and ornament associated with the arts of the RENAISSANCE. Popular in Europe and the US, it appeared in architecture from the 1820s, with buildings in the style of 16th-century Italian villas and town palaces. It remained in vogue until the 1880s as one of the main revivalist styles. In Britain the ELIZABETHAN REVIVAL is an adaptation of the Renaissance Revival style. It is distinguished by loose interpretation of Classical motifs such as scrolls, FLUTING, SWAGS, oval panels and STRAPWORK, often derived from MANNERIST and BAROQUE designs and combined with GOTHIC and ROCOCO motifs. The style was widely favoured in Italy, where it was known as "Dantesque". Italian furniture of the 1860s and 1870s often features IVORY and bone inlay and PIETRE DURE plaques inspired by 16th-century originals. Renaissance Revival furniture was also produced in France and the US. MEISSEN and SÈVRES Renaissance-inspired porcelain

features grey and white decoration of Classical figures, GROTESQUES and swags on coloured grounds imitating 16th-century LIMOGES ENAMELS. The Italian glassmaker Antonio SALVIATI made glass in the Venetian Renaissance style, featuring winged and serpent stems and lampwork decoration on TAZZAS, goblets and other wares. In jewellery, the HOLBEINESQUE style combined gold, ENAMEL and GARNETS.

Rennes potteries Lead-glazed EARTHENWARE was made here in Ille-et-Vilaine, France, from the 16th century. A FAIENCE factory called Manufacture Forasassi di Barberino, operated from 1748 to the end of the century. Statuettes of the Virgin Mary and local saints have been attributed to this factory. In 1749, François-Alexandre Tutrel founded another factory, Manufacture Tutrel, which closed in 1770.

Rent table See DRUM TABLE.

Rep (possibly from "rib") A corded textile used in curtains and upholstery.

Repairer The craftsperson who assembles the separately cast parts of a ceramic figure, such as the legs, arms, head and torso, before it is fired.

Repeater A mechanism in a clock or watch that repeats the strike of the past hour and sometimes the quarter hour. The mechanism is

Renaissance Revival relief-moulded plaque, late 19th-century [R]

activated by pulling a cord or lever or pressing a button and is found mainly on watches and CARRIAGE CLOCKS.

Repoussé work A French term for the relief decoration on malleable metals that have been chased and embossed. See also CHASING and EMBOSSING.

Repoussé work on a silver standing salt, English c.1664 [B]

¹Reserve An area of a design, especially in textiles and porcelain, that is left uncoloured or unworked. SÈVRES porcelain often features white reserve panels painted with figurative motifs such as birds or flowers.

²Reserve In auction parlance, the amount of money required by the seller, below which the auctioneer is not allowed to sell.

Resist lustre A ceramic decoration in which parts of an object are temporarily "resisted" with a wax or paper cut out so that the LUSTRE solution applied to the whole does not affect those areas.

Restauration style The decorative arts popular in France c.1815–1830 during the restoration of the monarchy under Louis XVIII (1814–24) and Charles X (1824–30). The French royal family continued to employ craftsmen such as Pierre FONTAINE and François JACOB-DESMALTER, who had enjoyed the patronage of Napoléon I. Furnishings made in this period are largely in the EMPIRE style, but in more restrained designs. Restauration furniture used light-coloured woods and eschewed elaborate mounts. On SÈVRES PORCELAIN, flowers, birds and views replaced scenes of battles and the life of Napoléon. The furniture of Pierre-Antoine BELLANGÉ gradually introduced RENAISSANCE and GOTHIC REVIVAL motifs.

Restoration style The decorative arts popular in England from the restoration of the monarchy in 1660 to the late 1680s, also known as the CAROLEAN style after Charles II (reigned 1660-85). The return of the King and his court from exile on the Continent led to the replacement of the Puritan severity of the CROMWELLIAN style with a taste for magnificence and opulence and to the introduction of Dutch and French artistic influences. These are evident in furniture in the use of floral MARQUETRY, walnut instead of oak, twisted turned supports and legs, exotic veneers, cane seats and backs on chairs, sumptuous tapestry and velvet upholstery and ornate carved and gilded scrolling bases for cabinets.

Restoration silver is characterized by embossed motifs of tulips and naturalistic fruit and leaves. New types of furniture introduced in this period include CABINETS-ON-STANDS, CHESTS-OF-DRAWERS, armchairs and WING CHAIRS, DAY BEDS and SETTEES. The growing power of the British EAST INDIA COMPANY resulted in increased imports of exotic commodities from China and Japan, including tea, porcelain and LACQUER, and chintzes from India. This led to a craze for CHINOISERIE, reflected in the development of imitation lacquer (JAPANNING), BLUE AND WHITE decoration on ceramics, flat-chased scenes of Chinese-style figures and landscapes on silver and new forms of silver such as teapots, as well as colourful Indian-style CREWELWORK bed-hangings and curtains. Other developments in the Restoration period were the emergence of the English glass industry, following the invention of lead glass by George RAVENSCROFT c.1676, and the manufacture of SLIPWARE by Thomas Toft. After the accession of William III and Mary II in 1689, Restoration style was superseded by WILLIAM AND MARY STYLE.

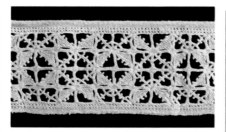

Reticella lace, Italian c.1880

Reticella (Italian) The name given to the decorative geometric grid designs created by drawing out and cutting away threads from a woven linen ground and then filling the spaces with complex designs worked in a variety of detached buttonhole stitches. The forerunner of NEEDLELACE, it was made popular in the 16th century by the fashion for heavily starched collars and ruffs. It is still made in the traditional way, mainly for domestic use, in Italy, Greece and Cyprus.

Reticello glass See LATTICINO.

Reticulated A pattern in the form of a network or web, either open (see PIERCED DECORATION) or filled in (blind reticulation). On glass, this pattern can be produced by blowing the GATHER into a wire network, decorating the piece with a latticework of embedded glass, cutting and engraving or constructing a piece from a network of fine glass strands.

Reticulated pattern glass, English c.1760 [M]

Réveillon, Jean-Baptiste (d.1811) An important French wallpaper designer and manufacturer. In 1763 he bought a site at Folie Titon and worked with original designs, specializing in flock. A great innovator and perfectionist, he used good quality paper and insoluble colours, producing wallpaper for three markets: elaborate luxury papers for the wealthy aristocracy, block-printed papers for the bourgeoisie and simple one-colour papers for those of humbler means. His factory was destroyed in the French Revolution.

Revere, Paul (the younger, 1734–1818) An American patriot, silversmith and folk hero of the War of Independence. He is famous for his dramatic midnight ride from Boston to Lexington in 1775, warning his countrymen that the British were on the march. Revere was the son of a French HUGUENOT silversmith, Apollos Rivoire. He began work as a silversmith in Boston before 1760, but was largely unsuccessful until after the War of Independence, supplementing his income with work as a print-engraver. His best pieces were made under the patronage of a wealthy American elite and can be compared to the work of contemporaries Joseph Richardson in Philadelphia and Myer MYERS in New York City. Revere's career spans the American COLONIAL and FEDERAL periods and his style changes accordingly. Pieces made before the War of Independence are rare and highly prized, typically plain and classical in style. His post-war work, much of which was carried out for wealthy Boston families, is generally more refined, featuring BRIGHT CUT DECORATION and engraved motifs. In the 1780s Revere became involved in other businesses including a foundry and a copper rolling mill.

Silver cream jug by Paul Revere, c.1765 [H]

Reverse painting See MIRROR PAINTING.

Revolver A repeating firearm with a multi-chambered cylinder rotating around a central axis, invented by SAMUEL COLT in 1836. In firing, each chamber is aligned and locked with the firing mechanism and barrel.

Revolving "Sheriff" chair, US c.1880 [o]

Revolving chair A type of revolving chair that was in use in the Gothic period, but became increasingly popular in the 18th century. The idea evolved in the mid-19th century with the taste for all things mechanical, but it was in the period after World War II that the revolving chair was fully developed by imaginative designers such as Charles EAMES, Eero SAARINEN and Arne JACOBSEN. Eames's lounge chair no. 670, a traditional armchair mounted on a metal swivel base, combined masculine good looks with comfort. Along with Saarinen's swivel "Tulip" chair, it remains popular and is still imitated today.

Rhoad, Frederick Hurten (1880–1942) An English-born potter active in the US from 1902, where he worked at the Weller Pottery, Zanesville, Ohio (1888–1948), and as artistic director of the ROSEVILLE Pottery. From 1913–17 he ran a pottery with his wife in Santa Barbara. He designed the extremely successful US tableware "Fiesta", first produced in 1936. He later concentrated on research, teaching and writing. His designs feature incised decoration and are signed with a monogram.

Rhead Family Three generations of English ceramicists. George Woolliscroft Rhead senior (1832–1908) worked for BROWN, WESTHEAD, MOORE & CO. and MINTON. He had three sons, George Woolliscroft (1855–1920) who worked at Minton Art Studio and FOLEY POTTERIES, Louis John (1858–1927) artist, illustrator and successful US poster artist, and Frederick Alfred (1857–1933). The latter, a potter, designer, teacher and writer, worked for W. Brownfield, Minton, WEDGWOOD, SHELLEY, Cauldon Potteries and ROYAL WORCESTER PORCELAIN CO. He had three children who followed in the family tradition: Frederick Hurten RHEAD, Harry G. Rhead (1881–1950), who worked for a number of potteries in the US before starting the Standard Tile Co., Zanesville, Ohio, in 1923, and Charlotte Rhead (1888–1947), who trained under her father and was a designer and skilled TUBE-LINE decorator for many potteries' ranges including CROWN DUCAL.

Rhineland stoneware (or Rhenish) Heavy salt-glazed wine jars and tankards made in several places along the River Rhine in Germany for the Rhenish wine trade, from the late 16th to the 18th century. Vessels often have a bearded mask near the rim, a small loop handle and are called BELLARMINES or Bartmanns.

Rhinestone Originally a type of clear quartz used for COSTUME JEWELLERY, it is now a commercial term usually referring to costume pieces mounted with colourless paste or rock crystal imitating diamonds. It can also broadly apply to many imitation gems in jewellery made after the 1930s.

Rhodium A brilliant silvery-white metal, similar to PLATINUM, discovered in 1803. It is durable, resistant to corrosion and is used mainly for plating metalwork and jewellery.

Night light by Frederick Alfred Rhead, c.1920 [N]

Rhyton A drinking horn or cup, in the form of a stag's antler. In early times they were made from horn but were later made all over Europe in silver, pottery and porcelain. There is a hole in the pointed end for drinking from.

Ribbing A ridged or raised line formed by introducing a coarser yarn into a woven textile. The term also describes the same effect on knitted fabric created by the alternation of plain and purl stitches.

Ribbon-back Decoration carved to resemble ribbons tied in bows. A popular ROCOCO motif for the SPLATS of chairbacks in CHIPPENDALE style.

Ribbon-back

Ribbon plate An inexpensive porcelain plate made widely in Europe in the late 19th and early 20th centuries with pierced rims, either for decorative fruit sets or to be threaded with a ribbon and hung on a wall. German and British examples often had lithographed views.

Rice-grain A perforated decoration used on porcelain in Asia from the 12th century and popular on 18th-century Chinese QIANLONG wares. The body is pierced with small holes resembling grains of rice. The transparent glaze that covers the vessel fills in and seals the pierced work, which remains faintly visible.

Richardson, Henry Hobson (1838–86)

An influential US architect and designer, active in New York City and Brookline, Massachusetts, from 1867. He studied at Harvard and in Paris, where he worked briefly for the Neo-classical architect Jacques-Ignace Hittorf (1792–1867). The "Richardsonian" style is comparable to the work of Edward William GODWIN.

Richardson, H.G. & Sons

An English glass factory established near STOURBRIDGE, West Midlands, c.1850, taken over c.1930 by Thomas WEBB & Sons. One of the first English manufacturers of IRIDESCENT glass, in the 1920s and 30s, Richardson's also produced a popular range of clear and coloured "Rich Cameo" glass.

Lucie Rie vase, 1970s [H]

Ricketts glasshouse

Two glasshouses in Bristol, owned by the Ricketts family that merged to form Henry Ricketts & Co. (closed 1923). The Phoenix (late 18th-century) specialized in cut glass; the Soapboilers' (acquired 1811) made bottles.

Ridgways

A factory set up by Job Ridgway (1759–1813) at Cauldon Place, Staffordshire, in 1802. It produced blue and white STONE CHINA ("Cauldon ware"). Job's sons John and William continued after his death, exporting quantities of Cauldon ware to the US, some of it decorated specially for this market. Rare porcelain marked "Ridgway & Sons" dates from 1808–14. The firm was run by the Ridgway family until 1964, when it was absorbed by Allied English Potteries.

Ridgway china dish from a dessert service, early Victorian [R]

Rie, Dame Lucie (1902–95)

A studio potter, who was born in Vienna and trained under Michael

POWOLNY at the Kunstgewerbeschule. She went to England as a refugee in 1938 and made glass buttons at a friend's workshop while setting up her own studio in London. Rie produced mainly domestic wares, in both stoneware and porcelain. She was a friend of Bernard LEACH, but her style is less Oriental and more European. Hans COPER began his career as Rie's assistant.

Riedel, Gottlieb Friedrich

(1724–84) A German porcelain painter of landscapes and birds, and designer of services and figures. He was a decorator at the MEISSEN factory from 1743–56, at FRANKENTHAL 1756–59, and from 1759–79 worked as chief decorator at LUDWIGSBURG, designing a set of miniature figures and stalls of the annual "Venetian Fair" in Württemberg. As an engraver, he published transfer patterns for porcelain decorators.

Riemerschmid, Richard

(1868–1957) A German painter, architect and designer of glass, metalware, furniture, ceramics and textiles. He was a founder of the Vereinigte Werksatten für Kunst im Handwerk, Munich (1897) and of the Deutsche Werkbund (1907), both institutes that encouraged artists, designers and manufacturers to work to the mutual benefit of all.

Riesener, Jean-Henri

(1734–1806) A German-born French furniture-maker celebrated for elegant design and exceptional craftsmanship. He joined the workshop of Jean-

François OEBEN after 1754, becoming the manager after his patron's death and marrying his widow. By 1767 he had been appointed a *maître ébéniste*, completing the famous "bureau de roi", originally commissioned from Oeben and now in Versailles. As well as being a gifted designer, he also made his own furniture. Hallmarks of his style include elaborate floral marquetry panels, richly sculptured gilt-bronze mounts and careful treatment of the carcass. Following his appointment as *ébéniste* to Louis XVI, he produced sumptuous COMMODES, secrétaires and mechanical furniture for an illustrious coterie of patrons. He began as an earnest advocate of the ROCOCO tradition, but also adopted the elegant, rectilinear style

Riesener writing table with marquetry, c.1780 [A]

becoming fashionable in architecture and the decorative arts. His ability to accommodate changes in taste served him well in the economy campaign of 1784. Many of his pieces made in the 1780s – plain mahogany veneers embellished with slender fillets of gilt bronze – seem austere by comparison to his earlier work. He survived the Revolution and was employed to remove royal emblems from furniture in 1794. He purchased many of his own pieces at the Revolutionary sales and continued in business until 1801. His work under the Directoire and Consulate lacked the originality and distinctive quality upon which his reputation rests.

Riessner & Kessel's Amphora porcelain

See AMPHORA PORCELAIN.

Rietveld, Gerrit

(1888–1964)
A Dutch architect and designer and member of the De Stijl group of painters and designers whose work was based on geometric shapes, the use of primary colours and the eschewing of all ornament. He is best known for his Red/Blue Chair (1918) and for the Trus Schroder-Schrader House (1924/1925) and its interior.

Rietveld stained and lacquered beechwood table, 1922–23 [K]

Rifle A firearm in which the bore is cut with spirally twisting grooves. On firing, the bullet engages with the grooves and this makes it spin, thus increasing its accuracy. Rifled firearms were known as early as the 16th century, but were not perfected until the mid-19th.

Rinceau A French term for a continuous spiralling or wavy ornament, usually comprised of scrolling vine foliage or ACANTHUS leaves. A popular decorative motif in the 18th century, the rinceau was adopted by ornamental designers for carved, moulded and painted decoration.

Rinceau

Ringler, Joseph Jacob (1730–1802)
An Austrian porcelain-maker who worked in the Imperial factory in VIENNA from 1744, where he became an ARCANIST, learning about making porcelain and building kilns. He left Vienna and was a porcelain-maker at HÖCHST in 1750, STRASBOURG in 1752, briefly in Neudeck, at NYMPHENBURG from 1753 until 1757 and Ellwangen from 1753 until 1758. He moved to LUDWIGSBURG in Germany in 1759 and settled there as director for over 40 years.

Rings One of the oldest forms of jewellery. As tokens of love and betrothal or visible symbols of status and authority, rings possess a powerful influence as potent today as ever in the past. They have largely conformed to well established designs through the centuries. Roman rings were generally plain and frequently mounted with a simple HARDSTONE, while medieval gold rings might contain an irregular polished gem such as a SAPPHIRE in a "pie-dish" setting. Wealth and rank were key elements in the 16th century; a prosperous merchant or nobleman would wear a heavy gold seal ring with the bezel – the top of the ring – engraved with an armorial device. Gemstones were invariably flat and two-dimensional in appearance; much of the embellishment was confined to the mount, which was often heavily scrolled or brightly enamelled. It was only by the 18th century that advances in gem-cutting meant that the beauty of the faceted stone could be properly appreciated, resulting in lines and clusters of diamonds and coloured gems often backed with tinfoil to enhance sparkle. By the early 1800s, the NEO-CLASSICAL influence inspired hardstone CAMEOS and INTAGLIOS in "Roman" seal settings or romantic gold "fede" rings in which two hands covered a heart below. Floral clusters of PEARLS and buckles of gold typified the mid-19th century taste. By the end of the century mass production had eroded individuality; enormous numbers of gold

Gold and garnet eternity ring, English 1770 [J]

rings were manufactured in cheap and popular designs with any combination of diamonds and coloured gems. The elegant garland designs of the early 20th century and inspired naturalism of the ART NOUVEAU style were rapidly replaced by the linear geometry of the ART DECO period. By the 1940s and 1950s, massive yellow and white gold dress rings, mounted with interesting combinations of diamonds and SEMI-PRECIOUS STONES, competed with traditonal single stones, clusters and half hoops, in which the value was in the gem rather than in the mount.

Sapphire, diamond, gold and platinum ring, French c.1905 [D]

Risenburgh II, Bernard van

(c.1700–1765/7) A French furniture-maker, who was the son of a *maître ébéniste* of Dutch origin. Until 1957, when his full name was discovered, he was known only by his stamp, BVRB. Risenburgh worked exclusively for Paris dealers, through whom his elegant and refined furniture was supplied to a distinguished clientele that included Louis XV, his mistress Madame de Pompadour, and the German courts. A *maître ébéniste* himself by 1730, Risenburgh specialized in furniture decorated with MARQUETRY designs of naturalistic flowers or veneered in Oriental or imitation Japanese gold and black LACQUER and occasionally in VERNIS MARTIN. He was the first furniture-maker to apply SÈVRES porcelain plaques to furniture, a practice popularly revived in the late 19th century.

Roanne potteries There were several FAIENCE factories in Roanne, France, the first documented of which was founded by Richard Teste c.1632. Its 17th-century products include tiles and large dishes. There were nine factories active in the area before the French Revolution making tablewares and larger pieces such as stoves and wall fountains. During the Revolution *faience patriotique* was made. One of the last factories to remain active was the Faiencerie Sebastian Nicolas, in operation from 1772 until 1866.

Robbia, Luca della The most important member of a family of Florentine RENAISSANCE sculptors, who were the first to use a ceramic medium for sculpture and gave their name to a type of TIN-GLAZED EARTHENWARE (della Robbia ware). They made many representations of the Virgin and Child and other religious subjects (often life-sized), in frames formed of wreaths of fruit, leaves and flowers. They also made vases with realistically modelled and coloured fruit and flowers for decorating churches and houses. Andrea della Robbia (1435–1528), nephew to Luca, worked exclusively in tin-glazed earthenware and made many RELIEFS, the most famous of which are the babies in swaddling clothes on the façade of Brunelleschi's Loggia degli Innocenti, in Florence.

Robineau, Adelaide Alsop (1865–1929) A US STUDIO POTTER, active mostly in Syracuse, New York, making porcelain from *c.*1903. Her work is rare and mostly consists of small, ovoid vessels decorated with pale, CRYSTALLINE GLAZES and stylized flora in the manner of the French ceramicist Taxile Doat (1851–1938). After 1911 she used Chinese and Mayan motifs. Prized examples feature RETICULATED decoration. Her company closed in 1928.

Robineau jar based on a Japanese tea caddy, c.1910 [L]

Robin's-egg glaze An opaque speckled pale blue or turquoise glaze used on Chinese porcelain from *c.*1720, particularly on wares of archaic form.

Robinson, Gerrard (1834–91) An English woodcarver who was born in Newcastle upon Tyne, where he remained for most of his working life. Robinson is best known for his massive, profusely carved oak SIDEBOARDS. His highly accomplished furniture was ideally suited to the popular taste and was displayed at numerous international exhibitions in the second half of the 19th century.

Robinson & Leadbeater A factory in Stoke-on-Trent from 1864 to 1924 that made inexpensive PARIAN WARE, figures and busts. Early examples are unmarked and are of better quality than the later ones, which from *c.*1885 were sometimes marked with R & L in an oval, or with the full name.

Robinson & Leadbeater child and dog group, c.1870 [N]

Robsjohn-Gibbings, Terence Harold (1905–76) An English-born furniture designer, writer and interior decorator who had his own showroom on Madison Avenue, New York, and designed furniture for John Widdicomb Co. (1943–56). He moved to Athens in 1964, where he designed the Classically inspired KLISMOS chair (1961).

Rocaille (French: "rockwork") The iconic decorative motif of the ROCOCO STYLE. It derives from the rock and shell forms used in grotto decoration. The jagged asymmetrical shapes provided the ideal backdrop for motifs such as scrollwork, CHINOISERIE, flowers and playful SINGERIES.

Rock & Gräner A toy manufacturer in Biberach, Germany, that was one of the earliest producers of TINPLATE toys. The company was established in 1813 by Christian Gottfried Rock and his brother-in-law, Gottfried Wilhelm Gräner. Rock and Gräner specialized in well crafted, hand-painted dolls' house furniture, forts and castles, railway locomotives, boats and dioramas. The company ceased production in 1904.

Rock and pop memorabilia Collectors' items connected to the world of rock and pop music such as autographs, instruments, presentation discs, clothing, rare recordings, unpublished photographs, concert programmes and posters. Items associated with legendary names such as Buddy Holly, Elvis Presley, Jimi Hendrix, The Rolling Stones and The Doors are especially sought after. There is a distinct focus on the 1960s, particularly on The Beatles, whose memorabilia leads the market and consistently achieves record prices. The first auction of rock and pop memorabilia took place in 1981.

The first LP featuring Buddy Holly as a member of The Crickets, 1957 [N]

Rock crystal The commonest mineral in existence, composed of pure silica. Found in crystal groups worldwide, it has been used in *objets d'art* and decorative ornaments for centuries.

Rocking-chair A chair mounted on curved BENDS between the front and back feet, introduced in the US and Britain in the 1760s. It was very popular in the US, with several unique types deriving from the WINDSOR CHAIR, such as the BOSTON ROCKER. It was adapted in the UK in the Victorian period in a diverse range of designs. A bentwood version was pioneered by THONET from the mid-19th century. A later version stands firmly on the floor while the seat rocks on springs.

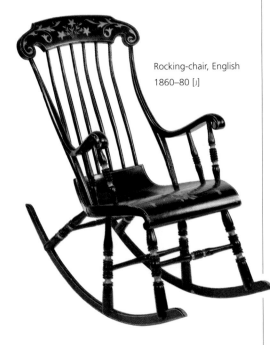

Rocking-chair, English 1860–80 [J]

Rockingham glaze The name given in the US to a rich, lustrous, brown glaze, sometimes called treacle glaze. It was obtained by the use of MANGANESE, and applied to US, British and other earthenware from about 1870 to 1920. The ware was produced at numerous potteries, but is particularly associated with the United States Pottery Co. of BENNINGTON, Vermont. Typical products in the glaze include pitchers, Toby jugs, mantelpiece dogs and other animals and spirit flasks.

Rockingham model of a setter, 1826–30 [O]

Rockingham pottery and porcelain factory Possibly founded as early as 1745 on the estate of the Marquess of Rockingham at Swinton in Yorkshire, England. In its early period, the factory produced EARTHENWARE similar to that of LEEDS and some with a treacle-like glaze, including the lidless CADOGAN TEAPOT. From 1826 until its closure in 1842, it produced high-quality BONE CHINA in ROCOCO REVIVAL style, especially tea and dessert services with rich floral decoration. It also produced well-modelled animal figures. The Rockingham mark (the griffin of the Rockingham family) was widely imitated.

Rockingham ware A name used generically in the US to describe earthenware decorated with a ROCKINGHAM GLAZE, made in several states, Britain, Australia and Canada from *c.*1830 to the end of the 19th century. The most valued items are pre-1840 US pieces of interesting form, such as bottles shaped as coachmen, attributable to specific factories, especially BENNINGTON.

Rococo Revival A style of decorative arts and interior design popular from the 1830s to 1860s throughout Europe and the US, reviving the forms and motifs of the 18th-century ROCOCO style. One of the most popular of the 19th-century revival styles, it emerged in the 1820s and 1830s as part of a vogue for "Old French" styles and remained popular for much of the century. All the decorative arts, but especially furniture, porcelain and metalwork, feature larger, heavier and more sinuous forms than in 18th-century originals, with a greater profusion of ornament, typically shells, flowers and scrollwork. The brighter colours and

shinier gilding distinguish Rococo Revival porcelain, made for example at MEISSEN and SÈVRES, from authentic Rococo pieces, even though at such leading factories 18th-century moulds were re-used for casting. In the US the style was popularized by John Henry BELTER in his patented moulded and laminated rosewood furniture, decorated with elaborate openwork and carving.

Rococo Revival peacock by Derby, *c.*1830 [L]

Rod A term used in glass-making for a cylindrical length of glass that can be monochrome, coloured or polychrome. It can vary in width and may be used in lengths, as decoration in glass STEMS, or cut into slices and used as decoration in PAPERWEIGHTS. Rods were first widely used in VENETIAN GLASS.

Rod bear An early TEDDY BEAR, made for only one year, 1904–5, by Richard STEIFF. Rod bears are jointed by means of two firm horizontal metal rods at shoulder and hip level and one vertical rod through the head, allowing the bear to stand on all fours. Rod bears can be identified by x-rays, or by a hand-sewn seam on the top of their head between the ears. DISC-jointing replaced rod-jointing in 1905.

Rodney decanter A type of glass decanter named after the British naval hero Admiral Rodney, who defeated the French fleet at Cape Saint Vincent in 1780. Typically, it is richly decorated and has a large flat base, suitable for the cabin of a ship's officer.

Rococo style

Originating in France in the early 18th century, the Rococo style swept Europe and then reached America. Seen in all branches of the decorative arts, its characteristics include ornaments of shells and other naturalistic forms, extravagantly carved and gilded.

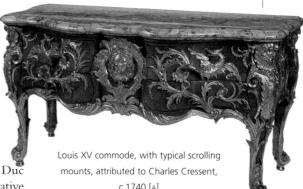

Louis XV commode, with typical scrolling mounts, attributed to Charles Cressent, c.1740 [A]

Shell-like curves

The beginnings of the Rococo style can be traced to the work of Jean BÉRAIN in the early years of the 18th century. By the RÉGENCE of the Duc d'Orleans in 1715 a new lightness and curvaceousness of form in the decorative arts was apparent. Designs by the French court silversmith Juste-Aurèle MEISSONNIER as early as 1724 are asymmetrical and soon afterward this had become a well defined feature of the new and rapidly evolving style which was to sweep Europe, arriving in England *c.*1735.

The term is probably derived from the French *rocaille* (rockwork) and *coquillage* (shellwork), referring to the scrolling ornament of shells and rockwork, which is one of the most distinctive features of the style. Other characteristics include complex arrangements of C- and S-scrolls, fantastic and exotic marine forms, naturalistic flowers and an emphasis on movement. Forms are small in scale, delicate and elegant, in sharp contrast to the massive, symmetrical shapes of the BAROQUE. Chinese and Indian motifs are also common.

Rococo furniture is relatively small-scale, with curving CABRIOLE legs, often inlaid with MARQUETRY of exotic woods, and embellished with pierced and gilded foliate and curving mounts. This style is exemplified by the work of Charles CRESSENT in France and Thomas CHIPPENDALE in England. The designs of the latter had a particularly strong influence on American cabinet-makers and carvers, especially Thomas AFFLECK, James Reynolds and Hercules Courtenay. The emergence of Rococo coincided with the development of the European porcelain industry, and the style was taken up enthusiastically by factories such as MEISSEN, NYMPHENBURG, SÈVRES, BOW and CHELSEA. Leading silversmiths such as Paul de LAMERIE produced tureens, candelabra and other wares with cast ornament of shells, flowers and fruit. During the mid-18th century a reaction against the Rococo style emerged, and it was gradually replaced by the more austere NEO-CLASSICAL style of the 1750s.

Louis XV bergère with typical serpentine front rail, c.1760 [H]

Recognizing the style

The Rococo style is characterized by linear curves in low relief of foliage, shells and other naturalistic forms. These may echo a Classical motif or, in their most extreme form, become semi-abstract.

Shell motif

Hop festoon

Diaper

Mirror with carved giltwood frame, c.1770 [H]

Roentgen, David (1743–1807)
A German furniture-maker who had outlets in Berlin, Vienna and Paris. His sumptuous, heavily Germanic furniture is characterized by *trompe l'oeil* pictorial MARQUETRY, elaborate mechanical devices and an architectural monumentality. His marquetry designs were celebrated for their technical virtuosity and skilled composition, using delicate INLAYS of variously coloured woods. Roentgen's Paris depot supplied finely crafted furniture to the French royal palaces and he was given the unique title of *ébéniste-méchanicien du roi et de la reine* by Louis XVI. He joined the Paris guild and was made a *maître* in

Silver tea and coffee set by Rogers Brothers, c.1910 [F]

Roentgen Imperial mahogany cabinet-on-stand, c.1790 [A]

1789, taking the stamp DAVID, although he rarely signed or stamped his work. Roentgen also supplied a vast quantity of furniture to the Empress Catherine II of Russia and in 1791 was appointed court furnisher to Frederick William II in Berlin. His fortunes as the most famous *ébéniste* in Europe came to an abrupt end with the French Revolution in 1789, when his workshops were pillaged and his Paris depot confiscated. Although he tried to re-establish his business in the early 19th century he was unsuccessful.

Rogers Brothers A firm of US silver plate manufacturers, active from 1847 in the silversmithing towns of Hartford and Meriden, Connecticut, which made the first successful ELECTROPLATE wares in the US. It was absorbed into the Meriden Britannia Co., the largest silver plate maker in the US, now known as the International Silver Co. although the name "Rogers" continued to be used for some years.

Rogers group An American plaster genre group made from designs by the sculptor John Rogers (1829–1904) in New York from 1859–93. Most were painted in pale grey, but some were polychromed in realistic colours.

Rohde, Johan (1856–1935)
A Danish painter and designer who commissioned Georg JENSEN to make some FLATWARE and HOLLOWWARE pieces (1905). He designed for Jensen from 1907, and his work included the popular Acorn pattern cutlery.

Rohlfs, Charles
(1853–1936) An American ARTS AND CRAFTS furniture designer who opened the Charles Rohlfs Workshop in Buffalo, New York State (1898–1928). He had a distinctive style that combined Arts and Crafts solidity with ART NOUVEAU ornament and Norwegian craft

influences. His furniture was mostly made from oak with fretwork decoration and sinuous carved motifs. It was also known in Europe and he made some pieces for Buckingham Palace, London.

Rolex A wristwatch manufacturing company set up in London by Hans Wilsdorf in 1905 and still going today. They specialized in importing watch movements from Switzerland. Wilsdorf was convinced that wristwatches would become popular and persisted in promoting them. The name Rolex was chosen in 1908 because it would sound more or less the same in many different languages. In 1926 the name Oyster was patented and used for the innovative water-resistant case that became the foundation of the Rolex success.

Rolled gold Imitation solid gold created by fusing a thin layer of gold to a base metal such as copper and then rolling it into sheets, in a method similar to that used for SHEFFIELD PLATE. It was used for inexpensive jewellery and small decorative objects in the 19th century.

Rolled paper work (or quillwork)
A decorative technique in which narrow lengths of tightly rolled coloured paper were glued to furniture and, in Catholic countries, onto reliquaries and religious pictorial souvenirs. It was a popular home craft in the 18th and 19th centuries. Tea-caddies and other small items were decorated by Napoleonic prisoners of war and others.

Oak fall front bureau by Rohlfs, 1907 [H]

Rolling ball clock
See CONGREVE CLOCK.

Romanesque Revival A 19th-century style inspired by ROMANESQUE architecture. It was largely confined to architecture, in particular the work of Henry H. RICHARDSON in the US, but it is also seen on furniture. Wardrobe and cabinet doors were decorated with carving of round-headed arches in the style of Romanesque buildings and, in the 19th century, jewellery featured brightly coloured CHAMPLEVÉ enamels. The style was also used by such eclectic 20th century designers as Piero FORNASETTI.

Romanesque style The architecture, painting, manuscript illumination, sculpture and decorative arts of the mid-11th century to the end of the 12th century, when it was supplanted by the GOTHIC style. Inspired by Classical Roman architecture, it is characterized by the use of round-headed arches, arcading, naturalistic birds and animals, geometric motifs such as CHEVRONs and LOZENGEs and CLOISONNÉ and CHAMPLEVÉ enamels.

Roman glass Made in the Roman Empire from c.100 BC until its collapse in the 4th century AD. Wares included quantities of CORE-FORMED, free and MOULD-BLOWN glass bottles, AMPHORAS and flasks, as well as luxurious CAMEO and MOSAIC glass.

Roman glass
wine jug, 2nd–3rd
century AD [K]

Roman pottery Ceramics produced in various parts of the Roman Empire from the 1st century BC until the 4th century AD. The most distinctive type of Roman pottery is Arretine ware and its provincial equivalent Terra Sigillata or Samian ware.

This red, glossy pottery was typically relief-moulded. In the provinces and in the later stages of the Roman Empire decoration gradually became more abstract and in Northern Europe took on a CELTIC flavour. The technique of lead glazing, introduced from Asia Minor to Italy, reached Southern Gaul by the middle of the 1st century AD and the Rhineland and England by the 3rd century AD, producing handsome jugs and other vessels with a greenish-yellow glaze. The eastern provinces of the Empire developed a type of pottery from powdered quartz that had originated in Egypt – characterized by glassy, brilliantly-coloured turquoise-blue glaze – which remained popular from the 1st until the 3rd century AD. Vessels made of each of these types of pottery were exported in great quantities to other parts of the Empire from their sites of manufacture.

Roman striking system A mechanism invented by the 17th century English clockmaker Joseph KNIBB. This system aimed to reduce the number of hammer blows and thus the power storage of the weight. One bell strikes for the Roman numeral I and another for V, e.g. the hour VII may be struck by one low note then two high ones.

Römer (roemer) A traditional German or Dutch drinking glass, usually of WALDGLAS. Derived from 15th-century BEAKERS, early examples took the form of a cup-shaped bowl on a hollow stem decorated with PRUNTS and a short coiled foot. On later examples the stem became shorter and the foot became longer.

Rookwood Pottery A US ART POTTERY founded by Maria Longworth Nichols (1849–1932) in 1880 in Cincinnati, Ohio, and named after her old childhood home. One of her decorators was her friend, Mary Louise McLAUGHLIN. William Watts Taylor

Waldglass römer,
Dutch c.1670 [L]

Rookwood "Vellum"
vase, 1924 [F]

joined Rookwood as a partner in 1883 and took over the pottery when Maria remarried in 1890. She had been impressed by the Japanese ceramics at the Philadelphia Centennial Exposition in 1876 and many Rookwood art wares have an Oriental feel. In 1888, a Japanese artist, Kataro Shirayamadani, was employed. The "Rookwood Standard Glaze" (colour applied with an atomizer) was the idea of one of Rookwood's artists, Laura Fry, in 1883; another popular glaze, "Tigers Eye" or "Goldstone" (streaks or flecks of gold), appeared in 1885. Recognizing the commercial potential for good glazes they employed a chemist, Karl Langenbeck, in the same year. Rookwood exhibited at the Exposition Universelle in Paris in 1889 and at the World Columbian Exposition in Chicago in 1893. Silver appliqué (overlay) was introduced in 1892. Portraits, figures, animals and birds were made from 1897 and tiles in 1901. Taylor died in 1913 and the pottery continued with a board of trustees until it failed in 1941.

After World War II Rookwood re-opened with new owners and less time was spent on art wares. After 1971 various owners came and went and revivals using old moulds were tried. In 1982 Arthur Townley of Michigan Center bought Rookwood and a limited number of pieces have been made from old moulds.

Rörstrand pottery and porcelain factory

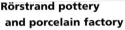

The most important Swedish FAIENCE factory, along with MARIEBERG, with which it merged in 1782. It was founded in 1726, near Stockholm, under royal patronage. The earliest wares were blue and white, based on German and DELFT models, and after 1745 it was one of the first northern European factories to use the BIANCO-SOPRA-BIANCO

Rörstrand Art Nouveau vase, c.1910 [L]

technique. By the 1760s, wares were influenced by French FAIENCE and mostly in ROCOCO style. By 1771 the factory was making CREAMWARE and faience manufacture was discontinued in 1797. In the 19th century Rörstrand produced a variety of ceramics, including copies of PARIANWARE and LIMOGES ENAMELS, as well as porcelain showing Swedish scenes. Under the direction of Alf Wallander, the factory embraced ART NOUVEAU, making use of PÂTE-SUR-PÂTE and FLAMBÉ glazes. In the 1920s and 1930s leading designers such as Edward Hald (see ORREFORS GLASBRUK) reflected contemporary Swedish design. A modern Swedish style was maintained through the 1940s and 1950s. In 1964 Rörstrand became part of the Upsala-Ekeby group.

Rose, John (1772–1841)

The founder of the porcelain factory that later became the COALPORT AND COALBROOKDALE PORCELAIN FACTORY. Both he and his brother Thomas trained at CAUGHLEY. In c.1796 he began porcelain production at nearby Coalport, and in 1799 acquired Caughley itself. Early Coalport wares were

mostly copies of Chinese patterns, but Rose also supplied independent china-painters with plain white porcelain. By 1803 John Rose & Co. was one of the leading porcelain manufacturers in England and in 1814 he also acquired the factory of Anstice, Horton and Thomas Rose, partly owned by his brother.

Rose amberina See AMBERINA.

Rose du Barry

A term used by 19th-century English porcelain factories for "rose Pompadour", a pink ground colour used on SÈVRES porcelain. It was not called by either of these names in the 18th century; the Sèvres factory records refer only to "roze" – a delicate rose-red ground said to have been discovered in 1757 by the decorator Xhrouet. Madame de Pompadour was the mistress of Louis XV and a patron of the factory – she died in 1764 and Madame du Barry became the King's mistress in 1768.

Rosenthal porcelain factory

Founded by Philipp Rosenthal (1855–1937) in 1879 as a decorating studio. In 1889 he opened a factory in Selb, Bavaria, to make his own ceramics to decorate. He also employed well-known designers and modellers and from 1900 a group of pieces with marbled and lustre finishes were designed by Adolf Oppel in the ART NOUVEAU style. In the 1920s and 1930s strong figurative designs were produced. In the 1950s, Rosenthal produced

pieces by Beate Kuhn and the American industrial designers, Raymond Loewy and Richard Latham. In 1961 Rosenthal introduced their "Studio Line" producing high quality pieces by leading designers (e.g. Tapio WIRKKALA). The company continues today,

Rosenthal porcelain vase, 1960s [O]

making some traditional but mostly modern pieces.

Rose Pompadour See ROSE DU BARRY.

Rosette

Rosette

A circular patera or disc ornament in the shape of a rose, sometimes with formalized rose-like petals. An ancient decorative motif, the rosette was adopted from the early Renaissance as a standard enrichment for architecture, furniture, metalwork and ceiling ornament. Occasionally rosettes cover the joins on lattice patterns and also feature in continuous patterns, such as ribbon mouldings, GUILLOCHES and frets.

Roseville Pottery Co.

Founded in 1890 at Roseville, Ohio, under the directorship of George F. Young, for the production of utilitarian STONEWARE. By 1910 the factory had moved to Zanesville, Ohio. The company's reputation is based on their art wares produced from 1900 to 1920, including vases with richly coloured glazes, marketed as "Rozane" ware. The factory closed in 1954.

Rosewood

Rosewood

A hard, heavy, evenly grained tropical wood from the *Dalbergia* tree, coloured from light hazel to rich reddish brown, and richly marked with dark streaks. From the 18th century it was used in fine European furniture for VENEERS, INLAYS and BANDINGS, frequently combined with other contrasting woods. Rosewood enjoyed wide popularity in the 19th century, especially during the Regency period when it was used to make solid pieces of furniture.

Rosso antico The name used by WEDGWOOD for the unglazed red stoneware that was an improvement on similar ware introduced by the ELERS brothers in the late 17th century. Decorations were based on Greek and Roman designs – hence the "antico".

Rouen faience dish, c.1760 [J]

Rouen potteries Rouen developed as a prominent French centre for FAIENCE by the end of the 17th century. This was due to its location on the banks of the Seine, its proximity to Paris and access to good local clays. The large-scale melting down of silver ordered by Louis XIV in 1709 to pay for foreign wars also promoted the production of pottery. The first phase of production dates from *c.*1530, when the potter Masseot Abaquesne produced fine, tin-glazed Italian-influenced wares until his death in 1564. The second phase began in 1644, when a 50-year monopoly for making faience in Normandy was granted to Nicolas Poirel, Lord of Granval, who transferred it to Edmé Poterat. This family maintained the monopoly until 1694, during which time typical wares were still Italian-influenced, decorated in blue and white or polychrome. When the monopoly ended, the industry expanded, with 18 factories working concurrently. At the height of its fame (*c.*1695-1725) Rouen produced a wide range of wares, some typically decorated with scrollwork in *style rayonnant* (literally, radiating style),

i.e. with a close-knit pattern radiating from a focal point. This was widely copied by other French manufacturers. Later wares are in the ROCOCO style and show Chinese influence. By the end of the 18th century, the industry was suffering from competition from England. The industry declined, the last factory closing in 1847. Today the manufacture of faience has been revived in Rouen, mostly for the tourist trade.

Rouleau vase The name for a Chinese porcelain vase with cylindrical body and neck of slightly smaller diameter than the body, made from the KANGXI period (1662–1722). The Dutch equivalent term is *rolwagen*.

Rousseau, François-Eugène (1827–91) A French glass retailer and designer who experimented with the effects of internal CRACKLING. He owned a combined workshop and retail outlet in Paris, where he sold ceramics and glass designed both by himself and other notable artists such as Marc-Louis SOLON, many reflecting the fashion for JAPONAISERIE.

Roux, Alexandre (active 1837–81) One of the most accomplished of 19th-century American furniture-makers, active in New York City. Many Roux pieces are of grand scale with rich marquetry and Louis XVI-style ormolu mounting, but those that show an understanding of the AESTHETIC MOVEMENT are more popular today.

Royal Copenhagen porcelain See COPENHAGEN PORCELAIN FACTORY.

Royal Crown Derby Porcelain Co. See CROWN DERBY.

Royal Dux "Spanish" lady, c.1930 [M]

Royal Dutch Glassworks (Koninklijke Nederlandse Glasfabrik) Founded in 1765, the factory's reputation is based on its 20th-century glass, in particular ART DECO pieces designed by Andries Dirk Copier (1901–91). The factory is still in existence.

Royal Dux A porcelain factory founded at Dux (or Duchcov) in Bohemia in 1860. The factory copied ROYAL WORCESTER, especially in its matt ivory and bronze finishes. Dux became part of Czechoslovakia in 1918, but continued to use "Bohemia" in the mark. The factory made some good ART DECO figures in the 1930s, and is still in existence.

Royal Winton The trade name for a group of potteries in Stoke on Trent including Grimwades, whose name was included in the Royal Winton mark until 1930. Royal Winton is particularly noted for its domestic wares and MAJOLICA, with bright colours and lustre glazes, and popular CHINTZ WARE. It has seen several changes of ownership since 1979, and is today based at Longton, Staffordshire.

Royal Winton "jazzette" coffee set, 1930 [M]

Royal Worcester porcelain See WORCESTER PORCELAIN CO.

Roycroft See HUBBARD, ELBERT.

Rozenburg pottery and porcelain factory Founded by Baron Wilhelm von Gudenberg in 1883 in The Hague, Netherlands. It first produced ART NOUVEAU earthenware and, from 1899, under the direction of Jurriaan Kok, EGGSHELL PORCELAIN, hand-painted with naturalistic motifs. It closed in 1916.

Rubber band mechanism A device in mechanical toys where a rubber band is wound up by hand and used to power items such as propellors on flying model aeroplanes and some plastic cars.

Ruby The red gem variety of corundum. The finest examples are found in Burma (Myanmar) where specimens of exceptional colour are called "pigeon's blood". Other sources are Thailand, Sri Lanka, Vietnam, Afghanistan and Africa. Ruby is one of the most valuable precious stones. Star rubies exhibit a six-rayed star effect called "asterism".

Ruby glass A red glass derived from GOLD-RUBY GLASS, including 19th-century Bohemian glass coloured with the red stain produced by Friedrich EGERMANN and the pinkish red and brilliant red glass developed by Frederick CARDER at STEUBEN GLASSWORKS.

Ruby glass wine glass by Stevens & Williams, c.1860 [R]

Ruhlmann, Jacques-Emile (1879–1933) One of the finest furniture-makers and designers of the 20th century and one of the most revered French ART DECO designers of his generation. His first

designs were shown at the Salon d'automne in Paris in 1913 (furniture, fabric and lamps) and in 1919 his firm merged with Pierre Laurent to become Ruhlmann & Laurent. In 1923 he opened his own cabinet-making company, employing the finest craftsmen and draughtsmen. His forms are modern, clean and sophisticated, exquisitely crafted in rich, exotic woods and other materials.

Rummer A 19th-century English drinking glass in the form of a goblet with a short stem, sometimes with a domed or square foot. The name probably derives from the German RÖMER (wine glass) as it was used for drinking wine rather than rum.

Rundell, Philip (1743–1827) An English silversmith, born at Widcombe, Bath, and apprenticed to William Rogers, a jeweller. He arrived in London c.1768 as shopman to Theed and Picket, silversmiths in Ludgate Hill, and acquired sole ownership of the business in 1772. He took John Bridge, then later his nephew Edmund Rundell, into partnership. From 1805 the firm was known as Rundell, Bridge and Rundell. In 1797 it was appointed Goldsmith and Jeweller to King George III and the royal family. Paul STORR came into the partnership from 1807–19. After his departure, the plate produced bears the marks of Philip Rundell until 1823, when he probably retired. The firm employed the French artist J.J. Boileau who introduced a severe Greek style to their work as well as the Egyptian motifs that were popular on French silver of the 1780s. Rundell's work,

"Morel", an ebony and ivory dressing table by Ruhlmann, 1921–22 [E]

Silver milk jug and sugar bowl by Philip Rundell, 1823 [C, for 3 pieces]

particularly during the REGENCY period, is characterized by outstanding craftsmanship and Classical design excellence.

[1]Runner The name given to long, narrow rugs. Designed by size, the length can vary but the width should not exceed 1.22m (4ft). They are made in most Eastern rug-producing countries in urban workshops as well as by tribal groups.

[2]Runner A strip of wood sliding in a groove in CASE FURNITURE. In the 16th and 17th centuries, a runner supported the leaves of DRAW-LEAF tables. The term also refers to the strips of wood added along the side or, in the 18th century, the bottom edge of a drawer, allowing it to slide. The runners that support the flaps of BUREAUX and SECRÉTAIRES when open are known as lopers.

Runner (or bar) foot A type of foot common for chairs and tables in the Renaissance. Horizontal side-bars connect the front and rear legs at ground level.

Running dog See VITRUVIAN SCROLL.

Rush work Plaited stems of marsh plants used to form seats for chairs and stools. The use of rush developed in the Netherlands in the late 16th century. Chair seats consisting of a square wooden frame in which rushes were wound from side to side were popular in France, England and the US from 1700. William MORRIS designed rush seat chairs and they are still popular today.

Ruskin, John See ARTS AND CRAFTS.

Ruskin Pottery Founded by William Howson Taylor (1876–1935) in 1901 in West Smethwick, England, this pottery was called Ruskin Pottery in honour of the ARTS AND CRAFTS champion John Ruskin after their work was on show at the 1903 Arts and Crafts Exhibition. Taylor was a glaze specialist and developed his own clay BODY to take his renowned high-fired glazes. He produced lustre, crystalline and high-fired glazes with vibrant colours. Shapes may be Chinese in inspiration. The pottery closed in 1935.

Stoneware vase by the Ruskin Pottery, 1914 [G]

Russell, Sir Gordon (1892–1980) An English furniture-maker who began his career c.1911. His firm became known as Russell & Sons after World War I. Russell was influenced by the work of Ernest GIMSON and the BARNSLEYS and he followed the ARTS AND CRAFTS ideal of handmade furniture. However, in the mid-1920s, he introduced machine tools and made some pieces in batches to reduce costs. The firm also offered a modern alternative to traditional design with the designs of Richard Drew Russell (Gordon Russell's younger brother), Eden Minns and Marion Pepler. Russell became a government adviser during World War II (working on Utility Furniture) and in 1947 he became director of the Council of Industrial Design.

Walnut and ebony bedside cabinet by Russell, 1930 [J]

Russet A technique for producing a brown finish on iron and steel by chemical action. Also known as browning, the subsequent finish is not only decorative but also impedes corrosion.

Rustic furniture Rough, handmade functional furniture, usually of common materials, for farmhouses and cottages. Pieces include kitchen dressers, benches and cupboards, and WINDSOR chairs or Yorkshire LADDER-BACK chairs. The term also refers to garden furniture carved in imitation of tree roots and branches, made in England from the mid-19th century. It was popularized in the designs of Thomas CHIPPENDALE and Robert Mainwaring, among others, and was intended to furnish arbours, hermitages and other follies in a landscape garden.

The most famous US rustic furniture was made in the late 19th century in the Adirondacks, in the north of New York State, including work by Ernest Stowe.

Rust spotting A blemish that develops when the layer of TINPLATING on steel oxidizes in moisture. LITHOGRAPHED or paint decoration offers little protection and the condition cannot be remedied.

Ru ware (formerly Ju ware) A Chinese northern SONG (960–1279) ware made for Imperial use from 1107–27. The most coveted of all Song ceramics, Ru wares have a grey-blue glaze with a close crackle and a buff stoneware body. Until a Ru kiln site was discovered in 1986, fewer than 40 examples were known.

Ryijy rug ("coarse haired") A coarsely knotted pile rug made in Scandinavia with a large number (5–20) of wefts between each row of knots, first mentioned in 1420 at Vastena Monastery in Sweden. The pile is thick and about 25mm (1in) long. Most examples are 18th and 19th century, made mainly in grey, black and white.

S

Saarinen, Eero (1910–61) A Finnish-born architect and designer who went to the US in 1923 with his parents, the architect Eliel Saarinen (1873–1951) and sculptor and textile designer, Loja Saarinen (1879–1968). He studied sculpture in Paris and architecture at Yale, and worked for a short time in Finland (1934–36). Eero Saarinen practised a Humanist approach to design, perhaps influenced by his Scandinavian heritage.

He worked with Charles EAMES and they won an award for their moulded plywood shell armchair in 1940. In 1948 he designed his now famous "Womb" chair (produced by KNOLL ASSOCIATES) and in 1956 the "Tulip" chair, an organic form in moulded fibreglass and aluminium mounted on a slender pedestal support of white lacquered cast metal. In 1957 he designed a group of elegant and uncluttered tables and chairs, again using pedestal bases. Saarinen also undertook some large architectural commissions, which he did in a grand organically modern way: the most famous is the TWA Terminal at New York's JFK Airport (1962). Some of his furniture designs are still made today.

Sabino, Marius-Ernest (1878–1961) An Italian-born French glass-maker who first trained as a wood-carver. He established a company to make light fitments c.1923 and began to work increasingly with glass. Sabino made a variety of lamps and small decorative objects in a range of techniques. He is best known for his OPALESCENT sculptures and vases in the ART DECO style. His company closed in 1939 but reproductions of his wares using original moulds have been made since 1960.

Sabot (French: "shoe") The metal shoe fitting the end of a CABRIOLE LEG.

Sabot

Sabre A sword primarily intended for cutting but also effective for thrusting. Blades are single-edged and are usually curved. Sabres have been in continuous use since the 7th century and were introduced into Western Europe from the East in the 15th century.

Sabre leg A chair leg with a gentle concave curve. A popular form in Western Europe – especially England – in the first half of the 19th century, the sabre leg commonly featured on chairs and sofas made during the REGENCY period and on the classical furniture evolved from the FEDERAL STYLE in America in the early 19th century.

Sabre leg

Saddle seat A wooden (usually elm) chair seat that has been scooped away at the sides and back from a central ridge resembling the pommel of a saddle. Shaped to prevent the sitter from sliding forward, the saddle seat was adopted for WINDSOR CHAIRS in the 18th century.

Sadler & Green A Liverpool-based company established in 1756 that decorated ceramics using a TRANSFER-PRINTING process invented by John Sadler (1720–89). Sadler and his partner Guy Green decorated pottery for several factories, notably WEDGWOOD, printing over the glaze in black, green and red. The company closed in 1799.

St Ives Pottery jug, c.1995 [R]

Sagger A box of fireproof clay designed to hold porcelain ware securely in the kiln – the saggers are stacked in layers in the kilns once they have been loaded with items for firing

Saint-Clément A French ceramics factory founded in 1757 by Jacques Chambrette as an offshoot of LUNÉVILLE. From 1772 it was run by the architect, Richard Mique. It produced FAIENCE and BISCUIT figures, but is best known for its tablewares with enamel decoration. The factory declined at the end of the 18th century, but was revived in 1824 by Germain Thomas and remained in production until the late 19th century.

Saint-Cloud A faience factory founded in 1666 by François Révérend. In 1674 it was rented by Pierre Chicaneau who discovered the process for soft-paste porcelain but died in 1677. In 1679 Berthe Coudray, his widow, married Henri Charles Trou and in 1702 Louis XIV granted a privilege to her and her children for the manufacture of porcelain. Saint-Cloud made the first commercially viable European porcelain. Much of their early ware is derived from Oriental porcelain, but later it produced more individual pieces, including wares with an over-lapping leaf pattern and teapots with animal head spouts. It also made small objects such as SNUFF-BOXES. It closed in 1766.

St Ives Pottery
A ceramics studio in St Ives, Cornwall, founded in 1920 by the English studio potter, Bernard LEACH in collaboration with the celebrated Japanese potter Shoji HAMADA. After Leach's death the pottery was run by his widow until 1999 and is still in operation today.

Saint-Louis Glassworks A French glassworks established at Saint-Louis, Alsace-Lorraine, in 1767. It underwent several changes of ownership and name and is now known as the Compagnie de Cristalleries de Saint-Louis. It developed a fine LEAD CRYSTAL in the late 18th century and during the 19th century was one of the leading producers of high-quality CUT-GLASS tablewares, in addition to OPALINE GLASS and PAPERWEIGHTS.

Plate from the "Military Service" made at the St Petersburg factory, 1841 [F]

St Petersburg Imperial porcelain factory A Russian factory, established c.1720 by Peter the Great. In the early years it was unsuccessful, but in 1744 the Empress Elizabeth engaged Christoph Hunger, an ARCANIST, who helped turn it into a viable concern. Hunger left in 1748, but the factory continued under the patronage of Catherine the Great. The earlier wares show MEISSEN influence, but Catherine encouraged Russian traditions. Its products included imposing NEO-CLASSICAL dinner services, porcelain with military motifs and a series of peasant figures and portrait busts. After the 1917 Revolution the factory became the property of the people. Since 1925 it has been called the Lomonosov State Porcelain Factory.

Saint-Porchaire A French ceramics factory near Bressuire, Deux-Sevres, from 1525. It produced elaborately ornamented ware formerly known as "Henri Deux". Fine white EARTHEN-WARE was decorated by

Goblet by the Saint-Louis glassworks, c.1900 [O]

impressing with book-binders stamps and then filling the hollows with a contrasting coloured clay, usually dark brown but occasionally green, black or blue. Saint-Porchaire made a variety of wares including TAZZE, CANDLESTICKS, SALTS, and EWERS. These are very rare – only around 50 pieces are known. The factory closed in 1560. It was much admired in the 19th century and was much copied – in France by AVISSEAU and in England by WEDGWOOD and also by Toft at MINTON.

Salem secretary An American form of the SECRETARY, comparable to a late George III bureau bookcase, made in Salem, Massachusetts, in the late 18th century. Features include a FALL FRONT writing surface concealing a pull-out desk compartment of a type known in Britain as a SECRETAIRE.

Silver salver, 1769 [I, pair]

Salopian The old name for Shropshire, England. Although the CAUGHLEY factory marked with the word "Salopian", it should not be confused with the Salopian Art Pottery Co., of Shropshire, working from 1882 to c.1912. They made EARTHENWARE and MAJOLICA and marked their wares "SALOPIAN", which they registered in 1882.

Salt A receptacle for table salt. The scarcity of salt during the Middle Ages gave it great social significance and the position of the salt container on the table separated the host and principal guests from less important diners. Salts have been produced in all materials from ceramics to silver gilt or gold.

Salt, Ralph (1782–1846) A potter active in Hanley, Staffordshire, in the late 18th and early 19th centuries with his son Charles (1810–64). They made brightly coloured naive figures, usually with

BOCAGE background, often marked with the word "SALT" on a small ribbon panel on the back of the base. Charles Salt also made Parian ware.

Salt glaze A thin, glassy coating on STONEWARE, produced by throwing common salt into the kiln at the end of the firing. The combination of salt and steam produces a gas that turns into natrium oxide and hydrochloric acid and the natrium oxide combines with silicic acid to form a glaze.

Salver A flat, handleless dish with a border, for serving food or drink. A salver usually, but not always, has small feet. When it is elevated on a single foot or pedestal it is known as a TAZZA or "footed salver". The term usually applies to silver or plated wares.

Salviati glasshouse A Venetian glasshouse established at MURANO in 1866 by Antonio Salviati (1816–90) at first with English financial backing. It specialized in VENETIAN GLASS in historical styles and in MOSAICS. Mass-produced pre-assembled mosaic tesserae were used in such prestigious projects as the Albert Memorial, London. The factory also produced reproductions of ancient Roman glass. In 1876, Salviati separated from his English associates and set up on his own. His company continues to be a leading glassworks.

Samadet Pottery A French FAIENCE factory founded in 1732 that made wares such as fountains, TUREENS, and jugs in the style of MOUSTIERS and MARSEILLES. After the Revolution (1789) it produced only simple village crockery. It closed in 1836.

Sampler (Latin *examplum*: "example" or "model") Originally a record of stitches and patterns made as a reference tool by professional and amateur needleworkers. Although few survive, 16th-century samplers included border patterns and spot motifs worked in coloured silks on linen. These were gradually superseded by printed pattern books and by the 17th century samplers were used to show the embroiderer's skill. Samplers still included border patterns and spot motifs, but WHITEWORK, DRAWN THREAD WORK and NEEDLELACE techniques and the occasional name and date also started to appear.

Increasingly, alphabets, inscriptions and pictorial elements began to feature and, with the exception of specific forms such as map or darning samplers, these elements became ubiquitous on 18th-century samplers. Many of the most detailed examples were stitched by young girls and include moral or religious verses.

During the 19th century the pictorial element became increasingly dominant and the variety of stitches reduced until often only CROSS STITCH featured. As education for women became more common, sampler making became less important, and in the 20th century it became primarily an adult leisure activity.

Sampler worked in coloured silks, 1838 [K]

Samson et Cie The French porcelain maker Edmé Samson (1810–91) began by working for collectors and museums, making exact copies of European and Oriental porcelain. His son Emile (1837–1913) also made reproductions of 18th-century SÈVRES, MEISSEN and CHINESE EXPORT ware. Wares carried Samson et Cie's own monogram, an entwined "S" or a dissected cross, alongside that of the factory they were imitating. The Samson et Cie factory openly sold reproductions that were often almost better than the originals and can still fool inexperienced collectors. Only when he copied English and French soft-paste pieces did the hard paste that Samson used betray the pieces' origins. He also made copies of pieces in ormolu, Delft, faience, and enamels. The firm closed in 1970.

Sancai burial figure, AD 618–906 [J]

Sancai ("three-coloured wares") Chinese TANG (618–906 AD) wares decorated with green, amber and cream lead glazes and other colours used for burial figures and boxes. The glazes might be splashed (streaky), mottled or controlled with RESIST designs. The term is also associated with MING (1368–1644) "Fahua" wares and enamel decoration on biscuit porcelain.

Sandblasting Fine grains of sand, crushed flint or powdered iron are "blasted" or propelled at high speed under compression onto glass on which a design has been masked out. Invented in America in 1870, the technique gradually

Samson imari pattern vase, late 19th century [I]

superseded ACID-ETCHING as a way of producing matt decoration, especially on tableware, in the 20th century.

Sanderson, Elijah (1751–1825) A US cabinet-maker who worked with his brother, Jacob (1757–1810), in Salem, Massachusetts. They began in the AMERICAN CHIPPENDALE period, but worked mainly in the FEDERAL style. Some pieces feature carving attributed to Samuel McINTIRE.

Sand glass See HOURGLASS.

Sand moulding (sand casting) A mould is created in damp, compacted sand, sometimes with a carved wooden block. Molten glass or metal is poured into the mould, removed when cool and treated to remove any residual marks.

Sand picture A picture made from coloured sands glued to a wooden or canvas surface and usually depicting a landscape. Benjamin Zobel was perhaps the best-known maker and worked for George III. They continued to be popular throughout the 19th century.

Sandwich glass A generic term given to US glass of a type made by the BOSTON & SANDWICH GLASS CO. and other New England factories from the 1820s until the 20th century. Most US coloured pressed and "fancy" glass of all types is referred to as "Sandwich". Famous designs include dolphin-stem candlesticks, which are widely reproduced.

Sang de boeuf (French: "ox blood") A brilliant red or plum-coloured glaze used for Chinese monochrome wares from the KANGXI period. It is derived from copper fired in a reducing atmosphere. It tends to run, collecting at the shoulders and foot of the object, leaving a streaky effect with pale greenish areas or pink markings.

Sanson, Nicolas (1600–67) The foremost French cartographer of the 17th century, Sanson laid the groundwork for his nation's future cartographic pre-eminence. His major work, the *Cartes Générales de Toutes les Parties du Monde* (General Maps of All Parts of the World), published in 1658, includes the first MAPS to show all of the North American Great Lakes and to name Lakes Superior and Ontario. Less ornamental than contemporary Dutch maps, Sanson's finely engraved maps are distinguished by their clarity, simplicity and elegant decorative title CARTOUCHES.

Sapphire The blue variety of corundum but it also occurs in several other colours of which pink, yellow and a rare peach shade called padparadschah are the most valuable. The highest prized of all sapphires come from Kashmir in Northern India. Other principal sources include Burma, Thailand, Sri Lanka, Australia and Africa.

Sapwood The wood from between the bark and heart of a tree trunk. Still living tissue when the tree was felled, it is softer than the heartwood and tends to be susceptible to attack by woodworm.

Sarcophagus An often richly decorated stone coffin from Classical antiquity. A common motif in funerary ornament in the late 18th century, the distinctive shape of the sarcophagus was adopted for wine coolers, cellarets and tea caddies from the Neo-classical period, but mainly for Regency and Greek Revival styles.

Mahogany sarcophagus-shaped box, c.1820 [L]

Sasha dolls Designed by the Swiss sculptor Sasha Morgenthaler in an attempt to produce a doll that would appeal to all children of all races. Sasha dolls have dark skin and calm, wistful expressions. First commercially produced by Trendon Toys in 1965, they are still manufactured today by the German toy company Götz.

Satin birch See BIRCH.

Satin glass Glass with a fine matt finish created by ACID-ETCHING or light SANDBLASTING. It is also known as *verre de soie* (silk glass), a term coined by STEUBEN GLASSWORKS for a popular range of clear glass with a silky, slightly iridescent finish made from 1905 to 1930.

Satinwood

Satinwood A hard-textured, fine-grained honey-coloured wood from several species of tree from the West Indies, Ceylon and India. From the late 18th century it was used as a VENEER and INLAY, as well as in the solid. It was suitable for furniture of the period between the solidity of CHIPPENDALE and the lighter designs of HEPPLEWHITE and ADAM. It was still used at the beginning of the 19th century, alongside less expensive alternatives, e.g. mahogany.

Satsuma potteries Established by immigrant Korean potters in the late 16th century in the Satsuma province of Kyushu island, Japan. They made simple wares in the Karatsu style for the tea ceremony, often with thick, dark glazes. It has since become a generic term for Japanese cream-coloured pottery made for export to the West from *c.*1850. With

Satsuma incense burner, c.1840 [G]

a clear, yellowish, finely crackled glaze, it is often decorated with figures, flowers and butterflies in polychrome enamels and gilding. Much of this later "Satsuma" was made at Kyoto and elsewhere. The quality varies enormously. See also JAPANESE POTTERY & PORCELAIN; KINKOZAN; MEIJI PERIOD.

Sauceboat Made in ceramic or silver to adorn the dining table and contain flavoured sauces or gravy. Early 18th century sauceboats were double-lipped, boat-shaped vessels with a handle on each side and raised on a central foot. By the 1730s these were superseded by single-lipped, single-handled examples, more usually on three feet.

Leaf ornament sauceboat, English late 19th century [R]

Savery, William (1721–87) A furniture-maker of the AMERICAN CHIPPENDALE period. His best pieces are among the most valuable of all American furniture, and feature high quality carving and sweeping ROCOCO lines. A chair specialist (who also made case furniture), he traded from "The Sign of the Chair" on Second Street, Philadelphia, from *c.*1740.

Savings banks These toy saving devices, usually of cast iron or tin, fall into two categories: the mechanical (which performs a function or trick) and the still bank. The first mechanical bank, the Hall's Excelsior,

appeared in the US in 1869, designed by John Hall of J.E. Stevens & Co. Other noted makers include Shepard Hardware Co., W.S. Reed, Charles A. Bailey and Ives. Many banks were made by companies as a side line or promotion to their main product. They were at their most popular

Beech and marquetry savings bank, English c.1890 [R]

from *c.*1869–*c.*1910 and in decline by the beginning of World War I, after which tinplate banks were popular in the US and in Europe (mainly Germany, the centre of tin production). Many reproductions have been made.

Savona potteries An Italian centre for MAIOLICA, which was made at Savona and at nearby Albisola from the 16th to 18th centuries. The earliest wares were in the BAROQUE STYLE with embossed ornament and blue painted decoration. In the second half of the 17th century APOTHECARY JARs and dishes were made, generally with Roman cavalry but also PUTTI, marine views and biblical subjects. The potteries were numerous and products are hard to distinguish. The shield mark of Savona is commonly used. Conrade of Albisola was an important potter; his initials beneath a ducal crown occur as a mark. At another factory G. Levantino used the lighthouse of Genoa, while a pentagram mark is known for Siccardi or Satomini.

Savonnerie carpet factory A French carpet factory at Chaillot, near Paris, from the early 17th century. Production under Louis XIII (1610–43) is characterized by blackish-brown grounds with rich, naturalistic floral patterns in various colours. The style was deliberately non-Oriental, reflecting instead contemporary French artistic tastes.

The factory's greatest success was under Louis XIV (1643–1715), when 13 carpets were made for the Apollo Gallery in the Louvre and 92 for the Great Gallery connecting the Louvre to the Tuileries Palace. Carpets were also made for the palaces at Versailles, Fontainebleau and Choisy-le-Roi. During the ROCOCO period, the designer Pierre Josse Perrot (active 1725–50) created bold patterns with exuberant colours. In the EMPIRE period (1804–15) designs were inspired by Classical antiquity and military emblems.

During the mid-19th century, under LOUIS PHILIPPE (1830–48), the carpets became more intricately patterned with stronger colours; during the SECOND EMPIRE (1848–70) the colours softened. The Savonnerie factory combined with the GOBELINS at their premises in 1826; the company is still producing carpets today.

Sawbuck table A US term for a rustic TRESTLE TABLE, made by communities such as the PENNSYLVANIA DUTCH, in which a long plank top rests on X-form supports like "sawbucks", or saw horses. Most are of 19th- or 20th-century origin.

Scagliola A hard plaster containing pieces of marble, ALABASTER, granite, PORPHYRY or other stones, sometimes used to imitate PIETRE DURE. It takes a high polish and is suitable for the tops of tables, chests and cabinets. Italian craftsmen revived scagliola in the early 17th century and carried it across Europe. It was favoured for English GEORGIAN furniture and was used by designers such as Robert ADAM.

Scale pattern Overlapping circles that resemble the scales of a fish. The pattern originated in Greco-Roman architecture,

Scale pattern on a Worcester porcelain saucer, c.1768 [L]

and reappeared during the Italian RENAISSANCE. It was used to decorate glass and MAIOLICA in the late 15th and early 16th centuries. It took a more delicate form on 18th-century European porcelain, moulded in relief at SAINT-CLOUD and enamelled on wares made at MEISSEN, BERLIN, VIENNA and WORCESTER. The pattern also features on 18th-century woodwork as carved or pierced surface decoration on chairs, settees and console tables in the style of William KENT.

Scales (balance) A horizontal beam supported at the middle, with a dish or hook hanging from each end, one for weights and the other for the item to be weighed. They vary in size from small sets in 18th-century medicine chests to large grocers' scales. Hand-held coin balances are known from the late 15th century. Apothecaries' balances are distinguished by glass pans and jewellers' are mounted on a stand. Chemical balances, made from c.1700, required high precision. Letter scales were used by the general postal service from 1840.

Scalloped An edge or border cut or modelled in a continuous series of curves, resembling the shape of a scallop

Scalloped

shell. The design has long been favoured for furniture, textiles, ceramics and metalwork and was particularly popular on Irish glass from c.1790.

Scallop shell See SHELL MOTIF.

Scarificator A medical instrument used to pierce the skin to aid blood-letting. Developed in the late 17th century but still available in the late 19th century, they are usually made out of BRASS or silvered metal. They have a series of horizontal slots from which four to 12 sharp blades protrude when triggered, to make several incisions at the same time. A screw governs the depth of the cut.

Sceaux pottery and porcelain factory The factory at Sceaux, near Paris, was managed from c.1748 by Jacques Chapelle, who was the proprietor 1759–1763 Originally, he made SOFT-PASTE porcelain but, due to the monopoly of VINCENNES, in 1749 he turned to

Sceaux porcelain cabbage tureen c.1765 [G]

making high quality FAIENCE, known as *faience japonnée*. Soft-paste porcelain making was re-established in 1763, when the factory was acquired by Joseph Jullien and Charles-Symphorien Jacques. Richard Glot, under the patronage of the Duc de Penthièvre, owned the factory from 1772 until the French Revolution and Antoine Cabaret from 1796. Its last years, in the early 19th century, produced only common household wares.

Scent bottles See PERFUME BOTTLES.

Schäper, Johann (1621–70)
A German pottery and glass decorator.
Born in Hamburg, he worked as a
HAUSMALER in Nuremberg, where
he developed SCHWARZLOT.

Schinkel, Karl Friedrich (1781–1841)
A German architect, painter and
designer. He settled in Berlin in 1805,
creating delicate furniture that anticipates
the BIEDERMEIER period.
His contemporary style drew on
historical motifs, but did not
overemphasize them. Among
his innovations were daring
designs in CAST IRON. The
outstanding qualitites of his
furniture were solidity, practicality,
comfort and simplicity.

Schleswig pottery A German faience
factory founded in 1755 by J.C.L. von
LÜCK and acquired by Johann Rambusch
in 1758, who ran it until 1773. Its best
products were made in this period. Wares
included bowls in the shape of a bishop's
mitre and ROCOCO tureens. Its marks are
"OS", "S" and "SR", often with the marks
of decorators such as Conrad Bade,
Abraham Leihamer and Johann C. Ewald.
The pottery closed in 1814.

Schmelzglas (German: "enamel
glass") A type of opaque glass with
a marbled surface that resembles
HARDSTONES. It was first made in Italy
in the late 14th century (where it was
known as *calcedonio*) and was imitated
in Germany from the 16th
century. See also AGATE glass.

Schneegas & Sons
A producer of high quality
wooden dolls' house furniture
in Waltershausen, Thuringia,
Germany. Manufacturing began in
the 1840s with BIEDERMEIER-style
pieces, often in imitation rosewood,
and continued with the addition of later
styles in various finishes, until World War I.
The furniture was available in up to
nine different sizes.

Schofield
candlestick, 1779
[c, set of 4]

Schnelle The German name for a
tall tapering TANKARD, usually made of
STONEWARE or FAIENCE, often with a
PEWTER cover. It was the typical shape
of the SIEGBURG potters of the 16th
century and was often decorated in
relief with biblical or mythical subjects.
Imitations were made in the 19th century.

Schofield, John A prominent English
silversmith who worked in London
from *c.*1776 to 1794, firstly in
partnership with Robert
Jones and then alone from
1778. His work displays a
classical elegance and he is best
known for his Adamesque cruets,
candlesticks and candelabra.

School of Nancy See NANCY.

Schreiberhau glasshouse A leading
German glasshouse (est. *c.*1840) at
Marienthal, near Schreiberhau. Directed
by Franz Pohl (1813–84), it produced
MILLEFIORI PAPERWEIGHTS, impressive
vases and enamelled and IRIDESCENT
GLASS. In 1923 it amalgamated with two
other glasshouses. Now based in Poland
the company is still active.

Miniature Schuco
teddy, c.1920 [R]

Schuco The
trademark of Schreyer
& Co. (1912–77), of
Nuremberg, makers
of high quality
mechanical toys
and teddy bears.
The Tricky (or
Yes/No) bear with
a moveable head
was introduced in
1921 and was soon
followed by a variety
of PLUSH animals
incorporating PERFUME
BOTTLES, compacts or lipstick holders.
The most successful products of the
1920s were reissued in the 1950s.

Schwarzburg porcelain factory
Founded in Schwarzburg-Rudolstadt,
Thuringia, in 1908 by Max Adolf Pfeiffer.
The factory was known for its white
porcelain Russian peasant figures, designed
by the sculptor Ernst Barlach. It merged
with a factory in Volkstedt in 1913.

Schwarzlot (German: "black lead")
A type of monochrome handpainted
decoration in black or brown enamels
applied to glass and ceramics and
especially popular on bowls and beakers
from *c.*1650–1750. The technique was
improved by Johann SCHÄPER in
Nuremberg in the mid-17th century, and
soon spread to Bohemia and Silesia where
it was used mainly for landscape and
battle scene designs on glass BEAKERS and
flasks and ceramic domestic ware by such
notable exponents as Ignaz Preissler
(1676–1741). Schwarzlot was revived at
the end of the 19th century.

Sconce A wall candleholder of silver
associated with the early 17th to early
18th centuries. It consisted of an arm or
bracket with a socket for a candle and a
backplate to magnify and reflect the light.
Although silver sconces were made in
quite large sets, few survive and none
seem to pre-date the English Civil War.

Scrapbook A book with colourful paper
images of a sentimental or souvenir value
fixed to the pages. First made in the early
19th century, by the mid- to late 19th
century making scrapbooks had become
such a popular pastime that printed and
often embossed scraps were
specially produced.
Scrapbooks are still
popular today.

Scratch blue A style
of decoration on early
18th-century English
STONEWARE. The
design is scratched onto
the surface with a
pointed tool and filled
in with blue pigment.

Scratch blue jug,
English c.1750 [M]

Screen Originating in China around the 2nd century AD and introduced into Japan in the 8th, screens appeared in Europe when it began trading with the East in the 16th century. Made in Europe from the 17th century, they served practical purposes to block out draughts, to protect modesty, or (the majority) to shield from the direct heat of fires (see FIRESCREEN and POLESCREEN). As decorative devices, screens were excellent for displaying carving and needlework. By the 18th century, screen panels decorated with prints, paintings, imported Chinese wallpapers, embroidery and filigree paper were highly fashionable; the ladies of the house also created BERLIN WOOLWORK and BEADWORK panels. From *c*.1750, it was considered *de rigueur* to match screen panels with the fabric of upholstery and wall hangings.

Screw Early screws, with hand-filed, uneven threads and uncentred slots, were made of brass and used together with brass pins to fasten hinges. From the late 17th century tapering metal screws with slotted heads appear in furniture construction. Lathe-made screws were introduced from *c*.1760, securing hinges of folding tables, including gate-leg tables. By the mid-19th century, machine-made screws with centred slots and milled threads were a common feature of furniture construction.

Scrimshaw A 19th-century art produced by craftsmen from the east coast of North America and British ports, in which the teeth and tusks of whales and walruses were used to make decorative objects. After extraction, the surface was scraped smooth and then a design was pricked out with a needle. The pricked out dots

were then joined together with black ink, soot or tar to reveal, for example, a whaling scene or portraits of ships. There are many replicas on the market. As a general rule, these are often heavier than originals with a milkier, whiter finish. They are often highly polished at the base and do not have a deep gorge inside.

Scroll foot The foot of a CABRIOLE LEG which terminates in a tight upturned scroll or spiral form. The "French" scroll foot, derived from the 17th-century French BAROQUE scroll leg, became fashionable on furniture in the mid-18th century, in imitation of the French taste that began to assert itself in the 1730s.

Scroll foot

Scroll handle The handle of a piece (for example a silver or pewter mug) which is curved and shaped to resemble either the letter S or C.

Scroll handle on a silver coffeepot, English 1853 [N]

Scroll top See SWAN-NECK PEDIMENT.

Scrutoire An enclosed desk for writing, originating with the FALL FRONT desk in the form of a box or portable fitted chest on a table. It evolved into the vertical SECRETARY or writing cabinet, mounted on a stand or CHEST-OF-DRAWERS. Coined *c*.17th century in England, by 1800 the term was nearly obsolete.

Scrimshawed walrus tusk cribbage board, 43cm (17in), 1909 [N]

Seal Used universally from ancient times, the seal is a relief image of an emblem, coat of arms or crest made in sealing wax and fixed to a document, letter or charter. It serves as a mark of authentification or a warrant. The term also applies to the matrix that is impressed into the wax on which the devices are engraved in reverse (or intaglio). Seal matrices can be cut from ivory, silver, gold or HARDSTONES. They may be for personal use, set into rings or handles, or may have wider importance, e.g. those used in a borough or corporation, or the Great Seal of Scotland.

Seal bottle A glass bottle used to serve wine, impressed with a moulded SEAL marked with a monogram, coat of arms or initials that identified either the owner, the glassworks where it was made, or the tavern and contents. Very dark freeblown "shaft and globe"-shaped seal bottles were made in Britain from *c*.1650, developing to "onion"-shaped examples in the early 1700s. Seal bottles remained popular until the mid-19th century, by which stage they were cylindrical in shape and were made in dark brown and dark green glass.

Seal box A box made to contain a SEAL when it is attached by a cord or ribbon to a document, protecting it from wear. They were used since the advent of seals, but circular silver or silver-gilt examples with detachable covers are associated with the 17th and 18th centuries. Royal seal boxes are invariably engraved and/or embossed with the royal coat of arms.

Seal-top spoon A silver or base metal spoon characterized by a SEAL-shaped terminal or finial soldered to the end of the stem. Early ones (late 15th-century) have squat finials whereas 17th-century examples have more elongated baluster terminals. By *c*.1670 they were unfashionable.

Seams The visible lines along which two separate pieces of a material (or two ends of the same) have been joined together. Seen, for example, on moulded glass and in silver when a sheet of silver is curved around to form a cylinder and joined to form a visible solder seam.

Seat rail The horizontal structural member of a chair supporting the seat. The seat rail can be situated across a chair seat at the back, front or sides.

Seaweed glass A term used to describe clear-cased glass with an internal decoration of air bubbles that resembles seaweed. Well-known exponents include Andries Dirk Copier (1901–91), who used the technique in the "Serica" limited edition range of vases he designed for the ROYAL DUTCH GLASSWORKS, and the Austrian glass factory LOETZ-WITWE.

William and Mary walnut and seaweed marquetry chest-of-drawers, c.1695 [D]

Seaweed marquetry A type of decoration consisting of a delicate design made up of intricate leaf patterns of richly-figured holly or boxwood on a walnut background, resembling seaweed. Originating in Italy, it was further developed in England and Holland in the late 17th century. It was frequently applied to the fronts of longcase clocks, chests-of-drawers, secrétaires and cabinets.

Secessionist Movement A society of avant-garde artists, designers and architects founded in 1897 as a breakaway group from the conservative academy of fine arts in Vienna. Its leading members included Josef HOFFMANN and Koloman MOSER, who founded the WIENER WERKSTÄTTE in 1903, architect-designer Otto Wagner and the painter Gustav Klimt. They exhibited the work of MACKINTOSH and the GLASGOW SCHOOL, whose rectilinear and geometric designs inspired those of the Wiener Werkstätte. The term is now used to describe the Austrian variant of ART NOUVEAU.

Second Empire A term describing the variety of styles popular in France during the reign of Emperor Napoleon III from 1848–70 (the Second Empire). It does not refer to a revival of the early 19th-century EMPIRE style of Napoleon I but to the increasingly eclectic mix of forms and ornament and overall effect of opulence, characteristic of late 19th-century French decorative arts. The LOUIS XVI style was dominant, owing to the Empress Eugénie's interest in the life and times of Queen Marie Antoinette, and was manifest in Classical forms with GILT-BRONZE mounts and BRASS INLAY. The RENAISSANCE REVIVAL was also popular, and high quality furniture in both styles was made by Louis-Auguste-Alfred Beurdeley (1808–82). Interiors were filled with large, richly upholstered and tasselled armchairs, sofas and ottomans. From the 1860s, with the opening up of trade between the West and Japan, the taste for JAPONAISERIE was also evident.

Secrétaire The French term for a freestanding writing cabinet. Popular from the late 18th century, the vertical-fronted cabinet of the secrétaire is enclosed by a deep top drawer that, when pulled out, drops down to create a smooth writing surface. Behind this FALL FRONT are recessed drawers, cupboards and pigeonholes where papers can be safely stored and locked away. Frequently the upper section of a secrétaire features a bookcase or a glazed display cabinet.

Secrétaire à abattant, French c.1800 [E]

Secrétaire à abattant A tall French writing cabinet, first made in the 17th century, and especially favoured in late 18th France. The *secrétaire à abattant* resembles a cupboard with a thin drawer at the top, a panel below and three drawers or a pair of cupboard doors enclosing drawers. The top usually has a FALL FRONT, which encloses small drawers and pigeonholes and provides a larger writing surface when open.

Secretary An American term for a tall writing desk, comparable to the English BUREAU bookcase. Popular from c.1750, they were made in two parts for ease of moving and often had brass carrying handles. Most are NEO-CLASSICAL in style.

Sedan chair An enclosed portable chair borne on two long poles for carrying. Sedan chairs first emerged in Italy at the end of the Middle Ages. The popular appeal of this mode of transport – often elaborately decorated and upholstered with luxurious fabrics – rapidly spread alongside a growing taste for luxury from the 16th until the 18th centuries.

Sedan clock A type of clock intended for use when travelling in a sedan chair or coach. Made mainly in the late 18th century, it is circular, square or octagonal in form with a metal or wooden case and fitted with a verge watch MOVEMENT.

Seddon, George (*c.*1727–1801) An English cabinet-maker. He established his workshop in London by 1760, which by the 1780s had become celebrated for a large and varied output of high quality furniture. His business, in partnership with his sons and son-in-law, flourished until the mid-19th century, following the opening of a new West End branch in 1826. From 1827 until 1833 the firm provided furniture for Windsor Castle, in partnership with Nicholas Morel.

Segmental pediment

Segmental pediment An unbroken, curved pediment formed from the arc of a circle, derived from debased Classical architecture. Toward the end of the 18th century, it was adopted for bureaux, cupboards, cabinets and bookcases, mirroring designs found illustrated in the *Drawing Book* of Thomas SHERATON.

Self-loading pistol A repeating pistol whose action relies on either recoil or gas operation to reload it after each CARTRIDGE has been fired. Effective self-loaders date from the 1890s and were readily adopted for military use by most of the major powers. They are still in use today and most are based on the patents of gunmaker John Moses Browning.

Selvedge The edge of a length of woven fabric that has been finished to prevent fraying. The term is also used for the over-bound edges on a rug, made by joining together one or more warp threads and then overcasting in wool, cotton or silk.

Semainier A French term for a narrow CHEST or CHIFFONIER made from the 18th century. With seven drawers, it was originally intended to hold a fresh supply of personal linen for every day of the week. The term is also applied to a case or rack with seven divisions or drawers.

Semi-flat A metal figure, e.g. a toy soldier, cast in a mould usually with lead, made by small factories in Europe and the US from the late 19th century. Often unpainted and with no maker's mark, they are classed today as the cheaper cousin to FLATS and HOLLOW-CAST FIGURES.

Ormolu-mounted kingwood and mahogany semainier, c.1750 [G, a pair]

Semi-precious stones A group of gemstones often occurring in large sizes and of a lesser value than PRECIOUS STONES. The term "semi-precious" is not precisely defined, but PERIDOT, AQUAMARINE, TOURMALINE, SPINEL and ZIRCON are usually included.

Senneh knot See PERSIAN KNOT.

Serpentine A wavy or undulating curved surface on a piece of furniture. From the mid-18th century, serpentine

Serpentine-fronted mahogany chest, c.1770 [F]

curves were adopted for furniture in place of rectangular shapes. The new style based on elegant outlines demanded the talents of highly skilled craftsmen for construction and the laying of VENEERS. COMMODES, CHESTS-OF-DRAWERS and clothes presses were made with serpentine fronts. The form was also applied to the seat-rails and stretchers and for the friezes of side tables through the 19th century. See also BOMBÉ.

Seto Potteries An early Japanese pottery centre around Seto in the Owari province, Honshu island. It is the earliest and the most important of the "Six Old Kilns" of Japan. The earliest wares of the Heian period (898–1184 AD) include large jars with natural ash glazes. In the Kamakura period (1185–1358 AD) Chinese CELADON wares were copied using a coarse STONEWARE body. From the same period is the celebrated "Flower Seto" incised or

Seto porcelain candlestand, Meiji period (1868–1912) [J]

stamped with floral designs, as well as TEMMOKU glazed wares. Toshiro in the 13th century was considered the greatest Seto potter, but very little is known of individual early kilns or potters. By the mid-15th century, Seto produced wares for TEA CEREMONY use. Throughout the 17th and 18th centuries wares for daily use continued to be produced. In the 19th century domestic and decorative porcelain, often of low quality, was made in large quantities for the export markets. Today, Seto has over 900 pottery factories. See also JAPANESE POTTERY & PORCELAIN.

Settee A light open seat with a back and open arms, sometimes with a padded seat, large enough for two or more persons. More comfortable than a settle and more formal than a SOFA – encouraging one to sit but not to lounge – it was adopted in England from the 17th century in various forms, from the LOVE SEAT to the French *causeuse*. In the first quarter of the 18th century, the hall settee – an enlarged hall chair featuring a solid wooden seat – became popular, although in general by the 19th century the form had largely been abandoned in favour of the more comfortable sofa.

Settle The earliest chair designed to seat two or more persons, comprised of a bench with a back and curved open arms. Constructed entirely of wood – generally oak – with solid ends and occasionally a wooden hood, the settle remained popular from Tudor times until the 19th century, mainly for taverns and farmhouses. Sometimes built solid to the floor with a hinged seat positioned over a box, it was the forerunner of the SETTEE. Valued for its rustic appeal, the settle was revived in the late 19th century by designers such as William MORRIS.

Seville potteries The Moors made well-heads, oil and water jars and vases in this Spanish town from the 11th century. After the Christian reconquest in 1248, TILES became the most important product. In the 15th century tiles were exported to other parts of Europe. Pictorial tile panels in Italian Renaissance style were made in the 16th century and in the 17th and 18th centuries colourful

domestic wares were also produced in an Italianate style, with later inspiration coming from CHINESE EXPORT PORCELAIN. In the 19th century several industrial potteries were founded. Around 1840, the English industrialist Charles Pickman built a pottery at the disused Cartuja Convent, producing "china opaca", TRANSFER-PRINTED wares and imitations of HISPANO-MORESQUE tiles. The pottery remained in operation on the same site until 1982, when it relocated to a new out-of-town factory.

Sèvres porcelain factory See pp.342–43.

Sewing table See WORK TABLE.

Sextant by Heath & Co., English 1895 [J]

Sextant A navigational instrument, still used today, in the form of a sixth of a circle, based on the concept of the OCTANT but introduced over a quarter of a century later in 1767. The arc has a scale divided from 0° to 120°, an index arm, vernier, filters, telescope and magnifier. Sextants often come in a wooden case with two additional telescopes. Earlier examples are made of brass, with later examples showing a black crackle finish.

Seymour, John (*c.*1738–1818) An important English-born American cabinet-maker of the FEDERAL period, active in Boston from 1794. Together with his son Thomas, he was patronized by wealthy New England merchants. His elaborate and complex furniture in the English NEO-CLASSICAL taste was inspired by George HEPPLEWHITE and Thomas SHERATON. The best pieces feature inlay, delicate banding and the use of exotic woods.

Sgraffito (Italian: "little scratch") A term that denotes inscriptions or drawings scratched or carved onto a pottery (or rock) surface. The pottery decoration is incised through a contrasted coating of slip to expose the colour of the body beneath. The term was used first in England in 1862 – Italian writers refer to such decoration as *a stecco*.

Shagreen-covered Art Deco box, French c.1925 [M]

Shagreen (Persian *saghari*: "ass's skin") This term occasionally refers to roughened animal skins, but usually describes a form of abrasive shark or ray skin with small, raised circular or lozenge shaped "scales". Used in the 17th, 18th and early 19th centuries as an inlay or to cover boxes, sword handles and other small articles, it is usually dyed green, although this can fade.

Mahogany work table by Seymour & Son, American 1796–1813 [D]

Sèvres porcelain factory

One of the most famous of all ceramic factories, Sèvres produced some of the most beautiful porcelain of the 18th century. It enjoyed the powerful patronage of Louis XV (reigned 1723–74) and the interest and encouragement of his influential mistress Madame de Pompadour.

Butter dish, cover and stand painted with flower sprays within honey-gilt rims, c.1760 [i]

Monopoly in France and a rich clientele

The factory started in VINCENNES, outside Paris, in the château of Orry de Fulvy in about 1738. In 1745 Louis XV showed his backing by prohibiting all foreign porcelain imports, except for Chinese goods. He even prohibited other French porcelain factories from decorating in more than one colour and forbade their use of gilding. In 1753, the king styled the factory *Manufacture Royale de Porcelaine*, cementing its privileges. Sèvres had the further advantage of the services of the best painters such as Jean-Jacques Bachelier (1724–1805) and modellers like the goldsmith Jean-Claude Duplessis (1690–1774).

In 1756 the factory was moved to Sèvres, at the King's instigation, where it is still in business to this day. It made a beautiful SOFT-PASTE PORCELAIN. In 1768 KAOLIN was discovered at St Yrieux near Limoges and HARD-PASTE PORCELAIN was made at Sèvres. Both types of porcelain were made after 1768 until soft paste was abandoned at the start of the 19th century.

The products of the 18th century are pure French ROCOCO style. They were made for aristocratic clients of the French court to blend in with their Rococo interior décor, furniture, other works of art and indeed their whole way of life. Vast services were made, not only for the French but also for the crowned heads of Europe. Delicate CABARETS, vases in startling colour combinations and JARDINIÈRES were among the ornaments made. Porcelain plaques were created to be inserted in pieces of furniture. BISCUIT figures were made after originals specially designed by sculptors such as Etienne-Maurice Falconet (1716–91). One of the many achievements of the factory was their wonderfully modelled flowers, which were attached to ORMOLU branches and put into vases. Roses, carnations, buttercups, lilies, narcissus, tulips, stocks, jonquils, violets and hyacinths were all portrayed. Madame de Pompadour had her rooms filled with these expensive objects and even had them sprayed with perfume.

Green ground vase and cover with strapwork and panels of fishermen, probably painted by Morin, 1764 [F]

Sèvres colours

The Sèvres factory is renowned for the brilliance of its ground colours. Chemist Jean Hellot (1685–1766) developed the first four. Gros bleu is a deep under-glaze blue used from 1749. Bleu celeste (turquoise) was introduced in 1752; yellow in 1753; pea-green in 1756. Pink, later called rose Pompadour, was developed in 1757. Outlined and scrolled with delicately tooled gilding, these colours surrounded cartouches of pastoral scenes, often in the style of the painter François Boucher. Once Sèvres started making hard-paste porcelain in 1768, new colours such as brown, black, tortoiseshell and another dark blue were developed.

Bulb pot with rose Pompadour ground and landscapes in cartouches, 1757 [c, a pair]

Sèvres had a comprehensive system of marking, with the entwined Ls for the King's initial enclosing the year of making as a letter (starting with "A" for 1753), the mark of the painter and that of the gilder.

New look for a new century

In 1780 the state monopoly was discontinued due to a recession and, with the French Revolution (1789–99), the factory lost its aristocratic custom and royal patronage. However, the new government looked upon Sèvres as an asset. In 1800 Alexandre Brongniart (1770–1847), a ceramicist and geologist, became the manager. His policies of selling off considerable quantities of old stock and retaining only the best workers, combined with orders from the Emperor Napoleon (in power 1804–15), started a new period of prosperity. It became the Imperial Factory in 1804 and received regular financial support. Brongniart also abandoned the tricky soft-paste porcelain. Fine services were made for Napoleon including the Egyptian service, later presented to the Duke of Wellington and now in Apsley House, London.

Bleu-nouveau-ground teapot with cartouches of exotic birds and bands of oeil de perdrix. The painter's mark is "N" for Aloncle, c.1771 [J]

After Brongniart's death in 1847, copies of 18th century pieces were made in hard-paste porcelain but soft-paste porcelain was also revived and FAIENCE and ENAMEL work on copper were introduced. The ceramist Joseph-Théodore DECK was director from 1887 to 1891. He had been one of the first ART POTTERS and this taste was reflected in some of the individualistic pieces created at the end of the 19th and in early 20th century. The 20th-century factory produced many services for diplomatic gifts that were imitations of earlier ware but also made ART DECO pieces in porcelain, designed by such artists as Suzanne Lalique. Sèvres from the 1940s is much collected, as are the specially commissioned works of the late 20th century, particularly under the directorship of S. Gauthier from 1964 to 1976. The factory still flourishes to this day.

Green-ground tea caddy with swags of flowers painted by Vincent Taillandier (at Sèvres 1753–90), c.1780 [G]

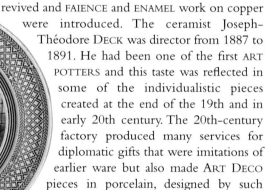

One of a set of plates depicting factory scenes, this shows the interior of a wallpaper factory, 1830–35 [E]

"Chinese monochrome" vase, early 20th century [O]

Sèvres marks

The early marks are much copied. Genuine Sèvres marks can be complete with date, decorator, gilder and with the name of the palace for which the piece was destined.

1753: date letter within two Ls

First Republic 1793–1804

Reign of Charles X 1824–28

20th-century dates and marks

Oak occasional
table, its form
based on a wine
table, c.1830–50 [K]

Shaker crafts

The Shaker community was a religious sect for whom furniture-making and other crafts sprang naturally from their spiritual approach to life. They left a lasting legacy in craft and design.

Plain and simple

The Shakers, so called because of a dance they performed in worship, or The United Society of Believers, as they were formally known, followed a path of peaceful, celibate co-existence inspired by the life of Christ. The community was founded by Ann Lee, a 39-year-old English woman who left Manchester, England, for America with eight founding followers in 1774. However, she did not live long enough to see the expansion of the Movement.

The greatest period, in terms of growth and therefore artifacts made, was from c.1820 to c.1860 and is known as the classic period with a total membership of over 5,000. The community was large enough to create a successful environment that was peaceful, fulfilling and efficient. Without any worldly distractions, the artisans of the Shakers were able to devote their time and energies to their crafts, either for the community or for trade or sale outside.

Because of their comparative isolation, Shakers were not dictated to by the vagaries of fashion and their work has a timeless quality. Their design is based on function, economy and proportion, with no added ornamentation. Any decoration was in the construction or making and in this sense is similar to the work of the ARTS AND CRAFTS designers. The Shaker way of life meant that every task, however small, was executed to the best of the individual's ability and without haste. Materials were simple, usually locally available timber, such as maple or oak, and usually unpainted although some were painted in muted shades of red, yellow, green or blue. The details of the joinery work were left visible and were regarded as beautiful in themselves, rather than being veneered over. The attention to detail meant that even small utilitarian pieces, like the oval steamed storage boxes and coat racks, were attractive. Other craft items included braided rag rugs, baskets, brooms and metalware.

Maple slat-back side chair,
late 19th or
early 20th century [M]

Shakerism declined in the late 19th century although there is still one surviving community today. The Shakers did not set out to create a "Shaker Style" and they were not design-conscious in the way that we would understand it. However, the simple elegance of their designs has beome increasingly popular and many reproductions are now available; some harmonize better than others with the original Shaker values.

Maple cupboard with chest-of-drawers
from Mount Lebanon,
New York, mid-19th century [F]

Shako A military hat, generally cylindrical with a peak, plume or pom-pom. Shakos appeared *c.*1800 and were superseded by the *képi* and spiked helmet at the end of the 19th century.

Shakudo A Japanese alloy of copper and small amounts of gold and silver, used for sword guards and fittings during the EDO period. Shakudo objects are generally inlaid with gold, silver or brass and have a rich black patina.

Shamshir (Persian: "lion's tail") A Middle-Eastern SABRE with a curved blade, often anglicized to "scimitar". They tend not to have a FULLER and are often decorated with calligraphic inscriptions from the Koran. Made from the Bronze Age onward, shamshirs became popular in Europe after Napoleon's campaign in Egypt from 1798 to 1801.

Shang dynasty The Chinese historical period (*c.*1500–1028 BC), following the Neolithic period and noted for the quality and variety of its bronze ritual vessels. Among the best known ritual shapes are the "ding", "tsun", "hu", "li", "ju" and "gu". They are decorated with complex designs often incorporating monster masks called "taotie". There are two notable types of Shang pottery – a high-fired ware with a FELDSPATHIC GLAZE, which represents a considerable technical advance for the time, as it made porous vessels watertight, and a thickly potted white ware. Wares include ritual vessels imitating

Shang fang yi (funerary bronze vessel) [A]

French infantryman's shako, c.1870 [I]

bronze shapes and decorative and domestic red-, grey- or buff-coloured pottery often continuing earlier Neolithic styles. The Shang dynasty was succeeded by the Zhou (Chou) (c.1028–221 BC).

Shearer, John (active *c.*1800–1817) An American furniture-maker in Martinsburg, West Virginia. Shearer's furniture was of provincial type, typically in walnut or cherry. His work is distinctive and identifiable by its carved or inlaid detail in which his British sympathy is shown in his use of the "federalist knot" (elongated quatrefoil), symbolic of presumed Federalist support of the British monarchy. Examples are extremely rare.

Sheffield plate Another term for Old Sheffield that refers to English fused plate made between *c.*1742 and *c.*1840. The process was invented by a Sheffield cutler, Thomas Bolsover, who discovered that a sheet of copper could be fused to a thin sheet of silver (or fused in a sandwich between two thin sheets of silver) and that articles could be constructed from this bi-metallic sheet giving the outward appearance of silver while reducing the cost of the raw materials. Seams and edges on these articles were disguised, to prevent the copper core being revealed, with silver wires and borders, by the lapping over of edges and by the judicious placing of handles, spouts and decoration. In continental Europe the products are referred to as fused plating, rather than Sheffield plate. With the advent of commercial ELECTROPLATING *c.*1840 the more skilled and labour-intensive Sheffield plate industry continued for a short period, then ceased.

Shelf clock A type of inexpensive, mass-produced American BRACKET CLOCK made from the early 19th century. The

Sheffield plate candlestick, c.1780 [N, a pair]

movements were initially made entirely of wood but later of thin rolled brass. Cases, made in a wide range of styles such as "steeple" and "acorn", were mostly of softwood with a mahogany veneer and decorative VERRE EGLOMISÉ panels.

Shellac A lacquer from Asia, derived from the secretion of an insect, *Coccus lacca*. It was used on bookbindings in Persia and India from the 15th century and as a protective or decorative coating for wood. In the 16th century, it was introduced to Europe via Venice, and from the 17th century was a key ingredient in coloured varnishes devised to imitate Oriental lacquer, such as VERNIS MARTIN, which originated in France. FRENCH POLISHING became widespread from the 1820s.

Shelley pottery A Staffordshire company originally Wileman & Co., then Foley pottery. Joseph Shelley joined the firm in 1872 and his son Percy Shelley continued the business. After 1925 the firm traded as Shelley's and from 1929 as Shelley Potteries Ltd. It closed in 1966. They became well known for their BONE CHINA tea sets and during the 1920s their ART DECO wares were known for their practicality and innovative design. The company's lasting popularity is owed largely to such designers as Susie COOPER and Eric Slater (*b.* 1902), who introduced two new Modernist ranges, to the illustrator MABEL LUCIE ATWELL and to painters Duncan Grant and Dame Laura Knight.

Shelley "Melody" pattern teacup and saucer with plate, c.1935 [S]

Mahogany open armchair with a reeded frame,
lion masks and paw feet,
c.1800 [A, for 12]

Mahogany breakfast table
cross-banded with satinwood c.1800 [F]

Thomas Sheraton (1751–1806)

English Georgian furniture reached its final phase of NEO-CLASSICAL refinement in the designs of Thomas Sheraton. His influential publications gave his name to furniture that is characterized by lightness, elegance and the extensive use of inlay.

Designs for living

Thomas Sheraton was born in Stockton-on-Tees, Durham, and settled in London in 1790. He had clearly trained as a cabinet-maker, although no furniture by him has been identified and it is unlikely that he owned a workshop. He is celebrated above all for his books of designs, especially the *Cabinet-Maker & Upholsterer's Drawing Book* of 1791–94. These were aimed at the trade, with practical advice and up-to-date designs for cabinet-makers. Although highly influential – his trade card promoted him as a teacher of "Perspective, Architecture, and Ornaments, makes designs for Cabinet-Makers and sells all kinds of Drawing Books &c" – he is not known to have furnished designs for any named piece of furniture except a grand piano constructed of satinwood and embellished with plaques by Josiah WEDGWOOD and James Tassie.

Much satinwood furniture made in England *c.*1790–*c.*1800 is labelled "Sheraton" and much has been erroneously attributed to him. He did not single-handedly invent the style that bears his name, but played a key role in its formation. Sheraton studied the furniture of the Louis XVI period and the work of Henry HOLLAND at Carlton House. The patterns in his *Drawing Book* show a preference for simple outlines delicately inlaid or painted and emphasize the qualities of wood grain VENEERS. He also freely adopted the antique ornaments favoured by Robert ADAM.

He produced two additional books: the *Cabinet Dictionary* in 1803 and the incomplete *Cabinet-Maker, Upholsterer and General Artist's Encyclopedia* in 1805. The latter celebrated the re-establishment of French influence and promoted popular REGENCY ornament such as the SPHINX, LION MASK and LION'S PAW FOOT, as well as antique forms such as the Greek KLISMOS-inspired SABRE LEG chair. After Sheraton's death, a selection of plates from the three pattern books was issued as *Designs for Household Furniture* in 1812.

Sheraton Revival

Sheraton's style returned to favour in the late 19th century, when the elegant forms of Neo-classicism were resurrected. By the 1880s satinwood or satin-birch furniture based on his designs was being produced, decorated with inlaid stringing lines and Classical motifs. The taste was encouraged by publications on interior design in the 1870s and by the 1891 reprinting of the *Cabinet-Maker & Upholsterer's Drawing Book*. Together with the designs of Adam and Hepplewhite, this gave birth to the Edwardian style. Inexpensive imitations existed alongside high-quality reproductions by firms such as Gillows of Lancaster and Edwards & Roberts of London.

Sheraton Revival satinwood dining-chair, c.1905 [P]

Shell motif

Shell motif

The scallop or cockleshell is the most common shell form used as ornament, especially for Italian and Spanish furniture from the Renaissance. The ROCOCO style is partially based on shell ornament, and the form was used in silver and ceramics for sauceboats, salt cellars, dishes and tureens throughout the 18th century. In furniture, the shell featured as carved ornament on Queen Anne CABRIOLE legs and as a central theme in the work of Thomas CHIPPENDALE. Inlaid wood furniture of the late 18th and early 19th centuries often features the conch shell.

Shellwork Octagonal cedarwood cases enclosing coloured shells arranged in geometric patterns, made in the late 18th and 19th centuries in the West Indies. Some examples have wording such as "Home again" or "Forget me not". Shellwork was often bought by English and US sailors as a memento for the loved ones they left behind.

Shellwork valentine, Barbadian c.1875 [L]

Shepherd's-crook arm The arm of a chair carved in a curving form, resembling a shepherd's crook. The form is found in English furniture of the QUEEN ANNE reign (officially 1702–14, but applied generally to the period up to the 1730s). The form is found in furniture made in both WALNUT and MAHOGANY.

Sherrat, Obadiah A master potter working in Burslem, Staffordshire, from c.1815 to the late 1830s; perhaps the maker of some of the unmarked pottery groups that bear his name. These are naive and brightly painted, with themes such as fairgrounds or bull-baiting.

Obadiah Sherratt group of Polito's Menagerie modelled as a stage, c.1830 [D]

Shibayama A type of Japanese INLAY developed by the farmer Onogi Senzo in 1770–80. Popular in the Meiji period (1868–1912), it uses a variety of materials (including tortoiseshell, ivory, glass and shell), carved and usually set into a gold lacquer or ivory ground. It was used on both *objets d'art* and furniture.

Shibuichi The Japanese name for an alloy of copper and silver (approximately 70% copper to 30% silver), inlaid with gold or silver and treated to produce a pewter grey patina. Like SHAKUDO, it was used for sword fittings in the EDO period, and for elaborate metalwork in the Meiji period (1868–1912) and up to the present day.

Shield A piece of defensive armour carried on the opposite arm to that holding a weapon such as a sword. Shields

were used worldwide from the Bronze Age onward. They became obsolete in European warfare from c.1450, but survived in such usage as riot equipment for police forces.

Shingle style A US vernacular style of architecture popular in the 1880s, making extensive use of shaped cedar shingles on walls and roofs.

Ship in a bottle A wood, bone or ivory ship model, complete with masts, sails and rigging, inserted into a bottle. The masts and sails are then erected by pulling strings. Popular in the 19th century but known earlier, these were commonly made by sailors.

Shiraz A historic city in south-west Iran whose name is used for rugs in the tribal tradition of the region, especially PRAYER RUGS. They are generally of medium pile and thickly knotted, in dark reds and blues, and motifs include stylized animals, birds and human figures. Examples are found from the early 19th century, and today Shiraz produces rugs using modern techniques.

Shirvan A rug-making district to the south of the Caucasus mountains, one of the most prolific weaving areas in the region during the 19th and 20th centuries. Products tend to be finely woven, incorporating a huge variety of stylized geometric, floral and animal motifs in jewel-like colours. The pile is close clipped with high knot counts.

Shi-shi See DOG OF FO.

Shoe A projecting bar rising from the back RAIL of a chair seat, into which the base of the central SPLAT has been slotted.

Shoulder The sloping part of a vase above the body and below the neck.

Shoulder head A type of doll where the head and shoulder are cast together, made from the 1830s to the 1880s.

Shoulder plate Part of the SHOULDER HEAD of a doll, comprising shoulders and front and back chest plates.

Sicilian potteries A group of potteries in Sicily, Italy, producing MAIOLICA wares from the late 16th century onward. The main centres were Caltagirone, Palermo, Sciacca and Trapani. At Caltagirone wares were made in the style of CASTEL DURANTE, with figures of saints, military arms and foliage in parti-coloured compartments. The style was continued into the 18th century. All the centres produced ALBARELLI of the typical tall, waisted shape and also large oviform jars in the Venetian style. Potteries still exist in Sicily today.

Sideboard A piece of dining furniture, comprising a number of drawers for the storage of cutlery, table linen and condiments, invented for use as a serving table in the early 1760s by Robert ADAM. In the late 18th and early 19th centuries, sideboards were frequently designed en suite with other dining furniture, and could incorporate knife boxes, plate-warmers and wine coolers.

Side cabinet See CHIFFONIER.

Side (single or upright) chair A chair without arms, designed to stand against a wall, frequently

Inlaid walnut side chair, Dutch c.1720 [J]

resembling a dining chair. Originating in the BACK STOOL and later having upholstered seats and backs, they were traditionally made in sets. Side chairs were made in the UK and Europe from the late 17th century and in the US from the early 18th century.

Sidereal time See MEANTIME.

Side table A simple table designed to stand against a wall. Dating from the 16th century, side tables were used for serving food, for writing, or as dressing tables. The LOWBOY was a form of side table popular in England c.1700–1760.

Siegburg potteries A group of potteries in the area of Siegburg, near Bonn, Germany, producing some of the best German STONEWARE from the 15th to the early 17th centuries. The most typical wares were *Schnellen*, tall tapered tankards decorated with shallow reliefs moulded separately and sealed onto the sides. Decorative motifs were often taken from contemporary engravings, or were modelled in German Renaissance style. The industry declined at the beginning of the 17th century, but Siegburg wares have been extensively copied from the 19th century.

Siegburg stoneware Schnelle, 1580s [I]

Sileh A type of FLATWEAVE carpet incorporating embroidery on a KILIM base. More specifically, the term refers to a design made up of S-motifs representing stylized dragons. Silehs were normally woven in two halves and joined together. They were made in vibrant colours, mainly during the 19th century, and were produced in the Caucasus. See also SOUMAK.

Silhouette of a girl by B. Gilbert, English c.1850 [M]

Silhouette A profile portrait, usually in black paper fixed to a white background, but it may also be painted. The earliest silhouettes are French and date from the late 17th century. The word is derived from the reputation for parsimony gained by one of Louis XV's finance ministers, Etienne de Silhouette. They were popular in the 18th and 19th centuries in the UK and the US until the arrival of photography. Makers included Augustin Edouart and John and W.H. Field, and the Americans William King and Charles Polk.

Silicon ware A hard, smooth, high-fired stoneware with a thin glaze made by the DOULTON POTTERY AND PORCELAIN FACTORY from c.1880 to 1912, with typical decoration of light blue and white on a buff and brown body.

Silk A natural fibre obtained from the cocoon of the mulberry silk-moth of China. Its cultivation originated in China around 4000 BC, and spread slowly westward along the Silk Road (the trading route between China and the West), arriving in the Byzantine empire around AD 300. By the 4th century, silk was being produced in Constantinople. Silk produced in the East was known in northern Europe by the 8th century. In the 11th century, silk-weaving was established in Europe, introduced first in southern Italy by the Arabs and then in Spain by the Moors. Silk was cultivated in Italy by the 13th century and by the 14th century had reached a high standard in the centres of Lucca, Florence and Venice. By the mid-17th century, French silk production had begun to challenge that of Italy and Spain and by the late 17th century and into the 18th the main silk workshops were in France and England.

Panel of silk, English c.1880

After the Napoleonic Wars (1799–1815), France continued to produce high quality silks; England concentrated on the lower end of the market. Experiments to manufacture artificial silk began at the end of the 19th century and, together with the economic, social and political changes of the early 20th century, this meant that by 1945 the European silk industry had effectively ended.

Silk-screen printing (or screen-printing) A 20th-century term for a printing technique in which ink is forced over a stencil that is supported on a mesh or screen (originally made of silk). The image can be built up by the application of a succession of different colours over a series of carefully aligned stencils.

Silver A brilliant, greyish-white element that is the most malleable and ductile metal after gold. It can be hammered, worked, shaped, stretched, beaten and cast, making it an extremely useful

commodity since early times. It is one of the least reactive of elements and therefore suitable for most domestic and culinary purposes. Since the 16th century, most silver has come from the Americas (largely Mexico and Peru). Pure silver is too soft for normal use and has to be alloyed, usually with COPPER and other trace elements. There has always been a close tie between silverware and silver coinage, one being easily converted into the other, particularly in times of political upheaval when the intrinsic value of silverware could always be realized by melting it down.

Silver-electroplated glass A type of ART GLASS, the surface of which was decorated with a design of silver deposits, using an electrical current. It enjoyed a period of popularity from c.1890 to c.1920, when it was made in Britain by companies such as STEVENS & WILLIAMS.

Silver gilt Silver that is covered with a thin film of gold. On antique pieces (and certainly on those before 1840), this was done by MERCURY GILDING, superseded c.1840 by electrogilding.

Silveria glass A type of English ART GLASS, in which silver foil was embedded between layers of clear or coloured glass to give a silvery effect. It was developed by John NORTHWOOD. In the early 20th century Silveria glass was made by STEVENS & WILLIAMS.

Silveria glass bonbon bowl, English 1930s [R]

Silvering A technique for decorating woodwork and furniture with silver leaf instead of gold. Used from ancient times, it was favoured in France and England from the mid-17th century for the lavishly carved BAROQUE furniture of the LOUIS XIV period. The term is also used to describe the method of backing mirror-glass with a deposit of silver. The technique was perfected by the Venetian glassmakers of the 19th century, by means of replacing an amalgam of tin and mercury with silver nitrate.

Silver table A square table with a galleried edging, first designed by Thomas CHIPPENDALE in 1754. Silver tables were used for serving tea or displaying objects. They were decorated on all four sides and were designed to stand in the centre of the room. See also TEA TABLE.

Simmance, Eliza See DOULTON POTTERY AND PORCELAIN FACTORY.

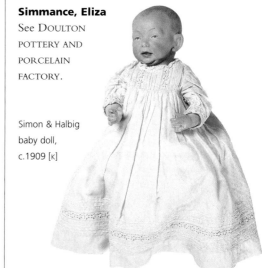

Simon & Halbig baby doll, c.1909 [K]

Simon & Halbig A porcelain factory founded in 1869 in Gräfenhain, Thuringia, which manufactured BISQUE dolls' heads. Its best product is a range of CHARACTER DOLLS and ethnic dolls, e.g. the Dolls of Four Races (1890–1910). Simon & Halbig also supplied dolls' heads to factories such as KÄMMER & REINHARDT. Most Simon & Halbig heads are incised with the factory's name or initials, as well as a mould number. It closed in 1940.

Singerie

Singerie An ornament incorporating monkeys, frequently dressed in clothes. Monkeys figured in European art from the Middle Ages, but were most popular in the 18th century, during the fashion for CHINOISERIE. They were painted on walls, porcelain and FAIENCE by *ornamentistes* such as Claude AUDRAN and Jean BÉRAIN, worked in PIQUÉ and MARQUETRY and embroidered and printed on textiles until the early 1800s.

Siphon barometer Invented in the late 17th century, this type of BAROMETER has its tube bent in a "J" with the short arm open to the atmosphere. Siphon barometers continued to be made, more often in Europe than in England, until superseded by the ANEROID barometer in the mid-19th century.

Sitzendorf porcelain
A 19th-century German porcelain factory making copies of MEISSEN porcelain. It was founded in Thuringia by the Voigt brothers, in 1850. Their marks include two parallel lines crossed by a third line, imitating the crossed swords of Meissen, and also a crown. They made vast quantities of decorative porcelain, such as large baskets encrusted with cupids and flowers in delicate pastel shades.

Size gilding
A technique used in early ceramic painting, of applying leaf gold to designs painted in gold size or animal glue, when it was partly dried. Usually seen on Italian MAIOLICA and some early FAIENCE, and on English SOFT-PASTE PORCELAIN such as BOW. It does not withstand wear.

Skean Dhu, c.1890 [M]

Skean Dhu (Gaelic: "black knife") A small knife, similar to a DIRK, worn in the top of the hose in Scottish Highland dress. This practice was unknown before the 19th century and is probably a Victorian affectation.

Skeleton clock A type of clock with a pierced or fretted frame, usually brass, revealing the movement. Intended to display the skill and ingenuity of the clockmaker, most examples date from the mid-19th century and are set on a marble or wood base. Some frames are modelled on well-known medieval cathedrals, with Gothic spires and arches.

Skillet A bronze, brass or ceramic medieval cooking vessel, in the form of a cylindrical or rounded bowl, with three or four short legs and a long handle. Some English silver examples surviving from the 17th century have a vertical scroll handle, similar to the one on a tankard.

Sitzendorf mantel clock, c.1880 [i]

Slag glass A type of inexpensive opaque coloured press-moulded glass, first made by SOWERBY of Newcastle-upon-Tyne and taken up by other glass-makers particularly in the north-east and in Derbyshire from *c.*1880–1900. It used an admixture of slag from local foundries, which resulted in a marbled appearance.

Slat back chair A type of simple chair made from the late 17th century, with horizontal slats across the back. The LADDER-BACK chair is a more elaborate derivative of it.

Sleeper A dealers' term used to describe a piece of either great interest or value, and often both, that has not been recognized as such by the owner, seller or auctioneer.

Sleeping eyes Dolls' eyes that can open and close. With dolls produced after 1880, this movement is usually mediated by a lead-weighted rod inside the head. The eyes are linked by a metal bar to which a weight is attached. If the doll is upright, the weight hangs down and the eyes are open. If the doll is moved into a horizontal position, gravity causes the weight to move backward, which allows the eyes to close.

Skeleton clock, English 1860–70 [K]

Doll with sleeping eyes, c.1900 [P]

Sleeve vase A type of Chinese vase with a cylindrical body and slightly waisted neck, popular in the TRANSITIONAL period *c.*1640.

Sleigh bed A type of bed based on the LIT EN BÂTEAU, with a scrolled head and foot, curved wooden sides and occasionally a canopy. The style was popular in Europe in the Regency and Empire periods, from *c.*1800 until *c.*1840.

¹Slip A homogeneous mixture of clay and water, usually finer and richer than the BODY it covers. Slips are used for coating clay bodies to give colour and a smooth textured surface.

²Slip An embroidered motif cut out and applied to a ground fabric, commonly on heavy silk and velvet bed and wall-hangings in the 17th century.

Slip-casting A technique for moulding pottery. Liquid clay is poured into plaster-of-Paris moulds that absorb some of the water from the slip. A layer of clay builds up to give a cast. When the excess slip is poured out, the cast is left in the mould. The cast is stiffened, removed from the mould and fired in the usual way.

Slip glaze A GLAZE that contains over 50 per cent clay and is applied as a slip to the raw ware.

Slip-trailing A type of ceramic decoration. Different coloured slips are trailed onto the first surface slip, when it is dry, in a similar way to icing a cake.

Slipware: Wrotham tyg, 1656 [C]

Slipware Pottery with one or more coatings of a more refined clay, which is then decorated with designs trailed on in different coloured SLIPS. The name of the potter and the date may be added. The lead glaze finish gives a characteristic yellowish colouring. The technique was used by the Romans and was widely popular from the 17th to the mid-19th century, for example in WROTHAM WARE. Imitations are still made.

Slit head A type of wax-over-composition SHOULDER HEAD in DOLLS, popular in England around the second quarter of the 19th century, produced by dipping a shoulder head in liquid wax. Slit heads, sometimes called "Crazy Alices", are named after the slit in the crown of their head into which strands of hair were inserted.

Slop bowl An uncovered bowl in 18th- and 19th-century tea services, to hold the used tea leaves from the teacup. They were used throughout Europe and made by all the major porcelain factories.

Meissen slop bowl, c.1730 [C]

Smallsword A light civilian sword that was worn from the 1680s to c.1790. Their HILTS are often lavishly decorated with engraving, chiselling, precious metals, stones and porcelain. See also RAPIER.

Smalt A type of silica glass coloured deep blue with cobalt oxide, the term is also used for the blue-coloured pigment made by crushing this glass – used in coloured enamels.

Smith, Benjamin (1764–c.1822) An English silversmith who worked in Birmingham with Matthew BOULTON as a chaser and silversmith. Smith entered his first mark in 1802 as partner to Digby Scott in London and then registered his own mark in 1807. He manufactured silver almost solely for Rundell, Bridge and Rundell (as did Paul STORR) including many fine pieces for the Royal Collection. His son, also Benjamin (1793–1850), continued the business.

Smith, George (1786–1826) An important English furniture designer of the REGENCY period who owned a sizable London cabinet-making business. Smith popularized the circular dining table and the OTTOMAN in England. His interpretations of the Grecian and Egyptian styles disseminated by Thomas HOPE emphasized comfort rather than historical accuracy but he used Classical motifs such as MONOPODIAE and claw feet. Smith published several volumes on design, including *A Collection of Designs for Household Furniture and Interior Decoration* (1808) and *A Collection of Ornamental Designs after the Antique* (1812).

Smith and Wesson (Horace Smith 1803–93 and Daniel Wesson 1825–1906) American firearms manufacturers remembered mainly for their REVOLVERS. The firm was founded in 1856 and is still in business today. They produced the first practical CARTRIDGE REVOLVER in 1857 and became a major rival of COLT. A small number of their revolvers were fitted with grips made by TIFFANY.

Smocking A decorative embroidery using a variety of stitches, commonly, chain, feather and herringbone, over a tightly pleated ground. Usually applied to shirts, shifts and childrens' clothes.

Snakewood A hard and durable pale brown wood from Brazil, with a serrated figure. Snakewood was used occasionally in the 17th century as an INLAY, in the 18th century primarily for MARQUETRY and BANDING and as a VENEER in Regency cabinet-work.

Sauce tureen by Benjamin Smith, Snr, 1811 [B, a pair]

Snaphaunce pistol, Italian c.1700 [I]

Snaphaunce A variant of the FLINTLOCK mechanism, dating from the mid-16th century, in which the flint was attached to a spring-loaded arm. Less expensive than the WHEEL LOCK, it was gradually superseded by the true flintlock during the 17th century.

Snuff bottle A small Chinese bottle for snuff, usually with a stopper to which a tiny spoon is attached. Typically cylindrical or of flattened ovoid form, they were made in porcelain, glass, lacquer, amber, coral, ivory, jade, agate and other hard stones. They were made throughout the 18th century, but most date from the Daoguang period (1821–50) and later.

Agate snuff bottle, late 18th–early 19th century [N]

Snuff-box by Nathaniel Mills, early Victorian [L]

Snuff-box A box for holding a small quantity of snuff (finely ground scented tobacco) and keeping it fresh and dry. Most snuff-boxes were small and portable, perhaps shaped to fit pockets, but larger presentation pieces were made for use at the table or ceremonies. They were made in porcelain, ivory, papier-mâché, tortoiseshell, treen and, particularly gold and silver (or silver gilt). Decoration varied from bright-cut engraving that sparkled as it caught the light to detailed depictions of hunting or pastoral scenes or Classical myths. They were fostered by the trend for taking snuff in Europe from the late 17th to the mid-19th century; after that, popularity declined.

Snuffer See CANDLE SNUFFER.

Soap box A silver box of spherical or rectangular form, sometimes on a spreading base with a hinged cover. They contained a soap ball and were part of toilet services from the early 18th century but are scarce today.

Soapstone A whitish material with a soapy texture used for small carvings. A variety of talc called steatite, it is soft enough in its purest form to scratch with a fingernail. Soapstone was used as a component of porcelain, notably at WORCESTER. It is found worldwide and was carved in ancient Egypt, China and India. It is still carved in Africa and by the Inuit in Greenland and northern Canada.

Soapstone writing set, Chinese late 19th century [R]

Soccer memorabilia See FOOTBALL MEMORABILIA.

Société Française de Fabrication de Bébés et Jouets (SFBJ) A syndicate founded by French dollmakers in 1899 in an attempt to compete with the fast-growing German doll industry. SFBJ's most common mould numbers are 60 and 301. Its 200 series of character dolls is the most sought-after of its products. The syndicate closed down in 1950.

Socket head A doll's head with a neck that ends in a ball shape. This ball neatly fits into a specially designed socket, a cup-shaped opening between the shoulders of the torso, thus enabling the head to rotate from side to side.

Soda glass A type of GLASS in which soda is used as the FLUX and lime is also added to the batch as a stabilizer. It was the earliest form of glass and various materials were used to provide the soda, including salt-marsh plants and seaweed. The resulting, often slightly yellowish or brown-tinged glass, is light and remains plastic for longer, which made it highly suited to the intricate designs as seen on early VENETIAN and FAÇON DE VENISE glass.

Soap box, English c.1712 [D]

Sofa A long informal fully upholstered SETTEE. Made from the 1690s, the sofa usually resembled a double chair until the mid-18th century, when it was lengthened. Unlike the settee, the sofa invited the user to lounge or recline upon it and this "comfort factor" gradually saw the sofa replacing the settee from the 19th century.

Sofa table A table for use while sitting on a sofa. Popular from the late 18th

Mahogany sofa table, English c.1825 [H]

century until the 1840s, the sofa table generally contained a drawer that was fitted with compartments for storing cards or gaming counters. Sofa tables had rectangular tops and hinged flaps and rested on trestle or plinth-type supports. During the early 19th century, elegant sofa tables were decorated with fine veneers of exotic woods and occasionally embellished with ebony or brass inlay. More elaborate specimens had lyre-shaped end supports, MONOPODIA or lion masks on the drawer handles.

Soft-paste porcelain
A substitute for true porcelain made of ground-up glass or FRIT (to give translucency) blended with white clay, soapstone and lime. It was fired at a relatively low temperature (1200°C/2192°F), was costly to produce and suffered heavy kiln losses.

Softwood Timber from coniferous trees, such as pine, hemlock and spruce. The wood is often, but not invariably, of a more open grain and softer than that of HARDWOOD.

Solar time See MEANTIME.

Solid China A term referring to an all-in-one porcelain doll's figure such as the FROZEN CHARLOTTE.

Solids Early lead toy figures cast completely solid. The process was superseded by HOLLOW-CAST figures. The term is usually applied to toy soldiers. See also FLATS.

Solitaire See CABARET.

Solon, Marc-Louis (1835–1912)
A French modeller and decorator who developed the technique of *pâte-sur-pâte* and *pâte d'application* at the SÈVRES factory from 1862 to 1871, when he went to England and worked at the MINTON factory.

Ding Yao bottle, Song dynasty [A]

Song dynasty A Chinese period (AD 960–1279) notable particularly for ceramics, especially stoneware in simple and elegant shapes with monochrome glazes. CELADON wares with semi-translucent greenish glazes were made for court. Some early pieces made when the court was at Kaifeng in northern China (960–1126) have moulded floral decoration. Later Song wares include ivory porcellaneous DING WARES, Qingbai wares with a pale-blue glassy glaze and CIZHOU WARES with bold incised or painted decoration in black and white slip. The simplicity of Song ceramics was influential on 20th century STUDIO POTTERY.

Sonneberg A town in Thuringia, Germany, a leading doll- and toy-producing centre in the 19th and early 20th centuries. Except for the porcelain heads, most components were made by outworkers and sold to the Sonneberg companies to be assembled. Many dolls, bears and toys were bought by American buyers to import to the US.

Sottsass Jnr, Ettore (b.1917)
An Austrian-born Italian architect and designer. He was one of the most influential figures of POST-MODERNISM in the 1980s and a major player in the establishment of the MEMPHIS group. He was a versatile designer, creating office machines for Olivetti (1957–69) as well as more expressive pieces of colourful furniture for Memphis (from 1981), especially in the "new" coloured plastic laminate materials and in MDF (medium density fibreboard).

Soumak A flat-woven rug with the weft wrapped round a number of warp threads. Made in the Caucasus, south-west Persia, Turkey and by the Baluch on the Afghan Persian borders from the 19th century to the present day by tribal groups or in village workshops. Designs tend to be geometric and finely woven.

South Jersey glass American glass made at small glasshouses in southern New Jersey, including that of Caspar WISTAR, from the mid-18th century through the 19th. The first products were crude, freeblown green glass, made by German immigrants and resembling Bohemian forms. Jugs (pitchers) and sugar bowls are typical. Early examples are rare and have been reproduced in the early 20th century.

South Jersey glass jug, c.1790 [P]

Southwark potteries London factories producing TIN-GLAZED EARTHENWARE in the 17th century. Production probably began with the Dutchman Christian Wilhelm (c.1595–1640) in the 1620s. He petitioned several times for a monopoly of the manufacture of smalt (cobalt pigment) and his pottery was known for BLUE AND WHITE wares similar to DELFT.

Souvenir ware A term mostly applied to inexpensive small objects in ceramics and glass, often with inscriptions naming the holiday resort in which they were purchased. It includes Bohemian glass trinkets sold in SPA TOWNS and engraved with the word *Andenken* ("souvenir" or "memory") and GOSS porcelain items with the town's name or coat of arms.

Sowerby Glass "Crane" apple pickers, c.1880 [Q]

Sowerby's Ellison An English glassworks established at Gateshead by John Sowerby in 1847. They introduced many new ranges, e.g. Vitro-porcelain and Queen's Ivory, and in the later 19th century were one of the leading manufacturers of PRESSED GLASS, SLAG and wares decorated with enamelling or iridized glass. Their mark was a moulded peacock's head. The factory supplied world markets with all types of domestic ware, including nursery wares inspired by the designs of Walter CRANE. It closed in 1972.

Soy frame A CRUET frame, made from c.1775–c.1830 usually of silver or Old Sheffield plate for stoppered, cut glass bottles for soy and other sauces.

Spade foot A rectangular form of foot that slightly tapers from the top – suggesting the outline of a spade. The spade foot was used in England from the latter part of the 18th century by such influential furniture designers as Thomas SHERATON and George HEPPLEWHITE.

Spandrel An architectural term referring to the triangular space on either side of a central arch, or the space between one arch and another in an ARCADE, which is frequently favoured for decorative ornament. Spandrels may be embellished with patterns or paired figures, such as angels, victories or cherubs.

Spanish colonial A term given to the art and architecture of the Spanish colonial Americas, including parts of the southern US, from the 16th to the 19th centuries. Decorative arts include painted wood "santos" (saints) figures and painted and carved primitive wooden furniture.

Spanish foot See BRAGANZA FOOT.

Spanish needle lace A style of lace influenced by VENETIAN and Moorish designs, often with sun and wheel motifs and using gold and silver threads. Traditional sun laces are still made in former Spanish and Portuguese colonies.

Sparrow-beak jug A small milk jug, part of a tea set, with a pear-shaped body and a pointed spout like a bird's beak, found in 18th-century pottery and porcelain – especially WORCESTER and CAUGHLEY porcelains.

Sparrow-beak jug, Worcester, c.1765 [L]

Spa towns In the 18th and 19th centuries "taking the waters" was fashionable in spas and resorts such as Carlsbad, Warmbrunn and Franzensbad in Bohemia, Baden-Baden and Wiesbaden in Germany, Aix-en-Provence in France and Bath and Tunbridge Wells in England and wares were made to cater for the taste of the visitors. The visitors were wealthy, often nobility or royalty, and the wares included spa glass, tumbler and carafe sets and vases. Many were decorated by distinguished engravers such as Dominik BIEMANN; others were made of coloured glass such as LITHYALIN, or of STAINED or CASED glass decorated with local views or suitable inscriptions.

Spatter (or spangled) glass Glass made in Europe and the US decorated with a pattern of multicoloured spots or blobs. Variations were made by the HOBBS, BROCKUNIER & CO., J.S. Irwin and SOWERBY'S ELLISON.

Spatterware See SPONGE WARE.

Specimen chest A chest designed to contain a collection of coins or other precious objects, such as shells, medals or semi-precious stones. The WELLINGTON CHEST, named after the Duke of Wellington, was originally created as a specimen chest in the early 19th century.

Speed map of Europe, early 17th century [Q]

Speed, John (1552–1629) An English cartographer of the early 17th century. Drawing on the work of Christopher Saxton (c.1543–c.1610) as well as his own research, Speed published an English county atlas, the *Theatre of the Empire of Great Britaine*, in 1611, which continued to be re-issued well into the 18th century. In 1627, he published *A Prospect of the Most Famous Parts of the World*, the first world atlas produced by an Englishman. Speed's maps are noted for their flowing script and rich decoration.

Spelter A term for zinc or an alloy of zinc and lead or aluminium, used as a substitute for bronze. It was popular in the 19th century for small mass-produced, inexpensive cast items, e.g. candlesticks, but also for larger pieces, such as figures.

Sphinx A mythological winged creature with the body of a lion and the head of a woman. Although a royal and religious symbol in ancient Egypt, it was the Classical interpretation of the sphinx that became popular throughout Europe. The original function of the sphinx as a guardian of temples and tombs inspired its use as a support for SARCOPHAGI during the Italian Renaissance and as a garden ornament from the BAROQUE period. In 18th-century France the sphinx – originating in the designs of Jean BÉRAIN and further popularized by Napoleon's Egyptian campaign – was even more widely adopted, ranging from overmantel decoration, gilt-bronze FIRE-DOGS and for images of court beauties. In the NEO-CLASSICAL period it was also used to decorate chair arms, vases, side tables and architectural brackets. In mid-18th century England porcelain figures of famous actresses as sphinxes were produced at CHELSEA and BOW. The sphinx continued to be used as a decorative motif throughout the 19th and 20th centuries and is still employed in the 21st.

Spice-box A small box or cupboard designed to contain exotic spices. In the 18th century, wooden spice cupboards were made as miniature cabinets. TREEN examples were made in the form of towers. Silver spice-boxes were made as dining table accessories, with several compartments and sometimes incorporating a nutmeg grater. Small examples were sometimes included in travelling dining sets. Porcelain spice-boxes were made from the early 18th century at SAINT-CLOUD and MENNECY.

Spider leg table A rectangular gateleg OCCASIONAL table popular from the late 18th century and made mainly in mahogany. The name "spider" derives from the six slender legs but they were also sometimes called Hogarth tables.

Spill vase A vase, usually cylindrical with a flared rim, used on the mantelshelf in pairs to hold "spills" of paper to light candles and lamps from the fire. They were made in many materials including ceramic, brass and papier-mâché.

Spindle A slender piece of wood turned on a lathe often used as an upright member or horizontal stretcher of a chair. Turned spindles sawn in half – called "split spindles" – were commonly applied as decoration to the flat framed faces of chests in the 17th century.
See also BALUSTER.

Sphinx in press-moulded glass by Molineaux, Webb & Co., 1875 [R]

Spinel A gemstone found in several colours – including red, blue and green – although red is the most used commercially. Found in Ceylon, Burma and Thailand, the stone was popular in India where it was particularly prized by the Mughal Emperors, and was frequently set in necklace and turban jewels. Synthetic blue spinel is a common imitation of AQUAMARINE.

Spinner, David (1758–1811) A US folk potter active in Buckinghamshire County, Pennsylvania. His work, with its animated decoration often depicting horses, is considered typical REDWARE of PENNSYLVANIA DUTCH type.

Spitalfields silk factories
In the East End of London, Spitalfields became the centre of the English silk industry from *c*.1700. Although silk-weaving was already known in England, it was

Spitalfields silk scarf, 19th century [O]

given new impetus from immigrant Huguenot weavers after the Revocation of the Edict of Nantes in 1685. In the first half of the 18th century, dress silk was the main product. Designers such as James Leman (1688–1745) and Anna Maria Garthwaite (1690–1763) contributed to the growth in both the home and export market. Government legislation, including the 1721 prohibition of printed calicoes and the 1766 ban on imported French silks, together with the Spitalfields Acts on rates of pay, helped the industry to prosper. Spitalfields continued to prosper until 1824, when legislation once again permitted free trade, and imported French silks flooded the market causing Spitalfields to go into a steep decline. In the late 19th century a number of new factories produced furnishing silks for the growing interior design market but the last one left the area in 1895.

Spittoon A receptacle for smokers to spit into, made in the 18th and 19th centuries in pottery, porcelain or metal (usually brass). They could either be small and hand-held, or larger and designed to rest on the floor. Examples from WORCESTER and CAUGHLEY have a spherical body and sloping rim. They were also made at SÈVRES and as CHINESE EXPORT WARE.

Worcester spittoon, c.1775 [L]

Splat The central vertical member of a chair back, generally shaped, and either left solid or decorated with carving, piercing, veneering or inlay. From the early 18th century, splat shapes were produced in a variety of designs.

Splint seat Thin interlaced strips of oak or hickory wood that have been woven into chair seats. An early American tradition that continues on rustic types of furniture, splint seats have been in use since the 18th century.

Spode From 1776, Josiah Spode of Stoke on Trent produced well-made pottery across a wide range: white STONEWARE with applied or sprigged designs in relief, black basaltes copying WEDGWOOD and, most importantly, blue printed EARTHENWARE. The "Caramanian" and "Indian Hunting" series of prints are famous and much collected. The pottery made high quality overglaze designs using the BAT-PRINTING technique. Early pieces have the mark SPODE impressed or painted with the pattern number.

Spode is generally credited with the invention of BONE CHINA around 1796–97. In tune with the Regency designs of the time, the pottery used brilliantly coloured Japanese patterns with excellent gilding. Harry Daniel was in charge of decoration but left in 1822 to set up his own factory. Spode continued its rich Regency patterns throughout the 1820s – pattern 1166 is well-known, with coloured sprays of flowers painted on a dark blue ground gilt with an all-over scale pattern. The PATTERN-BOOKS of the factory give information on shapes and decoration. As well as table wares, vases, desk sets, candlesticks, pastille burners and cabinet wares were produced.

In 1833 the firm was taken over by William Copeland and Thomas Garrett, who had been managers in Spode's

Spode blue and white transfer-printed dish, c.1825 [Q]

London retail shop. The firm traded as COPELAND & GARRETT and, aware of the growing competition, endeavoured to introduce up-to-date designs. Their "Statuary Porcelain" busts, figures and groups – better known as PARIANWARE, sold in vast quantities. In 1847, Garrett retired and Copeland took sole charge. He spent much time in London (becoming an Alderman and Lord Mayor) but still managed the factory. He retired in 1867, leaving the firm to his four sons. The factory continues today, having reverted to its name of Spode in 1970, and still makes its 19th-century patterns.

Sponge ware Cheaply decorated ware in which the colour was applied with a sponge, creating a blurred effect. This dates from the beginning of the 19th century and was common on Staffordshire pottery. Called SPATTERWARE in the US.

Spoon tray A small, shallow, usually silver or porcelain, tray often with fluted edges, made c.1700–60, before saucers were common. They held teaspoons and stopped tea drips soiling the furniture, people's clothing or tablecloths.

Spoon warmer A Victorian invention in the form of a vessel or container for hot water in which one or more serving spoons could balance with their bowls heating in the water. Often made from silver-plate or silver, these items exist in various novelty forms and often have a nautical theme or shape, e.g. shells or a life buoy. Before central heating was common, every effort was needed to ensure that hot food remained hot.

Sporting memorabilia

See AMERICAN FOOTBALL; ANGLING; BASEBALL; CRICKET; GOLF; RACQUET SPORTS, SOCCER.

Spot motif See SAMPLERS.

Sprig A decorative technique for ceramics, whereby ornament moulded or stamped separately is attached to the body of an object or vessel.

Yixing teapot with sprig decoration, c.1690 [K]

Sprimont, Nicholas (1716–70) A leading practitioner of English ROCOCO in silver and porcelain. A Flemish Huguenot, he was apprenticed as a silversmith and arrived in England in the early 1740s, entering his mark in London in 1743. He specialized in decoration inspired by, and in some cases cast from, sea creatures, such as shells, crabs and dolphins – even naturalistic crayfish salts, which he produced both in porcelain and silver. He also decorated objects with finely modelled human figures. In 1749 he became manager of the CHELSEA PORCELAIN FACTORY.

Spode porcelain punchbowl, c.1815 [K]

Spring clock See TABLE CLOCK.

Spun glass A technique for producing sheet glass in which a GATHER of glass is blown, transferred to an iron rod and spun into a disc. The disc is then cut into sheets, which will have a "bull's-eye". See also CROWN GLASS.

Spur mark The small mark on the underside of a plate left from the "spurs" or pegs that support them in the SAGGER in the kiln. They are noticeable on CHELSEA and JAPANESE PORCELAIN.

Squab cushion A removable stuffed cushion for a chair or stool. Originating in France, squab cushions were a popular feature of chairs and stools from the 17th and 18th centuries. Occasionally the term was used to designate a large padded seat.

S-scroll A decorative scroll form carved or applied in the shape of an S, continuous or broken. It commonly featured as an apron or corner ornament in the BAROQUE and ROCOCO styles. See also C-SCROLL and VOLUTE.

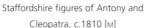

Staffordshire figures of Antony and Cleopatra, c.1810 [M]

Staffordshire figure A ceramic "portrait" figure, produced throughout the 19th century. The trend grew from c.1840 to the early 20th century for portraits of contemporary figures. Several factories in the "Five Towns" of the Potteries made portrait figures. They are a fascinating record of the Victorian period seen through the lives of the famous and the infamous. They depict people from all walks of life – from the royal families of Europe, politicians, soldiers and sailors, actors and actresses to circus performers,

sports personalities, people who achieved fame or notoriety and even famous animals. Many of the potters would never have seen these people but the likenesses were produced from prints in newspapers and show bills. It is also certain that many figures of soldiers and politicians had the same mould for the body but with a different head. Many of them were FLATBACKS designed to stand on the mantelshelf. Some have the name of the person depicted moulded on the base (not always correctly). Much research has been done to identify the figures. Queen Victoria and her family were popular. So were generals, such as Wellington, Napoleon and Garibaldi, the Italian patriot, who made two visits to England and captured the people's imagination.

The American circus performer van Amburgh featured in pottery after Queen Victoria went to see his wild animal act twice in 1838. The opera singers Jenny Lind (the Swedish Nightingale) and Maria Malibran were portrayed, and so were the perpetrators of the "Murder in the Red Barn". Even the elephant Jumbo, who was killed by a train and plunged the nation into mourning, was captured in a ceramic immortality.

Staffordshire creamware plate with underglazed oxide colours, made by Thomas Whieldon, c.1760 [O]

Staffordshire potteries
The "Five Towns" of the Potteries – Stoke, Burslem, Hanley, Longton and Tunstall – were the heartland of British ceramics. In the 19th century there were more than 1,000 firms working at various times, a few right through the period, such as WEDGWOOD, SPODE and RIDGWAY. These were the great "potting families", but innumerable small concerns made a fleeting appearance. There were factories at Longport, Fenton, Cobridge, Shelton, Lane Delph (now called Middle Fenton) and Lane End.

Largely thanks to Josiah Wedgwood and the canal system and, in the last half of the 19th century, the railways, English ceramics spread far and wide. The port of Liverpool also helped, supplying the vast export trade to the Americas and to India. Staffordshire became the pottery supplier to the world.

As well as figures, most factories made tea and dinner sets for everyday use, which were sold through china shops. These shops did not wish the makers to mark their products with their own names. Naturally, the shops wanted clients to go back to them for repeat orders and, in consequence, it is hard to attribute much Staffordshire pottery to specific makers.

Staffordshire teapot, c.1840 [R, restored]

Stained glass A term for coloured, stained or enamelled glass held together by lead strips in an abstract or figurative design, set in an iron framework and used in an architectural context, usually a window, or as a decorative panel. The process was used in the Middle Ages, when first monastic and then guild workshops made windows from glass – usually blue, green, gold and brown – coloured with metallic oxides. Details of drapery, features and decoration were painted onto the

Stained glass design with palm trees by Omega workshops, 1914 [K]

surface and then it was fired. Some of the finest stained glass cathedral windows from the 13th and 14th centuries were made using this technique.

From the late 15th and through the 16th century, stained glass windows were often made of rectangular panes of clear glass painted with coloured enamels. During the 17th and 18th centuries, the art of stained glass fell into abeyance, but it was revived in the 19th with the GOTHIC REVIVAL, under the influence of William MORRIS and the Pre-Raphaelite painters. Stained glass windows, doors and panels became a feature of ART NOUVEAU and ART DECO interiors. In the US, TIFFANY produced panels and screens for domestic interiors and adapted the technique for lampshades. In the 20th century, leading artists such as Henri Matisse (1869–1954), Marc Chagall (1887–1985) and Patrick Heron (b.1920) designed stained glass windows, while glass workshops and individual makers have used the technique for decorative pieces such as jewel boxes.

Staining Oil-based vegetable stains have been used to darken or colour the original appearance of some woods since the 17th century, sometimes with the intention to deceive. The green husks of

walnuts were used to stain beech to achieve the look of highly-prized walnut furniture. Pearwood was often ebonized during the Victorian period. In the 18th century, oxide of iron was applied to sycamore to produce the greenish-grey HAREWOOD. Mahogany was reddened and imitated using alkanet root. Staining was useful in INLAY and MARQUETRY work, where colours were used to render flower and foliage designs realistically.

Stainless steel A corrosion-resistant alloy of STEEL with chromium and nickel, developed simultaneously in Germany and Sheffield, England, in the early 20th century. Although used for cutlery and tableware before World War II, it was only after the war that it became the predominant material in cutlery manufacture.

Set of stainless steel cutlery, c.1960 [R]

Stalker, John, and George Parker The authors of *A Treatise on Japanning and Varnishing* produced at Oxford in 1688. It was a welcome source for European copiers – from female amateurs to well-established craftsmen – of the rare and highly expensive Chinese lacquered furniture that was fashionable from the late 17th century. With 24 plates of CHINOISERIE designs – bamboo foliage, rocks, temples, insects, cranes, HO-HO

birds and mandarins – Stalker and Parker's book illustrates a variety of patterns originating in Japanese LACQUERWORK, that have been adopted as decoration for a host of objects, including cabinet furniture, picture and mirror frames, and toilet articles.

Stam, Mart (Martinus Adrianus) (1899–1986) A Dutch architect and designer closely identified with the BAUHAUS designers in Germany, where he worked in the 1920s, and with Russian Constructivists. He is best known as the inventor of the tubular steel CANTILEVER CHAIR, celebrated for its simplicity of construction, with two supports rather than four legs that relied on the strength of tubular steel. His seminal design of 1924, which was not fully realized until 1926, coincided with a similar tubular steel cantilever chair produced by Ludwig MIES VAN DER ROHE. The pioneering form was adopted and popularized by designers such as Marcel BREUER.

Stamping The practice of impressing a mark into a piece of metalwork, ceramics or furniture with a stamp. Also describes pressing low-relief ornament onto a ceramic body.

Standing cup (or hanap) A silver or gold cup, usually with a cover, where the bowl is raised up or literally standing on a pedestal or extended foot. The term is mainly used for larger, important, ceremonial cups dating from the medieval period, right through the Reformation and up to and including certain examples from the early 18th century.

Standish See INK STAND.

Stanhope A small souvenir formed in metal, plastic or carved wood or bone, produced from the

Bone umbrella needlecase with Stanhope inset handle, English 1860–67 [S]

mid-19th to the mid-20th centuries in various novelty shapes. It is held close to the eye to view a tiny transparency showing one to 12 tourist scenes through a miniature lens (invented in the late 1700s by the 3rd Earl of Stanhope). David Brewster was the first to set these "micro-images" into jewellery in 1853.

Starck, Philippe (b.1949)

A French designer, trained at the Ecole Camondo in Paris as an interior architect. In 1969, employed by Pierre Cardin, he designed well over 50 pieces of furniture. Along with four other young designers he was asked to contribute designs (1983) for the President's private apartments at the Elysée Palace in Paris. This brought his work to a broader audience and since then he has achieved celebrity status. A good self-publicist with a strong personality, he established his own company, Starck Products, in 1980 to manufacture his own designs. In 1985 the French Government invited competitive entries to design the "street-furniture" for the Parc de la Villette in Paris; Starck won. His interiors for the Costes Café in Paris, the Starck Club nightclub in Dallas and the Royalton and Paramount Hotels in New York have all added to his reputation as one of the best designers of his generation. His work is modern, stylish and with hints of humour. In the 1990s he designed many smaller products such as a toothbrush, toilet brush, door handles and a "sci-fi" lemon squeezer that looks like an alien three-legged octopus. He has designed several works for which he took names from the science fiction novels of Philip K. Dick.

Steam mechanism

See LIVE STEAM MECHANISM.

Alessi lemon squeezer by Starck, 1990 [N]

Steel An alloy of IRON and carbon, valued for its extreme hardness that is produced by rapid cooling (quenching) and heating (tempering) during the manufacturing process. Steel has been used since prehistoric times for weapons, especially swords, and armour, as well as domestic cutting implements

Steel openwork perfume burner, Russian late 18th century [K]

such as knives and scissors. In the 16th and 17th centuries small, largely decorative, steel caskets, boxes and furniture were fashionable. Faceted steel studs, known as cut steel, became popular in the late 18th and early 19th centuries as decoration on buckles, buttons and plaques and for jewellery. Inexpensive, rust- and stain-proof STAINLESS STEEL revolutionized the manufacture of cutlery in the 20th century.

Steiff The Steiff factory was founded in 1884 by Margarete Steiff, a seamstress who sold felt clothing from her shop in Giengen, Germany. In 1880 she made a felt elephant pin cushion for a friend. An overwhelming success, this was soon produced on a larger scale in her workshop. In 1885, 600 elephants were made and in 1892 Steiff distributed her first catalogue. The Steiff soft toy business was registered in 1893. At the Leipzig spring trade fair of 1903, Steiff showed its first animals with movable limbs. One was a TEDDY BEAR called 55PB. Three thousand bears were ordered for export to the US and soon other orders followed. Bear 55PB was joined by 35PB in 1904 and 28PB in 1905.

Jointing evolved in these two years from twine to twisted wire over rods to disc joints. To distinguish its products from those of its competitors, Steiff devised its trademark "button in ear". At first,

in 1904, the button was embossed with an elephant. From 1905 onward, the button stated "Steiff". Until 1908, 90 per cent of Steiff's bears were exported to the US. Later, the English and the German markets followed, resulting in a teddy bear craze that lasted into the late 1930s. Some of Steiff's best known bears of that period are its "original" bear, the teddy clown, the Petsy bear and the teddy baby. Models often had a characteristic humped back. The firm also made other animal toys such as monkeys. World War II put a stop to the factory's output but production resumed in 1947. As MOHAIR was difficult to get, bears of artificial and wool plush were made. In the 1950s, some of the pre-war models were slightly modified and

Brown felt monkey skittles by Steiff, c.1930 [L, for 9]

produced again. The "original" bear was reintroduced with larger head, shorter snout, stubbier limbs and less pronounced hump. A typical Steiff bear of that time is the Zotty bear, a super soft bear with great appeal for children. In the following years, Steiff's bear designs were made safer, washable, more hygienic and child-friendly, but perhaps lost their appeal to grown-ups. In 1980, the factory started producing replicas of their old models, sometimes in limited editions for collectors.

Steiner, Herman A company making BISQUE-headed dolls, in SONNEBERG, south Germany, founded in 1911 and still producing toys. Most Steiner dolls are marked with the company's initials HS.

Steiner (Société) A Parisian maker of BISQUE-headed BÉBÉS, founded by Jules Nicholas Steiner, a former clockmaker, in 1855. The company patented over 24 innovations, many of them CLOCKWORK, including the *bébé premier pas*, which could walk while being held by one arm, a baby that kicked and cried and a dancing lady. Following Steiner's death in 1901, the company continued to use his name until 1903, when it was taken over by Edmond Daspres. It closed in 1908.

Steiner dolls
c.1880 [E]

Stem The structure that joins the bowl of a drinking vessel to the foot. Stems vary in length, thickness and decoration, from the PRUNTS on RÖMERS, to serpent-stemmed Venetian goblets or the types and combinations of KNOPS on BALUSTER and BALUSTROID glasses and the AIR TWIST stems on 18th-century English drinking glasses.

Stem cup
A Chinese ritual vessel, otherwise called a *gaozu*, with a wide shallow bowl raised on a tall slender stem that flares towards the base. Some of the best MING DYNASTY examples from the

Stem cup,
early Ming,
15th century [D]

Xuande reign (1426–35) are pure white, decorated with three fish painted in underglaze copper red. Stem cups were also made in LACQUER and decorated with Buddhist motifs.

Stencilling A method of decoration known from ancient times in which paint is dabbed through a design cut in a template that can be used repeatedly to reproduce the pattern. Stencilling can be done by hand on wall surfaces or furniture or as a form of printing on fabrics or wallpaper. It was widely adopted – especially in the US – in the 18th and 19th centuries and was also used to achieve the effects inspired by JAPONAISERIE and for the geometric shapes and heraldic ornament of the GOTHIC REVIVAL. The fashion also spawned imitations: fabrics, ceramics and wallpaper simulating stencilled designs were created by designers from the late 19th century.

Stereoscope A device for viewing two images (stereographs) placed side by side that appear to be identical but are in fact subtly different, each image having been taken from a slightly different viewpoint along the horizontal. Through a stereoscope, each eye is directed to one of the images and thus the combined single image gains depth and appears to be three-dimensional. Initially invented by the English scientist Charles Wheatstone in the 1830s, the idea was applied to photography by David Brewster in 1849 and presented at the 1851 GREAT EXHIBITION in London.

Sterling silver Silver with a standard of purity equal to 925 parts of silver to 75 parts alloy, or 92.5% pure. It is possibly named after "Easterlings" – mint workers from East Germany, brought to England by Henry II (1154–89) to improve the coinage of the realm. Sterling silver became the accepted purity or standard in Britain from 1300 (excluding the BRITANNIA period 1697–1720) and the standard for some other countries including the US. See also HALLMARKS.

Steuben Glassworks
A US glassworks founded in Corning, Steuben County, New York State, in 1903 and incorporated as a division of the CORNING GLASSWORKS. Under the directorship of Frederick Carder (1863–1963), an English glassmaker and chemist, they introduced an impressive range of artistic lines, many in response to contemporary US or European glassmakers. One of the most popular ranges was "Aurene", an IRIDESCENT GLASS, made from 1904 to 1930. They also made "CLUTHRA", inspired by Scottish CLUTHA, and Intarsia glass, which was similar to ORREFORS "Graal". From the 1930s Steuben concentrated on engraved, clear glass of high lead content, the most popular today being ART DECO designs made under the direction of the architect Sidney Waugh (1904–63). The company got into financial difficulties during the Great Depression but their fortunes were revived by Waugh, John Montieth Gates (an architect) and Robert J. Leary (manager). At the end of the 1930s, they began to commission designs from leading artists (Henri Matisse, Salvador Dali, Marie Laurencin, Jean Cocteau, Paul Manship and Eric Gill) and continued this practice through the 1950s. The company is still active.

Steuben glassworks
intaglio cut glass pitcher
by Carder, c.1910 [M]

Stevengraph A brightly coloured woven silk picture, depicting horse races, transport and famous people, used to decorate GREETINGS CARDS and bookmarks. Made in England on JACQUARD LOOMS from c.1879 to c.1938, they were named after their manufacturer Thomas Stevens (d.1888).

Stevens & Williams An English glasshouse established in 1847 at Brierley Hill, near STOURBRIDGE, West Midlands, and known as Royal Brierley after receiving a royal warrant in 1919. The company developed new types of ART GLASS such as ALEXANDRITE and SILVERIA, as well as making fine engraved glass (at the end of the 19th century) and CUT GLASS enhanced by the designs of Keith MURRAY in the 1930s. Royal Brierley still produces art glass today.

Stevens & Williams Silveria bowl, c.1900 [L]

Stick back A chair-back that is composed of SPINDLES or small members. The stick back form is a characteristic feature of the WINDSOR CHAIR.

Stick barometer The earliest and simplest type of barometer, made from c.1750 but largely dating from the 18th century, in which a glass tube of mercury ending in a cistern of mercury is contained in a narrow upright case (often walnut or mahogany) about 1m (3ft) high.

Stick furniture Rustic furniture, sometimes with the bark left on and possibly made from green (unseasoned) wood. The joints are usually MORTISE AND TENONS held in place by wedges. It still made in rural areas.

Stickley, Gustav (1857–1942) A prominent US ARTS AND CRAFTS furniture-maker. In the 1870s Gustav and his younger brothers Charles and Albert worked in their uncle Jacob Schlager's chair factory in Pennsylvania. After a visit to England, Gustav was converted to the ARTS AND CRAFTS style and in 1898 he founded the Gustav Stickley Company, making furniture inspired by William MORRIS. In 1901 he began to publish a monthly magazine, *The Craftsman,* and renamed his business United Crafts. In 1904 the name of the business changed again, to The Craftsman Workshops.

Most Stickley furniture is made of quarter-sawn oak with the MORTISE AND TENON joints exposed. It is solid and comfortable and generally without ornament. Panel and frame construction was also used and any metalwork was bold and hand-wrought. He employed the talented architect and designer Harvey Ellis from 1903 until his death in 1904, who introduced a slightly lighter style with small inlaid motifs. Gustav's business expansion in New York led him into difficulties at the beginning of World War I. In 1916 his other brothers, Leopold and John George, took over and ran the company as L & JG Stickley. In 1974 the company passed out of the family's hands, but it still retains the Stickley name. (See also MISSION STYLE and GRAND RAPIDS.)

Stickwork A term for small objects, similar to TUNBRIDGEWARE and TREEN, made in the 19th century. Sticks of coloured wood were glued together into rods that were then either sliced into veneers to decorate items or turned on a lathe to make eggcups, snuff-boxes, chessmen, pens and sewing implements.

Stiegel, Henry William See AMERICAN FLINT GLASSWORKS.

Stile The vertical member of a MORTISE AND TENONED framework of a chair-back or a piece of panelled furniture, such as a chest or a cupboard door. The stiles may be prolonged to form feet.

Stinton, Harry See WORCESTER PORCELAIN FACTORY.

Stipple engraving Engraved decoration on glass in which the design is built up from tiny shallow dots made by striking the surface with a diamond or other hard point. Glass is the perfect medium for this technique as the design is visible on both sides. The technique was developed c.1621 in Holland and Dutch craftsmen remained the major exponents of the technique in the 18th and 19th centuries, often on goblets imported from Newcastle, UK. In the 20th century, the technique was revived in Britain by Laurence Whistler (b.1912).

Stippling A decorative technique applied to ceramics where a detailed design is built up of dots of colour applied using the point of a brush. Examples include pieces from the Italian CAPODIMONTE factory. Also a technique used in TRANSFER-PRINTING where the design is built up of dots, not lines.

"Morris" chair by Stickley, 1902 [C]

Stirrup-cup A drinking vessel of silver, silver-gilt, glass, ceramic or Old SHEFFIELD PLATE, intended to be used on horseback. These cups have no base or foot, so they cannot be put down unless they are empty. Many silver examples are formed as fox, hare, boar or greyhound masks. They are still made today but were most popular between 1770 and 1820 and enjoyed a revival in the late 19th century.

Stobwasser und Söhn
The German japanner Johann Heinrich Stobwasser (1740–1829) was noted for his PAPIER-MÂCHÉ SNUFF-BOXES, which were often painted by great artists. His factory opened in Braunschweig in 1763 and closed just after World War I.

Papier-mâché snuff-box by Stobwasser, c.1830 [i]

Stone china A type of STONEWARE that approaches porcelain in hardness and may be slightly TRANSLUCENT. It was first developed by John TURNER around 1800. Turner sold the patent to Josiah SPODE who used the formula to make tableware. See also IRONSTONE CHINA.

Stoneware A type of ceramic that shares characteristics of EARTHENWARE and porcelain. The BODY is made of clay mixed with a fusible stone (i.e. one capable of being melted at sufficiently high temperatures, c.1300°C/2372°F), usually FELDSPAR. This vitrification renders the ware watertight, although salt glaze or LEAD

Relief-moulded stoneware jug by Charles Meigh, 1839 [R]

GLAZE are also added. It was produced in China in the SHANG DYNASTY but was developed independently in Germany in the Middle Ages and spread to other European countries. It was not known in England until the late 17th century and was at the height of its popularity with WEDGWOOD in the 18th century.

Stool The most common type of seat furniture until the 19th century, the stool was used in ancient Egypt, was adopted by the Greeks and later by the Romans. Unlike a bench, the stool seats only one person. It is distinguished from the chair as it lacks arms and a back. From antiquity the stool was constructed in two forms: supported on four straight legs, or on four legs arranged crosswise. It remained more or less unaltered until the late Middle Ages, when a three-legged version with a circular or polygonal top, known as the "Strozzi" stool, was introduced in Italy. Later stools are largely variants of the original two basic types, with the decoration of the supports and the treatment of the padded or hard top being the only innovations.

Stopper A shaped piece of glass, ceramic or metal that fits into, and so closes, the mouth of a vessel such as a DECANTER, bottle or CRUET, designed to hold liquid that might otherwise evaporate or become tainted. They were made in a wide variety of shapes and sizes, usually in a style that complements the vessel and may help to date it.

Storr, Paul (1771–1844) England's most celebrated 19th-century silversmith and a brilliant businessman. He was apprenticed to the Swedish-born NEO-CLASSICAL master, Andrew Fogelberg, in Soho, London. He had a short-lived partnership with William Frisbee from 1792 to 1793, when he entered his first mark alone.

By 1807, styled as Storr and Co. and now having registered his fourth mark, he was producing most of his work for the Royal Goldsmiths, Rundell, Bridge & Rundell, forming a sub-partnership with them in 1811. This partnership ended in 1819 when Storr took premises in Clerkenwell, London. In 1822 he went into partnership with John Mortimer, thus benefiting from his retail premises in New Bond Street, and succeeded in recruiting various excellent craftsmen who had previously worked for Rundell. Storr and Mortimer then employed Storr's nephew, John Hunt, as a chaser.

Storr retired in 1838 and the firm continued under the name Mortimer and Hunt. Storr's early silversmithing (before 1800) was generally unremarkable and rather domestic, both in design and quality, although the workshop produced some highly competent pieces. It was, perhaps, his apprenticeship with Fogelberg and his dalliance with Neo-classical ornamentation, coupled with the timing of Britain's Industrial Revolution and

Paul Storr entrée dish and cover, 1810 [G]

burgeoning wealth, that led to his success. Certainly, his astute association with the Royal Goldsmiths and his contact with some of the most eminent sculptors and artist–craftsmen of the period (including John FLAXMAN) helped to build the solid foundation of what became a mighty business. It was under Storr's direction that his business produced the vast array of magnificent Regency silver and silver-gilt that adorned the tables and sideboards of the wealthiest households in Britain, but it is not known for certain how much of the silver was made by Paul Storr himself.

Stourbridge glasshouses Glasshouses established near Stourbridge, UK, a major centre of glass production. The first were established in the area by HUGUENOT refugees in the early 17th century. They specialized in flat glass, but began to produce decorative and coloured glass in the mid-18th century, and by the 19th century Stourbridge had become home to many small decorating workshops as well as many of the major English manufacturers, including H.G. RICHARDSON & SONS, STEVENS & WILLIAMS, STUART & SONS and Thomas WEBB & SONS, who made all types of glass, including CAMEO GLASS.

Cameo glass vase by Stevens & Williams, Stourbridge, late 19th century [H]

Straightlace See BOBBIN LACE.

Straining spoon (or gravy spoon) A silver spoon with a pierced divider running down the centre of the bowl, used for straining vegetables or sauces. Most were made in Ireland in the late 18th century, but they were still being made in the late 19th century.

Strapwork An ornament reminiscent of leather straps or carved FRETWORK, used either alone in interlacing bands or teamed with GROTESQUES – as first

designed in the late 16th century by Rosso Fiorentino and Primaticcio to frame some paintings at Fontainebleau. Originating in antique motifs and distorted for expressive purposes by Italian RENAISSANCE artists, strapwork spread to the rest of Europe through the ENGRAVINGS of designers such as Hans Vredeman de Vries and Cornelis Floris. It was used extensively in the Netherlands, England, Germany and France for metalwork, furniture, mouldings in plaster and STUCCO, and for carved wooden panels. Strapwork appeared in increasingly elaborate variations throughout the 17th and 18th centuries, embellished with jewels, rosettes, pyramids and nailheads, or combined with foliage and scrollwork.

Strapwork

Strasbourg pottery and porcelain factories Carl Hannong founded a FAIENCE factory in Strasbourg, France, in 1721, together with Johann Wachenfeld, who left after a short time. The faience produced was particularly fine – well-painted plates, mugs and pots, some decorated with botanically accurate plants. They also made TROMPE L'OEIL plates applied with realistic models of fruit and vegetables, and specialized in large tureens in the form of wild boars' heads or fish. The Prince de Rohan had a palace in the city, so there was a rich market for such extravagant creations. In 1724 Hannong founded another faience factory in Haguenau, France, (near the source of the clay) and when he retired in 1732 he left the two factories to his sons. Balthasar ran Haguenau and Paul-Antoine took over

Strasbourg faience table centrepiece, c.1730 [E]

Strasbourg, where faience table services, and large clock cases, fountains and bidets were made, decorated in HIGH-TEMPERATURE COLOURS. In 1751 Paul-Antoine went into partnership with J.J. RINGLER. They were soon making fine quality porcelain, decorated in bright overglaze enamels. In 1754 Louis XV, determined to protect the monopoly of SÈVRES, passed a royal decree forbidding any other porcelain manufacturer to use gilding or more than one colour. As a result of this, the porcelain-making side of the business was moved to FRANKENTHAL, where Paul-Antoine enjoyed the patronage of the Elector, Carl Theodor von der Pfalz. Following Paul-Antoine's death in 1760, the faience factories at Haguenau and Strasbourg passed to his sons, Pierre-Antoine and Josef Adam, who resumed porcelain production in 1766. However, by 1781 the business was in financial ruin, Josef Adam was declared bankrupt and the factories were closed.

Strass, Georges Frédéric (1702–73) A Parisian jeweller who invented a form of PASTE (known as "strass") that effectively imitated precious gemstones, especially diamonds. He set up his own business in 1730 and made a fortune, becoming jeweller to Louis XV in 1734.

Strawberry-dish A silver, silver-gilt or ceramic bowl of shallow circular form with a scalloped rim, flat base and fluted, upcurved sides, associated with the serving of strawberries, particularly in England during the first half of the 18th century.

Strawberry Hill Gothic See GOTHIC STYLE and GOTHICK.

Straw marquetry A decorative technique mainly used on mirror frames, tea caddies, caskets and small pieces of furniture, in which strips of bleached and coloured straw are applied to create landscapes, figures, animals or geometric patterns. Also called straw work, it was practised in Europe from the 17th century. It was especially popular in France in the late 18th and 19th centuries as a veneer for tabletops and cabinets and for little boxes known as *petits boîtes de l'amitié*.

Stretcher The horizontal rail or bar joining the legs of tables, stools and chairs, designed to strengthen the construction. The stretchers may be left plain, or may be embellished by turning or decorative carving.

Striations Irregularities in glass in the form of fine parallel or swirling lines. They were usually caused when the glass was manipulated into shape by tools; these tool marks can be seen on early LEAD glass where the stem joins the bowl and on the flat-cut sections on CUT GLASS.

Strike/silent A device usually in the form of a lever or small handle set against a SUBSIDIARY dial marked "strike" and "silent" used to turn the striking mechanism of a clock on or off. Such devices are often set in the dial arch on the dials of 18th-century LONGCASE clocks.

Striking system Sounds made by the bell or gong of a clock to indicate the passing of the hours and often also the half or quarter hours. Before the late 17th century, the striking TRAIN was activated by the COUNT WHEEL, which enabled the hours to be sounded only in succession; if the mechanism was altered the strike was not synchronized with the hands on the dial. This problem was alleviated in 1676

by Edward Barlow who invented the rack-and-snail system, which linked hand movement with striking.

Stringing Fine inlaid lines of wood or metal inlay, applied as a decorative border for furniture – especially around the edges of tabletops or drawers. The technique was especially popular in the late 18th century, coinciding with the fashion for SATINWOOD veneers, which furnished an accommodating ground for this decorative device. American furniture produced in New England at this time featured stringing frequently composed of small, geometric patterns.

Strut clock A small travelling clock with a shallow case supported by an easel-like strut. Most date from the 1850s onward. They were a speciality of Thomas COLE.

Brass strut clock, English c.1860 [H]

Stuart, James (1713–88) An English architect and designer. Co-author of *The Antiquities of Athens* in 1762 with Nicholas Revett, James "Athenian" Stuart championed the GREEK REVIVAL in England. He worked only sporadically as an interior designer – at Kedleston Hall in Derbyshire and at Spencer House in London – in a florid interpretation of Classical style that influenced the early work of Robert ADAM. His greatest success was his ability to adapt Roman temple furniture, such as altars and tripods, to household use. See also ATHÉNIENNE.

Stuart & Sons Ltd An English glasshouse established in STOURBRIDGE in 1881 by

Frederick Stuart. It patented "medallion cameo" glass in 1887, but is best known for fine quality, clear cut glass made in the 1930s. It continues as a family business.

Stucco A slow-setting plaster used for interior mouldings, especially on ceilings, and for exterior rendering and sculptural purposes. Containing marble or stone dust, it comprises mainly gypsum, sand and lime. Stucco spread in the 18th century from Italy, where it had been used since the Classical Roman period.

Studio, The An English monthly art periodical published 1893–1988 (also in the US), subtitled *An Illustrated Magazine of Fine and Applied Arts*. In the early years it acted as a newsletter for the ARTS AND CRAFTS movement.

Studio glass One-off or limited edition glassware, designed and made by artists in small workshops, or under their direct supervision. Fine studio glass was made in France in the 19th and early 20th centuries by such designers as Maurice Marinot (1882–1960), François DECORCHEMONT and François-Eugène ROUSSEAU. Since the 1960s it has been produced in America, Dominick Labino (1910–87) and Dale Chihuly (b.1941) being notable makers, and throughout Europe.

Studio pottery The work of independent artist potters working in individual studios or with other like-minded potters wishing to express their own artistry without commercial pressures. Studio potters are responsible for all aspects of pottery production. Leaders of the trend include John Mason (b.1927), Peter Voulkos (b. 1924) and Betty Woodman (b.1930) in America, and in Europe Michael CARDEW, Bernard LEACH, Lucie RIE, Hans COPER, William Staite MURRAY and Raoul Dufy (1877–1953).

Studio pottery: ash-glazed stoneware vase by Katherine Pleydell-Bouverie, 1960s [Q]

English silk stumpwork, mid-17th century [H]

Stumpwork (or raised work) A term widely used for a form of 17th-century embroidery in which padded motifs are raised from a satin ground fabric to form a three-dimensional image. Frequently featuring a variety of stitches and materials, including glass beads, seed pearls, coral and mica, it was often the work of young girls. From *c*.1650 to *c*.1680, it was a fashionable decoration on small-scale pictures, caskets and mirror frames.

Style rayonnant A manner of ceramic decorative painting first developed in the late 17th century at ROUEN, France. The patterns – which on plates and dishes radiate inward from richly decorated borders – resemble engraved embroidery designs and are comprised of LAMBREQUINS, scrolls, FESTOONS of flowers and leaves, lacy ARABESQUES and FERRONNERIES. It was taken up at influential French factories for the decoration of faience, including NEVERS, MOUSTIERS and MARSEILLES, and for porcelain at SAINT CLOUD. A similar motif is seen on English silver cups *c*.1650–*c*.1750. It remained a popular decorative motif until the 1740s.

Subsidiary dial A small dial set in a clock's main DIAL PLATE, inside the CHAPTER RING or in the dial arch on break-arch dials, showing the seconds, date, phases of the moon or STRIKE/SILENT indication.

Sucket fork These delicate silver (and silver-gilt) utensils have two prongs or tines at one end and a spoon bowl (teaspoon size) at the other. They were used for sweetmeats and candied fruit. Either engraved or plain, they were produced during the second half of the 17th century but few fully hallmarked examples are extant from before 1670.

Sugar tongs (nips) Small silver utensils used for conveying sugar chips to a cup. The earliest type, resembling small ember tongs and dating from *c*.1680, were superseded around 1700 by tongs that had a pivot instead of a spring "U" section. As sugar became more affordable *c*.1770 sugar nips evolved into scissor-like items with ring handles and shell grips. Larger sugar nips were often made of brass for kitchen use. They still formed part of silver tea utensils in the 19th and into the 20th century.

Silver sugar tongs by Georg Jensen, *c*.1900 [O]

Sulphides Small ornaments, often medallions or cameo portraits, made of a white porcelain-like material and encased in clear glass. They were incorporated into pieces such as drinking glasses, perfume bottles, bowls, paperweights and plaques. First developed in France in the early 19th century, Apsley PELLATT patented his "cameo incrustations" in Britain in 1819. In the US fine sulphides were made from *c*.1814 by the Pittsburgh Flint Glass Manufactory.

Apsley Pellatt sulphide paperweight with portrait of George IV, 1820s [N]

Sumakh See SOUMAK.

Summers, Gerald (1899–1967) A British engineer and designer who worked for Marconi before forming his own company, Makers of Simple Furniture, in 1933, having designed the furniture for his own home. He made furniture from moulded sheets of plywood. The firm closed during World War II because of rationing of materials.

Sunburst motif A motif featuring the sun surrounded by rays. A popular theme for 17th-century Baroque ornament, it appears frequently in furniture and interior decoration, as the central point for ceiling decoration and the gilded surround for a mirror, clock or barometer. In the 19th century it was used for decorating light fittings and US mould-blown glass flasks. It was also favoured by ART DECO designers and later a more formalized sunrise motif was popular in the 1920s.

Sunderland ware Pottery made in Sunderland, north-east England, in the 19th century, mostly by Dixon, Austen & Co. (*c*.1800–65). Large jugs, plates and mugs, typically with pink and copper lustre borders, are transfer-printed with images of the iron bridge over the River Wear, ships and plaques with religious verses.

Sunderland pearlware jug, *c*.1850 [P]

Sundial An instrument for measuring the passage of time from the shadow of a pointer (the GNOMON) cast by the sun on a graduated plane. Sundials were the main method of judging time before the spread of mechanical clocks and watches in the 16th and 17th centuries. Portable sundials were often made of ivory.

Sunflower motif A symbol of remembrance, gratitude and constancy, widely used as a decorative device from the 17th century. In the early 1750s, sunflower-shaped dishes and lidded pots were produced in England by the CHELSEA porcelain factory. Sunflowers figure in the Queen Anne revival in the 1870s and in the Aesthetic Movement.

Supper set A set of four or five shaped dishes that fit together to form an oval or circle and stand on a tray. Popular in Britain from the late 18th century, they were made from silver, Sheffield plate, porcelain or pottery.

Suspension A means of attaching the PENDULUM of a clock to the arbor on which the escape wheel turns, e.g. by a spring or silk thread.

Sussex chair A rush-seated ARTS AND CRAFTS chair designed by MORRIS & CO. Made from *c.*1865, it had its roots in

Sussex chair, English
c.1875 [N]

the turned spindle-back country chair. Elegantly proportioned, this simple form was produced in a host of variations including a corner version, a settee and a "Rossetti" armchair. Its popularity continued well into the 20th century.

Sutherland table A small, narrow, lower version of the drop-leaf gate-leg dining table used for taking tea or card playing, the early equivalent of the coffee table. Made in England in great quantities from the 1880s until *c.*1914, it was reputedly named after the Duchess of Sutherland, who

Sutherland table,
English c.1870 [J]

served as Queen Victoria's Mistress of the Robes. Though practical, the Sutherland table enjoyed limited popularity. It was made mainly in mahogany or oak, and occasionally decorated with inlaid borders, foliage or formalized Neo-classical patterns.

Suzuribako A Japanese term for a writing box containing tools for calligraphy or writing, including brushes, an ink stick, a stone slab to rub the ink stick on to make ink and a pot for water.

Swag A decorative ornament similar to a FESTOON, made up of fruit, flowers, nuts, leaves (often laurel) or shells. Unlike the festoon, a swag may also be composed of a pendant loop of cloth drapery.

Swag

Originally a Classical motif, the swag was adopted in the NEO-CLASSICAL period for architecture as well as for silver and ceramics and carving or painting on items of furniture.

Swan-neck handle A curved, hanging brass handle introduced in the early 1760s on the drawers of CASE FURNITURE.

Swan-neck pediment (US: scroll top) A pediment, derived from Classical architecture, in which two S-curves almost meet in scrolls. They were a popular decorative feature on early 18th-century English furniture, especially for bookcases, cabinets, cupboards, mirrors and bureaux.

Swansea pottery and porcelain factories A pottery, which became known as the Cambrian Pottery, was established in the 1760s in Swansea by William Coles. He made salt-glazed stoneware and creamware resembling Wedgwood. Some of this was painted with realistic botanical designs by William Pardoe between 1795 and 1809. Coles died in 1779 and the factory was run by his descendants before being taken over by William Dillwyn in 1801 followed by his son Lewis Weston Dillwyn. Porcelain was produced in 1813 after William Billingsley

Swansea porcelain
tureen and cover,
c.1820 [D]

joined the factory from WORCESTER in 1813. He and his son-in-law Samuel Walker had worked at NANTGARW, then moved in 1814 to Swansea. Billingsley and Walker produced a beautiful porcelain but had severe kiln losses. The wares were finely decorated in the latest Paris fashion with figures, birds and flowers, in the factory and in London by OUTSIDE DECORATORS. Billingsley and Walker left in 1817 and the factory was taken over by Bevington Brothers, after which little or no porcelain was made. It finally closed in 1870.

Swastika (Sanskrit: "well-being") In many cultures, represents the sun's course and the rotation of the heavens. The swastika was widely used as a symbol of prosperity in early Greece and was adopted as a cross form in early Christian art. On Chinese ceramics the swastika – signifying longevity – appears in border patterns. The symbol fell into disrepute in the 20th century when it was adopted by the German National Socialists.

Sweetmeat dish A shallow silver, silver-gilt or ceramic dish, usually lightly constructed, with one or two handles, and with or without a stem. They could be decorated with fluting on the rim, or embossed or punched work. They were made in large numbers from the 1630s to the 19th century to hold candied fruits, preserves and pastries.

Silver sweetmeat dish by James Dixon, Sheffield c.1880 [K]

Sweetmeat set A central star-shaped or small circular dish surrounded by four or six shaped dishes. Known in English DELFT c.1730–60, and in saltglaze and creamware into the 19th century.

Sword and scabbard, English c.1880 [L]

Swivel-head A variation on the SHOULDER HEAD that allows the head of a doll to move from side to side, independently of the breastplate. The ball-shaped underside of the neck fits neatly into a cup-shaped indentation in the SHOULDER PLATE. This type of head was commonly used for PARISIENNES between 1860 and 1880.

Sword An edged weapon with a long blade, for cutting or thrusting or both. Swords first appeared in the Bronze Age and were used constantly in warfare until the beginning of the 20th century. Officers still carry dress swords as badges of rank today. Civilians once carried swords as well, for self-protection. Some swords were specifically designed for beheading criminals. Most swords are intended for use with one hand, but a few are designed for two. Types include the BROADSWORD, the CLAYMORE and the FIRANGI.

Sycamore (*Acer platanus*) A light-coloured, close-grained, durable wood from western Europe. A variety of maple, sycamore was used by turners and joiners from the Middle Ages, especially for the tops of country tables. The grain is interlocking, so that the wood does not split straight and is difficult to work. It was a popular VENEER in 18th-century England and was used for MARQUETRY in Europe. Sycamore veneer dyed greenish-grey is known as harewood and is often found alongside satinwood on late 18th-century furniture.

Syllabub glass A small glass vessel for drinking syllabub, first introduced into Britain in the early 18th century. A version of the jelly glass, it had a flared top (also known as a pan top) and either a single or no handle.

SylvaC Shaw and Copestake made earthenware in Staffordshire from 1901 bearing various printed marks with the trade name SylvaC. Most frequently seen pieces are moulded rabbits glazed in blue, brown or green. Production ceased in 1982.

SylvaC rabbit, English 1930s [R]

Syng, Philip (1703–89) An American silversmith of the COLONIAL period, active in Philadelphia. Syng was a personal friend of Benjamin Franklin and other prominent citizens, and made the inkstand used for the signing of the Declaration of Independence, on 4 July 1776. His work, with ROCOCO decorations, resembles George II silver and is extremely rare and historically significant.

Synthetic gem An affordable, artificially manufactured copy of a real gemstone. Almost every gem of any value has been synthesized, some more successfully than others. Synthetic gems tend to possess different internal characteristics from their natural counterparts. Synthetic ruby and sapphire provided a viable alternative to natural stones and were used extensively in jewellery of the 1920s and 1930s.

S.y.p. teapot Stands for "Simple yet Perfect", a novelty teapot made by WEDGWOOD from 1895, in which the leaves could be separated from the liquid. They were small pots on three peg feet with blue printed floral decoration.

T

Tabako-ire A Japanese tobacco pouch or box, usually on a cord with a NETSUKE counterweight. Metal or lacquerwork examples from the 19th century are sometimes highly ornate.

Tabernacle clock A type of early clock produced principally in Germany from the late 16th to the late 17th century. They had square brass cases encasing a movement made entirely of steel. Larger versions, often in elaborate GOTHIC architectural styles, feature dials or CHAPTER RINGS on all four sides.

Tabernacle mirror An American giltwood mirror form popular from the early FEDERAL period until the late 19th century. They were portrait shape, often with engaged half-columns, and the glass was divided into a large lower looking glass and an upper section resembling an entablature, with a moulded cornice (earlier examples with applied balls), and decorated (normally ÉGLOMISÉ) glass.

Table A furniture form used in two basic forms from early times – with a central support or with supports at either end. The single, large, communal dining table originated among the barbarians of northern Europe and continued in the Middle Ages. These simple tables were little more than boards resting on trestles. This type of dining table remained in use until the 18th century, but more elaborate tables for writing and game-playing were also produced. Purely decorative tables came into fashion during the Renaissance, becoming widespread in the late 17th century. Many small tables designed for specific uses – writing, reading, playing games, dressing, sewing or serving tea – were developed in the 18th and 19th centuries.

Table ambulante The French term for any small, portable table. From the mid-18th century, these were used for various comforts of domestic life, such as books or cups of tea.

Table centre (French: EPERGNE) An elaborate silver, porcelain or glass centrepiece for a dining table, often fitted with candle sockets and cruet bottles. They were popular in the 19th century.

Table clock A type of spring-driven clock produced from the late 16th century in Germany, with a drum-shaped, square or hexagonal case on which the dial was set horizontally. Such clocks usually have three or four elaborate feet; the case is of gilt brass decorated with silver, glass or rock crystal panels. The movement is also often ornately pierced and engraved.

Table clock in gilt metal, German 17th century [C]

Tabouret The French term for a low, upholstered footstool, originally drum-shaped. Tabourets played an important role during the reign of Louis XIV, as the rigid court etiquette – which dictated who was permitted to sit on a stool – made this privilege a distinction that was highly sought after. In the 18th century a tabouret referred to a stool of any shape with fixed upright legs.

Tabriz One of the leading centres of Persian carpet production in the 16th century. Production declined after *c*.1650 until the latter years of the 19th century when the industry was re-established on a massive workshop basis. The carpets are sometimes difficult to identify as their design repertoire is very varied, incorporating geometric and curvilinear patterns. Many pieces use a restricted colour palette with shades of terracotta, ivory and blue. The quality of the carpets varies enormously from extremely fine to rather coarse.

Talavera wall-tiles, Spanish late 18th/early 19th century [J]

Talavera de la Reina Potteries A group of factories producing tin-glazed earthenware in Castile, Spain, from the mid-16th century. The most important of the factories made 24,800 tiles for the Escorial (the palace of Philip II of Spain) in 1570. Although they also made large pictorial panels, tiles were the major product until the 17th century when an edict of 1601 restricted the use of silver and so increased the demand for household pottery. Small plates, helmet-shaped ewers and basins were decorated with hunting scenes and bull-fights. Modern wares are made in imitation of those of the 17th century.

Tabriz carpet, Persian *c*.1890 [C]

Talbert, Bruce James (1831–81)
An architect and designer of furniture, wallpaper and metalwork, born in Dundee, Scotland. His designs reflected the prevailing mid-19th century reaction against the Neo-Gothic excesses of William BURGES and Augustus PUGIN. His "GOTHIC dressoir" earned him a silver medal at the Paris Exhibition of 1867, which was closely followed that year by the publication of his *Gothic Forms Applied to Furniture, Metal Work and Decoration for Domestic Furniture*. Talbert is best known for his "reformed" Gothic style, combining massive rectilinear forms with shallow panels of geometric inlays and reliefs rather than the florid, deeply carved ornament favoured by Pugin, exemplified by Talbert's celebrated "Pet Sideboard", made by GILLOWS.

Talking doll A doll that makes sounds. The simplest method to make a doll squeak uses bellows in the doll's torso. These can be activated by exerting pressure on the belly or by pulling strings to the side. A more realistic sound can be produced by means of a phonograph, used from about 1890 onward.

Tallboy See CHEST and HIGHBOY.

Tallcase clock A term used in the US for a LONGCASE CLOCK. Produced from the late 18th century, tallcases are similar in style to European longcases, but are often distinguished by the

Tallcase clock,
early 19th century [G]

use of native woods such as maple for case veneers. As brass was a scarce commodity in the US, most dials are made of white-painted iron.

Tambour A flexible sliding shutter or door constructed of thin strips of wood laid side by side and glued to a piece of stiff fabric, such as linen or canvas, and with the ends slotting into grooves. Tambours were used as curved sliding tops for "roll-top" writing desks or for the sliding doors on the fronts of cupboards, mainly in furniture made in England, France and America from the last quarter of the 18th century.

Tambour hoop The name given to a frame of two concentric hoops over which fabric was stretched in order to make the hooked embroidery popular in the 18th century, known as TAMBOUR WORK.

Tambour work A fine chain-stitch embroidery produced originally on muslin stretched over a tambour or frame, using a very small hook to work threads from beneath. Imported from India in the late 18th century with muslin for ladies' aprons and sleeve ruffles and used on machine net for veils in Ireland, England and elsewhere throughout the 19th century. It was also produced by machine.

Tang A Chinese dynasty (AD 618–906) of great cultural and economic prosperity, when ceramic art achieved high status. The dynasty is famed for the pottery burial wares that revived traditions of

Sancai-glazed
horse, Tang
dynasty
Chinese [H]

the Han dynasty (206 BC–AD 220). Burial wares were made of a soft absorbent pottery (modern copies are usually harder). A wide variety of objects was produced, glazed or decorated with earth pigments. The best examples are powerfully modelled horses, camels and guardian figures decorated with SANCAI glazes, which are splashed or poured over the piece's upper section and allowed to drip and run. The use of SANCAI became widespread in the Tang dynasty. YINGQING, one of the earliest Chinese porcelains, was developed in this era.

Tankard A drinking vessel like a mug, but with a hinged cover. Tankards are made of silver, pewter-mounted ceramic, ivory, horn, wood, hardstone or glass and are generally used for beer or cider. The small silver-gilt tankards from the late 16th and early 17th century were sometimes used for wine.

Silver tankard, English
early 18th century [I]

Tantalus A silver-plated or mounted wooden frame fitted with two or three cut-glass spirit decanters that can be locked inside the frame to prevent theft but remain tantalizingly visible. Although still made today the design dates from the mid-19th and early 20th centuries.

Silver-plated tantalus, English c.1900 [L]

Taperstick A type of candlestick usually of silver and plated wares or brass, made from the end of the 17th century until the end of the 18th. Smaller than the candlesticks of the period, they were designed to hold a single taper or slender candle used to melt sealing wax at a desk.

Tapestry A weaving technique in which coloured weft threads are woven into an undyed warp thread to form a decorative or pictorial design. The different coloured weft threads are wound on bobbins and woven as far as the warp thread that marks the edge of a particular area of colour. Thus each part of the design is built up independently. The term also applies to the wall hangings and furnishings made by this method of weaving by factories such as GOBELINS and ARRAS.

Tapissier A French term for a tapestry weaver, also sometimes used in countries outside France.

Tarnishing The dulling or discolouration of silver or other metals including Old SHEFFIELD PLATE and ELECTROPLATE, caused by exposure to air or moisture, which provides the conditions necessary to allow the surface to oxidise slightly.

Tarsia See INTARSIA.

Tartan ware Small wooden domestic items such as boxes and napkin rings and small pieces of furniture decorated with a distinctive printed tartan pattern. As Scotland became a fashionable Victorian holiday destination, so this SOUVENIR WARE boomed in popularity from the 1850s. It was made primarily by the MAUCHLINE WARE manufacturer J & J Smith from the early 19th century.

Tartan ware needle case, Scottish c.1840 [o]

Tassie A portrait medallion, rather like a cameo moulded from glass paste, that was applied to a flat glass surface and was named after the Scotsman James Tassie (1735–99) who invented the technique.

French silver tastevin, 18th century [L]

Tastevin A French silver wine taster for sampling and examining the colour of wine, usually in the form of a small shallow circular bowl or cup. With a ring handle at one side, often formed as a coiled serpent, and sometimes with a thumbpiece, extant examples are known from the early 18th century and often have engraved or embossed decoration. Tastevins are still used today.

Tatami A woven rice straw mat used in the traditional Japanese house, a type of modular floor covering.

Tatting A technique for knotting thread, usually cotton or linen, to produce a type of lace, using a metal shuttle. Developed in the 19th century as a domestic craft, tatting was used to produce such items as collars and lace-edged handkerchiefs.

Tavern clock A type of English wall clock intended for use in taverns and other public buildings. Made from c.1720 to the early 19th century, it had a relatively large, square, shield-shaped or round wooden dial, with gilt numerals and sometimes CHINOISERIE, scroll or flower decoration. A long trunk houses the pendulum and weights. The case was sometimes decorated with appropriate vignette scenes. Such clocks are sometimes erroneously described as "Act of Parliament" clocks following a tax on clocks and watches instituted by the British Parliament in 1797.

Tazza From either Arabic *tassah* (basin) or the Italian *tazza* (cup). A form deriving from Venetian 15th and 16th century glass in which a shallow saucer-like drinking cup or bowl is raised up on a single pedestal foot.

Later examples were made of silver, ceramics or enamel as well as glass and found in Europe and America from the 16th to the 19th century. In the 19th century, the tazza form was used in heavy CUT GLASS and delicate VASELINE glass.

Tea bowl A small handleless bowl or cup, originally made in China and exported to the West, with Chinese tea. They were also produced by many European factories in the 18th century, with or without saucers. Tea drinking became fashionable in the late 17th and early 18th century and both tea and tea bowls were expensive. Portraits of people drinking tea show the various ways they held this handleless cup.

Tea caddy A metal or wood container for storing tea, often lined with lead foil. From the Malaysian word *kati* and used in China for a unit of weight, equal to about one and a half pounds (0.67kg). Caddies sometimes incorporated a small sugar bowl in the centre and some 18th century examples, dating from the period when tea was relatively expensive, also had locks. Wooden caddies were used in England, usually with two compartments to hold "Green" and "Bohea" tea, and flanking a central glass mixing or sugar bowl.

Tea canister A small ceramic container to hold tea, and an integral part of an 18th century tea service, in both Chinese and European porcelain. Early MEISSEN

Tazza by the Russian Imperial Porcelain Factory, mid-19th century [I]

examples are usually upright rectangular in shape but, from the latter part of the century, most are ovoid. Canisters were superseded by caddies during the late 18th century, although they continued to be made during the 19th century.

Pearlware tea canister, English late 18th century [R]

Tea ceremony ware Ceramic vessels used in the Japanese tea ceremony or *Cha no yu*. This Buddist ceremony, which is thought to have arrived in Japan from China in the 15th century, became an important part of Japan's social and cultural life. A specific protocol was developed by Tea Masters who favoured humble coarse pottery so as not to distract from the ceremony. From the 16th century, wares were produced to cater specifically for the tastes of the Tea Masters thus influencing most areas of Japanese ceramics as well as STUDIO POTTERY. Tea ceremony wares include tea bowls, jars, trays, dishes, flower vases, braziers, whisks and KOGO. See JAPANESE POTTERY AND PORCELAIN; BIZEN; KARATSU; KENZAN; RAKU; SATSUMA; SETO; TEMMOKU.

Tea dust glaze A brown opaque glaze with a speckled greenish appearance created when iron oxide is fired. It was used on Chinese porcelain from the QIANLONG period (1736–95) often for pieces in the SONG DYNASTY tradition.

Teague, Walter Dorwin (1883–1960) A leading US designer and founder of the American Society of Industrial Designers in 1944. An exponent of functionalism Teague's vast portfolio of designs ranged from furniture and glass to the motor-car.

Teak A brown, heavy, oily wood. Resistant to fungi and insects, teak was used for furniture – especially for the garden – from the 18th century onward.

Tea kettle A large silver vessel on a stand with a lamp or spirit burner beneath to provide boiling water for tea or coffee. First appearing during the late 17th century, early examples were plain with low separate stands later giving way to light, three-legged stands attached to the body of the kettle with a hinge to aid pouring. They were largely superseded by tea urns *c*.1760.

Teapot A pot in which tea is infused. In the late 17th century, teapots were made of silver, Chinese red stoneware and Chinese porcelain. By the beginning of the 18th century they were made of stoneware and porcelain in Europe. Teapots made in soft paste often cracked as boiling water caused the glaze to crack – many English factories experienced this difficulty as did SÈVRES. They have been made in many shapes, with different types of decoration over an extremely long period.

Mason's Ironstone teapot, *c*.1825 [L]

Teapoy A small tripod table or stand for the storage and mixing of tea. Popular during the first half of the 19th century, the teapoy was designed for use in the drawing room. The top was usually constructed as a lockable lidded wooden box above the pedestal base and often contained two small caddies and two glass bowls – one for sugar and one for mixing the leaves.

Tear A tear- or drop-shaped bubble of air accidentally or deliberately enclosed in a glass stem.

Rosewood tea table, English *c*.1815 [D]

Tea table A small table for the service of tea, popular in the 18th and 19th centuries. This fashionable beverage soon gave rise to an afternoon ceremony with a whole paraphernalia of equipment – including teakettle stands, TEAPOYS, and TEA CADDIES – that in turn needed a table to accommodate them.

Tea urn A large silver, plated or other metal urn-shaped vessel with two handles, a detachable cover, a pedestal base, a spigot or tap and a heating apparatus (often an internal compartment to take a red hot iron) These vessels, introduced in the mid-18th century, were more convenient than tea kettles but did not completely supplant them.

Teco Pottery A US ART POTTERY, founded in Terra Cotta, Illinois, in 1881 by William D. Gates (1852–*c*.1928). The Teco line (a shortened form of terracotta) was introduced in 1902 and produced until the mid-1920s. The French sculptor Frederick Moreau brought the ART NOUVEAU style to the pottery in 1904. Later wares were modern in style and included vases, tiles or garden ornaments of architectural form with a soft matt glaze, usually pale green, that is characteristic of Teco.

Teco earthenware vase, *c*.1902 [R]

Teddy bears

The teddy bear's ancestors are the late 19th-century rabbit-skin-covered clockwork animals produced by French toy companies such as Roullet and the wooden bears carved in the Black Forest in Germany and Tyrol, Austria.

Early bears

Two companies claim to have been the first to produce plush, jointed teddy bears, which appeared between 1902 and 1903. In 1902 Morris Michton, a Russian émigré in New York, was inspired by a cartoon in the Washington Post that showed Theodore "Teddy" Roosevelt refusing to shoot a bear cub. Michton's wife made a brown plush bear to display in the window of their shop, alongside the cartoon. The toy, labelled "Teddy's Bear", was an instant success. Michton went on to establish the IDEAL NOVELTY AND TOY COMPANY.

The German company STEIFF also claims to have invented the teddy bear. Around 1884, Margarete Steiff, a seamstress, included a bear standing on all fours in her range of toys, which she sold at local fairs. Her nephew Richard Steiff devised a jointed version, which was exhibited at the Leipzig spring trade fair in 1903. Although the toy was unpopular at first, Borgfeldt of New York ordered 3,000, fuelling a teddy bear craze in the US.

The ban on German imports during World War I helped to boost the English industry. Companies such as CHAD VALLEY and J.K. FARNELL added teddy bears to their ranges. However, by the 1920s the German companies had regained their position as leaders in teddy bear production and innovation. SCHUCO introduced miniature bears in unusual colours that concealed lipsticks, compacts and perfume bottles. They also made a bear that could shake its head and nod. Steiff created the dual plush teddy clown, the Petsy bear and the teddy baby. Gebrüder Süssenguth made a bear with rolling eyes and Helvetic's bears incorporated squeeze-operated musical boxes.

World War II disrupted toy production in Germany and England. MOHAIR, the principal material used for teddies, was scarce. Most bears made in the 1940s were sewn out of sheepskin, blankets or other substitutes.

In the 1950s, bear production recovered to its pre-war volume. New models appeared with rounder features, shorter snouts and stubbier limbs. Plastic eyes and noses and synthetic fibres like Dralon were introduced. Well-known products of the 1950s include Steiff's Jackie and Zotty bears, MERRYTHOUGHT's Cheeky bear and Dean's true-to-life. Unjointed bears, first introduced on a large scale by Wendy Boston, became popular in the 1960s, resulting in bears such as Steiff's Cosy Teddy and Schuco's Biggo Bello. In the 1970s, cheap bears made in the Far East flooded the market. Today, an increasing number of manufacturers are creating plush, jointed teddies in the traditional style, many as limited editions.

Early Steiff bear with boot button eyes, back hump, stitched nose, mouth and claws and elongated arms with upturned paws, German c.1909 [I]

Teddy bear made by the Ideal Novelty and Toy Company, US 1920s [K]

Large mohair teddy bear with plastic eyes, made by Dean's Rag Book Co. (founded in 1903), English c.1950s [Q]

Golden mohair teddy bear with glass eyes, made by Lefrey, English c.1950s [P]

Teheran A central Persian carpet-producing town. Few rugs were made here prior to 1900. Weaving is generally of fine quality displaying intense floral curvilinear designs similar to those rugs made in ISFAHAN. Colours are similar too, although many have a distinctive rust-red tone.

Tekke An important carpet-weaving tribal group in the 19th century in West Turkestan. They were prolific weavers whose products range from carpets to functional artifacts. Their carpets are often incorrectly described in the West as BOKHARA. Background colours range from a soft terracotta in earlier examples to shades of plum and bright red in early 20th-century examples. The pattern is characteristically made up of GUL motifs, sometimes known as "elephant's foot" motifs, arranged within a black grid.

Telescope An instrument for viewing distant objects. Of the two forms of telescope, the refracting telescope, which uses a series of lenses and is popularly credited to Galileo, was invented by a Dutch spectacle-maker, Sacharias Janssen, in 1608. The reflecting telescope, which uses polished metal mirrors and is ideal for astronomical uses, was first made by the English scientist Isaac Newton in 1668. Early refracting telescope lenses were affected by chromatic aberration distortions, which were corrected by the invention of the ACHROMATIC LENS in the 18th century. Both types of telescope are still made today.

Three draw telescope, c.1840 [P]

Temmoku glaze A Japanese term, used originally to describe the Chinese stoneware cups with a streaky black/brown glaze made at Jian (Fujian province) in the SONG DYNASTY. They were favoured by the Japanese as TEA CEREMONY WARES. Named after the Tianmu mountains in China, the term is now used to describe almost any pottery or stoneware with a thick black/brown glaze.

Tennis See RACQUET SPORTS MEMORABILIA.

Tenon See MORTISE AND TENON.

Tent stitch A plain diagonal stitch (also known as PETIT POINT) across one thread of ground fabric, usually canvas. The term is also used to describe tapestries using this stitch.

Terracotta (Italian: "fired earth") An unglazed EARTHENWARE of reddish clay, often used for architectural purposes, such as ornamentation, tiles and facing. It has been used throughout the world since ancient times, not only for practical items, but also for sculpture, toys, ritual objects, decorative pieces and even furniture. When glazed, it is known as FAIENCE.

Tester From the French word *tête*, meaning "head", this term originally described the headboard of a four-poster bed. From the 17th century it referred to the canopy above it. A half-tester has a canopy that extends only halfway down the bed. Known from the Middle Ages, the half-tester was reintroduced in the 17th century and remained popular until the 19th century.

Tête-à-tête See CABARET.

Thaumatrope A simple optical toy consisting of a circular disc either side of which are drawn two related images, such as a bird in a cage. The disc may be rotated rapidly by means of threads attached. As it spins, the eye sees the two images simultaneously and in the same place, creating the illusion of movement. It was introduced in 1826 and is generally attributed to Dr J.A. Paris of London.

Thebes stool A type of X-frame stool popular in the REGENCY period based on a prototype from Classical antiquity. Generally made of ROSEWOOD, the form appears in the design books of Thomas HOPE and George SMITH.

Theodolite An instrument used by surveyors for measuring both horizontal and vertical angles. The most common form is a transit theodolite in which a TELESCOPE is mounted over a circular plate marked with a scale and containing a COMPASS. The theodolite was invented in the 1500s, improved in the 18th century and in use today.

Thieme, Carl The founder of a porcelain factory in 1872 in Potschappel, Thuringia (near Dresden), which imitated MEISSEN. Typical wares were large vases, candelabra and clockcases, encrusted with bright flowers, fruit and birds. The original mark – a "T" over a cross – was similar to that of Meissen. From 1900 the factory became known as Sächsische Porzellanfabrik and in 1972 was reorganized as VEB Sächsische Porzellanmanufaktur Dresden.

Clockcase by Thieme, late 19th century [M]

Thimble A cap worn since Roman times to protect the finger when sewing. Many silver examples are found in 18th-century ÉTUIS. Earliest known porcelain examples were made by MEISSEN c.1725–30, decorated with CHINOISERIES in the style of HÖROLDT.

Meissen thimble, c.1730 [I]

Thompson, Robert (1876–1955) An English furniture-maker from Kilburn, Yorkshire, who is often known as the "Mouseman" because his work is signed with the carved figure of a mouse. He used oak for well-made pieces with a distinctive adzed finish that gives a subtle rippled effect to the surface. The firm he founded still exists today.

Thonet Brothers A family of German furniture-makers, comprising Michael Thonet (1796–1871) and his four sons, who perfected the BENTWOOD process for chair-making and pioneered the mass production of standardized furniture. Born in Boppard, southern Germany, Thonet established a cabinet-making business, specializing in parquetry, in 1819. By the 1830s his experiments with bentwood led to the invention of a revolutionary process where solid lengths of beechwood were boiled or steamed in water, then bent to form long curved rods for chair frames. Inexpensive, light and flexible, yet remarkably durable, Thonet's chair eliminated the need for hand-carved joints. By the time he had perfected the mechanized process in 1859, the landmark design, with its elegant, flowing curves, was lacking in ornament of any kind. Thonet was granted international patents for his bentwood process and he established salerooms and factories throughout Europe and the US. The firm still exists in Austria, making modern and traditional bentwood furniture.

Thonet bentwood hallstand, c.1904 [J]

Thread and shell pattern A decorative popular variant of FIDDLE and OLD ENGLISH PATTERN flatware, made in silver and plated ware since the early 19th century. It is similar to these patterns, with a border of THREADING and a shell in relief at the top of the stem.

Threading A decorative motif on silver, also known as a threaded edge, which consists of fine lines that have been engraved around the border of the handle of a fork, spoon or other small article of silver. It was common from the early 19th century.

Throne A ceremonial seat, primarily for a sovereign or an ecclesiastical dignitary. The term derives from the Greek (*thronos*) and Latin (*thronus*) meaning an elevated seat, and as such its main purpose was to raise the occupant above the level of other people, designating a function rather than a form.

Throwing A term used in potting to describe making a vessel by hand on the potter's wheel. A lump of well-kneaded and prepared clay is placed in the centre of the revolving wheel. It is then sprinkled with water to keep it pliable and shaped by hand by the potter as it revolves.

Thumb-piece An area where the thumb can be placed to aid in holding or steadying an article, e.g. a silver TASTEVIN. On a drinking vessel it is usually on top of the handle. On a SNUFF-BOX it takes the form of a protruding lip designed to give the thumb purchase for the rapid opening of the box, or a vertical protrusion on the cover.

Thuyawood A golden brown or brown-red close-grained wood from North Africa with a mottled, bird's-eye figure. Used in the 18th and 19th centuries for small turned ware and veneer.

Moonstone, sapphire and silver tiara, c.1900 [H]

Tiara A woman's semicircular jewelled headdress for formal occasions, popular from the 18th century onward. The tiara was probably the most significant of all the jewels in a collection and often the finest gems were reserved for such a piece. Mid- to late 19th-century tiaras could usually be broken down and converted into individual brooches or a necklace; the original fittings are an important element when assessing tiaras today. Firms such as GARRARD and CARTIER produced tiaras for an aristocratic clientele from the 1880s to the 1950s. The tiara is also an item of papal regalia.

Tie pin (or stick pin) An accessory worn principally by men since the 18th century and still made today. The tendency is that the more unusual the pin, the higher the value – hence, diamond-studded animals, rare fancy coloured gemstones and novelty or political subjects are keenly sought after. Many late Victorian designs were mass-produced in Britain.

Tiffany, Louis Comfort See TIFFANY.

Tigerware A word used in Elizabethan England for Rhenish stoneware, especially jugs with a mottled brown glaze over a greyish-coloured body. Similar ware was made by John DWIGHT who started a factory in Fulham, London, toward the end of the 17th century.

Tigerwood See ZEBRAWOOD.

Tiffany

Founded in 1837, Tiffany & Co. of New York became America's leading manufacturer of silver, jewellery and glass. The designing genius of the founder's son, Louis Comfort Tiffany, has given the name "Tiffany Style" to American Art Nouveau.

From "fancy goods" to Favrile

Charles Louis Tiffany was born in 1812 in Connecticut and started his career with a "fancy goods" store at 259 Broadway, New York. A manufacturer with a keen sense of the spending power of America's burgeoning wealthy class, he expanded his business rapidly, especially into the areas of jewellery and SILVER. He instigated buying trips to Europe, resulting in some famous purchases from the estate of the deposed French Empress Eugènie, and in 1848 he opened shops in Paris and London. In 1851 he secured the services of one of America's finest silversmiths, John C. Moore, and subsequently his son Edward C. Moore. Tiffany's expansion led to some spectacular pieces such as the "Magnolia Vase" shown in 1893 at the World's Fair in Chicago.

On his father's death in 1902, Louis Comfort TIFFANY (1848–1933) became Vice-President of Tiffany & Co. (as the company was called after 1853) and its first artistic director. He had trained as an artist, and when he joined the firm he brought an artist's eye and an enthusiasm for the emerging Art Nouveau style. He became a master designer of GLASS, jewellery, STAINED GLASS, silver, METAL and CERAMICS, and the creator of magnificent lamps and windows whose luminous colours are revered as much today as in his own lifetime.

Louis Tiffany's first business venture had been as an interior designer and in 1880 he founded Louis C. Tiffany & Associated Artists, whose commissions included interiors for the White House. Increasingly, he had been experimenting with innovative glass-making methods and in the same year he patented his famous glass, sold under the trade name of "Favrile" (from the Old English "fabrile" meaning "belonging to a craftsman or his craft") with its characteristic iridescent finish. His reputation and business grew and his lamps and other bronze and metal items were made at, and marked, Tiffany Studios. He received international acclaim after he exhibited wares at the Exposition Universelle in Paris in 1900.

Tiffany Studios closed in 1932, but during the interwar years the original company, Tiffany & Co., continued to produce silver, jewellery and glass of outstanding quality. In the 1950s there was a move to simpler forms from innovative contemporary artists, which continues today. The French designer Jean Schlumberger, who had worked for Elsa Schiaparelli, joined the company in 1956; Elsa Peretti designed jewellery from 1974 and Paloma Picasso from 1981.

Tiffany Studios lamp with typical leaded glass shade and ceramic base, early 20th century [c]

Tiffany gold and diamond bow brooch, showing the romantic, traditional design of the 1890s [H]

Art Nouveau imitation jade ceramic bowl embossed with leaves, stems and berries, c.1905 [H]

Tiffany Favrile sweetmeat dish, with characteristic iridescent finish, c.1900 [I]

A simple, elegant silver vase, made at Louis Tiffany's Tiffany Studios, 1910 [K]

Tiles Earthenware tiles with various types of decoration and glazes have a long history. In Islamic countries they were used from the 8th century for walls, floors and the domes of mosques. In Europe they were made by Cistercian monks, often using the ENCAUSTIC method. In Spain, the *cuerda seca* (literally: "dry cord") method was used to produce tiles with coloured glazes enclosed by lines of grease. In Portugal, tilemaking has been an important industry from the Middle Ages and still is. FAIENCE tiles (*azulejos*) were built up into large panoramic views on walls. Tiles were a huge part of Delft production in Holland, either made to form a continuous pattern, or with a single motif on each tile. The Dutch workmen who came to England with William and Mary *c.*1680 brought their tilemaking techniques with them.

Seventeenth-century tiles were usually hand-painted both in blue and in polychrome, often with naïve renderings of biblical and mythological subjects. Toward the end of the 18th-century, English tiles were also TRANSFER-PRINTED with NEO-CLASSICAL subjects (see SADLER & GREEN) and theatrical images. During the 19th and early 20th centuries, tiles became popular again. They were decorated with Japanese themes, inspired by Japanese exhibitions in London and Paris in the mid-19th century, by designers of the AESTHETIC MOVEMENT such as William DE MORGAN. Designers in the ART NOUVEAU and ART DECO STYLES also created tiles and, in Staffordshire, factories such as MINTON and DOULTON made them industrially. Tile factories also flourished in the US, such as the LOW ART TILE WORKS in Massachusetts.

Tilt-top table A table with a top hinged to the base or pedestal so that it can be tipped to a vertical position. Originating

Earthenware tile, English early 20th century [S]

in medieval times, the tilt-top had become highly developed by the 18th century and was popular in Britain and America. The ingenious construction allowed the decorative features of the top to be displayed and also enabled the table to be stored neatly against a wall when not in use – it even meant that the table could act as a firescreen when necessary.

Timepiece A clock or watch that shows the passing of time but does not have a striking or chiming mechanism.

Tin A brittle and soft white metal, the main constituent of PEWTER and, alloyed with COPPER, of BRONZE. Tin has also been used as a protective coating to prevent oxidization or corrosion on objects made from other base metals such as iron and steel and on the interiors of copper and BRASS cooking vessels.

Oak tilt-top table, English c.1770 [L]

Tinderbox A small metal box used from the 15th to the 19th century that held a piece of flint, a section of steel and tinder (such as dry wood). Striking the flint against the steel produced sparks that ignited the tinder. Later tinderboxes were sometimes decorative and quite elaborate in mechanism. The tinderbox was the forerunner of the lighter (invented in the late 19th century).

"Pistol" tinderbox, English 1790 [I]

Ting A Chinese ceramic or bronze cooking vessel made from the SHANG and early Zhou dynasties (*c.*1500–1000 BC) onward. It generally comprises a rounded or rectangular bowl set on three or four feet with loop handles on the rim.

Tin glaze The process by which MAIOLICA, FAIENCE and DELFT were produced. After a first firing, the pottery was dipped into a glaze of oxides of lead and tin, which produced a porous white surface. It was then decorated with HIGH-TEMPERATURE COLOURS, which were absorbed by the glaze, and fired again, possibly with the addition of a lead glaze. The decoration was therefore fused into the substance of the piece and could not be altered.

The technique was first used in the Middle East in the 9th century and was brought to Europe via Spain in the 13th century by the Moors. In the 18th century, in Germany, ENAMEL COLOURS were used over the tin glaze.

Tin-glazed charger, English c.1690 [E]

Tinplate toy A plaything made from thin sheet steel that was coated with tin or a tin alloy to counter rust. Early tinplate toys were painted by hand, but from around 1908 they were decorated using LITHOGRAPHY.

Tinsel picture Formed from coloured metallic foil, often for portrait engravings. First sold in 1808, they were especially popular in the 1830s and 40s, depicting actors and actresses. These were often sold in sets, with maple frames.

Tinworth, George See DOULTON POTTERY AND PORCELAIN FACTORY.

Tired An expressive term used to describe a piece, often with a practical function, that is in poor or worn condition due to heavy usage through the years.

Toasting fork Usually made of silver or Sheffield plate with a long, turned wooden handle (sometimes these could be telescopic or collapsible) and deeply curved tines that allowed a slice of bread or the muffin to be held vertically in front of an open fire so that it toasted evenly. Silver examples exist from the late 17th century.

Toasting glass A tall GLASS with a small trumpet bowl and a thin, elongated stem, introduced in the 17th century and much used in the 18th century in England and Holland. Tradition has it that such wineglasses were used to drink the ladies' health, after which the stem was snapped to ensure the toast could not be broken.

Toastmaster's glass A drinking GLASS used throughout the 18th and early 19th century. The apparently full-size bowl was,

Tinplate fire engine, German c.1920 [R]

in fact, made of very thick glass, in order to reduce capacity and thus allow the toastmaster to repeatedly down the contents in one and still remain sober.

Tobey Furniture Company A furniture-making and decorating firm founded in Chicago by Charles and Frank Tobey in 1875, producing architectural-style furniture inspired by the work of local architects Louis Sullivan and Frank Lloyd WRIGHT. The company closed in 1954.

Toby jug The name given to the pottery jugs that were first made by Ralph WOOD in the 1760s, and imitated throughout Staffordshire and elsewhere in England, from the late 18th century until the present time. The name probably comes from the title of an engraving of an obese drinker "Sir Toby Philpott", who was depicted sitting down holding a mug of foaming ale in one hand and a glass or a pipe in the other. There were many variations, including the Squire, the Thin Man, Martha Gunn, the Brighton Bathing Machine Lady and The Snuff Taker.

Creamware Toby jug, c.1785 [J]

Toddy lifter A glass vessel used for transferring liquid such as punch from a large bowl to a small drinking glass, made in Britain in the 18th and 19th centuries. A toddy lifter was shaped like a small,

long-necked decanter with a small hole in the base. The lifter was plunged into the punch bowl and the liquid entered through the hole. The punch was held in place by closing off the neck opening with the thumb to create a vacuum, and then released into the drinking glass by removing the thumb and allowing the liquid to flow out.

Toftware Slip-decorated earthenware dishes bearing the names of James Toft (d.1673), Ralph Toft (d.1638) or Thomas Toft (d.1689). Some examples have dates as well as the names, on the front of the dishes. On some dishes the name of the potter is part of the decoration. Thomas Toft's work is the most common – over 30 signed examples are recorded. It is the only known SLIPWARE of this kind that displays the potter's name in such a way. The dishes are usually large, some bear the Royal Arms in the centre and the rims have a trellis border.

Toile (French: "cloth") A term given to single-colour designs printed onto cotton. First made in the 18th century, early toiles were printed on cloth imported from India. In 1759 the French textile designer and industrialist Christophe-Philippe Oberkampf set up his factory in Jouy-en-Josas, near Versailles, producing what have become the best known toiles, *toiles de jouy*. These were roller-printed off copper plates engraved with scenes.

Piece of toile 91.5cm (36in) square, French early 19th century [O]

Tokoname potteries A large and productive Japanese pottery, one of the celebrated "Six Ancient Kilns". Located south of Nagoya, the potteries' early phase – along with SETO, Shigaraki, Tamba, BIZEN and Echizen – was from the 12th until the late 16th century. Their production consisted of wares unevenly formed and undecorated – either partially or entirely covered with natural wood-ash glazes – as well as the highly prized vessels associated with the TEA CEREMONY. In the late 19th and early 20th centuries, the potteries produced accomplished imitations of early Japanese wares and Chinese YIXING teapots.

Toleware tray, English c.1810 [J]

Toleware A term for *tôle peinte*, or painted (JAPANNED) tinware, used for lampshades and hollowware. Most toleware in the US was imported during the 19th century, but some was made as Pennsylvania tinware.

Tomimoto, Kenkichi (1886–1963) A Japanese potter who studied under Kenzan VI with Bernard LEACH, then established his own workshop at Ando (Nara) in 1915. He is best known for his very pure white porcelain decorated, especially with landscapes, in underglaze blue or enamel colours. One of the leaders of the Mingei movement – founded to foster an appreciation of traditional Japanese folk art – Tomimoto was a very influential teacher and from 1958 was principal of the Municipal College of Fine Arts in Kyoto.

Tompion, Thomas (1639–1715) An English clockmaker, admitted to the Clockmakers' Company in 1671. He was the leading London maker of ebony-veneered LONGCASE and BRACKET CLOCKS and watches in the late 17th century. Tompion introduced a number of features in clockmaking such as a wider, more legible CHAPTER RING and larger hour hand, small subsidiary dials for striking mechanisms and the locking of the pendulum while the clock was transported.

Ebony and ormolu Tompion clock, c.1680 [C]

Tongue and groove A method of creating panelling by jointing boards side by side with a tongue on one fitting into a groove on the adjacent one.

Tooling A technique employed to give ornamental decoration to LEATHER and employed on bookbindings on leather-topped furniture. This includes various techniques such as stamping, gilding, punching or incising.

Tootsietoys A US toy company established by Samuel Dowst in Chicago in 1876, making lead novelties and toy vehicles. The range of road vehicles and aeroplanes, called Tootsietoys after a small child in the family, started in 1921. They had the DIECAST field to themselves and introduced mazac (an alloy of zinc) in 1933. Their best-known achievements were cars, including the Graham Paige. They are still in business.

Topaz A gemstone found in several colours, although brown is the most desirable and a rich, golden brown from Brazil called "Imperial" or "sherry" topaz is the most valuable. Topaz was used extensively in 18th and 19th century jewellery, particularly sets of pink topaz and chrysolite in CANNETILLE frames.

Top plate A term used to describe the plate uppermost when looking into the back of a WATCH. This is usually where the maker signs their name and puts any relevant information. All the wheels are held between the top and bottom plate.

Toprail The highest horizontal bar on the back of a chair.

Topsy-turvy A type of RAG DOLL, popular in the early 20th century, with two heads, one on each side of the torso. One head is concealed by clothing while the other is on view.

Torchère (or candle stand) A portable stand for a candle or lamp, usually a tall table with a small top. From the mid-17th century, they were frequently made en suite to flank a SIDE TABLE with a mirror above. They are found in many 18th-century design books and the form was especially suited to the NEO-CLASSICAL style of Robert ADAM.

Giltwood Adam-style torchère, c.1790 [G]

Torquay Terracotta Company Figures, plaques and vases were made at Hele Cross, Torquay, Devon, in the local terracotta from 1875 to 1909. They used an impressed or printed mark of the name in full and from 1900–09 the name within a double circle.

Tortoiseshell A shiny, translucent material from the shells of the Hawksbill turtle. The shells are flattened by heat and pressure and smoothed. The material can be heat-moulded and carved and used for jewellery, boxes, objects of vertu and inlay for centuries. Now tortoiseshell is more often imitated in celluloid.

Tortoiseshell tea caddy with ivory banding, English c.1790 [E]

Tortoiseshell glass A type of 19th- and 20th-century clear cased ART GLASS, in which a layer of brown mottling was enclosed between two layers of clear glass, made throughout Europe and in the US.

Tostrup, Jacob (1806–90) A Norwegian silversmith working in Christiania (now Oslo) from the early 19th century who promoted mechanized production and manufacturing techniques to compete within the European marketplace. In the 1830s, he installed powered machinery in his workshops and thus stimulated the revival of silversmithing in Norway. The company made pieces in historical revival and ART NOUVEAU styles.

Touch mark The maker's mark of a pewterer, stamped on his wares. From the 16th century, most European pewterers were required to register their mark on a touch plate held by the local guild. Some pewterers added imitation HALLMARKS.

Touch mark

Touchpiece A coin or medal given out by a monarch when curing the disease of scrofula (TB of the lymph glands), known as "the king's evil". From medieval times, it was thought that the monarch could cure this disease by touching the sufferer. In England, King Henry VII introduced the giving of a token after "touching".

Toulouse-Lautrec, Henri de (1864–1901) A French artist and printmaker renowned for his paintings and posters, which usually depict the circuses, night clubs, music halls and theatres of *fin-de-siècle* Paris, especially the Montmartre area. *Moulin Rouge: La Goulue* (1891) was his first LITHOGRAPH poster and in his lifetime he was better known for these than for his painting.

Tourmaline A gemstone found in a range of colours of which a dark bluish-green and deep pink variety (known as rubellite) are the most popular. Tourmaline was rarely used before 1900 but, in the 20th century, was used extensively, mounted in bold gold and silver jewellery.

Tournai porcelain A factory founded in Tournai, in the Netherlands (now Belgium) by François-Joseph Peterinck in 1751, under the patronage of the Holy Roman Empress Maria Theresa. They made a creamy soft paste, resembling that of SÈVRES and the products are completely French in tone. They employed Henri-Joseph Duvivier as chief decorator from 1763–71. He also later worked in England. In 1787 they made a famous service for the Duc d'Orléans, painted with birds after Buffon's *Natural History*, probably painted by Jean-Ghislain Mayer. But they also produced a great deal of cheap blue and white tableware. The factory closed but was re-opened in 1840 by

Tournai plate, c.1770 [R]

Maximilian Bettignies, who moved it to St Armand les Eaux where he made good copies of SÈVRES, CHELSEA and WORCESTER until the factory closed in the mid-19th century.

Tournai tapestry factories Weaving was known in Tournai from the 13th century and it became an important tapestry-weaving centre in the 15th century. Through merchants such as the highly influential Pasquier Grenier (working in Tournai *c.*1447–77) high quality tapestries were sold to the Dukes of Burgundy and to the church, as well as to European royalty. Competition from Brussels together with the plague of 1513 saw a marked decline in Tournai's fortunes, although fine tapestries were still being produced. They are often recognizable because from 1544 weavers were obliged to include the city arms in the design. During the 16th and 17th centuries Tounai's continued use of old cartoons meant Brussels and Antwerp became more fashionable and in 1712 the last workshop in Tournai closed.

¹Toy See AUTOMATA, DIECAST, DOLLS, TEDDY BEAR, TINPLATE, TRAIN.

²Toy A small inexpensive item made in the 18th and 19th centuries in various materials, but especially in porcelain. Items included cane handles, SCENT BOTTLES and ÉTUIS.

Toy: St Cloud cane handle, c.1740 [I]

Tracery Delicate lattice shapes consisting of lines and bars with spaces for glass or openings.

Tracery

Derived from GOTHIC windows and ornament, tracery was used in architecture and adapted for use in furniture, especially during the GOTHIC REVIVAL of the 19th centuries.

Trailing A type of decoration on glass in which softened circular strands of plain or coloured glass are trailed or wound onto the handle, foot or body. The technique, first employed on ROMAN GLASS, is still used.

Train A set of interlocking toothed wheels and pinions in the MOVEMENT of a clock or watch. TIMEPIECES have only one train, but other clocks require a separate train for striking the hours. A third train is used to activate more complex striking.

Trailing on a glass bottle, English 19th century [R]

Train (model) Replicas made to common scales, e.g. 0-gauge and 00-gauge, and usually powered by steam, clockwork or electric motors contained within the locomotives. Production started in the 1860s with rather crude examples. Accurate representations followed by 1900. MÄRKLIN, BASSETT-LOWKE and HORNBY are the best known makers. The focus has been on smaller gauges since 1950. Many early examples in TINPLATE or cast iron were unmotorized.

Transfer printing A process for decorating ceramics in which an engraved copper plate is covered with ink, prepared with metallic oxides. The engraved design is then transferred to paper, which while wet with pigment is pressed onto the surface of the object. The design is then fixed by firing. Transfer printing was much used at the BATTERSEA ENAMEL FACTORY (c.1753), BOW (c.1756), WORCESTER (from 1756) and on earthenware at LIVERPOOL by John Sadler from 1756. Subsequently, most English factories used the process. In the rest of Europe it was not popular as a commercial means of decoration until FAIENCE had been abandoned for cream-coloured earthenware. One exception was at RÖRSTRAND where Anders Stenman, who discovered the process independently, used it from 1766. He took it to MARIEBERG. Berthevin tried it at FRANKENTHAL but without much success. At the end of the 18th century it became common on earthenware at many factories, including CREIL, Sarreguemines, Montereau, ZURICH, Proskau, ALCORA, Sargadelos and METTLACH.

Transitional ware Chinese porcelain made around the transition from the MING DYNASTY to the QING DYNASTY (c.1620–50). The blue and white Transitional style is characteristically well painted with naturalistic images of flowers, foliage, animals and figures. Narrative subjects illustrating scenes from Chinese Classical literature were also popular. Pieces often have flat unglazed bases and ANHUA border designs.

Chinese Transitional ware porcelain bottle vase, c.1640 [L]

Transfer-printed porcelain saucer, c.1780 [P]

WUCAI, BLANC-DE-CHINE, KRAAK PORCELAIN and ko-sometsuke wares (for the Japanese market) were also made in this period.

Translucency True porcelain allows light to pass through to some extent; most pottery does not. Translucency depends on the thickness of the porcelain and on the firing temperature, which produces a degree of vitrification.

Tranter, William (1816–90) An English FIREARMS designer and manufacturer. Active from 1840, Tranter was granted some 16 patents for improvements to firearms. He is best known for his REVOLVERS, which were well made and reliable. His factory at Aston Cross near Birmingham produced all types of firearms, many of which were for the armed forces and other services.

Treen (Old English word: "tree" or "wood") Small wooden objects, often of domestic use, turned on a lathe or carved in a variety of woods, including FRUITWOOD and HOLLY. Pieces include LOVE SPOONS and small boxes. Early pieces date from the 17th century.

Treen fruitwood snuff-box, c.1780 [J]

Trefid (or trifid) A silver FLATWARE pattern probably derived from the TREFOIL, developed during the 1660s and popular until c.1700. The terminals of forks and spoons are hammered out and given either two projections or two notches, making a tripartite splay visually dividing the end of the piece into three sections.

Trefoil A GOTHIC decorative motif consisting of three lobes and resembling a stylized clover leaf. Occasionally used as a symbol of the Christian Trinity – like other three-part devices – the trefoil was widely adopted in the late 19th century for geometric GOTHIC REVIVAL designs for metalwork, wall decorations and furniture inlays.

Trefoil

Trek A painted outline in dark blue, sometimes in black or manganese, on Dutch DELFTWARE, filled in with blue or other colours.

Trelliswork (French: *treillage*) An elaborate trellis motif constructed with a false perspective, giving the illusion of a building, archway or niche. Well-known examples of trelliswork include garden screen niches at Versailles in France and at Sans Souci at Potsdam.

Trembler (tremblant) Naturalistic diamond and gem-set spray brooches worn in the 18th and 19th centuries in which the principal flower-head was mounted on a coiled spring causing the brooch to "tremble" when worn. Such a mechanism was described as *en tremblant*.

Trembleuse A saucer with a circular pierced gallery in the centre to hold the cup and prevent it "trembling" or spilling the contents.

Trencher A medieval term for a slab of wood or bread from which food was eaten. Post-medieval receptacles made in silver which served the same purpose were also known as trenchers, but the term became outmoded. By the 16th century they were known as plates. See also CHARGER.

Trencher salt A small low open receptacle without feet having a hollowed top section to contain salt.

They were designed for use by individual diners, originally accompanying the TRENCHER. They were often made in sets from silver, ceramic or enamel from the early 17th century to *c*.1730 until super-seded by SALTS, sometimes in CRUETs.

Trestle table The earliest type of dining table – made of massive boards of oak or elm resting upon a series of "trestles", or central supports. The tops were detachable, making it easier to remove the entire table following a meal. Trestle tables were made for dining from the Middle Ages through to the 17th century.

Triang In 1919, William, Walter and Arthur Lines left their father's firm (LINES BROS) to set up on their own in Merton, near London, and adopted a triangular trade mark. They made everything for children: Pedigree prams, dolls and soft toys, pedal cars, Fairy Cycles, nursery furniture, ships, Frog Planes, dolls' houses, tinplate clockwork vehicles and more. By emphasizing finish and quality, they became Britain's most successful general

toymaker, even rescuing MECCANO in 1964 before succumbing to poor trade conditions in 1971.

Tricoteuse A term used in the 19th century to designate a small WORK TABLE. Originally the term referred to a table at which one could *tricoter*, or knit.

Tridarn A type of Welsh PRESS cupboard constructed in three stages. The two lower stages are enclosed by doors, while the upper stage remains open.

Triang pressed-steel truck, pre-World War II [R]

Tripod table A small OCCASIONAL table often with a round top supported on a slender central three-legged pillar. Derived from the 17th-century CANDLE STAND, the tripod table was widely adopted in the second half of the 18th century for the informal serving of tea, supper, desserts and other refreshments. Many tripod tables have a TILT-TOP and sometimes a BIRDCAGE SUPPORT.

Tripod table, mahogany, British 1740s–60s [i]

Trivet A stand with three legs (sometimes four) usually made of wrought iron, but may be of brass or bronze, for supporting cooking vessels and other domestic utensils such as a kettle, in front of an open fire. In use from early times, the trivet commonly has a decorative pierced top, a long wooden handle and may also have hooks for attaching it to the bars of a firegrate.

Trompe l'oeil (French: "trick the eye")
A type of decoration designed to imitate
a surface or texture, or to create the
impression of three-dimensional objects
or patterns in two dimensions. Different
effects – such as MARBLING or GRISAILLE –
were used to transform wood, stone or
plaster. Quodlibet, another form,
produced an image of objects lying on a
surface. In the mid-18th century, some
influential German porcelain was painted
with flowers with *trompe l'oeil* shadows.

Trophy A motif that originated as a
memento celebrating a victory and
consisting of arms and armour. In the
17th century, it was popularly adopted as
decoration for related themes such as
hunting. Its usage expanded throughout
the 18th century, particularly in France, to
embrace a variety of themes – love, music,
the seasons, astronomy and ecclesiastical
designs. No longer confined to architectural
ornament, the trophy was applied to
MARQUETRY, textiles and embroidered
patterns. In the NEO-CLASSICAL period it
returned to its roots as a military motif.

Trophies on a Brussels tapestry fragment
depicting war, c.1700 [H]

Troubadour style A French variant of
the GOTHIC REVIVAL style, popular from
c.1815 to the 1840s. It was introduced
during the RESTAURATION period as it
was favoured by the Duchesse de Berry, a
member of the French royal family, and
was popularized by the translations into
French of Sir Walter Scott's historical

novels at this time. Elements of Gothic
architecture such as pinnacles, CROCKETS
and arches were applied to furniture,
tapestries, mirrors, glass, clocks and
ceramics, often combined with other
classically inspired components of the
RESTAURATION such as ACANTHUS scrolls
and LAUREL wreaths. In this way the style
was a continuation of the ornamental
GOTHICK rather than the
historically accurate
GOTHIC REVIVAL. The
Troubadour fashion
declined in the mid-19th
century with the growing
enthusiasm for the
RENAISSANCE REVIVAL.

Troy weight A unit of
measurement used for
weighing precious metals,
e.g. silver, gold and platinum,
named after the town of
Troyes, France. One troy pound
equals 5760 grams, 240 penny
weight or 12 ounces. One troy
ounce equals 31.3 grams. It is
slightly heavier than the ordinary
(avoirdupois) weight measurement where
one ounce equals 28.3 grams.

Trumpeter clock A variant of the
CUCKOO CLOCK featuring mechanically
propelled figures of trumpeters instead of
a cuckoo and with the hour (and
sometimes the quarter hour) sounded on
a tiny trumpet operated by bellows.

Tsuba The plate mounted on a Japanese
sword between the blade and the handle
acting as both a counterbalance to the
blade weight and a hand guard. Most
commonly made from metal, they are
often highly decorated.

Tube-lining A ceramic decoration in
which thin trails of slip are applied as
outlines to areas of coloured glaze, a
technique used extensively at
MOORCROFT. See also SLIP-TRAILING.

Tubular bell See BELL.

Tucker porcelain
pitcher, 1828–38 [H]

Tucker porcelain factory A US
porcelain works founded in 1827 and the
earliest to enjoy commercial success.
Established by William Ellis Tucker
(1800–32) in Philadelphia, the factory
produced a wide range of hard-paste
porcelain comparable to contemporary
French porcelain. Most
Tucker is sparsely
decorated, but may
be painted with
floral sprays or
simple landscapes
in polychrome,
sepia or gilt. Some
decoration can be
attributed to Thomas
Tucker (1812–90), the
chief decorator. Few
pieces are signed but may
be attributed by form,
painting style and distinctive
foot rims. Ambitious pieces
include pairs of scenic vases or
pieces with historically
significant decoration. The firm
became Tucker & Hulme in
1828 and Tucker and Hemphill
in 1831; the factory closed in 1838.

Tudor Revival A revival of forms and
motifs of the 16th-century TUDOR style
in 19th-century English decorative arts.
Typical elements include richly carved
bulbous supports on tables and other
furniture, the use of the stylized Tudor
rose and LINENFOLD panelling, as well as
Renaissance and Mannerist motifs such as
STRAPWORK, GROTESQUES, ARABESQUES
and roundels. Thus the Tudor Revival was
closely related to, and often combined
with, the GOTHIC, ELIZABETHAN and
RENAISSANCE REVIVALS, and integrated
with Elizabethan and Jacobean ornament
to create the eclectic JACOBETHAN STYLE.

Tudor style The architecture and applied
arts dominant in England during the 16th
century, named after the ruling Tudor
dynasty (1485–1603). The style is
characterized by medieval English forms
combined with Renaissance and

Mannerist ornament, introduced by continental European artists working at the court of Henry VIII (for example Hans Holbein) and later, with the advent of printing, derived from Flemish, French and German pattern-books.

Typical ornament includes portrait roundels, ARABESQUES and GROTESQUES and, in the late 16th century, STRAPWORK and cherubs. Such motifs are found on oak furniture characterized by large, rectilinear forms with rich carving, ceremonial silver, such as STANDING CUPS and salt cellars, and silver and silver-gilt mounts on exotic items such as coconuts and hardstones.

ELIZABETHAN style specifically denotes the Tudor style of the reign of Elizabeth I (1558–1603).

Tudric pewter clock by Knox, c.1905 [c]

Tudric The trade name for table and decorative ware made from 1903 in a type of pewter with a high proportion of silver, marketed by LIBERTY & Co. to accompany its silver CYMRIC range. Made by William Hair Haseler of Birmingham, it was inspired by the CELTIC and ART NOUVEAU styles and featured ENTRELACS, stylized leaves and flower heads and vitreous enamel in blueish-green. Forms include chalices, clocks and vases. Many pieces were designed by Archibald KNOX.

Tula work Steel furniture, candlesticks, caskets and fireplace furnishings made at the ironworks at Tula, near Moscow, founded by Tsar Peter the Great in 1705. Made in traditional Russian and Western NEO-classical styles, these items feature cut-steel and inlaid metal decoration. The term also applies to small silver and NIELLO objects, e.g. snuff-boxes, made at other Russian factories from the early 19th century.

Tulip ware plate, US 19th century [K]

Tulip ware A generic term given to American pottery of PENNSYLVANIA DUTCH origin, decorated with stylized tulips in SGRAFFITO through a yellow or green glaze. Originally made by 18th and 19th century German immigrants, tulip ware has been widely reproduced.

Tulipière A vase, especially Dutch Delft, specifically meant to hold tulip bulbs while they were growing. Such vases were ancillary to the bulb-growing trade. Tulips had been imported from Turkey in the 17th century and "Tulipmania" became an obsession with rare species reaching astronomically high prices.

Tulipwood A hard, dense, light-coloured wood with a pronounced red grain similar in appearance to striped tulips. Related to ROSEWOOD, it was imported to Europe from Brazil and Peru in the 18th century and often used by French furniture-makers with amaranth. In France it is called *bois de rose*.

Tulwar A name for the Indian SABRE, particularly the type with a curved blade. The most common of Indian swords, its HILT generally features a disc-shaped pommel.

Tumbler A type of domestic drinking glass without a handle and with a cylindrical, tapering, waisted or barrel-shaped body on a flat base. They were

made in various sizes, styles and decoration, and in ceramic, horn and metal as well as glass. See also MILDNER GLASS; KOTHGASSER; ZWISCHENGOLDGLAS.

Tunbridgeware Small wooden domestic objects such as stamp- and workboxes, rulers, picture frames and games boards, and also, rarely, work tables. The surfaces are decorated with patterns created from an intricate mosaic of coloured woods. Although the technique was used from the late 17th century, most Tunbridgeware seen today was produced from the 1830s until the end of the 19th century. It was made in and near Tunbridge Wells, England, often as souvenirs of this spa town, a popular resort in the 19th century. Geometric borders surrounded flora and fauna designs, people, buildings and views.

Tunbridgeware box, c.1880 [o]

Tureen A deep vessel with a lid, two handles and an oval or circular outline. Large tureens are for soup and small for sauce. They were made in sets or pairs. Originally ceramic, soup tureens appeared in silver in the 1720s and sauce tureens from *c*.1760.

Silver sauce tureen, English 1795 [E, for 4]

Turin pottery and porcelain factories There were several MAIOLICA factories in Turin, Italy, whose typical products were pierced baskets of BIANCO DI FAENZA made in the 1570s. The first factory, founded before 1562, employed painters from URBINO. The Regio Parco factory (est. 1646), run by workmen from Liguria, was notable in the 17th century for BLUE AND WHITE wares similar to those of SAVONA.

A factory founded in 1725 by Giorgio Rossetti di Macello and his two nephews peaked in the 1750s. It made good French FAIENCE-style wares painted in HIGH TEMPERATURE COLOURS with ROCOCO subjects. Similar wares were also made in the factory of Giovanni Antonio Ardizzone from c.1765–1771. Rossetti experimented with porcelain-making from 1757 but very few examples are known. Two busts are in the Museo Civico in Turin. In 1824 his factory was bought by Jacques-François Richard and Frédéric-Louis Dortu. It made porcelain printed with landscapes until it closed in 1878.

Turkey work A type of needlework, fashionable in England in the late 16th century, simulating the pile rugs imported from the Near East. It was made by pulling heavy wool through canvas or coarse linen, knotting it and cutting the ends to form a pile. Rare carpets were used as table-covers in the same way as Oriental rugs of the same period. It was also used for cushions, bed hangings and upholstery.

Turkish (or Ghiordes) knot
A type of symmetrical knot used for making the pile in handmade rugs, named after Ghiordes, an Anatolian town. It is used throughout Turkey, in Persia, the Caucasus and Europe, and is well suited to creating geometric patterns.

Turkish style From the 16th century, Turkish architecture and art inspired a style of decorative arts and interior design throughout Europe. The Turkish style

Turkish style charger by Joseph-Théodore Deck, 1876 [H, for 2]

reflects Western fascination with exotic motifs and decoration and was later combined with CHINOISERIE and the ARABIAN STYLE. The influence of Turkish art was a result of the proximity of the Ottoman Empire (which at its height in the 16th century extended from Hungary to Egypt to Western Europe) as well as the introduction in the 16th century of imported TURKISH CARPETS. These were highly prized and feature in many TUDOR portraits. European carpet-makers adapted the predominantly geometric motifs for use in their own work, while TURKEY WORK was popular until the late 17th century.

In the 18th and early 19th centuries publications such as Charles de Ferriol's *Les Différents Nations du Levant* (1714) stimulated growing interest in Ottoman art. A fashion for entire rooms decorated in the Turkish style, with richly tasselled and fringed upholstery and ornament such as crescents, stars and stylized flowers, became popular among royalty and aristocracy, especially in France.

Turkish knot

Similarly, the growth of smoking in the mid-19th century led to the development of smoking rooms furnished with divans and OTTOMANS, upholstered in richly figured and coloured materials. Some artists attempted to produce wares based more closely on Turkish originals, in particular William DE MORGAN, who in the late 19th century designed tiles with intertwined floral patterns, long serrated leaves and rich colouring of blue, turquoise, red, green and purple, adapted from IZNIK pottery.

Turkoman carpets A collective term for the carpets woven by the tribes of West Turkestan, an area bordered by Persia, Afghanistan and China. The best known tribes are the Tekke, Yomut, Salor, Ersari, Beshir, Saryk and the Baluch. Most products seen date from the 18th century or later and as a group are relatively easy to recognise. They have a limited colour palette. Red is used as a background in shades ranging from bright terracotta through burgundy, brown and aubergine.

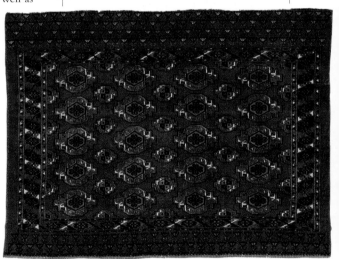

Silk and cotton Turkoman juval, mid-19th century [J]

The geometric patterns are defined in shades of white, brown, blue, yellow, crimson and green. The GUL motif is a distinguishing feature. By the end of the 19th century, colours are less harmonic and designs more stereotyped.

Turkish carpets

Turkey is an important country for the production of rugs and carpets. The tradition of carpet-weaving established during the 15th–17th centuries under the Ottoman rule formed the basis and inspiration of carpet production in the 18th and 19th centuries. Production in the 20th century was prolific and continues in the 21st century.

Design and influences

With its beginnings in the 16th century, an industry emerged producing carpets on a large scale, mainly to fuel Western demand and a growing export market. Carpets woven in Turkish towns are similar to Persian carpets, using floral curvilinear designs in a formal format. Wool, as opposed to cotton, is often used for the foundation. Ghiordes was one of the main towns in the 19th century, making prayer rugs with patterns recreated from earlier classical designs. Ladik and Konya were also important centres for prayer rugs. Extremely fine carpets were made in Hereke and in the Armenian quarter of Istanbul, known as Kum Kapi, from the end of the 19th century and into the second quarter of the 20th. Designs were inspired by the Ottoman court style and the classical 16th-century Persian rugs of the Safavid period (1501–1732). Many such pieces were signed by master weavers whose names include Zareh Penyamian, Hagop Kapoudjian and Toussonian. These rugs are mostly small and are woven in fine silk. Some include metal thread brocading. The PRAYER RUG format is frequently seen.

West Anatolian Cannabale rug, first half of the 19th century [I]

Anatolian prayer rug from the town of Konya, c.1750 [D]

Large decorative carpets were produced on a huge scale toward the end of the 19th century, particularly at USHAK. Carpets from here and other towns were often made to order by stores such as LIBERTY & Co. in London; some carpets still bear the labels of the store. The quality of town-produced carpets varies. Some are extremely fine and compare favourably with their Persian counterparts; others can be extremely coarse and loosely woven. Colour combinations range from monochromatic to brightly coloured.

Products of village-based or cooperative rug-making are similar to CAUCASIAN and some Persian rugs in design inspiration, construction and tradition. Geometric design elements are predominant, woven on a woollen foundation and made with the TURKISH knot. The medallions or GULS are similar to those found in TURKOMAN rugs. Influence of the earlier classical pieces is seen in rugs that display Holbein medallions. Production by nomadic groups is virtually non-existent; only the Yoruk and the Kurds weave while on migration. Rugs woven by these two groups share similarities with their Caucasian neighbours, using strong colours and bold geometric designs. Human forms are not seen in either village or nomadic carpets.

Turkish rug woven by Yoruk/Kurd nomadic group, mid-19th century [J]

Oval drainer by Turner & Co, c.1810 [Q]

Turner & Co. A Staffordshire pottery started by John Turner (d.1786) who was apprenticed to Thomas WHIELDON. He set up on his own in 1755 making JASPER, CREAMWARE and BASALTES WARE. He exported to Holland and France, but his sons John and William were ruined in 1806 by the repercussions from the French Revolution. John (Jnr) developed STONE CHINA c.1800.

Turning A technique of cutting legs, spindles and other members of pieces of furniture in the round that enables similar pieces to be cut easily and also in various decorative ways, such as BARLEY SUGAR TWISTS or BALUSTER shapes.

If the piece of wood is turned on a face-plate, hollow items such as bowls and small boxes with or without lids, like TREEN, can be made. Pole lathes, in which the power was supplied by the spring action of a whippy pole, and treadle lathes have been widely used since the Middle Ages, especially by country chair bodgers who worked on green wood. As these pieces dry they often distort to an oval rather than a round section. In various eastern and North African countries, craftsmen still use lathes powered by their feet while they sit on the ground and ISLAMIC woodwork includes great quantities of elaborate turnings. Treadle lathes

were superseded by electric-powered lathes at the end of the 19th century. In the late 20th century, computer-controlled lathes enabled turners to produce unlimited runs of exactly similar pieces.

Improvements in cutting tools and in the speed of revolution attainable on the lathe meant that wood fixings such as screws and bolts could also be made on lathes from the mid-18th century.

English turquoise, diamond and gold earrings, c.1880 [E]

Turquoise An opaque, waxy gemstone that varies in colour from sky-blue to pale green. Turqoise has been used in jewellery and ornament since ancient times. The finest turquoise is found in Iran; other sites include New Mexico, the Sinai Peninsula and Egypt. Turquoise was used extensively in 19th-century jewellery, such as sentimental rings and lockets where it represented forget-me-not, or gold serpent necklaces studded with turquoise CABOCHONS.

Spirally turned legs on an English walnut cabinet-on-stand, c.1690 [D]

Turret clock A type of weight-driven wall clock, developed from the earliest medieval mechanical clocks, usually made of iron and named from its being mounted on the tower of a church or other public building.

Twist stem A type of drinking GLASS stem made by twisting a glass rod embedded with bubbles of air, threads of opaque or coloured glass, or a combination of these. Introduced c.1735, the twist stem was popular until c.1780.

Two-faced doll See MULTI-FACE DOLL.

Tyg A large earthenware mug with three or more handles dividing the rim into sections for several drinkers. A favourite drinking vessel in the 16th and 17th centuries, it is known in both SLIPWARE and LEAD-GLAZED examples. Tygs were made in quantities at WROTHAM in Kent and in many STAFFORDSHIRE POTTERIES.

Moulded tyg by W.H. Goss, c.1880 [R]

Tyneside potteries The earliest EARTHENWARE factory on the River Tyne, near Newcastle, was founded by John Warburton c.1730, making BROWN WARE until 1750 when he moved to Gateshead. By 1827 there were around 20 factories, producing household wares in blue-printed earthenware, LUSTREWARE, CREAMWARE and MOCHA.

In the early 19th century C.T. Maling (d.1901) moved his factory to Tyneside from Sunderland, where the Maling factory had been established c.1762. Maling was very successful and produced enormous quantities of earthenware, including pink-splashed lustre, until the factory closed in 1963. Other factories include Richard Davis, making tiles in the 1830s, and Thomas Fell & Co. (1817–90).

U

Unaker The Cherokee name for a form of KAOLIN from colonial Virginia and used for the earliest COLONIAL porcelain in the 17th century, of which very little survives. It was also imported to England for early English porcelain made at BOW.

Undercut A type of carving on wood that is hollowed out, or cut away. The technique, perfected on furniture in the 17th and 18th centuries by carvers such as Grinling GIBBONS, was used on mirrors and other furniture to give a light, refined impression.

Underglaze Decoration painted onto a BISCUIT body. As the colours have to withstand the full heat of the kiln, the palette is restricted. Cobalt blue is the main colour, although chrome, nickel and iron oxides can also be used. After the decoration has been put onto the body, it is glazed and then fired again. The Chinese used copper oxide for red, but it was not discovered in Europe until the end of the l8th century. See also HIGH-TEMPERATURE COLOURS.

American lead glass and brass lamp by Union Glass Co., 1835–40 [L]

Union Glass Company A large American glassworks that began as a factory founded in Somerville, Massachusetts, in 1851 by Amory and Francis Houghton. They failed in 1860 and the factory became the Union Glass Company, specializing in clear CUT and PRESSED glass until the its closure in 1924.

Union Porcelain Works oyster plate, c.1865 [N]

Union Porcelain Works A large US porcelain works founded in 1861 by Thomas Carll Smith (1815–1901) in Brooklyn, New York, on the site of earlier works operated by William Boch & Brothers (and close to the rival works of Charles Cartlidge 1848–56). Much of the porcelain was of a continental HARD-PASTE type with a German feel to the decoration. Union produced inexpensive robust ware, including door plates and knobs, but is best known for the "Century" commemorative vases made for the CENTENNIAL Exposition in 1876, a range of innovative and whimsical ware, modelled by Karl L.H. Müller (1820–87) and oyster plates. Some pieces are marked U.P.W. The factory closed in the 1920s.

United States Pottery Co. See BENNINGTON POTTERY.

Upholstery This term has specifically come to mean the covering and padding of seat furniture, but originally it referred to all the textile decoration and furnishings in a room. By around 1600 some chairs began to be upholstered in the more modern sense. Padded furniture was often commissioned from saddlers. In the late 16th century craftsmen known as "upholsterers" were employed in large households as decorators. Independent upholsterers in cities and large towns soon followed. By the 18th century, most seat furniture was upholstered (CHIPPENDALE gives guidelines in his *Director*). Upholstery with springs was introduced in the early 19th century; patents were obtained in Vienna in 1822 by Georg Junigl and in London by Samuel Pratt in 1825. BUTTONING, characteristic of Victorian furniture, was also introduced early in the 19th century.

Uranium glass Glass with a yellow tint made by adding uranium oxide. It was first made in the 1830s by Josef Riedl (active 1830–48) in Bohemia (see BOHEMIAN GLASS), who developed Annagrün (greenish-yellow) and Annagelb (yellowish-green) glass, named after his wife. It was subsequently made by other glassworks, including STOURBRIDGE. Uranium was used in the 19th century for VASELINE GLASS. Uranium glass was later found to be mildly radioactive and the process was abandoned. See also PEACHBLOW.

English uranium glass lampshade by Thomas Webb & Sons, c.1880 [K, for 2]

Urban, Joseph (1871–1933) An Austrian architect and furniture designer, trained in Vienna, active in the US from 1911. He opened the New York WIENER WERKSTÄTTE showrooms in 1922. His architecture, including the New School building on West 12th Street, Manhattan, distinctively shows its roots in modern Vienna. His luxury furniture is considered among the best American ART DECO.

Urbino maiolica "Prodigal Son" dish, c.1570 [E]

Urbino potteries An important group of Italian MAIOLICA potteries from 1477, patronized by the Dukes of Urbino. Known 16th-century potters include Guido Durantino, Francesco Xanto Avelli, the Patanazzi family and Nicola da Urbino. From the 1520s Urbino specialized in ISTORIATO wares painted in blues, yellows and oranges. Also typical are *Belle donne* dishes, from *c.*1520, depicting the heads of women. From the 1560s GROTESQUE decoration after Raphael was used. In 18th-century Urbino, maiolica was made on a smaller scale, as other pottery centres in Europe became more important.

Urn stand A small table for a tea kettle and burner, often with a pull-out teapot stand, made *c.*1720–80.

Ushak A Turkish weaving centre, known for 16th- and 17th-century (see OTTOMAN) and late 19th-century (see TURKISH) carpets. The best examples have soft colour palettes; the worst are harsh and abrasive.

Utility A British government scheme of 1942. Designed by Sir Gordon RUSSELL, "utility" furniture had clean, modern lines and was made in only 20 styles to refurnish bombed-out houses.

V

Valadier, Luigi (1726–85) An Italian bronze-founder and official silversmith to Pope Pius VI from the late 1770s. He produced a variety of ecclesiastical and domestic silver, in particular ornate ÉPERGNES with representations of Classical sculpture and architecture. He also made NEO-CLASSICAL BRONZE MOUNTS for furniture and CAMEOS. His mark was LV with three FLEURS-DE-LIS.

Valencia potteries A Spanish centre of LUSTREWARE making. Before 1400 it was based in MALAGA. The finest 15th-century lustrewares are thought to have been made in the Valencia suburb of Manises. No marked pieces are known and, as designs remained unchanged throughout the 15th century, chronology and origin are difficult. The finest examples are dishes (40–50cm/16–20in diameter) made for the aristocracies of France, Italy and Spain, decorated with coats of arms and prancing beasts on a ground of foliage or DIAPER in rich golden lustre, with touches of blue. ALBARELLI and jugs were also made and are seen in paintings of the time, e.g. a Hugo van der Goes painting in the Uffizi Gallery, Florence, shows a lustred albarello. Tiles were also made in considerable quantities, with heraldry, arabesques and inscriptions in Arabic or Gothic script. The wares continued to be made at Valencia, but by the 16th century they were beginning to lose status as Italy was already beginning to make its own MAIOLICA. In the 17th and 18th centuries the quality of the

Mahogany urn stand, English 1770 [F]

painting declined. The lustre has a harsh burnished copper tone, while on early wares it ranges from soft gold to rich reddish-purple. There are still potteries at Valencia.

Valenciennes A French BOBBIN LACE centre that made very fine STRAIGHTLACE, typically with no raised threads. In the early 18th century it was densely patterned with flowers, snowflakes and OEIL DE PERDRIX, and was used for high fashion LAPPETS and ruffles. Later, the pattern had a plaited round mesh ground. In the 19th century, it was sparsely patterned with a diamond mesh and was used for ladies' underwear and children's clothes. It was also made by machine.

Valenciennes linen thread lace lappets, 1750 [O]

Valentine card Commercial examples first appeared in Britain *c.*1800 and derived from the centuries-old custom of sending love verses. By the middle of the 19th century the simplistic cards had developed into highly decorative items often made of fine paper, satin and lace. They were sentimental, hugely popular and collected in Britain and the US.

Val-Saint-Lambert glasshouse Belgium's most important glasshouse, founded just outside Liège in 1825 to make bottles and flat glass. The chemist François Kemlin expanded it and began producing decorative wares and table glass, and, from the 1830s, PRESSED GLASS. In 1836 it was incorporated into a large group of Belgian glass factories. It embraced the ART NOUVEAU and ART DECO styles and later used designs by the US glass designers Samuel Herman and Harvey K. Littleton. It is still active today.

Van Briggle, Artus (1869–1904)

A US ART POTTER active as a decorator at the ROOKWOOD POTTERY, but best known as the founder of a pottery in Colorado Springs in 1899 where he made a range of ART NOUVEAU, matt-glazed vessels. His widow sold the factory in 1912 but it is still in operation making copies of his original wares.

Val-Saint-Lambert cut-glass vase, c.1925 [H]

Van Cleef & Arpels

A French firm of jewellery designers and manufacturers active from the early 20th century. They produced elegant and colourful diamond and gem-set jewels including innovative calibré-cut (cut to fit a particular shape) sapphire and ruby flower studies with no apparent setting between the stones, which are described as "invisible setting".

Van de Velde, Henry

(1863–1957) A Belgian architect and ART NOUVEAU designer, with ideals midway between ARTS AND CRAFTS craftsmanship and the industrial severity of the MODERN MOVEMENT. Originally a painter, he turned to the decorative arts and architecture c.1893, influenced by the writings of William MORRIS. In 1894 he designed his own house, Bloemenwerf, near Brussels, creating all the furniture, fixtures, silver and cutlery

in an undecorated, elegant style, influenced by C.F.A. VOYSEY. His 1896 interior design for Samuel BING's Paris shop *L'Art Nouveau* brought him European renown. He became director of the School of Arts and Crafts at Weimar in 1908, the precursor of Walter GROPIUS's BAUHAUS in 1919. His furniture is sculptural with little applied decoration; chairs have slender splats, out-curving legs and studded UPHOLSTERY.

Van Doren, Harold (1895–1957)

A US industrial designer working from the late 1920s. Along with Raymond LOEWY, Norman BEL GEDDES and others, his designs were concerned with "streamlining", i.e. finding the function of an item, representing it aesthetically and creating an attractive product. He was a pioneer of plastics. In 1940 he published *Streamlining in Industrial Design*. Two examples of his designs are the "skyscraper" Air King radio and the Ensign Ful-Vue camera.

Vandyke rim

A decorative scalloped rim used on glass and ceramics (often on MONTEITHS) and named after the scalloped lace collars depicted in portraits by Anthony van Dyck (1599–1641).

Vandyke rim on an Anglo-Irish glass bowl, 1810 [O]

Van Erp, Dirk (1860–1933)

A Dutch-born ARTS AND CRAFTS metalworker, active in Oakland, near San Francisco, California, from 1908. He worked in the Dutch medieval style, specializing in hammered copper with exposed riveting. Typical products include vases, writing table equipment, and table lamps with conical shades of mica panels, which are highly prized today. His son William carried on his studio until 1944. Modern reproductions are now common.

Van Erp table lamp with mica panelled shade, c.1920 [D]

Van Vianen, Christian

(1598–1667) A Dutch silversmith, born in Utrecht into a family of silversmiths. His uncle Paul and father Adam famously developed the AURICULAR style. Christian worked in the same style, publishing a book of his father's designs in 1650, which spread the style. His work for Charles I and II brought the style to England.

Van de Velde desk and chair, c.1898 [A]

Vargueño A type of Spanish drop-front writing cabinet, also called a bargueño, that rests on a chest or a trestle stand. The interior was often elaborately carved, painted with red and gold, or decorated with TORTOISESHELL, IVORY, EBONY or other INLAYS in a variety of intricate geometric patterns. The vargueño was popular throughout the 16th and 17th centuries.

Varnish A wood-finishing material consisting of gum dissolved in linseed oil that is applied in layers by brush or spray to protect and enhance the appearance of wood surfaces. The technique of varnishing, which had been known in ancient times, was lost during the medieval period and replaced by oil and wax that was absorbed into the wood. Although no reliable records exist to indicate that varnish was made again prior to the mid-19th century, in some form it was probably the basis of VERNIS MARTIN. Early varnishes had a sticky, glazed appearance, but improved quality today produces a fine, satiny gloss.

Vasart See YSART, SALVADOR & SONS.

Vaseline glass A type of opalescent glass with a "greasy" appearance, hence the name. It was first made in Britain by James Powell at the WHITEFRIARS glassworks in 1877 and then by several other manufacturers until the 1930s, for such items as vases, candlesticks and beads. Blue, yellow, green and the very rare red Vaseline glass were made by adding tiny quantities of

Whitefriars vaseline glass perfume bottle, c.1880 [M]

uranium and metal oxides to the batch. When it was reheated in a gas jet, the clear glass turned opaque and milky.

Vauxhall glasshouses A group of English glasshouses active in Vauxhall, London, from the mid-17th century and throughout the 18th. The first firmly documented Vauxhall glasshouse was that founded by the Duke of Buckingham, c.1663, which produced MIRROR glass.

Vauxhall porcelain sauceboat, c.1760 [H]

Vauxhall porcelain factory An early English porcelain factory at Vauxhall, London, founded in 1752 by Nicholas Crisp, which was not officially recognized until 1988, when the Museum of London excavated the site. In 1753, Crisp, a jeweller and one of the founders of the Society of Arts, joined John Sanders, a Lambeth DELFTWARE potter, and together they advertised "Porcelain Ware made of English materials" (they used a soap-rock formula similar to that used by WORCESTER) for sale in Vauxhall. They made BLUE AND WHITE wares that were influenced by CHINESE EXPORT PORCELAIN. Some polychrome examples with CHINOISERIE decoration are known, but these are very rare. It closed in 1763.

Vechte, Antoine (1799–1868) A French artist-craftsman who was exceptionally talented and skilled at REPOUSSÉ WORK, producing highly complex silver designs in very high relief, in the MANNERIST and Classical styles. Originally working in Paris, Vechte left France to work in London for Hunt and Roskell

Silversmiths who received a medal at the GREAT EXHIBITION of 1851 for work executed by him. He was commissioned to produce silverware for Queen Victoria and taught many pupils, some of whom went on to become great silversmiths in their own right, such as L. Morel-Ladeuil (see ELKINGTON).

Veilleuse A receptacle designed to keep food or drink warm on a bedside table. It consists of a cylindrical stand that holds a dish for a nightlight and a lipped bowl or teapot and cover that rests on the top of the stand, over the flame. Known in POTTERY and PORCELAIN, WEDGWOOD and CREAMWARE, the veilleuse was popular in the 18th and early 19th centuries, especially in Paris.

Veneer A thin layer of fine wood applied to the surface of a furniture CARCASS made of a coarser, cheaper wood. Widely used from the second half of the 17th century, the technique of veneering was used to decorate all kinds of furniture in a wide range of imaginative designs. Originally, veneers were cut by hand, but from the early 19th century machine-cutting has been employed.

Venetian glass perfume bottles, c.1870 [P, each]

Venetian glass Glass made in Venice and the neighbouring island of MURANO. Although glass had been made in Venice from the 5th century AD, the industry really began to develop in the 13th century, with the establishment of a glass-makers' guild. This was followed by an ordinance in 1292 that prohibited Venetian glass-makers from divulging their trade secrets and, to protect Venice from the fire risk posed by the furnaces, relocated many glasshouses to Murano. In the 15th century, the sacking of Damascus led to an influx of skilled Syrian glass-makers. By mid-century, the development of CRISTALLO glass, new and revived techniques such as GILDING, ENAMELLING, TRAILING and thread decoration (see FILIGRANA, LATTICINO) and the use of AGATE, IRIDESCENT and ICE GLASS, had made Venice the world's leading glass-making centre. Despite their guild restrictions, many Venetian glass-makers travelled widely in the 16th and 17th centuries and as a result FAÇON DE VENISE ("Venetian-style") glassware was made throughout Europe in forms such as TAZZE, serpent-stemmed drinking glasses and covered goblets. In the 18th and 19th centuries, Venetian glassware was overshadowed by the new LEAD glass, but its fortunes revived in the 20th century through the efforts of leading companies such as SALVIATI & CO. and designers and makers such as Paolo VENINI, who revived and introduced forms,

Venetian latticino bottle, c.1930s [P]

colour and decoration – much as the early Venetian glass-makers had done – and did much to restablish the reputation of Venetian glass.

Venetian needlelace The name given to various types of NEEDLELACE made in Venice from the 17th century. The most flamboyant of these is GROS POINT, which has large flower and foliage motifs linked

Venetian gros point needlelace, 1690 [I]

by rows of buttonhole stitching, decorated with bars, with padding and raised picots. POINT DE NEIGE, made between 1650 and 1700, is the most intricately worked of all laces and is also the rarest and most highly sought after. Other types of Venetian needlelace include *point de Rose*, a fine 17th-century lace that was revived in the 19th century, and *point de Venise à Reseau*, a flat, mesh-based lace that was made in the 18th century.

Venice porcelain Venice was a centre of porcelain-making from the 18th century. Important factories include VEZZI, COZZI, Le NOVE, ESTE and Trevison. Porcelain was also made by Nathanial and Maria Dorothea Hewelcke, who came to the Udine, in Venetian territory from MEISSEN. In 1757 they petitioned for a monopoly for making porcelain; this was granted in 1758. They worked at Udine from 1758–61 and in Venice from 1761–63. The Cozzi factory was the last to produce porcelain c.1812.

Venice pottery MAIOLICA was made in Venice from c.1515. Early wares were inspired by imported Chinese BLUE AND WHITE porcelain and use a tin glaze stained with cobalt to a pale lavender-grey decorated in dark blue or opaque white. This unique glaze, known as "berettino", distinguishes Venetian pottery from other Italian pottery of the time. From c.1540

there were many workshops producing maiolica in various styles, including ARMORIAL WARES and ISTORIATO pieces. Important workshops include those of Maestro Lodovico at San Polo, Iacomo da Pesaro at San Barnabas, Domenigo da Venezia and the Bertolini and Manardi brothers. In the 17th and early 18th centuries, wares were produced, decorated with Classical PUTTI and Roman ruins.

Venini, Paolo (1895–1959) A Venetian glass-maker who became a partner in a Venetian glassworks in 1921, known from c.1925 as Venini & Co. This was the leading post-war Italian glassworks, producing decorative coloured glassware. It revived many traditional Venetian techniques and Venini and other leading designers, including Gio PONTI, developed new forms and decoration in glassware. From 1959 the firm was run by Venini's widow and son-in-law, but in 1985 it was sold to the Ferruzzi and Gardini families. Since 1988 it has traded as Venini S.p.a.

Venturi, Robert (b.1925) A US architect and designer, popular mainly in the 1980s. He pioneered POST-MODERNISM in furniture, produced by KNOLL International, and housewares, including tea kettles and silver plate made by Alessi.

"Chippendale" chair with "Grandmother's Tablecloth" pattern by Robert Venturi, 1984 [K]

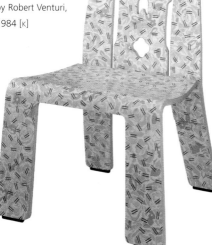

Victorian style

The term Victorian style describes the characteristics of architecture and the decorative arts during the reign of Queen Victoria (1837–1901) in Great Britain. It is sometimes used more broadly to refer to similar trends in 19th-century European and American decorative arts and to encompass the revival of NEO-CLASSICISM in the reign of Edward VII (1901–10).

Revival styles and advances in technology

As a result of the Industrial Revolution, the Victorian era was dominated by the growth of industrialization and mass-production for the increasingly prosperous middle classes. There was no one definable Victorian style, but instead a general fascination with a range of historical styles and exotic motifs derived from INDIAN, Chinese, Japanese, PERSIAN, TURKISH and ISLAMIC art, among others, combined with a fashion for extremely realistic depictions of nature. A greater emphasis on comfort and the display of wealth, required by the newly affluent industrialists and entrepreneurs, resulted in heavier, more curvaceous and richly upholstered, braided and tasselled furniture, together with a liberal sprinkling of ornamentation.

Inexpensive reproductions and imitations were made possible by new industrial techniques such as ELECTROTYPING and LAMINATION. Motifs from a variety of styles were often bizarrely combined in one piece (see ECLECTICISM) without regard for their origin, scale or function. The most popular revival styles were the Gothic, Renaissance and particularly the Rococo. In Britain, the GOTHIC REVIVAL was considered the "national" style for architecture, interior decoration and furnishings after it was used for the Houses of Parliament (rebuilt from 1836). The designer A.W.N. PUGIN inspired a more archeologically exact approach to furnishings inspired by medieval styles from the 1830s. Closely related to the Gothic Revival was the RENAISSANCE REVIVAL, particularly popular in France and Italy, and characterized by the use of ornament such as GROTESQUES, STRAPWORK,

Silver tea caddy with Rococo-inspired ornament, 1849 [I]

Copeland bust in Parian, sometimes referred to as "Statuary Porcelain", mid-19th century [N]

Work table inlaid with walnut, with machine-turned legs, c.1850 [I]

Minton majolica vase with applied naturalistic flowers, c.1850 [H]

Recognizing the style

Crockets (hook shapes outlining wood and metalwork), pinnacles, cluster columns and trefoils, which derived from medieval church architecture, proliferated in the Gothic Revival style. Flowers were popular throughout the era.

Pointed Gothic Revival arch

Honeysuckle motif

Arcading on cabinet

GRISAILLE panels, SWAGS and FLUTING. In France, some lead-glazed earthenware was made in the style of 16th-century pieces by Bernard PALISSY, while in Italy the glassmaker Antonio SALVIATI was responsible for reviving 15th- and 16th-century styles of VENETIAN GLASS. From the 1830s the ROCOCO REVIVAL was evident in exaggerated curving shapes, generous use of carved scrolls and rich gilding. Naturalistic flowers, fruit, birds and shells were often applied as decoration, for example in the moulded and laminated furniture of the American John Henry BELTER and in the manufacture of Rococo Revival ceramics by the MEISSEN porcelain factory.

Technology leapt forward in the Victorian period. A wide range of oil, gas and eventually electric lighting was produced, with lamps made in the various revival styles. Glass was manufactured in a vast array of colours and unusual materials such as moulded PAPIER MÂCHÉ were used for furniture. This Victorian mastery of technology, combined with the expansion of international trade, encouraged the development of international exhibitions showcasing industrial products from around the world and the most up-to-date trends in design and mass-production. The first, and most important, was the GREAT EXHIBITION held at the purpose-built Crystal Palace in London in 1851 and organized by Prince Albert and Sir Henry COLE. A number of objects from the exhibition – dominated by virtuoso items such as centrepieces with hyper-naturalistic decoration – were bought to form the basis of the collections of the South Kensington, later the Victoria and Albert Museum, in London. Throughout the second half of the 19th century and the early 20th there were numerous successive international exhibitions in Paris, Vienna, Italy and the US.

Buttoned chair designed for comfort, c.1870 [L]

Machine production versus hand craftsmanship

A reaction against the prevalence of historical styles and the poor quality of industrial manufacturers emerged in the second half of the 19th century, led by design reformers such as Sir Henry Cole and critics such as John Ruskin. They advocated the use of ornament appropriate to the function of the object, and an emphasis on simplicity and honesty in the use of materials. From this the ARTS AND CRAFTS MOVEMENT led by William MORRIS emerged. Inspired by medieval art, the movement rejected slick machine production in favour of a return to the high standards of hand craftsmanship.

Similarly, toward the end of the 19th century, exponents of the ART NOUVEAU style repudiated the use of historical motifs and instead aimed to create a wholly new style appropriate for a dawning century. The designers of the AESTHETIC MOVEMENT, particularly E.W. GODWIN, were inspired by the simplicity of Japanese design. The widespread fashion for JAPONAISERIE had developed after the re-opening of trade between Japan and the West in 1858 and the display of Japanese artifacts at the International Exhibition in London of 1862.

However, the manufacture of pieces in historical styles continued into the 20th century. But, even in mass-produced items there was a trend during the first decade after Queen Victoria's death for a lighter style of furnishings, influenced partly by the design reform movements. This new taste was particularly evident in the revival of elegant, restrained forms of late 18th-century NEO-CLASSICISM. Most pieces were mass-produced, but some high quality, exact reproductions were made by firms such as GILLOWS of Lancaster.

Renaissance Revival machine-turned walnut armchair, c.1880 [M]

Verdigris (Old French: "green of Greece") The greenish, powdery deposit that forms naturally on the surface of copper or brass articles. It can be removed by polishing. Verdigris is also produced artificially and used as a pigment.

Verge escapement A type of ESCAPEMENT used in most clocks until the invention of the more accurate ANCHOR ESCAPEMENT in the 1670s. It was first drawn up by Giovanni da Dondi, a Paduan professor, in 1364. It comprises a toothed wheel and a verge (shaft), with two pallets released in turn by a foliot (large horizontal bar) or balance (wheel).

Vermiculé (Latin *vermis*: "worm") A type of decoration, usually gilding, that is wavy and sinuous and reminiscent of worm tracks. It is often seen on the gilding of SÈVRES porcelain.

Vernier scale A graduated scale of units with an auxiliary sliding scale, allowing further subdivision of the reading from the principal scale to tenths and then hundredths. Used to show minute sections of an arc on navigational instruments such as a SEXTANT, or vertically beside the mercury tube on a BAROMETER. Pierre Vernier is credited with its invention in 1631.

Vernis Martin A generic name to describe an 18th-century French JAPANNING method on wood. Named after Guillaume Martin and his brothers –

French wooden box with vernis Martin c.1870–80 [N]

but covering similar work by other craftsmen as well – this varnishing technique was invented during the reign of Louis XIV (1643–1715). Although less durable than the Oriental lacquering that inspired it, the attractive brilliancy and depth of vernis Martin made it highly fashionable during the 18th and 19th centuries for indoor panelling, furniture, small boxes and even carriages.

Verre de fougère (French: "fern" or "bracken glass") An early type of glass in which potash from burnt bracken or ferns was used as the FLUX. The French equivalent of WALDGLAS, it shares the same green/brown/yellow colour, and was used for simple forms, often with shallow cut decoration.

Verre églomisé A type of glass decorated with a layer of gold or silver leaf on the back. A design is engraved on the leaf, sometimes accompanied by REVERSE PAINTING, and covered with a protective layer of varnish or glass. The technique dates from the 13th century, but is named after a Parisian framemaker, Jean-Baptist Glomy (d.1786), who used it in the 18th century.

Gold pendant with painting of The Flight into Egypt in verre églomisé, Spanish or Italian, early 17th century [C]

Vesta case A small portable box made in a great variety of forms with snap-shut covers to contain vestas (short matches) and keep them dry. Produced extensively from *c*.1890 to 1920, they coincided with an explosion in the popularity of smoking. Most were

Silver combined vesta and sovereign case c.1898 [M]

made of inexpensive materials but some were made in precious metals or enamelled.

Vetro latteo See MILK GLASS.

Vezzi porcelain factory The Venetian goldsmiths Francesco and Giuseppe Vezzi, perhaps helped by C.C. Hunger from MEISSEN, first made porcelain *c*.1720 with KAOLIN smuggled from Aue in Germany. Hunger returned to Meissen in 1725. Vezzi made translucent HARD-PASTE PORCELAIN, with a clear, wet-looking glaze, often using silver shapes, until 1727. Decoration included CHINOISERIES and coats of arms. Some wares have BLANC-DE-CHINE style Prunus blossom. A distinctive Venetian shape is a gondola lamp, with Bérainesque designs.

Victorian style See pp.392–93.

Vienna regulator A type of REGULATOR produced in Austria during the first half of the 19th century. Generally weight-driven, it is either of the LONGCASE or wall-mounted type, with a wooden case with glass panels on the front and sides and a pediment at the top. The movement is finely made, with a compensated PENDULUM. In the late 19th century poorer imitations were produced in the US and in the BLACK FOREST region of Germany.

Vienna Secession An alliance of artists, designers and architects who broke from the Viennese Society of Visual Artists in 1897. Josef HOFFMANN was a founder; the group included Otto Wagner and Gustav Klimt. They favoured symbolism and ART NOUVEAU. The Secession still survives.

Vienna porcelain

The story of Viennese porcelain is not that of a single factory over a limited time, but of a number of enterprises. Many of these used the Bindenschild mark taken from the arms of the ruling Hapsburgs, although it should only rightfully have been used by the first Austrian porcelain factory. This was founded in 1718 by Claudius du Paquier (d.1751).

Enticing workers from Meissen leads to success

Du Paquier had tried but failed to make porcelain in 1716. In 1717 he lured Christoph Conrad Hunger, an enameller and gilder, from MEISSEN. In 1719 Samuel Stolzel, another defector from Meissen who had the secret of the ARCANUM, joined him. Consequently, they produced porcelain similar to that of BÖTTGER in Meissen, with shapes based on silver. Stolzel and Hunger soon absconded, but du Paquier continued alone until 1744, when he sold the factory to the State, stayed as director for a year and left. In 1749 KAOLIN was discovered nearby in Schmolnitz in Hungary, which was a great advantage.

Beaker and trembleuse stand with pierced gallery, decorated with the Arms of a Cardinal, c.1730 [B, a pair]

Under State ownership from 1744 to 1784, the factory shows Baroque influence and then that of Sèvres. The painters during the "Viennese Baroque" period were J. Danhofer and Jakob Helchis. The artist Klinger and a few others from Meissen were also engaged. From 1747 the master modeller was Josef Niedermayer. In 1784, due to financial difficulties, the directorship was transferred to Konrad Sorgenthal, a textile manufacturer who brought a flurry of success with pieces in NEO-CLASSICAL styles, figures modelled by Anton Grassi and plaques superbly painted by Josef Nigg and Joseph Fischer. However, by 1820 the factory was beginning to decline and in 1864 the Emperor closed the factory. Moulds from the factory were sold in 1900 to the enterprising retailer Ernst Wahliss and to HEREND in Hungary.

Other porcelain factories in Vienna

Augarten was founded in 1922 to carry on the tradition of the State-owned factory. They used the shield mark of the original factory, with various additions. The Bock factory was founded in 1828 and made table, coffee and tea services until 1933. From c.1880–1930, Franz Dorfl ran a studio decorating porcelain. In 1885, the GOLDSCHEIDER porcelain and majolica factory was founded and made metallized TERRA-COTTA in the ART NOUVEAU style. It closed in 1953. There were several other factories and decorating studios, some of which used forms of the Vienna banded shield mark, taken from Hapsburg armorial bearings. See also Michael POWOLNY.

Cabinet cup and saucer from the golden age of Vienna porcelain, c.1800 [I]

Vienna's marks

In the mid-1740s this mark was sometimes impressed on wares from the du Paquier factory and from c.1749 it appeared in underglaze blue. The last two digits of the year were impressed from 1783; the last three digits from 1800.

Banded shield

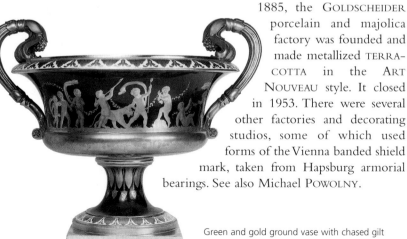

Green and gold ground vase with chased gilt putti playing musical instruments, 1813 [c]

Vietnamese pottery and porcelain
Ware made at Annam, modern Vietnam, usually referred to as "Annamese" ware. For over 1,000 years (3rd century BC to the 10th century AD) Annam's major cultural influence was China. Excavations in North Vietnam have uncovered pottery contemporary with China's Han and SONG DYNASTIES variously decorated using SLIP, CELADON or brown glazes. The finest Annamese wares date from the 12th–15th centuries and closely follow the Chinese YUAN and MING originals. Annamese wares have a coarse, heavily potted, greyish body, usually painted in UNDERGLAZE blue or occasionally in polychrome enamels. Wares include bowls, vases, KENDI and boxes that were exported throughout south-east Asia. They are similar in type to the Thai ceramics of Sawankhalok.

Vignette (French: *vigne* "vine") A carved ornament – traditionally dating to the medieval period – featuring a continuous design of grapevine leaves and tendrils. The term also refers to a photograph or drawing in which the edges are shaded off.

Vile & Cobb Leading English furniture-makers of the mid-18th century. William Vile (*c.*1700–1767) established a London workshop in partnership with John COBB (*c.*1715–78). They did interior decorating and made some of the highest-quality ROCOCO and ADAM-style furniture produced in England for, among others, George III and Queen Charlotte.

Villeroy & Boch See METTLACH POTTERY.

Vinaigrette A small box produced from *c.*1770 up to *c.*1900, generally of silver with a hinged cover and grille, behind which was a sponge soaked in aromatic vinegar that could be inhaled to mask bad smells or counteract faintness.

Silver-gilt vinaigrette, English c.1817 [L]

Vincennes The "nursery" of the SÈVRES factory. Orry de Fulvy, an official at the Treasury, helped by the Dubois brothers from CHANTILLY, started experiments in porcelain-making in the Château de Vincennes, France, *c.*1740. By 1745 their

Vincennes bowl, c.1750 [B]

wares had become commercially acceptable. Typically, decoration was rather sparse, consisting mainly of scattered sprigs of flowers – a far cry from the sumptuous colours and gilding of later Sèvres porcelain. In 1755 the company moved to its new factory at Sèvres but, from then on, it belonged to King Louis XV.

Vinovo porcelain factory Founded under royal patronage by Giovanni Vittorio Brodel and Paul Anton Hannong in 1776, in the castle of Vinovo near Turin, in Italy. When Hannong left in 1780, Vittorio Amadeo Gioannetti took over and the factory began to produce useful wares and a variety of figures and groups, especially COMMEDIA DELL'ARTE. The French invasion of 1796 ended the prosperous period and the factory never recovered. It closed in 1826.

Vinyl A durable, flexible and in its time revolutionary PLASTIC developed in the 1940s and used since then for toys, flooring, tubing, and coverings on items where less durable materials or rubber would have been used before.

Violet wood See KINGWOOD.

Vitrifiable colours A term applied to glazed colours primarily with enamels but also on porcelain, earthenware or glass when they become hard, fixed and glassy once fired. This happens at 500–900°C (930–1650°F) for enamels and at 800–1000°C (1470–1830°F) for pottery and porcelain.

Vitrine A cupboard with large glazed panels. Originally made in the 18th century as bookcases, vitrines designed especially for the display of ornaments did not become common until the latter part of the 19th century. Vitrines with mirror backs were popular from the mid-19th century, as they made it possible to view both sides of the objects displayed.

Walnut-veneered vitrine, English c.1860 [L]

Vitro-porcelain A shiny, opaque glass that resembles porcelain. It was produced in several colours and was a popular medium for late-19th century inexpensive press-moulded domestic glass and novelties. See also MILK GLASS.

Vitruvian scroll A Classical ornament of repeated VOLUTES, usually on a frieze. Also known as a running dog or wavescroll, it was revived in the early

Vitruvian scroll

Renaissance and was used extensively to embellish 18th-century architecture and silver and early Georgian furniture.

Vizagapatnam A town in south-east India producing Anglo-Indian furniture and smaller pieces for the British market in the 18th and 19th centuries. Hardwood was inlaid or covered with panels of ivory. The pieces are essentially English in form, but the decoration fuses Indian and English styles.

Vizagapatnam ivory sewing-box, c.1810 [D]

Volkmar, Charles (1841–1914) An American studio potter who trained in France as a *barbotine* (underglaze painting) artist. He founded a studio in Brooklyn, New York, in 1895 moving to Metuchen, New Jersey, in 1903. Volkmar's work is technically and artistically advanced and may be marked with an incised V or CV.

Volkstedt A porcelain-making centre in Thuringia, Germany. The oldest factory, founded in 1762 under the protection of the Prince of Schwarzburg-Rudolstadt, used crossed hayforks as a mark. In the 19th century many new factories sprang up, making ornamental porcelain now often called "DRESDEN". Among them was Richard Eckert & Co., who revived the hayfork mark in 1895. Many of these factories continue today.

Volkstedt figure of St Jerome, c.1765 [I]

Volute A spiral scroll typically found on an Ionic CAPITAL, supposedly derived from the horns of the ram. The volute was taken up from the Renaissance for ornament and architecture and used on on ceramics, silver and furniture.

Voyeuse A French term for a low seated chair with a padded top at the back. First made in France in the 1740s and later in England – where it was called a conversation chair – the occupant sat astride the seat to watch card playing. A special *voyeuse à genoux* was invented for women to kneel on.

Voysey, Charles Francis Annesley (1857–1941) An English architect and designer, central to the ARTS AND CRAFTS Movement. He joined the ART WORKERS GUILD in 1884 and showed furniture with the Arts and Crafts Exhibition Society in 1893. His furniture, mainly in oak, has a simple, almost rustic appeal. Regarded as one of England's leading designers of the period, he also designed metalwork, wallpaper, textiles and pottery.

Vulcanite A substitute for JET often used in Victorian MOURNING JEWELLERY. Also known as "gutta-percha", it is a form of hardened rubber and sulphur which, unlike jet, has a deep brown tone.

Donegal wool carpet designed by Voysey, c.1900 [B]

Vulliamy family An English family of clockmakers. The earliest known member, Justin Vulliamy (1712–97), arrived in London from Switzerland in 1730. Justin's son Benjamin (1747–1811) made the regulator for George III's observatory at Kew, London, as well as LONGCASE and BRACKET CLOCKS. His son, Benjamin Lewis (1780–1854), was a leading London clockmaker in the early 19th century.

W

Postcard designed by Louis Wain, 1920s [S]

Wain, Louis William (1860–1939) An English illustrator famous for his cat drawings. His work was immensely popular and from 1901 to 1925 he published a *Louis Wain Annual*. Averaging 600 drawings a year, many for postcards, the market for his work became flooded and eventually declined. He was certified insane in 1924 and later died in poverty in an institution.

Wainscot chair (Germanic *wain*: "wagon" and *schot*: "crossbar") A 17th-century oak-joined chair with arms. The wainscot chair originated in Britain, although variations were made throughout northern Europe. The panelled back was often decorated with carved leaves, LOZENGES, roundels and LUNETTES. The scroll-carved TOP RAIL might be inscribed with names and dates. The solid seat would have been fitted with a SQUAB CUSHION. The front supports were ring-turned – a popular decorative technique at that time – and the legs were joined by STRETCHERS. Wainscot chairs were made until the end of the 17th century and they survive in some numbers today.

Waiter See SALVER.

Waldglas (German: "forest glass") A type of early glass in which burnt wood provided the potash FLUX. Known also sometimes as "green glass" – a colour resulting from natural impurities in the ingredients or batch – it was made in the heavily wooded areas of central and Northern Europe.

Wall clock Any type of clock that can be mounted on a wall. One of the earliest domestic wall clocks was the LANTERN CLOCK. From the mid-18th century, simple DIAL CLOCKS were used in public buildings and offices. Other types of wall clock include French CARTEL CLOCKS with elaborate brass or bronze cases, TAVERN CLOCKS and many types of REGULATOR clock.

Wall pocket A flat-backed vase, made in pottery and porcelain and pierced to hang on the wall to hold flowers, made widely in Europe from the beginning of the 18th century until the present.

Wall pocket,
English 1930s [R]

Walnut A hardwood ranging from light golden to dark brown in colour. Burr walnut is highly prized for veneers and for turning. In Europe, walnut was popular for furniture-making – both solid and as a veneer – from the mid-17th century until the introduction of

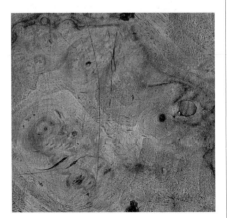

Burr walnut

mahogany in the early 18th century. In the early 18th century, walnut was exported to Europe from Virginia, US.

Walter, Alméric (1859–1942) A French glass artist renowned for his PÂTE-DE-VERRE work which he made at first for DAUM FRÈRES, with whose support he introduced more colour into his work. He also produced sculptural pieces and plaques. Some pieces were created in collaboration with the glass technician Henri Bergé (1868–1936). In 1919 he set up his own studio at Nancy.

Waltham Watch Company A US watch-making company in Waltham, Massachusetts, from 1854 which merged in 1859 with Appleton, Tracy and Co. It underwent several name changes, re-emerging as the Waltham Watch Co. in 1925. It was the first to mass-produce watches and by 1957, when manufacture ceased, had made over 34 million watches.

Wanli porcelain Chinese porcelain made in the reign of the MING DYNASTY emperor Wanli (1573–1619). Large quantities of blue and white KRAAK PORCELAIN were made for export to Europe. The finest porcelain decorated in the WUCAI palette was made in this reign. See also CHINESE EXPORT PORCELAIN.

Wanli porcelain box and cover, c.1600 [H]

Wardrobe A closed cupboard for the storage of clothes. Usually fitted with drawers, shelves, and pegs or hooks for hanging, wardrobes began to replace the PRESS, with its horizontal sliding trays, by the mid-19th century. Although Thomas SHERATON had designed a cupboard with

a rail and "arms to hang clothes on" in the 1790s, rails and coat-hangers did not appear until the 1870s, and were not universally used until after 1900. From the late 19th century, wardrobes were usually made as part of bedroom suites, often with a fitted mirror.

Waring & Gillow See GILLOWS.

Warming pan A circular brass or copper pan to contain hot embers, for warming a bed. Made from the 15th century, it usually has a long, carved or turned wooden handle and a decorative pierced, embossed or engraved hinged lid. It was superseded in the 19th century by copper or earthenware hot-water bottles.

Warwick cruet frame An English silver condiment stand with a cinquefoil (five-lobed) base and central handle, fitted with three silver casters and two cut-glass bottles, made from c.1750 and probably named after the Earl of Warwick.

Warwick vase A large ancient Greek marble vase, purchased by the Earl of Warwick after it was unearthed at Hadrian's villa, Rome, c.1770. Scaled-down copies were produced in bronze, silver and ceramics by such people as Paul STORR and RUNDELL & Bridge.

Washstand Although known from the medieval period, the washstand was not common until the mid-18th century. Washstands vary in shape from simple tripod stands to small cabinets holding wash basins and jugs, with drawers for toiletries. During the late 19th century large washstands with marble tops were made en suite with bedroom furniture.

Watch See POCKET WATCH; WRIST WATCH.

Watch stand A small stand made in both pottery and porcelain, often with figures, to hold a watch, either at night or on a mantelpiece as a substitute for a clock. They were popular in Staffordshire pottery but were also made in fine porcelain, for example at SÈVRES.

Watcombe Pottery A pottery founded near Torquay, Devon, in 1867 by G.J. Allen to make use of the local red clay. Christopher DRESSER provided some designs for their ware, which included terracotta pieces for domestic use, often SLIP-CAST and sometimes decorated with turquoise enamels. In 1901 it merged to become Royal Aller Vale & Watcombe Potteries and finally closed in 1962.

Water clock A type of clock used in ancient Egypt, Greece and Rome in which time is measured by the flow of water into or out of a calibrated container. In the 17th and 18th centuries water clocks with a drum filled with mercury or water and mounted on an axle were produced, the falling weight of the drum driving the clock.

Waterford Glasshouse Irish glasshouse founded in 1783 at Waterford, County Wexford. One of the best-known producers of IRISH GLASS, the company's international reputation was built on its high quality, heavy, deep-cut glassware that included decanters, fruit bowls, honey jars, finger bowls and jugs. The company was relaunched in 1951 as Waterford Crystal and is still active today.

Waterford glass fingerbowl, c.1820 [L]

Water gilding A type of wood GILDING in which the gold leaf is laid onto damp GESSO and is exceptionally smooth.

Watteau figures Pastoral lovers, based on the paintings of the French ROCOCO artist Jean-Antoine Watteau (1684–1721). These were copied by MEISSEN and SÈVRES, amongst others, in the 18th century and called "Watteau pictures".

Poured wax Pierotti Baby, c.1860 [M]

Wax dolls The heads and sometimes the limbs of dolls have been made from wax, either poured into a mould or carved, throughout Europe since ancient times. The process was commercialized around the middle of the 19th century by firms such as PIEROTTI and MONTANARI. The SHOULDER HEADS may either be of solid or hollow wax. Solid heads with moulded hair and black bead eyes were popular in the early 19th century. After 1840, hollow heads were favoured, with inserted glass eyes and rooted hair. The fashion for wax dolls began to wane c.1870.

Wax jack (or taper stand) A silver or Old Sheffield plated frame to hold a coil of wax taper, the end of which is secured between spring-loaded grips. They were made in various forms from c.1680–1820.

Wax over composition A doll-making technique in which SHOULDER HEADS of a material such as papier mâché are dipped into molten wax to create a skin-like effect, popular in the mid-19th century.

Waywiser An instrument consisting of a wheel attached to an arm, handle and a dial with scales used to measure distance on the ground. Also known as an odometer, perambulator or surveyor's wheel, it was used by the Romans and reintroduced in the 17th century.

Weathervane (or windvane) A metal construction mounted on a building for showing wind direction with an arrow. Since the 18th century, most arrow pointers are balanced with a larger flag or motif to point upwind. Motifs include cocks, ships, mottos and figures.

Webb, Philip (1831–1915) English architect and designer who opened his architectural practice in 1856. He designed the Red House, in Bexley, Kent, for William MORRIS in 1860. He was the chief designer for Morris, Marshall & Faulkner and then Morris & Co. until 1900 and was responsible for many interiors, particularly the furniture. He also designed a suite of glass tableware for James POWELL & Sons, c.1860.

Webb, Thomas & Sons English glassworks founded by Thomas Webb (1802–69) in 1837 near Stourbridge, West Midlands. From 1863, it was managed by his sons and produced an exciting range of decorative glass. The range included

Thomas Webb salt cellars, c.1885 [K, a set of 4]

CAMEO GLASS by John NORTHWOOD (1836–1902), Thomas Woodall (1849–1926) and George Woodall (1850–1925), and new types of art glass such as ALEXANDRITE, IRIDESCENT GLASS and QUEEN'S BURMESE. After various takeovers and mergers the company closed in 1990.

Wedgwood pottery

Josiah Wedgwood (1730–95) was an extraordinary man, with great commercial sense and foresight allied to an enquiring, perfectionist mind and a thorough understanding of ceramics. In 1759 he founded a pottery factory at Burslem in Staffordshire and the firm bears his name today.

Creamware plate with green frog crest
from a service made for
Catherine the Great, 1773 [E]

How it all began

Josiah was the 13th (and youngest) child of a family of potters. His father died when he was nine and he was sent to work for his brother at the Churchyard Pottery. When he was 12 he caught smallpox, which left him with a weakness in his right leg. He was apprenticed as a potter in 1744 but a year later ill-health forced him to quit the thrower's bench. Instead, Josiah began to learn to mould wares and to experiment with different clays and metallic oxides. In 1754 he joined Thomas WHIELDON, devoting himself to improving coloured glazes and, in 1759, he started on his own in the Ivy House, Burslem. At this stage Josiah made all kinds of pottery similar to contemporary STAFFORDSHIRE wares.

Josiah extended his business and in 1764 took over larger premises in the Brick House Works, later known as Bell House. In 1762 he met Thomas Bentley, a Liverpool merchant who imbued him with a love of the classical. They became partners in 1768 and went on to build a new factory, house and village on the Ridge House Estate, which Josiah named Etruria (most GREEK vases were then thought to be ETRUSCAN). The partnership with Bentley related to "vases and ornamental wares" – useful wares were made at Bell House until 1771–73 when the workmen and plant were gradually moved to Etruria. Bentley died in 1780. In 1790 Josiah took his own sons John, Josiah and Thomas and his nephew Thomas Byerley into partnership. Josiah Wedgwood died in 1795, having been made a Fellow of the Royal Society and having secured a worldwide market for his own wares and those of his fellow Staffordshire potters.

Sucrier and cover in green jasper ware,
a body developed by Wedgwood and
also found in blue,
c.1820 [K]

Wedgwood's marks

Most Wedgwood pieces are marked. The date codes used in the 19th and early 20th centuries can be confused if the three letters are not arranged in a group but scattered on the underside of a piece. Later, the last numbers of the year were used as a date mark.

Wedgwood + Bentley
1768–80

1769–80

WEDGWOOD
Standard mark
from 1780

Types of pottery

Cauliflower and pineapple wares were the first products made at Burslem, ten years before Etruria opened and for a few years after that. They were similar to those of Wedgwood's former partner Thomas Whieldon, differing only in their finer finish, because of Wedgwood's attention to detail, and the standardization of shapes and materials. The first efforts at the new factory were to improve black EARTHENWARE, which Josiah called black BASALTES and used for imitations of Greek vases. He also strove to improve marbled wares and find new materials to make the white reliefs he used to decorate the jasper grounds. JASPER WARE contained barium sulphate in the form of a Derbyshire mineral known as "cawk" and was perfected in 1774–75. All manner of articles were made from jasper ware – cameos, portrait medallions, SEALS, beads, BUTTONS and tableware. William Hackwood was the principal modeller

Blue-painted creamware vegetable tureen
and cover, c.1830 [Q]

from 1769 to 1832. From the outset Wedgwood also produced AGATE WARE knife handles, SALT-GLAZED STONEWARE and green-glazed wares with relief-moulded leaves. Josiah Wedgwood also created CREAMWARE. It was fired to stoneware hardness by adding Cornish CHINA STONE. Creamware was used for table wares, kitchen and dairy equipment and every kind of household utensil. Wedgwood named it QUEENSWARE, after securing the patronage of Queen Charlotte. His creamware swept Europe, completely swamping the DELFT and FAIENCE markets. In PEARLWARE, created *c.*1779, the cream tinge of creamware was counteracted by a minute quantity of cobalt blue. It was sometimes translucent, although Wedgwood never made porcelain in Josiah's lifetime.

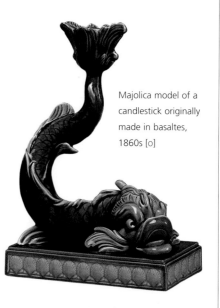

Majolica model of a candlestick originally made in basaltes, 1860s [o]

NEO-CLASSICAL forms were all the rage by 1775. The first catalogue of Queensware *c.*1775 had nine pages of austere and graceful engraved designs influenced by contemporary silver. Creamware was decorated outside the factory, including a large service made for Catherine II (the Great) of Russia, known as the Frog Service because it was intended for the palace of La Grenouillère ("The Froggery") in St Petersburg. This was painted at CHELSEA with views of named English landscapes and country houses.

Wedgwood's great wish was to make vases in the style of the classical antique. Designs for vases were taken from Sir William Hamilton's *Catalogue of Etruscan Specimens*. He made a copy of the PORTLAND VASE, which aroused great interest. His vases were decorated with lathe-cutting and restrained enamelling and gilding. He is said to have installed an engine-turning lathe at Burslem as early as 1763. Black basaltes, red and cane-coloured stoneware vases were made. In *c.*1767 the first specimens of library busts (life-sized) of classical and modern authors were created. From 1769 the factory produced bronze and painted Etruscan wares. Tiles were first made at this time. The animal and portrait painter George Stubbs persuaded Wedgwood to make large plaques too.

Matt green Art Deco earthenware bowl by the 20th-century designer Keith Murray, 1930s [o]

Wedgwood in the 19th and 20th centuries

After Thomas Byerley's death in 1810, the factory continued in the charge of Josiah Wedgwood II until 1841. When he retired, his son Josiah Wedgwood III succeeded him. Francis, the younger son of Josiah II, was in charge in 1844, followed by his son Godfrey who was head of the firm in 1870. Francis Hamilton Wedgwood, nephew to Godfrey, joined the firm in 1899 and was senior partner until 1930. After the death of Thomas Byerley in 1810 the firm revived and continued old styles and patterns of the 18th century but gradually lost its leadership of the Staffordshire industry. In the early 19th century LUSTRE decoration began to be used, as well as RESIST and incised patterns in silver, and pink mottled lustre (so-called MOONLIGHT). Chinese FAMILLE-ROSE style painting on black basaltes (Capri ware) was in vogue from 1804–10 and Wedgwood made BONE CHINA from 1812–16.

20th-century designers

Wedgwood responded to Art Deco by employing the architect Keith Murray (1892–1981), who designed plain geometric forms, and the sculptor John Skeaping (1901–80) who designed stylized animals and birds.

Art Deco earthenware seal by John S. Skeaping, 1930s [L]

In the 20th century, Wedgwood employed many innovative designers, including Daisy Makeig-Jones, who produced FAIRYLAND LUSTRE; Keith MURRAY, who designed some CELADON green and cream tableware in the 1930s; and Eric RAVILIOUS, whose 1930s designs were produced in the 1950s. Traditional ware was still produced alongside these more modern designs, for example jasper ware is still made in copies of 18th-century originals. A new factory was built at Barlaston, Staffordshire, which opened in 1940. In 1989, Wedgwood merged wth WATERFORD GLASS to form the Waterford-Wedgwood Group.

Weesp porcelain factory The first successful Dutch porcelain factory, founded in 1757 by the Irish ARCANIST D. McCarthy and taken over in 1759 by Count Gronsveldt-Diepenbroek, helped by the German arcanist Nikolaus Paul. The factory, which made good quality HARD-PASTE porcelain with a clear glaze, moved to Oude Loosdrecht in 1771, to AMSTEL in 1784, and closed in 1820.

Weisweiler, Adam (1744–1820) A German furniture-maker who began his career in the workshop of David ROENTGEN. He moved to Paris, becoming a *maître ébéniste* by 1778 and worked primarily for furniture dealers, such as Dominique Daguerre, who supplied furniture for Marie Antoinette and the Prince of Wales. Weisweiler specialized in small, light pieces, such as BONHEURS-DU-JOUR, CONSOLES and SECRÉTAIRES, and is celebrated for clean, elegant lines, flawless construction, and delicate floral mounts. He used plain mahogany veneers, lacquer, SÈVRES plaques or PIETRE DURE panels. His furniture features tapering legs with barley-sugar inlay, interlaced stretchers and legs shaped like spinning tops.

Weller Pottery See RHEAD, F.H.

Wellings, Norah An English rag doll maker. After working for CHAD VALLEY, she ran her own soft toy company with her brother in Wellington, Shropshire, from 1926 to1960. Her dolls have characteristic moulded fabric faces and are marked with a label on one limb.

Wellington chest A narrow CHEST-OF-DRAWERS popular in England and France

Wellington chest, in satin-wood, English c.1840 [H]

from 1820. They have up to twelve drawers and a single locking mechanism, in which a hinged flap runs down one side of the chest and locks over the drawers. See also CAMPAIGN CHEST and SPECIMEN CHEST.

Welsh dresser See DRESSER.

Wemyss ware Distinctive pottery from the Fife Pottery in Kirkcaldy, Scotland (est. *c.*1790). It was run by Robert Methver Heron from 1833–1906, the main period of production of Wemyss ware (named after Wemyss castle, Fife). In 1883 he put Karel Nekola from Bohemia in charge of the painting shop, who introduced the brightly coloured underglaze motifs typical of Wemyss.

Wemyss ware pig by Nekola, c.1930 [J]

Wares include jug-and-basin sets, large pig doorstops, tablewares, inkstands and candlesticks, hand-painted with fruit, cabbage roses, birds and cats. Nekola made commemorative souvenirs for Queen Victoria's Diamond Jubilee and George V's coronation. Some wares were commissioned by Thomas Goode & Co. In 1930 the rights and moulds were sold to the Bovey Tracey pottery, Devon, where Nekola's son Joseph continued to paint traditional Wemyss ware until his death in 1942.

Westerwald potteries A group of German stoneware factories at Adendorf, Grenzau, Grenzhausen and Höhr established in the Middle

Westerwald bulbous tankard, 1691 [J]

Ages in the Rhineland. In the 17th century a distinctive type of jug appeared with oviform body and narrow neck, stamped with reliefs of lion masks, flowers and rosettes and with cobalt blue or manganese purple glaze. They had an extensive export trade, especially with England. Stoneware continued to be made in the area throughout the 19th century and is still made there today.

Whatnot See ÉTAGÈRE.

Wheat-ear motif A symbol of fecundity and fertility since ancient times, the wheat ear was a popular decorative motif from the 17th to the 19th centuries. It was used on glassware and ceramics as well as furniture, particularly chairbacks, and on bread platters and knives.

Wheat ear motif on ale tankard c.1770 [O]

Wheel barometer Invented *c.*1650 by the British scientist Robert Hooke. It comprises a U-shaped tube filled with mercury, with a float attached to a pointer on a dial which measures changes in atmospheric pressure. See also BANJO BAROMETER.

Wheel engraving A technique for decorating glass and metal. The piece is held up to a rotating wheel using discs of stone or copper and a fine abrasive paste to create an incised design. It was known in Roman times, revived by Caspar Lehmann for use on BOHEMIAN GLASS and remained popular until it was superseded by ACID ETCHING.

Wheel lock A gunlock that was the first to strike its own sparks to ignite gunpowder. The mechanism was invented in southern Germany, *c.*1500, and was used until the mid-18th century. A notched steel wheel, held by a spring, is released by the trigger against a flint to create a spark.

Whieldon, Thomas (1719–95) A Staffordshire potter, apprentice to John ASTBURY. From 1740 he made stoneware and agate ware, cauliflower and pineapple-moulded vessels, and animal and human figures, using semi-translucent green and yellow as well as tortoiseshell glazes. In 1749 he employed Josiah SPODE and *c.*1755 was in partnership with Josiah WEDGWOOD.

Whitby jet See JET.

Whitefriars Glassworks vases, 1967–80 [S]

Whitefriars Glassworks A London glasshouse founded in the 17th century. In 1834 it was acquired by James Powell (1774–1840) and was known as James Powell & Sons until 1962, when it reverted to Whitefriars Glassworks before closing in 1980. In the 19th century, production included designs for William MORRIS, windows for Pre-Raphaelite painters and handblown glass in historical styles. In the 20th-century, glass was made in ART DECO designs and innovative coloured and textured glass, designed by Geoffrey Baxter (b.1922) in the 1960s.

White metal See BRITANNIA METAL.

Whitework A technique, known from medieval times, in which white linen thread is embroidered onto a white linen ground. The term also describes SAMPLERS worked solely in white, which often include NEEDLE-LACE techniques.

Wickerwork The weaving of flexible rods or shoots, usually of willow, cane or rattan, known from ancient times. Surviving examples prior to the 17th century are rare. It was fashionable for outdoor use in the 18th century, but achieved greater recognition through the SECESSION designers of the 19th century. LLOYD LOOM created a surge in its popularity from 1920–40.

Wiener Werkstätte (1903–32) Workshops founded in Vienna by Josef HOFFMANN, Koloman MOSER and Fritz Wärndorfer as an association of craftsmen based on C.R. ASHBEE's Guild. By 1910 they had been joined by Joseph Olbrich, Gustav Klimt, Dagobert Peche and Otto Prutscher. The 100 workers (including 40 "masters") made a wide range of furniture, metalwork and glass of progressive design.

Wig aperture An opening in the crown of a BISQUE doll's head into which the PATE is inserted. It allows access for stringing and the insertion of the SLEEPING EYE mechanism.

Wiener Werkstätte knife and fork by Hoffmann, c.1925 [H, for set of 6]

Wig stand A shaped wooden support for storing wigs, made from the 17th to early 19th centuries.

Wilkinson, A.J. Ltd A pottery founded in Burslem, Staffordshire, in 1885, making earthenware and ironstone ornamental pieces and tablewares. It took over the Newport Pottery in 1920 and is best known for Clarice CLIFF's work. In 1964 it was taken over by Midwinter and in 1970 became part of the WEDGWOOD group.

Wilkinson, Norman (1878–1971) An English marine painter, poster artist and printmaker. He illustrated travel posters in the 1920s and 30s for British railway companies. He also developed camouflage techniques during both world wars and painted a series of pictures about the war at sea for the nation.

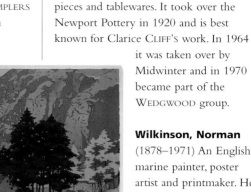

Norman Wilkinson poster, c.1930 [N]

William & Mary style Decorative arts and architecture associated with the reign of William III and Mary II in England (1688–1702). It was influenced by the French LOUIS XIV style due to the HUGUENOT refugees coming to England via the Netherlands (where William ruled as Stadholder). The designer Daniel MAROT created unified schemes of interior decoration featuring motifs such as LAMBREQUINS and ACANTHUS. Developments in furniture included the introduction of BOULLE marquetry, silver furniture and JAPANNING. Huguenot silversmiths introduced new types of decoration, such as CUT-CARD WORK, and new wares, e.g. tureens, ECUELLES and HELMET-SHAPED EWERS.

Willow A flexible and tough wood that was chiefly used in Europe for basket and furniture-making from early times to the present. It was also dyed black to imitate EBONY in the 17th and 18th centuries, for inlay as well as for applied ornament. Willow pegs were also used in early English oak and country furniture.

Willow pattern on a creamware plate,
English early 19th century [R]

Willow pattern A CHINOISERIE design
designed by Thomas MINTON for printing
on ceramics c.1780, probably for the
CAUGHLEY pottery, and soon used by a
large number of STAFFORDSHIRE factories
throughout the 19th and 20th century. It
comprised a willow tree, a Chinese
temple, a bridge with figures on it, a boat,
birds in flight and a distant island.

Wilson, Henry (1864–1934) An English
ARTS AND CRAFTS goldsmith and
metalworker. He used polychrome
enamel in jewellery and *objets d'art*
influenced by ecclesiastic or medieval
style. He employed major Arts and Crafts
figures such as John Paul Cooper and
H.G. Murphy.

Wilton A centre for carpet production in
Wiltshire, England, from the second half
of 19th century and still active today.
After a fire destroyed the AXMINSTER
factory, their looms were transferred to
Wilton in the 1830s. Designs were
inspired by the French carpets of the
period – AUBUSSON and SAVONNERIE –
though the quality and colours were
generally less sophisticated.

Wincanton Delft Pottery Founded in
the small town of Wincanton, near
Bristol, by Nathaniel Ireson (1686–1769)
and Thomas Lindslee (1725–50). Apart

from a few marked pieces, ranging in date
from 1737 (on a plate in Edinburgh
Museum) to 1748 (a jug in the Glaisher
Collection, Cambridge), the
products of this factory
cannot be differentiated
from those of a number
of others. However, a
particular lilac-
manganese
"powdered" border
with reserved panels
decorated in blue is
often attributed to it.

Winchester, Oliver F.
(1810–80) A US gunmaker and
entrepreneur. He was a successful
shirt manufacturer who invested
his profits in the Volcanic Repeating Arms
Company. He hired
B. Tyler Henry as his expert designer and
in 1866 the first Winchester repeating
rifle was born. Operated by a lever and
fed by a tubular magazine, the Winchester
rapidly became an American icon and
was in heavy demand during the Civil
War. In 1866 the company was renamed
the Winchester Repeating Arms
Company. It is still in production today.

Wincanton delftware
plate, c.1745 [L]

Winchester 32 calibre lever action rifle, 1873 [O]

Winding mechanism Mechanical
clocks and watches rely on a spring to
power the MOVEMENT. The earliest watch
springs were wound directly with a key.
In the 1650s the FUSEE was introduced,
connected to the spring barrel by a cord
or chain. This remained until 1822 when
Thomas Prest invented the KEYLESS
winding mechanism.

Window seat A bench, usually with low
arms and sometimes upholstered, that was
designed to fit into the recess beneath a
window. Fashionable from c.1825,
especailly in the US, the window seat
most often stood on high legs or scrolled
DOLPHIN supports.

Windsor chair A provincial wooden chair
with the legs, arms and spindle back
dowelled into the shaped seat. Made in
Britain from the early 18th century,
they were traditionally created
by wood-turners using ash,
yew, beech and birch,
with an elm seat. Early
examples were painted
and intended for
outdoor use. So-named
because they were said
to have originated
round Windsor and the
Thames Valley, the main
centre of the industry was High
Wycombe, Buckinghamshire,
although the form was adopted
for provincial chairs throughout
Britain and the US. Since the
late 19th century, Windsor
chairs and their variant
styles have been mass-
produced.

Windsor armchair,
c.1880 [K]

Wine cooler A container, made from the
15th century, in silver, wood with a lead
liner (CELLARET), or porcelain, in which
bottles of wine may be stood in ice. In
English porcelain they were generally of a
deep U-shape with small handles. In
SÈVRES they might be oval and were
called *seaux à bouteilles* or *seaux à liqueurs
ovales* to cool pairs of liqueur bottles.

Wine funnel Made from ceramics but more commonly silver and plated wares, these funnels had a strainer bowl or provision for a muslin strainer and were used for decanting wine. They were made in quantity from *c*.1775 to 1825, but earlier examples are known.

Silver wine funnel, English 1810 [K]

Wineglass cooler See MONTEITH.

Silver wine label, English 1837 [R]

Wine label (or bottle ticket) A small label made from *c*.1745 in vast numbers and in an infinite variety of forms in silver, Old Sheffield plate, enamels and porcelain. They hung by a chain or wire around the neck of a bottle or decanter to display its contents, e.g. sherry or rum.

Wine table (or hunt table) A small occasional table in the form of a tray on a stand for the informal serving of wine, produced from the mid-18th century. It was usually a semi-circular horseshoe shape, sometimes with drop leaves. It was fitted with a pivoted arm and coaster that could swing across to pass the bottles to any point of its radius.

Wine taster A small silver and parcel-gilt saucer-like bowl, usually with two wire handles and with a polished domed centre, for tasting and examining the clarity and colour of wine. It is the English form of a TASTEVIN. Sometimes decorated with punched work, wine tasters date from the 17th century.

Wine waiter An open wagon or case supported on legs, designed to contain bottles or decanters of spirits or wine. Possibly of Irish origin, the wine waiter was sometimes fitted with a CELLARET and castors to enable easy movement about the room.

Wing chair A fully upholstered armchair with "wings" added at the sides of the chair back to keep out draughts, originally designed for the eldery and infirm. Derived from French sleeping chairs with adjustable backs dating to the 1670s, they were first made in England in the late 17th century and described in contemporary inventories as "easie" chairs. They have been made ever since.

Winston, Harry (1896–1978) A US jeweller, one of the most successful of the 20th century. He worked in New York City where he quickly established a reputation for buying antique estate jewellery, remounting the stones into superb new settings and selling to a clientele that included royalty, film stars and millionaires.

Winter, Friedrich (*fl*.1685–*c*.1710) A German glass-engraver working at the end of the 17th and beginning of the 18th centuries. He used a water-powered cutting mill to produce cameo reliefs (HOCHSCHNITT) in bold baroque designs, exclusively for his patron Graf Christopher Schaffgotsch.

Wirework A technique whereby small articles such as fruit baskets or toast racks are formed from wire, usually silver or gold, of different sizes bent into a lattice.

Wirkkala, Tapio (1915–85) A Finnish designer in wood and glass who worked for factories in Finland and other European countries, such as the ROSENTHAL porcelain factory in Bavaria and the CHRISTOFLE silver factory in France. His work is characterized by a respect for the intrinsic nature of his materials.

Wistar, Caspar (1696–1752) A German-born American glass-maker, founder of the SOUTH JERSEY GLASSHOUSE at Wistarburg, New Jersey, in 1739. Products resembled German WALDGLAS, and are difficult to attribute. The works closed in 1780 but former employees, the Stanger Brothers, established an important works in nearby Glassboro, New Jersey.

Wit, Federick de (1630–1706) A prominent map engraver and publisher in Amsterdam, Federick de Wit produced sea charts, world ATLASES and "town books" of European town and city plans. He was known for the high quality of his engravings and his use of colour.

WMF (Württemberg Metalwork Factory) A German firm founded in 1853 by Daniel Straub in Geislingen but renamed in 1888 as WMF as an amalgamation of several firms. Particularly known for its ART NOUVEAU metalware and the Art Nouveau maiden that decorated some of the most popular pieces. In the 1920s it introduced ART DECO style "Ikora" metalware and a range of glass including

WMF electroplate tea and coffee set, c.1900 [K]

iridescent "Myra" glass and heavier "Ikora" glass decorated with colours and bubbles. WMF is still producing metal-ware but glass production ceased in 1984.

Wogden, Robert (1734–1813) An English gunmaker active from 1748, famous for his high quality and innovative FLINTLOCK DUELLING PISTOLS.

Sauceboat painted in underglaze blue
with a typical chinoiserie design of a fishing scene,
c.1760 [o]

Plate decorated in the embossed
"Blind Earl" pattern, made for the blind
Earl of Coventry, c.1770 [L]

Plate transfer-printed with the
popular "Pine Cone" pattern,
reintroduced in the 1920s,
c.1770 [Q]

Worcester porcelain factory

Founded in Worcester, England, in 1751, by Dr John Wall and the apothecary William Davis, this company has survived the turmoil of two and a half centuries of change.

An English success

The cathedral city of Worcester was not perhaps the most obvious location for a major British porcelain manufacturer to be established, because there were no local deposits of clay or coal; these had to be brought in by river. Nevertheless, it was there in 1751 that Dr John Wall, "an eminent Physician", and the apothecary William Davis, with the financial help of some local businessmen, invested in a new porcelain factory. After some initial failures, the partners also bought the BRISTOL porcelain factory, giving them a source of SOAPSTONE and new kilns, and by 1752 they were making PORCELAIN. They had to compete with Chinese imports and the London factories of BOW and CHELSEA, and started by making useful wares, decorated in UNDERGLAZE blue in Chinese style.

The use of soapstone gave Worcester porcelain great durability and the ability to withstand hot liquids; a problem that other English factories had difficulty in overcoming. A great variety of shapes – creamboats, sauceboats, bowls, mugs and tea wares – were produced and Worcester also copied the Chinese wares that were arriving in England in great quantities. Following the custom of the time, much porcelain was sold by auction in London and the first recorded auction sale, of about 40,000 pieces, took place on 15 March 1774. In its first ten years, Worcester produced wares that were finely potted and decorated in both underglaze blue and colours. They restricted themselves to what they knew they could sell, making a limited range of plates, dishes and vases, but not figures.

From the mid-18th century, Worcester pioneered the technique of TRANSFER-PRINTING on porcelain. Two of the original backers, Joseph Holdship and his brother Richard, made some early attempts. The engraver Robert HANCOCK probably produced some of the earliest prints (called "Smoky Primitives") before his arrival in Worcester in 1756. His prints of rustic scenes, inspired by contemporary paintings, have great

The Stinton family

A typical early 20th-century Royal Worcester Porcelain Company piece is an item decorated by John Stinton (1854–1956), his brother James (1870–1961) or his son Harry (1883–1962). John and Harry painted scenes of Highland cattle against a backdrop of atmospheric mountains and brooding skies. Neither are known to have visited Scotland; their subjects were copied from postcards. James Stinton's pieces often depict game birds.

Vase painted by Harry Stinton, 1925 [J]

charm and appear on a wide variety of wares until his departure from Worcester in 1774. In the 1760s Worcester also made polychrome designs in Chinese FAMILLE-ROSE style to compete with imported MEISSEN wares. They also introduced coloured grounds, such as deep blue and SCALE blue.

In spite of a severe economic recession in England in the early 1770s, the Worcester factory survived, taking on new painters such as John Donaldson and Jefferyes Hamett O'Neale. Worcester porcelain was also decorated in London by James Giles for a short period. The defection of Thomas Turner in the mid-1770s to run his factory at CAUGHLEY was a blow, but Worcester struggled on until it was bought by Thomas Flight in 1783 for his sons. Young John Flight managed the company through the next difficult seven or eight years and abandoned the unprofitable blue and white in favour of the latest French styles.

In 1789 the CHAMBERLAIN family, who had supervised the decoration at Worcester, also left to set up their own business. When John Flight died in 1791 his brother Joseph was joined in 1792 by Martin Barr and the firm traded as Flight & Barr, making the best products for the top end of the market. Rich Regency designs enhanced with the finest gilding attracted royalty and the nobility. Although initially successful, the factory once again fell behind current fashion in the 1820s and 1830s. In 1840 it was forced to merge with its rivals and the partnership traded as Chamberlain & Co. When W. H. Kerr, a china dealer from Dublin, joined the factory in 1852, the firm was briefly named Kerr & Binns, but in 1863 was reborn as the Worcester Royal Porcelain Company.

Products of the Victorian period were elaborate and often richly gilded and painted. Reticulated pieces by George Owen (1845–1917) imitated pierced ivory. The 1870s and 1880s expressed the fashion for JAPONAISERIE, for example in figures modelled by James Hadley (1837–1903). After 1901 there was a greater output of everyday wares, but grand painted porcelains such as those by the Stinton family were still made. The great achievement of the 1930s and 1940s was the production of a series of ceramic sculptures that enjoyed widespread commercial success. Outstanding amongst these are the American and English bird figures modelled by Dorothy Doughty (1892–1962), and the equestrian portraits by the sculptor Doris Lindner. In 1978 the company merged with SPODE. It continues its tradition of producing high-quality porcelain, in both historical and contemporary styles.

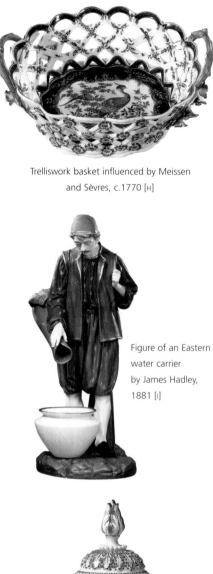

Trelliswork basket influenced by Meissen and Sèvres, c.1770 [H]

Figure of an Eastern water carrier by James Hadley, 1881 [I]

Reticulated vase and cover by George Owen, imitating Chinese pierced ivory, c.1910 [D]

Worcester marks

Pieces exhibit an array of marks from the numerous periods:

751–74	Dr Wall	1813–40	Flight, Barr & Barr
1774–83	Davis	1840–52	Chamberlain & Co.
1783–92	Flight	1852–62	Kerr & Binns
1792–1804	Flight & Barr	From 1863	Worcester Royal Porcelain Co.
1804–13	Barr, Flight & Barr		

1783–92   1852–62   From 1863

Wolfsohn, Helena (d.*c.*1872) A porcelain decorator whose workshop in Dresden (est.1843) used seconds from MEISSEN and white porcelain from other factories. One of her specialities was imitating the Meissen pattern of WATTEAU FIGURES alternating with flower patterns. Her workshop marked wares with the Meissen AR until 1881, when stopped by legal action; after that a crown over a D was used. The firm was bought by a Walter Stephan in 1919 but little is known of its later history.

Porcelain group by Wolfsohn, late 19th century [R]

Wood, Aaron (1717–85) A Staffordshire ceramics modeller, brother of Ralph WOOD I. He worked for WHIELDON and other factories and made models for household wares and ornaments.

Wood, Enoch (1759–1840) The son of Aaron WOOD. He ran a factory with his cousin Ralph WOOD II from 1783–90 and with James CALDWELL from 1790–1818. His wares included blue printed ware, BASALTES, and JASPER WARE. He was joined by his sons until his death; they continued the business until 1846.

Wood, Ralph I (1715–72) The most important member of a distinguished family of Staffordshire potters. He owned the Hilltop factory, Burslem, and made figures – some modelled by John Voyez, others adapted from the Belgian modeller Paul-Louis Cyfflé – as well as TOBY JUGS and models such as the "Vicar" and "Moses".

Wood, Ralph II (1748–95) The son of Ralph Wood I, who inherited his factory and continued making figures. He initiated the use of ENAMEL COLOURS.

Woodcut A type of printing that originated in the East *c.*860. It developed in Europe *c.*1400 and was the earliest way of printing illustrations. The image is cut in low relief on the wood with a sharp knife. Ink is applied to the remaining relief image and the paper is pressed down onto it.

Wooden doll Dolls have made from wood by most civilizations since earliest times. In early English examples the heads and torsos are turned or carved out of one piece of wood to which arms are nailed or tied and legs are jointed. In the 18th century, doll-carving centres emerged in Austria and Germany at GRÖDNERTAL, SONNEBERG, Oberammergau and Berchtesgaden. Mass production resulted in the PENNY WOODEN.

Wool picture A picture in which the chief embroidery thread is wool. Good examples of the genre are 19th-century pictures of boats embroidered by sailors and BERLIN WOOLWORK pictures popular from the mid-19th century.

Worcester porcelain factory See pp.406–07.

Staffordshire figure designed by Ralph Wood II, c.1785 [C]

Mahogany work table, English c.1790 [G]

Work (or sewing) table A small low table used by ladies to store needlework, made from the mid-18th century and popular in France, England and the US. They were fitted with drawers or shelves and a pouch for silks, bobbins and needles. Some had hinged lids, others a hinged flap top and pullout sides.

Wreathing Spiral marks in the "paste" of a ceramic BODY made by the vessel twisting in the heat of the kiln, particularly seen on BRISTOL hard-paste porcelain.

Wrigglework A form of engraved zigzag or wriggly lines as border decoration on metals, particularly PEWTER and SILVER boxes and HOLLOWWARE. It was widely used in the NEO-CLASSICAL period.

Wright, Russel (1904–76) A US designer who, with his wife Mary, championed an informal approach to design. His furniture, e.g. the "Pony Skin chair", was deliberately more comfortable and organic than the International Modern style. He is best known for his ceramic dinnerware "American Modern", made from 1939 by the STEUBENVILLE POTTERY, which sold in huge quantities. He later designed "Casual China", which was promoted for its durability; if it chipped or broke it was replaced free of charge. "Flair", his blown glass range, was produced by Imperial Glass (est. 1901) in 1949.

Russel Wright jug, 1939 [S]

Wristwatch Although earlier bracelet-type watches exist, the wristwatch did not begin to supersede the POCKET WATCH until World War I. It was promoted as a sports watch by such makers as CARTIER. The basic design of watch with strap or bracelet has changed little in 100 years.

Frank Lloyd Wright (1867–1959)

One of the giants of 20th-century Western architecture, Wright believed in designing a house and its interior as an entity that was integrated with its surroundings. His contribution to the decorative arts in the first half of the 20th century includes an influential range of furniture, stained glass, ceramics and metalwork.

Cherrywood and stained walnut table, 1899 [H]

From architecture to furniture

Wright studied architecture and, briefly, engineering and worked in the Chicago practice of Louis Sullivan, himself one of the finest American architects of his generation. For Adler & Sullivan, Wright became the practice specialist in designing homes. In 1893 he started his own practice in Chicago and evolved his own particular style that became the cornerstone of the so-called Prairie School. In this period, at the turn of the century, Wright designed houses mostly round Chicago and particularly the suburb of Oak Park. Influenced by the surrounding prairie and his appreciation of Japanese design, many of these houses have a dominant horizontal line that mirrors the contours of the land. His stained glass designs for the "Prairie Houses" also have echoes of the Japanese paper screen. His reputation as a furniture designer derives largely from the pieces he designed for these buildings. Wright felt that a house had its own "grammar" and that this influenced every aspect of it.

Oak side chair covered in yellow oil cloth for the Imperial Hotel, Tokyo, c.1916–22 [G]

Wright was a major supporter of the Chicago Arts and Crafts Society that he helped to found in 1897. His interior designs at this time were in the ARTS AND CRAFTS style, and his high-backed chairs were probably influenced by British examples. Where he, and American Arts and Crafts in general, differed from the British movement was in the use of machines. Craftsmen in Britain were opposed to machinery; in the US they took the view that, if used judiciously, machines could ease the heavy labour, leaving the artisan more time to use finer skills. Wright positively endorsed the use of machinery and designed for mass production. Along with other leading designers of his generation (including Charles Rennie MACKINTOSH and Josef HOFFMANN) his work relied on geometric forms and this, coupled with his positive attitude toward the machine, anticipated the MODERN MOVEMENT.

As Wright's reputation grew so did the range of his commissions. His early liking for geometric forms resulted in cube-shaped and polygonal furniture. In 1916 the Imperial Hotel in Tokyo was built, for which he designed the furniture and tableware (made by NORITAKE). This was followed by the stunning house Fallingwater in Bear Run, Pennsylvania, built over a waterfall. From 1936–39 he masterminded the S.C. Johnson Administration Building in Racine, Wisconsin. His final building was the Solomon R. Guggenheim Museum in New York, with its distinctive spiral focal point.

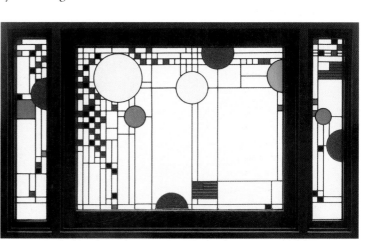

Stained glass window based on the flags, balloons and ticker tape of a parade, made for the Avery Coonley Playhouse, Riverside, Illinois, 1912 [A]

Writing table A flat-topped desk, inspired by the French BUREAU PLAT. Various types were made, with drawers and with baize or leather-covered tops. Desks with two pedestal chests of drawers came into use in the late 17th century and were popular from the 1740s. Writing tables of this and other types continued to be made through the 19th century to the present. See also CARLTON HOUSE DESK and PEDESTAL DESK.

Wrotham pottery
A small village pottery in Kent, England, making simple SLIPWARE in the late 17th century, with trailed decoration in yellow on a dark brown ground. Potters include Henry Ifield, George Richardson, John Green and Nicholas Hubble. Most objects are mugs and TYGS.

Wrotham pottery tyg, c.1690 [C]

Wrythen ale glass, early 19th century [O]

Wrythening A type of decoration consisting of diagonally twisted ribbing, used on early Venetian glass and 18th-century ALE GLASSES. It was revived in the late 19th century, notably by the WHITEFRIARS GLASSWORKS. Wrythening was also used in metalwork, for example to make cutlery handles.

Wucai ("five coloured") A type of decoration on Chinese porcelain related to the earlier DOUCAI style but with washes of under-glaze blue and overglaze coloured enamels. Outlines are usually in red or black. The finest pieces date from the WANLI period.

Württemberg Metalwork Factory See WMF.

X

X-chair Chairs with X-shaped frames were known in Ancient Egypt, Rome and Greece. A type of folding chair with a frame like an "X" viewed from the front or the side originated in medieval Italy. Also known as a Savonarola or Dante chair in Italy, or a Luther chair in Germany, the X-chair was a light and practical form that spread through Renaissance Europe. In England, the GLASTONBURY CHAIR made an X-shape by crossing the front and back legs, while in Spain X-chairs were inlaid with ivory and metals in Moorish designs.

The woodwork was nearly always completely covered with silk or velvet, and the seat was made up of loose cushions resting on webbing between the side rails of the frames. The form was revived in the NEO-CLASSICAL period and features in Thomas SHERATON's *Cabinet Directory*. It continued through the 19th century as a folding portable chair, for use during campaigns or other outdoor pursuits. (See also THEBES STOOL.)

X-frame campaign chair, Italian c.1870 [L]

Y

Yangshao culture The Neolithic culture in China *c.*5000–*c.*1500 BC, noted for coiled bulbous earthenware in red, black and white, with impressed cord patterns or purple or black geometric designs, possibly for gifts for the dead.

Yew A hard and close-grained wood of reddish-brown colour, used from an early period for small work and TREEN and for the backs of WINDSOR CHAIRS.

Yingqing (Qingbai) Early Chinese porcelain made in the JINGDEZHEN area. Literally "shadowy blue", from the bluish tinge of the glaze, it was introduced in the TANG and made throughout the SONG dynasty. Wares included bowls and vases with naturalistic carved, moulded or incised decoration.

Yixing Chinese kilns in the Jiangsu province dating back to the SONG DYNASTY. They produced red and brown STONEWARES, tea wares and other small items, usually unglazed, known in China as *zisha* ware. From the 17th century they were exported to Europe.

Yomut A prolific carpet-weaving tribal group in the 19th century from West Turkestan. Designs often have geometric motifs. Their distinguishing GUL often has hooked edges, arranged in diagonals. Colours include shades of brown, aubergine with bright reds, yellows, blue and ivory.

Yongzheng porcelain Chinese porcelain made in the reign of the QING emperor Yongzheng (1723–35), including some of the most technically perfect Chinese porcelain. SONG DYNASTY and MING DYNASTY shapes and styles were revived, REIGN MARKS were written using seal (*zhuanshu*) script alongside the regular (*kaishu*) script. The FAMILLE ROSE palette was widely adopted.

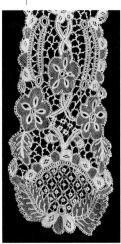

Youghal Irish NEEDLELACE inspired by a fragment of Italian lace, unpicked and copied at the Convent School, Youghal, creating an industry at the time of the potato famine in the mid-19th century.

Yougal needlelace tie, c.1880 [s]

Ysart, Salvador (& Sons) (1878–1955) A Spanish-born glass-maker who with his son Paul created MONART glass at the MONCRIEFF GLASSWORKS. In 1948, with his sons Augustine and Vincent, he set up Ysart Bros, Perth, Scotland, making "Vasart", a coloured glass range. Specialities were vases, bowls, miniature baskets and some paperweights. The company became Strathearn Glass in 1965 and production of coloured glass stopped in the late 1970s.

Yu (or you) A Chinese bronze jar and cover with bulbous body and swing handle, made for carrying wine in the 13th–9th centuries BC. See also SHANG DYNASTY.

Yuan The Chinese Mongol dynasty (1260–1368) founded by Kublai Khan. Production of ceramics at JINGDEZHEN flourished, with CELADON wares exported to the Middle East, and the introduction of UNDERGLAZE blue.

Yuruk (Yoruk) A widespread Turkish nomadic tribal group, weavers of rugs whose design repertoire is close to those of the CAUCASUS. Designs are essentially geometric, based on stylized floral forms, with sombre colour combinations. Rugs tend to be relatively narrow.

Z

Zebra wood A general term used for several tropical hardwoods with vivid and pronounced dark brown stripes. Zebra wood was used mainly as a veneer in the late 18th and early 19th centuries.

Ziegler A British/Swiss firm making carpets in Sultanabad in north-west Persia, c.1885. It responded to the needs of European clients and created a new and distinctive style. The carpets tend to have large-scale motifs in a vine lattice, usually with an overall repeat pattern within large borders. Terracotta shades and ivory are most frequently seen for the main field colour and pale or dark blue for the borders. They are not finely woven, but tend to use lustrous fine-quality wool.

Zircon A gemstone with a high degree of brilliance, which in its colourless state can be mistaken for diamond. Blue and brown zircons were used in late 19th-century jewellery, particularly in bold rings and stylized spray brooches in the 1940s–50s.

Zoetrope (Greek: "life" and "turn") An optical toy also called the "Wheel of Life", one of the forerunners of the art of animation. It was first described by William George Horner in 1834, who called it a "Daedatelus", but was not properly introduced until the 1860s by the French inventor Pierre Desvignes, who named it. It is a modification of the slotted disc device in which a series of images on a strip of paper

Yuruk rug, late 19th century [c]

are placed in hollow drum that can be rotated about a vertical axis. The images are viewed through slots in the side of the drum. The eye sees a succession of momentary images, which together give the impression of movement.

Zürich pottery and porcelain factory Started in 1763 as a joint stock company in Schönen on Lake Zurich, directed by Adam Spengler (d.1790) who had been at HÖCHST. At first it made FAIENCE and SOFT-PASTE porcelain. From c.1765 it made finely painted tablewares in HARD-PASTE, typically with elaborate scrolled handles. The chief modeller in the 1780s was Valentin Sonnenschein (1749–1828), who created charming models of Swiss people. A series of figures of street vendors was called "The Cries of Zürich". The painter Heinrich Fussli worked at the factory from 1771–81. In 1793 the factory was bought by Spengler's son-in-law, Mathias Nehracher (d.1800), the first of several changes of ownership until closure in 1897. Production in the 19th century was of faience and cream-coloured earthenware. The factory mark was a "Z".

Zurich porcelain figure of a sportswoman, c.1770 [i]

Zwischengoldglas (German: "gold between glass") A type of decorative glass in which gold leaf was applied to the outside of a glass, engraved and then sandwiched between two layers of clear glass by a close fitting outer sleeve, which was sealed at the top and bottom. The technique, developed in Bohemia and popular in the 1730s–40s, was used primarily on beakers and goblets. It was revived at the end of the 18th century by Johann Josef MILDNER.

Further reading

General and Miscellaneous

Fleming, John and Hugh Honour *Penguin Dictionary of Decorative Arts* Viking, London, 1989

Lewis, P. and G. Darley *Dictionary of Ornament* Cameron & Hollis/David & Charles, Newton Abbot, UK, 1986

Mallalieu, Huon *The Illustrated History of Antiques* Running Press, Philadelphia, Pa, 1999

Miller, J. (ed.) *Miller's Antiques Encyclopedia* Mitchell Beazley, London, 1998

Miller, J. *A Closer Look at Antiques* Marshall Publishing, London, 2000

Thornton, Peter *Authentic Decor: the domestic interior 1620-1920* Viking, New York, 1984

Trench, Lucy (ed.) *Materials and Techniques in the Decorative Arts* John Murray, London, 2000

Turk, Frank A. *Japanese Objets d'Art* Sterling Publications, New York, 1962

Turner, J. (ed.) *The Dictionary of Art* Macmillan, London, 1996

Waterer, John D. *Leather Craftsmanship* G. Bell & Sons, London, 1968

Wright, Michael, ed. *Treasures in your home* Reader's Digest, London, 1993

Cameras and Optical instruments

Matanle, Ivor *Collecting and Using Classic Cameras*, Thames & Hudson, London, 1992

McKeown, James M. and Joan C. McKeown, *Collector's Guide to Kodak Cameras* Centennial Photo Service, Grantsburg, Wis., 1981

Sartorius, Ghester *Identifying Leica Cameras: The Complete Pocket Guide to Buying and Selling Leicas*, Amphoto, New York, 1997

Carpets

Bennett, Ian *Rugs and carpets of the world* Grange, London, 1997

Day, Susan (ed.) *Great carpets of the world* Thames & Hudson, London, 1996

Middleton, Andrew *Rugs and carpets: techniques, traditions and designs* Mitchell Beazley, London, 1996

Wright, Richard E. *Caucasian carpets and covers: the weaving culture* Hali: Lawrence King, London, 1995

Ceramics

Atterbury, Paul et al. *Twentieth-century ceramics* Mitchell Beazley, London, 1999

Battie, David *Sotheby's Concise Encyclopedia of Porcelain* Conran Octopus, London, 1990

Boger, Louise *The Dictionary of World Pottery and Porcelain* Scribners, New York, 1971

Bourne, Jonathan et al. *Lacquer – An International History and Collector's Guide* Crowood Press, Marlborough, UK, 1984

Charleston, Robert *World Ceramics – An Illustrated History* Hamlyn, London, 1968

Cushion, J.P. *Handbook of Pottery & Porcelain Marks*, 4th ed., Faber & Faber, London, 1980

Frelinghuysen, Alice Cooney *American Porcelain 1770–1920* The Metropolitan Museum of Art, New York, 1989

Godden, Geoffrey *Encyclopaedia of British Pottery and Porcelain Marks*, rev. ed. Barrie & Jenkins, London, 1991

Godden, Geoffrey *Godden's Guide to European Porcelain* Barrie & Jenkins, London, 1993

Gompertz, G. S. and G. M. Gompertz *Chinese Celadon Wares* Faber & Faber, London, 1958

Hansford, Howard *A Glossary of Chinese Art and Archaeology* The China Society, London, 1972

Harris, Victor *Japanese Imperial Craftsmen – Meiji Art from the Khalili Collection* British Museum Press, London, 1994

Jenyns, Soame *Japanese Pottery* Faber & Faber, London, 1971

Kerr, Rose *Chinese Ceramics – Porcelain of Qing Dynasty 1644–1911* Victoria and Albert Museum, London, 1986

Kovel, Ralph and Terry Kovel *Kovels' American Art Pottery* Crown Publishers Inc., New York, 1993

Lawrence, Louis *Satsuma; masterpieces of the world's important collections* Dauphin Publishing, London, 1991

Levin, Elaine *The History of American Ceramics* Harry N. Abrams Inc., New York, 1988

Lewis, Griselda *A Collector's History of English Pottery* Antique Collectors' Club, Woodbridge, UK, 1999

Manners, Errol *Ceramics Sourcebook – A Visual Guide to a Century of Antiques* Chartwell Books, Secaucus, NJ, 1997

Medley, Margaret *Illustrated Catalogue of Ming and Qing Monochrome Wares* University of London, London, 1973

Medley, Margaret *Illustrated Catalogue of Ming Polychrome Wares* University of London, London, 1978

Medley, Margaret *Illustrated Dictionary of Celadon Wares* University of London, London, 1997

Reilly, Robin and George Savage *The Dictionary of Wedgwood* Antique Collectors' Club, Woodbridge, UK, 1980

Rinaldi, Maura *Kraak Porcelain* Bamboo, London, 1989

Sandon, John *Antique Porcelain* Antique Collectors' Club, Woodbridge, UK, 1997

Sandon, John *Dictionary of Worcester Porcelain* Antique Collectors' Club, Woodbridge, UK, 1993

Savage, George and Harold Newman *An Illustrated Dictionary of Ceramics* Thames & Hudson, London, 1985

Schiffer, Nancy *Japanese Porcelain 1800–1950* Schiffer Publications, Atglen, Pa, 1999

Scott, Rosemary E. *Elegant Form and Harmonious Decoration – Four Dynasties of Jingdezhen Porcelain* Suntree Publishing, London, 1992

Scott, Rosemary E. and Stacey Pierson *Flawless Porcelains: Imperial Ceramics from the Reign of the Chenghua Emperor* Percival David Foundation of Chinese Art: Suntree Publishing, London 1995

Stanley-Baker, Joan *Japanese Art* Thames & Hudson, London, 1984

Vainker, S. J. *Chinese Pottery and Porcelain – From Prehistory to the Present* British Museum Press, London, 1991

Watson, William *The Great Japan Exhibition – Art of the Edo Period 1600–1868* Royal Academy of Arts: Weidenfeld & Nicolson, London, 1981

Clocks and Watches

Allix, Charles and Peter Bonnert *Carriage Clocks* Antique Collectors' Club, Woodbridge, UK, 1974.

Bailey, Chris H. *Two hundred years of American clocks and watches* Prentice-Hall, Englewood Cliffs, NJ, 1975

Baillie, G.H. *Watchmakers & Clockmakers of the World* vol.1. N.A.G. Press, London, 1947 (and later editions)

Ball, Robert W.D. *American shelf and wall clocks: a pictorial history for collectors* Schiffer Publications, Atglen, Pa, 1999

Barder, Richard *The Georgian Bracket Clock* Antique Collectors' Club, Woodbridge, UK, 1993

Dawson, Percy G., C.B. Drover and D.W. Parkes *Early English Clocks* Antique Collectors' Club, Woodbridge, UK, 1982

Faber, Edward *American wristwatches: five decades of style and design* Schiffer Publications, Westchester, Pa, 1988

Harris, Henry Gordon *Nineteenth-century American clocks* Emerson Books, Buchanan, New York, 1981

Lee, R.A. *The Knibb Family* Manor House Press, Byfleet, UK, 1964

Lengelle-Tardy *French Clocks from their origin to the present* Tardy, Paris, 1949 (and later editions)

Loomes, Brian *Watchmakers & Clockmakers of the World*, vol.2. N.A.G. Press, Colchester, UK, 1976 (and later editions)

Ord-Hume, Arthur *The Musical Clock* Mayfield Books, Ashbourne, UK, 1995

Roberts, Derek *British Longcase Clocks* Schiffer Publications, Westchester, Pa, 1990

Roberts, Derek *Continental and American skeleton clocks* Schiffer Publications, Westchester, Pa, 1989

Roberts, Derek *Mystery, Novelty and Fantasy Clocks* Schiffer Publications, Atglen, Pa, 1999

Robinson, Tom *The Longcase Clock* Antique Collectors' Club, Woodbridge, UK, 1981

Rose, Ronald *English Dial Clocks* Antique Collectors' Club, Woodbridge, UK, 1978 (and a later edition)

Royer-Collard, F. B. *Skeleton Clocks* N.A.G. Press, Colchester, UK, 1969 (and a later edition)

Symonds, R.W. *Thomas Tompion* Batsford, London, 1951

Thorpe, Nicholas *The French Marble Clock* N.A.G. Press, Colchester, UK, 1990

White, George *English Lantern Clocks* Antique Collectors' Club, Woodbridge, UK, 1989

Dolls and Teddy Bears

Beckett, Alison *Collecting Teddy Bears & Dolls: The Facts at your Fingertips* Miller's/Reed International, London, 1996

Goodfellow, Caroline *The Ultimate Doll Book* Dorling Kindersley, London, 1993

Kay, Hilary *Antiques Roadshow Pocket Guide to Dolls, Toys & Games* BBC Books, London, 1995

King, Constance *The Century of the Teddy Bear* Antique Collectors' Club, Woodbridge, UK, 1997

Furniture

Aronson, J. *The Encyclopedia of Furniture* Batsford, London, 1996

Beard, G. *The National Trust Book of English Furniture* Penguin, Harmondsworth, UK, 1986

Beard, G. *Upholsterers and Interior Furnishing in England, 1530–1840* Yale University Press, New Haven and London, 1997

Bly, J. *Discovering English Furniture* Shire Publications, Princes Risborough, UK, 1993

Chinnery, V. *Oak Furniture* Antique Collectors' Club, Woodbridge, UK, 1986

Collard, F. *Regency Furniture* Antique Collectors' Club, Woodbridge, UK, 1995

Cooper, Jeremy *Victorian and Edwardian Furniture and Interiors* Thames & Hudson, London, 1987

Dallas Museum of Art, *China and Glass in America 1880–1980* Harry N. Abrams Inc., New York, 2000

Davidson, R. *Miller's Furniture Antiques Checklist* Mitchell Beazley, London, 1994

Edwards, Ralph *The Dictionary of English Furniture from the Middle Ages to the Late Georgian Period I–III* Antique Collectors' Club, Woodbridge, UK, 1983

Edwards, Ralph *The Shorter Dictionary of English Furniture* Country Life, London, 1964

Fastnedge, R. *Sheraton Furniture* Antique Collectors' Club, Woodbridge, UK, 1983

Filbee, M. *Dictionary of Country Furniture* The Connoisseur, London, 1977

Fry, P. S. *The Handbook of Antique Furniture* Barrie & Jenkins, London, 1992

Gloag, J. *A Short Dictionary of Furniture* (revised edition) Allen & Unwin, London, 1969

Greene, Jeffrey P. *American Furniture of the 18th Century* Taunton Press, Newtown, CT, 1996

Heckscher, Morrison H. *American Furniture in the Metropolitan Museum of Art* Metropolitan Museum of Art/Random House, New York, 1985

Hurst, Roland C. and Jonathan Prown *Southern Furniture 1680–1830: The Colonial Williamsburg Collection* Harry N. Abrams Inc., New York, 1997

Jarry, M. *Chinoiserie* Vendome, New York, Sotheby's, London, 1981

Jervis, S. *The Penguin Dictionary of Design and Designers* Allen Lane, London, 1984

Johnson, Peter *The Phillips Guide to Chairs* Merehurst Press, London, 1993

Joy, E. *English Furniture 1800–1851* Ward Lock, London, 1977

Morley, John *The History of Furniture: Twenty-Five Centuries of Style and Design in the Western Tradition*, Bulfinch Press, Boston, 1999

Oates, Phyllis Bennett *The Story of Western Furniture* Herbert Press, London, 1993

Payne, C. (ed.) *Sotheby's Concise Encyclopedia of Furniture* Conran Octopus, London, 1989

Philp, P., G. Walkling and J. Bly *Antique Furniture Expert* Century, London, 1991

Pradère, A. *French Furniture Makers* Sotheby's, London, 1989

Riccardi-Cubbit, Monique *The Art of the Cabinet* Thames & Hudson, London, 1992

Sack, Albert *The New Fine Points of Furniture – Early American* Crown Publishers, New York, 1993

Sassone, Adriana Boidi et al. *Furniture from Rococo to Art Deco*, Evergreen/Benedikt Taschen Verlag, Cologne, 1988

Strange, Thomas *English Furniture: Decoration, Woodwork and Allied Arts* Studio Arts, London, 1986

Symonds, R.W. *Masterpieces of English Furniture and Clocks* Studio Arts, London, 1986

Thornton, Peter *Form and Decoration: Innovation in the Decorative Arts, 1470–1870* Weidenfeld & Nicolson, London, 1998

Thornton, Peter *Seventeenth Century Interior Decoration in England, France and Holland* Yale University Press, New Haven, 1978

Ward, Gerald W.R. *American Case Furniture* Yale University Art Gallery, New Haven, 1988

Yorke, James *English Furniture* Gallery Books, New York, 1990

Glass

Arwas, V. *Glass: Art Nouveau to Art Deco* Academy Editions, London, 1977

Battie, D. and S. Cottle (eds) *Sotheby's Concise Encyclopedia of Glass* Sotheby's, London, 1991

Elville, E.M. *The Collector's Dictionary of Glass* Country Life, London, 1969

Newman, H. *An Illustrated Dictionary of Glass* Thames & Hudson, London, 1977

Palmer, Arlene *Glass in Early America* Winterthur Museum, Delaware/W. W. Norton, New York, 1993

Polak, A. *Glass: Its Makers and Its Public* Weidenfeld & Nicolson, London, 1975

Jewellery

Becker, V. *Antique and 20th Century Jewellery* N.A.G. Press Ltd, London, 1980

Becker, V. *Art Nouveau Jewellery* Thames & Hudson, London, 1985

Bennett, David and Daniela Mascetti *Understanding Jewellery* Antique Collectors' Club, Woodbridge, UK, 1994

Fales, Martha Gandy *Jewelry in America, 1600–1900* Antique Collectors' Club, Woodbridge, UK, 1995

Flower, M. *Victorian Jewellery* Cassell, London, 1967

Gere, Rudoe, Tait and Wilson *The Art of the Jeweller; A Catalogue of the Hull Grundy Gift to the British Museum* British Museum Publications, London, 1984

Snowman, A. K. *The Art of Carl Fabergé* Faber & Faber, London, 1974

Maps

Manasek, Francis J. *Collecting Old Maps* Terra Nova Press, Norwich, Vt., 1998

More, Carl and David Bannister *Antique Maps* Phaidon, Oxford, 1983

Potter, Jonathan *Country Life Book of Antique Maps* Country Life, London, 1988

Skelton, Raleigh *Maps: a historical survey of their study and collecting* University of Chicago Press, Chicago, 1972

Prints and Posters

Castleman, Riva *Prints of the Twentieth Century: a History* Thames & Hudson, London, 1988

Gascoigne, Bamber *How to Identify Prints* Thames & Hudson, London, 1986

Gascoigne, Bamber *Milestones in Colour Printing 1457–1859* Cambridge University Press, Cambridge, UK, 1997

Heyman, Theresa Thau *Posters American Style* National Museum of American Art/Harry N. Abrams Inc., New York, 1998

National Railway Museum, York *Railway Posters 1923–47* Lawrence King, London, 1992

Simmons, Rosemary *Collecting Original Prints* Quiller Press, London, 1883

Scientific Instruments

Bennion, Elizabeth *Antique Medical Instruments* Philip Wilson Publishers for Sotheby Parke Bernet Publications, London, 1979

Mills, John FitzMaurice *Encyclopedia of Antique Scientific Instruments* Aurum Press, London, 1983

Turner, Gerard L'E *Scientific Instruments 1500–1900: An Introduction* Philip Wilson Publishers, London, 1998

Warren, David J. *Old Medical and Dental Instruments* Shire Publications, Princes Risborough, UK, 1994

Silver

Bace, Jill *Collecting Silver: The Facts at your Fingertips* Miller's/Mitchell Beazley, London, 1999

Blair, Claude *History of Silver* Macdonald Orbis, London, 1987

Bones, Frances *The standard encyclopedia of American silverplate, flatware and hollow ware* Collectors' Books, Paducah, KY, 1998

Clayton, Michael *The Collector's Dictionary of Silver and Gold of Great Britain and North America* Antique Collectors' Club, Woodbridge, UK, 1885

Fennimore, Donald L. *Silver and pewter* Chanticleer Press, Knopf, New York, 1984

Forrest, Tim *Bulfinch anatomy of antique china and silver* Bulfinch Press, Boston, 1998

Grimwade, A.G. *London Goldsmiths, (1697–1837)* Faber & Faber, London, 1976

Helliwell, Stephen *Small silver tableware* Bulfinch Press, Boston, 1996

Langford, Joel *Silver: A Practical Guide to Collecting Silverware and Identifying Hallmarks* Apple Press/Quintet Publishing, London, 1991

Newman, Harold *An illustrated dictionary of silverware … from c.1500 to the present* Thames & Hudson, New York, 1987

Pickford, I. *Silver Flatware English, Irish and Scottish, 1660–1980* Antique Collectors' Club, Woodbridge, UK, 1983

Wills, Geoffrey *The Guinness Book of Silver* Guinness Publishing, London, 1983

Sporting Memorabilia

Baddiel, Sarah Fabian *Beyond the links: golfing stories, collectibles and ephemera* Studio Editions, London, 1992

Baddiel, Sarah Fabian *Miller's golfing memorabilia* Mitchell Beazley, London, 1994

Horne, Nicky *The Complete American Football Book* Robson Books, London, 1987

Kewley, Charles and Howard Farrar *Fishing Tackle for Collectors* Sotheby's Publications, New York, 1987

Steel, Allan Gibson and the Hon. R. Lyttelton *The Badmington Library: Cricket* Ashford, Southampton, UK,1985

Styles

Hiesinger, Kathryn B. and George H. Marcus *Landmarks of Twentieth Century Design – An Illustrated Handbbok*, Abbeville Press, New York, 1993

Johnson, J. Stewart *American Modern – 1925–1940, Design for a New Age* Harry N. Abrams Inc., New York, 2000

Klein, Dan, Nancy A. McClelland and Malcolm Haslam *In the Deco Style* Thames & Hudson, London,1987

Rudoe, Judy *Decorative Arts 1850–1950: A Catalogue of the British Museum Collection*, British Museum Press, London, 1991

Textiles

Dillmont, T. de *The Complete Encyclopedia of Needlework* (3rd ed.) Courage Books, Philadelphia, 1996

Huish, Marcus B. *Samplers and Tapestry Embroideries* Longmans, London, 1990

Levey, Santina M. *Lace – A History* Victoria and Albert Museum/W.S. Maney & Son London, 1983

Phillips, Barty *Tapestry* Phaidon, London, 1994

Sebba, Anne *Samplers – Five Centuries of a Gentle Craft* Weidenfeld & Nicolson, London, 1979

Synge, Lanto *Antique Needlework* Blandford Press, London, 1982

Toys

Baeker and Väterlein (eds) *Germany's Forgotten Toymakers* Michael Kohl, Frankfurt, Germany, 1982

Fawdry, Marguerite *British Tin Toys* New Cavendish Books, London, 1990

Gottschalk, Lillian *American Motortoys* New Cavendish Books, London, 1986

O'Brien, Richard *The Story of American Toys* New Cavendish Books, London, 1990

Pressland, David *The Art of the Tin Toy* New Cavendish Books, London, 1976

Randall, Peter *The Products of Binns Road* (Hornby Companion 1) New Cavendish Books, London, 1977

Remise, Jac and Jean Fondin *The Golden Age of Toys* Edita Lausanne, Lausanne, 1967

Richardson, Mike and Sue *The Great Book of Dinky Toys* New Cavendish Books, London, 2000

Weapons

Blackmore, Howard *A Dictionary of London Gunmakers* Phaidon, Christie's, London, 1986

Dufty, Arthur *European Armour in the Tower of London* HMSO, London, 1968

Dufty, Arthur *European Swords in the Tower of London* HMSO, London, 1974

Reid, William *The Lore of Arms* Mitchell Beazley, London, 1976

Stone, George *A Glossary of the Construction, Decoration and Use of Arms and Armour* Jack Brussel, New York, 1961

Tarassuk, Leonid and Blair, Claude *The Complete Encyclopaedia of Arms and Weapons* Simon & Schuster, New York, 1982

Value codes

Beside every antique featured is a value code, which gives the approximate value of the item. These are broad price ranges and should only be seen as a guide, as prices for antiques vary depending on the condition of the piece, where it is sold and market trends.

[A] Over £30,000 Over $45,000	[K] £750–1,000 $1125–$1500
[B] £20,000–30,000 $30,000–$45,000	[L] £550–750 $825–$1125
[C] £10,000–20,000 $15,000–$30,000	[M] £450–550 $675–$825
[B] £7,500–10,000 $11,250–$15,000	[N] £350–450 $525–$675
[E] £5,000–7,500 $7500–$11,250	[O] £250–350 $375–$525
[F] £4,000–5,000 $6000–$7500	[P] £200–250 $300–$375
[G] £3,000–4,000 $4500–$6000	[Q] £150–200 $225–$300
[H] £2,000–3,000 $3000–$4500	[R] £75–150 $112.50–$225
[I] £1,500–2,000 $2250–$3000	[S] Under £75 Under $112.50
[J] £1,000–1,500 $1500–$2250	

Credits

The publishers would like to thank the following people and organizations for supplying pictures for use in this book or for allowing their pieces to be photographed.

AA The Art Archive **AB** Alisdair Brown, The Cranewell, Chelsea SW6 **AH** Angelo Hornak Photograph Library **AJ** A & J Photographics **AKG** AKG London **AL** Andrew Lineham, The Mall, Camden Passage, London, N1 **AM** American Museum, Claverton Manor, Bath BA2 7BD **ART** Artemis **AS** Andrew Sydenham **ASH** The Ashmolean Museum, Oxford OX1 2PU **AU** Andrew R Ullmann Ltd, 10 Hatton Garden, London EC1N 8AH **B** Beverley, 30 Church Street, London NW8 **BA** Beth Adams, Alfies, 13–25 Church Street, London NW8 **BAL** The Bridgeman Art Library, London W2 **BAZ** Bazaat, 51 Ledbury Road, London W11 **BD** Barry Davies Oriental Art Ltd, 1 Davies Street, London W1 **BIZ** Bizarre, 24 Church Street, London NW8 **BON** Bonhams **BROWNS** Brown's Antique Furniture, The Furniture Cave, 533 King's Road, SW10 **BS** B. Silverman, 26 The London Silver Vaults London WC2A **BV** Barbara Veith **C** Cristobal, Alfies, 13–15 Church Street, London NW8 **C&C** Cohen & Cohen, 101B Kensington Church Street W8 **CC** Caroline Carrier, 1 Pierrepont Arcade, Camden Passage, London N1 **CC Ltd** The Clock Clinic Ltd, 85 Lower Richmond Road, SW15 **CC/ME** Clive Corless/Marshall Editions **C&D** Cathers & Dembrosky, 43 E10th Street, New York **CG** Chelsea Gallery, The Plaza, 535 Kings Road, SW10 **CDM** Colin D. Monk, 58–60 Kensington Church Street, London W8 **CI** Christie's Images 1 Langley Lane, London SW8 **CK** Caroline de Kerangal, Antiquités le Grand Mare, Brittany, France **CL** Chris Linton **CO** Corbis Images 12 Regents Wharf, All Saints Street, London N1 **CW** Chris Wilde Antiques, The Courtyard, Mowbray Square, Harrogate HG1 5AU **DL** David Love, 10 Royal Parade, Harrogate, HG1 2SZ **DN** Dreweatt Neate, Donnington Priory, Donnington, Newbury, Berks RG14 2JE **DR** David Rago Auctions, Lamberville, New Jersey, USA **DS** David Seidenburg, 836 Broadway, New York, NY **Duggan** Stuart Duggan, The Furniture Cave, 533 Kings Road, SW10 **E** Esto Photographics Inc, 222 Valley Place, Mamaroneck NY 10543 **EH** English Heritage Photographic Library, 23 Savile Row London W1X 1AB **EP** Elaine Phillips Antiques Ltd, 1 & 2 Royal Parade, HG1 2SZ **F** Forza, 143–149 Great Portland Street, London W1 **FG** Francesca Galloway, 21 Cornwall Gardens London SW7 **FGH** French Glasshouse, Antiquarius Antiques Market, 135 Kings Road, London SW3 **FL** Fay Lucas Gallery, 50 Kensington Church Street, London W8 **French M.** French Metalworks, Antiquarius Antiques Market, 135 Kings Road, London SW3 **G11** Gallery Eleven, 11 West Street Dorking, RH4 1BL **G & G** Guest & Gray, 1 7 David Mews, London W1IL **GA** Garry Atkins, 107 Kensington Church Street, London W8 **GACT** Gallery of Antique Costumes & Textiles, 2 Church Street, London NW8 **GEMA** Gem Antiques, 1088 Madison Avenue, New York **GN** Gillian Neale Antiques, PO Box 247, Aylesbury, HP20 1JZ **GR** Graham Rae **GV** Grosvenor Antiques, 27 Holland Street, London W8 **Harpur** Harpur Dearden, The Furniture Cave, 533

Kings Road, London SW10 **H & Co** Holts & Co.
98 Hatton Gardens, London EC1 **Holt** Holt & Co.
5 Rickett Street, West Brompton, London SW6
H & W Haslam & Whiteway, 105 Kensington
Church Street London W8 **H of D** Hampshires of
Dorking, 50/52 West Street, Dorking, Surrey RH4
HD Halcyon Days, 14 Brook Street, London W1Y
IS Courtesy of Israel Sacks Inc., New York **JB** John
Barlow **JBULL** John Bull Ltd, 139A New Bond
Street, London W1Y **JH** Jeanette Hayhurst, 32A
Kensington Church Street London W8 **JHO**
Jonathan Horne Antiques, 66 Kensington Church
Street London W8 **JJ** John Jesse, 160 Kensington
Church St, W8 **JF** Jubilee Fotographica Pierpoint
Row, Camden Passage, Islington N1 **JM** Jill Metcalf,
The Furniture Cave, 533 Kings Road, SW10
JTS June & Tony Stone Fine Antique Boxes, 75
Portobello Road, London W11 **K & Y** K & Y
Oriental Art, South Molton Street, W1K **KB** Karl
Bartley **KW** Kiki Werth, 185 Westbourne Grove,
London W11 **L** Legacy, Alfie's Antique Market,
13–25 Church Street, NW8 **LA** Lunn Antiques, 86
New Kings Road SW6 **LFA** Law Fine Art, Firs
Cottage, Church Lane, Brimpton, Berkshire RG&
4TJ **Loveless** Clive Loveless, 54 St Quintin Avenue,
London W10 **LK** Leigh Keno, 980 Madison Avenue,
New York, NY **LN** Lillian Nassau, 220 E57th Street,
New York, NY **M** Morris & Co. 387 The Arches,
Geffrye Street, London E2 8HZ **MA** Manic Attic,
Alfie's Antique Market, 13–25 Church Street, NW8
MG Michael German, 38B Kensington Church
Street, London W8 4BX **ML** Marion Langham, 41a
Lower Belgrave Street, London SW1 **MN** Mike
Newton **NB** Norman Brand **NBOSTON** Nicolaus
Boston, Kensington Church Street Antiques Centre,
58–60 Kensington Church Street, W8 **NC** New
Century, 69 Kensington Church Street, London W8
ND Nicholas M. Dawes, 67 E11th Street, New York
Pearson Sue Pearson, Antique Dolls and Teddy
Bears, 13¹/2 Prince Albert Street, Brighton BN1 1HE
PB Philip de Bay **PC** Private Collection
PG Pruskin Gallery, 73 Kensington Church Street
W8 **PH** Paul Howard, Bourgan-Hanby Antiques
Centre, 151 Sydney Street London SW3 **Phillips**
Phillips Fine Art Auctioneers, London **Pinn** W.A.
Pinn & Sons, 124 Swan Street, Sible Hedingham, Essex
CO9 3HP **PS** Peta Smyth Antique Textiles, 42
Moreton Street London SW1V **RA** Rare Art,
London Silver Vaults WC2 **RD** Richard Dennis, 144
Kensington Church Street, London W8 **RJ** Roderick
Jellicoe, 3a Camden Street, London W8 **RR** Rogers
de Rin Antiques, 76 Royal Hospital Road, London
SW3 **RW** Raffety & Walwyn, 79 Kensington Church
Street, London W8 **S** Scala **SA** Sean Arnold, 21–22
Chepstow Corner, London W2 **SAS** Special Auction
Services The Coach House, Midgham Park, Reading,
Berks RG7 5UG **SC** Sandra Cronan 18 Burlington
Arcade, London W1V **SD** S. Durrant, The Flea
Market, 7 Pierrepont Arcade, Camden Passage,
London N1 **SF** The Silver Fund, 40 Bury Street,
London SW1Y **SJP** S.J. Phillips Ltd, 139A New
Bond Street, London W1Y **SM** S. Marchant & Son,
120 Kensington Church Street, London W8 LN
Smiths Smiths, Dragon Road, Harrogate HG1 5DR
SO Somervale Antiques, 6 Radstock Road,
Midsomer Norton, Bath BA3 2AJ **Sotheby's**
Sotheby's 34-35 New Bond Street, London W1A
SSPL Science & Society Picture Library **SPL**
Sotheby's Picture Library **SS** Simon Spero, 109
Kensington Church Street London W8 **ST** Steve
Tanner **STR** Stradlings, 1225 Park Avenue, New
York **T** Trio, Grays Mews Antique Market, London
W1K **TH** Thorntons of Harrogate, 1 Montpellier

Gardens, Harrogate HG1 2TF **TMG** Terrence
McGinniss **V&A** Victoria & Albert Museum, South
Kensington, London SW7 **V&APL** V & A Picture
Library, London SW7 **VH** Valerie Howard, 4
Campden Street, London W8 **W** Woodage Antiques,
7 Lower Mall Camden Passage, Islington, London
WA Witney Antiques, 96/100 Corn Street, Witney
OX8 7BU **WHA** Weatherell's of Harrogate Antiques
and Fine Arts, 29 Montpellier Parade, Harrogate HG1
2TG **YW** York Whiting, 533 Kings Road, London
SW10 **Z** Zeitgeist, 58 Kensington Church Street,
London W8

KEY
b bottom; **c** centre; **l** left; **r** right; **t** top

6 bl L/CL, br CI, c BON/ST, t C &C/CL;
7 b MA/CL, c BAL/PC, tl FGH/CL, tr CI; **10** b & t
SPL; **11** b JH/ST, t S/Museo Mosca; **12** b EH,
c BAL/PC, t EH; **13** bl JJ/A & J, br CI, t DN/A & J;
14 c CI; **15** cl CI, cr BAZ/AJ, l JH/GR, r CC/ME;
16 c DN/A & J, l & t CI, r JH/GR; **17** b CO,
l LA/ST, t JH/GR; **18** bl SC/CL, br & t S/National
Museum of Nuremberg; **19** bl CI, br CI, t E;
20 b PH/CL, c LFA/MN, t CI; **21** b SPL, c SA/CL,
t CC/CL; **22** b CI, t BAL/PC; **23** GACT/ST,
c CG/CL, tl Christie's/AJ, tr RMN/M.Beck-
Coppola; **24** b H&W/AJ, b SAS/ST; **25** b Z/PB,
br BD/AJ, t RA/ST; **26** b B/CL, c PG/A & J, t CI;
27 bl B/AJ, br GA/TMG, tl JH/GR, tr SPL;
28 bl SPL, br DL/AJ, t CI; **29** tl CI, tr AL/CL;
30 b AL/AJ, c MG/AJ, t CW/AJ; **31** bl C/GR,
br JJ/A & J, t CI; **32** b CW/AJ, c ND/TMG, t JJ/A
& J; **33** b JJ/A & J, l RD/CL; **34** bl CC/ME,
br BAL/Musée des Arts Décoratifs, Lyon, tl RA/AJ,
tr SPL; **35** bl B/AJ, br SPL, t CI; **36** bl SJP/ST, br CI,
t AKG/Erich Lessing; **37** bl BON/MN, br JH/A & J;
38 c B/AJ, l SPL, t AL/CL; **39** b SPL, r CI,
t RW/CL; **40** bl CI, br B/AJ, t AL/CL; **41** bl CC
Ltd/CL, br AB/AJ, t CI; **42** b G&G/CL, t V&APL;
43 bl CC/ME, br CI; **44** b & c CO, t CK/A & J;
45 b CI, tl C/GR, tr DN/MN; **46** b BON/MN,
r C&C/CL, t CI; **47** c HD/ST, l FG/ST, r E;
48 b & c SPL, br Z/PB, t CI; **49** bl V&APL, br
CK/AJ, t CI; **50** b SPL, l GACT/ST, r CI; **51** b SPL,
tl BON/ST, tr SO/MN; **52** b DN/MN,
c BAL/Metropolitan Museum, tl SPL, tr ML/AJ;
53 b E, t CI; **54** b E, c E, t E; **55** b CK/A & J, l E;
56 b LFA/MN, c SPL, t SPL; **57** b DR, r CI, t
DL/AJ; **58** b CI, tl CI, tr BAL/Corning Museum of
Glass; **59** b W/CL, c AH, t SPL; **60** bl CI, br
Bonhams, Chelsea, c BAL/V & A, t BAL/PC;
61 b SD/CL, l JJ/A & J, t DN/AJ; **62** b K & Y/CL,
c CI, tl BON/ST, tr CW/AJ; **63** b BS/ST,
tl Sotheby's, tr CI; **64** b CDM/MN, b GN/AJ,
c DN/AJ, t PC/GR; **65** b MG/CL, c Z/PB, tl
GA/CL, tr Sotheby's/KB; **66** bl PC/CL, br CI,
cl AL/CL, tl AL/AJ; **67** b DN/MN, tl
RMN/Arnaudet/J.Schormans, tr BAL/SPL;
68 b VH/CL, t DN/MN; **69** b STR/TMG, c
Sotheby's; **70** b RMN/Louvre/Arnaudet, tl
C&C/CL, tr CI; **71** bl GN/AJ, br CI, t Christie's/AJ;
72 b CI, l JF/CL; **73** b AA/Museo Correr
Venice/Dagli Orti, t SJP/ST; **74** b CI, t H & W/A &
J; **75** b RJ/CL, cl HD/ST, cr GA/CL, t BON/MN;
76 b GACT/ST, c CK/ST, t MG/CL; **77** b T/CL,
c SC/CL, t MG/CL; **78** bl LA/ST, br E, t CI;
79 b BIZ/CL, c RA/ST, t BAL/Bonhams, London;
80 b RD/CL, c AL/AJ, t Smiths/AJ; **81** b CI, tc CI,
tl CI, tr SPL; **82** bc CC/ME, br V&APL, t CC/ME;
83 bl RA/ST, br SC/CL, t JF/CL; **84** b

BROWNS/AJ, c YW/AJ, t AL/CL; **85** b Harpur/AJ,
t SF/GR; **86** b BAZ/AJ, bl CDM/MN, t C & C/CL;
87 bl Pinn/AJ, br YW/AJ, c CI, t B/AJ; **88** b TH/AJ,
l EP/AJ, t LA/ST; **89** b SC/CL, t CC Ltd/CL;
90 b CI, tl H of D/ST, tr SJP/ST; **91** b BON/MN, c
JBULL/ST, tl CI, tr DR; **92** b BS/ST, c CI, l SJP/ST;
93 b Duggan/AJ, c DN/A & J, t LFA/MN;
94 b V&APL, c E, t BAL/Royal Scottish Museum;
95 t SPL; **96** b CI, tl VH/PB, tr JH/GR; **97** bl SPL,
br FL/CL, t CI; **98** b RJ/CL, c RJ/CL, t RJ/CL; **99** b
CI, c V&APL, t V&APL.

100 b LK, t CK/A & J; **101** b RD, c BON/ST;
102 b C & C/CL, c LFA/ST, t C & C/CL;
103 b CDM/MN, c LFA/ST, tl C&C/CL, tr
C&C/CL; **104** b CI, c CI, t CI; **105** b LFA/ST, tl CI,
tr LFA/ST; **106** b BAL/V&A, c BAL/PC, t SPL;
107 bl PG/AJ, br JJ/AJ, cl B/CL, cr Phillips;
108 b BAL/Mallet & Son, c V&APL/P.Barnard, t CI;
109 bl CI, br CI, tl CI, tr CI; **110** c FL/CL, l
CC/ME, r E, t L/CL; **111** bl CI, br E, tr SC/CL;
112 bl B/AJ, br B/AJ, cl CI, cr B/AJ, t AL/CL;
114 b BAL/G.Gros-Galliner Collection, c V&APL, c
CI; **115** b DN/A J, r DL/AJ, tl LFA/MN; **116** b AM,
t AM; **117** b CI, l CI, tr CI; **118** b CI/AJ, c LFA/MN,
t EP/AJ; **119** c PC/GR, tl BAL/BON, tr MG/CL;
120 bl CI, br PH/CL, cr CI, tl DN/MN, tr B/AJ;
121 b DN/AJ, c B/AJ, t SO/MN; **122** b French
M./MN, c PC/GR, t LFA/MN; **123** b BON/MN,
c SO/MN; **124** b C/GR, cl C/GR, cr C/GR,
t C/GR; **125** bl B/AJ, br CI, t SPL; **126** b AL/CL,
r TMG/ND, t CI; **127** b Crafts Council, c CI,
l V&APL, t CI; **128** b SPL, t CI, t DN/A & J;
129 b FG/ST, t PS/ST; **130** b B/AJ, c SO/MN,
tc B/AJ, tl DN/A & J; **131** b AB/AJ, r MG/CL, t CI;
132 b Smiths/AJ, c DN/A & J, tl Holt/ST, tr FG/ST;
134 c SPL; **135** b DN/AJ, c JHO/GR, t DN/MN;
136 b E, r MG/CL, t H & W/A & J; **137** bl
LFA/MN, br GV/AJ, t SPL; **138** l E, r CI; **139** c JH/A
J, t Bonhams, Chelsea/MN; **140** b BON/ST, cl
BON/ST, cr BON/ST, t BON/ST; **141** b BON/ST,
cr CC/ME, l CC/ME, t BON/ST; **142** b LK/TMG,
c CI/AJ, t BON/MN; **143** bl DN/A J, br SF/GR,
c BON/ST, t CI; **144** bl BON/MN, br BAL/PC,
c BON, t BON; **145** b BON, cb BON, ct BON,
t MA/CL; **146** b Royal Doulton, cl CC/ME, cr B/AJ,
t LFA/ST; **147** l SO/MN, r BON/ST; **148** b CW/AJ,
c JJ/A J, t DN/A J; **149** b G11/ST, c H of D/ST,
tl JBULL/ST, tr MG/CL; **150** b Z/PB, br SPL,
t V&APL; **151** b CO/Philadelphia Museum of Art,
t V&APL; **152** b CI, c M/MN, t SPL; **153** b CI,
c SPL, t CC/ME; **154** b V&APL, c C&C/CL, t CI;
155 b B/AJ, t V&APL; **156** b V&APL, c SF/GR,
t V&APL; **157** b PS/ST, cl WA, cr WA, t FG/ST;
158 bcr SC/CL, bl RD/CL, br PC/ST, c W/AJ,
t CK/AJ; **159** b DN/MN, cl DL/AJ, cr SF/ST, t CI;
160 l T/CL, r RA/ST, t RA/ST; **161** r W/AJ, t L/CL;
162 bl BON/ST, br SC/CL, c BAL/PC, t BON/PC;
163 b CI, cl CK/AJ, cr BAL/PC, t SO/MN;
164 b LN/TMG, c HD/ST, tl AJ,tr BON/MN;
165 l GA, r BON/MN; **166** c E, t CI; **167** bl IS,
br CO/Peter Harholdt, c CO/Peter Harholdt, t CI;
168 b MG/CL, c SJP/ST; **169** bl CK/ST, br
C&C/CL, t LFA/ST; **170** bl BAL/Imperial War
Museum, br Sotheby's/KB, t CC Ltd/CL;
171 t Holt/ST; **172** bl GA/CL, br SAS/ST, t JH/ST;
173 b CI, tl CI, tr JJ/A & J; **174** l FG/ST, r DN/MN;
175 b DR, c JH/GR, t CC/ME; **178** b H of D/ST,
c CI, t CC/ME; **179** b ART/AJ, c JJ/AJ, t CC/ME;
180 b CI, cl Sotheby's/AJ, cr AA/Nicholas Sapieha,
t C & C/CL; **181** H & Co./ST; **182** b JH/AJ,
tl TH/AJ, tr BS/AJ; **183** b CK/AJ, l Sotheby's/KB,
r SPL; **184** l JH/GR, r G&G/CL, t SC/CL; **186** b CI,